Doctrine *of* Conditions

JCL Studies in Comparative Law: Second Series

Series Editors

Professor William E. Butler

Professor Michael Palmer

1. W. E. Butler and O. V. Kresin (eds.), *Discovering the Unexpected: Comparative Legal Studies in Eastern and Central Europe* (Clark, New Jersey, Talbot Publishing, 2021). ISBN 9781616196554

2. Simon Palmer and Zhai Xiaobo (eds.), *Bentham Around the World* (Clark, New Jersey, Talbot Publishing, 2021). ISBN 9781616196561

3. O. V. Kresin, *Comparative Law in Warsaw: 1800-1835,* transl. W. E. Butler (Clark, New Jersey, Talbot Publishing, 2022) ISBN 9781616196585

4. W. E. Butler and O. V. Kresin (eds.) *The Comparative Method in the Science of Law* by Lev Rebet (Clark, New Jersey, Talbot Publishing, 2022) ISBN 9781616196653

5. Horst Dippel, *Modern Constitutionalism,* 2 vols. (Clark, New Jersey, Talbot Publishing, 2022) ISBN 9781616196769

6. Stephan Meder, *Legal Machines* (Clark, New Jersey, Talbot Publishing, 2023) ISBN 9781616196813

7. Ama F. Hammond, Folashade Rose Adegbite, Maame Yaa A. Mensa-Bonsu, Prosper Batariwah (eds.), *Family Law in Africa: Perspectives on Selected Systems of Marriage* (Clark, New Jersey, Talbot Publishing, 2023) ISBN 9781616196844

8. William E. Butler and Oleksiy V. Kresin (eds.), *The World Picture of Comparative Law* (Clark, New Jersey, Talbot Publishing, 2024) ISBN 9781616196905

9. Carmelo Massimo De Iuliis (ed. & trans.), *Gottfried Wilhelm Leibniz: Model of Certainty or Demonstrations in Law, Expounded in the Doctrine of Conditions* (Clark, New Jersey, Talbot Publishing, 2025) ISBN 978-1-61619-693-6

Model *of* Certainty *or*
Demonstrations *in* Law
Expounded *in the*

Doctrine *of* Conditions

Gottfried Wilhelm Leibniz

INTRODUCTORY ESSAY,
TRANSLATION, AND NOTES BY
Carmelo Massimo de Iuliis

TALBOT
PUBLISHING
Clark, New Jersey
2025

ISBN: 978-1-61619-693-6

TALBOT PUBLISHING

AN IMPRINT OF
The Lawbook Exchange, Ltd.
33 Terminal Avenue
Clark, New Jersey 07066-1321

Please see our website for a selection of our other publications and fine facsimile reprints of classic works of legal history www.lawbookexchange.com

Library of Congress Cataloging-in-Publication Data

Names: Leibniz, Gottfried Wilhelm, Freiherr von, 1646-1716 author. | De Iuliis, Carmelo Massimo, translator.
Title: Model of certainty or demonstrations in law expounded in the doctrine of conditions / Gottfried Wilhelm Leibniz ; introductory essay, translation, and notes by Carmelo Massimo de Iuliis.
Other titles: Doctrina conditionum. English
Description: First edition. | Clark : Talbot Publishing, an Imprint of The Lawbook Exchange, Ltd., 2024. | Series: JCL studies in comparative law. Second series ; no. 9 | Includes bibliographical references and index. | Summary: "An English translation of Gottfried Wilhelm Leibniz's 1669 compilation Doctrina Conditionum"-- Provided by publisher.
Identifiers: LCCN 2024043994 | ISBN 9781616196936 (hardcover)
Subjects: LCSH: Law--Methodology. | Law--Philosophy. | Conditionals (Logic)
Classification: LCC K213 .L4513 2024 | DDC 340/.1--dc23/eng/20240918
LC record available at https://lccn.loc.gov/2024043994

Printed in the United States of America on acid-free paper

Table of Contents

INTRODUCTION

Leibniz and the Rules of Law Geometrically Demonstrated

The *Doctrina Conditionum* presents a harmonious structure of rules relating to conditions in legal acts, previously scattered throughout the *Corpus Juris* and canon law, which constitute the so-called *ius commune*.[1] As no other text provides such an elegant and comprehensive summary of the cultural foundation of European continental codifications on this topic, translating Leibniz's *Doctrine* becomes essential for the following reasons.

First, it offers a powerful tool for a broader audience of jurists, not confined to historians and legal philosophers, to understand the cultural context that nourishes the applicable norms in similar cases. Second, it allows us to evaluate the success of the author's intent: to render the opinions of ancient Roman jurists on conditions in legal acts into "the most certain and almost mathematical demonstrations"[2] using the Euclidean demon-

[1] *Ius commune* was then in force by unanimous consent (*consensus omnium*) in almost all continental Europe. See *Ratio Corporis Juris Reconcinnandi* (1668) (AA VI, 2), "§. 1. We call Roman Law that which comes from Roman Emperor Justinian, as that which comes from Roman Pontiffs; the first is called Justinianean, the latter Papal. §. 2. Both have authority throughout almost all of Europe, by voluntary acceptance of the force of *Jus Commune*, and as if of *Jus Gentium Christianorum*, so that it is applied every time that it is not deviated by specific laws, statutes, or customs of particular states, regions, provinces, or places" [italics added; e.t.].

[2] AA VI, 1, 330, *Preface*. "Hic illud saltem praeterire non possum, tanto ingenio tantaque profunditate in reddendo jure versatos esse Juris Consultos veteres, ut in certissimas ac pene mathematicas demonstrationes eorum responsa redigendi laboris potius sit in digerendo, quam in supplendo ingenii.". [I cannot even be silent here that the ancient jurisconsults did justice with so much acumen and so much depth that it concerns more of working to order their opinions in certain and almost mathematical demonstrations than of integrating them with acumen. (e.t.)].

strative method.[3] Third, this work is crucial for the general study of law both historically and in contemporary times, particularly in its connection to the field of comparative law.

Leibniz's Bio-Bibliographical Profile until 1669: Influence of Euclid in his Education

Gottfried Wilhelm Leibniz was born at Leipzig in 1646[4] into a family of Lutheran jurists. His father, Frederic Leibniz (1597–1652), served as a lawyer, notary, and professor of moral philosophy at the local university. Similarly, his maternal grandfather, Wilhelm Schmuck (1575-1634), was a law professor at the same university, while his uncle, Johann Strauch (1612-1679), held a prominent position as the secretary of the city of Brunswick and was also an eminent jurist.

At the age of six,[5] Leibniz tragically lost his father and received his primary education at home. While the specific educational program and timeline remain unknown, it is evident that his remarkable breadth of reading contributed significantly to his exceptional intellectual development. By the age of twelve, he could

[3] Franco Cordero (1928-2020), in his work *Riti e sapienza del diritto* [Rituals and Wisdom of Law] (Rome, Bari, 1981), p. 137, talks about the "Euclidean tastes" exhibited by the young Leibniz in a treatise titled "Specimen certitudinis seu demonstrationuum in jure: Doctrina de Conditionibus pars quaedam est Logicae Juridicae, agens de propositionibus Hypotheticis in jure" (e. t.).

[4] Gottfried Wilhelm Leibniz, born in Leipzig on either 1 July (Gregorian calendar) or 21 June (Julian calendar), 1646. The introduction of the Gregorian calendar in the Protestant countries during the eighteenth century caused a shift in Leibniz's birthdate from the previously recorded Julian calendar date. Maria Rosa Antognazza, *Leibniz. An Intellectual Biography* (Cambridge, 2009), p. 27.

[5] "Vita Leibnitii a se ipso breviter delineata", in Alexandre Foucher de Careil (1826–1891) (ed.), *Nouvelle lettres et opuscules inédits de Leibniz* (Paris, 1857), p. 379: "Natus sum illi jam quinquennario et vix sexenni amisi patrem" (hereinafter *Vita Leibnitii*).

write 300 hexameters in Latin,[6] a feat that generated public praise from his tutors.[7]

Titus Livy (59 BC – AD 17) exerted a strong influence on the young Leibniz, and he made notable discoveries in his father's library, encountering the works of Cicero, Quintilian, Seneca, Pliny, Herodotus, Xenophon, Plato, and historians from the Augustan era.[8] Among the "modern" intellectuals he cites in his autobiography, Leibniz mentions the names of Jacopo Zabarella (1533-1539), a prominent Aristotelian philosopher and logician at the University of Padua, as well as Antonio Rubio (1548-1615), Pedro de Fonseca (1528-1599), and Francisco Suarez (1548-1617), all esteemed Jesuit thinkers.[9]

In April 1661, a few months before turning fifteen years old, he enrolled at the University of Leipzig. There, he tells us, "I was fortunate to have the famous Jacob Thomasius (1622–1684) as a teacher",[10] who played a decisive role in the study of philosophy, encouraging him to read the philosophers directly, especially Aristotle, to gain a better understanding of the works of this philosopher without the interpretations of the First and Second Scholastica.[11] On 2 December 1662, Leibniz

[6] Antognazza, note 4 above, p. 37.

[7] "versus 300 hexametros praeceptores laudatos, et quod affectaveram, sine ulla elisione, quos publice stata die pronuntiavi", *Vita Leibnitii*, p, 382.

[8] *Vita Leibnitii*, p. 381.

[9] *Vita Leibnitii*, p. 382, "Interea in Zabarella et Rubio et Fonseca et aliisque scholasticis non minori, quam antea in Historicis voluptate versabar et eousque profeceram, ut Suaresium non minore facilitatem legerem, quam Milesias fabulas solemus, quas vulgo Romanos vocant" [Meanwhile, I was engrossed no less in Zabarella, Rubio, Fonseca, and other scholastics than I had previously been in historians, and I had advanced so far that I read Suarez with no less ease than we are accustomed to read the Milesian tales, which are commonly called Roman].

[10] Leibniz's note (1660s?) in Foucher de Careil (ed.), *Mémoire sur la philosophie de Leibniz* (Paris: F. R. de Rudeval, 1905), Part I, p. 6.

[11] Christia Mercer, "Aristotelism at the Core of Leibniz's Philosophy",

received his bachelor's degree in philosophy, and six months later, he defended a *Disputatio metaphysica de principio individui*[12] with a preface by Thomasius himself.

In the following ten days (20 June 1663), he enrolled in the summer semester at the University of Jena. The mathematics lessons held there by Erhard Weigel (1625–1699) attracted[13] the young student who, influenced by the Euclidean demonstrative method applied by Weigel to Aristotelian thought,[14] decided to apply it to law. On 15 July 1665, he published the first part of his law degree dissertation *Disputatio Juridica de conditionibus* (that is, *De conditionibus I*),[15] and on the next 17 August, always in Leipzig, the *Disputatio Juridica de conditionibus posterior* (that is, *De conditionibus II*),[16] where *the ius commune*[17] of the conditionals is reduced to theorems and geometric-style demonstrations.[18]

The influence of algebra and geometry, along with the belief in achieving the solution to any gnoseological problem through "calculemus" (let's calculate!) instead of "disputemus (let's dispute!), stimulated the writing

in Cees Leijenhorst, L. Christoph, and Johannes M. M. H. Thijssen (eds.), *The Dynamics of Aristotelian Natural Philosophy from Antiquity to the Seventeenth Century* (Leiden: Brill, 2002).

12 AA VI, 1, p. 3.

13 On the influence of Weigel in the cultural formation of Leibniz, see Christia Mercer, *Leibniz's Metaphyisics. Its Origins and Development* (Cambridge, 2001), in particular pp. 38-39.

14 Erhard Weigel (1625-1699), *Analysis Aristotelica ex Euclide Restituta* (Jenae: apud Grosium, 1658); German transl. Thomas Behme (Stuttgart: Frommann-holzboog, 2008), with parallel Latin text.

15 Lipsiae: Typis Johannis Wittigau, AA VI, 1, p. 99.

16 Lipsiae: Typis Johannis Wittigau, AA VI, 1, p. 127.

17 See note 1 above.

18 AA VI, 1, p. 367. See on *De Conditionibus I and II* Pol Boucher's Introduction in *Des Conditions* (Paris: Vrin, 2002), the French translation of the aforementioned works, edited by Boucher himself.

of the famous *Ars Combinatoria* (1666),[19] which Leibniz developed for his philosophy degree in March 1666.

[19] AA VI, 1, p. 170 ff, *Dissertatio de arte combinatoria* (of which there is a complete translation into English by Massimo Mugnai, Han van Ruler, and Martin Wilson (eds.), *Leibniz. Dissertation on Combinatorial Art* (Oxford, 2020); in Spanish, by Manuel Antonio Correia (ed.), *Leibniz. Dissertacion acerca del Arte Combinatorio* (Santiago de Chile, 1992). For the premises of the operation of "legal calculation", see in the same work, AA VI, 1, Prob. II, VIII usus, 40, where

> *Ars casuum formandorum.* Porro Ars casuum formandorum fundatur in doctrina nostra de Complexionibus. Jurisprudentia enim cum in aliis Geometriae similis est, tum in hoc quod utraque habet Elementa, utraque casus. Elementa sunt simplicia, in Geometria figurae triangulis, circulus etc., in Jurisprudentia actus promissio, alienatio etc. compexiones horum sunt infinities. Elementa Geometriae composuit Euclides, Elementa juris in eius corpore continetur, utrobique tamen admiscentur Casus insignores. Terminos autem in jure simplices, quorum mixtione caeteri oriuntur, et quasi Locos communes, summaque colligere institutit Bernardus de Lavinheta Monacus ordinis Minorum Com. in Lullii Artem Magnam, quem vide. Nobis sic visum: Termini quorum complicatione oritur in Jure diversitas casuum, sunt: Personae, Res, Actus, Jura [*Art of forming cases.* Art of forming cases is founded on our doctrine of *Complexionibus* (Combinations). Jurisprudence is similar to Geometry in other respects, as both have Elements and Cases. The Elements are simple; in Geometry, they are figures like triangles, circles, etc., while in Jurisprudence, they are acts, promises, alienations, etc. The Cases are combinations of these elements, which are infinitely variable in both fields. Euclid composed the Elements of Geometry, and the Elements of Jurisprudence are contained in its body; however, significant Cases are mixed in both fields. The simple terms in law, from which others originate through mixing, are like common places, and Bernhardus Lavinheta, a Franciscan monk, in his Commentary on Lull's Ars Magna, includes the highest collection of these terms. For us, it appears as follows: The terms from which the diversity of cases arises in law are: Persons, Things (Property), Actions, and Rights.

The process of identifying the *elementa simplicia* in law, referred to in this passage, suggests that it is one of the most exemplary passages expressing, in Leibniz's legal works, the theoretical premises for the later development of Jurisprudence in the nineteenth century. For more details, refer mainly to Maximilian Herberger, *Dogmatik* (Frankfurt am Main, 1981), IV, especially chapters 7 and 8; Tullio Ascarelli (1903-1959), "Hobbes e Leibniz e la dogmatica giuridica", in *Testi per la storia del pensiero giuridico* [Texts for the History of Legal Thought] (Milano, 1960), I, p. 161, fn. 182.

In this book, Leibniz tries to build a system[20] based on Ramon Lull's (c. 1233–1315) *Ars magna* (1305), whose basic idea was to resolve complex ideas into their component simple concepts, and then combine them, through some mechanism, to generate complex concepts or propositions — possibly even ones that had not previously been thought of, as Leibniz suggests. By choosing an appropriate mechanism, moreover, one could combine concepts into valid arguments, thus leading to propositions that express true and certain knowledge.

However, in the doctoral dissertation in jurisprudence, *De casibus perplexis in jure*[21], discussed at the University of Altdorf in 1666[22], he was already aware that

[20] Richard T. Arthur, *Leibniz* (Cambridge MA: Polity, 2014), p. 30, which underlines how Lull's aim of obtaining true propositions through combinatorial calculus had been taken up by the scholars of the so called Herborn school, in particular by Johann Heinrich Alsted (1588-1638), who, together with his students Johann Heinrich Bisterfeld (c. 1605-1655) and Jan Amos Comenius (1592-1670), was, for Leibniz, an immediate source of inspiration; but above all, on the Herborn school and its influence on young Leibniz, see Antognazza, note 4 above, pp. 40-45; Leroy E. Loemker, "Leibniz and the Herborn Encyclopedist", *Journal of the History of Ideas* (1961), pp. 323-338.

[21] AA, VI, 1, p. 234.

[22] It is still a "mystery" why Leibniz received his doctorate in law from the University of Altdorf instead of from Leipzig. His "truth" is in the following passage of *Vita Leibnitii*, p. 384,

> The law faculty of Leipzig consists of twelve assessors who are different from the professors. They are occupied more with giving answers and advice than with lectures and debates. All Doctors of law in Leipzig are received in order of their doctorate, when a vacancy occurs due to the death of one of them. I saw that if I were to be promptly created a doctor, I would be among the first, and my fortune would be assured. However, at that time, a huge dispute arose when some wanted only senior doctors to be created, excluding the junior ones and postponing their promotion. Many in the faculty favored them. Observing the intrigue of rivals, I changed my plan and turned my mind towards traveling, considering it unworthy for a young man to be fixed in one place like a nail: for my mind had long been burning for the greater glory of studies, foreign knowledge, and mathematical disciplines. (…) Shortly after, at the age of twenty-one, I obtained the degree of Doctor at the

the mathematical or geometrical demonstrations in law are not always possible.[23]

The following year (1667) saw the anonymous publication of *Nova methodus discendae docendaeque jurisprudentiae* (NM), although the initials of the author's name are impressed on the frontispiece. This work was

> Nuremberg Academy, to the greatest applause of all. (e.t.)

In any case, this version of events does not seem very convincing because Leibniz could boast of numerous connections and protections. As we said, his maternal grandfather was the great jurist Wilhelm Schmuck, and his uncle, Johann Strauch, was also an eminent jurist. Additionally, he had a network of friends in the academic world, as mentioned in *Vita Leibnitii*, 383. The first biography of his life was published 20 years after his death by M. L. de Neufville, *Histoire de la Vie et des Ouvrages de Mr. Leibnitz* (Amsterdam, chez François Changuion, 1734). However, regarding this matter, it offers nothing more than gossip,

> Monsieur de Fontanelle, who appears to have had some excellent recollections, solely attributes the cause of this refusal to the Dean of the Law Faculty of Leipzig. The woman, angered with Mr. Leibniz, easily convinced her husband to postpone his doctorate under the pretext of his young age. Whatever the reason for this woman's bad mood, which could only be understood by knowing the character of her temperament, it is always certain that Mr. Leibniz was deeply affected by the rejection of this small favor. This led him to make the decision to leave a homeland where his true worth and talents were so little appreciated, and where people could have benefitted greatly from his abilities. (e.t). [M. de Fontanelle qui paroît avoir eu d'excellens Mémoires, rejecte uniquement la cause de ce refuse sur le Doyen del la Faculté de Droit. La Femme irritée contre M. Leibnitz, obtint aisément de son Epoux qu'il le renvoyât sous prétexte de sa jeuness. Quelle que soit la cause de la mauvaise humeur de cette femme, ce qu'on ne pourroit bien démêler qu'en connoissant le caractere de son génie, il est toujours certain que M. Leibnitz fut fort sensible au refus de cette legere grace, et que cela lui fit prendre la résolution d'abandonner une Patrie, où l'on connoissoit si peu ce qu'il valoit, et ce qu'on pouvoit se promettre de ses talens.]

[23] AA, VI,1,235, "§.II, Unde problemata eorum ...similia sunt controversiis jurisconsultorum... distintione expediendis, et impossibilia casibus perplexis, in quibus pro solutione est advertere et demonstrare impossibilitatem, quod algebra praestat." [Hence, their problems are similar to the controversies of jurists, which must be resolved through distinctions, and to the impossible perplexing cases, in which the solution requires recognizing and demonstrating the impossibility, as algebra does.] (e.t.).

written during a journey from Mainz to Frankfurt, "amidst the uncertainties of travel, the noise of inns, and the lack of books".[24] The main purpose of the booklet was to secure an appointment by Johann Philipp von Schönborn (1605-1673), elector and prince-archbishop of Mainz as collaborator of his court counselor Hermann Lasser, who was engaged in reforming the code of the Mainz Electorate. Leibniz hoped that by showcasing his boundless erudition in law and history (exemplified in NM, II, §§28-41), he could attain this position, which he achieved in 1669 when he released the final version of *Doctrina Conditionum.*

Cultural Context of the De conditionibus I and II.

The influence of German mathematician Erhard Weigel's teachings on Leibniz, particularly his work *Analysis Aristotelica ex Euclide Restituta* (1658), which reduces Aristotle's philosophy into theorems and demonstrations in geometrical order (*more geometrico*), has been noted above.

This "geometrization" of knowledge, which involves applying the Euclidean method to every field of knowledge to attain an unquestionable and indisputable "mathematical" certainty of the truthfulness of each cognitive result, is well delineated in the European cultural context in which Leibniz formulates his early legal works.

In 1665, the Latin translation of Euclid's "Elementa", prepared by Isaac Barrow (1630-1677), Newton's mentor and a theologian and mathematician at Cambridge University, was published.

Our ambitious university student of philosophy and jurisprudence, aligning himself with the cutting edge of intellectual thought of the time, decided to

24 AA VI, 1, 263, *NM*, Dedication.

apply the Euclidean method to the *ius commune* of conditions, the topic of his degree dissertation in law at Leipzig University. This undertaking had never been done before. Moreover, just as the Euclidean method had never been applied to ethics, another giant of philosophical thought, Baruch Spinoza (1632-1677), did so in those years.[25] Spinoza began writing his *Ethica more geometrico demonstrata,* published posthumously in 1677 at Amsterdam, around the same time that Leibniz was reviewing the essays that would later be compiled into *Doctrina Conditionum.*

In the philosophical and legal culture of the seventeenth century,[26] there emerged an immanent desire for "certainty", following the exhaustive juridical and theological debates of previous centuries. It is, therefore, not surprising that Leibniz was also influenced by this cultural attitude and attempted to "innovate" by adeptly applying this method of articulating ideas in the domain most prone to disputes: the field of law.

Publication History of Doctrina Conditionum

As noted above, the work was published in two parts, due to time constraints, under the supervision of his mentor, Bartholomaeus Leonhardus Schwendendörffer (1631-1705). The second part appeared in August 1665, probably because Leibniz was unable to

[25] Baruch Spinoza, *Ethica ordine geometrico demonstrate,* (Amsterdam, 1677); published anonymously), in the *Opera posthuman;* by Spinoza's own will, the author's name appeared only with the initials B.d.S., and to avoid risks to the publishers, the real name of the publisher, Jan Rieuwertsz (1617-1687), and the place of printing, Amsterdam, were not mentioned.

[26] Leibniz himself, in *NM*, II, §. 6, points out that, "... in imitation of Euclid, who followed in the titles of their books Thomas Hobbes in *Elementa de Cive* (Parisiis, 1642); Johann von Felden in *Elementa juris universi, et in species publici Justinianei* (Francofurti et Lipsiae, 1664) and Samuel Pufendorf in *Elementorum Jurisprudentiae universalis Libri Duo,* (Hagae Comitis, 1660).

complete the work within the expected time frame.[27] Schwendendörffer became a professor at the faculty of law in Leipzig and in 1659 obtained the chair of *De Verborum Significatione et Regulis Iuris*, and in 1660 that of *Institutiones*. He held these positions until 1669 when he was given the chairs of *Digest* and, later the same year, of *Codex*.[28] Consequently, Leibniz attended courses on Institutiones, the book of "principles" of Roman law, and therefore the most concise and essential in structure.

If we consider his professor's books, what immediately stands out is the essential and dry style, quite distant from the pompous academic dissertations that certainly do not provide the basic and undisputed mental structures necessary to master the fundamentals of law. Above all, they do not lend themselves to the clear and undisputed clarity that Leibniz always pursued. Surely, Schwendendörffer's style of writing and teaching must have left its imprint on Leibniz's conception of law.[29]

27 See Matthias Armgard, *Das rechtslogische System der 'Doctrina Conditionum' von Gottfried Wilhelm Leibniz* [The Legal-Logical System of the 'Doctrine of Conditions' by Gottfried Wilhelm Leibniz], (Marburg: Elwert, 2001), pp. 6 ff., also the fortunate events surrounding the publication of the work.

28 Carl Günther Ludovici (1707-1778), *Grosses vollständiges Universal-Lexicon Aller Wissenschafften und Künste* (Halle, 1743), p. 396.

29 Bartholomaeus Leonhardus Schwendendörffer, *Exercitationes academicae ad VI libros Institutionum Imperialium* (Lipsiae, 1661),Tit. XV, §. 9, "Legitimate guardianship, which directly descends from the Laws of the Twelve Tables, follows testamentary guardianship. It is either openly assigned, as to agnates, or through interpretation, as to cognates, patrons, parents, and brothers. Agnates and cognates differ as genus and species: genus being cognates, and agnates being a species of cognates. [...] Agnates are cognates connected through male lineage, as if by the father; but doesn't this definition also include emancipated persons? Indeed, when inspecting its words closely, there is no doubt." Leibniz style in *De conditionibus* id very close to that of his master: AA VI 1, p. 102, "1. Propositio conditionalis est, quae hoc continet: Si illa Propositio vera est, haec vera est." [A conditional proposition is one that is formed like this: if that proposition is true, then this one is true]. "2. Illa Conditio dicitur, 3. haec Conditionatum" [2 That is called the condition. 3 This one is conditionatum.]. "4 Terminus est earum alterutra" [The term is either one of the two] »; 105, "62 Propositio est Conditionalis (Pura) figura, id est sola dispositione verborum, vel expresse et figura et sensu, vel tacite

In 1667, he revised the work and published it in a single volume through a printer in Miltenberg. After the printer's death, the manuscript was lost, and only a few copies were sold. Johann Heinrich Pape (d. 1700),[30] a friend of Leibniz, managed to obtain a copy and presented it to Leibniz, who then revised the book and included it, under the title *Specimen certitudinis seu demonstrationum in Jure, exhibitum in Doctrina conditionum*, along with two other early juridical works.[31]

Place of the Translated Work in his Complete Oeuvre

The *Doctrina conditionum* in the context of Leibniz's overall work is among those that most significantly exemplify the attempt to apply the tools of "mathematical-logic" to a field not strictly mathematical, such as law. Whether the attempt to reduce the *ius commune* to theorems was successful is a matter that we will examine in subsequent sections. Here, however, it is important to highlight that the work in question represents a fundamental milestone, along with the *Ars combinatoria* (1666), in Leibniz's thought on logic. Other legal works do not contain attempts in this direction. In *De casibus perplexis in jure*, Leibniz, as we have seen, is fully aware that logical calculus does not solve all

solo sensu" [A proposition is a conditional (pure) form, that is, solely by the arrangement of words, or expressly both in form and meaning, or tacitly only by meaning].

30 Armgardt, note 27 above, ibid.

31 That is, *Specimen Difficulatatis in Jure, Seu Dissertatio De casibus Perplexis in jure*, already published in 1666 without location, but printed by the widow of George Hagen in Altdorf (see note 4, AA VI, 1, p. 233), and *Specimen Enciclopaediae in Jure, seu Quaestiones Philosophicae Amoeniores, ex Jure Collectae*, published in 1664 in Leipzig by Johannis Wittigau [AA VI,2, p. 70]. Both are available in English translation by Alberto Artosi, Giovanni Sartor, Bernardo Pieri (eds.), *Leibniz: Logico-Philosophical Puzzles in the Law: Philosophical Questions and Perplexing Cases in the Law* (Berlin: Springer, 2013).

problems;[32] and in *Nova methodus discendae docendaeque jurisprudentiae* published in 1667 in Frankfurt,[33] he writes that "Euclid is not believed because he makes statements, but because he proves, which is otherwise in divine and human laws, where the will stands in place of reason";[34] furthermore, in the same work, the same Leibniz does not furnish any instances of applying logical-mathematical calculations to norms, nor does he illustrate his theory of legal reasoning with practical examples.

Therefore, the myth of Leibniz as a pure logician who solves everything with logical reasoning needs to be re-evaluated. I have sought to demonstrate this in my earlier work, derived from a lecture at a conference held in Hannover in 2014.[35] Hence, the *Doctrina conditionum* remains a significant milestone, not so much for the use of logic to solve legal problems, but more for its method of organizing the legal system.[36]

Structure of Doctrine and Challenges of the Translation

The work is divided into ten untitled chapters. I have deemed it appropriate to insert the subject matter of

[32] Note 23, AA, VI, 1, 35, II.

[33] AA, VI, 1, 261; in English translation Leibniz, *The New Method of Learning and Teaching Jurisprudence*, transl. Carmelo Massimo de Iuliis (Clark NJ: Talbot, 2017).

[34] AA, VI, 1, §. 4, p. 294, "*Euclidi* non creditur quia dicit, sed quia probat, quod secus est in Legibus Divinis Humanisque, ubi stat pro ratione voluntas.".

[35] Carmelo Massimo de Iuliis, "Leibniz and Legal Logic: A Myth to Resize", in Wenchao Li (ed.), *Das Recht kann nicht ungerecht sein* (Stuttgart, 2015), p. 109-117.

[36] Carmelo Massimo de Iuliis, "Leibniz e la scienza giuridica tra topica e Dogmatica", in *Europa e diritto privato* (2010), pp. 711-748, but see also, diffusely, the Introduction to my English translation of *NM*, note 33 above; Scott Brewer, "Law, Logic, and Leibniz. A Contemporary Perspective", in Artosi and others (eds.), see note 31 above, p. 206.

each chapter in square brackets to provide the reader with a conceptual map of the work, which is organized as follows:

CHAPTER I [Conditional Propositions in Law]

CHAPTER II [Nature and Effect of the Condition]

CHAPTER III. [Express Condition]

CHAPTER IV [Partial Propositions]

CHAPTER V [Multiplication of the Terms and Interpretation of Quantity]

CHAPTER VI [Form of the Partial Propositions]

CHAPTER VII [Subject Matter of The Partial Propositions: Persons]

CHAPTER VIII [Subject Matter of The Partial Propositions: Things]

CHAPTER IX [The State or Motion that Must Occur or Fail in Conditioned Part]

CHAPTER X [Legal Effectiveness of the Conditional Disposition]

Each chapter is divided, as in the original text, into definitions and subsequent theorems in the geometric manner. The theorems are nothing more than the reduction to a single rule of the impressive number of passages from Justinian's Roman law and canon law on a specific subject.

Because Leibniz states in the *Preface* to the work, that "the ancient legal experts rendered justice with such acumen and depth that it is more a matter of organizing their opinions into certain and almost mathematical demonstrations than of integrating them with further acumen",[37] it was essential to include all citations of passages from the *Corpus Juris* and canon law within

[37] See note 2 above.

the main text rather than in footnotes. This approach makes the cited normative data immediately available to the reader, allowing one to easily verify how Leibniz organized the Roman jurists' opinions into clear and "mathematical demonstrations".

Moreover, the immediate visual impact of the Roman sources offers another significant benefit: it provides a comprehensive overview of conditional law in the *ius commune*. This overview, presented as a category, represents a monograph on the topic that no one before Leibniz had ever created in so perfect structure.

As for the challenges in translation, the main one is related to the Latin term *demonstratio* in definition 17. The legal meaning of *demonstratio* in Roman law, especially in the context of testamentary matters, is that of "precise indication".[38] Leibniz utilizes the word with a different meaning: as a logical term that does not denote proof[39], but rather as a logical term for designating the subject of a necessary universal categorical proposition (*Subiectum propositionis categoricae universalis necessariae*)[40]. It is worth quoting the entire passage:

38 Vincenzo Arangio-Ruiz (1884-1964), *Istituzioni di diritto romano* [Institutions of Roman Law] (Napoli, 14th ed. 1978), p. 526; Adolf Berger (1882-1962), *Enciclopedic dictionary of Roman law* (Philadelphia, 1991, repr.), *ad vocem Demonstrare*, "To denote, to explain, describe, define (a thing, a term, a plot of land etc.). It refers primarily to testamentary clauses by which the testator defined the persons or things mentioned in his testament.". Alan Watson (1933-2018), *The Digest of Justinian*, 4 vols., (revised edition Philadelphia, 2009), translates *demonstration* as Particularizations, e.g., D.35.1.77. pr., 35.1.*De condicionibus et demonstrationibus et causis et modis eorum, quae in testamento scribuntur (Conditions, particularizations, explanations for and modalities of provisions in wills)*.

39 Heinrich Schepers (1925-2000), "Leibniz Disputationen 'De conditionibus': Ansätze zu einer juristischen Aussagenlogik" [Leibniz's Disputations 'De conditionibus': Approaches to a Legal Propositional Logic], in: *Akten des II. Internationalen Leibnizkongresses in Hannover, Wiesbaden, Studia Leibnitiana Supplementa* (1975), Vol. IV, p. 9.

40 AA, VI, 1, *De conditionibus I*, p. 104: "52. Demonstratio est proprium loco subjecti positum." [The designation is precisely what is indicated in place of the subject or as the subject.]

17. DESIGNATION (DEMONSTRATIO) (whose signs "Who" and "Who-ever" indicate direct designation, and "That" indicates indirect designation as seen in D.28.7.10, .], and "This" in D.30.3, 6; and the sign of a condition is "If anyone", which contains both a condition and a direct designation, as seen in D.30.17.1, D.34.5.5, 11., which I define as the subject of a necessary universal categorical proposition, such as "He who marries my daughter shall have the Cornelian estate for himself." This proposition is universal and necessary not because of the nature of the thing, but because of the will of the testator. Therefore, the precise designation is the subject of the one who marries my daughter, by means of which the person who will possess that estate is determined and can be verified.

Another term, although not a challenge for translation, aroused curiosity about its origin in a juridical context: *condicio moralis*,[41] moral condition. Nowadays, to refer to a legally significant condition in a law, contract, or will, we say "legal condition" or "juridical condition". Here, the term "legal" or "juridical" is replaced by the adjective "moral" or "ethical". Precise references have not been found on this point in the literature, only that in the second scholasticism, law was considered a part of moral philosophy. This would explain the use of the term "moral" in relation to aspects of law. Franco Todescan[42] underlines that this nomenclature has a pre-

[41] AA VI 1, p. 105, "63. Conditionatum morale est, in quod deductum est jus aliquod, subjectum autem deducti persona" [The *conditionatum* is moral, <when> some right is deduced in it, but the subject of the deducted, is a person]. "64. Conditio moralis est a conditionato." [A condition is moral by virtue of a conditioned]. "66. Propositio conditionalis Moralis, cujus nempe conditio et conditionatum sunt moralia, dicetur a nobis imposterum Dispositio in specie." [A moral conditional proposition, of which precisely the condition and the conditioned are moral, will be called by us hereinafter disposition in the particular case]".

[42] Franco Todescan, *Le radici teologiche del giusnaturalismo laico. Il*

cise source in Francisco Suarez, who wrote: "The term "right" is typically used to refer to a certain *moral* faculty that each person has concerning their own property or regarding something owed to them".[43] So *conditio moralis* is the condition, juridically relevant, which is imposed by choice of a testator or of a part of a contract. However, let us not overlook Hugo Grotius (1583-1645), according to whom "*ius* is a *moral* quality of a person enabling one to have or do something justly".[44] Leibniz is certainly influenced by Grotius's definition of right and related terminology.[45]

What is the Euclidean Method and If It Has Been Correctly Applied

We return to the central theme of the *Doctrina*

problema della secolarizzazione nel pensiero giuridico di Samuel Pufendorf. [The theological roots of the laic law of nature. The problem of the secularization in the juridical thought of Samuel Pufendorf]. III (Milano: Giuffré, 2001), Chap. I, p. 14 ff., mostly pp. 18-22

[43] Francisco Suarez (1548 – 1617), *Tractatus de legibus*. (Conimbriæ, 1612), I, II, 5, p. 24, "Solet proprie jus vocari facultas quaedam moralis, quam unusquisque habet circa rem suam, vel ad rem sibi debitam.".

[44] Hugo Grotius (1583-1645), *De iure belli ac pacis* (Amsterdam, 1625), 1.1.4.2., "quo sensu ius est qualitas moralis personae, competens ad aliquid juste habendum vel agendum". See also Johannes Coccejus (1603-1669), *Opera Anecdota Theologica et Philologica* (Amstelodami, 1706), Tomus Alter, pp. 132-133, "Aliud est conditio logica, aliud moralis. Logica conditio veritatem enunciati non determinat simpliciter, sed a signo & argumento quovis suspendit, ut, si asinus volat, habet pennas. Ibi conditio volandi est habere pennas. Conditio moralis est fundamentum a qua suspenditur obligatio alterius erga alterum" [(...) Moral condition is the ground in force of which the obligation of someone toward another one is suspended].

[45] See in AA, VI, I, NM, II, § 14[a], "Moralitas autem, seu Justitia, vel Injustitia actionis oritur, ex qualitate personae agentis in ordine ad actionem, ex actionibus preacedentibus orta, quae dicitur Qualitas moralis. Ut autem Qualitas realis in ordine ad actionem duplex est: Potentia agendi, et necessitas agenda; ita potentia moralis dicitur Jus, necessitas moralis dicitur Obligatio." [Morality, that is, the justice or injustice of an act, derives however from the quality of the acting person in relation to the action springing from previous actions, which is described as moral quality. But just as the real quality is twofold in relation to action: the power of acting, and the necessity of acting; so, the moral power is called right, the moral necessity is called obligation.].

conditionum; namely, whether the Euclidean method has been correctly applied to the subject matter dealt with in the book. However, we must first clarify what the Euclidean method constitutes. Sofia Vanni Rovighi (1908-1990) explained it masterfully.[46] It is, in essence, an *inductive investigative procedure* to which Leibniz conforms in his treatise to achieve the goal of "ordering opinions [of the Roman jurists reported in the Digest, e.n.] in the most certain and almost mathematical demonstrations"[47] (*Proemio*). In Definition 9 of chapter I, he declares, "We will also observe, always this rule, to add to the definitions, that is to the explanation of the terms, theorems or demonstrable rules based on the definitions".

After reading the work, we can conclude that, at least formally, the Euclidean method is respected. Therefore, it represents a novelty in the treatment of conditions in the legal field. However, it is necessary to verify whether the form corresponds to the substance of a correct application of the same method and whether the opinions of the veteran jurists are suitable for

[46] Sofia Vanni Rovighi (1908-1990), *Istituzioni di filosofia.*, (Brescia, 2015), p. 31.

> For the ancients, for Aristotle [384 BC or 383–322 BC] in species, there is only one kind of scientific knowledge. Aristotle distinguishes yes, in the sixth book of METAPHYSICS, three theoretical sciences: physics, mathematics and theology (rational theology, that is, metaphysics), these are three degrees of a single knowledge, distinguished on the basis of the minor or major abstraction. And when Aristotle in the Second Analytical describes the process of scientific knowledge, *he has as a model the process of geometry - of that geometry which will then become part of the Elements of Euclid* [330 BC? - 275a.C.?] -. *Scientific knowledge is an "if" demonstrated*, and the proof must start from real immediate propositions, universal and necessary: *axioms*. The axioms in turn are based on *definitions, that is on the concepts that we derive from experience*. The procedure is therefore *from experience to definition, from this to the axiom, from the axiom to the theorem, that is to the proven conclusion. Process that gives rise to a fully successful science: Euclidean geometry*. (italics added; e. t.)

[47] See note 2 above.

being ordered in "certain and almost mathematical demonstrations".

It seems that this is not possible because the Roman jurist does not follow the analytical method, but instead employs a topical approach to solve the cases presented to him. That is, he does not start from premises to infer consequences but rather compares situations to find a balance in the proportional exchange of values between the involved parties.[48]

[48] For example, among many, D.35.1. *De condicionibus et demonstrationibus et causis et modis eorum, quae in testament scribuntur (Conditions, designations, causes, ways in which they are found in the provisions written in the will).* 73 Papinian, *in the nineteenth book of Questions*: A testator bequeathed a property to Titius under the condition that he does not go to Asia, and he also bequeathed the same property to Sempronius if he goes to Asia. Just as in all conditions that end with the death of the legatee, it has been established that the Mucian bond be provided, so the heir received this bond from Titius and gave him the property. If Titius then went to Asia, the heir will be compelled, through an equitable action, to provide Sempronius with everything he can obtain through the stipulated bond. However, if the bond becomes void in the meantime, even though it was exacted with the utmost diligence, the heir will not be obliged to pay from his own funds. But if he is not at fault and the bond has failed, it will be sufficient for him to provide his own remedies. Furthermore, if Sempronius died after Titius went to Asia but before receiving the bequest, the heir would have to pay to his heir what the deceased could have claimed. D.30. *De legatis et fideicommissis (Legacies and fideicommissa).*12 Pomponius, *in the third book to Sabinus*: If the same thing has been bequeathed to me and to you, and then I, after the moment when the legacy became due to me, have become your heir due to your death, Labeo asserts that there is freedom for me to acquire what has been bequeathed to me based on the legacy left to me or based on the fact that I am your heir. If I wish to own that thing based on the legacy left to me, I can request it under the hereditary legacy to make it entirely mine. 17 Ulpian, *in the fifteenth book to Sabinus*: If someone left a legacy to his daughters, and in some part of the will, he mentioned a posthumous child, it is considered that he has also included the posthumous child in the legacy to the daughters. If someone has bequeathed as follows: "if I have a daughter, my heir shall give her one hundred," and several daughters are born, it is considered that he has bequeathed the same to each of them, unless there is clear evidence of a contrary intention of the testator. 104 Julian, *in the first book to Urseius Ferox*: It was bequeathed upon all the heirs as follows: "Whoever becomes my heir shall be obliged to give one hundred to Titius." Later on, it was stated that one of the heirs should not give him anything. The question arises whether the other heirs should give the full amount of one hundred, or whether they should give the amount deducted from the hereditary share of that one. <Julian> replied that it was truer that the other heirs should give the full one hundred, both because the meaning of the words does not con-

Leibniz does not seem to realize that the Roman legal system is a complex array of solutions tailored to individual problems,[49] making it irreducible to a unified system. The jurists employed the topical method, where the syllogism starts from premises that are treated as true opinions[50] in relation to specific cases.[51] As a result, the conclusions, as seen in passages from the Authors reported in the Digest, sometimes appear trivial.[52]

Attempts to reduce various opinions on a given topic to a common factor may serve for the purpose of "ordering", but they cannot establish a valid theoretical rule indefinitely, as the Digest often presents contradictions on the same case, as pointed out by Leibniz himself.[53] It is essential to note that the Roman

tradict this opinion and because it is in line with the testator's intention.

[49] Luigi Raggi (1930-1968), Alessandro Mancinelli (ed.), *Il metodo della giurisprudenza romana.* [The method of Roman jurisprudence], (Torino, 2007), p. 32-33; previously in *Scritti* (Milano, 1975), pp. 165-254.

[50] Aristoteles (384–322 BC), Graece, *ΤΟΠΙΚΩΝ Α.*, ex recensione Immanuelis Bekkeri. Edidit Academia Regia Borussica, I (Berolini, apud Reimerum, 1831), 100 "ένδοξα δ'ὴ τὰ δοκοῦντα πᾶσιν 'ὴ τοῖς πλείστοις 'ὴ τοῖς σοφοῖς, καὶ τούτοις 'ὴ πᾶσιν 'ὴ τοῖς πλείστοις 'ὴ τοῖς μάλιστα γνωρίμοις καὶ 'ενδόξοις", A. Zadro, in *Aristotle. Topica,* It. tr., intr. and comment by Zadro himself, (Napoli, 1974), I, 100 b 21-23, p. 83, points out the following translations, ft. 3 to the quoted passage, p. 309,"ex endoxon, Pickad-Cambridge from opinions that are generally accepted, Tricot de premisses probable, Forster from generally accepted opinions.".

[51] Raggi, note 49 above, p. 55, states, "The argumentative scheme, the topos, always works closely with these figures. It is not an abstract mechanism that can be used in various ways. Instead, the topos always operates in conjunction with these typifications of legal reality and is 'colored' precisely by their presence." (e.t.).

[52] D.18.6.8.1 [D.18.6. *De periculo et commodo rei venditae (Risk and benefit of the thing sold).* 8 Paul, *in the thirty-third book to the Edict*: 1. If a sale of this kind was made: "that slave is bought whether the ship has arrived from Asia or not," Julian considers the sale to be immediately valid, because it is certain that it has beenc ontracted.].

[53] See, e.g., infra, Theorem 49 (Chap. VIII); Theorem 68, (Chap. X).

jurists lacked normative premises from which they could derive case solutions.[54]

Regarding the correct application of the Euclidean method, it is evident that, in many cases, the answer is negative. Simple observations confirm this. For instance, Teorem 30 (Chap. V) ["A part of a condition orderly conjunctive or disjunctive, disorderly fulfilled does not lighten the burden of the condition"] is contradicted by the final "demonstration": "When a partial payment is allowed, it does not divide the disposition, but, however, it lightens the condition, see D.40.7.3.5". A theorem, in itself, cannot have exceptions; otherwise, it would cease to be a theorem.

Likewise, in Theorem 68 (Cap. X), Leibniz acknowledges the evidence of the contradiction between the norms: "[...] The Doctors derive this argument *a contrario sensu* (argument from the contrary), which often leads to antinomies, but indirect authority is of no importance as it yields to direct authority".

[54] Raggi, see note 49 above, pp. 39-40,
The concept of law, in the sense of a general and abstract norm, is something unknown to primitive societies; it represents a more evolved stage in the history of human thought. In primitive societies, the common focus is essentially on the pronouncement of particular cases, the judicial pronunciation, or "legem dicere." This original meaning of the law has little to do with the modern understanding of law as a result of a certain procedure, within the competence of specific organs, and containing general and abstract precepts.
Initially, legislative activity itself, in many cases, lacked the characteristics of generality and abstractness: the most recent types of legislative activity can be traced back to the consideration of particular cases. This suggests an interpretation of the historical origin of the law as arising precisely from "legem dicere," the pronouncement on particular cases. This intermediate phase is exemplified, for instance, by the legislative activity of *the comitia curiata*, the *lex de imperio*, the *adrogatio*, and the *testamentum calatis comitiis*. These are all acts that can be categorized as law, yet they still pertain to specific cases.
The reason for this characterization of Roman legal speculation as essentially casuistic may be rooted in various components of cultural, social, and ethnological order. However, delving into this discourse is beyond our current limits, as it involves imagination and a broad exploration.

In such cases, the "calculation of the rule" is not possible. In formulating Theorem 27_1, Chapter V (as seen in the translated text below), Leibniz reduced the provisions of D.30.33, 79, 85; D.31.88.6; D.32.80; D.45.1.56 to Celso's sentence:[55] "The odds are determined by the competition of the parties" (*concursu parte fiunt*). However, this is a mediocre operation, considering that the formula *concursu parte fiunt* had been firmly established as a maxim and was never doubted by anyone unless the testator had disposed of it differently.

The next demonstration is more "critical" from a gnoseological perspective. Leibniz claims that the theorem in question was "subtly deduced by the ancient jurisconsults from the same natural law"[56], but he fails

[55] D.32.80. [D.32. *De legatis et fideicommissis (Legacies and fideicommissa)* 80. Celsus, *in the thirty-fifth book of the Digests*: Being appointed heirs jointly or receiving a legacy jointly means this: that the entire inheritance or all the legacies are attributed to each, while the shares are determined by their concurrence.].

[56] Pol Boucher, *Gottfried Wilhelm Leibniz. Doctrina conditionum* (Paris: Institut M. Villey, 1998), Presentation, p. 10, ft. 18, cites a letter to Hobbes dated July 13/22, 1670, where Leibniz writes: "...above all, I dare to assert that half of Roman law is pure natural law and that it is evident that almost all of Europe uses this law when it has not been expressly overridden by local customs."; p. 11, Boucher himself notes how "Roman positive law and its natural law roots are inseparable in the eyes of Leibniz because they come from the same source and complement each other.".
About the natural law in general, Leibniz writes in the NM, "The principles of decision-making are reason based on natural law and similarity based on certain civil law" (NM, II, §. 70). He places natural law, which he continues to claim has a divine foundation, among the sources of law (NM, II, §§. 75). In an attempt to reconcile the speculative results of Grotius and Hobbes, particularly concerning what Leibniz refers to as the third degree of natural law, namely rigid right (the other two being *aequitas* - equity - and piety, NM, II, §. 73), he organically reconstructs the principles of the latter. This reconstruction is driven by a disenchanted pragmatism regarding the verification of primitive human instincts (aggression and self-defense) that support such principles. Let us now turn to the Author for further insights

> The rigid or pure law derives from the intrinsic the definition of the terms, and if assessed, it can be seen to be nothing other than the law of war and peace. In fact, between person and person the law of peace is in force, as long as the other does not begin the war or engage in harmful conduct. Between person and thing, however, there is a perpetual law of war, because a thing has

to specify the precise "norm" of natural law from which the theorem would have been derived. Instead, Leibniz invented this norm of natural law from scratch, positing that the contest of parties contains a certain physical principle arising from the nature of motion.

Leibniz then applies, *a posteriori* and seemingly arbitrarily, the laws of motion of bodies to the juridical competing forces of each person entitled to the same good. In one context (*Doctrina*), these forces on a good (whether movable or immovable) physically push

> no intelligence. And it is lawful for a lion to tear a man and for a mountain to crush a man by a landslide; equally, it is lawful for a man to restrain a lion, break down a mountain. But the victory of a person over a thing and the captivity of the thing is called possession. Thus, possession endows the person with a right over the thing, by law of war, provided that the thing belongs to no-one. If, however, the thing belongs to someone, then no man is allowed to damage it or to appropriate it, any more than he is allowed to kill the slaves of others or give shelter to fugitives. Therefore, if one damages another either in his person or in his things, this gives him the same right as that which he has over a thing, namely, the right of war. And even malicious deception is counted among the species of damage, because the damage is inflicted on the mind, from which there derives the need for keeping promises. It is therefore clear that the only true precept of natural law is: never injure, hurt, or damage anyone (*neminem laedere*); in this manner you will ensure that no person can claim the right of war against you. To this belongs commutative justice, and the right that Grotius calls faculty. (NM, II, §. 73, e.t.).

The theologically grounded divine foundation of natural law will be reiterated by the same Leibniz in the preface to the *Codex iuris gentium diplomaticus*, (Hannover, 1693) pp. 9-10: "Now from this source [of the Christian precepts of universal justice, e.n.] natural law springs forth, of which there are three degrees: strict right in commutative justice; equity (or charity in the strict sense) in distributive justice; and finally piety (or probity) in universal justice, from which the most general and common precepts of the Law descend: do no harm, give each one his due, live honestly (or piously).".

On the natural law in Leibniz thought, see Hubertus Busche (2015), Leibniz' Lehre von den drei Stufen des Naturrecht [Leibniz's Doctrine of the Three Levels of Natural Law], in Wenchao Li (Hg.), see note 35 above, p. 29; Stefanie Ertz (2015), *Pietas, Aequitas, Caritas*: Einige Bemerkungen zur Terminologie und historischen (Übergang-) von Leibniz' Naturrecht [*Pietas, Aequitas, Caritas*: Some Remarks on the Terminology and Historical (Transitional) Context of Leibniz's Natural Law], ibid., p. 69.

forward until bisecting the angle derived from uniform and contrary thrusts. In another context (*De casibus perplexis*),[57] concerning possession of a movable good, such as a jar grabbed by opposed handles, the same opposite forces push backward. According to Leibniz, the resultant of these equal and opposing forces would be the "stasis" of the body, meaning it would remain in equilibrium even in the event of abandonment by one of the two contenders. Doubts, however, remain about the detachment of the force impressed in the opposite direction on the jar by the rival, potentially causing the other to fall backward due to the backlash. Ultimately, the logical-mathematical argument supporting the theorem and its practical benefits to the right are not entirely clear.

Our graduate student, unable to "close the circle", is forced to resort to *aequitas* (equity).[58] He chooses the

[57] AA VI, 1, §. XXV, p. 248.

[58] On the concept of *aequitas* in Roman law, see Adolf Berger note 38 above, *ad vocem Aequitas*, "Related to justice (*iustitia, iustum*) but distinguished from the positive law, *ius*. One of the fundamental principles which direct or should direct the development of law; it is the corrective and creative element in such development. A law which is guided by *aequitas* is *ius aequum*, its antonym is *ius iniquum*. In the legal sphere *aequitas* may be realized either by interpreting the existing law or by supplementing it where an exact legal provision is missing."; Leibniz considers equity the first degree of natural law (NM, II, §. 73); but about this judgment rule, some years later, with greater disenchantment, Lodovico Antonio Muratori (1672-1750), *Dei difetti della Giurisprudenza*. [On the Defects of Jurisprudence], (Venezia, 1742), pp. 102-103,

> Secondly, *Judges should not murder Justice with the pretext of equity*. It is certain that in Christian courts, equity must prevail, its dominion being so extensive that Giulio Cesare Calvino wrote a vast Tome about it. Its strength and authority are such that it sometimes moderates laws, reforms wills, abolishes contracts, and brings the wishes and actions of people into the best possible proportion.
> However, since most things established or permitted in the world have their right and their reverse, the privilege of equity, justly granted to Judges, can easily be abused, leading to the detriment of Justice itself. There have been, and always will be, those who, by virtue of their position in the courts, believe they are above all laws and contracts because they can judge according to equity.
> In their hands, every last will, every contract, every pact is in danger. While it may be true that a person intended something,

case of Theorem 49 (Chap. VIII), according to which, "Heir and legatee can collude in fraud of the honored, unless the last is co-heir". He admits that

> We cannot provide a reason for this theorem because, if we consider strict law, there seems to be no privilege for the coheir in this regard. However, I believe that equity (*aequitas*) should provide assistance even to an outsider (*extraneus*). But this is how it was deemed right by the Jurisconsult. Consider the following scenario: The testator wrote: "My heir must give 100 to Titius if Titius gives 50 to Maevius". Titius and the heir make an agreement in which the legatee returns the bequest to the heir and, for another reason or pretext, they stipulate that 80 should be given to Titius unconditionally, disregarding the original condition. In this way, the heir gains 20, and Titius gains 30. The question arises whether Maevius has any remedy against this stratagem. The answer is no, as stated in D.35.1.57, where it is considered a wise action (this is similar to what Christ said, that the sons of the world are wiser in their generation than the sons of light). The situation is different when a coheir is involved D.40.7.3.4. However, D.12.4.3.9 contradicts this idea. In that law, an *actio in factum* is granted

these esteemed individuals may assert that the person should have intended and acted differently, imposing their judgment in the end. This is an evil that must be added to the other inconveniences of the courts, as it makes Jurisprudence more uncertain, and its Judgments doubtful, ultimately undermining Justice entirely.
To interpose equity to lessen the rigor of penalties in the majority of cases is commendable. To aid the deceived, to lead the contracts of the ignorant back to good faith, to establish dowries, maintain fair wages, and rectify missing formalities, along with similar equitable provisions, are all praiseworthy actions.
However, when in many other cases, the Judge believes they are allowed to reform the written law and acts using unwritten fairness, simply because it seems better or more appropriate to do so, this is no longer equity but rather iniquity. It becomes a remedy that turns into poison." [italics added; e.t.].

to the injured party against the heir, without making any distinction based on greater equity. As for reconciling these laws, let others work on that.

The final sentence ("But the D.12.4.3.9 contrasts, etc...") disavows the theorem: if the contrast between norms is irremediable, then even here the theorem does not hold. A theorem, by definition, as already observed, does not admit exceptions.[59] The medieval rule of "distinction" ("unless, etc.") is not overcome.

Another maxim reduced to theorem is "Legitimate acts are unconditionable" (Theorem 52, Chapter VIII). The entire theorem is encompassed in D.50.17.77, which states: "Legal acts which do not involve a day or a condition, such as emancipation, acceptilation, entry into an inheritance, option on a slave, grant of tutor are entirely vitiated by the addition of a time or a condition. [....]". The purpose of constructing such a theorem based on explicit and unequivocal statements contained in the law itself may seem redundant. The theoretical phrase merely summarizes other statements of equal significance found in the law, thus not providing any new demonstration; rather, it serves to acknowledge that in some cases, the law dictates so.

In the demonstration of Theorem 67 (Chapter X), common sense is employed instead of logical-formal arguments:

[59] With reference to the theorems in the *Ars Combinatoria,* Manuel Antonio Correia, ft. 19, states:

> Although the definitions may not have all the axiomatic articulations that we would expect today, it is undeniable that Leibniz accomplishes his fundamental mission. The theorems, on their part, are presented almost as corollaries of the solution to the proposed problems, and it is natural that, in this strict sense, *many of them cannot be defined as theorems* (emphasis added). In reality, what Leibniz calls a theorem here is the reason (τὸ διότι) for the solution to the proposed problem... (e.t.).

Another essential aspect in evaluating a conditional right is the conditioned factor. Here, the rule is that all other things being equal, a conditional right is greater when the conditioned factor is more significant. For example, suppose there are two bequests: If the ship comes from Asia, I leave a legacy of 100 to Seius and 200 to Caio. It is evident that Caio's right is greater, although it is possible that the difference in the conditions may make a conditioned factor with a higher nominal value of lesser practical value. For instance, consider two more legacies: I leave a legacy of 100 to Titius if he ascends to Capitolium, and I leave a legacy of 200 to Caio if my cousin, captured by Tripolitanians, returns. In this case, I affirm that the legatee of Titius is greater than that of Caio.

Logic of the Doctrina conditionum *and Its Place in Juridical Work of Leibniz: omparison with the Nova Methodus: The Former Inductive, the Latter Deductive*

In the NM, written two years after *De conditionibus I* and *II*, Leibniz revisited the theme of using logic to settle disputes regarding rights. Without repeating what was already written in the two prefaces, to which the reader is referred, in my Italian and English translations of the NM,[60] Leibniz, in NM, II, §56 stated: "We, however, by abstraction, have thus summarized the universals,[61] so that it is permissible to derive all the laws of the title based on our rules." [62].

60 See note 33 above.

61 From the 78 *leges* of which the third title of the third book of the *Digest* is composed, D. 3.3. *De procuratoribus et defensoribus*.

62 Already in his degree dissertation (*De casibus perplexis in jure*, see note 21, above), Leibniz introduces the essential idea that doubtful cases can be solved by a logical calculation of juridical statements, although

Having established the "system" in principle, one can move from inductive to deductive logic to resolve the dispute. However, apart from an admirable synthesis of the procurator's discipline (NM §56), Leibniz did not provide any example of logical-mathematical calculation of the norm or illustrate his theory of legal inferences with examples, as pointed out by one of the founders of deontic logic, George Kalinowski (1929-2000).[63] This is what the practitioner jurist, judge, lawyer, or notary would expect and legitimately ask to find in the text, including "innovative" indications even with respect to classical logic, after reading such statements of intent. In this booklet, instead, the rules of logic essentially refer to the good old Aristotelian syllogism[64] and the

he does not fully achieve this goal. In the *Dissertatio de arte combinatoria* (see note 19, above), *Probl. II, 40,* he states "Elementa juris in eius corpore continetur" (The elements of law are contained in its body). Furthermore, in a letter dated 1696 to Gabriel Wagner, he reiterates that "By logic or the art of reasoning I understand the art of using the understanding not only to judge proposed truth but also to discover hidden" (Leibniz to Gabriel Wagner, 1696) in Leroy Earl Loemker (1900-1985) (ed.), *Leibniz, Philosophical Papers and Selected Letters* (Dordrecht, Boston, London, 1989), p. 463.

[63] George Kalinowski, "La Logique juridique de Leibniz " in *Studia Leibnitiana* (1977) Band IX / 2, p. 187, points out that in NM, as well as in other juvenile juridical works, "Leibniz n'a pas illustré sa théorie des inferences juridiques par des exemples" and nevertheless he believes that

> Si l'on laisse de côté le einseignement d'Aristote sur le syllogisme practique, einsegnement plutôt philosophique que Logique, et quelques idées de détails touchant directement ou indirectement à la Logique des normes qu'on trouve chez de certains auteurs du l'antiquitè et du moyen **âge**, Leibniz apparaît, à la lumière de nos connaissance historique actuelle (...), comme l'auteur d'une premier ébauche de la logique des normes, ébauche assez avancée puisque comportant deux parties: la théorie de l'opposition des normes et le modèles aléthiques, comme on les appelle depuis An essay in modal logic de G. H. von Wright, Amsterdam 1951.

See also George Kalinowski, Jean-Louis Gardies (1925–2004), "A logicien déontique avant la lettre Gottfried Wilhelm Leibniz", in *Archiv für Rechts und Sozialphilosophie* (1974), pp. 60-79 ss.

[64] In NM, I, §22, Leibniz stated, in adherence to Aristotle 's Organon scheme, that "topics and analytics are included in the single lemma of logic".

loci[65] by Quintilian. Leibniz did indeed mention logic and metaphysics (NM, II, §50), reconciliation of the antinomies (NM, II, §51), and "interpretation of the law" (§52), but he did not specifically or extensively delve into these topics. He provides the reader with nothing more than a bibliography on the subject, warning that the authors he quoted, François Hotman (1524-1590), Johann Thomas Freige (1543-1583), and above all Martin Schickard (1579-1636), treat "certain philosophical rules that must be respected in law, but which are commonly mixed inappropriately with the rules of law" (NM, II, §50). Moreover, in the *Preface* he invited the reader

> to bear in mind that everything we will say must be done or learned; in no way have we ourselves done or said those things; far from us this presumption, since long ago we had no knowledge of it; but believe me that we have acted as the whetstone that sharpens the iron, but the same by itself has no power to cut.

In this work too, the promises of the *calculemus* remain wishful thinking.

[65] Quintilian (35-100 A.D.) *Institutio Oratoria* in Donald Andrew Russel (ed.), *Quintilian, The Orator's Education* (Cambridge MA, London: Harvard University Press, 2001), pp. 5, 10, 20,

> Let us now investigate the Places where Arguments are found, though some hold that these are identical with the topics I have just been discussing. By 'Places' I do not mean what are nowadays commonly meant by loci, namely set pieces against luxury, adultery and the like, but the areas in which Arguments lurk and from which they have to be drown.

Heinrich Lausberg (1912-1992), in David E. Orton, R. Dean Anderson (eds.), *Handbook of Literary Rhetoric: a Foundation for Literary Study*, (Leiden, 1998), p. 171:

> [loci] the formal analysis and classification of the argumenta presupposes the content of the arguments. It is precisely the task of rhetorical invention, however, to provide instructions for the discovery of ideas that correspond with the issue and the party, that is, for the discovery of the content.

Logic in Leibnizian Thought

If the NM with the *Doctrina Conditionum* constitutes an early attempt[66] to confer systematic order upon Roman law, and above all, if they are evidence of the importance that Leibniz attributed to the logic applied to law[67] as an indispensable tool for finding solutions to perplexing cases, then in the mature phase of his thought, the Philosopher undertook a significant rethinking of the function of logic in general. In the Letter to Gabriel Wagner (c. 1660-c. 1717),[68] he wrote that logic is "a bag full of good memories".[69]

Leibniz points out, however, that

> If logic is nothing but a bag full of good reminders, it is certainly not futile. I have no praise for the new logicians who condemn the old rather than improve it. It is not always in our power to find the truth when not enough data

[66] Antonio Padoa Schioppa, "Il giurista" [The Jurist], in Massimo Mori (ed.), *Leibniz e la cultura enciclopedica* [Leibniz and the Encyclopedic Culture], (Bologna, 2018), pp.174-177; Italo Birocchi, *Alla ricerca dell'ordine. Fonti e cultura giuridica nell'età moderna* [In Search of Order: Sources and Legal Culture in the Modern Age], (Torino, 2002), p. 211 ff.; as well as Adriano Cavanna (1938-2002), *Storia del diritto moderno in Europa* [History of Modern Law in Europe], 1., (Milano, 1982), p. 337 ff.

[67] The philosophical attitude in this regard has not changed today: "If a law is contradictory, everything that is done in relation to it is also contradictory - and it is also illegal, given that logic is the basis of law" [italics added], as stated by the philosopher Emanuele Severino (1929 –2020) in "Equivoci e rigore nei patti Lateranensi" [Misunderstandings and Rigor in the Lateran Pacts], *Corriere della Sera,* 26 May 2001. It is hardly necessary to add that in this context, the term "illegal" does not seem to be used in the conventional sense. Unfortunately, illogical rules, even when they exist, do not necessarily cease to be in force.

[68] Leibniz, note 51 above, p. 470. This is the original German text, in Carl Immanuel Gherardt (1816–1899), *Die Philosophischen Shriften von Leibniz* (Leipzig, 1931), VII, 526, Leibniz an Gabriel Wagner (1696): "15. Ist die Logick ein sackh voll guther erinnerungen, so ist sie ja nicht vergeblich. [...]".

[69] As evidenced by Luigi Mengoni (1922-2001) "Dogmatica giuridica" [Legal dogmatics] in by the same author, *Ermeneutica e dogmatica giuridica* [Hermeneutics and legal dogmatics], (Milan, 1996), p. 51.

are at hand, but we can always guard against error if we have time to think about a matter and to discover everything possible from the data—if we bring logic to full perfection. I have brought matters so far with my infinitesimal calculus of differences and sums that many problems can now be solved in mathematical physics which one could not even venture to try before. *Even when data are lacking, we can at least observe what data we do need*[70] (italics added).

Leibniz then turned his attention to constructing a logic of the probable, which was new in comparison to Aristotle's, but this "construction" likewise remained mere wishful thinking:[71]

In any case call it what you will, the study of the degrees of probability would be very valuable; we do not yet have such a study, and this a serious shortcoming in our logic text-books. For when one cannot definitively settle the question of whether P is the case or not, one could still establish how likely P is on the evidence, enabling one to form a reasonable opinion about which side—·P or not-P·—is the more plausible. And when our wisest moralists (I refer to the wisest among them, like the current general of the Jesuits[72]), bring in the question of what is

[70] Leibniz, note 51 above, p. 470.

[71] In the original French, the posthumous *Nouveaux Essais sur l'Entendement Humain*, published by Rudolf Erich Raspe (1736–1794) in, *Leibnitz's Oeuvres philosophiques Latines & François*. (Amsterdam and Leipzig, 1765). The *Nouveaux Essais* are now available in the critical edition by André Robinet (1922-2016) and Heinrich Schepers, AA VI, 6, IV, 2, §14, (1962, 1990, 2006), pp. 372-73. The following quote is from the English translation by Peter Remnant and Jonathan Bennet (eds.), titled Leibniz: *New Essays on Human Understanding* (Cambridge 1996).

[72] In the original French text, the sentence in brackets is omitted by the English translators (see note 71, above). The "current" General of the Jesuits referred to by Leibniz is Tyrso Gonzalez (1624–1705) *Synopsis Tactatus Teologici de Recto usu Opinionum Probabilium, cui accessit logistica*

probabilitatum [Synopsis of the Theological Treatise on the Correct Use of Probable Opinions, with the addition of the logistics of probabilities.] (Tyrnaviae, 1696), §XX, pp. 83-85,

> If a merchant were to ask me whether it is permissible for him to enter into such a contract or not, I cannot respond: 'It is permissible.' Because in doing so, I would affirm by this very statement that it is absolutely permissible, which I absolutely believe to be usury; and I would lead him to do something that I consider to be evil and prohibited. This would be an entirely illicit act. It is not enough that a probable opinion exists, affirming that the contract is permissible; because as long as I do not approve of that opinion, I cannot act or give advice according to it. To prove that the contrary opinion is probable indeed proves that its proponents, and all those who consider it to be true, can act and give advice according to it; however, not those who disapprove of it and reject it as false. For above all, to absolutely affirm outwardly as permissible what I judge inwardly to be absolutely illicit is a lie, which is intrinsically illicit, as it is contrary to the commerce and society of humans. Furthermore, to induce someone to do what is gravely prohibited by the law of God is a serious sin. And although I do not know with certainty and evidence that such a law exists, I judiciously believe it exists, and I am convinced of it [...]. Therefore, in the said case, I must either absolutely respond that the contract is not permissible, or at least say: Indeed, there are doctors who affirm that this contract is permissible; however, I believe their opinion to be false, and therefore I cannot absolutely tell you that this contract is permissible, because I consider it illicit. Consult other scholars; if they affirm it to be permissible, and you prudently believe so, you can embrace their opinion rather than being deceived by me. [*Si mercator a me roget, an sibi liceat talem contractum celebrare, non-possum respondere: Licet: quia hoc ipso affirmarem, esse absolute licitum, quod absolute censeo esse usuram; et inducere illum ad faciendum, quod iudico esse malum, et prohibitum: quae res est omnino illicita. Nec sufficit, quod detur sententia probabilis affirmans, illum contractum esse licitum; quia quamdiu illa sententia a me non approbatur, non possum secundum illam operari, et consilium dare. Sententiam contrariam esse probabilem, probat quidem, Suos Authores, et omnes, qui illam veram esse existimant, posse secundum illam operari et consilium dare; non autem eos, qui illam improbant, et ut falsam rejiciunt. In primis enim absolute affirmare exterius ut licitum, quod interius judico esse absolute illicitum est mendacium quod est intrinsece illicitum, utpote contrarium commercio et societati hominum. Deinde inducere ad faciendum, quod lege Dei est graviter prohibitum, est grave peccatum. Et quamvis ego non cognosca certo & evidenter talem legem existere, tamen prudenter judico existere, idque mihi persuasum habeo [...]. Quare in dicto casu, vel debeo absolute respondere, non esse licitum illum contractum, vel saltem dicere: Dantur quidem doctores affirmantes contractum istum esse licitum; caeterum ego illorum falsam esse existimo sententiam, ac proinde tibi absolute respondere ego non possum, esse licitum istum contractum; quia censeo illicitum. Tu alios doctiores consule; si illi affirmaverint esse licitum, & tu prudenter censeas, me potius quam illos decipi, eorum sententiam amplecti poteris.*].

> even put safety ahead of probability *thus they are not really abandoning the most probable.* For here the question of safety is the question of the improbability of an impending evil. Moralists who are lax about this have gone wrong largely because they have had an inadequate and *unduly-narrow notion of probability,* which they have confused with Aristotle's "*acceptability*": in his Topics Aristotle aimed only to conform to the opinions of other people, so that for him what is "acceptable" is ... *whatever is accepted by the greatest number of people or by the most authoritative people.* He *was wrong to restrict his Topics to that;* this approach meant that he only concerned himself there with accepted maxims, *most of them vague—as though he wanted to reason by means of nothing but old jokes and proverbs!* But probability or *likelihood is broader ·than that: it must be drawn from the nature of things;* and the opinion of weighty authorities is one of the things that can contribute to the likelihood of an opinion, but it does not produce the entire likelihood by itself. At the time when Copernicus was almost alone in his opinion ·that the earth goes around the sun·, it was still incomparably more likely than the opinion of all the rest of humans, namely that the sun goes around the earth. I *suspect that establishment of techniques for estimating likelihoods would be more useful than a good proportion of our demonstrative sciences, and I have more than once thought of trying it* (italics added).

It is a different Leibniz who abandons the fashions and whims of his youth concerning the cases solution *more geometrico demonstrati*. However, given the remarks in *De Casibus Perplexis in jure* and in the NM, doubts arise: was he truly convinced?

Did Reformulation of De conditionum *I and II in the* Doctrina conditionum *Give Practical Benefits for the Correct Application of the Rules?*

Here, too, the answer is negative.[73] The results obtained by Leibniz through the reduction of conditions in the *ius commune* to Euclidean theorems are rather obvious.[74] In this respect, there is nothing new when compared to the interpretive elegance of other jurists of his time, to whom Leibniz paid deferential homage.[75] Similarly, the late medieval canonists, with their brilliant minds, seem to suggest solutions to famous "perplexing" cases, perhaps with a touch of subtle irony.[76]

[73] As highlighted by Alexandre Thiercelin, "On two Argumentative Uses of the Notion of Uncertainty in Law in Leibniz 's Juridical Dissertations about Conditions", in Marcelo Dascal (1949-2018) (ed.), *Leibniz: What Kind of Rationalist?*, (Dordrecht, Heidelberg, London, New York, 2008), p. 251.

[74] Alexandre Thiercelin, "Epistemic and practical Aspects of Conditionals in Dov M. Gabbay, Patrice Canivez, Shahid Rahman, Alexandre Thiercelin (eds.), *Leibniz 's Legal Theory of Conditions, Approaches to legal Rationality*, (Dordrecht, Heidelberg, London, New York, 2010), p. 211.

> Leibniz 's legal theory of conditions has *obvious* legal results [italics added]. Based upon the logical theory of conditionals, It provides many answers given by the Roman jurisconsults with 'very certain and almost mathematical demonstrations' Insofar as It provides them with general and systematic Reasons [italics added]. To put it more directly, Leibniz's logical approach to law enables him to make it notably more explicit.

[75] I am referring to "Mr. Carpzov [Benedikt Carpzov, 1595-1666] Of pious memory, the illustrious light of Saxon law here in Leipzig was extinguished a few months ago, to the greatest pain of all of us. (e.t.)", cite §. XX *De Casibus Perplexis in Jure* (note 21 above AA VI, p. 244), where the same L. cites the Carpzov's, *Jurisprudentia forensis romano-saxonica* (Francofurti, 1638).

[76] So much in the response of the Ostiense, Henricus de Segusio Hostiensis (1200-1271), *Henrici De Segusio Hostiensis, Iuris utriusque Monarchae Celeberrimi. In sexutm Decretalium librum Commentar*ia (Venetiis: Apud Iuntas 1581) 13-14, "De eo qui mittitur in possessionem causa rei servanda, n. 7 where the juridical solution on the dispute between two litigants about an ecclesiastical benefit, when neither of them proves his right fully or partially or in any other way; in that case: whereas that (...) neque tolerabilis est diuturna vacatio (...) quid ergo erit? Respondeo: Consulas Papam, quia in hoc casu non est expressum ius.". [nor a long

The most conspicuous result that Leibniz obtains is that of organizing the norms of the Digest related to the subject under discussion. As already pointed out,[77] Leibniz utilizes formal (here inductive) logic as a simple instrument of order, always aware that algebra serves to demonstrate that if a case is impossible, it remains so.[78] We have seen also that he acknowledges that Euclid method is not good in divine and human laws, because they depend on human will.[79] This awareness leads Leibniz to insist on *calculemus* in the juridical sphere in the *NM*, but with less conviction.

German doctrine[80] has undertaken the task of expressing Leibnizian "demonstrations" in logical symbols and demonstrates how it foreshadows many of the new logics developed in the twentieth century, but it remains unclear what practical advantages this operation brings to the interpreter for deciding cases.[81] For example, the Italian Civil Code, Article 2384, paragraph two, provides that: "The limitations on the powers of directors arising under the statutes or from a decision of the competent organs may not be relied on as against third parties, even if they have been disclosed, unless it is proven that these third parties have intentionally acted to the detriment of the company.".

suspension is tolerable [...] what will be, therefore, the norm? I answer: let consult the Pope because for this case there is no express norm].

[77] See note 36 above.

[78] See note 23 above.

[79] See note 34 above.

[80] Armgardt, note 27 above.

[81] Moreover, in descriptive terms, Amedeo G. Conte (1934-2019) discusses aspects of the relevance of Leibniz for today's deontic logic in Italian literature. In his work titled "Parega leibnitiana" in *Informatica e Diritto* (1978), n. 2, pp. 217-255, he particularly focuses on the so-called paradox of the rhetorian (pp. 227-231), which Leibniz addresses in §XVI of *De Casibus Perplexis in Jure* (AA VI, p. 241).

Do the limitations on the powers of directors, which the company cannot rely on as against third parties, also include acts that are beyond the company's purpose (*ultra vires* acts)? There are conflicting rulings from the Court of Cassation. Some interpret the Article to mean that a director can also perform an act outside the company's purpose with the prior unanimous consent of the assembly, and without the need for a statutory amendment to expand the corporate purpose in advance;[82] another ruling holds the opposite view.[83] Who is right? How can one "mathematically" determine which opinion is certain and compliant with the norm? Leibniz does not help, and this is precisely the assistance the jurist seeks: to know what the certain law is.

Relevance of the **Doctrina Conditionum** *as a Roman Law Course: The Absence of Dialogue Between Legal Philosophers and Professional Jurists*

Although Leibniz may not have fulfilled his promise to offer practitioners a secure method for deducing rules from the legal "system", he does, nevertheless, present us with an elegant synthesis of Justinian and Canon law concerning conditions in acts *mortis causa* and *inter vivos*. For this reason alone, it would be desirable for the *Doctrine* to be included in specialized university courses on Roman law focused on these subjects, serving as a guide for comparison with the current discipline in place. Having a comprehensive overview of ancient and modern law on this matter would "compensate" legal professionals for the perceived "shortcomings" of the Philosopher's work and the attempts to fit law within

[82] See, in this regard, Cass., 11 December 2006, no. 26325, in *Giur. It.*, 2007, 1437.

[83] Cass., 4 October 2010, no. 20597, in *RDS*, 2111, 1 ff., commentary by De Iuliis.

the frameworks of formal logic[84] (applied *a posteriori* to Leibniz's Doctrine),[85] for which we await practical guidance in crafting judgments or opinions that are "mathematically" certain. However, we must confront reality: the philosophy of law (including legal logic)[86] and positive law are two distinct sciences. This was well understood by Hegel, who imparts this understanding in his Philosophy of Right.[87]

Experience confirms the Hegelian insight: "every normative body is a complicated device ... and similar matters require *syntax-conscious* readers"

[84] I refer especially to George Kalinowski, *La logique des norms* (Paris: Presses universitaires de France 1972); Miguel Sánchez-Mazas (1925-1995), *Calculo de las normas* (Barcelona, 1973); Amedeo G. Conte (note 81).

[85] Schepers (note 39 above) Armgardt (note 27 above).

[86] Natalino Irti, *Un diritto incalcolabile* [An incalculable right] (Torino, 2016).

[87] Georg Wilhelm Friedrich Hegel (1770-1831), *Grundlinien der Philosophie des Rechts* (Berlin 1821); English translation, from which I quote, by Allen W. Wood (ed.) and H. B. Nisbet (transl.), *Hegel. Elements of the Philosophy of Right*, (Cambridge, 2003), pp. 26-27,

> According to the formal, non-philosophical method of the sciences, the first thing which is sought and required, at least for the sake of external scientific form, is the definition [essential element of theorems, e.n.]. The positive science of right cannot be much concerned with this, however, since its chief aim is to state what is the right and legal [*Rechtetns*], i.e. what the particular legal determinations are. This is the reason for the warning: 'omnis definitio in iure civili periculosa.'[D.50.17.202, in civil law all definitions are hazardous, e.n.]. And in fact, the more incoherent and internally contradictory the determinations of a [system of] right are, the less possible it will be to make definitions within it; for definitions should contain universal determinations, but in the present context, these would immediately make the contradictory element – in this case, what is unjust [*das Unrechtliche*] – visible in all its nakedness. Thus, in Roman law, for example, no definition of a human being would be possible, for the slave could not be subsumed under it; indeed, the status of the slave does violence to that concept. The definitions of 'property' and 'proprietor' would seem equally hazardous in many situations. - But the deduction of the definition may perhaps be reached by means of etymology, or chiefly by abstraction from particular cases, so that it is ultimately based on the feelings and ideas [*Vorstellung*] of human beings. The correctness of the definition is then made to depend on its agreement with prevailing ideas [*Vorstellungen*].

[emphasis added]. When it comes to interpretation, syntax remains the most valuable tool for practical application".[88] However, it assumes that "**the ideal** [for every interpreter, emphasis added] would be an apprenticeship guided by two principles. First: master the utilization of legal texts; knowing which articles are relevant to a case is already substantial progress. Second: convey all essential information using authentic language, employing concise and clear expressions; though it demands effort, the benefits are substantial".[89]

All this, while always bearing in mind that "once the words [of a norm] become part of the system, they interact with other words, forming an independent semantic cycle, detached from their authors",[90] and that "a legal rule cannot be comprehended by detaching it from the issue it was intended to address".[91]

Finally, there exists the possibility that the so-called "question of the just", which the positive jurist must address, may emerge. It takes the form of: "which among the conceivable solutions for the case, compatible with the letter of the law and the overarching logic of the system, is nearer to justice and better aligns with it".[92] These considerations are true also for Anglo-American legal systems to the extent that the law of these countries is increasingly filled with written rules and codes, and in this scenario, rhetorical argumentation becomes a significant factor.

[88] Franco Cordero, *Procedura Penale* [Criminal procedure] (Milano, 1993), Preface to the first edition.

[89] Cordero, note 88 above, p. 124 (e.t.).

[90] Cordero, note 88 above, p. 253 (e.t.); Cordero, note 3 above, p. 534 (e.t.).

[91] Italian Constitutional Court, Judgment of June 2, 1993, No. 207, drafting judge of the judgment Judge Mengoni, in *Foro it.*, 1994, I, 2034.

[92] Luigi Mengoni, "Interpretazione e nuova dogmatica", in *Ermeneutica ecc.*, note 69 above, pp. 79-81.

In any case, the problem of a legal calculation is utopian because the logic in law is and cannot be otherwise the "old" Aristotelian syllogism.[93] The real problem is: how to build the premises of the syllogism: "In particular, how the judge constructs the premises of the syllogism. What matters are, as always, only the premises, in the determination of which the judge is always 'free'".[94] Logic remains, of course, an important tool of verification of the inherent consistency of the argument used to support the conclusion reached.[95]

The "New" Relevance of the Leibniz Doctrine

A recurring phenomenon is noticeable: we experience archetypal psychological flows that repeat cyclically in the development of law. This cycle embraces:

(a) axiomatic rules: initially, laws are based on clear, straightforward axioms. Examples include:

- The Code of Hammurabi: "6. If anyone steals the property of a temple or of the court, he shall be

[93] I see no other tool to check the consistency of a judgment, even though, according to the Nobel laureate in economics, 1978, Herbert Simon (1916-2001), "Aristotle is barely alive-and certainly his scientific works are not, and his logic hardly." Id. *The reason in human affairs* (Stanford, 1983), p. 33, whose reading has also made me aware that "There is a final difficulty, first pointed out by Godel, that rich systems of logic are never complete-there always exist true theorems that cannot be reached as outputs by applying the legal transformations to the inputs." (ibid. 7).

[94] Guido Calogero (1904-1986), *La logica del giudice e il suo controllo in Cassazione* [The logic of the judge and its review in the Court of Cassation] (Padova, 1964), p. 99, but diffusely.

[95] Theodor Viehweg (1907–1988), *Topik und Jurisprudenz* (Frankfurt am Main, 1953); English translation by W. Cole Durham Jr. (Frankfurt am Main, New York, 1993), from which I quote: "On closer consideration of dialectical inferences, which as we have seen are the subject matter of Topics, we recognize the following: such as inferences cannot be differentiated from apodictic inferences in a formal sense (...). Dialectical inferences differ from the other types, rather—and this characterizes the entire way of thinking— according to the nature of their premises.".

put to death, and also the one who receives the stolen thing from him shall be put to death";[96]

- The Ten Commandments: "16. Thou shalt not bear false witness against thy neighbor";[97]
- The Twelve Tables of Rome: "Table VI. Ownership and Possession: 1. When a person makes a bond and conveyance, according as he specified with his tongue so shall be the law";[98]

(b) rules based on explanations: over time, laws evolve to include explanations and reasons behind them, reflecting a deeper understanding and rationalization. Examples include:

- Roman-Justinian Law:[99] laws were elaborated with comprehensive explanations and commentaries; for example, C.8.17.*Qui potiores in pignore habeantur* [Who are preferred creditors when property is pledged].12,[100]

[96] *The Code of Hammurabi* (1755–1750 BC) Translated by L. W. King (available online).

[97] The ten commandments Exodus 20: 3-17. The proposed dates range from the 15th century BCE, according to a traditional interpretation, to the 6th or 5th century BCE, according to a modern critical interpretation. The dating of the Book of Exodus is a topic of considerable debate among scholars, see about Michael D. Coogan (ed.), *The Oxford History of the Biblical World* (Oxford 2001).

[98] The twelve tables (451-450 BC) the earliest attempt by the Romans to create a code of law (available online).

[99] Code of Justinian (529-534) (available online).

[100] C.8.17.*Qui potiores in pignore habeantur* [Who are preferred creditors when property is pledged.].12, «*Imperator Justinianus* . We are continually annoyed by the persistent applications of women who complain that they have lost their dowries because the property of their husbands has been seized by creditors whose claims are prior to their own. 1. Hence, we have examined the ancient laws, and, with reference to personal actions, find that the *Actio rei uxoriae,* which we have abolished, was granted by them to the wife, and that they conferred the great privilege of precedence over all other personal actions, as well as over other creditors, even though the claims of the latter were prior in point of time. 2. And, while this related to personal actions, when these laws came to discuss the hypothecary action, they at once relaxed the severity of justice

- Canon Law: following the structure of Roman law, Canon law often included a normative part preceded by the "ratio", explaining why certain behaviors were made obligatory, for example, X. V. 24, 1[101]; Constitution "Cum inter nonnullos"[102]:

and excluded the recent hypothecations of women, if they had any rights of action, in favor of creditors who held prior ones, without having any regard to the weakness of the sex, and the fact that husbands made use of their wives' bodies, property, and entire lives, since almost the entire fortune of a woman is included in her dowry. 3. It was proper to decree that husbands should satisfy their creditors out of their own property, and not out of the dowries of their wives, as a woman possesses the dowry for the purpose of her subsistence, whether it was given by herself or by someone else for her benefit. 4. (1) After having carefully examined and considered all these matters, as well as the other two Constitutions which we have promulgated concerning dowries, we, for the purpose of coming to the relief of women and to consolidate all these rules into one, hereby decree an action on the ground of stipulation, which we have already granted to women with reference to their dowries, and in favor of whom we have permitted a tacit hypothecation on the property of their husbands, as well as the preference over all other creditors of the latter, even though the said creditors may enjoy the advantage of priority of time.]

101 X [*Decretales Gregorii IX compilatio, sive Liber extravagantium* in *Corpus Iuris Canonici*, Aemilius Friedberg (1837-1910), pars secunda, (Graz, 1955). X. V. 24, 1, Although the prelates of churches are constituted by apostolic authority, and their excesses are frequently corrected by the apostolic see, some complain reasonably against them but cannot obtain justice unless they appeal to us.
We decree that if anyone has a complaint against their bishop or another ecclesiastical prelate, they shall bring it to the apostolic see and find justice there. And if a serious question arises against him that the ordinary judge cannot duly resolve, we will have it examined and decided by suitable men. (e.t.)

102 Constitution "Cum inter nonnullos" On the Error of the Spirituals Concerning the Poverty of Christ - Pope John XXII
November 12, 1323
1.Since among not a few scholarly men it often happens that there is called into doubt, whether to affirm pertinaciously, that Our Redeemer and Lord Jesus Christ and His Apostles did not have anything individually, nor even in common, is to be censured as heretical, diverse and opposite things being opined concerning it, We, desiring to put an end to this contest, after [having taken] the counsel of our brothers [the cardinals] by this perpetual edict do declare that a pertinacious assertion of this kind, when sacred scriptures, which assert in very many places that they had not a few things, expressly contradict it, and when it supposes openly that the same sacred scripture, through which certainly the articles of orthodox faith are proven in regards to the aforesaid things, contains the ferment of falsehood, and consequently, as much as regards these things, emptying all faith in them, it renders the Catholic Faith doubtful and

(c) return to axiomatic rules: legal reasoning often cycles back to a more axiomatic structure, emphasizing clarity and brevity. This can be seen in:

- The Napoleonic Codes (1804): Civil code, "Art. 711: La propriété des biens s'acquiert et se transmet par succession, par donation entre vifs ou testamentaire, et par l'effet des obligations." [The ownership of property is acquired and transmitted through succession, inter vivos donation, or testamentary, and by the effect of obligations].

Subsequent codifications in Austria (1811), Italy (1865), Japan (1898), Germany (1900), and Switzerland (1912).

(d) legislation based on explanations: currently, we are witnessing a return to laws that are heavily based on explanations and principles. An example is European Union law, which governs the legal systems of twenty-seven States:

uncertain, taking away its demonstration, is respectively to be censured erroneous and heretical.
2. Again to pertinaciously affirm in the preceding [matter], that the right to use would not by any means have pertained to Our aforesaid Redeemer [and] to His Apostles for those [things], which sacred scripture testifies they had had, or that they would not have had the right to sell or given them away, or on account of these [the right] to acquire them, which things nevertheless sacred scripture testifies that they did in regard to the aforesaid things, or supposes expressly that they could have acted thus, since such an assertion evidently would constrain that their use [of things] and their conduct, as regards the aforesaid things [were] not just, which certainly as regards the use, conduct or deeds of Our Redeemer, the Son of God, is wicked to opine, We do delcare, after [having taken] the counsel of our brothers [the cardinals], this pertinacious assertion to be deservedly censured as contrary to sacred scripture, inimical to Catholic doctrine, and heretical.
Certainly, therefore to no man it is lawful to infringe this page of our declarations, or by rash daring to oppose it. If anyone however [should do so, let him know that he has incurred the rath of the Omnipotent God and of His Apostles, Peter and Paul.]
Given at Avignon, two days before the Ides of November, in the Seventh year [of Our Pontificate]. [i.e. 1323 A.D.] (available online).

- Regulation (EU) 2020/852,[103] which includes detailed explanations to ensure clarity and coherence across member States.

Leibniz's doctrine is situated in the period when European civilization sought certain rules and therefore made attempts to extract *more geometrico* from the immense normative production of *ius commune*, in a way elaborating certain and logically undisputed

[103] Regulation (EU) 2020/852 of the European Parliament and of the Council of 18 June 2020 on the establishment of a framework to facilitate sustainable investment, and amending Regulation (EU) 2019/2088, in Whereas: (1) Article 3(3) of the Treaty on European Union aims to establish an internal market that works for the sustainable development of Europe, based, among other things, on balanced economic growth and a high level of protection and the improvement of the quality of the environment.
(2) On 25 September 2015, the United Nations General Assembly adopted a new global sustainable development framework: the 2030 Agenda for Sustainable Development (the '2030 Agenda'). The 2030 Agenda has at its core the Sustainable Development Goals (SDGs) and covers the three dimensions of sustainability: economic, social and environmental. The Commission communication of 22 November 2016 on the next steps for a sustainable European future links the SDGs to the Union policy framework to ensure that all Union actions and policy initiatives, both within the Union and globally, take the SDGs on board at the outset. In its conclusions of 20 June 2017, the Council confirmed the commitment of the Union and its Member States to the implementation of the 2030 Agenda in a full, coherent, comprehensive, integrated and effective manner, in close cooperation with partners and other stakeholders. On 11 December 2019, the Commission published its communication on 'The European Green Deal'.
3) The Paris Agreement adopted under the United Nations Framework Convention on Climate Change (the 'Paris Agreement') was approved by the Union on 5 October 2016 (3). Article 2(1)(c) of the Paris Agreement aims to strengthen the response to climate change by making finance flows consistent with a pathway towards low greenhouse gas emissions and climate-resilient development, among other means. In that context, on 12 December 2019, the European Council adopted conclusions on climate change. In light thereof, this Regulation represents a key step towards the objective of achieving a climate-neutral Union by 2050.
(4) Sustainability and the transition to a safe, climate-neutral, climate-resilient, more resource-efficient and circular economy are crucial to ensuring the long-term competitiveness of the Union economy. Sustainability has long been central to the Union project, and the Treaty on European Union and the Treaty on the Functioning of the European Union (TFEU) reflect its social and environmental dimensions.
Other 57 "whereas" follow before the actual regulatory text made up of 27 articles.
https://eur-lex.europa.eu/legal-content/EN/TXT/PDF/?uri=CELEX:32020R0852

principles. It is widely believed that Leibniz paved the way for dogmatics.[104] The present writer, on the other hand, is of the opinion that Leibniz's doctrine was better represented by the drafting of modern codes, particularly the Napoleonic codes, which are an example of great synthetic expressive elegance.[105]

Although it is true that Leibniz's doctrine, for the considerations expressed above, largely loses its effectiveness in the structure of modern codes, drafted in axiomatic terms, it regains great utility today *as a model for extracting rules* in the overwhelming normative production of the European Union and its member States, as well as in the federal legislation and that of each state of the United States of America. By way of example, we illustrate some possible application contexts of the Leibnizian model, obviously to be used *with the aid of AI.*

AI systems can be developed using Leibniz's logical methods to analyze legal texts and extract relevant rules and conditions, thereby assisting lawyers and judges in their work. At the same time, *AI* tools based on Leibniz's frameworks can enhance legal research by identifying and synthesizing relevant legal principles from vast databases of case law and statutes.

104 See note 19 above.

105 I would like to recall here the phrase that Stendhal wrote to Balzac: "En composant *La Chartreuse* pour prendre le ton, je lisais chaque matin deux ou trois pages du Code civil, afin d'être toujours naturel; je ne veux pas, par des moyens factices, fasciner l'âme du lecteur. Ce pauvre lecteur laisse passer les mots ambitieux, par exemple, le vent qui déracine les vagues; mais ils lui reviennent après l'instant de l'émotion. Je veux que si le lecteur pense au comte Mosca, il ne trouve rien à rabattre" Lettre de Stendhal à Balzac, Civitavecchia, 30 octobre 1840, *http://www.maremurex.net/stendhal2.html* [While composing The Charterhouse to capture the tone, I would read two or three pages of the Civil Code every morning, in order to always be natural; I do not want, through artificial means, to captivate the reader's soul. This poor reader lets ambitious words pass by, for example, the wind that uproots waves; but they return to him after the moment of emotion. I want that if the reader thinks of Count Mosca, he finds nothing to subtract.]

Utilizing Leibniz's Method from his Doctrina conditionum in Comparative Law

European civil law countries

The Leibniz doctrines can be particularly useful in a comparative milieu as an example to synthesize the immense feature of law. European Union law and national law, including in America, are increasingly shaped not by rigid categories but by overarching principles and values. This shift reflects a broader trend towards flexibility and adaptability in legal systems, addressing the complexities of modern society. For instance, the European Union legal framework often emphasizes principles like proportionality and the protection of fundamental rights, guiding both legislation and judicial decisions. Similarly, American law frequently revolves around principles such as equality and liberty, which underpin various doctrines and case law.

The capacity to derive specific rules from these broader principles is crucial in contemporary legislation. This skill involves identifying the rule necessary to safeguard a given value or principle. Modern legal education thus emphasizes critical and contextual thinking, preparing lawyers and judges to apply laws in a manner that aligns with underlying values. The traditional structure of legal rules, characterized by "if A, then B" (for example, if there is reciprocal consent, then there is a contract), is evolving. Now, actions such as forming a contract must also consider and uphold broader values, such as environmental protection.

For example, environmental laws often require businesses to align their practices with sustainability goals, integrating the principle of environmental stewardship into legal compliance. Environmental legislation, instead of merely prohibiting certain emissions, might require that business practices promote ecological sustainability. This approach demonstrates how modern laws are designed to address the broader social and economic impacts, ensuring that legal frameworks remain relevant and effective.

In Europe today, for example, companies face the challenge of reconciling CO2 reduction with human rights and business profitability.[106] How many tons of CO2 would one trade for a reduction of one unit of child labor? This kind of problem can be approached by systematically analyzing the conditions under which these interests coexist and conflict, leading to balanced and principled legal solutions. Of relevance is Article 1.3 of a European Parliament resolution regarding the Corporate Sustainability Due Diligence directive:[107] "If a provision of this Directive conflicts with a provision of another Union legislative act pursuing the same objectives and providing for more extensive or more specific obligations, the provision of that other Union legislative act shall prevail to the extent of the conflict and shall apply as regards those specific obligations".

[106] Regulation (EU) 2020/852, see note 81 above, Article *18* Minimum safeguards 1.The minimum safeguards referred to in point (c) of Article 3 [Article 3 Criteria for environmentally sustainable economic activities For the purposes of establishing the degree to which an investment is environmentally sustainable, an economic activity shall qualify as environmentally sustainable where that economic activity: (a) contributes substantially to one or more of the environmental objectives set out in Article 9 in accordance with Articles 10 to 16; (b) does not significantly harm any of the environmental objectives set out in Article 9 in accordance with Article 17; (c) is carried out in compliance with the minimum safeguards laid down in Article 18] shall be procedures implemented by an undertaking that is carrying out an economic activity to ensure the alignment with the OECD Guidelines for Multinational Enterprises and the UN Guiding Principles on Business and Human Rights, including the principles and rights set out in the eight fundamental conventions identified in the Declaration of the International Labour Organisation on Fundamental Principles and Rights at Work and the International Bill of Human Rights.

[107] European Parliament legislative resolution of 24 April 2024 on the proposal for a directive of the European Parliament and of the Council on Corporate Sustainability Due Diligence and amending Directive (EU),2019/1937, in *https://eur-lex.europa.eu/legalcontent/IT/TXT/?uri=CONSIL:ST_6145_2024_INIT*.

We thus return to a sort of *ius commune* and will probably be engaged in solving problems to determine which Union legislative act will prevail, thus highlighting the need for order. Leibniz provided a masterful example of order in addressing *ius commune* issues, organizing the legal conditions that were chaotically scattered in the *Corpus Juris* and canon law. Today, his example could only be replicated with the help of AI, which ultimately stems from the binary calculation devised by Leibniz.[108]

American legal system

The American legal system is characterized by a complex interplay of federal and state laws. Leibniz's heuristic model doctrine of conditions can help in:

- interpreting and reconciling laws: by providing a logical framework, Leibniz's approach can assist in interpreting and reconciling conflicts between federal and state laws, ensuring that legal principles are applied consistently.
- streamlining legal reasoning: legal practitioners can use Leibniz's method to systematically analyze and clarify complex legal issues, making the law more accessible and understandable.

Leibniz's emphasis on logical structure and coherence can improve judicial decision-making by:

- enhancing consistency: judges can use Leibniz's logical frameworks to ensure that their decisions are consistent with established legal principles and precedents.
- supporting detailed reasoning: Leibniz's approach can help judges articulate the conditions and reasoning behind their decisions more clearly, which is crucial for maintaining

108 Leibniz, "Explication de l'Arithmétique Binaire", in *Memoires de l'Academie Royale des Sciences* (1705), now in AA, VII, pp. 223-227.

the integrity of the judicial system and for setting clear precedents.

In all cases, keeping the Leibnizian model of data insertion and processing in mind to find the common thread that unites them or creates discrepancies can be truly useful. The same *Doctrine of Conditions,* if read alongside the passages from the *Digest* and the cited canonical decretals in their entirety (as done in the present translation), provides today's jurist with insights on how to harmonize and distill contemporary European and Anglo-American normative production into a few essential lines.

ABBREVIATIONS AND CAUTION TO READERS

AA VI, 1: Paulus Ritter (1872-1954), Willy Kabitz (1876-1942), and Heinrich Schepers (1925-2020) (eds.), *Leibniz, Philosophische Schriften.* Band 1: 1663-1672, (Berlin: Akademie Verlag, repr. 2006), pp. 369-430, the critical text of the *Doctrina conditionum* followed by the translation.

AA VI, 2: Paulus Ritter (1872-1954), Willy Kabitz (1876-1942), and Heinrich Schepers (1925-2020) (eds.), *Leibniz, Philosophische Schriften.* Band 2: 1663-1672, (Berlin: Akademie Verlag, 1966).

AA VI, 6: André Robinet (1922-2016) and Heinrich Schepers (1925-2020) (eds.), *Leibniz, Philosophische Schriften. Noveaux essays sur l'entendement humain.* Band 6. (Berlin: Akademie Verlag, repr. 2006).

DC: *Doctrina Conditionum.*

NM: *Nova Methodus Discendae Docendaeque Jurisprudentiae*

The birth and death dates of the authors cited in the text are enclosed in round brackets () when mentioned in the text or when preceding the publication date of the cited work in the footnotes.

Berger, *ad vocem*...: for a better understanding of certain concepts of Roman law, I have utilized entries, transcribed in their original form, which in some cases are clearer than domestic manuals. These entries were authored by Adolf Berger (1882-1962) (1991, repr.), *Encyclopedic Dictionary of Roman Law,* Philadelphia, 1991;

Watson, *Glossary*: Alan Watson (1933-2018), *The Digest of Justinian*. Philadelphia, 2009. 4 vols.

In the text, I have provided passages from Justinian's Corpus Juris cited by Leibniz, translated for a better understanding of the Leibnizian context:

- for Justinian's I.[nstitutes] translated into English by D. B. Moyle, D.C.L. of Lincoln's Inn, *https://clyx.com/books/moyle/the_institutes_of_justinian/*.
- for D.[igest], the translation is mine.
- for the C.[ode] and the Nov.[els], translated by Justice Fred Blume, *https://www.uwyo.edu/lawlib/blume-justinian/ajc-edition-2/books/; https://www.uwyo.edu/lawlib/blume-justinian/ajc-edition-2/novels/index.html,*
- for Frag.[menta] Ulpiani, from Gustavus Hugo (1764-1844) (ed.), *Domitii Ulpiani Fragmenta Libri Regularum Singularis, uti videtur, vulgo XXIX Tituli ex Corpore Ulpiani,* (Berlin, 1811), the translation is mine
- for the Ministries (e.g., c.[anon] 1, D.[istinctio] 8), (e.g., C.[ase] 23, q.[uestion] 5, c.[anon] 25) Sacraments (D.[istinctio] de cons.[ecratione], i.e., name of the distinctio, c.[anon] 3) from *Gratian's Decretum* in Aemilius E. Friedberg (1837-1910) (ed.), *Corpus Iuris Canonici,* Pars prior (Graz, 1955). In the cited passages, the translation is mine.
- for the X. [Decretales Gregorii IX sive Liber extravagantium decretalium sive Decretalium Gregorii IX compilatio]; Clem.[entine] Constitutions of Pope Clement V; VI [Sextus decretalium] in Aemilius E. Friedberg (1837-1910) (ed.), *Corpus Iuris Canonici,* Pars secunda, (Graz, 1955). In the cited passages of the sources of Canon law, the translation is mine.

As for the citations of the Digest, they have been expanded in brackets with the relevant titles and the names of the Roman jurists who authored the passages. For example, a citation such as D.12.1.8 is expanded as follows: [D.12.1. *De rebus creditis si certum petetur et de condictione* (On things credited giving rise to fixed claims and the *condictio*). 8. **Pomponius**, *in the sixth book From Plautius*: Consequently, sometimes a loan is in a state of pending, so that it can be confirmed by a subsequent event, as, for example, if I lend you some coins with the condition that they become yours if...]. I believe that this method of including the full text of the cited passages from the Digest and inserting them in smaller characters within brackets in Leibniz's translated text, where he merely cites the references and directs the reader to a laborious verification in the Corpus Juris Civilis, greatly helps the reader to better understand the synthesis made by Leibniz himself.

It seemed appropriate to typographically highlight the names of the Roman jurists by putting them in bold for the following reason: the editor considers it important that the non-specialist reader is made aware of the names of the ancient authors, whose rigorous exposition is praised by Leibniz in the preface.

The same criteria have been followed for the citation of passages from the Justinian Code and the rules of canon law, ensuring that each reference is clearly expanded and contextualized for the reader's convenience. Although the passages from the Justinian Code and canon law do not include the names of authors, they are also inserted in brackets with reduced text size to maintain consistency.

Finally, I added titles to chapters that were without them in the original text to clarify the topics of each chapter for the readers.

TRANSLATIONS OF DOCTRINA CONDITIONUM

There are three translations of *Doctrina conditionum* into modern languages:

- In French: Gottfried Wilhelm Leibniz, *Doctrina conditionum,* transl. Pol Boucher (Paris: Institut M. Villey, 1998);
- In German: *Das Rechtlogische System of the "Doctrina Conditionum" von Gottfried Wilhelm Leibniz,* transl. Matthias Armgardt (Marburg: Elwert, 2001);
- In Italian: Gottfried Wilhelm Leibniz, *Doctrina conditionum* (Dottrina delle condizioni*),* transl. Carmelo Massimo de Iuliis (Milano: Giuffré Francis Lefebvre, 2020).

Model of Certainty or Demonstrations in Law

Expounded in the

DOCTRINE OF CONDITIONS

By

Gottfried Wilhelm Leibniz

Preface

I would have gladly abstained from writing a preface, but my brevity in the following pages will testify to the fact that I have observed it more firmly than was necessary for someone who presents many new ideas.

Now, my fear of criticism compels me to say something, as I feel the judgments of examiners reaching me either through sympathy or impatience. Indeed, some will attribute my parsimony of words to a deficiency, while others will attribute it to the lack of citations from the Doctors, with which pages are commonly inflated.

Still, others will attribute my curiosity to a deficiency, as they themselves define the way in which I explain the many different aspects of a fact. To these critics, let this same booklet be the answer, and let the first critics be persuaded that it would have been easier to produce a volume with expanded and quoted words from other authors and with cases from laws than a treatise with essential words.

Those who, on the contrary, are annoyed to observe a prince without a retinue, that is, a work without authoritative citations, should consider how frequent this subject is, how many null conditions have been passed over in silence or in summary. Therefore, either it will be necessary to cite all [the Doctors], an infinite task, or some before others, which is odious, or none, except when it contains something not treated by ancient writers, a circumstance of very rare glory. Nor do I really fear admitting that I have chosen such a common subject: in most cases, in fact, what is very common is at the same time very useful; I certainly do not envy the notoriety of those who, while treating unimaginable subjects, maintain only the title in rarity: what follows is either vacuous or banal.

It seems to me much more worthy to work to give prestige to my work, since celebrated men put zeal into illustrating such a subject. It is prominent, as I learned from the incomparable person whom I name for the sake of honor, Johann Strauch[1], that the "Tractatus de Conditionibus" by Philibert Brussel, royal counselor of Charles V and Philip II king of Spain, published in Leuven in the year 1560[2]; I have discovered that Leandro Galganetti's "De Conditionum Demonstratione, Modo, Causa et Poena" was also published in Venice in 1609 [3], as well as Paolo Duran's "De Conditionibus et Modis Impossibilibus et Prohibitis Contractibus et Testamentis Adscriptis," edited in Venice in folio in 1616[4].

Oswald Hilliger also gave a dissertation on conditions at Jena in 1618[5]. In addition, there are also circulating the "Tractatus de Conditionibus" by Lochmann[6], "De Conditionibus Sponsalium" by Signor Bechstedt[7], and the recently held inaugural dispute of the distinguished and illustrious Mr. Ziegler[8].

1 Johann Strauch (1612-1679), an eminent jurist, and the acquired uncle of Leibniz: Strauch was the husband of Catharina Smuck (1621-1664), Leibniz's mother's sister, see Maria Rosa Antognazza, *Leibniz* (Cambridge, 2009), p. 27.

2 Philibert Brussel (1518-1570), *De conditionibus libri quat[t]uor* (Lovanii,1560).

3 Leandro Galganetti (second half of sixteenth century), *De conditionibus et demonstrationib[us] modo, causa & poena tractatus* (Venetiis, 1609).

4 Pablo Duran (1580-1650), *Tractatus de Conditionibus, Et Modis Impossibilibus, Et Jure Prohibitis Contractibus, Et Testamentis Adscriptis* (Venetiis, 1612).

5 Oswald Hilliger (1583-1619), *Disputatio solemnis de conditionibus* (Jenæ, 1618).

6 Philipp Lochmann, *Disputatio solemnis de conditionibus* (Jena, 1618). It is the same book cited in note 5 above; the *disputatio* was held by Lochmann for the attainment of a doctorate in both civil and canon laws [*in utroque*] under the supervision of Hilliger.

7 Johann Bechstedt (Bechstadius) (1572-1635), *De conditionibus sponsalium.* (Coburgi, 1660).

8 Kaspar Ziegler (Zieglerus) (1621-1690), *De conditionibus: diatriba*

To try to surpass such masters would be foolish, or to try to emulate them would be senseless. However, I believe it should be allowed for those seeking a different path to attempt to access that same peak from another side. And thus, I come to my own method, which the work itself would defend from criticism. Here, I cannot help but mention that the ancient legal experts rendered justice with such acumen and depth that it is more a matter of organizing their opinions into certain and almost mathematical demonstrations than of integrating them with further acumen.

This is something that not only the great Hermann Conring indicated in the preface to Hopper's "De Vera Jurisprudentia",[9] but was also attempted by Matteo Gribaldi,[10] Gilkenius in his work "Quod Jurisprudentia sit proprie dicta Scientia"[11] and Ant. Faber in Papinianea Jurisprudentia.[12] More recently, the esteemed Felden attempted this in his Elements of Jurisprudence[13] (using the method he had previously shown in the appendix to the manuscript *On the Use of Aristotelian Topics*,[14] on the method of demonstrating (14)). Thus, a justification of the work is sufficiently congruous. For those who do not

iuridica (Jenae, 1655).

[9] Joachim Hopper (1523-1576) and Hermann Conring (1606-1681), *Seduardus sive de vera iurisprudentia Editio nova cura H. Coringii* (Brunsvigae, 1656).

[10] Matteo Gribaldi Mofa (1504-1564), *De ratione ac methodo studendi* (Lugduni, 1541).

[11] Peter Gilkens (Gilkenius) (ca. 1558-1608), *Quod Jurisprudentia sit proprie dicta scientia* (Francofurti,1602).

[12] Antoine Favre (Faber) (1557-1624), *Jurisprudentia Papinianea scientia* (Lugduni, 1607).

[13] Johann Von Felden (d. 1668), *Elementa juris universi et in specie justinianei* (Fancofurti et Lipsiae, 1664).

[14] Johann Von Felden's bibliography only mentions a direct reference to Aristotle, found in his work "Analysis of Aristotle's Politics Books", published at Frankfurt in 1654.

give any importance to the opinions of such men, they will be much less disturbed by my words.

Preliminary Remarks

The doctrine of conditions is a certain part of legal logic that deals with hypothetical propositions in law. Its places in the body of law are: the entire title of *de Condit. Instit.*[15] (C.I., as we will cite later), *de Cond. et Demonstr.*[16] (C.D.), *de Statu Liberis*[17] (St. L.), as well as C. *de Inst. et Subst. sub Cond.*[18] and C. *de Cond. Insert. Legat.*,[19] etc., and *Extra d. Cond. Appos.*[20] (C.A.).

Furthermore, since the field of topics is immense, we will not be occupied much by nominal issues. The etymology of "conditio" (condition) if written with "t"[21] comes from "condendo", which at the same time comes from "dando" and "adjiciendo" as for "redditio", it derives from "reddendo". If, however, you spell it as in the *Pandectae Florentinae*[22] with a "c", "condicio" derives

15 D.[igesta] 28.7. *De condicionibus institutionum* [Conditions on institutions].

16 D.35.1. *De condicionibus et demonstrationibus et causis et modis eorum, quae in testamento scribuntur* (C.D.) [Conditions and designations, their reasons and kinds, which are written in wills].

17 D.40.7. *De statuliberis* (Statuliberi).

18 C.[odex].6.25. *De institutionibus seu substitutionibus sub condicione factis* (Concerning appointments, substitutions or trusts, made upon condition).

19 C.6.46. *De condicionibus insertis tam legatis quam fideicommissis et libertatibus* (Concerning conditions attached to legacies, trusts and manumissions).

20 X [*Decretales Gregorii IX sive Liber extravagantium decretalium sive Decretalium Gregorii IX compilatio*].4.5. *De conditionibus appositis in desponsatione vel in aliis contractibus* (Conditions attached in promises of marriage and in other contracts).

21 See *Thesaurus linguae latinae* (Lipsiae, 1906-1909), IV, ad vocem, 70, «Condicio, (cf. c. condicere) Lex imposita (...) in permultis libris (non in INSCR.) forma per *t* invenitur, sed scribi per *c* oportere evincunt Corssen, Ausspr. u. Vokal. I2 p. 52 etc.».

22 Berger, *ad vocem Florentina*, (Sc. *Littera*), "The oldest and most authoritative manuscript of the Digest, written in the late sixth or early

from "condicendo", a term familiar to legal experts, in the sense of something that was said and added simultaneously to other clauses. Therefore, correctly, Duaren defines a condition as an addition, in the title of *C. I. c. I.*[23]

German "Bedingung" is almost "Ben-Dingung", that which is added in a discussion or agreement. Hence the formula: the condition is not an addition, see Theorem 17, and later we will demonstrate that the condition is an accessory to the main condition. Therefore, we immediately come to the definition, or rather the explanation of the term (it is not useful to hunt for synonyms in books, and Mr. Rebhan, whose volumes we do not want to plagiarize, abundantly collected homonyms in *Hodegeta juris*),[24] and it is not really lacking, what we will add of our own, not to mention that a precise definition is the measure of all distinctions and explanations of homonymy, as Thomas Hobbes noted in *Element. de Corpore, parte prima Logica, c.*

seventh century. The manuscript was preserved in Pisa during the twelfth and thirteenth centuries (hence named Littera Pisana). From the beginning of the fifteenth century, it has been in Florence".

[23] Françoise Duarenus (1509-1559), *Omnia quae quidem hactenus edita fuerunt opera* (Francofurti, 1598), in Tit. VII, De conditionibus institutionum, p. 411, c. II Quid sit conditio, "Conditionem ita solitus sum definire: Conditio est adiectio [corsivo mio], qua legatum, vel institutio heredis suspenditur in futurum eventum.". [Certainly, I am accustomed to defining a condition as an addition, by which a legacy or the institution of an heir is suspended until a future event].

[24] Johann Rebhann (1604-1689), *Hodegeta juris* (Argentorati, 1656), pp. 474-494, therein an extensive review of the meanings of *conditio*.

6 art. 15 propriet. 1[25], Cujas, in *Paratitla de C. I.*[26], defined it as limit [*modus*], Vulteius[27] *J. R. 1.7*, cause, Antoine Favre[28] and after him Frantzk in *ad L. Gallus 11.4.11*[29],

[25] Thomas Hobbes (1588–1679), (Londinium 1655), 51, Pars Prima, *Computatio sive Logica*, Caput 6 De methodo, art. 15, Proprietatis definitionis sunt: I. Quod tollit aequivocum, adeoque omnem illam distinctionum multitudinem quibus utuntur ii qui Philofophiam acquiri posse putant disputationibus. Nam natura definitionis est ut definiant, id est, determinet nominis definiti fignificationem, eamque abscindat ab omni alia fignificatione quam quae in definitione ontinetur; & propterea distinctionum quotquot esse possunt circa definitum una definitio omnium locum obtinet. Engl. transl. London 1656; William Molesworth (1810–1855) (1839), *The English Works of Thomas Hobbes of Malmesbury*. I, (London, 1839), p. 84: 15. The properties of a definition are: First, that it takes away equivocation, as also all that multitude of distinctions, which are used by such as think they may learn philosophy by disputation. For the nature of a definition is to define, that is, to determine the signification of the defined name, and to pare from it all other signification besides what is contained in the definition itself; and therefore, one definition does as much, as all the distinctions (however many) that can be used about the name defined.

[26] Jacques Cujas (1522-1590), *Paratitla in Libros Quinquaginta Digestorum, seu Pandectarum Imperatoris Iustiniani*. (Lugduni, 1587), 153, "Condicio est modus qui suspendit id quod agitur quoad ex postfacto confirmetur.". [The condition is a way that keeps suspended what is concluded until it has been confirmed in light of subsequent events].

[27] Hermann Vulteius (1555-1634), *Jurisprudentiae Romanae a Justiniano compositae libri duo*. (Marpurgi: Typis Pauli Egenolphi Typography Acad.,1598), 25, De Facto. CAP. VII., "Conditio est causa, rem, quae agitur, ita suspendens, ut antequam illa existat, neque ipsum factum, neque effectus eius exstitisse videatur. [The condition is the cause that suspends the transaction that has been concluded, so that before it occurs, it seems that neither the fact itself nor its legal effectiveness existed]."

[28] Antoine Favre (Faber) (1557-1624), *De erroribus pragmaticorum et interpretum iuris. Hemischilias seu Pars secunda* (Lugduni, 1604), Decad. XXVI, Error. I, 4-5, "Nam sive quid conditio sit, ispiciamus, constat nihil aliud eam esse, quam privationem, ut ita dicam, puritatis, hoc est, suspensionem actus, qui alioquin purus esset, ac proinde nihil, quia & privatio ipsa qualibet nihil est, licet tale nihil sit, quod efficit ut actus conditionalis, quandiu conditio pendet, pro nullo sit." [If we carefully observe what a condition is, it consists of nothing more than a lack, so to speak, of purity, that is, the suspension of an act that would otherwise be pure, and therefore it is a void. And since any kind of lack is also a void, despite it being a void, this causes a conditional act, as long as the condition is pending, to be considered null].

[29] Georg Von Frantzke (1594-1659), *Georgii Frantzkii Jc. Commentarius in difficilem & intricatam L. Gallus Aquilius, 29. D. de liber. & postum. heredibus instituend. & c. Quinque disputationibus publicis olim in Academia Ienensi*

lack of purity (as if purity is not rather defined by the absence or lack of what is foreign), Ludwell in §9 I. *de H.I.*[30] calls it a quality. However, since quality is rather conditionality, that is, a concatenation of propositions, the condition itself is actually a preceding proposition: for example, "If the ship comes from Asia, I will give you 100." Hence, that same proposition "the ship will come from Asia" is a condition, not a quality of it; and it either must be fulfilled or must be lacking.

exhibitus. Prodit nunc secunda cura priori correctior. (Argentorati, 1653), pp. 111-112, "11. Conditio enim nihil aliud est privatio quaedam puritatis [corsivo mio], hoc est suspensio alicuius actus, qui alioquin purus esset, in hunc finem adscripta, ut existens eundem quasi retro purum, deficiens nullum fuisse declaret. 12. Ergo in se uti conditio est, nihil est, etsi suo modo existens vel deficiens effectum aliquem habere videatur, uti multis disputant Ant. Fab. 26 error pragm. I. & II.". [In fact, a condition is nothing but a certain lack of purity, that is, the suspension of some act that would otherwise be pure, inserted for the purpose of declaring that the same act was pure from the beginning when the condition is met, and if it doesn't occur, it would be void. 12 Therefore, in itself as a condition, it is nothing, although in its own way, whether it occurs or not, it seems to produce some effect, as many argue Ant. Fab. 26 error pragm. I. & II.].

30 Wilhelm Ludwell (1589-1663), *Commentarii in IV libros Institutionum Justiniani* (Altdorfii Noricorum, 1656), p. 226, [sub I.2.14.9], "Et Pure et Sub Condicione & C. Tertia (...) pars modum, sive qualitatem institutionis [corsivo mio] continet, quod ea vel pure, vel sub conditione fieri possit." [Both purely and under conditions, etc. The third (...) part contains the manner, that is, the quality of the institution, what it can become either purely or under conditions.].

CHAPTER I

[Conditional Propositions in Law]

DEFINITIONS

1. A CONDITIONAL PROPOSITION[31], (opposed to the pure[32]): for example, "if man is an animal, Peter perceives sensations; if the ship arrives, Titius will have 100", is that which consists of two

2. PARTIAL PROPOSITIONS, both in terms of subject matter and connection as well as form, and this connection, or rather

[31] AA VI 1, 102, "1. Propositio conditionalis est, quae hoc continet: Si illa Propositio vera est, haec vera est.". [A conditional proposition is one that is formed like this: if that proposition is true, then this one is true]. "2. Illa Conditio dicitur, 3. haec Conditionatum" [2 That is called the condition. 3 This one is conditionatum.]. "4 Terminus est earum alterutra" [The term is either one of the two]; 105, "62. Propositio est Conditionalis (Pura) figura, id est sola dispositione verborum, vel expresse et figura et sensu, vel tacite solo sensu" [A proposition is a conditional (pure) form, that is, solely by the arrangement of words, or expressly both in form and meaning, or tacitly only by meaning].

[32] Egidio Forcellini (1688-1768), *Lexicon Totius Latinitatis* (1965 anast. quartae edit. Patavii 1864 – 1926), *ad vocem Purus*, "Apud JCtos pura sunt, quae simpliciter & absolutae fiunt, nulla exceptione, aut conditione adjecta.". [Among Juriconsults it is pure everithing which is born simply and perfect, without any exception or condition added, e.t.] Justinian. Institution. 3.15.2. Omnis stipulatio aut pure aut in diem aut sub condicione fit. Paul. D. 35.2.45. In lege Falcidia non habetur pro puro, quod in diem relictum est. Scaevola D.40.4.59.1. Puram et directam domini sui testamento libertatem Stichus acceperat. *Adde* Ulpian. D.46.3.5. Gravior videtur, quae et sub satisdatione videtur, quam ea quae pura est."; *A Latin dictionary* (1984 repr. 1879), Founded on Andrews' edition of Freund's Latin dictionary, revised, enlarged, and in great part rewritten by Charlton Thomas Lewis (1834–1904). Oxford, *ad vocem Purus*, "B. in juridical language, unconditional". Vincenzo Arangio-Ruiz (1884 – 1964), *Istituzioni di Diritto Romano*, Napoli, (14th ed. 1978), p. 85, "...al negozio giuridico principale, inteso come puro (non condizionato) ...". Alan Watson (1933-2018), *The Digest of Justinian*, 4 voll. (Philadelphia, 2009), follows this translation, see for example, in vol. 2, D.18.2.2. Peter Birks (1941–2004), *The Roman Law of Obligations*. (Oxford, 2014)76, maintains "...contract is pure...".

3. CONDITIONALITY[33], affirms at least that: if the first partial proposition, namely, the

4. CONDITION (which we will henceforth write[34] as Co, *Conditionatum* as Ctum, *Conditionale* as Cle, *Conditionatorem*[35] as Ctorem, and *Conditionarium*[36] as Crium), exactly the one that is expressed not in the indicative form, but in the subjunctive, is true (e.g., if man is an animal, if the ship arrives), then the subsequent one is also true, namely

5. the CONDITIONATUM, which is already expressed directly, that is, in indicative tense (Peter perceives

[33] AA VI 1, p. 102, "5. Conditionalitas est Connexio Termini ad terminum." [Conditionality is the connection of one term to another]. "6 Connexio est necessitas unius ad alterum, connexa sunt, quae ad se invicem requiruntur." [Connection is the necessity of one to another; connected are those things that require each other]; p. 105. "56. Conditionalitas vel est Veritatis, et diem habet, id est nihil aliud dicit quam justa d. 1: Si conditio vera est, verum est conditionatum; vel est Existentiae, cum tempus existentiae Conditionati adjectum est, definitum existentia Conditionis, seu hoc dicit: Si Conditio existit, tum etiam existet Conditionatum, ea dicitur diem habere ". [Conditionality either concerns the truth and has a term, that is, nothing else says that what is in definition 1: if the condition is true, the conditioned is true; or concerns existence, when the time of existence of the conditioned is added, defined by the existence of the condition, that is, it says that: if the condition exists, the conditioned also exists, then it is said that it has a term].

[34] I will avoid using the abbreviations used by Leibniz in order to not burden the reading.

[35] AA VI 1, p. 105, "67. Disponens Persona est Conditionator, cujus ultimo actu voluntatis declarativo valida est dispositio." [The person making the disposition (the one who puts a condition) is the *Conditionator*, and the validity of the disposition is determined by their final declarative act of will.].

[36] AA VI 1, p. 105, "68. Conditionarius est subjectum deducti in Conditionatum, seu persona, cui jus, quod Conditionatoris fuit, Dispositione tribuitur." [The *conditionarius* is the subject placed in the conditioned, or rather the person, to which according to a provision, is assigned the right that belonged to the *conditionator*, e. transl.]. "69. Uterque [the Conditionator and the Conditionarius, e.n.] Persona Principalis in hoc argumento, alius ab his Tertius dicitur." [Both (the Conditionator and the Conditionarius, e.n.), are the Foremost Person in this argument, a different from these is said Third].

sensations, Titus will have 100) and we call this affirmative connection of words with a single word

6. INFERENCE[37]. On the other hand, a negative connection is called

7. SUSPENSION[38], which affirms that: if that is not true, then this is not true either; see about D.12.1.8,37 [D.12.1. *De rebus creditis si certum petetur et de condictione* (Things credited giving rise to fixed claims and the condictio). 8 **Pomponius**, *in the sixth book From Plautius*: Consequently, sometimes a loan is in a state of pending, so that it can be confirmed by a subsequent event, as, for example, if I lend you some coins with the condition that they become yours if a certain condition occurs, and you are obligated towards me for their return. Similarly, if the heir has lent the sum of money left to the legatee as a legacy in real terms, and then the legatee refuses to accept such a sum as a legacy, it can be judicially claimed as money lent, namely through the action of repetition by notice, because it is considered to have belonged to the heir from the day of accepting the inheritance. Indeed, Julianus asserts that even the transfer deliveries made by the heir should be attributed to the time when the inheritance was entered into, whether the legacy was refused or lost. 37. **Papinianus**, *in the first book of Definitions*: When the condition refers to the present time, the stipulation is not suspended, and if the event referred to in the condition is true, the stipulation binds, even if the parties involved are unaware that the condition has occurred; for example: 'If the king of the Parthians is alive, do you promise to give me a hundred?' The same things must be said when the condition refers to the past.]; D.35.1.79.pr. [D.35.1. *De condicionibus et demonstrationibus et causis et modis eorum, quae in testamento scribuntur* (On conditions, designations, reasons, and the ways they appear in provisions written in the will]. 79 **Papinianus**, *in the first book of Definitions*: "My heir, when Titius dies, will give him a hundred; this legacy is pure because it is suspended

[37] AA VI 1, p. 102, "7. Illatio est necessitas illati ad inferens seu ut dato inferente detur illatum" [A logical inference is the necessary connection between what is inferred and what is inferred from, such that given the inferring, the inferred must follow.].

[38] AA VI 1, p. 102, "8. Suspensio est necessitas suspendendi ad suspensum, seu ut dato suspenso detur suspendens, sine suspendente non detur suspensum" [A suspension is the unavoidable consequence of suspending for a suspended, i.e. that as a suspension is given, a suspending is given, no suspension is given without suspending]; Egidio Forcellini, note 32 above, *ad vocem Suspensio*, "pro animi fluctuazione, dubitatione.".

not by a condition but by a delay; because such a condition cannot exist.]; D.40.4.44 [D.40.4.*De manumissis testamento* (Testamentary manumission). 44 **Modestinus**, *in the tenth book On Responses*: Mevia, upon her death, left freedom conditionally to her slaves Sacco, Eutichia, and Irene with these words: "Sacco, my slave, and Eutichia and Irene, my slaves, shall all be free under this condition, that one month one of them and one month the other alternately shall light the lamp at my monument and perform the funeral rites." The question was whether Sacco, Eutichia, and Irene can be considered free if they do not diligently attend Mevia's monument. Modestinus replied: "Neither the context of the words in the entire writing, nor the intention of the testatrix, who wanted the freed persons to be present at the monument, lead to the conclusion that freedom should be suspended under a condition. However, the judge must, on his own initiative, compel them to obey the testatrix's command.]; see *infra* definition 52.

Here, by dealing with it immediately, we will explain the division of the conditional proposition into logic[39] and moral[40], that is, as *Bachovius* in *Tr. II, 27.6, lit. d*[41]

[39] AA VI 1, p. 105, "65. Logica, quae non est moralis, quam nos inposterum a nostra tractatione removemus, et cum hactenus etiam logicis Conditionibus communia dixerimus, nunc ad morales pertractandas accingimur." [‹The logical condition›, which is not moral, we exclude it from our discussion, and since up to now we have talked about things that are common even to logical conditions, now we are going to deal in depth with moral conditions].

[40] AA VI 1, p. 105, "63. Conditionatum morale est, in quod deductum est jus aliquod, subjectum autem deducti persona"
[The *conditionatum* is moral, <when> some right is deduced in it, but the subject of the deducted, is a person]. "64. Conditio moralis est a conditionato." [A condition is moral by virtue of a conditioned] "66. Propositio conditionalis Moralis, cujus nempe conditio et conditionatum sunt moralia, dicetur a nobis imposterum Dispositio in specie." [A moral conditional proposition, of which precisely the condition and the conditioned are moral, will be called by us hereinafter disposition in the particular case]. On the use of term moralis in juridical contest, see, Franco Todescan, in *Introduction*.

[41] Reinhard Bachoff von Echt (1575-1640), Hieronymus Treutler (1565–1607), *Bachovius augmentatus i. e. Cl. V. Reinhardi Bachovii Echtii Notae et animadversiones ad Hieron. Treutleri.* (Coloniae Agrippinae, 1688), II, pars posterior, disp. XXVII, 6, lit. D, "Docendi causa conditio distingui potest, quod alia sit secundum dici, alia secundum esse." [For educational purposes, a condition can be distinguished, due to the fact that one is according to the word, another according to the nature of the thing]. This is the "common medieval distinction between relations merely according to speech (relationes secundum dici) and relations according

prefers to call it, according to the word (*secundum dici*) and according to the nature of being (*secundum esse*).

This division, although it arises from the effect, nevertheless produces for us a great concern about the effect due to an infinite variety of causes, to the extent that some causes are to be considered appropriate and others, on the contrary, are to be rejected as inadequate.

A conditional proposition, therefore, is either considered in itself, based on its form and content, or based on its legal effect, which is relevant to our legal purpose. It either lacks the conditional effect of the law (meaning it is in an intermediate position between unconditional law and nullity), and is called by us

8. LOGIC, or it has <such a legal effect>, and is said

9. MORAL.

However, I do not deny that from time to time logical conditions are also used in law. For example, if someone conditionally threatens (that is, promises harm instead of a benefit), it is not a moral condition, because one of the two will never exert pressure through legal action to obtain the promised harm.

Nevertheless, with regard to these conditions in law, it should be noted that whoever threatens under a condition, meeting the other requirements for harm[42], is punished as a true threatener, as if they had purely

to nature of being (relationes secundum esse)."; J. Brown (First published Tue May 29, 2001; substantive revision Mon Nov 30, 2015), *Medieval Theories of Relations*, in *Stanford Encyclopedia of Philosophy*, https://plato.stanford.edu/entries/relations-medieval/, Introduction (accessed 10th Sept. 2018). It seems the distinction, commonly made by St. Thomas and the ancient scholastics, of relations into "relation according to [existence] (secundum esse)" and "relation according to be-spoken (secundum dici)." See S[umma] T[heologiae] I q.13 a.7 ad 1.

[42] Charles Fresne Du Cange (1610–1688) and others, *Glossarium mediae et infimae latinitatis*. (Niort, 1883–1887), *ad vocem Diffidatio*, "Damnum quodvis".

threatened[43], *Daniel Moller, Ad Constit. Elect., p. IV, c. 15*[44], to name just a few examples.

We will always observe the practice of adding to the definitions, theorems, or demonstrable rules by providing further explanation according to the definitions. Therefore, we should now expound

Theorems

(1) A Condition generates a Conditioned [part].

For, if the condition is true, the conditioned is true, according to the definition 3. Therefore, there is an illation according to definition 6. This is what they commonly say: once the condition is satisfied, the testamentary disposition is due, as stated in D.35.1.41, 44.10 [D.35.1. *De condicionibus et demonstrationibus et causis et modis eorum, quae in testamento scribuntur* (Conditions, designations, explanations for and modalities of provisions in wills). 41 **Ulpianus**, *in the thirty-fourth book to the Edict*: Legacies left under a condition become due, not forthwith but when the condition is satisfied; it follows that they cannot be delegated in the interim. 44 **Paulus**, *in the ninth book to Plautius*: 10. I left an estate to one of my heirs, if he gave one hundred to the heirs; he may deduct his hereditary share [of the money] and give the remainder to his co-heirs in their proportionate shares. But should an heir be instituted in part on the terms that he gives one hundred to the heirs, he will become heir only if he gives the full sum to his co-heirs; he is not admitted to the inheritance until he has handed over the whole amount. For equally if a slave be freed by the will and instituted heir in part with the requirement that he should give ten to the heirs, it is settled that he becomes free and heir only if he has given the full ten to his co-heirs. Paulus: such is the law which we apply.]; D.36.1.65(63).1 [D.36.1. *Ad senatus consultum Trebellianum (Regarding the Senatus Consultum Trebellianum). 65 (63)* **Gaius**, *in the second book On Fideicommissa*: 1. If the fideicommissary has taken a stipulation for the restitution of the inheritance from the heir and the inheritance were restored to him when he sued on the stipulation, it is clear that the actions pass nonetheless, that is, if the defendant re-

[43] Fresne Du Cange, note 42 above, *ad vocem Diffidator*, "Qui ad certamen evocat.".

[44] Daniel Moller (d. 1600), *Commentarius in Ordinationem et Costitutionem Augusti Electoris Saxoniae*. (Lipsiae, 1599).

store the inheritance. If, on the other hand, he were condemned to pay the value of the inheritance because he did not restore, the actions belonging to the inheritance remain with the defendant, who was condemned, and the plaintiff recovers a sum of money.]; D.40.5.14 [D.40.5.*De fideicommissariis libertatibus* (On Fideicommissary Freedoms). 14 **Modestinus**, *in the tenth book On Responses:* Lucius Titius, in his will, appointed his wife Seia and their common daughter Titia as heirs in equal shares. In another clause of the will, he stated the following: "I want my slave Erote (also known as Psillus) to be free if my wife pleases." Seia, the wife of Lucius Titius, abstained from the inheritance, and by the substitution, her share passed to the daughter of Titius. It is asked whether, by those words in the will, Erote, also called Psillus, is entitled to freedom. Modestinus replied that Erote is not prevented from freedom because the testator's wife abstained from the inheritance. It is also asked whether Seia, who abstained from the inheritance, can rightfully oppose Erote's request for freedom. Modestinus replied: Seia's objection is of no consequence.]; D.24.3.58 [D.24.3. *Soluto matrimonio dos quemadmodum petatur* (How the dowry is judicially claimed after the dissolution of the marriage). 58 **Modestinus**, *in the single book On Legal Remedies:* A dowry slave, appointed as an heir by someone, must either accept or reject the inheritance by order of the husband. However, to ensure that the husband, by either rejecting an unknown succession too easily or accepting it rashly, is not obligated under the dowry action to his own wife, it is advisable for the husband to ask the wife, in the presence of witnesses, whether she wants to forgo or acquire the inheritance. If she says she wants to reject it, the slave will reject it at once by order of the husband. If she prefers to accept the inheritance, the slave must be returned by the husband to the wife on the condition that, after he has accepted the inheritance at her command, he is then returned to the husband himself. In this way, the husband's concerns will be addressed, and the wife's desires will be accommodated.]; D.45.1.10 [D.45.1.*De verborum obligationibus* (Verbal obligations). 10 **Pomponius**, *in the third book to Sabinus:* Let us apply this principle, that under this stipulation, "Do you promise to give ten if Lucius Titius does not come to Italy before the Kalends of May?" nothing can be demanded until it is certain that Titius cannot come to Italy before that day, whether he arrives alive or is deceased.]; D.28.5.93(92) [D.28.5.*De heredibus instituendis* (The institution of heir). 93 (92) **Paulus**, *in the first of the six books On Imperial Decisions Rendered in Cognitions or in the second book On Decrees*: Pattumeius Androstenes had appointed Pattumeia Magna, the daughter of Pattumeius Magnus, as the sole heir and had substituted her father for her. After the death of Pattumeius Magnus and rumors circulating that the daughter had also died, the testator changed his will and appointed Novius Rufus as the heir with this provision: "Since I could not have the heirs I had wanted for myself, let Novius Rufus be the heir." Pattumeia Magna appealed to our emperors, and upon receiving knowledge of this, even though the institution of heir contained a reason, which, if false, does not usually harm, the emperor deemed it necessary to come to her aid based on the testator's intention. Therefore, it was ruled that the inheritance belonged to Pattumeia Magna, but she was required to fulfill the legacies specified in the second will, as if in the second set of tablets, she herself had been designated as the heir in writing.]; D.28.7.2.1, 8.7, 28 [D.28.7.*De conditionibus institutionum* (Conditions on institutions). 2 **Ulpianus**, *in the sixth book to Sabinus*: 1. But if two slaves have been appointed as heirs in this manner: "First and Second, if they are mine when I die, be free and heirs," and one of them has been sold, Celsus correctly believes that it should be understood that the testator had appointed the individual slaves separately under the same condition. 8 **Ulpianus**, *in the fiftieth book To the Edict*: 7. If Stichus died or was incapacitated while the testator was still alive, and the person who has been appointed as heir in this manner, if he swore that he would incapacitate Stichus, he will not be considered to have failed the condition, even though it is true that he must be compelled to incapacitate Stichus if he is still alive. The same applies if someone were appointed as heir in this way: "Titius is the heir so that he incapacitates Stichus," or: "I bequeath a hundred to Titius, so that he incapacitates Stichus." In fact, when Stichus dies, no one will say that he should be removed from the designation, because he is not considered to have failed the condition unless he cannot fulfill it; the testator's intent, after all, must be fulfilled if it is possible. 28 **Papinianus**, *in the thirteenth book On Questions*: If a child is appointed as an heir under a condition, and grandchildren born from him are substituted, as it is not sufficient for the validity of the will that the child is appointed as heir under any condition, but the will is valid only if the fulfillment of the condition is within the child's power, we must consider whether it matters what type of condition was imposed. For example, whether it is a condition that, if the child had found himself on his deathbed, could not have been fulfilled, such as: "If he goes to Alexandria, my child shall be the heir," and he died in Rome. Or it could be a condition that could have been fulfilled even in the last moments of life, such as: "If he gives ten to Titius, my child shall be the heir," a condition that can be fulfilled by another person on behalf of the child. Indeed, the first type of condition allows the grandchildren to inherit while the child is still alive. If there were no substitutes, when the child dies without having fulfilled the condition, he would become the legitimate heir for the father. This is confirmed by what is also reported in Servius: he mentions that someone had been appointed as heir under the condition that if he had ascended the Capitoline Hill, but if he hadn't, a legacy would be given to him, and this person had died before ascending. In relation to this case, Servius provided a response that, with the death of the person, the condition had not been fulfilled, and because of this, the right to the legacy had arisen for him as he was dying. However, the second type of condition does not admit the grandchildren to the inheritance while the child is alive. If they were not named as substitutes, they would become heirs to the deceased grandfather intestate. In fact, the child is not considered to be an obstacle, after whose death the father's will remains without an heir, just as if the child had been disinherited, and the grandchildren had been appointed heirs.].

It is sufficient that fulfillment of the condition has occurred only once, C.6.25.1 [C.6.25. *De institutionibus seu substitutionibus sub condicione factis* (Concerning appointments, substitutions or trusts, made upon condition).1. Since you state that your maternal grandfather appointed your daughter his heir upon condition that she should marry the son of Anthyllus, it is clear that she does not become heir till she shall have fulfilled the condition or the son of Anthyllus, by refusal, prevents the marriage.]; D.35.1.11.1 [D.35.1. *De condicionibus et demonstrationibus et causis et modis eorum, quae in testamento scribuntur* (Conditions, designations, explanations for and modalities of provisions in wills). 11 **Paulus**, *in the fourth book to Sabinus*: 1. You should also be aware that general conditions, such as "if he shall ascend the Capitol" and similar ones, must be fulfilled after the death of the testator, provided that they are present in the will for compliance. Conditions that are specific, for instance, "if Titius shall have become consul," can be fulfilled even during the testator's lifetime.].

(2) A conditioned suspends the condition.

For, if the condition is true, the conditioned is true, according to the definition 3 and the theorem 1, so if it is not true the conditioned, it is not true the condition (in fact if it were true, the conditioned would also be true, in the contrary to the hypothesis).

Therefore, the conditioned suspends the condition, according to definition 7, for example if you haven't yet been given 100, it means that the ship is not yet coming from Asia.

(3) *The condition of a condition is the condition of the conditioned.*

Let A be the first condition, B the second, and C the conditioned. Suppose A is the condition of B; <A> infers B according to the theorem 1, and for the same reason B infers C. Therefore, also A infers C, if A exists, C will exist, according to the definition 6 (similarly also if they suspend). Thus, A is the condition of C, according to the definition 4.

This theorem is applied in the circular provisions which follow, where we will compare the condition and the conditioned, as in the theorem 4.

From this, it follows that when a condition is added to freedom, it applies also to the institution of heir and the legacy (*legatum*) of that slave who is granted the freedom, D.35.1.52 [but 53, e.n.; D.35.1. *De condicionibus et demonstrationibus et causis et modis eorum, quae in testamento scribuntur* (Conditions, designations, explanations for and modalities of provisions in wills). 53 **Modestinus**, *in the single book On Eurematici*: If someone has commanded that a slave be freed if he has settled accounts with the heir, and subsequently has forbidden settling accounts, to make the freedom unconditional, freedom is granted to the slave according to the will.].

The same freedom is almost always a condition of the legacy and the institution of heir in the slavers belonging to the testator.

Differently as for the slaves not belonging to the testator since the master receives in the place of them.

So, if a certain slave ceases to belong to the testator or become common to another (That slave in fact is considered as *extraneus* D.28.5.7)[45],the bequest is uncondi-

[45] I prefer to footnote this long parenthetical sentence placed by the Author in the text, for better readability of the theorem: "That slave in fact is considered as extraneus D.28.5.7, [D.28.5. *De heredibus instituendis* (The institution of heirs). 7 **Julianus**, *in the thirtieth book On the Digest*: If a common slave, appointed as an heir under a condition, acquires his freedom while the testator is alive, he can still enter into the inheritance

tional, nor does the condition of freedom be observed, D.28.5.3.1, 38.2, 3, 4 [D.28.5.*De heredibus instituendis* (The institution of heir). 3 **Ulpianus,** *in the third book To Sabinus*: 1. If I have designated my slave in writing purely and simply, and as free under a condition, the institution is deferred until the moment when freedom has been granted. 38 **Julianus,** *in the thirtieth book On the Digest*: 2. If someone has written in the will that his own slave is to be free under a condition and the heir purely and simply, and then sold the slave while the condition is pending, the slave can enter into the inheritance upon the order of the buyer because the institution still stands, and there is someone with the right to order him to accept it. 3. However, if the slave were sold after the condition had not been fulfilled, he cannot enter into the inheritance upon the order of the buyer because the inheritance has already passed to him when the institution had already become extinct and without effect. 4. Therefore, if it is ordered that the slave is to be free under a condition and

while the condition regarding his freedom specified in the will is pending. 1.Similarly, whether the testator has sold him or whether the heir has sold him after the testator's death, the appointed heir will enter into the inheritance upon the order of the master.]". Berger, *ad vocem Extraneus, Extraneus heres,* "An outside heir who is not subject to the testator's power at his death, and therefore is neither his *heres suus et necessarius* nor his *heres necessarius*. [...]. An *extraneus heres* was given an opportunity to deliberate (*deliberare, ius deliberandi*) whether to accept the inheritance or not. Therefore, an explicit declaration of acceptance was required from him." For this reason, he also is called *heres voluntarius*. But if the *extraneus* were a slave he could only accept at the direction of the master. No need declaration of acceptance of the inheritance for *heredes sui et necessarii* (i.e. the descendants of the testator) and *heredes necessarii* (his own slaves). They were heirs *ipso iure*. (See also Arangio-Ruiz, note 32 above, pp. 551-553). *Ad vocem Heres suus et necessarius,* "A person under the paternal power (or *manus*) of the deceased who after his death becomes *sui iuris* (head of a family). If appointed as an heir in a testament or succeeding at intestacy he has no power to refuse the inheritance and becomes heir at once after the testator's death whether he wishes or not. Such heirs are sons, daughters, and the widow of the deceased; grandsons and granddaughters are *heredes sui* only in the event that their father is dead or no longer under the paternal power of the deceased. The praetorian law granted the *heredes sui et necessarii* the right to refuse the acceptance of an insolvent inheritance (*Ius Abstinendi*).". *ad vocem Heres suus,* "An heir who at the death of a person was under his paternal power (patria potestas). This is a technical term to be distinguished from *suus heres* (—his heir) which refers to the heir of a specific person.—". Biondo Biondi (1888-1966), *Istituzioni di diritto romano,* (Milano, 1972[4] repr.), p. 634 "*Heres necessarius* is the slave manumitted in will by his master and in the same time appointed as heir. He is called *necessarius* because he gets freedom at testator's death, and becomes automatically heir, with no need of acceptance, without the chance to refuse the inheritance; i.e. he becomes heir whether he wants or does not want (*sive velit, sive nolit*)" (e.t.).

he receives a bequest purely and simply, if he had been incapacitated or sold while the condition is pending, he will either receive the bequest or acquire it for the master, even if at the time of the death of the testator, the condition for the grant of freedom has become extinct. However, if he has been incapacitated or sold after the condition has not been fulfilled, the bequest becomes void.]; D.35.1.47 [D.35.1. *De condicionibus et demonstrationibus et causis et modis eorum, quae in testamento scribuntur* (*Conditions, designations, explanations for and modalities of provisions in wills*). 47 **Marcellus**, *in the fourteenth book of Digest*: Freedom was granted to the slave in the following manner: "He who is free if he becomes mine." The testator gave him the bequest or the inheritance without any condition; then he sold him. The bequest or inheritance will be given to his new master, and it can be accepted upon the order of this master. Because the expression "if he becomes mine" in the grant of freedom allows for the future possibility of an impediment to freedom, even though this is not explicitly stated. Often, however, the effect of something is changed, and even if the testator had represented that effect, what he had not represented is nevertheless implied.].

D.35.1.68[46] contrasts on point [D.35.1. *De condicionibus et demonstrationibus et causis et modis eorum, quae in testamento scribuntur* (Conditions, designations, explanations for and modalities of provisions in wills). **Javolenus**, *in the second book On Extracts from Cassius*: If someone was bequeathed in this manner: "When she gets married," and she was already married, and the testator knew it, one should wait for another marriage. It will be irrelevant whether the legatee gets married before or after the death of the testator.].

I respond, regarding this contrast, that there the rule is established in favor of the dowry.

Similarly, the condition of institution [as heir] in a slave, to whom the freedom is given and in the same time the inheritance of an estate, draws together also the freedom C.6.51.6 [C. 6.51.*De caducis tollendis* (Concerning abolishing lapses (escheats.).1.6. Manumissions, of course, which, on account of their nature, have to wait the acceptance of the inheritance by the heir, and bequests left to slaves manumitted in the will or to slaves bequeathed to others, vest from the time that the inheritance is accepted. 6a. A usufruct, too, which by reason of its nature cannot

[46] Not D.35.1.86, such as in text, which seems an evident misprint and has nothing to do with the subsequent Leibniz'argument, because D.35.1.86 does not deal about dowry e.n.

be transmitted to the heirs of a legatee, vests, so far as transmission is concerned, neither at the time of the testator's death, not when the inheritance is entered on. 6b. All these provisions apply, according to the specified terms, to bequests which are left unconditionally or are due at a definite time.].

All these provisions apply, according to the specified terms, to bequests which are left unconditionally or are due at a definite time, since the day of freedoms is only once the inheritance is accepted, *adde* D.28.5.21.1, 22 [D.28.5.*De heredibus instituendis* (The institution of heirs).21 **Pomponius**, *in the first book To Sabinus*: 1. I believe it to be absolutely true that freedom can be granted to a slave purely and simply, and the inheritance conditionally, so that both are dependent on the condition. 22. **Julianus**, *in the thirtieth book On the Digests*: And, once the condition is fulfilled, he will be free and an heir, regardless of when the condition is fulfilled. If, on the other hand, the condition is not fulfilled, it is as if freedom had been granted without the inheritance.].

Otherwise, if he is coheir, freedom is due to the slave unconditionally, but he must wait for the condition of the inheritance to be fulfilled, as stated in D.28.5.9.17, 18 [D.28.5.*De heredibus instituendis* (The institution of heirs).9 **Ulpianus**, *in the fifth book To Sabinus*: 17. If a slave has received freedom with a specific term and the inheritance purely and simply, and then has been sold or incapacitated, let us see if the institution as an heir is valid. Indeed, if he has not been sold, it can be argued that the institution is valid since, once the term for acquiring freedom, which delays the acquisition of the inheritance, has expired, and once freedom is acquired, the slave also becomes a *necessarius heres*. 18. However, if freedom is granted with a specific term, and yet the inheritance is conditional, if the condition is fulfilled after the expiration of the term, the slave will be free and an heir.]; D.40.4.2, 14, 26 [D.40.4.*De manumissis testament* (Testamentary manumissions).2 **Ulpianus**, *in the fifth book To Sabinus*: If a testator appointed the heir in the following manner: "Titius is the heir; if Titius is not the heir, Stichus is the heir; Stichus is to be free", Atrius says that Stichus will not be free if Titius becomes the heir. It seems to me that it can be said that he will be free, as if freedom had not been granted to him in one degree only but in both. And this is the legal principle we rely on. 14 **Ulpianus**, *in the eighth book On Disputes*: If freedom is granted to a slave purely and an heir is appointed conditionally, in the absence of the condition, it is established that the slave is free. 26 **Marcianus**, *in the first book On Rules*: The Emperor Pius and the brothers-emperors favorably decreed that if a slave was substituted with freedom, and a bequest was made to him in case he was not the heir, without expressly granting him freedom, it will be understood as if freedom was also attached to the bequest.]; D.42.5.4pr. [D.42.5.*De rebus auctoritate iudicis possidendis seu vendundis*. (On things to be possessed or sold by the authority of the judge). 4 **Paulus**, *in the fifty-seventh book To the Edict*: pr. If a slave is appointed as an heir conditionally, or if there is doubt whether he will become the heir and be set free, it will not be unfair to establish, upon the request of creditors, that if he does not become the heir before a certain time, everything proceeds as if he had not been so appointed as heir. This often happens when an heir is appointed conditionally to give money to someone, and the time has not been specified. However, this should be observed regarding the assets. Moreover, freedom belongs to him at any time, and the praetor must preserve it for him, even if it is certain that there will be neither an heir nor a possessor of the assets. If, though, someone undertake the defense of a person deceased by declaring himself heir and submitting to legal proceedings, the property of the deceased is not to be sold.].

Even by a Justinian's constitution, if the freedom is given to the slave under non-potestative condition [i.e. it is not in the power of the slave to unfulfill the condition, e.n.], <and> the inheritance unconditionally, was introduced that, on contrary, it must be understood that the freedom is given unconditionally, the inheritance under condition, C.6.27.6 [C.6.27.*De necessariis et servis heredibus instituendis vel* substituendis (Concerning the appointment and substitution of slaves, as compulsory heirs). 6. Leaving in force the constitution which we enacted, and by which we ordained that a slave who is appointed heir by his master without liberty should be considered as having been also granted his liberty, if anyone appoints his slave as his unconditional heir, but gives him liberty upon condition, then if the condition is such as is in the power of the slave to fulfill but the latter disregards it and fails to fulfill it, he will, through his own fault, be deprived of both liberty and his inheritance. But if the fulfillment of the condition depends upon fortuitous circumstances and does not take place by reason of the snares of fortune, then, he shall, out of humanitarian consideration, be entitled to his liberty, but the inheritance, if solvent, shall go to the intestate heirs, if no one else is substituted. If the estate is not, however, solvent, the slave shall, as compulsory heir, have both liberty and the inheritance. For in such case, he becomes free as well as compulsory heir, both under the provisions of ancient law, as well as that of our own.].

In the first case, therefore, the slave receives freedom from himself when the condition of the inheritance occurs, D.28.5.6.4 [D.28.5. *De heredibus instituendis* (The institution of heirs). 6. **Ulpianus**, *in the fourth book To Sabinus*: 4. However, if he has been appointed with freedom, in the opinion of Julianus, the question arises whether the grant of freedom can be revoked by a codicil. And he believes that in the case where he becomes a necessary heir, the revocation cannot be valid so that freedom is not revoked by himself. The slave appointed as an heir, in fact, acquires freedom for himself. This opinion has its reasoning: just as no one can make a bequest to his own detriment, he also cannot revoke it.]; D.40.7.2.2 [D.40.7. *De statuliberis (Statuliberi).* 2 **Ulpianus**, *in the fourth book To Sabinus*: 2. Julianus also wrote that if a slave is bequeathed by the heir of the father and is ordered to be free in the will made for a minor, the granting of freedom prevails.].

On the ground of these rules <he> is not properly *orcinus*[47] [i.e. free from the burdens of *patronatus*[48] towards his former master, e.n.], but freedman (*libertus*[49]) of his ex-master (*suus libertus*[50]).

[47] Berger, *ad vocem Libertus Orcinus*, "A freedman manumitted in the testament of his master. In classical law he was free from patronage since his former master was dead. In Justinian's law, however, the manumitter's son became his patron with all rights of patronage.".

[48] Matteo Marrone (transl.) in D.28.5.8, Sandro Schipani (ed.), *Iustiniani Augusti Digesta seu Pandectae* (Milano, 2013), V, 40., *ad vocem Patronatus*, "The relationship between the former master and his freedman.". *Ad vocem Patronus*, "The master of a slave became after manumitting him the patronus of the freedman (libertus). The freedman had various duties towards his manumissor: vedi obsequium, reverentia The person of a patron should always appear honorable and sacred to the freedman and his son."(D. 37.15.9).[...]. (e.t.).

[49] Berger, *ad vocem Libertus*, "A freedman. The term is used of a freedman in relation to the person who manumitted him (patronus, manumissor). A freedman is libertinus, but *libertus* of his ex-master. In a few texts libertus is used in sense of *libertinus*. *Liberta* is a freedwoman.".

[50] Lorenzo Valla (c.1407–1457), *De Linguae latinae elegantia, libri sex* (Parisiis, 1529). IV, pp. 103–104, "Igitur libertinus relativum est ingenui, libertus relativum est patroni, licet unus idemque sit et libertinus et libertus. Per libertinum significamus conditionem hominis, ficut per ingenuum: Per libertum significamus privatum quendam respectum, sicut per patronum. [...]. Ideoque interrogamus hic ingenuus est, an libertinus? Non autem an libertus, et quum responsum est libertinus interrogamus cuius libertus? Non autem cuius libertinus. Respodeturque est libertus meus, aut tuus, aut illius, aut Catonis, aut nullius." [Therefore, the libertine is the relationship of the freeborn, freedman

That freedom is also the cause for which, strictly according to the law, this <kind of> institution (*haec institutio*) does not resist: Stichus free, and afterward, or if he shall being free, be him the heir (*ex asse* [51]), for the favour of the freedom nevertheless that: "and afterward", should be taken off D.28.5.9.14, 52(51) [D.28.5.*De heredibus instituendis* (The institution of heirs).9 **Ulpianus**, *in the fifth book To Sabinus*: 14. If someone has written as follows: "Stichus is to be free, and, after becoming free, is to be the heir," Labeo, Neratius, and Aristo are of the opinion that, with the word "after" removed, both freedom and inheritance take effect simultaneously. This opinion also seems true to me. 52 (51) **Marcianus**, *in the third book On Rules*: Some authorities did not consider the following institution valid: "Stichus is to be free, and, if he becomes free, he is to be the heir." However, the deified Marcus Aurelius established through a rescript that this institution is valid, as if the clause "if he becomes free" had not been added. 1. f someone has written as follows: "Stichus, if he is mine at the moment of my death, is to be free and the heir," once he is alienated, Stichus cannot inherit upon the order of the buyer. Even if it had not been expressly written, he could not have become free and the heir unless he had remained the property of the testator. However, if the testator has manumitted him during his lifetime, Celso writes in the fifteenth book of the Digest that Stichus becomes the heir. It is not clear that the testator intended to exclude him in this case, nor do the words used in the will entirely oppose this; indeed, even if he is not "his" as a slave, he is "his" as a freedman.]; *adde* our *De casibus perplexis in iure*, §. 15[52].

is the relationship of the patron, although only one is both libertine and freedman at the same time. By libertine we mean the condition of a man, as well as for the freeborn: by libertine we mean a certain private respect, as for the patron (...). Therefore, we ask, is he freeman, or libertine? Not "or freedman": and when the answer is "libertine" we ask, whose freedman? Not instead "libertine of whom". And answer is my freedman, or yours, or of that one, or of Cato, or of anyone].

[51] Berger, *ad vocem Ex asse haeres*, "An heir to the whole estate".

[52] This is a perplexed case illustrated by Leibniz in the work quoted in text, A VI 1, 241. "XV. Of similar flour is the VII: "Stichus liber esto et, posteaquam liber erit, heres esto" ["Stichus is to be free, and, after becoming free, is to be the heir"]. That institution and the attribution of freedom, strictly according to the law, is uncertain, but for the favour of the freedom that "after" has been taken off D.28.5.9.14, 52 (51). Not everyone will, perhaps, recognize the perplexity, so we will show it. The ancients jureconsults wanted, in fact, that slave appointed heir had to be considered firstly as heir and succeed in the person of the testator and, therefore, slave would acquire the freedom on his own, D.28.5.6.4 [see

In addition, our theorem implies also that in a *legatum praecipuum*[53] [i.e. when something has been

above in theorem 3], D.40.7.2 [see in definition 70], because the slave is *necessarius heres*; on contrary, nobody which is *liber* and *extraneus* is *heres necessarius*; therefore, if [the slave] were *liber* soon at the master's death, would be in his own power to accept of being heir or not; consequently, in order that the slave has not the power of acceptance of the inheritance, he has to be heir immediately [without need of acceptance, e.n.]. From it flows that, since according to law the acquisition of freedom depends on the acquisition of the inheritance, the perplexity will be evident, where, on the contrary, by the will of the testator the acquisition of the inheritance depends on the acquisition of freedom. The D.28.5.21.1 [see above in theorem 3] with D.28.5.22 [see above in theorem 3] pertains to this case, where it is said: *freedom can be given to slave without condition, the inheritance with condition, so that both depend on one condition*. In which way, therefore, and for what reason, you ask me, do both depend on condition? I answer because in legates of freedom the term [of acquisition of liberty, n.d.t.] starts exactly from the moment in which the inheritance has been accepted, so that, when the institution of the designated heir in writing is suspended, the inheritance cannot be accepted; it is therefore not surprising that even the freedom granted without condition must be suspended until the condition of the institution of [heir] has been fulfilled according to C.6.51.6 [see above in theorem 3]; for if this condition is not fulfilled, it will be as if freedom were granted without inheritance; in other words, according to the distinction, [one wonders] whether another heir appointed in this succession accepts the inheritance, or does no, and in the first case, indeed, [the slave] gets the inheritance, but not in the second according to the aforesaid C.6.51.6. (e. t.)].

[53] Berger, *ad vocem Legatum per praeceptionem*, "A legacy expressed in the follow form: "X shall take a thing beforehand". The nature of this kind of *legatum* was controversial among the jurists. The problem was wether it could be appplied only in case of an heir to whom the testator wanted to leave a specific thing over and above his share in the inheritance, or wether it could be left to anyone with the effect of a *legatum per vindicationem*. The secon view prevailed.". See also Paul du Plessis, *Borkowski's Textbook on Roman Law* (Cambrigde, 2005), p. 228. Arangio-Ruiz, note 32 above, p. 568 ff., point out that this kind of *legatum*, could be given only in case of coheirs, cose it was not consistant that only one heir can be debtor of himself. A *legatum*, indeed, is always a burden of the inheritance, so when it is provided in a will it has to be calculated on the whole *relictum*, before the division of the inheritance. This is the reason for Leibniz says that in case of an heir which had a *prelegatum* but can't accept inheritance or it is not fulfilled a casual condition to whom the testator submitted that share of inheritance, the jurist has to be not strict, cose on his view the situation is such as that of a *legatum* of which are charged ther heirs.
However, here Leibniz is not consistant with the strict logic reconstruction of the system in terms of teorem and demostration of it. He draws up the rule (the teorem) by the cases law in the Digest, so he does not demonstrate a teoreme but construcs a rule on the basis of the common factors of the cases. Differently, we write a general norm in which we verify if the case can be subdued. Also, in this case we dont "calculate"

bequeathed to the heir as legate beforehand than to the others co-heirs] there is a condition of institution as heir, as in D.28.7.18 [D.28.7.*De conditionibus institutionum* (Conditions on institutions).18 **Marcianus**, *in the seventh book On Institutions*: When a slave has been made free without conditions and designated as an heir in writing under a condition, and if he had not become an heir, he would have received a legacy, the deified Marcus Aurelius established through a rescript that the condition is considered repeated in the legacy.]; D.35.1.70, 77 [D.35.1.*De condicionibus et demonstrationibus et causis et modis eorum, quae in testamento scribuntur*. (Conditions, designations, explanations for and modalities of provisions in wills). 70 **Papinianus**, *in the sixteenth book On Questions:* A mother appointed her two sons as heirs in parts under the condition of emancipation and gave them various things to be taken purely. They accepted the inheritance. Their father must be deprived of the legacies made to them, also for the reason that he, by emancipating them according to his wife's will, is considered to have wanted the last will of his wife to be executed. 77 **Papinianus**, *in the seventh book On Responses*: A grandmother who had appointed her grandchild as an heir in part under the condition of emancipation, later wrote in her codicils: Besides appointing him as an heir, I bequeath to my grandchildren the mentioned properties. The condition of emancipation is considered repeated, even though the grandmother did not add the substitution in the legacies that she had added in the inheritance. Because even when a slave has been left free purely and appointed as an heir under a condition, and a legacy has been left to him if he is not an heir, the deified Marcus Aurelius wrote that the freedom is considered repeated in the legacy.]; D.40.4.26 [D.40.4.*De manumissis testamentis* (Testamentary manumissions).26 **Marcianus**, *in the first book On Rules*: The Emperor Pius and the brothers who were emperors favorably rewrote that if a slave was substituted with freedom, and a legacy was given to him in case he is not an heir, without granting him freedom separately, it shall be understood as if freedom is also attached to the legacy.].

In the above-mentioned passages of Digest, the law 18 and the law 26, explain themselves to each other, likewise law 70 e 77. Because someone who (evidently through his fault) is ousted from the inheritance

the rule at all, but only we make a syllogism.

(think about the fact that he refused or did not fulfill a potestative condition) has not *praelegatum*[54] .

However, if he cannot be heir, or a casual condition is not fulfilled, I would consider that we should behave more benevolently toward him and that the legacy is due, because the legacy was left in consideration of the inheritance, and it should be considered as if it were a bequest to an heir. By the same reason, a condition of instituting an heir made by the person who left the legacy produces the same conditional legacy, even if the nature of such legacy is not moral but extrinsic, as in D.35.1.107 [D.35.1. *De condicionibus et demonstrationibus et causis et modis eorum, quae in testamento scribuntur* (Conditions, designations, explanations for and modalities of provisions in wills). 107 **Gaius**, *in the single book of Cases*: see above in theorem 3.].

Hence <it follows >also that, if I made do a promise (*stipulatio*[55]) to me or to another, the condition added to me is deemed as added also to the other, because the other receives according to a right of mine. Indeed, I can demand; to the same can only be paid. D.45.1.141.7, 8 [D.45.1.*De verborum obligationibus* (Verbal obligations).141 **Gaius**, *in the second book On Verbal Obligations*: 7. Furthermore, I can stipulate for myself purely, or for Titius under a condition. Conversely, if I stipulate for myself under a condition or for Titius purely, the entire stipulation will be useless if the condition is not fulfilled concerning my person, in other words, because the addition cannot be valid

[54] Berger, *ad vocem Praelegare (praelegatio).* "To make a legacy in favor of an heir who, in addition to his share in the inheritance, receives a specific thing as a legacy. The term *praelegatum* used in the literature, is not of Roman coinage. See *legatum per praeceptionem."* (note 53 above).

[55] See Berger, *ad vocem Stipulatio.* "An oral, solemn contract concluded in the form of a question (interrogatio by the creditor: '*spondesne centum dare*?' = 'do you promise to pay one hundred?') and an affirming answer (responsio) of the debtor ('*spondeo*'= 'I promise'). The answer had to agree perfectly with the question; any difference or restriction (addition of a condition) made the stipuiatio void. Presence of both parties was required, and any interruption between question and answer was inadmissible. Stipuiatio was used for any kind of obligation, from die payment of asum of money to the most complicated performances.". See also Watson, note 32 above, Glossary: item *Stipulatio* "The appropriate action on a stipulation was usually a condictio [q.v.], although for some purposes there was an *actio ex stipulatu*."

unless the obligation had gained force for me. Therefore, it cannot be decided in this way if it is evident that Titius's person is purely added. When someone stipulates like this: "Do you promise to give if the ship arrives from Africa to me and Titius?" Titius's person is also considered added under a condition. 8. From this, it is seen that if a different condition is placed concerning my person than concerning Titius's person, and the condition concerning my person is not fulfilled, the entire stipulation is of no value. When my condition is met, if Titius's condition is also met, it can be paid to Titius. Still, if the condition concerning his person fails, it should be considered as not added].

In short: all the conditioned who have tacit conditions (on which see the whole Chapter 2) are suspended and inferred because of what infers and suspends; in other words, the condition of an implied condition is the condition of the conditioned.

(4) A condition does not put into effect anything.

In fact, a conditional sentence is abstract, nothing else preaching that a connection of words, i.e. partial propositions, according to definition 1, the abstract propositions, on the other hand, can be true, indeed they are, with terms that do not exist (e.g. every man is an animal, although no man, nay even humanity exists).

Although I don't ignore the disputes of summulists about the constancy of the thing [*constantia subiecti*[56]]. So, when I say: if a donkey flies, it has wings, I do not assert directly, nor I deny that donkey flies.

[56] Lambertus Marie De Rijk (1924-2012) (ed.), *Giraldus Odonis OFM. Opera Philosophica. I Logica* (Leiden, New York, Köln, 1997), p. 53, "In fourteenth-century logic and semantics the term 'constantia' is frequently used in the technical expression 'constantia subiecti', 'constantia rei', constantia terminorum', and the like, meaning the actual existence of the things referred to by (the subject or predicate) term of a statement or argument.". Summulae are compendiums of theology, philosophy, and canon law that served as textbooks in medieval schools and as reference books. See, for example, John Buridan (1292-1360) in Niels Jørgen Green-Pedersen (1942-2017) (ed.), *Johannes Buridanus: Summulae de locis dialecticis, Artistarium* (Turnhout: Brepols, 2013) 10-6.

For this reason, partly the unlearned, partly the learned scholars are misled.

The unlearned are deceived, if someone arguing with them supposes something possible, that, however, doesn't exist, and ask for what could happen, object: the question is inappropriate, since what is assumed does not exist; as if those who are careful in examining even the things that can happen, must not be right. But men accustomed to their senses cannot raise their minds from matter.

The learned are often deceived by negative conclusions and are too subtle. I do not deny that it is often rightly inferred in ordinary conversation, for example, they say that Owen, a young man with neglected attire, boldly ran up to Queen Elizabeth's passing carriage, so as to present the appearance of a beggar to the Queen.

Then, since she was both kind and learned, she said: "The poor man lies everywhere". This sentence was immediately refuted by Owen's clever retort: "If that were true, then I would be sleeping in your chamber tonight, my queen". This young man, with his intelligence and frankness, deserved the highest favor of the queen and the freest access to the palace.

But to get to the point, there is a negative proposition here: that the poor do not lie everywhere, and this is shown by leading to an absurd conclusion.

However, this should only be said when it is clear that the speaker intends to refute the condition based on the absurdity of the conditioned. Hence, an illustrious question was decided: whether children who are named (*positi*) in a condition (e.g., if he shall die without children) are deemed to be named in a testamentary disposition (as heirs).

Although this question must be answered affirmatively according to natural law (*ius gentium*) (due to the argument from the contrary), it must be answered negatively according to civil law, which requires that children be expressly and clearly either established or disinherited for the sake of a better distinction between what is directly and indirectly given, *adde* D.28.5.19 [D.28.5.*De heredibus instituendis* (The institution of heirs).19 **Ulpianus**, *in the seventh book To Sabinus*: Pomponius and Arrianus also reported a discussion about someone who, leaving a share vacant, instituted an heir in the following manner: "If Seius," who had not been instituted, "will not be my heir, let Sempronius be the heir." This raises the question of whether Sempronius can occupy the vacant share. Pegasus believes that he can be admitted to that share, while Ariston believes the opposite because a share that does not exist would have been assigned to Sempronius. This opinion is also approved by Gaius, Pomponius, and Arrianus, and we rely on this rule.]; D.29.4.8 [D.29.4. *Si quis omissa causa testamenti ab intestato vel alio modo possideat hereditatem* (Where someone, passing over a will, takes possession of an inheritance on intestacy or in some other way). 8. **Ulpianus**, *in the fiftieth book To the Edict*: If someone, instituted as an heir under the condition of giving ten to someone or under some other condition of giving or doing something, neglects the testamentary cause of the succession, and possesses the inheritance ab intestato, it must be considered whether assistance should be provided in favor of the person for whom the condition is intended. It is preferable that assistance should not be provided for them because they are not a legatee.]; D.28.6.2.5 [D.28.6. *De vulgari et pupillari substitutione* (Normal and pupillary substitution). 2 **Ulpianus**, *in the sixth book To Sabinus*: 5. If someone has made a will in this way: "If my son dies within the fourteenth year, let Seius be the heir," and then added: "My son is the heir," the substitution is valid, even though the will has been formulated in this manner.].

From the quoted passages of Digest, above all on the basis of the law D.29.4.8 the distinction between honored (*honoratus* [57]) and legatee is evident. Similarly, if something is taken away under condition, it is deemed

[57] Berger, *ad vocem Honoratus*, "In the law of succession, a person 'honored' by a legacy in a testament See honor. Syn. legatarius. Ant. oneratus = an heir appointed in a testament and charged with the payment of a *legatum* or *fideicommissum* to the beneficiary".

not stably given under a contrary condition D.40.4.59.2 [D.40.4. *De manumissis testamento* (Testamentary manumissions).59 **Scaevola**, *in the twenty-third book of the Digest*: 2. Lucius Titius made the following provision in his will: "Onesiphorus is not to be free, unless you have carefully examined his account." Might Onesiphorus claim freedom on the basis of these words? He replied that the words quoted appeared to withhold rather than to grant freedom.]. If you do not deliver the slave Pamphilus, do you promise to give such and such? He cannot be claimed in court, according to D.45.1.115.2 [D.45.1. *De verborum obligationibus* (Verbal obligations). 115 **Papinianus**, *in the second book of Questions*: 2. Similarly, if someone stipulates as follows, "You promise to give one hundred if you do not give Pamphilus?" Pegaso expressed the opinion that the obligation to give one hundred takes effect only when it is no longer possible to give Pamphilus. But Sabinus believed, based on the intentions of the parties, that once the slave could be given, action could be taken immediately, and one could not act only until it was within the promisor's power to give that slave. He supported this opinion with the example of a bequest of provisions. Mucio wrote that if an heir could sell the provisions and did not do so, he could be immediately required to give the money for the bequest. This is accepted for the sake of utility, considering the intention of the deceased and the nature of the object. Sabinus's opinion can therefore be accepted, provided that the stipulation is framed in a non-conditional manner, as it would be if it were stated, "If you do not give Pamphilus, you promise to pay this much?" But if it is framed as follows, "You promise to give Pamphilus? If you do not give him, you promise to give this much?" This is undoubtedly true when it is proven that it was agreed that if the slave is not given, both the slave and the amount are owed. However, the same solution can be argued even if it was agreed that in case of a failure to transfer the slave, only the money is due because it is proven that the intention of the parties was for the slave to be given or for the amount to be demanded.].

Also, the circular arrangement: if Titius is to be the heir (or not), let Seius be the heir; if Seius is to be the heir (or not), let Titius be the heir, according to D.28.7.16 [D.28.7.*De conditionibus institutionum* (Conditions on institutions).16 **Marcianus**, *in the fourth book of the Institutions*: "If Titius will be the heir, let Seius be the heir; if Seius will be the heir, let Titius be the heir." Julianus writes that the institution of the heir formulated in this way is useless because the condition cannot be fulfilled.].

It would not be puzzled if in this case one of the two could be deemed unconditionally appointed; although this would be totally fair; since it is evident that the testator's intention in appointing them jointly was not for the purpose of mutual suspension, but of mutual implication.

Certainly, in a similar case, according to D.45.1.9 on several contractors stipulating separately, it is said that if you do not give it to them, do you promise to give it to me? [D.45.1. *De verborum obligationibus* (Verbal obligations). 9 **Pomponius**, *in the second book addressed to Sabinus*: If Titius and Seius separately stipulated as follows: "If you don't give that plot of land to that person, do you promise to give it to me?" The purpose was to give it to the other person once the judgment is accepted, and therefore, the action of the occupant is applicable.]. They are considered almost like two creditors (*reos credendi*) and the stipulation of who occupies the first place is unconditional. Therefore, I have often been curious why sometimes jurists deviate from strict law in cases of strict law, such as the *stipulatio* in this case, and sometimes they follow it in cases of good faith, such as in circular institutions of inheritance. It is not far-fetched to say that they also often composed their responses for friendship rather than truth, as stated in definition 32.

(5) *The Conditional logic proposition because of the effect is subject to the common rules of the conditions; the Moral condition has both these, and certain his own and special rules.*

I.e., an argument from Logics to Morals is valid in an affirmative way, not the opposite.

From Morals to Logics it's valid in a negative way, not the opposite. But this must be limited to the effect, not to the terms or nature, e.g. the logical condition infers the conditioned, see supra (above) theorem 1, therefore the moral condition also implies the conditioned.

But not the opposite, in fact the moral suspends the conditioned, see theorem 6, which logic does not. But if you depart from the effect, it does not proceed, e.g. a logical condition can be uncertain, not however the moral. On the contrary, the moral must be uncertain, not indeed the logical, see theorem 17. The demonstration of our theorem, at this point, is clear: all the rules of the conditions are either logical or moral. The logical rules are based on the nature of the terms, while the moral rules flow from the legal effect. Regardless of whether the legal effect adds something, it does not detract from or cancel the nature of the conditions. Logical rules that lack legal effect, as in definition 8, remain within the nature of the conditions. Moral rules, which have that effect as in definition 9, also require legal rules.

(6) The moral condition suspends the conditioned.

(And consequently, by the argument of demonstration of theorem 2, from which it is inferred, from the conjunction of the theorems 1, 2, and 7, it is clear that the Moral conditional proposition is convertible.).

D.4.8.23 [D.4.8. *De receptis: qui arbitrium receperint ut sententiam decant* (Matters referred to arbitration and those who have undertaken to arbitrate in order to make an award). 23 **Ulpianus**, *in the thirteenth book On Edict*: Celsus affirms that if the arbitrator has ordered something to be given by the Kalends of September and it hasn't been given, even if an offer has been made later, the penalty specified in the arbitration clause, once it becomes effective, doesn't go away, because it remains true that it wasn't given by the Kalends of the month; however, if he has accepted what was offered to him, he cannot judicially demand the penalty, as it would be rejected with the exception of fraud. The opposite holds true if something was simply ordered to be given.]; D.12.1.8, 37, 39 [D.12.1. *De rebus creditis si certum petetur et de condictiones* (Things credited giving rise to fixed claims and the *condictio).* 8 **Pomponius**, *in the sixth book From Plautius*, see above in definition 6; 37 **Papinianus**, *in the first book of Definitions*, see above in definition 7; 39 **Papinianus**, *in the first book of Definitions*: Hence, the effect of conditions is really felt when they relate to the future.]; D.12.6.16, 18, 56 [D.12.6. *De condictione indebiti* (The *con-*

dictio[58] for money not owed). 16 **Pomponius**, *in the fifteenth book To Sabinus*: A debt under a suspensive condition, if paid by mistake while the condition is still pending, shall be recoverable. However, once the condition has been fulfilled, it cannot be reclaimed. 18 **Ulpianus**, *in the in the forty-seventh book To Sabinus*: If, on the other hand, a payment has been made under a condition that will certainly be fulfilled, it cannot be reclaimed, even though what is owed under another condition, where it is uncertain whether it will be fulfilled, can be reclaimed. 56 **Papinianus**, *in the eighth book of Questions*: As a cause of undue payment, it is sufficient that it is uncertain whether the defense provided by the exception is temporary or without a time limit. For instance, if someone agrees not to be sued until Titius becomes a consul, because this exception, which is temporary, can become unlimited in time with the death of Titius, it will be quite reasonable to say that what has been paid in the meantime can be recovered. Just as an agreement not to claim, which has been set for a fixed term, does not allow the exercise of the recovery action through demand more than if the debtor pays when the term has expired, similarly, the protection of the right that has a cause that is uncertain if it will occur is realized through the recovery action.]; D.13.5.19 [D.13.5. *De pecunia constituta* (Regarding a sum of money set or established). 19 **Paulus**, *in the twenty-ninth book to the Edict*: What is owed under a condition, whether the payment is agreed upon with a fixed deadline purely and simply or <under a condition> with a certain deadline, remains suspended under the same condition, so that, if this condition is fulfilled, the debtor is obligated; if it is not fulfilled, both actions are extinguished.]; D.17.1.22 [D.17.1.*Mandati vel contra* (The action on mandate or the counteraction). 22 **Paulus**, *in the thirty-second book to the Edict*: If I have given you a mandate to provide surety with an initial term in my favor, and you have provided surety purely and simply and have paid, the most beneficial decision is that, during the interval, you are not entitled to a mandate action, but only when the term has expired.]; D.21.1.43 [but, it seems a misquote, e.n., D.21.1.*De aedilicio edicto et redhibitione et quanti minoris* (The edict of the aedile, rescission, and the action for diminution).43 **Paulus**, *in the first book to the Edict of the Curule Aediles*: The majority of jurists say that an ox that gores is considered flawed, as well as mules that kick; it is also said that horses

[58] Watson, note 32 above, Glossary: *Condictio*. A type of action alleging a civil law [ius civile q.v.] debt without mentioning any cause of action, available not only as a contractual remedy, but also on a quasi-contractual basis, where unjustified enrichment could be shown. Although its form was always the same, its name varied according to the situation involved, for example, the *condictio* for money not due [*indebiti*, that is, money paid in error.]

that become wild without reason and tear off their harnesses by themselves are considered flawed.]; D.20.1.13 [D.20.1. *De pignoribus et hypothecis et qualiter ea contrahantur et de pactis eorum* (On pledges and mortgages, how they are contracted, and the agreements related to them). 13 **Marcianus**, *in the single book On the Mortgage Action*: Once the herd has been pledged, even the animals born subsequently are bound; but even if the previous animals have died and the entire herd has been renewed, it will still be held as a pledge.]; D.28.7.8.6; [D.28.7.*De conditionibus institutionum* (Conditions on institutions). 8. **Ulpianus**, *in the fiftieth book to the Edict*: 6. Whenever an heir receives the order to swear that they will give or do something that is not objectionable, they will have the hereditary actions only if they have given or done what they were ordered to swear.]; D.32.14 [D.32.*De legatis et fideicommissa* (Legacies and fideicommissa).14 **Gaius**, *in the first book On Fideicommissa*: There is no doubt that, if a legacy has been left to a wife under the condition "if she does not get married", and if she has been asked "for a fideicommissum, in case she gets married" to give to another person what "was left to her", if she gets married, she must be compelled to give.]; D.35.1.26, 40.2, 41 [D.35.1.*De condicionibus et demonstrationibus et causis et modis eorum, quae in testamento scribuntur* (Conditions, designations, explanations for and modalities of provisions in wills). 26 **Julianus**, *in the eighty-second book of the Digests*: pr. These words: "if he swears to give twenty or to do such a thing", express a condition with two parts. Therefore, if someone was instituted as an heir under this condition: "if he swears to give ten or to make a monument"; even though, according to the words of the edict, he is admitted to the inheritance or legacy; nevertheless, he is obliged to do what he was ordered to swear that he will do, and he is only exempted from the oath. 40 **Gaius**, *in the second book of Extracts from the Posterior Works of Labeo*: 2. Someone bequeathed the sum of one hundred to Tiberius, adding: 'My heir shall give the sums of money to those to whom I bequeathed, if my mother dies.' The testator died before Tiberius, and Tiberius died before the mother. After the mother's death, Offilius replied that the bequest is due to Tiberius's heirs because the bequest was not conditional; it was made purely and then the payment deadline was set. Let's examine (says Labeo) whether this opinion is erroneous, as there is no difference between this expression: "My heir shall give the sums of money to those to whom I bequeathed if my mother dies", and this other expression: "He shall not give if my mother does not die". Now, in both cases, the bequest is given or taken under a condition. I approve Labeo's response. 41 **Ulpianus**, *In the thirty-fourth book to the Edict*, see above in theorem 1.]; D.36.2.4, 5, 13, 21, 25 [D.36.2. *Quando dies legatorum vel fidei-*

commissorum cedat. (When legacies and *fideicommissa*[59] become due). 4 **Ulpianus**, *in the nineteenth book to Sabinus*: If the testator has bequeathed that when the heir dies, they shall give the sum of ten to Lucius Tiberius, with the time of the expiration being uncertain, it does not pass to the heirs of the legatee if the legatee dies before the heir. 5 **Ulpianus**, *in the twentieth book, to Sabinus*: 4. The law is the same in case of an impossible condition; for the legacy is treated as unconditional. 13 **Pomponius**, *in the sixth book to Sabinus*: A legacy in these terms "whether such a thing be done or be not done, I give and bequeath" does not pass to the heir unless one or other event have happened in the life of the legatee; for nothing can be due before there is some ground upon which it is due, nor will the legacy be due in all events merely because one or other must happen; for a legacy such as "let my heir give when he shall die" is certain to be due; yet it does not pass to the heir of the legatee if he die in the life of the heir. 21 **Paulus**, *in the second book to Vitellio*: If a legacy be not made payable at a future date, it is due at once or at once belongs to him to whom it was given. If a date be named, though a distant one, if it be certain, as upon the Kalends of January a hundred years hence, the legacy vests at once, though it cannot be demanded before the date; but if it be uncertain, as "when he shall attain puberty" or "when he shall marry one of my family" or "when he shall become a magistrate" or indeed "when he shall do anything which the writer of the testament sees fit to express," the thing cannot belong to him nor can the legacy vest unless the date come or the condition happen. 1. If a legacy be left to Titius upon the same condition upon which I have instituted you my heir, Pomponius thinks that this legacy vests in the same manner as if it were left unconditionally; for it was certain to be due if the heir took the inheritance; for legacies do not become uncertain if the heirs be conditionally instituted, and that legacy does not much differ from this: "If he be heir, let him give.". 25. **Papinianus**, *in the eighteenth book of Questions*: When this or that thing is bequeathed, the enumeration of multiple things disjunctively does not create multiple legacies. And it cannot be approved otherwise if one has bequeathed purely and simply one estate or another under condition: indeed, while the condition is pending, the choice cannot take place, and if he dies, it will not be considered that the legacy has passed to the heir.]; D.40.5.61.1.2 [D.40.5.*De fideicommissariis liber-*

[59] "A trust created by will", Andrew M. Riggsby, *Roman Law and Legal World of the Romans* (Cambridge: Cambridge University Press, 2010), p. 119; "It may be noted that a Roman form of trust is the *fideicommissum*, but this was a device of law of succession which made possible the settlement of property within the prevailing notion of ownership.", David Carey Miller, "Property", in Ernest Metzger (1998), "Actions", in Id. (ed.), *A Companion to Justinians's Institutes* (Ithaca NY: Cornell University Press, 1998), p. 67.

tatibus (Grants of freedom by fideicommissa). 61.1. [does not exists; misquote? (e.n.)]; D.42.4.7.14 [D.42.4.*Quibus ex causis in possessionem eatur* (For what reasons possession may be obtained). 7 **Ulpianus**, *in the fifty-ninth book to the Edict*: 14. If a debtor is in hiding at a specified time or under a condition, before the expiration of the term or the fulfillment of the condition, his assets cannot be sold. Because there is no difference between not being a debtor and not being able to be sued yet. We will say the same even if he is not a debtor. The same will also be said if one indeed has the action but in a way that it can be rejected by an exception.]; D.44.7.42 [D.44.7.*De obligationibus et actionibus* (Obligations and actions). 42 **Ulpianus**, *in the twenty-first book to the Edict*: One to whom something has been bequeathed under a condition is not a creditor during the pending of the condition, but becomes one when the condition is fulfilled. However, it has been decided that the person who stipulated under a condition is a creditor even while the condition is pending.]; D.45.1.116 [D.45.1.*De verborum obligationibus* (Verbal obligations). 116 **Papinianus**, *in the fourth book On Questions*: If, after stipulating with Tiberius for a sum of ten, you stipulated with Maevius for as much as less than ten you could obtain from Tiberius, there is no doubt that Maevius is exposed to endure all the risk. However, even if you had asked Tiberius for the sum of ten, Maevius will not pay unless Tiberius has failed to satisfy the judgment. In fact, as Pedius observes, Maevius and Tiberius are not two debtors of the same obligation, but Maevius must do so under the condition that it cannot be recovered from Tiberius. Therefore, Maevius is not released from being called to trial by Tiberius, as he is uncertain if he will be a debtor, nor is Maevius released by Tiberius' payment, as he was not obligated due to the condition of the stipulation; nor can Maevius be rightly sued during the pending of the condition because it is not right to demand from Maevius before Tiberius has been pursued.]; I.3.15.4 [I.3.15. *De Verborum Obligatione* (Of verbal obligation).4 A stipulation is conditional, when performance is made to depend on some uncertain event in the future, so that it become actionable only on something being done or omitted: for instance, 'Do you promise to give five aurei if Titius is made consul?' If, however, a man stipulates in the form 'Do you promise to give so and so, if I do not go up to the Capitol?' the effect is the same as if he had stipulated for payment to himself at the time of his death. The immediate effect of a conditional stipulation is not a debt, but merely the expectation that at some time there will be a debt: and this expectation devolves on the stipulator's heir, supposing he dies himself before fulfilment of the condition.]; D.46.1.16.5 [D.46.1.*De fideiussoribus et mandatoribus* (On sureties and mandators). 16 **Julianus**, *in the fifty-third book of the Digests*: 5. If a stipulation is made with a time limit, and a surety has been accepted under a condition, their right remains pending, so that if the condition is met before the scheduled time, they are not obligated. If both a condition and a time limit are involved, or even if the condition follows the time limit, they are obliged.]; D.50.16.213 [D.50.16.*De verborum significatione* (Meaning of expressions). 213 **Ulpianus**, *in the first book of the Rules*: *Cedere diem* means that a sum of money is starting to be due; *venire diem* means that the day has arrived when the sum of money can be demanded. When it was stipulated purely, it is said *cedit et venit dies*; when it was stipulated for a specific day, it is said *cedit dies, sed nondum venit*; when it was stipulated under a condition, during the pending of this, it is said: *neque cessit, neque venit dies*.]; D.50.17.169 [D.50.17.*De diversis regulis iuris antiqui* (Of the different rules of ancient law). 169 **Paulus**, *in the second book to Plautius*: The one who orders to do something causes harm: there is no fault for the one who is required to obey.]; C.6.46.3 [C.6.46. *De condicionibus insertis tam legatis quam fideicommissis et libertatibus*. (Concerning conditions attached to legacies, trusts and manumissions.).3. If Auluzanus wanted the legacy left in the will to be paid only upon condition that the legatee should stay with his housekeeper and her mother, and it was the legatee's fault that the testator's wish was not complied with, purposely failing to obey it, he will not be permitted to claim the legacy.]; C.6.25.1 [C.6.25.*De institutionibus seu substitutionibus sub condicione factis* (Concerning appointments, substitutions or trusts, made upon condition)1, see above in this theorem 1]; C.6.51.2 [C.6.51.*De caducis tollendis* (Concerning abolishing lapses (escheats).1. Since you state that your maternal grandfather appointed your daughter his heir upon condition that she should marry the son of Anthyllus, it is clear that she does not become heir till she shall have fulfilled the condition or the son of Anthyllus, by refusal, prevents the marriage. 2. If you did not fulfill the condition under which you were appointed as heir in the testament of your mother, the substitute takes your place. Nor does it appear that she attempted to pledge you to widowhood under pretense of arranging a dishonorable marriage, since her purpose in wanting to join you in marriage to the son of her sister, your cousin, was entirely commendable. 1. Nor are you entitled to special relief, since it appears form the contents of your petition, that it is not your cousin's fault that the last wish of your mother, the testatrix, has not been complied with.].

Or rather, in conditions, an argument from the contrary is valid, as stated by *Everh. Loc. Legal. arg. a contr. sens. n. 36*[60]. And with the cessation of the cause in them, namely the condition, the effect ceases, that is, the conditionated, see *Andr. Tiraq. tr. peculiari quando cessante causa cesset effectus*[61]. For example, if a ship comes from Asia, let Seius be the heir: before it comes, he is not the heir. Indeed, a moral conditional proposition has the efficacy of conditional right, or rather, if a condition exists, a certain right is produced in another subject, which right is conditioned, according to definition 9. Hence, if the condition exists, the right also exists in another subject, according to theorem 1.

However, a right cannot exist in another subject unless it is by the will of the person to whom the right belongs from the beginning (since no one's right can be taken away without their consent), see definition 77 below. On the other hand, if a person has not otherwise declared their willingness, a right cannot exist in another person, if the condition, by hypothesis, does not exist. Therefore, a conditioned right will not exist if a condition does not exist, or rather, a moral condition suspends the conditioned, according to definition 7.

This was what needed to be demonstrated.

[60] Nicolaus Everardi (1462-1532), *Loci argumentorum legales* (Venetiis, 1567), Locus a contrario sensu, n. 36, p. 513.

[61] Andreas Tiraquellus (1488-1558), *Cessante causa cessat effectus*, in *Tractatus varii* (Lugduni, 1615), n. 1.

CHAPTER II

[Nature and Effect of the Condition]

Definitions

Furthermore, the special handling of conditional propositions is divided into nature and effect.

Nature pertains to the fact that we know when a condition exists; effect pertains to the law, so that we know what is considered a condition according to what has been established, which is what matters in law.

Therefore, the nature of conditions is determined partly by necessary consequences and partly by the presumed intention of the person whose intention should serve as the rule, or, better said, is resolved through interpretation.

The purpose of the interpretation is to gather through signs the thought of someone in a probable way. On the other hand, signs are words, or something else, such as facts, circumstances, etc., and indeed one explains the other when more signs are simultaneous.

All these things depend on rules of interpretation that either the reason or the law prescribe. And if the rules of law are not founded on reason (e.g. when the laws want us to presume an impossible condition in the last wills by an almost dormant and unconscious testator, added beyond his will) then one has an interpretation that is not true but fictitious.

That is not real, but legal.

Similarly, also *Bachovius*[62] divides the true into legal and real.

[62] Reinhard Bachoff von Echt (c. 1575–1640). The complete quotation of the text is not included.

Nature, moreover, is divided into form and matter, or rather into partial propositions.

Form is either internal or external, with the latter referred to as "appearance" or "force" in D.28.5.70(69) [D.28.5. *De heredibus instituendis* (The institution of heirs). 70 (69) **Proculus**, *in the second book of the Letters*: "Cornelius and Maevius, whoever of them wishes to be an heir," they both want to. Trebatius believes that neither of the two will be an heir, Cartilius thinks that they both will be heirs: to whom do you give reason? Proculus: I agree with Cartilius and consider that addition "whoever of them wishes" to be superfluous. It would have been the same even if it had not been added, so that whoever wanted it would not be an heir. Because if the two were among the necessary heirs, then this would not have been added unnecessarily, and it would have not only the appearance but also the effect of a condition: I would say, therefore, that if both of them wish to be heirs, they will both be heirs.] or as "effect" in D.12.1.39 [D.12.1. *De rebus creditis si certum petetur et de condictione* (Things credited giving rise to fixed claims and the *condictio*). 39 **Papinianus**, *in the first book of Definitions*: Therefore, the clause has the force of a condition only when referring to the future.].

The internal aspect, or conditionality, has rightly been emphasized and we discussed it in general in theorems 1, 2, 3, 4; we will now discuss it in detail.

Conditionality can be either affirmative or

10. ILLATION only, e.g. if that is a man, it follows that it is an animal; if he is not a man, then he is not even an animal, that is

11. ILLATION AND SUSPENSION, e.g. if that is a man, Christ died for him, if on the contrary, he is not a man, Christ did not die for him.

Theorem

(7) *If a condition implies and suspends the conditioned party, the conditioned party will also suspend and imply the same condition.*

Or rather, if conditionality is affirmative and negative, the partial propositions are changeable.

Indeed, the conditioned suspends the condition, according to theorem 2, and is suspended from this, for the hypothesis here examined; each suspended, on the other hand, implies a suspending, since there cannot be a suspension without a suspender, according to definition 7, for which if a suspended exists, a suspending one exists, which is to infer according to definition 6. For this definition also the conditioned implies a condition, e.g. in the next example we can also say: if Christ died for that, he will be a man; and if Christ did not die for that, he will not be a man.

Definitions

Conditionality, therefore, (as a sign) derives either from the nature of the thing, which the Jurisconsults call

12. EXTRINSIC, v. D.35.1.99 [D.35.1. *De condicionibus et demonstrationibus et causis et modis eorum, quae in testamento scribuntur* (Conditions, designations, explanations for and modalities of provisions in wills). 99 **Papinianus**, *in the eighteenth book On Questions*: Conditions that arise from an external cause and not from the will, meaning those that are implicitly related to the provision, do not make legacies conditional.]; D.36.2.6.1, 25.1 [D.36.2. *Quando dies legatorum vel fideicommissorum cedat* (When a legacy or a *fideicommissum* vests). 6 **Paulus**, *in the third book to Sabinus*: 1. But if the legacy is suspended by an external cause, not by the same will, even if the legatee dies first, we will say that he transmits the legacy to his heir. For example, if a husband bequeathed to a stranger the dowry, leaving the wife a sum instead of the dowry, and while the woman was deliberating whether she should choose the dowry or the bequest, the legatee died, and then the woman chose the bequest; it was decided that the legacy passes to the legatee's heir. The same response was given by Julianus, because it is considered that the legacy contains

more of a delay than a condition. 25 **Papinianus**, *in the eighteenth book On Questions*: 1. "My heir shall give Tiberius what Sextus owes me." If Sextus, as a minor without the authorization of his guardian, received money and became wealthier, and the claimant refers to this debt; since the minor owes nothing, the bequest will have no effect. However, if by the term 'debt' he meant to signify a natural obligation and a future payment, Tiberius, in the meantime, can demand nothing, just as if a condition had been implicitly inserted, no different from if he had said this: "Give Tiberius what the minor will pay"; or if he had bequeathed the offspring to be born from Aretusa; or the fruits that will be produced from a certain estate. And it cannot be objected that if the legatee were to die in the interim, and then the offspring were born or the fruits were gathered, or the minor paid the money, the legatee's heir would have a claim. Since the bequest with no explicitly stated condition immediately expires, even though the disposition is suspended for an external cause.], and exists for the effect, D.35.1.pr. [D.35.1.*De condicionibus et demonstrationibus et causis et modis eorum, quae in testamento scribuntur* (Conditions, designations, explanations for and modalities of provisions in wills). 99 **Papinianus**, *in the eighteenth book On Questions*: Conditions that arise from an external cause and not from the will, namely those that are implicitly related to the provision, do not make legacies conditional.], of the right, D.35.1.21 [D.35.1. *De condicionibus et demonstrationibus et causis et modis eorum, quae in testamento scribuntur* (Conditions, designations, explanations for and modalities of provisions in wills). 21 **Julianus**, *in the thirty-first book of the Digests*: There is a significant difference between a condition of fact and a condition of law. Because conditions like "if the ship arrives from Asia" or "if Tiberius becomes consul," even if they are fulfilled, prevent the heir from claiming the inheritance until he is unaware of their fulfillment. However, when conditions of law are fulfilled, they are not required. For example, if someone believes themselves to be a minor when they are actually an adult, they can still inherit. For the same reason, the heir can claim the inheritance in part even if they do not know whether the will has been opened.], not of the fact, D.35.1.60 [D.35.1. *De condicionibus et demonstrationibus et causis et modis eorum, quae in testamento scribuntur* (Conditions, designations, explanations for and modalities of provisions in wills). 60 **Paulus**, *in the seventh book On the Lex Julia and Papia*: Conditions that consist of an act are various and are somehow susceptible to a triple division: that something is given; that something is done; that something happens; or conversely: that nothing is given, nothing is done, nothing happens. The conditions of giving or doing depend on those to whom it was left, or on other people; the conditions of the third type depend on an event.], and an example can be found in D.35.1.107

[D.35.1. *De condicionibus et demonstrationibus et causis et modis eorum, quae in testamento scribuntur* (Conditions, designations, explanations for and modalities of provisions in wills). 107 **Gaius**, in the single book of Cases: see above in theorem 3.]; D.45.1.74 [D.45.1.*De verborum obligationibus* (Verbal obligations). 74 **Gaius**, *in the eighth book on the Provincial Edict*: Some stipulations are certain, others are uncertain. What is certain is what appears from the same expression to be a thing, such as what it is, what kind it is, and how much, like ten gold coins, the Tusculan estate, the slave Stichus, a hundred bushels of excellent wheat, a hundred amphorae of fine Campanian wine.], (such as a supervening will that comes from outside of man, but the Doctors call it intrinsic, which seems more accurate, and whose connection derives from the nature of the thing; extrinsic, whose connection derives from the will, see *Negusantius* de *pignor. V. 3.2.11*[63]);

or from the nature of the will of the person which has the thing in their own power, or rather

13. from the DISPOSER, whose conditional proposition is called

14. DISPOSITION. (Otherwise in D.35.1.21 [D.35.1. *De condicionibus et demonstrationibus.* (Conditions, designations, explanations for and modalities of provisions in wills).21 **Julianus**, *in the thirty-first book of the Digests*: see above in definition 12.] where the estrinsic is called <condition> of law, the disposition <condition> of fact). Although later we will utilize the word disposition such as conditional moral proposition.

In EXTRINSIC conditionality, whose examples are found in theorem 10, theorem 14 at the end, and theorem 17, according to its own nature, either the condition is necessary for the conditioned and suspends it, in which case the disposition is unconditional in efficacy, or the conditioned is necessary for the condition, meaning

[63] Antonius Negusantius (1465–1508), *Tractatus de pignoribus et hypothecis.* (Lugduni, 1606, first ed.1549), V, 3, 2, [Secunda pars tertii membri quintae partis principalis, e.n.], 11, "Sed quando in oblatione & dispositione apponitur conditio extrinseca, tunc talis oblatio & dispositio nullum effectum operatur" [but when an extrinsic condition is inserted in the payment and disposition, then that payment and disposition produce no effect].

that it is inferred by the same condition or suspends the condition, and in that case, the disposition in legal effect is null; see below theorem 17.

The EXTERNAL FORM is either implicit or explicit.

People often use implicit conditions, see *Grotius, de J. B. P. XI. 6*[64].

I do not want to delve here into the equivocations by which the Society of Jesus is commonly discredited; if nothing else, what is more Machiavellian and more suitable for subverting the tranquility of humankind than that witty maxim of the Great King of France, Henry IV? According to reports by *Forstner, Tac., lib omissis, p. 10*[65], he claimed that all the promises of princes contain an implicit condition: if it proves useful. The same as *Joh. De Laet. Hist. Univ. p. 405*[66] attributes to Mary of

[64] Hugo Grotius (1583– 1645], *De Jure Belli ac Pacis* (Parisiis, 1625), Lib. II, Cap. IX, VI, "Quando autem lex in tali praesumtione sit fundata, ex legis materia, verbis & circumstantiis colligendum. Similiter ergo dicemus, si promissio fundata sit in praesumtione quadam facti quod non ita se habeat, naturaliter nullam eius esse vim: quia omnino promissor non consensit in promiffum, nisi sub quadam conditione quae reipsa non extitit.". Engl. transl. in *https://lonang.com/library/reference/grotius-law-war-and-peace/gro-211/* (accessed on July, 20 2024) The decision when a law has been based on such a presumption must be inferred from the substance, words, and circumstances of the law. In like manner, then, we shall say that, if a promise has been based on a certain presumption of fact which does not so obtain, by the law of nature it has no force. For the promisor did not consent to the promise except under a certain condition which, in fact, did not exist.

[65] Christoph Forstner (d. 1667), *Omissorum in notis ad Tacitum liber I.* (Argentorati, 1631), p. 9 [not 10 such as in the text; the quote in the text is to be referred to Clemens VIII, not to Henry IV of France, e.n.], "Clemens VIII Pontifex Henrico IV, Galliae Regi foedus, cum Elisabecha Angliae Regina alleganti, respondit Principes sibi omnia permittere quae sibi utilia putant: et eo rem devenisse: ut ob foedus neglectum nemo reprehendatur." [Clement VIII Pontiff replied to Henry IV, king of France who had recalled a treaty with Queen Elizabeth of England: Princes can afford whatever they think is useful to themself: and that the question be submitted to him [to the Pope, e.n.] so that nobody could be reprimanded for the forgotten treaty].

[66] Johannes De Laet (1581–1649), *Compendium historiae universalis civilis & ecclesiaticae: tam Romanae quam Protestantium selectissimis rebus refertissimum ab Augusto ad annum usq[ue] Christi Iesu M DC XL. Deductum,* (Amstelaedami, 1653, first ed. 1643), p. 405.

Scotland. Briefly, according to our customary, premised the distinction of cases, we will contain the matter in rules. In fact, one wonders either when in speaking it would be allowed to reserve some condition in the mind; or when it would be allowed to assume something in the interpretation; the first case is more casuistic and belongs to the forum of conscience (internal justice); the latter more juridical and belongs to the external forum (external justice). And the first indeed must be subdistinct, in fact some condition is reserved either in a simple agreement, or in an oath. Hence two rules.

Theorems

(8) *In a simple statement is permitted to reserve in mind some condition only whenever it is lawful to circumvent.*

Indeed, just this is to deceive, knowingly to state something different from what we think. Although it is rejected by Augustine, by most moralists it is nevertheless accepted that sometimes it is allowed to deceive, s. *Mr. Hanchius* widely in some *Dissert. de Simulat. et Dissimulat.*[67] Then

(9) *Whilst on the other hand, it is permitted to reserve something in the mind only when deceiving is necessary.*

For in the oath it is allowed to deceive only when it is necessary to evidently preserve the glory of God. So, the promise of an illegal thing, e.g. of an assassination or murder, not even by an oath is corroborated. Even in these cases it is only allowed to imply a condition. One wonders now, moreover, when it seems implied by the fact, or by the interpretation.

(10) *In interpreting, a tacit condition must be implied, if the laws want it to be implied.*

[67] Martin Hanke (d.1709), *De simulatione et dissimulatione disputatio preliminaris secunda et tertia* (Jenae: Typis Johannis Nisii, 1656-57).

For example, a legacy contains a tacit condition that the person who receives it will become the heir (or will take what has been assigned to them), and they will be the one who has to pay the legate, according to D.30.126.1 [D.30.*De legatis et fidecommissis* (Legacies and *fideicommissa)*.126. **Paulus**, *in the single book On the Twelve Tables*: 1. If legacies "if he becomes the heir" are established to the detriment of a posthumous child, and, the posthumous child not having been born, substitutes take their place, it must be held.].

However, this condition does not arise so much from the presumed intention of the testator as it does from the nature of the legacy itself (since it is a matter of civil law) regulated by the laws.

Therefore, it is not a moral but rather an extrinsic condition, as implied by D.30.3 [D.30.*De legatis et fidecommissis* (Legacies and *fideicommissa)*. 3 **Ulpianus**, *in the fourth book to Sabinus*: These words of the testator: "whoever, among those who have been written down, will be my heir", or "if Tiberius becomes the heir", or "if he accepts the inheritance", do not make the legacy or the fideicommissum conditional.]; D.35.1.19.1 [D.35.1.*De condicionibus et demonstrationibus. et causis et modis eorum, quae in testamento scribuntur (Conditions, designations, explanations for and modalities of provisions in wills)*. 19. **Ulpianus**, *in the fifth book of Disputations*: 1. The clause "if he shall be the first heir, you shall be obliged to give" should not be treated as a condition, for the testator has more so indicated when the legacy should be given rather than inserting a condition, unless perhaps the testator had intended to make it a condition. Therefore, it should not be said that he has made a condition like this: "I bequeath whatever must be given to me in Ephesus." But if he bequeaths it in this manner: "if the first heir to me shall not be, you shall be obliged to give to the second," and the first heir exists, the legacy shall not be due. If the first heir comes in together with the second, there should be no doubt at all that the condition did not come into existence]; D.36.2.21.1, 22.2 [D.36.2. *Quando dies legatorum vel fideicommissorum cedat* (When a legacy or a *fideicommissum* vests) 21 **Paulus**, *in the second book to Vitellius*: 1. If it was bequeathed to Tiberius under the same condition under which you were instituted as an heir, Pomponius thinks that this bequest expires as if it had been made purely because it is certain that it will be due as soon as there is an heir. Indeed, the condition imposed on instituted heirs does not make legacies uncertain, and such a bequest is not much different from this: "If he becomes an heir, he shall give.".

22 **Pomponius**, *in the fifth book to Quintus Mucius*: 2. If, however, I appoint two heirs and charge them with a bequest in case one of them claims the inheritance, such a condition will not be entirely superfluous: it will be valid for the portion of the co-heir, and will be useless for the portion of the one mentioned in the condition, as it would be if he were bequeathed in this way when only the co-heir is instituted.].

Likewise, for the same reason, among annual legacies, the first year's legacy is considered pure (unconditional), while the others are conditional. In regard to the legatee's heirs, the legacy is understood under the tacit legal condition that it will pass to them only if the legatee is alive in the first year, as stated in D.33.1.4, 5 [D. 33.1 *De annuis legatis et fideicommissis* (Annual legacies and *fideicommissa*). 4 **Paulus**, *in the sixty-second book to the Edict*: If something was bequeathed to someone for each year, according to the opinion of Sabinus, which is correct, there are multiple bequests; the one for the first year purely, and those for the subsequent years conditionally. Because the condition is considered inherent if the legatee is alive; and therefore, after his death, the bequest will not pass to the heir. 5 **Modestinus**, *in the first book On Responses*: I also request my other heirs to give to my wife, as long as she lives, ten gold coins every year. The wife outlived the husband for five years and four months. I ask whether her heirs are entitled to the entire bequest for the sixth year. Modestinus replied: The entire bequest for the sixth year is due.]. Otherwise, it will not be transmitted to the heirs. Other examples can be found in theorem 3.

(11) *Likewise, whether it is probable that the settlor and the acceptor at the same time (e.g. the* promisor *and the* stipulator*) or, if there is no acceptor, that only the settlor (e.g. the testator) implied a condition.*

Because the testament e.g. and similar acts (in which there is no acceptance, but a revocable right is acquired only) depend purely on the mind of one; instead, where there is acceptance, the consensus of two concurs.

And such a testament maintains [evid. its validity, e.n.] when the settlor, if he had not implied, would be very foolish, nobody in fact is presumed foolish.

Examples of this situation occur every day, so we will mention only one: the dowry (and the donation due to marriage, is constituted with this tacit condition, if the marriage will be followed, I.2.7.3 [I.2.7. *De donationibus* (Concerning gifts).3. There is another specific kind of gift between the living, with which the earlier jurists were quite unacquainted, and which owed its later introduction to more recent emperors. It was called gift before marriage, and was subject to the implied condition that it should not be binding until the marriage had taken place; its name being due to the fact that it was always made before the union of the parties, and could never take place after the marriage had once been celebrated. The first change in this matter was made by our imperial father Justin, who, as it had been allowed to increase dowries even after marriage, issued a constitution authorizing the increase of gifts before marriage during the continuance of the marriage tie in cases where an increase had been made to the dowry. The name 'gift before marriage' was, however, still retained, though now inappropriate, because the increase was made to it after the marriage. We, however, in our desire to perfect the law, and to make names suit the things which they are used to denote, have by a constitution permitted such gifts to be first made, and not merely increased, after the celebration of the marriage, and have directed that they shall be called gifts 'on account of' (and not 'before') marriage, thereby assimilating them to dowries; for as dowries are not only increased, but actually constituted, during marriage, so now gifts on account of marriage may be not only made before the union of the parties, but may be first made as well as increased during the continuance of that union.]); D.23.3.21, 41 [D. 23.3.*De iure dotium* (The law of dowry). 21 **Ulpianus**, *in the thirty-fifth book to Sabinus*: It is certain that the stipulation made for the purpose of a dowry has the implicit condition "if, subsequently, the marriage will have taken place"; and therefore, it is certain that if the marriage subsequently occurs (although the condition was not expressed), one can take action based on the stipulation; therefore, if the notice of the dissolution of the engagement is sent, it is considered that the condition of the stipulation has been removed. 41 **Paulus**, *in the thirty-fifth book To the Edict*: By promising with a stipulation the dowry, all obligate themselves, of whatever gender or condition they may be.].

(12) Likewise, if the context persuades.

(In which case, the condition is partly tacit, namely in this instance, and partly expressed, in similar cases). This can happen in an infinite number of ways, but we will only mention two of the most prominent: the condition of the premise has been recalled in the agreement (the same act is in fact divided by the words), D.45.1.134.1 [D.45.1.*De verborum obligationibus* (Verbal obligations).

134 **Paulus**, *in the fifteenth book On Responses*: 1. He replied the same: In most cases, the things agreed upon in performance are also understood to be repeated in stipulations, in such a way that this repetition does not render the stipulation useless.].

And whatever agreement or contract is made, it is contained in the same way as stated in D.2.14.4.3, at the end, regarding agreements, [D.2.14.*De pactis* (Pacts). 4 **Paulus**, *in the third book To the Edict*: 3. He also provided an opinion for a specific case in which it had been agreed not to demand the principal amount until the interest had been paid. He expressed the view that, even though the stipulation had been formulated without a condition, the condition is inherent in the stipulation, as if it had been expressly agreed upon.].

Furthermore, if a condition of one thing is called for in relation to another different thing in the same sentence, and a connecting particle intervenes (e.g. "moreover"), it would have no effect otherwise, D.28.7.18.1 [D.28.7.*De condicionibus institutionum et causis et modis eorum, quae in testamento scribuntur* (Conditions on institutions). 18 **Marcianus**, *in the seventh book On Institutes*: 1. In accordance with this reasoning, Papinianus also writes that when a grandmother instituted her grandson as heir for a share under the condition that he be emancipated, and subsequently, in drawing up codicils, bequeathed to him more than what she had left him as instituted heir, the condition of emancipation is considered to be repeated in the bequest, even though she had not made any substitution in the bequest, as she had done in the inheritance.]; D.32.54, 63 [D.32.*De legatis et fideicommissis* (Legacies and *fideicommissa*). 54 **Pomponius**, *in the seventh book to Sabinius*: If I have bequeathed to you purely and simply and later write as follows: "And in addition, if the ship has arrived from Asia, my heir shall give you a plot of land," it is truer that with those words "in addition," the previous intentions are considered confirmed, just as when we say "Lucius Titius shall give the people five thousand, and Scaevola shall additionally distribute meat," we mean that Scaevola must also give the five thousand; and when we say "Titius received five, and Scaevola additionally a plot of land" we mean that Scaevola has also received the five. 63 **Julianus**, *in the first book to Urseius Ferox*: Sabinius gave the response that in repeating the bequests, these words that are usually added: "likewise, he shall be obliged to give," refer to the repetition of the same conditions and terms of the previous bequests.]; D.35.1.77.pr., 108 [D.35.1.*De condicionibus et demonstrationibus et causis et modis eorum, quae in testamento scribuntur* (Conditions, designations, explanations for and modalities of provisions in wills). 77 **Papinianus**, [see above in theorem 3]. 108 **Scevola**, *in the first book of the Digest*: A person bequeathed a house to all his freedmen, adding: So that the freedmen may live in it, to prevent it from ceasing to belong to the family and passing to whoever survives all the others. And, furthermore, I want the Sosian estate to be given to my aforementioned freedmen. It was asked whether the condition of not ceasing to belong to the family also applies to the second bequest. He replied: It applies.].

If a legacy is transferred from one person to another, the condition attached to the former is understood to belong to the latter, unless it is personal, that is, suitable only for the former person, purely physical, relating to a fact of doing or suffering, individual, as in definition 72; not moral, pertaining to law, of giving, general, see D.34.4.24 [*D.34.4.De adimendis vel transferendis legatis vel fideicommissis* (The ademption of legacies and *fideicommissa*). 24 **Papinianus**, *in the eighth book of Replies*: When a bequest given under a condition is transferred, it is considered transferred under the same condition, provided that this condition is not inherent to the first person. Because if someone had bequeathed to his wife "if she has children and raises them," this condition is not considered repeated, as it was necessary in the wife's case.]; D.35.1.95 [D.35.1.*De condicionibus et demonstrationibus et causis et modis eorum, quae in testamento scribuntur* (Conditions, designations, explanations for and modalities of provisions in wills). 95 **Hermogenianus**, *in the fourth book of Legal Compendiums*: A bequest left under a condition and transferred to another, if the condition is not inherent to the person, is considered transferred under the same condition.].

Similarly, in the case of a stipulation, it seems that there is an implied condition in the addition, as stated in D.45.1.141.7 [D.45.1.*De verborum obligationibus* (Verbal obligations). 141 **Gaius**, *in the second book on Verbal Obligations*: 7. see above in theorem 3.]. For example, "you promise to give to me or to Titius, if a ship shall come from Asia." The promise is invalid if given to Titius before the ship has arrived.

And regularly that Repetition of Conditions takes place (except for the cases which we will propose individually), unless it arises from a null act, for example, there is no repetition from a prior will into a subsequent one, *Galganettus, Treatise on Conditions, pars 2, cap. 1, q.14*[68], or from an institution into a substitution D.28.5.73 [D.28.5. *De heredibus instituendis* (The institution of heirs). 74 (73) **Gaius**, *in the thirteenth book On the Lex Julia and Papia*: If we were to appoint a substitute for an heir instituted under a condition and we did not repeat the same condition, it is understood that he substitutes the heir purely and simply.], since there is no place for substitution unless the institution falls.

Likewise, unless the reason for placing a condition here, for which it was placed there, is absent, see D.35.1.81.pr. [D. 35.1.*De condicionibus et demonstrationibus et causis et modis eorum, quae in testamento scribuntur* (Conditions, designations, explanations for and modalities of provisions in wills). 81 **Paulus**, *in the second book of Questions*: Pr. Julius Paulus to Nunfidius: You inquire whether, as provided in the will: "StichusStichus, if he renders accounts, shall be free together with his concubine, and the heir shall give them ten," when StichusStichus dies (whether he owes anything or not), the woman must be set free, and whether she should also obtain the legacy. Given that freedom is granted if he renders accounts, this condition should be understood as if it were ordained for the slave to return any surpluses he has as a result of his management. If he has none, it is considered that they have received freedom purely, and if he dies after accepting the inheritance, with freedom being due to them, they will also receive

[68] Leandro Galganetti, see note 3 above in *Preface, Pars 2, Caput 1, quaestio* 14, p. 121, "Utrum conditio apposita in primo testamento intelligatur repetita in secundo. Et apposita in primo testamento intelligatur repetita in Codicillis? Et quoad primam partem quaestionis sunt variae Doctorum opiniones." [Whether the condition inserted in the first will should be considered repeated in the second one. And that inserted in the first one will be considered as inserted in the codicils? And regarding the first part of the question, there are different opinions of the Doctors]. Therein opinion of several jurists, about the topic.

the legacy. But if he died indebted for surpluses, it is considered that his concubine has also received freedom purely, and the condition is considered as having failed. However, it could be said not without reason that Stichus was indeed manumitted under a condition, but his concubine was manumitted purely, and that this conjunction is not made to connect the condition but to show the bond that exists between those two slaves.].

Likewise, if it has been improperly inferred, D.30.113.4 [D.30. *De legatis et fideicommissis* (Legacies and *fideicommissa)*. 113 **Marcianus,** *in the seventh book of the Institutes*: 4. If a legacy has been left to a minor, under the condition "if he reaches the age of puberty," and the same legacy has been repeated to the substitute, the condition that would make the legacy invalid is not considered to be repeated.]; D.34.5.24 [D.34.4.*De adimendis vel transferendis legatis vel fideicommissis* (The ademption of legacies and *fideicommissa)*.24 **Papinianus,** *in the eighth book of Replies,* see above in this theorem 12.]. See below [in Chapter IX, definition 72, e.n.], what we will say about personal conditions and naked fact, C.6.51.9 [C. 6.51.*De caducis tollendis* (Concerning abolishing lapses, (escheats) .9 In order, moreover, that we may not over what Ulpianus, a man of the greatest genius, elegantly and with acumen stated in this connection, we shall make that plainer by this law. 9a. For since we have already decided, that a person who benefits by a bequest must take it with all its burdens, we ordain that if a condition or a burden directing something to be given is annexed thereto, all the parties who are benefited must bear the burden in proper proportion. 9b. If the burden consists of something to be done, even though this can be done by another, each beneficiary must, in like manner, do his part; as, for instance, where the person honored is ordered to construct a lodging house, monument or other structure, or the heir, legatee or some other person for whom the testator wished it to be constructed, or to purchase certain property from the heir of the testator or to make a lease or become a surety, or to do anything else similar to this; for it makes no difference in such case whether this is done by the person named by the testator or by another who succeeds to the bequest. 9c. But if the meaning of the direction given and the nature of the act to be done, are such that what was directed to be done cannot be done through another, then through the benefit accrues to such other, the burden, nevertheless, does not follow, since the nature of the act does not permit it and the testator did not wish it. For how could it be otherwise if the testator, for instance, had ordered a party to go to a certain place, or to devote himself to the liberal arts, or to build a house with his own hands, or to paint, or to marry? The testator must be considered to have intended all these things for the person only to whom he left his bounty in the first place. 9d. The general rule in all these cases is that all the parties who are benefited shall bear their proportionate burden, when the duties imposed are possible to be carried out. 9e. And this shall apply to situations which give rise to lapses proper an terminations equivalent to lapses, as stated above; but this shall apply to bequests (of the first class above mentioned) which are considered as not given at all only in certain cases. Some of them, though considered as not given at all (*etsi talia sunt*), are, nevertheless, taken over with the burdens annexed thereto. We have ordered such cases to be specially enumerated in our new compilation of laws, so that no one may reintroduce the prolixity of the ancient law as necessary on the subject or for the purpose of study thereof.].

Likewise, if a condition is placed between two dispositions and pertains to the former, it is not repeated in the latter, D.31.89.2 [D.31.*De legatis et fideicommissis* (Legacies and *fideicommissa*). 89 **Scaevola**, *in the fourth book of Replies*: 2. A certain individual bequeathed to Seius, who had been substituted for the heir: 'I want fifteen pounds of silver to be given to Seius, if he is not my heir, and to his wife Marcella.' I pose the question of whether, since Seius has become the heir, half of the legacy is due to Marcella. I answered that, according to what has been explained, it was due.].

Finally, if several words are joined together, they are not necessarily understood as joined by a condition, D.31.89.2, D.35.1.81 [D.35.1.*De condicionibus et demonstrationibus et causis et modis eorum, quae in testamento scribuntur* (Conditions, designations, explanations for and modalities of provisions in wills). 81 **Paulus**, *in the second book of Questions*: see above in this theorem 12.], C.6.51.11 [C.6.51.*De caducis tollendis* Concerning abolishing lapses (escheats).11, When there are, perchance, two or more legatees or trust-beneficiaries, to whom anything was bequeathed, and this is left to them jointly and all accept, each one receives his proportion. 11a. And if the part of one of them lapses, it, with its burden, goes to all in proportion to their bequest, if all want to accept; if none want to accept, then it remains the property of the party directed to pay it in the first instance; if some want to accept and other not, then the whole goes to those who want to accept. 11b. If the property was left severally and all can and wish to accept, each receives his proportional share and they need not expect one of them to take the property, while the others should receive their proportion of the value thereof. When such avarice appeared, antiquity treated it variously, permitting it in connection with some legacies, but rejecting it in connection with others. But we do not permit it at all, and treat all legacies and trusts alike, creating harmony out of ancient discord. 11c. These provisions shall apply, if the testator has not clearly and expressly provided that the property shall go to one, and the proportionate value thereof to the others severally. 11d. If all the legatees, to whom property has been left severally, do not concur in accepting the lapsed portion, but one of them, perchance, accepts, the whole shall belong to him; because the provision of the testator appears, prima facie, to give all of it to each, but in also providing for and joining others, diminishes the portion of the first to that extent. So, if no one else accepts or can accept, no one's part lapses or accrues to anyoneelse, so that the party first receiving a legacy would seem to be increased, but his legacy, all of which was given him in the first place, is simply not diminished by the addition of anyone else. 11e. Thus, if a burden is imposed on the person, with whom the whole legacy so remains, he must bear such burden and obey the testator's wish. 11f. But if the burden was imposed on the person, whose right lapsed, it need not be borne by one who simply receives his own without being diminished by someone else. 11g. The reason for the distinction is not obscure, because the testator appears to have left the property severally, so that each might bear his own burden without being compelled to bear that of another, for if he had wanted the contrary, he might easily have given it jointly.].

CHAPTER III

[Express Condition]

Definitions

An express condition has formal words, which are signs and copulas. SIGNS are conjunctions, for example, "If," "Unless," "With," "As long as," and so on.

Pronouns include "Who," "Whoever," and so on, and their complete treatment is expected from *Mr. Strauchius*[69] in *Particulis juris*.

The two ablatives are also included.

A COPULA is either the word "Follow" or a similar word. For example, if every man is an animal, it follows that Peter perceives sensations. Another copula is the word "is" or "Be!" which is especially common in Last Wills where the testator speaks imperatively. For instance, if Titius shall have ascended to the Capitol, let Seius be the heir! This copula is often absorbed by the verb, for example, if Titius shall have been appointed consul, I promise to give such and such, or I give or leave as a legacy 100, or have 100. An EXPRESS CONDITION is one that is stated either explicitly in direct language, which is called

15. EXPLICIT; or implicitly as a necessary consequence, which is called

16. IMPLICIT. The sign of an explicit condition is the word "if", as seen in D.36.2.22 [D.36.2. *Quando dies legatorum vel fideicommissorum cedat* (When a legacy or a *fideicommissum* vests). 22 **Pomponius**, *in the fifth book concerning Quintus Mucius*: If a legacy was made to Titius for when he reaches the age of fourteen, and

[69] Johann Strauch (1612-1679), *Lexicon particularum juris* (Francofurti, 1671).

Titius died before reaching his fourteenth year, the legacy will not pass to his heir. This is because this legacy contains not only a term but also the condition that he must be of the age of fourteen. Since the individual no longer exists, it cannot be considered that he is of the age of fourteen. It doesn't matter whether it is written "if he reaches the age of fourteen" or "when"; in the first provision, time is indicated through the condition, and in the second, the condition is indicated through time. However, there is the same condition in both.]; D.45.1.45.3, 46.2.3 [D.45.1.*De verborum obligationibus* (Verbal obligations). 45 **Ulpianus**, *in the fiftieth book to Sabinus*: 3. We can stipulate not only in this way: "when you die" but also "if you die", because there is no difference between these formulations: "when you come" or "if you come", and likewise, here, there is no difference between "if you die" and "when you die". 46 **Paulus**, *in the twelfth book to Sabinus*: 2. If I stipulate in this way, "when you wish", some say it's an ineffective stipulation; others say it's ineffective, but only if you die before making your decision; which is true. 3. It's clear that the stipulation 'if you wish that it be given' is ineffective, isn't it?]. An IMPLICIT condition can also be found in

17. DESIGNATION (*DEMONSTRATIO*) (whose signs "Who" and "Who-ever" indicate direct designation, and

"That" indicates indirect designation, as seen in D.28.7.10 [D.28.7.*De conditionibus institutionum* (Conditions on institutions).10 **Ulpianus**, *in the eighth book on Disputes*: Such an institution, "If I have designated Seius in writing as heir in the codicils, may he be the heir", is not ineffective with respect to any instituted heir, except for it being a child: it is, indeed, a conditional institution. The inheritance mentioned in the codicils is not considered to be the inheritance, something that is prohibited, but this conditional institution is given in the will. For this reason, even if it is written, "Whoever's name I have written in the codicils, may that person be my heir", for the same reason, it must be said that the institution is valid, as there is no right that prevents it.], and

"This" in D.30.3, 6 [D. 30.*De legatis et fideicommissis (Legacies and fideicommissa)*.3 **Ulpianus**, *in the fourth book to Sabinus*: These words of the testator, "whomever, among those who have been named, will be my heir", or "if Seius will be the heir", or "if he accepts the inheritance", do not make the subordinate legacy or fideicommissum conditional. 6. **Julianus**, *in the thirty-third book of the*

Digests: "My heir shall give Stichus Stichus, who will be mine when I die." The fact that the head of the household intended to impose a condition on the legacy, rather than making a clarification, is evident from the expression used. If this had been meant for clarification, it would have been phrased as "StichusStichus, who is mine", rather than "ho will be mine." This condition should be understood as "to the extent that he will be mine". Therefore, if he has completely alienated the property, the legacy would be extinguished; if he has alienated a portion, it would be due for the share that remained with the testator at the time of their death.], and

the sign of a condition is "If anyone", which contains both a condition and a direct designation, as seen in D.30.17.1 [D.30.*De legatis et fideicommissis* (Legacies and *fideicommissa*).17 **Ulpianus**, *in the fifteenth book to Sabinus*: 1. If someone has bequeathed as follows: "If I have a daughter, let my heir give her one hundred", and multiple daughters are born, it is considered that they have bequeathed an equal amount to each one. This is to be understood unless there is clear evidence of a contrary intention of the testator.]; D.34.5.5, 11 [D.34.5.*De rebus dubiis* (Dubious cases).5 (6) **Gaius**, *in the first book On Fideicommissa*: pr. In a certain will, after the institution of an heir and various legacies, the testator added the following: "If anyone among my appointed heirs or friends mentioned in this will, or any other person, obtains my restitution from the emperor, and I die before being able to thank them, I want my other heirs to give as many gold coins to the person who did this". One of the appointed heirs obtained the restitution, and the testator died before knowing about it. A question arose regarding whether the fideicommissum is due or not. Consulted on this matter, Julianus responded affirmatively, even if it were not the heir or legatee, but any other friend, who had sought his restitution. 11 (12) **Julianus**, *in the thirty-sixth book On the Digest*: Whenever a usufruct the usufruct of a piece of property is legated to a number of freedmen and ownership of it to the last survivor of the group, the legacy is valid; for I regard ownership as having been given to all the freedmen under the condition: "if he be the last survivor."],

which I define as the subject of a necessary universal categorical proposition, such as "He who marries my daughter shall have the Cornelian estate for himself.". This proposition is universal and necessary not because of the nature of the thing, but because of the will of the testator. Therefore, the precise designation is the subject of the one who marries my daughter, by means of which the person who will possess that estate is determined and can be verified. An implicit condition can also be found in a

18. TERM (*DIES*), that is, in a "when," or rather at a moment in "time" (thus, in this context, a term is used not for any part of time which we commonly call either natural or artificial day).

19. TIME, on the other hand, is a "how long" or more precisely, a "duration of time." And it can be either definite or indefinite, as stated in D.35.1.91 [D.35.1.*De condicionibus et demonstrationibus. et causis et modis eorum, quae in testamento scribuntur* (Conditions, designations, explanations for and modalities of provisions in wills). 91. **Maecianus**, *in the second book On Fideicommissa*: Conditions that relate to the future come in three varieties: some pertain to the time when the testator is alive, some to the time after the testator's death, and some to both. The time encompassed can be either determinate or indeterminate. These things typically occur not only in fideicommissa but also in instituting and bequeathing. For example, the condition "If Tiberius marries me" can only happen during the testator's lifetime; the condition "If he attends my funeral" can only happen after the testator's death; and the condition "If he marries my son" can happen both before and after. The first and third conditions consider an indeterminate time because they can occur at any time the marriage takes place; however, the second is limited to a specific time.].

The sign of the term and condition at the same time is "when," according to D.36.2.22 [D.36.2. *Quando dies legatorum vel fideicommissorum cedat* (When a legacy or a fideicommissum vests). 22 **Pomponius**, *in the fifth book concerning Quintus Mucius*: see above, in definition 16.], D.12.6.48 [D.12.6. *De condictione indebiti* (The *condictio* for money not owed). 48. **Celsus**, *in the sixth book of the Digest*: Anyone who has promised in a stipulation to give ten [units of currency], if he had done something or if such a thing had been done, if he has given the ten he had promised before such a thing had been done, it will not be considered that he has done what he promised, and therefore, he can claim it back.].

"Then" is used in D.35.1.4.1 [D.35.1.*De condicionibus et demonstrationibus. et causis et modis eorum, quae in testamento scribuntur* (Conditions, designations, explanations for and modalities of provisions in wills). 4. **Pomponius**, *in the third book to Sabinus*: 1. If a bequest was written like this: "If in the next five years, a child is not born to Tiberius, then the heir shall give ten to Seia". If Tiberius died before, the sum of ten is not immediately due to Seia, because in this context, the specification 'then'[*tum*] signifies the last day of the five-year period.] and the commentary by Gothofredus[70] in the same passage, and "after this" is used in D.28.5.9.14 [D.28.5. *De heredibus instituendis* (The institution of heirs). 9. **Ulpianus**, *in the fifth book to Sabinus*: 14. If someone has written the following: "Stichus-Stichus should be free and, after becoming free, should be the heir", Labeo, Neratius, and Aristo are of the opinion that, after canceling the word "after" inserted in between, both freedom and inheritance should be effective at the same time. This opinion, which also seems true to me.].

Two ablatives used in sequence indicate the consequence, as stated in D.35.1.109 [D.35.1.*De condicionibus et demonstrationibus. et causis et modis eorum, quae in testamento scribuntur* (Conditions, designations, explanations for and modalities of provisions in wills). 109. **Scaevola**, *in the twentieth book of the Digest*: An heir charged by the testator with returning the inheritance, after receiving one hundred coins, to Titia, his co-heir, died after taking possession of the same inheritance. Titia also died before giving back the one hundred coins. The question arose as to whether the heir of Titia, by offering the one hundred coins, could obtain a share of the inheritance. The response was: The heir cannot fulfill the condition. Claudius, that great legal mind, responded regarding what is evident in the law, although there may be doubt as to whether there is a condition in the present case.]. Furthermore,

20. The term can be as CERTAIN or UNCERTAIN as "if" (it is going to be) and "when" (it is going to be), or "if and when" (it is going to be), as noted by *Hahn in Wesembec's tit. De C.D. n. 3*[71]. Finally, there is an implied condition in the limit or duty (*modus*).

[70] Denis Godefroy (1549–1622) (1583), *Corpus Juris Civilis in IIII partes distinctum* (Lugduni, but Augusta Allobrogum, 1593) t. I, c. 1092, "adde de particula Tum legem penultimam in de testamentaria tutela", i.e. D.26.2.*De testamentaria tutela* (Testamentary tutelage). 33. **Javolenus** *in the eighth book, from the posthumous works of Labeo*: Tutors were appointed in the following manner: "I appoint Lucius Titius as tutor; if he is not alive, then I appoint Gaius Plautius as Tutor". Titius had lived and managed the tutelage; subsequently, he had died. Trebatius denies that the tutelage belongs to Plautius, while Labeo holds the opposite opinion, and Proculus follows Labeo. I approve of Trebatius's opinion because those words refer to the time of the testator's death.

[71] Heinrich Hahn [d. 1669], *Observata theoretico-practica ad M. Wesembecii*

21. The 'LIMIT OR DUTY'[72] (*modus*) (on which see all the titles of D.18.2 *In diem addictio*; D.18.3. *De lege commissoria* (De forfeiture clause); D.12.4. *De condictione causa data causa non secuta* (The *condictio* for non reciprocation); C.6.45. *De his quae sub modo legata vel fideicommissa relinquuntur* (Concerning legacies and trusts which are left subject to a duty (*sub modo*); C.8.53. *De donationibus* (Concerning gifts); C.8.54. *Si* mancipium *ita venierit ne prostituatur* (If a slave is sold upon condition not to be prostituted); in a different meaning the word *modus* in D.44.7.44.3 [D.44.7.*De obligationibus et actionibus* (Obligations and actions). 44. **Paulus**, *in the seventy-fourth book on the Praetor's Edict*: 3. A restriction in an obligation exists when we stipulate a sum of ten or a slave because the payment of one thing or the other extinguishes the entire obligation, and one cannot demand either of these as long as both persist.].

The limit it is something added to the disposition, by which the settlor specifies that if the recipient of the disposition or acceptor fails to carry out a certain action,

in 50 libros Digestorum commentarios et in hos editas R. Bachovii notas et animadversiones, 2 voll. (Helmaestadii, 1668), pars posterior, p. 222, N. III, "(Dies autem incertus) Dicitur ita fere tripliciter, (1) an & quando; ut cum alicui legatur si consul factus fuerit. (2) Tantum an : ut lego Titio 100 ubi natus erit 70 annos: potest enim mori antequam ad eam perveniat aetatem. (3) Tantum quando; ut quando is morietur. Hic itaque incertus est dies quando, & adscribitur ille non solum haeredi, de quo casu loquitur Wesenb. h. sed etiam tertio, & proinde etiam legatario; vid. Bachov. in not. h." [On the other hand, we speak of an uncertain term in roughly three ways. (1) If and when, as when it is left a legate to someone if it will be appointed as consul; (2) Only if: I leave 100 to Titius as soon as he turns 70: he can, in fact, die before he reaches that age; (3) Only when: when he dies. In this case, the term is therefore uncertain when, and it refers not only to the heir, a hypothesis referred to by Wesembech here but also to the third party and therefore also to the legatee].

[72] Berger, *ad vocem Modus*, "A measure, a limit. In the meaning of a burden, a duty imposed in acts of liberality (donations, legacies, manumissions) on a beneficiary, the term is of late origin. It appears in the language of the chancery of later emperors, and in the language of Justinian and his compilers. Sometimes the term covers what was a *condicio* (condition) in the classical language. In the classical law it was disputable whether a duty imposed as a *modus* created on the part of the beneficiary a binding obligation. The emperor Gordian set a general rule that the person interested in the fulfilment of modus of pecuniary value could sue the heir or the legatee for fulfillment. D.35.1.; C. 6.45.".

the right to the disposition will return to the giver or disposer. For example, 'I bequeath 1000 to Titius as a legacy, so that he may build me a sepulcher.' In this case, the legatee will receive the 1000 unconditionally D.35.1.80 [D.35.1. *De condicionibus et demonstrationibus. et causis et modis eorum, quae in testamento scribuntur* (Conditions, designations, explanations for and modalities of provisions in wills). 80 **Scaevola,** *in the eighth book of Questions*: In cases where the petition is immediately rejected, fedecommissi should be considered conditional. But when there is a time interval in addition to the expense, the petition is allowed, subject to security. Indeed, we should not consider the legacy left to someone if they build a monument to be the same as the one left for the purpose of building a monument (*ut monumentum faciat*).]; D.18.2.2pr., D.18.3.1, 2 [D.18.2 *In diem addictio*. 2 **Ulpianus,** *in the twenty-eighth book to Sabinius*: When a property is awarded within a certain period, it is debated whether it is a pure sale that is resolved under a condition or whether it is, indeed, a conditional sale. It seems to me that the most accurate solution is to consider what has been agreed upon in practice: if it has been agreed that, once a better offer is presented, one can withdraw, it will be a pure sale that is resolved under a condition. However, if it has been concluded in practice that the sale is perfected if a better offer is not presented, it will be a conditional sale. D.18.3. *De lege commissoria* (The forfeiture clause). 1. **Ulpianus,** *in the twenty-eighth book to Sabinius*: If a property has been sold with the condition of resolving the sale due to the non-payment of the price within a certain period, it is preferable to consider that the sale is resolved under a condition rather than it being concluded with a condition. 2. **Pomponius,** *in the thirty-fifth book to Sabinius*: In the case where the seller has included the following clause for security: "If, within the term, the money has not been paid, let the property no longer be considered purchased," the property is considered no longer purchased if the seller wishes it, as this is assured for the seller's benefit. If it were otherwise, it would be in the power of the buyer, in the event that the rural villa has been destroyed by fire, to dissolve the sale without paying the money, and the destruction would have been at their risk and peril.].

There is no contrast to rule C.6.43.3 [C.6.43.*Communia de legatis et fideicommissis et de in rem missione tollenda* (Common rules concerning legacies and trusts and concerning abolishing the granting of the right to enter on an inheritance.). 3b. We direct that this shall, similarly, apply to cases when legacies are bequeathed unconditionally or for a certain time, or conditionally or for an uncertain time, and in all these cases the legatee or beneficiary of a trust shall have every right to claim the property and have it assigned to himself; and no obstacle shall be put in his way by those who have the property.].

If a slave is given to him under a condition, the slave is free under that condition (see all of Title D.40.8. *Qui sine manumissione ad libertatem perveniunt* (Persons who obtain freedom without manumission), and the theorem 38 which concerns the *condicio iurisiurandi*[73] that is not remitted to the same legatee).

However, if the legatee does not build the sepulcher, he is required to return the bequest. In this case, the construction of the sepulcher is a limit (*modus*), the sign of the limit: "so that" (*ut*), as stated in D.35.1.80 [see above in this definition 21.].

The opposite of the limit is the condition, which is the failure to build the sepulcher.

Such a condition is commonly called resolutive, as it causes the right of the recipient to cease again D.20.6.3 [D.20.6.*Quibus modis pignus vel hypotheca solvitur* (Ending a pignus or hypotheca).3 **Ulpianus**, *in the eighth book of Legal Disputes*: If something has been sold in a manner that, within a specific period, no better terms are offered, and it has been delivered, and, by chance, the buyer, before better terms are offered, has given that thing in pledge, Marcellus, in the fifth book of the Digest, asserts that if better terms have been offered, the pledge is extinguished, although he believes that the pledge is not extinguished when the thing was sold with the clause: "if it is not to the liking of the buyer".],

or will be declared the resolution D.18.2.2pr. [see above in this definition 21.] and is opposed to suspensive conditions.

However, upon closer examination, resolutive and suspensive conditions differ only in one respect. If the settlor adds a clause to the transfer of the right, which

[73] Berger, *ad vocem Condicio iurisiurandi*, "A testamentary condition imposed on an heir or legatee to take an oath that he would fulfill the testator's wish. Such conditions were usual in testamentary munumissions. When added to other dispositions such a condition might be dispensed with by the praetor or replaced by a cautio.".

states that if something happens (in this case, the failure to build the sepulcher) the transferred right returns to the settlor, and the right of the recipient ceases again, and the thing is returned to its previous state, then the condition is called

22. RESOLUTIVE[74], indicated by the phrase "As long as", in D.26.10.3.7 [D.26.10.*De suspectis tutoribus et curatoribus* (On Guardians and Curators Suspected of Being Untrustworthy).3 **Ulpianus**, *in the thirty-fifth book to the Edict*: 7. Even if you suppose that someone has ceased to be a tutor and later resumed the role (for instance, if they had been appointed until the expiration of a term or the occurrence of a condition, then they were appointed again due to a subsequent testamentary condition or even by the praetor), the same question must be raised: can they be accused of being suspected of being untrustworthy? And since there are two tutelages, if someone brings an action on tutelage, it would be very fair to assert that the charge of being untrustworthy no longer applies.].

[74] A necessary premise, Arangio-Ruiz, see note 32 above, pp. 84-85, "It is called a condition (*condicio*) a clause of the legal transaction, under which the effectiveness of it, or the cessation of such effectiveness, depends on the occurrence of a future and uncertain event; less rigorously, but for an easily explainable transposition, the event is also called condition from which the effects of the transaction depend, or its cessation. According to whether the condition has regard to the beginning of the effects or to their cessation, we call it suspensive or resolutive: the condition of my promise to give a hundred is suspensive, when I say that I will give them if I win the lot; it is decisive, in the doctrine that prevailed, the condition for which the contract of sale will not have occurred if within a certain time the seller will receive a better offer (*in diem addictio*). But the distinction is modern. The practical needs analogous to those to which our resolutive condition succeded were felt by the Romans too, but their juridical technique knew only the suspensive condition [italics mine], and so we would say that they were forced to choose within this alternative: either to transform the condition into the opposite suspensive, or admit that to the main legal transaction, understood as pura (unconditioned), a pact was added direct to its resolution, subjected to this condition (suspensive)." [e.t. from Italian] Leibniz, remains adherent to the Roman legal thought. See also William Warwick Buckland (1859 – 1946), Peter Stein (1926 – 2016) (rev), *Text book of Roman Law* (Cambridge, V ed. 2007), 425-26; Berger, *ad vocem Condicio*, "[...] Until the fulfillment of the condition (*pendente condicione*) there is a state of uncertainty about the effects attached to its realization, to wit, as to wether the transaction will enter into force (suspensive condition) or be dissolved (resolutive condition).".

However, it appears that there is an implied *repromissio*[75] on the part of the recipient, wherein they promise the giver that if something (referred to as the resolutive condition) occurs, they will give back the thing that has been given to them (except in the case where a female slave is sold to someone with the condition that she not be prostituted, and yet she is indeed prostituted, the freedom of the slave is granted, and it does not revert to the seller, as stated in D.40.8.6.1; 7 [D.40.8. *Qui sine manumissione ad libertatem perveniunt (Persons who obtain freedom without manumission)*. 6 **Marcianus**, *in the sole book on the Hypothecary Formula*: 1. The same should be said of a female slave bought under the condition of not prostituting her, and the purchaser prostituted her. 7 **Paulus**, *in the sole book On Gifts of Freedom*: Our emperor, along with his father, established that he wished to set free a female slave whom her owner had sold for money while they could have saved her from prostitution. There is no distinction between prostituting the female slave and accepting money to allow her to engage in prostitution when they could have rescued her from such a fate.]) it is called

23. SUSPENSIVE, [that is, the return of the property to the settlor is placed under a suspensive condition e.n.]; and it only differs in terms of the relationship. Therefore, in the *repromissio*, the recipient is the *conditionator*, while in the resolutive, the giver is the *conditionarius* [the person to whom the conditioned right belongs, e.n.], adding theorem 47. However, when we speak of the suspensive condition, we will use the phrase:

24. UNDER CONDITION (*sub condicione*); if resolutive, we say

[75] Berger, *ad vocem Repromissio*, "A kind of *cautio* by which a debtor promises through stipulatio the performance of an already existing obligation or of an obligation not suable under the law."; Vincenzo Arangio-Ruiz, see note 32 above, pp. 143-44, "Certain solemn promises that citizens may be forced to make before the magistrate's court are said stipulationes praetoriae, either for the purpose of strengthening an existing legal obligation. Or - and more often - to create a new obligation to defend an interest not otherwise protected. When they consist only of the promise of those who must keep the desired behavior, they are called repromissiones; when guarantors intervene, satisdationes; the name of cautio applies equally to both hypotheses." [e.t. from Italian].

25. ON CONDITION (*ad condicionem*) the right was given. See D.8.1.4 [D.8.1.*De Servitutibus* (Servitudes).4 **Papinianus**, *in the seventh book On Legal Questions*: Servitudes, strictly speaking, cannot be established from or until a certain date, or subject to a suspensive condition, or until the fulfillment of a specific condition (for example, "for as long as I desire"). Nevertheless, if these elements are added, with the exception of fraud or deceit, the law will come to the aid of those who claim the servitude in accordance with the agreements. Cassius reported that Sabinus had also responded in this way, and that this seemed reasonable to him as well.], in a different sense the phrase is employed in D.45.1.8 [D.45.1. *De verborum obligationibus* (Verbal obligations). 8 **Paulus**, *in the second book to Sabinus*: In a stipulation that goes like this: "If you do not promise to give Stichus on the first day of the month, do you promise to give ten?" If such a slave dies, a question arises: can action be taken before the first of the month? Sabinus and Proclus believe that the term should be awaited, which is more accurate because the entire obligation is both conditional and with a term. Although it may seem that the condition is fulfilled, the term remains. However, against someone who promised in this way, if they do not touch the sky with their finger before the calends, an immediate action can be taken. Marcellus also approves of this.].

It is indeed a unique type of addition, mixed with limit and condition, which includes the following: as long as this will be, let that be; and when it will not be, let this not be; and when it will be again, let this be again, D.27.1.45.1 [D.27.1.*De excusationibus* (Excuses). 45 **Tryphoninus**, *in the thirteenth book of Disputes*: 1. If it has been written in the will as follows: "Titius is a tutor; when he has been absent in the interest of the republic, he is no longer a tutor; when he returns, he is a tutor again," let's see what can be said regarding the justification for absence in the interest of the republic or for any other subsequently arisen reason. However, first, we should examine another question, namely, whether tutors appointed by will with an initial term or under a condition should necessarily seek dispensation before the term expires or the condition is fulfilled, and, above all, if the fifty days, within which one must present reasons for dispensation, apply to them. But it is true that he is not a tutor until the term is completed, and certainly not before the inheritance is accepted. Since the tutelage was already being managed based on the same will, even one who has been exempted because he would have been elsewhere in the interest of the republic, once he returns, is immediately bound to the tutelage initially assumed, even within a year from his return. However, this person had ceased to be a tutor based on the same will and, therefore, he can assert exemptions with respect to the second tutelage.]. Moreover, these theorems arise:

Theorems

(13) *Any determination of a term through an existing thing in that term is a designation* (demonstratio).

For example, when a ship arrives from Asia, Titius will receive 100. Since it can be resolved into a necessary universal categorical proposition (e.g., every moment of the ship's arrival is the time in which 100 will be received by Titius), that is, into a designation, according to definition 17.

(14) *Every designation is a condition.*

Since a designation is the subject of a necessary universal categorical proposition[76], according to definition 17, such a proposition can be resolved into a hypothetical one. For example, every man is an animal, or rather: if someone is a man, that person is an animal, as *Thomas Hobbes* observed with precision in his book *De Corpore*[77];

[76] As is widely known, the categorical proposition in Aristotelian logic consists of a subject, a predicate, and a copula (e.g., "man is an animal"). The same categorical proposition becomes universal when accompanied by the quantifiers "each" or "everyone," and it becomes necessary when it is true or apodictic. However, the example provided by L. is erroneous and represents a paralogism. This is because the subject of the legal designation is not the time (such as "whenever" or "when a ship arrives from Asia"), but rather only Titius, who will receive 100 whenever a ship has arrived from Asia. Furthermore, the disposition is conditional, which prevents it from being resolved into a necessary universal categorical proposition. For Leibniz's method of utilizing universal quantifiers, refer to Massimo Mugnai, *Leibniz e la logica simbolica* (Firenze: Sansoni, 1973), p. 53, ft. 2.

[77] Thomas Hobbes (1588–1679), *Elementa Philosophiae 1, De corpore,* see note 25, in *Preliminary Remaks* above, p. 33 "13. Sicut autem in propositionibus necessariis ante ostensum est Categoricam et Hypothethicam aequipollens esse; ita quoque syllogismus Categoricum & Hypotheticum aequivalere manifestum est.
Omnis Homo est animal,
Omne Animal est corpus, Ergo,
Omnis Homo est corpus.

in this resolution, in a hypothetical proposition, the subject becomes the antecedent, and the antecedent is a condition, as defined in definition 4.

Therefore, each precise indication through resolution becomes a condition.

However, as we mentioned before in definition 8, it is not sufficient for our requirement that something implies a condition if it does not imply a moral condition. Additionally, for a moral condition, it is necessary that it is uncertain or rather uncertain if it is about to happen, as stated in theorem 17.

Based on this, it follows that a precise indication has a condition with moral effect only when it is also uncertain if it will occur. For example, it is not uncertain if this holds: whoever of my children will die first, will receive 100; but it is uncertain if this holds: whoever of my children will die first during my life, as it is possible that nobody will die during my life D.28.5.2.pr., 9.11 [D.28.5. *De heredibus instituendis* (The institution of heirs). 2 **Ulpianus**, *in the second book to Sabinus*: pr. Regarding those who have been instituted heirs in the following manner: "for the shares I will have designated in writing," Marcellus, as the shares are not designated, does not consider them heirs, just like if they were instituted as heirs like this: "if I have designated the shares in writing for them." But it is preferable to understand both of these institutions, provided the deceased's intention is not contradicted, in this way: "for the shares

Eandem habet vim quam Hypotheticus hic,
Si quid est homo, illud est animal.
Si quid est animal illud est corpus. Ergo,
Si quid est homo, illud est corpus. [...]",
Engl. transl. by William Molesworth, see note 25 above, in *Preliminary Remarks*, p. 33, "13. As it was showed before, that in necessary proposition a categorical and hypothetical proposition are equipollent: so likewise, it is manifest that a categorical and hypothetical syllogism are equivalent. For every categorical syllogism, as this,
Every man is a living creature,
every living creature is a body,
Therefore, every man is a body,
is of equal force with this hypothetical syllogism:
If ant thing be a man, the same is also a living creature,
If any thing be a living creature, the same is a body,
Therefore, if any thing be a man, the same is a body.[...].".

I will have designated in writing, otherwise in equal shares," as if a double institution had been made. This view is approved by Celsus in the sixteenth book of the Digests. It is different, however, in what he approves of concerning the following institution: "Seius is to be the heir for the share for which Titius designated me as heir in writing." In this case, if the testator has not been designated as an heir in writing by Titius, Seius has not been designated as an heir by the testator, and it is not in vain that Celso does not approve of it being as if it has been assigned in equal shares. Here, in fact, it is believed to involve a condition. But Marcello considers these two cases similar. 9 **Ulpianus**, *in the fifth book to Sabinus*: Clearly, this institution is similar to the case where the institution has been arranged like this: "whichever of my aforementioned brothers who takes Seia in marriage shall be the heir." I believe that this institution is also valid, as if arranged under a condition.]; D.28.7.10 [D.28.7.*De conditionibus institutionum* (Conditions on institutions). 10 **Ulpianus**, *in the eighth book of Disputes*: see above in definition 17.]; D.30.6, 17.1 [D. 30.*De legatis et fideicommissis* (Legacies and *fideicommissa*). 6 **Julianus**, *in the thirty-third book of the Digest*: "My heir shall give Stichus, the slave, who will be mine when I die." The head of the household (the testator) must have intended to attach a condition to the legacy, rather than making a clarification, as is evident from the fact that if this expression had been made for clarification, it would have been conceived as: "Stichus, who is mine," not "who will be mine." However, this condition must be understood as "to the extent that he will be mine," so if the testator has completely alienated him, the legacy would be extinguished. If, on the other hand, the testator had alienated him partially, the legacy would be due for the portion that was still owned by the testator at the time of his death.; 17 **Ulpianus**, *in the fifteenth book To Sabinus*: 1. If someone has bequeathed in this manner: "if I have a daughter, my heir shall give her a hundred," and multiple daughters are born, it is considered that he has bequeathed an equal amount to each of them. This should be understood in such a way, unless there is clear contrary intent on the part of the testator.]; D.32.85 [D.32.*De legatis et fideicommissis* (Legacies and *fideicommissa*).85 **Pomponius**, *in the second book To Quintus Mucius*: The emperor has recently decided that if someone bequeaths something to another person without adding "my" and intends that it be lent only if it belongs to them, the bequest is valid in a way that gives preference to the intention of the one making the bequest rather than the word "my." An elegant distinction is thus made: when a specific object is bequeathed, the word "my" referring to the present moment does not create a condition. However, if an indeterminate object is bequeathed, such as "my wines" or "my clothing," the word "my" is considered a condition, and only those things that belong to the testator are considered bequeathed. I do not think this position can be held with great certainty. Even if clothing or wine is bequeathed without the word "my," only those items that the testator owned should be considered bequeathed. For example, it was stated that even wine that has gone bad would be part of the bequest of wine if the testator had included it in their wine inventory. Certainly, the phrase "the clothing that will be mine" must be understood without a doubt as a condition. I also believe that the phrase "the slave Stichus who will be mine" should be understood as a condition, and there is no difference between "who will be mine" and "if he will be mine" because it represents a condition in both cases. However, Labeo writes that even the phrase "who will be mine" referring to a future moment should be understood as a determination rather than a condition, but the legal concept we apply is different.]; D.34.5.5pr., 11 [D.34.5.*De rebus dubiis* (Dubious cases).5 (6) **Gaius**, *in the first book On Fideicommissa*: A certain individual, who had been exiled, in his will, after appointing an heir and making various bequests, added the following provision: "If anyone among my heirs or friends mentioned in this will or any other person obtains my restoration from the emperor, and I die before being able to thank them, I want my other heirs to give as many gold coins to the person who did this." One of the nominated heirs secured the restoration before the testator was aware of it and passed away. There was a question of whether the trust was still binding. Julianus was consulted, and he answered that it was, even if someone other than the heir or legatee had procured the restoration. 11 **Julianus**, *in the thirty-sixth book of the Digests*: Whenever a usufruct of a piece of property is legated to a number of freedmen, and the ownership is left to the last one surviving, the legacy is valid. I believe that ownership is granted to each of the freedmen under the condition that it will belong to the last one surviving.], although at some other time, a designation is opposed to a condition, D.30.6 [D. 30.*De legatis et fideicommissis* (Legacies and *fideicommissa*). 6 **Julianus**, *in the thirty-third book of the Digest,* see above in this theorem 14]; D.35.1.19.1, 34.1 [D.35.1.*De condicionibus et demonstrationibus et causis et modis eorum, quae in testamento scribuntur* (Conditions, designations, explanations for and modalities of provisions in wills) 19. **Ulpianus**, *in the fifth book of Disputations*: see above in theorem 10. 34 **Florentinus**, *in the eleventh book of Institutions*: 1. The difference between a demonstration and a condition is that a demonstration usually indicates a thing that has been done, while a condition pertains to something to be done in the future.].

Since, on the other hand, a term contains a designation, according to theorem 11, the consequence is that even the uncertain day whether it will come at all (*incertus an*) contains a condition, D.12.6.56 [D.12.6.*De condictione indebiti* (Condictio *for money not owed).* 56 **Papinianus,** *in the eighth book of Questions*: As a cause for undue payment, it is sufficient for there to be uncertainty regarding whether the defense provided by the exception is temporary or without time limits. For example, if someone stipulates that they cannot be sued until Titius becomes a consul, and since this exception, which is time-limited, may become indefinite with the death of Titius, it is perfectly reasonable to say that what has been paid in the meantime can be claimed back. In the same way, just as an agreement not to demand payment, which is linked to a fixed term, does not allow the exercise of the action for recovery until the debtor pays after the term has expired, the protection of a right that has an uncertain cause is achieved through an action for recovery.]; D.30.30.4 [D.30.*De legatis et fideicommissis* (Legacies and *fideicommissa*).30 **Ulpianus**, *in the nineteenth book to Sabinus*: 4. But even if a legacy has been left under a condition, it can be said that the addition of a one-year period becomes void because the condition is designated as an "uncertain term."]; D.35.1.1.2, 75 [D.35.1. *De condicionibus et demonstrationibus et causis et modis eorum, quae in testamento scribuntur* (Conditions, designations, explanations for and modalities of provisions in wills).1 **Pomponius**, *in the third book to Quintus Mucius*: 2. A day, however, is uncertain when it is written as follows: "My heir, give ten when he dies," for death has an uncertain day. Therefore, if the legatee dies before the testator, the legacy does not pass to his heir because the day did not lapse during his lifetime, even though it was certain that the heir would die. 75 **Papinianus**, *in the thirty-fourth book of Questions*: An uncertain day constitutes a condition in a will.]; D.36.1.46 (48) [D.36.1.*Ad senatus consultum Trebellianum (The senatus consultum Trebellianum)*.48 (46) **Javolenus**, *in the eleventh book of Letters*: Seius Saturninus, a chief pilot of the British fleet, by his testament left Valerius Maximus, a captain, his fiduciary heir and demanded of him that he restore the inheritance to Seius Oceanus, the testator's son, on his attaining the age of sixteen. Seius Oceanus died before he had attained that age. Now Mallius Seneca, who claims to be the maternal uncle of Seius Oceanus, demands these goods by right of relationship, but Maximus, the captain, claims them for himself on the ground that he to whom he was to restore them is dead. So, I ask whether these assets belong to Valerius Maximus, the fiduciary heir, or to Mallius Seneca, who claims to be the maternal uncle of the dead boy. I replied: If Seius Oceanus to whom the fideicommissary inheritance should have been restored under the testament of Seius Saturninus at his age of sixteen by Valerius Maximus, the fiduciary heir, has died before he attained the prescribed age, the fiduciary inheritance belongs to him who was entitled to the other goods of Oceanus; for the fideicommissum vested in the life of Oceanus, that is, if he be deemed by deferring the time of payment to have allowed the fiduciary heir the guardianship of the goods, rather than to have made the fideicommissum payable upon an uncertain day.]; C.7.2.8 [C.7.2.*De testamentaria manumissione* (Concerning testamentary manumission).8. When the testator ordered freedom to be given when his son or daughter should be married, he did not fix the time of the grant of freedom, but rather fixed the condition thereof, so that if no such marriage takes place, freedom cannot be rightfully demanded.].

However, in other cases, an uncertain date and a condition are opposed to each other, D.12.6.16.1 [D.12.6.*De condictione indebiti (Condictio* for money not owed). 16 **Pomponius**, *in fifteenth book to Sabinus*: 1. But what is owed on an uncertain date, cannot be demanded on the day when it becomes certain.]; D.35.1.1.pr. [D.35.1. *De condicionibus et demonstrationibus et causis et modis eorum, quae in testamento scribuntur* (Conditions, designations, explanations for and modalities of provisions in wills). 1 **Pomponius**, *in the third book to Quintus Mucius*: 1. When a specific vesting date is set down, the legacies can be discharged forthwith, although that date has not yet arrived, because it is certain that they will become due.]; C.6.51.7 [C. 6.51.*De caducis tollendis* (Concerning abolishing lapses, (escheats).7: If any bequest is left on condition, which either depends on chance, or on the will of the donee, or is mixed, that is to say, the outcome of which depends on a chance-event of nature, on the wish of the person honored, or on both, or on the arrival of an uncertain day, the outcome of the condition under which it was left or the arrival of the uncertain day, must be awaited, so that it may vest when the condition is fulfilled or the uncertain day arrives. And if he too who receives a benefit under a testament dies in the meantime, or if the condition fails during his lifetime, such bequest which on that account did not remain in force, we direct, become the property of those who were directed to pay it, unless a substitute or joint beneficiary, whether that is an heir or legatee, has been appointed; for in such event, the latter will receive it, since the law is certain that a substitute may be appointed in instituting heirs, giving a trust, or making gifts in anticipation of death.].

It is undoubted that a day of which one is certain that it will come (*certus an*) and when it will come (*certus quando*) does not constitute a condition according to D.35.1.1.1 [see above in this theorem 14.], D.36.2.21 [D.36.2. *Quando dies legatorum vel fideicommissorum cedat* (When a legacy or a *fideicommissum* vests) 21 **Paulus**, *in the second book to Vitellius*: If no term is attached to a legacy, it is owed immediately or belongs immediately to the person to whom it is given. If a term is added, no matter how long, if it is certain, such as "the first day of January in one hundred <years>", the legacy begins to be owed immediately, but it cannot be claimed in court before the term; but if it is uncertain, such as "when he will be of age," "when she will have entered a family as a bride," "when he will have assumed office," or finally "when he will have done" something that the writer conveniently includes, if the uncertain time or condition has not been met, neither the thing can belong nor <the legacy> begins to be owed.]; see however, D.35.1.40.2 [D.35.1. *De condicionibus et demonstrationibus et causis et modis eorum, quae in testamento scribuntur* (Conditions, designations, explanations for and modalities of provisions in wills).40 **Javolenus**, *in the second book of Excerpts from Labeo's Posterior Works*: 2. A person bequeathed a sum of one hundred to Titius, adding: "My heir shall give the money to those to whom I bequeathed it, if my mother dies." The testator died before Titius, and Titius died before the mother. After the mother's death, Ofilius responded that the legacy is due to Titius' heirs because the legacy was not conditional; it was made purely and later the payment term was fixed. Let's examine (says Labeo) whether this opinion is incorrect because there is no real difference between this expression: "My heir shall give the money to those to whom I bequeathed it if my mother dies," and this other expression: "He shall not give it if my mother does not die." In both cases, the legacy is given or taken under a condition. I approve Labeo's response.].

But there is controversy regarding the day of which one is certain that it will come (*certus an*) and the day uncertain as to when it will come (*incertus quando*). They believe that it certainly does not constitute a condition in contracts, rightly so, according to D.12.6.48 [D.12.6. *De condictione indebiti* (The *condictio* for money not owed). 48. **Celsus**, *in the sixth book of the Digest*: see above in definition 19]; D.45.1.45.3, 46 [D.45.1.*De verborum obligationibus* (Verbal obligations). 45 **Ulpianus**, *in the fiftieth book to Sabinus*: 3 45.1, see above in definition 16. 46 **Paulus**, *in book twelfth to Sabinus*: "That it should be given on the hundredth Kalends" is a valid stipulation for us, since the obligation is immediate, but the payment is deferred to that date.]; D.46.3.70 [D.46.3.*De solutionibus et liberationibus* (Performances and releases). 70 **Celsus**, *in twenty-sixth book of Digest*: What is promised for a certain day may indeed be given at once; for the whole intervening period is regarded as open to the debtor for paying.].

There is no doubt that it does not constitute a condition in provisions of last wills, based on D.30.30.4 [D.30.*De legatis et fideicommissis* (Legacies and *fideicommissa*).30 **Ulpianus**, *in the nineteenth book to Sabinus:* 4, see above in this theorem 14.] D.36.2.4 [D.36.2. *Quando dies legatorum vel fideicommissorum cedat* (When legacies and *fideicommissa* become due). 4 **Ulpianus**, *in the nineteenth book to Sabinus*: see above in theorem 6.]; D.35.1.1.2, 75 [D.35.1. *De condicionibus et demonstrationibus et causis et modis eorum, quae in testamento scribuntur* (Conditions, designations, explanations for and modalities of provisions in wills).1 **Pomponius**, *in the third book to Quintus Mucius*: 2. 1.2, see above in this theorem 14. 75 **Papinianus**, *in the thirty-fourth book of Questions*: An uncertain day creates a condition in a will.].

However, not quite righteously, as stated in D.40.4.16 [D.40.4.*De manumissis testamento* (Testamentary manumissions).16 **Julianus**, *In the fifty-sixth book of the Digests*: "When Titius reaches the age of thirty, Stichus will be free, and my heir will give him that property" - and Titius died before reaching the age of thirty, Stichus will be entitled to freedom, but not to the legacy. This is because, in the case of freedom, it is accepted that time continues to run even after Titius' death, after which freedom is due. However, concerning the legacy, it is considered that the condition has not been fulfilled.]; D.40.5.18.2, 23.3 [D.40.5.*De fideicommissariis libertatibus* (Grants of freedom by *fideicommissa*).18 **Scaevola**, *in the twenty-third book of Digests*: In a testament, it was stipulated as follows: "Pamphilus, if he conducts himself properly in managing my affairs, shall be free." The question arose, given that the same testament remained unchanged for several years and Pamphilus passed away without any complaints regarding the management of his patron's affairs, whether he had acquired freedom as stipulated in the testament. The response was that there is no reason why he would not have obtained it (but there is not a §2, e.n.). 23 **Papinianus**, *in the ninth book of Responses*: 3. Even if a son was entrusted with a *fideicommissum* of freedom to be granted when he reaches a certain age, and he died before reaching that age, his heir must fulfill the *fideicommissum* on the specified day. This decision, made for a specific case, was determined not to be applicable to other *fideicommissa*.]; D.40.7.19.3 [D.40.7.*De statuliberis* (Statuliberi). 19 **Ulpianus**, *in the nineteenth book to the Edict*: If freedom was left to a slave and a legacy if the son reaches the fourteenth year of age, and the son died before that; freedom will be granted by favor upon the expiry of that term, but the condition of the legacy has failed. (There is not a §.3, e.n.)]; C.6.53.5 [C.6.53. *Quando dies legati vel fideicommissi cedit* (When a legacy or trust vests.). 5. By the words: "I give and bequeath to Aelia Severina my daughter by Secunda 10 (Sestertia), which she shall have when she arrives at legal age," no condition is imposed on the trust or legacy, but the claim therefore appears to be postponed to the day of her legal age. 1. And, therefore, if Aelia Severina, daughter of the testator, to whom the legacy was left, died after the legacy vested, she transmitted her right of action (to claim the legacy) to her heir, and payment should be made as if the time that Severina, if she had not died, would have been twenty-five years of age. 2. For the jurists are agreed that as far as the profits arising from a trust-bequest is concerned, the completed year, and not the beginning thereof, is to be awaited.].

For example, when Titius dies, my heir must give 100 to Seius. They argue that this bequest is conditional and contains the following condition: if Titius dies before Seius. Because if Seius dies later, it is evident that the bequest is not transferred to the heirs. But this condition is extrinsic [it is in the nature of the thing, see definition 12, endnote], both if it is appropriately named and if it is called moral. All the legacies would be conditional, as they all contain this condition: if the term of the legacy falls before the death of the legatee; otherwise, it will not be transmitted to the heirs. The impulsive cause (*causa compulsiva*[78]) also has the effect of a condition, evidently when it was conceived to be configured as a condition, D.30.12, 17.3, 104 [D. 30.*De legatis et fidecommissis (Legacies and fideicommissa)*. 12 **Pomponius**, *in the third book to Sabinus*: If the same thing has been bequeathed to me and to you, and then I, after the moment when the legacy became due to me, have become your heir due to your death, Labeo asserts that there is freedom for me to acquire what has been bequeathed to me based on the legacy left to me or based on the fact that I am your heir. If I wish to own that thing based on the legacy left to me, I can request it under the hereditary legacy to make it entirely mine. 17 **Ulpianus**, *in the fifteenth book to Sabinus*: If someone left a legacy to his daughters, and in some part of the will, he mentioned a posthumous child, it is considered that he has also included the posthumous child in the legacy to the daughters. If someone has bequeathed as follows: "if I have a daughter, my heir shall give her one hundred," and several daughters are born,

[78] A VI, 110, "Causa impulsiva (D.35.1.12) est, quam si nesciremus, quod agimus, non ageremus." [The impulsive cause is one that if we ignored it, we wouldn't do what we do].

it is considered that he has bequeathed the same to each of them, unless there is clear evidence of a contrary intention of the testator. [l. 17 has not §3 such as quoted in text, e.n.]. 104 **Julianus**, *in the first book to Urseius Ferox*: It was bequeathed upon all the heirs as follows: "Whoever becomes my heir shall be obliged to give one hundred to Titius." Later on, it was stated that one of the heirs should not give him anything. The question arises whether the other heirs should give the full amount of one hundred, or whether they should give the amount deducted from the hereditary share of that one. <Julianus> replied that it was truer that the other heirs should give the full one hundred, both because the meaning of the words does not contradict this opinion and because it is in line with the testator's intention.]; D.36.2.30, 6 [D.36.2. *Quando dies legatorum vel fideicommissorum cedat* (When a legacy or a *fideicommissum* vests).30 **Labeo**, *in the third book excerpted from the Posteriori by Javolenus*: A bequest made to a female minor for when she gets married; if she gets married while still a minor, it will not be due to her until she becomes of marriageable age, because a female who is not eligible for marriage cannot be considered married. [l. 30 has not paragraph, e.n.].6 **Paulus**, *in the third book to Sabinus*: If something that was left purely is later taken away under a condition, it is considered as if it were bequeathed under a condition.]; D.35.1.106, 107 [D.35.1. *De condicionibus et demonstrationibus et causis et modis eorum, quae in testamento scribuntur* (Conditions, designations, explanations for and modalities of provisions in wills). 106 **Julianus**, *in the twenty-fifth book of the Digest*: A bequest made to a woman with the condition that she does not marry Titius should be regarded as if it were left to take effect after the death of Titius. Consequently, the bequest cannot be obtained beforehand, nor can the Mucian bond be interposed. The woman also cannot obtain it by marrying another. 107 **Gaius**, *in the sole book on Legal Cases*, see above in theorem 3.]; D.40.5.43.1 [D.40.5. *De fideicommissariis libertatibus* (Grants of freedom by *fideicommissa*).43 **Paulus**, *in the first book to Sabinus*: Fideicommissary freedom is not due to a slave whom the master later placed in bonds. [l.43 has not paragraph 1, such as in the text, e.n.].

(15) *A purely negative moral condition, which is within the power of the conditionarius to fulfill, likewise, the object of the condicio iurisiurandi*[79] *in a disposition of last will, is considered as a limit or duty (modus).*

[79] Berger, note 73 above.

For example, if Titius will not have ascended the Capitol, let him be the heir! Thus, this provision is considered just as if he had said: "Let Titius be the heir but let him not ascend the Capitolium.". Hence, he immediately becomes the heir if he gives security (*cautio*) that he is not going to act against this condition, D.28.7.4.1 [D.28.7.*De conditionibus institutionum (Conditions on institutions)*. 4 **Ulpianus** *in the eighth book to Sabinus*: 1. The same Giulianus writes that the person who has been instituted as an heir under this condition, if he has not alienated a slave from the inheritance, fulfills the condition by providing a guarantee by stipulation to the co-heir. Otherwise, if he is designated in writing in the will as the sole heir, he is considered instituted as an heir under an impossible condition, and this opinion is correct.]; D.35.1.7, 18, 67, 73, 79.2, 107 [D.35.1. *De condicionibus et demonstrationibus et causis et modis eorum, quae in testamento scribuntur* (Conditions, designations, explanations for and modalities of provisions in wills). 7 **Ulpianus**, *in the eighteenth book to Sabinus*: The Mucian stipulation is effectively applied to conditions that consist of not doing something, for example, if someone says, "If he does not ascend the Capitoline Hill" or "If he does not harm Stichus" and similar conditions. Aristo, Neratius, and Julianus have decided this, and this opinion is confirmed by the constitution of the deified Pius. This remedy was not only applicable to legacies but also accepted for inheritances. 18 **Gaius**, *in the eighteenth book, On the Provincial Edict*: If someone is left something under the condition of not doing something, they must provide the Mucian security to the person to whom, under civil law, that legacy or inheritance would belong if the condition were not met. 67 **Javolenus**, *in the eleventh book of Letters*: To one person, a property was bequeathed under the condition that they would not harm a particular slave. If, in the event they did harm the slave, the legacy of the property would transfer to Maevius. The legatee provided security not to harm the slave, received the legacy, and then harmed the slave. The question is whether Maevius is entitled to anything. The response is as follows: The person to whom the property was bequeathed under the condition of not harming the slave, by providing security, can receive the legacy from the heir. If they subsequently harm the slave, they will have to return either the property or its value to the heir, in which case the heir will return what they received to the person entitled to the legacy under the second condition. 73 **Papinianus**, *in the nineteenth book of Questions*: A testator bequeathed a property to Titius under the condition that he does not go to Asia, and he also bequeathed the same property to Sempronius if he goes to Asia. Just as in all conditions that end with the death of the legatee, it has been established that the Mucian bond be provided, so the heir received this bond from Titius and gave him the property. If Titius then went to Asia, the heir will be compelled, through an equitable action, to provide Sempronius with everything he can obtain through the stipulated bond. However, if the bond becomes void in the meantime, even though it was exacted with the utmost diligence, the heir will not be obliged to pay from his own funds. But if he is not at fault and the bond has failed, it will be sufficient for him to provide his own remedies. Furthermore, if Sempronius died after Titius went to Asia but before receiving the bequest, the heir would have to pay to his heir what the deceased could have claimed. 79 **Papinianus**, *in the first book of Definitions*: 2. If the person who, after the Mucian bond has been provided, received a legacy and then did something contrary to what he promised, the stipulation will take effect, and he must also return the fruits to the heir because the legatee is obliged to make the promise from the outset. 107 **Gaius,** see above in theorem 3.]; D.35.1.37 [D.35.1. *De condicionibus et demonstrationibus et causis et modis eorum, quae in testamento scribuntur* (Conditions, designations, explanations for and modalities of provisions in wills). 37 **Paulus**, *in the single book on the Fufia Caninia Law*: If someone bequeathed a slave who could not be manumitted with the intention that the legatee would manumit him, even though the legatee is not deprived of the legacy, he is still not obliged to manumit the slave. This is because one must only fulfill the testator's intent when it is not contrary to the law. Neratius stated that the legacy should not be denied because the testator intended that the legatee, rather than the heir, should derive some benefit from this slave.]; C.8.56.4 [C.8.56. *De mortis causa donationibus* (Concerning gifts in contemplation of death).4. Since there was a doubt as to a gift in contemplation of death, some considering it as a last wish, in the nature of a legacy, others, however, considering it more in the nature of a gift between the living, we settle their doubt and ordain that all gifts in contemplation of death, whether made just before the death of the giver or sometime before, with the thought of (subsequent) death, shall not require registration, nor await the presence of public officials nor anything else usually observed in connection with such documents (which require entry on the public records). But the matter may be done so that if a man wants to make a gift in contemplation of death, in the presence of five witnesses, either in writing or without writing, the transaction shall, without the accession of a (written) memorial be fully valid and not subject to any attack. Nor shall it be considered inefficacious or useless because not entered on the public records, but it shall have the same effect as gifts under a last will and shall not be considered different in any respect.].

This caution is to be applied in almost all circumstances, and in negative conditions, it is specifically referred to as "Muciana"[80], by Mucius Scaevola, when they are transformed into a duty, D.35.1.77 [D.35.1.*De condicionibus et demonstrationibus et causis et modis eorum, quae in testamento scribuntur* (Conditions, designations, explanations for and modalities of provisions in wills). 77 **Papinianus**: see above in theorem 3.]. Nov. 22.43 [Nov.22. *De iis qui secundas nuptias contractent* (Concerning those who marry a second time.). c.43. What follows herein is old, has often been corrected not only by others but also by us, yet has not been perfected, as we propose to do now. The ancient Miscellaneous Julianus Law, which favored the procreation of children, permitted women, although second marriage was forbidden by the (first) husband, who left them property on condition that they would not remarry, nevertheless, to remarry as well as to receive the property left them upon taking an oath that the remarriage was for the sake of procreation of children. This opportunity was given to women for a year; if that period elapsed, they were not permitted to receive what had left them (upon the foregoing condition) unless they first gave a promise (caution) not to remarry. This addition was not first found in said Miscellaneous Julianus Law, but O. Mucius Scaevola had stated that to be the rule, he, indeed having proposed such a bond in all cases in which anything had been prohibited. Now, since we have noticed that many women take said oath and marry and disregard the wishes of the decedent, not for the purpose of procreating children, but by reason of the impelling force of nature, we think that we should in the first place look after the holy portion of said law and curb perjury by not permitting women to take said oath, in which perjury is so easy. The law provided not only that the oath should be taken by women without children, but also by women with children; and such oath gave offense not only to God but also to the spirit of the decedent, for perjury was easy, and the procreation of children is dependent on the fortunes of fate. We have provided by this law that women may take property left them without taking such oath, which is abolished. But we have not considered one matter, namely, that the wish of the deceased

[80] Berger, *ad vocem Cautio Muciana*, "A security given by a legatee (extended later to heirs) to whom a legacy was bequeathed under a negative condition that he would not do a certain thing. The fulfillment of such a condition could be established only at the death of the legatee. In order to give the legatee the opportunity of receiving the legacy during his lifetime this cautio was introduced (by republican jurist Q. Mucius Scaevola) by which he obligated himself not to act against the condition imposed. If, despite this promise, he did the act forbidden, he was compelled to return all that he benefited by the legacy including the profits (fructus).".

should be carried out. We enact the present law for that reason; for we do not want the wishes of decedents, if they are not absurd, to come to naught. If we should provide that a woman should never be permitted to remarry, if the husband should forbid it, such law, perhaps, would be harsh. But since there is another remedy, namely, that the woman shall not receive the property left her if she wishes to remarry, it would be absurd to disregard the wish of the decedent by permitting her to remarry as well as to receive such property, and thus to do hurt to the former husband in everything.].

It is given to those to the bequest would belong in the event that condition is not fulfilled D.35.1.18 [D.35.1. *De condicionibus et demonstrationibus et causis et modis eorum, quae in testamento scribuntur* (Conditions, designations, explanations for and modalities of provisions in wills). 18 **Gaius**, *in eighteenth book concerning the provincial Edict*: He to whom something is bequeathed under the condition of not doing something, that is, he must provide the Mucian caution to the person to whom, according to civil law, if the condition fails, this legacy or even the inheritance can pertain.]; D.36.1.67(65) [D.36.1.*Ad senatus consultum Trebellianum (The senatus consultum Trebellianum)*.67 (65) **Maecianus**, *in the fifth book of Fideicommissa*: When the slave acts without the master's consent or knowledge, the inheritance shall not be returned correctly. But if, subsequently, he approves of it, the return will be confirmed, but the legal actions will accrue to the master. It is not necessary for this restitution to precede an order, but as mentioned, ratification can also follow, similar to the example of the acquisition of bonorum possessio. Concerning the issue at hand, it does not matter whether the master or the slave is asked to return the inheritance, and no consent or action of the slave is required in this matter. However, in the case of acquiring bonorum possessio or entering the inheritance, his consent is necessary. Thus, if anyone declares the inheritance to be suspect, they shall be compelled to approach the inheritance and return it at the request of the master.], (not, however, to those who succeed in case of intestacy, *Bachovius* in *Tr. II. 13, 60, lit. f, l.4§1, l. 7 C. I.*[81]), by means of a *satis-*

[81] Reinhard Bachoff von Echt (c. 1575–1640), *Notae et animadversiones ad Hieronimus Treutleri disputationes*, 2 voll., (Heidelbergae, 1617-18), II. 13, 6 [not 60 such as in the text, e.n.], lit. g .[not f; under letter f are discussed the different kinds of confitions, e.n.] "[…] Altera controversia est, cui præstetur hæc cautio: et constat quod legatarius heredi, hic coheredi cavere teneatur l. 4. §.1. de condit. instit. [D.28.7.4.1.], l. 7. §. 1. de condit. & demonftrat [D.35.1.7.1.]. Sed quid si solus et ex asse quis heres fit? Et est textus generalis in l. is cui 18 de condit. et demonstrat. [D.35.1.18]. Cavendum esse ei, ad quem jure civilideficiente conditione

datio[82], D.35.1.67, 107 [35.1. *De condicionibus et demonstrationibus et causis et modis eorum, quae in testamento scribuntur* (Conditions, designations, explanations for and modalities of provisions in wills). 67 **Javolenus**, *in the eleventh book of Letters* see above in this theorem 15; 107 **Gaius**: see above in theorem 3.] i.e., guarantors D.35.1.97

hereditas pertinere poteft. Atquin deficiente alias conditione hereditas ad proximos cognatos ab intestato pertinet: ergo his quoque cavendum erit. Cui conclusioni duo adversantur textus in l.7.§.1. in f. de condit. et demonstrat. [D.35.1.7.1.] et in l. 4. §.1. de condit. instit. [D.28.7.4.1], Et ad illam responsio non est difficilis, causam in eo esse, quod conditio haec ibi proponitur, ne h[a]eres aliquid peteret: cum autem quod defunctus debuit, non nisi a testamentario h[a]erede peti possit, nemo a se ipso quid petere potest, & frustra adeo desideratur cautio Muciana, cum a legitimo h[a]erede nihil peti possit. (...)." [Another controversy is, to whom this guarantee should be given: and it is established that the legatee is bound to the heir, the heir to the co-heir, [D.28.7.4.1.], [D.35.1.7.1.]. But what right <applies> if only one of the whole hereditary compendium becomes heir? And the reference text is in [D.35.1.18] < **Gaius**, *in the eighteenth book On the Provincial Edict*: The person to whom a legacy or inheritance has been left under the condition of not doing something must certainly provide the Mucian stipulation of guarantee to the one to whom, by civil law, such legacy or inheritance may belong if the condition fails. >. Well, in the absence of the condition for other circumstances, the inheritance belongs to the next consanguineous relatives ab intestato: therefore they will also be given a guarantee. Two texts in D.35.1.7.1, in the end, [see infra] and in D.28.7.4.1 oppose this conclusion. And the answer is not difficult for the reason that lies in this, <that is> that there the condition is that the heir should not ask for anything: being able, on the other hand, what the deceased owed <to an heir>, be asked only to a testamentary heir, no one can ask anything of himself <sole heir> and the cautio Muciana is requested in vain at this point, as nothing can be asked of a legitimate heir] D.35.1. *De condicionibus et demonstrationibus et causis et modis eorum, quae in testamento scribuntur* (Conditions, designations, explanations for and modalities of provisions in wills). 7 **Ulpian**, *in the eighteenth book to Sabinus*: 1. Thus, if a wife has appointed her husband as heir for a share, to whom she had promised the dowry, as follows: "in the case that he has neither requested nor collected the dowry that I promised him," it seemed appropriate that he may declare to the co-heir that he is willing to make a formal renunciation of the dowry or provide a stipulation of guarantee, and thus he may accept the inheritance. But where the husband has been appointed heir for the entirety under such a condition, since there is no one to whom he can provide the stipulation of guarantee, it does not prevent him from accepting the inheritance: indeed, the condition is considered fulfilled ipso iure, because there is no one whom the husband himself, by accepting the inheritance, could sue for the dowry. D.28.7.*De conditionibus institutionum (Conditions on institutions)*.4 **Ulpian**, *in the eighth book to Sabinus*: 1, see above in this theorem 15.

[82] Berger, *ad vocem Satisdatio*, "Security given to the creditor by a debtor through a personal guaranty assumed by a surety (sponsor, fideiussor). Satisdatio is opposed to a simple promise (nuda promissio, repromissio) by the principal debtor and to a security given in form of pledge.".

[D.35.1. *De condicionibus et demonstrationibus et causis et modis eorum, quae in testamento scribuntur* (Conditions, designations, explanations for and modalities of provisions in wills).97 **Paulus**, *in the second book to Neratius*: A legacy was left to the municipal authorities, if they took an oath. The condition is not impossible of fulfillment. As Paulus says, it can be fulfilled through them. Therefore, they will swear by the individuals who conduct the affairs of the municipality.]; Nov. 22.43 [see above in this theorem 15]; C.6.40.2 [C. 6.40. *De indicta viduitate et de lege Julia Miscella tollenda* (Concerning enforced widowhood and repeal of the law Julia Miscella (Miscellaneous Julianus law).2. Dispelling all obscurities of the Miscellaneous Julianus law, we permit no one to take an oath according to the aforesaid law, but this law, together with the provisions for the Mucianian promise in connection therewith, shall be utterly void. Women shall be permitted, despite the threat of their husbands by which widowhood is enjoined on them, to enter into another marriage without taking an oath that they do so for the purpose of procreating children. The penalty fixed for such case shall no longer be enforced, and she may have the property left her by her husband, whether she have children or not, lest perjury be committed through legal compulsion and a colorable oath. They will not, however, in such case, receive the ownership of the property left them, if there are children, but only the usufruct thereof. The proprietary right belongs to the children of the first marriage according to the provisions enacted concerning second marriages and the benefits accruing to women in connection therewith.], if an offence (*peccatum*[83]) is committed, for the return of the thing, with interest and profits, at the value of the thing at the time of judgment (*quanti ea res*[84]), D.31.67.2 [D.31.*De legatis et fideicommissis* (Legacies and *fideicommissa*). 67 **Papinianus**, *in the nineteenth book of Questions*: Therefore, if, for example, there are three members of the same or different degrees in the family of the one who left the fideicommissum, it will be sufficient to have left it to one of them. In this way, after having complied with the testator's will, the others forfeit the condition of

[83] Berger, *ad vocem Peccatum*, "In classical law a violation of a somewhat criminal nature of a legal norm.".

[84] Berger, *ad vocem Quanti ea res est*, "What is the value of the thing. This clause, connected with the object of a pending civil trial, occurred in the part of the procedural formula called condemnatio. It referred to the evaluation of the object of the controversy. In certain formulae the clause referred to the past (quanti ea res fuit), i.e. to the time when the wrong was committed (e.g., in actio furti or actio legis Aquiliae), in others to the present (est), i.e. to the time of the litis contestatio (which was the normal case), or to the future (quanti et res erit), i.e., when the evaluation was to be made at the time of the judgment.".

being able to be chosen.]; D.35.1.67, 79.2 [D.35.1. *De condicionibus et demonstrationibus et causis et modis eorum, quae in testamento scribuntur* (Conditions, designations, explanations for and modalities of provisions in wills). 67 **Javolenus,** *in the eleventh book of Letters*: see above in this theorem 15. 79 **Papinianus,** *in the first book of Definitions*: 2: 2 see above in this theorem 15.].

If an agreement has been made (*committere stipulationem*), or rather if an offense has been committed, not only is an *actio ex stipulatu*[85] given, but also the claim for the thing (*rei vindicatio*[86]) is granted. If, indeed, the one to whom the bequest was made does not want to provide surety, his claim is rejected through the defense of fraud (*exceptio doli*[87]), Nov. 22.44.6 [Nov.22. *De iis qui secundas nuptias contractent* (Concerning those who marry a second time).44.6. But as soon as he remarried, the property shall be reclaimed, no matter in whose possession it may be and shall be considered as never having been bequeathed at all. This shall apply to every case of restitution, whether the property is movable or immovable.].

If, indeed, the person to whom the bequest was made does not want to provide surety, his claim is rejected through the defense of fraud, D.34.4.3.4 [D.34.4.*De adimendis vel transferendis legatis vel fideicommissis* (The ademption of legacies and *fideicommissa*). 3 **Ulpianus,** *in the twenty-fourth book to Sabinus*: 4. If someone has bequeathed in this manner: "My heir shall give the specified property to Titius, and if Titius has alienated that property, my heir shall give it to Seius," the heir is burdened. Since Titius has not already been charged with a *fideicommissum* in case of the alienation of the property, but the heir is charged with the legacy. Consequently, the heir must, by raising the exception of fraud, provide for himself, obtaining security from Titius that he will not alienate the property.]; D. 44.4.5 [D.44.4.*De doli mali et metus exceptione* (The defense of fraud and that of duress).5 **Paulus,** *in the seventy-first book of the Edict,*: You also owe me ten, which I

85 Berger, see note 55 above.

86 Berger, *ad vocem Rei vindicatio,* "An action served for the protection of quiritary ownership. Under this action the owner of a thing sued the possessor of his thing for its recovery. The victorious plaintiff regained possession of the object claimed. […].".

87 Berger, *ad vocem Exceptio doli,* "[A defense] opposed by the defendant sued for the fulfillment of an obligation that plaintiff had acted fraudolently (dolo). […]".

have bequeathed to you under this condition. In the meantime, if the heir demands it, he should not be removed by the exception of fraud since the condition can also fail. Thus, he should interpose the stipulation of the legacies. But if the heir does not provide for it, he will be removed by the exception of fraud. It is advantageous for the legatee to retain the sum, which will be added to the possession of the hereditary property.]. Unless it is waived by the testator, which the testator can do, D.35.1.72.2 and e 3, 77.3. [D.35.1. *De condicionibus et demonstrationibus et causis et modis eorum, quae in testamento scribuntur* (Conditions, designations, explanations for and modalities of provisions in wills).72 **Papinianus**, *in the eighteenth book of Questions*: 2. Titius demanded his instituted heir to restore the inheritance after his death, if the trust undertaking was not sought. He could not allow the precedent of the Mucian undertaking to take effect before the effecting of the remission of the other undertaking; for the condition could be satisfied within the lifespan of the intended beneficiary. 3. What say we then of the provision, "I ask you to make over the inheritance after your death," should no security of the trust be sought nor an account be required? Beyond any doubt, these words impose no condition of interposing an undertaking; the modality is restricted to the remission of negligence in the exacting of an account, not of bad faith. Such was the burden of a rescript in respect of one who conducted another's affairs and whose duty to account therefor was waived by the will. 77 **Papinianus**, *in his seventh book of Responses*: 3. A father disinherited his daughter and appointed tutors for her, instructing them to take charge of her affairs if her mother, with the daughter still a minor, were to pass away. The mother was also instructed to return tenfold the amount to the daughter upon her death. The appointment of the tutors is not subject to any condition, and they will not be prevented from managing the daughter's affairs even if she seeks something else in the meantime. However, the guarantee of the fideicommissa is waived for the mother. Any indication of the testator's intent can be used to determine whether the guarantee of legatees or fideicommissa can be waived. Therefore, if a condition is prescribed in the bequest or fideicommissa that the guarantee should not be sought, this condition will not be effective. It will not fail even if someone desires to provide a guarantee, given that, under public law today, the burden of a guarantee cannot be enforced against an unwilling party after it has been determined that a guarantee can be waived.]; D.36.3.12 [D.36.3.*Ut legatorum seu fideicommissorum servandorum causa caveatur* (That a *cautio* be given for the security of legacies or *fideicommissa*).12 **Marcianus**, *in the seventh book of the Institutes* : Even if a condition is written in the will that a surety is not to be required, it does not seem like a condition. Therefore, even if someone wishes to have a surety provided, they do not appear to be lacking a condition. This is because after it was legally established that such surety can be waived, neither the burden of surety follows, nor does the condition itself appear to exist.]; C.6.46.2 [C.6.46. *De condicionibus insertis tam legatis quam fideicommissis et libertatibus* (Concerning conditions attached to legacies, trusts and manumissions).2. Since you state that a father directed that his daughter if she should not separate from her husband, should furnish a bond to pay a trust, which the former had left to someone, to be paid at a certain time in the future, the praetorian law (requiring her to furnish a bond) must be complied with, as though the testator had not mentioned the matter. Nor is the example of a legacy or an inheritance, in which the fulfillment of the condition as to a divorce is a times remitted to be compared here, since it would be absurd to neglect the rule of the perpetual edict (in reference to giving a bond) because of non-compliance with the father's wish.]; Nov.15 [Nov.15. *De defensoribus. Concerning defenders (of the people)* (it seems a misquote, e.n.)]; Nov.22.44.9 [Nov.22. *De iis qui secundas nuptias contractent* (Concerning those who marry a second time.) c.44.9. The assurances (oath, pledge and surety) provided to be given by us, must be given, in case the property is left as a trust or legacy, to the heirs or their substitute or those, in a ward, by whom the property is to be delivered (to the beneficiary); in case of a gift in contemplation of death they must be given to the heirs. But if anyone is appointed as heir, upon the foregoing condition, for a whole inheritance, he must give such assurances to his substitutes, if any, or to the intestate heirs, so that the law may be perfect in every respect. If the testator, however, has provided that the party whom he appoints as heir, either for part or for all of his property, or to whom he leaves a legacy or trust or makes a gift in anticipation of death, then the wish of the decedent shall be followed; for it is our special desire to carry out the wishes of testators when not in conflict with law.].

But this theorem holds only in the case of last wills, certainly not in agreements, I.3.15.4 [see above in theorem 6], D.2.14.39 [D.2.14.*De pactis.* (Pacts).39 **Papinianus**, *in the fifth book of Questions*: The ancient jurists were of the opinion that an obscure or ambiguous provision is detrimental to the seller and the lessor [locator], who had the power to draft the contractual agreement more clearly.], D.45.1.99, 109, 115 [D.45.1.*De verborum obligationibus* (Verbal obligations).99 **Celsus**, *in the thirty-eighth book of the Digests*: Anything that pertains to creating an obligation should be considered omitted unless it is clearly expressed in words. We usually interpret it in favor of the promisor because the stipulator had the freedom to use broad language. And the promisor should not be burdened again if it is more in his interest to act with certain vessels or individuals by chance 109 **Pomponius**, *in the third book to Quintus Mucius*: If I have stipulated as follows: "Will you give ten or fifteen?" then ten are due. Likewise, if it is stipulated as follows: "Will you give after a year or two?" then it's due after two years, because in stipulations, it is observed that the lesser and the more extended period are considered to be included in the obligation. 115 **Papinianus**, *in the second book of Questions*: If I have stipulated in this manner: "Do you promise to place yourself in a specific location, and if you do not stand, do you undertake to pay fifty gold coins?" If, by mistake, the specific day was omitted in the stipulation when the intent was for you to stand on a certain day, the stipulation will be incomplete. It is the same as if I had stipulated to measure something by weight, number, or dimension without specifying the weight, number, or dimension, or if I had stipulated for the construction of a city block without specifying its site or for the delivery of a plot of land without specifying its name. But if, from the beginning, it was intended that you could stand on any day, and if you did not, you would pay the money, as if any stipulation were formulated under a condition, then such a stipulation will be valid, and it will not be enforced before it is determined that the promisor cannot fulfill their promise by standing.]; D.46.1.44 [D.46.1. *De fideiussoribus et mandatoribus (Sureties and mandators)*. 44 **Javolenus**, *in the eleventh book of Letters*: You stipulated that a certain work should be done at your discretion before a specific date. If the work was not completed and you had contracted for the same work to be done by others at a price equal to the price at which you would have arranged for the work to be done, you took sureties for that amount. Since the work had not been completed, you contracted with another person, and when the later contractor did not provide sufficient security, you performed the work yourself. My question is whether the surety is bound. He responded: According to the words of the stipulation that you presented, the sureties are not bound. You did not do what was agreed upon in the stipulation, which is that you did not arrange for the work to be done by someone else, even though you subsequently did so. The arrangement you made afterward is as if it had not been made, and as if you had immediately begun the work yourself.].

It is indeed extended due to the identity of purpose from negative conditions to other indefinite contiguous ones, D.35.1.73 [D.35.1. *De condicionibus et demonstrationibus et causis et modis eorum, quae in testamento scribuntur* (Conditions, designations, explanations for and modalities of provisions in wills).73 **Papinianus**, [see above in this theorem 15.], see, however, law 42 in the same title [D.35.1. *De condicionibus et demonstrationibus et causis et modis eorum, quae in testamento scribuntur*

(Conditions, designations, explanations for and modalities of provisions in wills).42 **Africanus**, *in the second book of the Questions*: Africano, in his second book of Questions: A legacy was made to a son-in-power under this condition: if he remains under the authority of his father. He says that the legacy is considered to be made to the father, and the father can claim it in his own name. The same would apply if it were left to a slave with a similar condition. Indeed, even if food was left to Titius' slaves, there is no doubt that the legacy was made to the master and not the slaves.].

We will now provide the proof of this theorem.

A purely negative condition cannot be fulfilled unless through the death of the subject, as stated in theorem 43. In the case of the *conditionarius*, in a hypothetical scenario (thus, it will be as if it had been left: "when you will be dead" as mentioned in I.3.15.4 [see above in theorem 6]), and in other cases where this does not apply D.35.1.72, 77.2, 101.3, 106 [D.35.1. *De condicionibus et demonstrationibus et causis et modis eorum, quae in testamento scribuntur* (Conditions, designations, explanations for and modalities of provisions in wills). 72 **Papinianus**, *in the eighteenth book of Questions*: Given that it was left to Titius that he should not abandon his children, some jurists argued that she could not give security because the condition could be fulfilled through the death of the legatee's children. However, this opinion was not accepted because such an unlucky interpretation should not be applied to the mother to prevent her from providing security.77 **Papinianus**, *in the seventh book of Responses*: 2. My heir will give one hundred to Titius if my wife does not remarry, and Titius was tasked with returning this sum to the wife. If the woman remarries, upon the expiry of the bequest, she can claim the trust. But if there were no trust, the legatee would not have the benefit of the Mucian security. 101 **Papinianus**, *in the eighth book of Replies*: 3. A mother-in-law left a trust to her daughter-in-law if she continues to live in marriage with my son. After the death of the mother-in-law, divorce occurred without the husband's fault. I replied that the condition failed, and the trust does not expire until the day of the wife's or husband's death. Consequently, the Mucian security does not apply, as the condition can be fulfilled by the husband's death. 106 **Julianus**, *in the twenty-fifth book of the Digest*: see above in theorem 14.], our theorem is not valid.

See for further reference D.28.7.4.1 [D.28.7.*De conditionibus institutionum* (Conditions on institutions).4 **Ulpianus**, *Sabinus, book 8*: 1, see above in theorem 14.]; D.35.1.7, 67 [D.35.1.

De condicionibus et demonstrationibus et causis et modis eorum, quae in testamento scribuntur (Conditions, designations, explanations for and modalities of provisions in wills).7 **Ulpianus**, *in the eighteenth book to Sabinus*: see above in theorem 14. 67 **Javolenus**, *in the eleventh book of Letters*: see above in this theorem 15.]. Consequently, the same *conditionarius* will not benefit from the testator's provisions, but only the testator's heirs, which is very harsh and goes against the testator's intention. The Last Will should be interpreted in the most benevolent manner, as stated in theorem 20. Therefore, in order for the *conditionarius* to enjoy the testator's benefit, he unconditionally receives it. However, to ensure that the testator's intended condition is not violated, the *conditionarius* is obligated to respect and provide assurances for it. This is equivalent to stating that a condition has become a limit, according to definitions 21 and following. What was to be demonstrated.

I will add only one theorem to this, which has not been observed by anyone so far, namely that the *Cautio Muciana* arises in negative conditions that are transformed into a limit, although there is much discussion on other aspects of this *cautio*. For the same reason, the object of the *condicio iurisiurandi* is transformed into a limit.

CHAPTER IV

[Partial Propositions]

So much about conditionality.

We will now examine the PARTIAL PROPOSITIONS, specifically the condition itself and the conditioned, about which we will discuss either fully or comparatively. FULLY, either in a general sense of interpretation or in a specific sense, based on the FORM and MATTER.

Let's consider both the object of interpretation and the effect.

The object can be either the terms of partial propositions or the partial propositions themselves in a simple manner, or repetition (*multiplicatio*).

In terms of the effect, interpretation can be either diminutive and extensive, whereby the condition or the conditioned can be satisfied in several ways, or intensive and augmentative, which requires more for their satisfaction, according to argument from D.42.4.2.4 [D.42.4. *Quibus ex causis in possessionem eatur* (The grounds on which *missio in possessionem* is granted). 2 **Ulpianus**, *in the fifth book to Edict*: 4. The phrase "defended" is intentionally phrased broadly to imply that it's not adequate to simply initiate a defense; one must also maintain it. Moreover, it won't be held against someone if they hadn't defended before but now choose to present a defense.]. The former determines a disjunction, the latter a conjunction. Hence, the

Theorems

(16) *Whatever is stipulated in a condition or for the conditioned and is hindered by the party for whom it is in their interest to have it stipulated, is considered in moral disposition as if it had not been added.*

The reason for this is evident, as anyone can renounce their own rights and is unworthy of the benefit they have despised. Provided that it is due to their fault and not by chance.

From this it follows that the debtor is freed from the obligation of giving if the honored party does not want to receive it.

This applies to both the less important honored party, whom I specifically refer to as honored, as seen below in definition 67. For example, if Stichus gives 10 to my heir, he is free if the honored party does not want to accept it, as per D.33.2.30 [D.33.2.*De usu et de usu fructu et reditu et habitatione et operis per legatum vel fideicommissum datis* (Right of use, usufruct, income, right of habitation, and services given by legacy or *fideicommissum*). 30 **Javolenus**, *in the second book from the Posthumous Works of Labeo*: If a woman was bequeathed the usufruct of a property until she received her entire dowry, and one of the heirs provided security for her share, even if the others did not, Labeo holds the opinion that, nevertheless, the woman would cease to have that portion of the usufruct. The same would happen if the woman herself delayed in receiving her security.]; D.28.7.3, 11, 20, 23.pr. [D.28.7.*De condicionibus institutionum* (Conditions on institutions).3 **Paulus**, *in the first book to Sabinus*: If I have been instituted as heir in this manner: "if I give ten," and the one to whom I received the order to give does not want to receive, the condition is considered as fulfilled. 11 **Julianus**, *in the twenty-ninth book of the Digest*. If someone has written in the will as follows: "My son, if he adopts Titius, should be the heir; if he does not adopt him, he should be disinherited," and Titius does not want to be adopted by the son who is ready to adopt him, the son will be the heir as if the condition had been fulfilled. 20 **Labeo**, *in the second book, from the Posthumous Works epitomized by Javolenus*: A woman who owed her husband money promised by stipulation as a dowry had appointed her husband himself as the heir in the following terms, if she had not requested or claimed that money she had promised as a dowry. I consider that if the husband had communicated to all the other heirs that he would not become the heir until the solemn remission of what was owed to him as a dowry had been made, he will immediately become the heir. If, on the other hand, he had been appointed as the sole heir under such a condition, I consider that, despite the condition, he will immediately become the heir, because an impossible condition is considered as unwritten. 23 **Marcellus**, *in* *the twelfth book of the Digest*: "Whichever of my brothers marries our cousin shall be the heir for three-quarters, and the one who does not marry her shall be the heir for one quarter." The cousin either marries one of them or refuses to marry either of them. If one of them marries the cousin, he will inherit three-quarters, and the other will inherit one quarter. If neither of them marries her, not because they themselves did not want to, but because she did not want to marry them, they are both admitted to the inheritance in equal shares. In general, this condition, "if he marries," "if he gives," "if he does," should be understood as meaning that it does not depend on him not to marry, not to give, or not to do.]; D.30.81.5 [D.30.*De legatis et fideicommissis* (Legacies and *fideicommissa*). 81 **Julianus**, *in the thirty-second book of the Digest*: "I give and bequeath to Titius that estate if he gives ten to my heir." If the heir owed ten to Titius, and Titius granted him a formal release of the debt, he can claim the estate.]; D.35.1.6, 45, 84 [D.35.1. *De condicionibus et demonstrationibus et causis et modis eorum, quae in testamento scribuntur* (Conditions, designations, explanations for and modalities of provisions in wills).6 **Pomponius**, *in the third book to Sabinus*: The heir and the legatee, or anyone who benefits from the last will, when entrusted to erect a monument at the discretion of someone else, will not incur the penalty imposed in the will if the person upon whose discretion it should be done is no longer alive, unavailable, or unwilling to make the decision.45 **Paulus**, *in the sixteenth book to Plautius*: According to Julianus, if a legatee, who was bequeathed a legacy with the condition to give ten to the heir, releases the heir from what the heir owes to them, it is not considered that the condition has been fulfilled as if the legatee has given the amount. The legatee can still demand the legacy as if the condition has been met because the heir prevented the fulfillment. 84 **Paulus**, *in his fourteenth book of Replies,* presented the following case: "I want one hundred denarii per month and clothing to be given to these freedmen for their maintenance if they reside with my son." The freedmen remained with the son until he reached adulthood and joined the military. Afterward, the son left for a journey, and he died while in the field. The question arose regarding whether his heirs should continue to provide maintenance to the freedmen. Paulus' response was as follows: "Since the testator's son has passed away, the condition is not considered unfulfilled for the freedmen who continued to reside with him or for those whose residence was not contingent on his actions. However, if the testator intended that maintenance be provided to the freedmen for the benefit of his son while they resided with him, their request should not be entertained because it contradicts the deceased's wishes.]; D.36.2.5, 5 [D.36.2. *Quando dies legatorum vel fideicommissorum cedat* (When a legacy or a *fideicommissum* vests). 5 **Ulpianus**, *in the twentieth book to Sabinus*: If there is a condition in a legacy that the legatee cannot fulfill, and instead, it is within the power of the heir or another person in whose hands the condition should be fulfilled, the legacy becomes void because the condition is considered to be fulfilled. For example, if someone was tasked with giving ten coins to the heir, and the heir refuses to accept them, the legacy fails. Similarly, if there was a condition that the legatee should marry Seia, but Seia refuses to marry the legatee, it must be said that the legacy becomes void. This is because the legatee cannot fulfill the condition, and it is another person who prevents its fulfillment.], D.40.7.34.1 [D.40.7. *De statuliberis* (Statuliberi). 34 **Papinianus**: The Emperor Antoninus issued a rescript regarding a slave conditionally granted freedom, provided they settle their accounts, and if the heir refuses to accept the accounts, the slave will be free nonetheless. This rescript should be understood as follows: If the slave does not owe any outstanding amounts, they will be free. However, if they are indeed a debtor, freedom will be granted only when they offer the actual amount they owe. In reality, for a slave to obtain freedom, it is not sufficient for the heir to be in default; the slave must have taken actions that would have led to their freedom if there had been no delay. For example, if a slave is manumitted with a condition such as, "Dama will be free if they go to Spain and collect next year's fruits," but the heir in Rome prevents the slave from leaving and carrying out this condition, it cannot be claimed that the slave is immediately free before the fruits are collected. Similarly, when something is stipulated in Rome, like, "Do you promise to give a hundred in Spain?" it was determined that the stipulation is contingent on the time when one can go to Spain, and a valid action cannot be exercised beforehand. But if the heir, after receiving the accounts and settling the debt owed by the statuliber, who had no means to pay, publicly states or communicates in written letters that he is giving it away, the condition of freedom will be considered as fulfilled. What if the slave claims not to owe any outstanding amounts and became free because the heir refused to accept the accounts, while the heir insists that there was no delay and the statuliber owes outstanding amounts? It will be determined by the person responsible for deciding on the freedom whether the condition has been fulfilled. It will be their duty to examine the delay, calculate the accounts, and pronounce that the slave is not free if they appear to owe outstanding amounts. However, if the slave does not deny the debt, instead takes the heir to court and declares their readiness to present the accounts and reimburse everything they are found to owe, offering a solvent person ready to pay that amount, and the heir is in default, the judgment should be in favor of freedom.].

Likewise (see however D.35.1.101.4 [D.35.1. *De condicionibus et demonstrationibus et causis et modis eorum, quae in testamento scribuntur* (Conditions, designations, explanations for and modalities of provisions in wills).101 **Papinianus**, *in the eighth book of Responses*: 4. Even though the monthly and yearly legacies left to the freed person under this condition: "As long as they manage the affairs of the patron's daughter," should be provided when the daughter does not want the legatee to manage them; however, if the daughter changes her mind, the condition regains its force because there are multiple legacies.]), this applies to the principal honored party, whom I specifically refer to as the *conditionarius*, as seen in the aforementioned D.35.1.6. Thus, if the honored party rejects the conditioned things and prevents them from reaching him, he receives nothing D.28.5.9.6 [D.28.5.*De heredibus instituendis* (The institution of heirs).9 **Ulpianus**, *in the fifth book*, to Sabinus: 6. Similarly, Marcello also explains that if the drafter of the will, against the testator's will, has removed or changed the condition, the instituted heir does not become an heir, but should be considered as if not instituted.], compare, however D.31.45.1 [D.31.*De legatis et fideicommissis* (Legacies and *fideicommissa*).45 **Pomponius**, *in the eighth book to Quintus Mucius*: 1. If a legacy has been left to us subject to a condition or a specific term, we cannot reject it before the condition or term is fulfilled. In fact, it does not even belong to us before the term arrives or the condition is met.]; D.29.2.13, 70.3 [D.29.2.*De adquirenda vel omittenda hereditate* (Taking up or failing to take up an inheritance).13 **Ulpianus**, *in the seventh book to Sabinus*: A person who is instituted as an heir or for whom there is a legal inheritance, loses the inheritance by renunciation. This is true if the inheritance was in a condition to be accepted. However, an heir instituted under a condition does not do anything if they renounce before the condition is fulfilled, regardless of the type of condition, even if it depended on their mere will. Section 70.3 does not exist; it might be Section 70 **Paulus**, *in the fifty-seventh book To the Edict*: If the heir responded that he does not wish to receive either of the two inheritances, the assets of the deceased must be taken over by the creditors. (e.n.)].

Hence, it also arises that if the debtor, to whom it is in their interest that the condition be added (according to theorem 46), prevents its fulfillment, the condition is deemed as not added, as stated in D.35.1.24 [D.35.1. *De condicionibus et demonstrationibus et causis et modis eorum, quae in testamento scribuntur* (Conditions, designations, explanations for and modalities of provisions in wills).24 **Julianus**, *in the fifty-fifth book* of *Digest*: It has been established in civil law that whenever, through the fault of the party for whom it is essential that a condition be fulfilled, the condition is prevented from being fulfilled, it should be treated as if the condition had indeed been fulfilled. Many have applied this principle to both legacies and the institution of heirs. Some have also rightly argued that in cases like these, stipulations may be imposed when the promisor's actions prevent the stipulator from complying with the condition.].

This principle is reiterated in D.50.17.161 [D.50.17. *De diversis regulis iuris antiqui* (Various rules of early law). 161 **Ulpianus**, *in the seventieth book To the Edict*: In civil law, it is established that whenever someone's actions, in whom it is in their interest for a condition not to be fulfilled, prevent the condition from being fulfilled, it is treated as if the condition had indeed been fulfilled. This principle applies to matters of freedom, legacies, and the institution of heirs. In these cases, stipulations may also be imposed when the promisor's actions prevent the stipulator from complying with the condition.], where Hotman[88] reads: "it is not to be treated as (*not fit*)," but incorrectly, arg. *promissorem* (promisor) in the end, adde D.35.1.81.1 [D.35.1. *De condicionibus et demonstrationibus et causis et modis eorum, quae in testamento scribuntur* (Conditions, designations, explanations for and modalities of provisions in wills).81 **Paulus**, *in the second book of Questions*: The condition is considered fulfilled when its execution is prevented by the person who would be liable if it had been satisfied.]; D.40.7.3.7, 34.1, 38 [D.40.7.*De statuliberis* (Statuliberi).3 **Ulpianus**, *in book twenty-seventh to Sabinus*: 7. If anyone has ordered a slave to pay ten

[88] François Hotman (1524-1590), *Observationum liber IIII*, (Basileae: Episcopius, 1575), p. 57, cap. XXVII, *Particula* NON apud *Iulianum restituta*.
This is the original: D.35.1.*De condicionibus et demonstrationibus et causis et modis eorum, quae in testamento scribuntur* (Conditions, designations, explanations for and modalities of provisions in wills). 24 **Julianus**, *in the fifty-fifth book of Digest*: Iure civili receptum est, quotiens per eum, cuius interest condicionem impleri, *fit*, quo minus impleatur, ut perinde habeatur, ac si impleta condicio fuisset: quod plerique et ad legata et ad heredum institutiones perduxerunt. Quibus exemplis stipulationes quoque committi quidam recte putaverunt, cum per *promissorem* factum esset, quo minus stipulator condicioni pareret. [It is accepted in civil law that whenever it happens through the person whose interest it is that the condition be fulfilled, that it is not fulfilled, it is considered as if the condition had been fulfilled: many have extended this to legacies and to the institution of heirs. Following these examples, some have rightly thought that stipulations are also committed, when it happens through the promisor's action that the stipulator does not meet the condition.].

and has sold him as a free person without any assets, whether he is immediately free (as if prevented from giving money because he was sold without assets) or if he is prevented from using his assets? And I think he will only be free when he is prevented from willingly giving, not immediately upon arrival. 34 **Papinianus**, *in the twenty-first book of Questions*: 1, see above in this theorem 16. 38 **Paulus**, *in the first book to Neratius*: It is not every hindrance put in the way of the statuliber from the heir's side that counts as fulfillment of a condition, but only such as have been designed to hinder freedom.]; D.45.1.85.7 [D.45.1. *De verborum obligationibus* (Verbal obligations). 85 **Paulus**, *In the seventy-fifth book on Edict*: 7. Whoever, while obliged conditionally, took steps to see that the condition would not be fulfilled is nonetheless bound.]; D.50.17.39 [D.50.17. *De diversis regulis iuris antiqui* (Various rules of early law).39 **Pomponius**, *in the thirty-second book to Sabinus*: In all cases, something is regarded as done if someone else is responsible for any delay in its occurrence.]. For example, if the testator has stated: "If Seius ascends to the Capitol within a decade after my death, let Titius be the heir." If indeed Seius remains bedridden during that entire period, Titius will never become the heir (different rules apply when it comes to freedom, see Theorem 60). This condition, although potestative, is not imposed on the *conditionarius*, as stated in theorem 60. However, if Seius prepares himself to ascend the Capitol and someone who would be the heir in the absence of Titius's designation, such as the next agnate, substitute, or co-heir, whom we can call Caius, attacks Seius as he leaves his house and inflicts beatings on him to the extent that he remains bedridden for the entire decade, there is no doubt that Titius, as if fulfilling the condition, would be the heir. The intention here is to prevent the unscrupulous from obstructing the realization of the testator's will through various machinations, violence, or deception for their own advantage.

However, if the condition is in the power of the debtor, for example, "Let Titius be the heir if Titius marries Mevia, let Seius be the heir," then Titius is allowed to prevent the fulfillment of the condition and not marry Mevia. Unless a different rule has been introduced to protect freedom. For example, if freedom has been granted to Stichus in the following manner: "If the heir ascends to the Capitol within a year after the testator's death, the heir is deemed to be commanded to ascend the Capitolium," and if the heir delays it without a valid reason, the slave is still considered free, D.40.5.41.1 [D.40.5.*De fideicommissariis libertatibus* (Grants of freedom by *fideicommissa*).41 **Scaevola**, *in the fourth book of Replies*: 1. Lucius Titius made the following provision: "My dearest son, Maevius, I request you not to let Stichus, Damas, and Pamphilus be your slaves any longer, if they have deserved well of you and you have discharged your debts"; if it was the heir's responsibility that he did not discharge the debts, could they obtain freedom by fideicommissum? He replied that the heir incurred no blame if he was rather slow in discharging his debts for the advantages to be gained in administration of his estate; but if it were proved beyond doubt that his purpose in not making payment was to delay the grants of freedom, the grants should be duly made.]; D.40.7.20.1 [D.40.7.*De statuliberis* (Statuliberi).20 **Paulus**, *in the in the sixteenth book to Plautius*: 1. Suppose he gives against the wish of the heir or without his knowledge; would he give title to the recipient? Julianus actually thinks that in this case statuliberi are apparently allowed to alienate the coins, even against the wish of the heir, and thereby to give title to the recipients.].

In this matter, jurists commonly use the phrase "if it depends on someone or does not depend (*si per aliquem stet, vel non stet*)". It appears that it depends not only on the one who hinders but also on the one who fails to do what they understand they are capable of doing D.33.1.13 [D. 33.1 *De annuis legatis et fideicommissis (Annual legacies and fideicommissa)*13 **Scaevola** *in the fourth book of Replies*: Maevia instituted as her heir her adult grandson born to Maevius and made a legacy to Lucius Titius as follows: "To Lucius Titius, a good man, for whose obsequium I offer thanks, I want to be given ten aurei a year for as long as he lives, if he attends to the affairs of my grandson and takes the full administration of them under his care." I ask, when Lucius Titius has for some time managed the affairs of Maevius and has made no objection to continuing to do so, but Publius Maevius is unwilling for him to administer them, whether the fideicommissum need be paid. I replied that if it was not on account of fraud or any just cause for criticizing his services that he had been removed from affairs which he was willing to administer in accordance with the wish of the deceased, he should receive the legacy. 1. A man appointed his wife as his heir and provided as follows: "I want twelve denarii a year each to be given to all my freedmen for maintenance, if they remain with my wife." I ask, since the head of the household was reluctant to leave the town of his own accord, whereas she traveled constantly, whether the freedmen should accompany her. I answered that no unconditional reply was possible, since many considerations might arise which should be judged on their merits; therefore, these various possibilities should be settled by the arbitration of a good man. Likewise, it is asked whether the legacy is owed when on setting out she offered them nothing extra and, therefore, they did not accompany her. He replied that this too should be judged with regard to the length or brevity of the journeys and the amount of the legacy.]; D.40.7.34.1 [D.40.7.*De statuliberis* (Statuliberi). 34 **Papinianus**, *in the twenty-first book of Questions*: 1, see above in this theorem 16.]; D.45.1.50, 83 [D.45.1.*De verborum obligationibus* (Verbal obligations).50 **Ulpianus**, *in the fiftieth book To the Edict*: In the context of the stipulation, "that nothing will be done by you," it doesn't imply that you won't take any action to hinder your ability to act. Instead, it signifies that you will make sure you can act as required. 83 **Paulus**, in *book seventy-second To the Edict*: Between the stipulator and the one making the promise, a legal transaction is formed. Therefore, when one person makes a promise on behalf of another, they are not personally obligated to give or do something because each individual should make promises concerning themselves. And when someone guarantees, "to be without evil intent and to ensure it will be absent," they are not merely making a simple negation but rather committing to ensuring that there is no evil intent. The same applies to stipulations such as "being permitted" and "neither by you nor by your heir shall it be done so as to prevent it.], as stated in definition 75.

(17) What for the same nature and necessarily exists is deemed as not added in a moral proposition.

Indeed, what exists unnecessarily is separately expressed, D.30.4 [D.30.*De legatis et fideicommissis* (Legacies and *fideicommissa*).4 **Ulpianus**, *in the fifth book to Sabinus*: If someone made a mistake in designating a property and named the Sempronian property as Cornelian, the Sempronian property will be due. But if there was an error regarding the object, it will not be due. Therefore, if someone, wanting to bequeath a garment, wrote "a household item," thinking that the garment was included under this designation, Pomponius wrote that the garment is not due, just as it would be if someone thought that under the designation of gold, electrum, or bronze were included, or, which would be even more foolish, that under the designation of a garment, silver was also included. The names of things are unchangeable, while those used by people are subject to change.]; D.35.1.19.1, 52 [D.35.1. *De condicionibus et demonstrationibus et causis et modis eorum, quae in testamento scribuntur* (Conditions, designations, explanations for and modalities of provisions in wills).19 **Ulpianus**, *in the fifth book of Disputations*: see above in theorem 10. 52 **Modestinus**, *in the seventh book of Differences*: It sometimes happens that certain things explicitly expressed are harmful, which, if omitted, would have been implied and would not have been harmful. This would occur if someone bequeathed as follows: "If Maevius ascends the Capitoline Hill, I give and bequeath ten to Titius." Because even though it is in Maevius's discretion to ascend the Capitoline Hill, and thus to cause the legacy to be due to Titius, it still cannot be validly bequeathed with other words: "I give ten to Titius if Maevius wishes," because a legacy cannot be conferred in someone else's will. Hence the maxim: "What is expressed is harmful, what is implied is not harmful.]; D.36.2.21.1, 22.1 [D.36.2. *Quando dies legatorum vel fideicommissorum cedat* (When a legacy or a *fideicommissum* vests).21 **Paulus**, *Vitellius, book* 2: see above in theorem 10. 22 **Pomponius**, *Quintus Mucius, book 5*: seabove in theorem 10.].

The other rule does not preclude: what is expressed is harmful, what is not expressed does not harm, D.17.1.47, 56 [D.17.1.*Mandati vel contra* (The action on mandate or the counteraction).47 **Pomponius**, *in the third book from Plautius*: Julianus asserts that if a wife has promised to her husband's surety in her dowry the amount he owes as a surety, immediately after the wedding, he can exercise a mandate against the debtor because he is considered to lack the money to support the obligations of marriage. 56 **Papinianus**, *in the third book of Replies*: The person who has given a mandate to lend money can be chosen to be sued while leaving out the principal debtor and without selling the pledges. This is allowed even if the written document of the mandate contract explicitly states that "even if the pledges are sold," the creditor may proceed against him. In fact, everything that is included by the parties in contracts to eliminate doubts does not derogate from common law.]; D.28.5.52(51).1, 68 [D.28.5. *De heredibus instituendis* (The institution of heirs). 52 (51) **Marcianus**, *in the third book of Rules*: If someone has written as follows: "Stichus, if he is mine at the moment of my death, shall be free and heir," once alienated, Stichus cannot claim the inheritance at the order of the buyer. However, even if this were not expressly written, he would not have been able to become free and heir unless he had remained the property of the testator. But if the testator manumitted him during his lifetime, Celsus writes in the fifteenth book of the Digest that Stichus becomes the heir. It is not clear, after all, that the testator intended to exclude him in this case, and the words used in the will do not completely oppose this; even if he is not "his" as a slave, he is as a freedman. 69 (69) **Pomponius**, *in the seventh book to Quintus Mucius*: If someone has appointed Sempronius as an heir under the condition "if Titius ascends the Capitoline Hill," even though Sempronius cannot be an heir in any other way unless Titius ascends the Capitoline Hill, and this very act is within Titius's power, because the intention of Titius is not expressly stated, this institution will be valid. However, if someone has written as follows: "If Titius wishes, let Sempronius be the heir," the institution is not valid. For in wills, certain matters, if expressly stated, have no effect when they would have the same meaning if covered by words and will have some significance. Thus, the disinheritance of sons is effective when someone may be an heir. Nevertheless, no one doubts that if someone were to disinherit his son as follows: "Titius, be the heir: when Titius becomes the heir, let the son be disinherited," the disinheriting of the son would have no effect.]; D.30.65.1 [D.30.*De legatis et fideicommissis* (Legacies and *fideicommissa*).65 **Gaius**, *in the first book on Legacies, To the Edict of the Praetor*: If someone has bequeathed as follows: "I give to Seius ten slaves, excluding those ten that I bequeathed to Titius," if indeed in the inheritance, there are only ten slaves, the legacy is useless. However, if there are more slaves found in the inheritance, beyond those chosen by Titius, the legacy is valid concerning the others but not for more than the ten slaves that were bequeathed. If there are fewer slaves, it is valid for as many as there are.]; D.50.17.77, 195 [D.50.17.*De diversis regulis iuris antiqui* (Various rules of early law).77 **Papinianus**, *in the twenty-eighth book of Questions*: Legitimate acts that include a term or condition, such as emancipation, acceptilation, entry into an inheritance, option on a slave, grant of tutor, are vitiated by the addition of the term or condition. Nevertheless, sometimes these aforementioned acts implicitly allow for the term or condition that, when explicitly inserted, would render the acts themselves invalid. For instance, if I accept an inheritance from someone who promised it under a condition, the acceptance is considered to have taken effect only if the condition of the obligation has been fulfilled. However, if this acceptance is expressly included in the wording of the acceptance, it renders the act null and void. 195 **Modestinus**, *in the seventh book of Distinctions*: Express provisions damage; implicit provisions do not damage.].

In fact, we must distinguish if the things that exist are superfluous, meaning they contain nothing else than what exists.

Even what is expressed does not harm, D.45.1.65 [D.45.1.*De verborum obligationibus* (Verbal obligations).65. **Florentinus**, *in the eighth book of the Institutions*: External matters and things unrelated to the present transaction that you add to a stipulation will be considered as superfluous and will not vitiate the obligation. For example, if you say, "I sing of arms and a man: I promise," it is still valid.]; D.50.17.94 [D.50.17.*De diversis regulis iuris antiqui* (Various rules of early law). 94 **Ulpianus**, *in the second book of Fideicommissa*: Things which abound do not usually vitiate writings.]; C.6.23.17 [C.6.23. *De testamentis: quemadmodum testamenta ordinantur* (Concerning testaments: In what manner testaments are executed).17. A testament ought not to be held invalid, because the decedent called it by different names, since superfluous matters are not prejudicial. For only the omission of necessary requirements, not abundant caution, renders contracts ineffective and thwart the testatorís wishes.].

However, what is useless is considered as not added in legal effect.

Hence it follows that a condition is not added if it is absolutely necessary in itself. For example, if 'While Titius is alive, he will eat, let him be the heir,' is equivalent to "Let Titius be the heir", I.2.14.10 [I.2.14.*De heredibus instituendis* (Of the institution of the heir).10 If the institution of an heir, a legacy, a fiduciary bequest, or a testamentary manumission is made to depend on an impossible condition, the condition is deemed unwritten, and the disposition absolute.]; I.3.19.11 [I.3.19. *De inutilibus stipulationibus* (Of invalid stipulations).11. An impossible condition annexed to an obligation invalidates the stipulation. An impossible condition is one which, according to the course of nature, cannot be fulfilled, as, for instance, if one says: 'Do you promise to give if I touch the sky with my finger?' But if the stipulation runs: 'Do you promise to give if I do not touch the sky with my finger?' it is considered unconditional, and accordingly can be sued upon at once.]; D.28.5.50 [D.28.5. *De heredibus instituendis* (The institution of heirs). 51 (50) **Ulpianus**, *in the sixth book of the Rules*: If in my lifetime I sold my slave, whom I instituted heir with a grant of freedom, to a person with whom there is no *testamenti factio*[89] and later I buy him back, he can still become my heir from

[89] Berger, *ad vocem Testamenti factio*, "The legal capacity of a person to make a testament (*ius testamenti faciendi*). This testamenti factio (called in the literature by the non-Roman term, *testamenti factio activa*) is to be

the will, and the intervening time he spent with the buyer does not invalidate the institution. This is because, during both the time of making the will and the time of my death, he was truly mine. Therefore, if he remains with the buyer, the institution is invalidated, or if the testamentary authority exists with the buyer, he will acquire the inheritance from him by his order.]; D.35.1.56 [D.35.1. *De condicionibus et demonstrationibus et causis et modis eorum, quae in testamento scribuntur* (Conditions, designations, explanations for and modalities of provisions in wills*)*.56 **Javolenus,** *in the fourteenth book of the Letters*: The one to whom a plot of land has been bequeathed if he is worth ten cannot obtain a part of the land unless he has paid the entire amount. But the situation is different when the same thing has been bequeathed to two people under a condition. In this case, the condition imposed on multiple individuals is considered, from the moment the will is made, divided among the individual persons. Therefore, each one can fulfill the condition for their part and receive the bequest. Although the entire condition is imposed as a whole, it can be considered divided by enumerating the persons. If, however, a legacy has been left to a person under a condition, the condition for that person must be accidentally divided, and all those who are substituted must be considered as one person.]; D.45.1.7

distinguished from the capacity - to be instituted heir in a testament or to be rewarded with a legacy (*testamenti factio passiva*). For active testamenti factio the Roman juristic language used the expression testator habet testamenti factionem cum aliquo (*cum herede, cum legatario*) for the so-called testamenti factio passiva: heres (legatarius) habet testamenti factionem cum testatore. Testamenti factio also refers to the ability to witness a testament of a specific person. Testamenti factio was required on the part of the testator both when the testament was being made at the time of his death. A testament made by a person without capacity did not become valid if he later acquired it. See Fictio Legis Corneliae. Those unable to make a testament were slaves (except public slaves, servi publici, who could dispose of half their peculium by a last will), persons alieni iuris as long as they were under paternal power, persons below the age of puberty, lunatics (see *Furiosus*), spendthrifts (see *Prodigus*) and women (see *Coemptio fiduciae causa*). From the time of Hadrian women were permitted to make a testament with the consent of their guardians (see *Tutela mulierum*). In later postclassical law apostates and heretics were excluded from making a testament (see *Apostata, Haeretici)* and from taking under one. Only Roman citizens could be instituted heirs in the testament of a Roman dtizen. For restrictions concerning women, see Lex Voconia. Persons alieni iuris could be heirs and legatees, but whatever they acquired went to their pater familias. A testator's slave could be instituted as an heir only cum libertate, i.e. if he was freed in the same testament. Another man's slave acquired all that he received from a testament for his master, provided that the latter had testamenti factio passiva. The institution of "uncertain persons" (see *Personae incertae*) was not permitted. Exceptions in favor of the state, municipalities, charitable institutions (see *Piae causae*) and collegia, were gradually admitted.".

[D.45.1.*De verborum obligationibus* (Verbal obligtions).7 **Ulpianus**, *in the sixth book to Sabinus*: When an impossible condition is conceived for an act, it stands in the way of stipulations. It is different if such a condition is included in a stipulation like "if they do not ascend to heaven," for it is valid, present, and includes the money lent.].

From this, it also follows that a condition is considered as not added if it is necessary for the conditioned according to the nature of the thing itself (which is called extrinsic, as defined above in definition 12), for example, if laws permit, let Titius be the heir, D.30.3 [D.30.*De legatis et fideicommissis* (Legacies and *fideicommissa*). 4 **Ulpianus**, *in the fourth book to Sabinus*: The words of the testator, such as "Whoever will be my heir from the above writings" or "If Seius will be the heir" or "If he enters into the inheritance," do not create a conditional legacy or trust provision.]; D.36.2.6, 25.1 [D.36.2. *Quando dies legatorum vel fideicommissorum cedat* (When a legacy or a *fideicommissum* vests). 6 **Paulus**, *in the third book to Sabinus*: But if the legacy is postponed due to an extrinsic cause, not in the same will, even though the legatee died earlier, we will say that it passes to his heir. For example, if a husband bequeathed the dowry to a stranger, leaving the wife a sum instead of the dowry, and while the woman was considering whether to choose the dowry or the bequeathed sum, the legatee died, and then the woman chose the bequeathed sum; it was decided that the legacy passes to the legatee's heir. Julianus also gave the same answer because it is considered that the legacy contains more of a delay than a condition.25 **Papinianus**, *in the eighteenth book of Questions*: 1. "Let my heir be given to Titius what Seius owes me." If Seius, being a minor, received money without the authorization of a guardian and did not become wealthier and the creditor mentioned nothing about the current debt, because Seius owes nothing, the legacy will be of no consequence. If, however, through the wording, he intended to establish a natural obligation of the debt and future payment, Titius will not be able to demand anything in the meantime, as if an implicit condition were inserted, just as if he had said: "Given to Titius, what the minor will pay," or if he had bequeathed "what will be born from the arethusa" or "the fruits that will grow on that land." It is not different that if, in the meantime, the legatee dies and later a child is born, and the fruits are received, the minor pays the money, the heir of the legatee has a claim. For the day of the legacy, to which no condition is attached, even though it must be awaited from outside, takes precedence.]; D.35.1.99 [D.35.1. *De condicionibus et demonstrationibus et causis et modis eorum, quae in testamento scribuntur* (Conditions, designations, explanations for and modalities of provisions in wills). 99 **Papinianus**, *in the eighteenth* *book On Questions*, see above in definition 12. 107 **Gaius**, *in the single book of Cases.* see above in theorem 3.].

Similarly, the conditioned is also considered as not added, and consequently, according to theorem 69, the disposition is null when it [the conditioned] is necessary. For example, when I bequeath something as a legacy to someone that already belongs to him D.30.29 [D.30.*De legatis et fideicommissis* (Legacies and *fideicommissa*).29 **Paulus**, *in the sixth book on the Lex Julia et Papia*: But if the debt is neither deferred in terms of manner, time, condition, nor place, the legacy is void.], likewise when it [the conditioned] is necessary for the condition, refer to theorem 69.

(18) *Likewise, whatever is unintentionally added. εὔδηλον [This theorem is evident].*

(19) *If it is evident that what has been expressed has been added for a certain purpose, the extensive interpretation is admitted, meaning that anything can be substituted in support which is equivalent in effectiveness to that purpose.*

εὔδηλον, D.35.1.26 [D.35.1. *De condicionibus et demonstrationibus et causis et modis eorum, quae in testamento scribuntur* (Conditions, designations, explanations for and modalities of provisions in wills).26 **Julianus**, *in the eighty-second book of the Digests*: see above in theorem 6.]; D.36.1.17.7, 57.1 [D.36.1.*Ad senatus consultum Trebellianum* (The senatus consultum Trebellianum).18 (17) **Ulpianus**, *in the seventh book on Fideicommissa*: 7. A person is considered to have died without children if they had acknowledged or adopted a child but lost them before their own death. However, if the child perished together with their parent in a shipwreck, we must consider whether the condition has failed. I am of the opinion that it has not failed because it cannot be said that the child survived. So either the child outlived the parent and the condition of the fideicommissum was extinguished, or the child did not survive, and the condition has been fulfilled. When it is unclear who died first, it should be rather said that the condition of the fideicommissum was fulfilled. 59 (57) **Papinianus**, *In the eighth book On Replies*: 1. A provision was expressed in the following terms: "I entrust to the loyalty of my sons that whoever among them passes away before the other without offspring should return his share to the surviving brother. And if both of them die without offspring, I want my entire inheritance to go to my niece Claudia." One of the sons has died, leaving a son, and the other has died without offspring. It appeared at first that, based on the wording of the condition, the niece should not be admitted to the inheritance. However, since fideicommissa must take into account the testator's intent, I replied that it would be absurd to deny the niece the right to claim her share when the first substitution has failed, especially when the testator wanted her to receive the whole if the second brother obtained the portion of the first.]; D.46.3.31 [D.46.3.*De solutionibus et liberationibus* (Performances and releases).31 **Ulpianus**, *in the seventh book on Disputes*: Among craftsmen, there is a vast distinction in intelligence, nature, education, and experience. Consequently, if someone promises to personally build a ship or a house or dig a ditch, and this is specifically stipulated, meaning to do it with their own work, the surety, without the consent of the stipulator, by constructing or digging the ditch themselves, will not release the promisor. Therefore, even if a surety agrees to such stipulations like "you shall not pass; it shall not be lawful for me to cross or act," the surety, by blocking the passage, does not enter into a stipulation. And if they express tolerance, it does not prevent the stipulation from becoming effective.], C.6.2.29.4 [C.6.29. *De postumis heredibus instituendis vel exheredandis vel praeteritis* (Concerning appointing posthumous children as heirs or disinheriting them or passing them over).4. Someone, in making his testament, used these words: "If a son or daughter of mine shall be born within ten months after my death, let them be heirs," or stated as follows: "A son or daughter of mine, who is born within ten months next after my death, shall be my heirs." A dispute arose among the ancient interpreters of the law, whether (children born during the lifetime of the testator) would seem not to have been contemplated in the testament, and that this would be broken (by their birth). Since we have made many laws aiding the wishes of testators, we, in deciding this dispute, direct that the testament shall be effective, notwithstanding the use of either of these phrases, and the testator's intention shall be upheld whether a son or daughter are born during the testator's lifetime or within ten months from the time of the testator's death, so that no testator who did not in fact overlook his children, suffer the penalty of doing so.]. Hence, if it does not matter who fulfills it, the condition is attributed to the named individual or to anyone acting on their behalf because the named individual can transfer money through others or engage others to carry out the assigned task. D.1.5.15 [D.1.5.*De statu hominum* (Human status).15. **Tryphoninus**, *in the tenth book on Disputes*: Arescusa, in whose favor freedom had been ordained by will if she gave birth to three children, initially gave birth to one with her first delivery and then three more with her second. The question was raised about the freedom of these children. For the condition attached to freedom to apply, it must have already been fulfilled by the woman. In this case, there should be no doubt that the last one to be born is free. Nature does not allow two infants to emerge from the mother's womb at the exact same time with a single push, making it uncertain which is born first, in servitude or freedom. Therefore, when the condition has already been fulfilled before the beginning of the birth of the fourth child, it ensures that the one born afterward is brought into the world by a free woman, as if any other condition were attached to her freedom, and it had already been met when she gave birth. For example, it is considered that she gave birth as a free woman if, subject to the condition of giving ten thousand to the heir or to Titius, she had fulfilled the condition at the time of delivery through someone else.]; D.28.7.28 [D.28.7.*De condicionibus institutionum* (Conditions on institutions). 28 **Papinianus**, *in the in the thirteenth book on Questions*: see above in theorem 1.]; D. 32.11.25 [D.32.*De legatis et fideicommissis* (Legacies and *fideicommissa*).11 **Ulpianus**, *in the second book of Fideicommissa, book* 2: 25. If someone, who has been directed to carry out a specific work, is willing to give a sum of money to the city community so that they themselves may accomplish it, they will not be listened to, for the testator intended that this should be done directly by them; this was established by the divine Marcus in a rescript.]; D.40.7.39.5 [D.40.7.*De statuliberis* (Statuliberi).39 **Javolenus**, *in the fourth book of the Posthumous Works of Labeo*: 5. If a slave was ordered to provide services to a stranger, no one can free him by providing their own services on behalf of the slave; this is observed differently concerning money, as a stranger, by giving money for that slave, liberates him from the obligation.]; C.6.51.9 [C. 6.51.*De caducis tollendis* (Concerning abolishing lapses escheats).9: see above in theorem 12.]; D.46.3.31 [D.46.3.*De solutionibus et liberationibus* (Performances and releases).31 **Ulpianus**, *in the seventh book on Disputes*: see above in this theorem 19.].

Furthermore, concerning the fulfillment of a condition, the *pupillus*[90] can fulfill it without the

[90] Berger, *ad vocem Pupillus*, "One below the age of puberty (impuber) who ceased to be under the power of his father by the latter's death or through emancipation'(D. 50.16.239 pr.). An impubes who became sui iuris was under guardianship (tutela impuberum). In a broader sense pupillus is used of all who are below the age of puberty, hence aetas pupillaris — the age below puberty. A pupillus could not alienate property or assume an obligation without the consent of his guardian

authority of the guardian, D.28.7.26 [D.28.7.*De condicionibus institutionum* (Conditions on institutions).26 **Pomponius**, *in the second book to Quintus Mucius*: If a ward has been instituted heir under a condition, he can fulfill the condition even without the guardian's authorization. The same applies if a legacy has been left to him under a condition because, once the condition is fulfilled, it is, for him, as if the inheritance or the legacy were left to him purely and simply.]; D.35.1.5 [D. 35.1. *De condicionibus et demonstrationibus et causis et modis eorum, quae in testamento scribuntur* (Conditions, designations, explanations for and modalities of provisions in wills).5 **Paulus**, *in the second book to Sabinus*: A ward can fulfill the conditions even without the authorization of the guardian. Nor can it be argued to the contrary that, once the condition is fulfilled, he may sometimes become a necessary heir; because this depends on the law of paternal power and not on the fulfillment of the condition.]; as he can improve his own legal position, I.1.21.pr.[I.1.21. *De auctoritate tutorum* (Of the authority of guardians). pr. In some cases, a pupil cannot lawfully act without the authority of his guardian, in others he can. Such authority, for instance, is not necessary when a pupil stipulates for the delivery of property, though it is otherwise where he is the promisor; for it is an established rule that the guardian's authority is not necessary for any act by which the pupil simply improves his own position, though it cannot be dispensed with where he proposes to make it worse. Consequently, unless the guardian authorizes all transactions generating bilateral obligations, such as sale, hire, agency, and deposit. the pupil is not bound, though he can compel the other contracting party to discharge his own obligation.].

It is currently unclear how a *pupillus* could worsen his condition. Even if a potestative condition has been fulfilled, the *suus*[91] makes himself *necessarius*[92] heir, but he still retains the right to refuse acceptance of an insolvent inheritance (*abstinendi potestas*), C.2.38.1.2 [C.2.38. *Si ut se hereditate abstineat.* (If restitution of rights is

(auctoritas tutoris). The opinions of the jurists were divergent as to whether a pupillus could acquire possession; some required the guardian's cooperation. Justinian declared the acquisition valid when the pupillus was beyond the age of infancy. In Justinian's Law. the property of a pupillus was not accessible to usucaption. —D. 26.8; 27.2; C 5.49; 50.".

[91] See note 45 above.

[92] See note 45 above.

demanded by a minor so that he may abstain from an inheritance). 1. If you refrained from having anything to do with your paternal inheritance, a declaration before witnesses (that you did not want it) it was not necessary, since in such case the truth needs no support of words. But if you acted as heirs or received the right of possession of the inheritance, you should receive the aid of restitution of rights on account of your age, to which aid is customarily given. 2. If, when your grandfathers had appointed you heir by testament, you did not enter upon their inheritance, you are at liberty, after repudiating the paternal succession, by the aid of restitution of rights, by which you say you are protected in virtue of your age, to obtain the inheritance of our forebears now, though you did not previously enter upon it.].

Similarly, someone who is under the power of another, such as a son or a slave, can fulfill the condition of freedom without the consent of the one who holds power over them, D.35.1.5.1 [D.35.1. *De condicionibus et demonstrationibus et causis et modis eorum, quae in testamento scribuntur* (Conditions, designations, explanations for and modalities of provisions in wills). 5 **Paulus**, *in the second book to Sabinus*: 1. Similarly, a slave or son-inpower can satisfy a condition without authorization by his master or head of household, since no one comes to harm thereby.]; D.28.7.25 contrasts [D.28.7. *De condicionibus institutionum* (Conditions on institutions).25 **Modestinus**, *in ninth book of the Rules*: A slave instituted heir under a condition cannot meet the condition without the authorization of his master.]. *Cujacius* eliminates the word: "Not"[93].

However, *Albericus Gentilis* distinguishes reasonably between a legacy and the institution of an heir[94]. In a

[93] Jacques Cujas (1578-98), *Observationum et emendationum libri XXVIII.* Coloniae Agrippinae, Lib. II, Lect. (but Cap.) XVI (not 14 such as in the text, e.n.), pp. 57-58, "[…] et ita Modestinum, quia scribere debuit, etiam scripsisse, Sub condicione heres servus institutus, sine iussu domini condicioni parere potest, quod a me iampridem animadversum & publice saepius demonstratum est.".

[94] Alberico Gentili (1552 –1608), *Lectionum et epistolarum ad jus civile pertinenentes liber IV.* (Londonii, 1583-84), lib. I, Lect. (but Cap.) V, Conciliatur l. 5. de cond & dem. cum l. sub condicione de cond. inst., pp. 15-17. "[...], In legato nec id fiat, nec moveremur, si fieret, quia recte in legato dicitur, similibusque, fraudari neminem posse ex implemento; in hereditate recte, l. legatum 36 de leg. 2, l. si hereditatem mand., etc. Ita ergo, cum possit in casu hereditatis dominus fraudari, probe Modestinus in l. 25 denegat illam servo facultatem". [In the legate this does not happen (that is, that the owner must authorize the fulfillment of the condition, e.n.), nor would it make us change our opinion if it happened, since it

legacy, there is no risk once the condition is fulfilled. But in the institution of an heir, although the condition is fulfilled, the person under power is not yet the heir. The period for deliberation begins from the day the condition has been fulfilled, determining whether to accept the inheritance or not.

Finally, when the power to fulfill the condition transfers to the heirs, refer to *François Douaren* in *Scaevola, inserto Com. de V. O. fol. Opp. 794-795*[95] and also, to the definition 72 below (the same applies to the person being honored, that is, the one to whom something must be given in order to fulfill the condition. In this case, the object of the bequest can be given to the guardian or curator D.35.1.13 [D.35.1. *De condicionibus et demonstrationibus et causis et modis eorum, quae in testamento scribuntur* (Conditions, designations, explanations for and modalities of provisions in wills). 13 **Paulus**, *in the fifth book to Sabinus,*: Where land is left to someone if he shall have given money to a pupillus or to a lunatic, he will be deemed to have satisfied the condition by giving to the tutor or curator.]; D.46.3.68, 95 [D.46.3.*De solutionibus et liberationibus* (Performances and releases).68 **Marcellus**, *in the thirteenth book of the Digest*: Consider the case in which a slave was ordered to give ten (something) to a ward and to be free if the ward is an heir or if the condition concerns only the slave; will the slave obtain freedom by giving to the ward even when the guardian of

is rightly said that in the legate, and in similar situations, no one can be harmed by the fulfillment of <the condition>. Thus, therefore, since the master may be damaged in the event of inheritance, Modestino in D.28.7.25 (s. *supra*) rightly denies the slave that faculty]. It should indeed be borne in mind that in any case "the institution of another's slave finds its implementation in an act of acceptance that the slave himself performs following the authorization (iussus) of the person with power over him, and the latter becomes the owner of the assets ", Arangio-Ruiz, note 32 above, pp. 531-32 (e.t.), and if the master authorizes the slave to accept the inheritance "it will draw with it all the hereditary burdens" in the patrimony of the master, Donatantonio de Marinis (e.and t.), *Istituzioni del Dritto Civile dell'Imperador Giustiniano* (Napoli,1829) T. 1, pp. 156-57, n..3, see also D.45.3.15 e I.3.28.pr., 1 and 2.

[95] François Douaren (1509–1559), *Scaevola: Francisci Duareni iureconsulti. libellus qui inscribitur Scevola, interpretationem continens cuiusdam Cervidii Scaevolae replies,* cap. CXXII tit. de verborum obbligation. lib. XLV Pandect. (Parisiis, 1551), pp. 32-35, subsequentely inserted in Id., *D. Francisci Dvareni IC celeberrimi Omnia Quae Quidem Hactenus Edita Fuerunt Opera.* (Francofurti, 1592), pp. 794, 795, such as quoted in the text.

the latter is not present? The consideration here is based on the condition that involves an act, for example, 'if he will be the slave of the ward,' which can be carried out even without the intervention of the guardian. And what right, you may add, if there is a curator and the slave was ordered to give to the insane person, will he gain freedom by paying the curator? Let's assume that the land is left in an inheritance to someone, if he gives it to the ward or to the insane person. It should be known that in all these cases, the actual payment is made to the guardian or the curator; but the payment is not correctly made to the beneficiaries themselves, that is, the ward or the insane person, in order not to lose what is given due to their incompetence, because the testator did not intend that the condition be considered satisfied by giving it in any way. 95 **Papinianus**, *in the eighth book of Questions*: You promise to give either Stichus or Pamphilus, whichever of the two I choose. When one of them dies, the one who is alive shall be asked for, unless there has been a delay for the one who died, which the plaintiff chose. In that case, only the one who passed away is given as if he were the only one brought into the obligation.], but it cannot be given to the master in place of the slave D.35.1.44 [D.35.1. *De condicionibus et demonstrationibus et causis et modis eorum, quae in testamento scribuntur* (Conditions, designations, explanations for and modalities of provisions in wills).44 **Paulus**, *in the ninth book to Plautius*: Whoever is charged with giving to the heir, if a slave belonging to another has been instituted as heir, must give it to the slave and not the owner. Indeed, even if the testator, having instituted any other heir, had ordered to give it to the slave of Titius, it would be necessary to give it to that very slave, because things in fact do not pass to the owner; in the same way that if I had made a stipulation for something to me or to Titius's slave, it could be given not to Titius but to the slave. These statements are correct.]; D.45.1.38.6 [D.45.1. *De verborum obligationibus* (Verbal obligations).38 **Ulpianus**, *in the forty-ninth book to Sabinus*: Those who are in the power of others can stipulate in the name of those in whose power they are that it should be permissible to have things in that manner, and they can stipulate other things on their behalf. But if a slave stipulates that it should be permitted for him to have things for himself, it was asked whether it appears that he stipulated properly. In the fifty-second book of the Digest, Julianus says: If a slave stipulates that it should be lawful for him to have, or promises that nothing should be done by him to prevent the stipulator from having, he does not, he says, incur a stipulation, although the thing can be taken from him, and likewise he can take it from himself, for in this stipulation there is no question of fact but of law. But when it is stipulated that nothing should be done by the promissor to prevent the right of way from being granted, it is not, he says, the right of stipulation which is in question, but a fact.

To me, however, it seems that although this stipulation contains the legal expression "it should be permissible to have," still it must be understood that it is regarded as keeping possession or not taking it away for the slave and the son of a family, and therefore it has the force of a stipulation.], except in the case of a statuliber, aforementioned D.35.1.44.2 [D.35.1. *De condicionibus et demonstrationibus et causis et modis eorum, quae in testamento scribuntur* (Conditions, designations, explanations for and modalities of provisions in wills).44. **Paulus**, *in the ninth book to Plautius*: 2. It is beyond doubt that a statuliber should make delivery to his master.].

Not to the slave without command in place of the master D.35.1.44.3, 94 [D.35.1. *De condicionibus et demonstrationibus et causis et modis eorum, quae in testamento scribuntur* (Conditions, designations, explanations for and modalities of provisions in wills).44 **Paulus,** *in the ninth book to Plautius*: 3. Conversely, one who should give to the master cannot satisfy the condition by giving to the slave, unless the master agree. For in such a case, no one can satisfy a condition, if the other party be in ignorance or unwilling. 94 **Hermogenianus**, *in the first book of the Epitome of Law*: When freedom is left to a slave if he gives to Titius (who is not an heir) a sum of ten, the person is determined, and the condition, as a consequence, can only be fulfilled in that person. Certainly, if on the day of maturity, the statuliber had the money included in the condition due to a special right, he retains his freedom even without giving the money to anyone. It would be different for a legatee, in whose person it was decided that the condition is considered failed if, before the legatee has given, Titius dies.]).

However, this substitution takes effect only as long as the principal [*principalis*, see below definition 54, e.n.] is alive; it ceases upon their death. Because when another person fulfills or receives on behalf of the principal, it is deemed as if the principal themselves is acting, but such a fiction requires suitable conditions; concerning the person fulfilling see D.30.104.1 [D.30.*De legatis et fideicommissis* (Legacies and *fideicommissa*).104 **Julianus**, *in the first book to Urseius Ferox*: 1. In a will, it was written as follows: "One hundred shall be given to Lucius Tiberius if he shall have given my heir the tablets with which I had promised him the money owed to him." Later, Tiberius died before returning the tablets to the heir. The question arose as to whether this bequest was due to his heir. Cassius gave the response that it was not due if the tablets existed because, as these had not been returned, the bequest had not yet come into existence. Julianus notes: for one reason only can it be said that the bequest is due to Tiberius, if at the time of drafting the will, the tablets did not exist because an impossible condition is considered as if it were not written.]; D.35.1.31, 69, 109 [D.35.1. *De condicionibus et demonstrationibus et causis et modis eorum, quae in testamento scribuntur* (Conditions, designations, explanations for and modalities of provisions in wills).31 **Africanus**, *in the second book of Questions*: In a will, it was written as follows: "Stichus and Pamphilus shall be free, and if they marry, my heir shall be obliged to give them one hundred." Stichus died before the will was opened. [Julianus] responded that Stichus's share had lapsed. Even for Pamphilus, it seemed that the condition had lapsed, so her share would go to the heir. Even if both of them were alive and Stichus did not wish to marry her while she was ready to marry, she was entitled to the bequest, but Stichus's portion became void. Because when someone was bequeathed as follows: to Tiberius, if he marries Seia, my heir shall give one hundred, if Seia dies, the condition is deemed to have lapsed. But if he dies, he transmits nothing to his heir because, in the event of his death, the condition is considered to have lapsed. However, if both of them are alive, and if he doesn't want to marry her, because the condition has lapsed due to his own actions, he receives nothing from the bequest. But if the woman doesn't want to marry, and he is willing, then the bequest is owed to him. 69 **Gaius**, *in the thirteenth book on the Lex Julia and Papia*: If the provision is expressed as follows: "I give, I bequeath to Tiberius if he desires," Proculus on Labeo observes that the thing bequeathed only passes to the heir of the legatee to the extent that the legatee himself has willed it to belong to him because it is considered as a condition imposed on the person. 109 **Scaevola**, *in the twentieth book of the Digest*: "An heir, instructed by the testator to return the inheritance, having received one hundred coins, to his co-heir Titia, died after entering upon the inheritance, and Titia also died before returning the one hundred coins. The question arose whether Titia's heir, by offering the one hundred coins, could obtain a share of the inheritance. Scevola's response was that the heir could not fulfill the condition. Cladius added that this eminent legal mind responded on a matter of clear law, although there could be doubt in the present case as to whether there is a condition.]; D.45.1.48 [D.45.1.*De verborum obligationibus* (Verbal obligations).48 **Ulpianus**, *in the twenty-sixth on Edict*: If I have stipulated that ten [items] should be given 'when I request,' the stipulation has more of a reminder for prompt delivery and, as it were, without delay, than a condition. Therefore, even if I should die before requesting, the condition does not seem to have failed.]; concerning the honored, D.35.1.31, 51.1, 94, 109 [D.35.1. *De condicionibus et demonstrationibus et causis et modis eorum, quae in testamento scribuntur* (Conditions, designations, explanations for and modalities of provisions in wills). 31 **Africanus**, *Questions*, *book 2*: see above. 51 **Modestinus**, *in the fifth book of Distinctions*: 1. A slave who was entrusted with giving ten [units] to the heir to gain his freedom, will also obtain his freedom by giving it to the heir of the heir. Publicius writes that the same does not apply to the person of the legatee. 94 **Hermogenianus**, *in the first book of the Epitome of Law*: see above in this theorem 19. 109 **Scaevola**, *in the twentieth book of the Digest*: see above in this theorem 19.]; D.9.2.23.2 [D.9.2.*Ad legem Aquiliam* (The lex Aquilia).23 **Ulpianus**, *in the eighteenth book to the Edict*: 2. The same Julianus writes that, if I have been appointed an heir under the condition "if I have harmed Stichus," and Stichus is killed after the testator's death, I will obtain the value of the estate in the estimate: indeed, the condition cannot be fulfilled due to the killing. If, however, he was killed while the testator was still alive, the estimate of the estate is void because the greater value is considered during the earlier period, and during that period, he was not an heir.].

D.30.54.2 [D.30.*De legatis et fideicommissis* (Legacies and *fideicommissa*).54 **Pomponius**, *in the eighth book to Sabinus*: 2. But if the death of a slave has prevented his manumission, when a legacy has been made to you on condition that you manumit him, the legacy will be due to you all the same. For it is not your fault that he did not obtain his freedom.] is not contradictory, as in that case, the principal died while the testator was still alive, according to the previous §1 of the same law. The statuliberi, with perpetual privilege, was commanded to be free if he had given 10 to the heir, including the heir of the heir, and even if he had given himself to his master to whom the heir had sold him. The statuliberi obtains freedom because the very power of dominion (*potestas dominica*) over slaves is considered honorable in itself, which passes on to the successors, as stated in D.35.1.51.1 [D.35.1.*De condicionibus et demonstrationibus.* (Conditions, designations, explanations for and modalities of provisions in wills). 51 **Modestinus**, *in the fifth book of Distinctions*: 1, see above in this theorem 19.]; D.37.5.15.4 [D.37.5.*De legatis praestandis contra tabulas bonorum possessione petita* (Payment of legacies where application for bonorum possessio contrary to will has been made).15. **Paulus**, *in the forty-first book To the Edict*: 4. If, while a stranger has been instituted as heir, a bequest was made to one of the people exempted under the condition that he shall give ten to the heir, the legatee will not be entitled to the action of legacies unless he has given ten to the person who received possession of the property against the testamentary tablets; and he shall not give to the instituted heir because it would be absurd for one to have the profits of the inheritance and another to bear the burdens in fulfilling the legacy. But even if it was ordered to the legatee to give to Titius, he must not give to him, but to the son. [who has received *bonorum possessio* contrary to the terms of a will.]; D.40.5.4.6 [D.40.5.*De fideicommissariis libertatibus* (Grants of freedom by *fideicommissa*).4 **Ulpianus**, *in the sixtieth book To the Edict*: 6. If grant of freedom is given under the condition of giving ten, whether he was ordered to give it to the heir who received freedom or whether it was not said to whom, one may inquire whether he, by giving it to the person to whom the property is to be assigned, attains to freedom, and it is more likely that he should give it to the one to whom the property is assigned, as if the condition were considered as transferred. Certainly, if he was ordered to give it to someone other than the heir, he shall give it to the one to whom he was ordered.]; D.40.7.22 [D.40.7.*De statuliberis* (Statuliberi).22 **Paulus**, *in the third book to Vitellius*: 22. One to whom it was ordered to give a sum, if it is not specified to whom he should give it, shall give it to the creditors in proportion to the hereditary shares; because each of them should receive a portion proportionate to the share of ownership they have.].

It is akin to when we abstractly speak of a legacy to a specific honorary office or to a person, where if any legacy, such as an annual annuity, passes on to the successors of that honorary office, as mentioned by *Menochius 4. praesumt. 121*[96]. If the *extraneus* to whom the slave was supposed to pay dies, the slave becomes free without paying anyone, as stated in D.35.1.94 [D.35.1. *De condicionibus et demonstrationibus et causis et modis eorum, quae in testamento scribuntur* (Conditions, designations, explanations for and

[96] Giacomo Menochio (1532–1607), *De praesumptionibus, conjecturis, signis et indiciis commentaria* (Coloniae Allobrogum: Sumptibus Iacobi Crispin,1636), lib. IV, preasumpt. CXXI, "Dubitari solet quando legatum est alicui sub nomine dignitatis puta si testator reliquit Pontifici Maximo vel Caesari Augusto, vel Episcopo, an legatum transeat etiam ad successorem in ea dignitate, si decessit laegatarius antequam cedat dies legati? Et certum est transire, quia praesumitur testatorem voluisse relinquere non illi certae personae existenti tunc in dignitate, sed ipsimet dignitati". [It is often a subject of doubt when a bequest is made to someone under the name of a dignified office. For example, if the testator bequeathed something to the Pontiff Maximus or to Caesar Augustus, or to a Bishop, it is questioned whether the bequest also passes to the successor in that office if the legatee dies before the deadline for claiming the legacy. And it is certain that it does pass, because it is presumed that the testator intended to leave the bequest not to the specific person currently holding the office, but to the office itself.].

modalities of provisions in wills). 94 **Hermogenianus**, *in the first book of Epitome of Law*: see above in this theorem 19.].

Therefore, the person who is the object of the condition of giving, referred to as "honored," allows for an extensive interpretation, unlike the person who is the object of the condition of doing. For example, if Titius were to teach music, let him have 100! Even if Titius desires it, the sum cannot be given to another, as stated in D.46.3.31 [D.46.3.*De solutionibus et liberationibus* (Performances and releases).31 **Ulpianus**, *Disputations, book* 7:see above in this theorem 19.]; D.35.1.44.pr [D.35.1.*De condicionibus et demonstrationibus et causis et modis eorum, quae in testamento scribuntur* (Conditions, designations, explanations for and modalities of provisions in wills).44 **Paulus**, *in the ninth book to Plautius*: pr.see above in this theorem 19.].

Finally, it should be noted that a condition, where the conditional person (the person to whom the condition refers) has a substitute, can also exist when that person is dying D.28.7.28 [D.28.7.*De condicionibus institutionum* (Conditions on institutions). 28 **Papinianus**, *in the in the thirteenth book on Question*, see above in theorem 1.]. While they are alive, they can exist in another person, as we will explain shortly. However, even when they are dying, at the very moment of death, they still live, *Gell. VI, 13*[97], D.39.6.42.1 [D.39.6. *De mortis causa donationibus et capionibus* (Gifts and acquisitions mortis causa).42 **Papinianus**, *in the thirteenth book of Responses*: 1. A father, finding himself in the final stages of life, gave some property to his emancipated son without any condition of return; and the brothers and co-heirs wanted these gifts to be included in the property subject to the Falcidian law. I replied

[97] Aulus Gellius [130–180 AD], *Noctes Atticae*. VI, 21 §§ 1 and 3 [not 13 such as in the text, e.n.], in John C. Rolfe (ed.), *Aulus Gellius. Attic Nights*, Books VI-XIII. (Cambridge (MA): Harvard University Press, 1927), p. 85, "Why it is that the phrases quoad vivet and quoad morietur indicate the very same time, although based upon opposite things. When the expressions quoad vivet, or "so long as he shall live," and quoad morietur, or "until he shall die," are used, two opposite things really seem to be said, but the two expressions indicate one and the same time. Also, when we say "as long as the senate shall be in session," and "until the senate shall adjourn," although "be in session" and "adjourn" are opposites, yet one and the same idea is expressed by both phrases.".

that the ancient law should be observed; because those gifts could not be referred to any constitution other than that of gifts made under a specific condition; and since death had occurred, the gifted properties do not return, as the hope of recovering them with the donor has been extinguished; but the one who had given absolutely would have given rather in death than due to death.]; D.40.4.18.1 [D.40.4.*De manumissis testamento* (Testamentary manumissions).18 **Julianus**, *in the second book to Urseius Ferox*: 1. This condition: 'Be free when I die,' pertains to a time during life, and therefore seems to be useless. But it is better to interpret these words more favorably and assume that freedom was left by the testator for after his death.].

(20) A condition admits an extensive interpretation in last wills, while the thing conditioned admits an intensive interpretation. On the contrary, in contracts, a condition admits an intensive or augmentative interpretation, while the thing conditioned admits an extensive or diminutive interpretation.

(Each of the two is useful for the debitor; detrimental for the *conditionarius*, according to theorem 46). For in the interpretation of last wills, it is necessary to favor the honored, as this does not harm the declarant; rather, it appears to be appreciated by the declarant if we interpret their wills in a very broad sense. On the contrary, in interpreting contracts, it is necessary to favor the giver, as in contracts, the giver and the declarant coincide. It is presumed, on the other hand, that each intended to minimize harm to themselves with their own words. In cases of doubt, an unconditional provision is assumed rather than a conditional one, according to *Menochius, 6, presumption 4*[98]. The use of this theorem has been of great importance throughout our entire dissertation, see theorem 29.

[98] Giacomo Menochio, see note 96 above, lib. 6, praesumpt. IV, *Actum quemlibet ita praesumi factum, ut valeat diligenter et copiosa explanatio.* [Any act is to be presumed to have been done in such a way that it may be valid with a careful and full explanation.].

(21) A necessary condition for the act admits a diminutive interpretation.

Because what we do necessarily, we do it to the utmost against our own will. If, therefore, the *conditionarius* willingly disregards the whole condition, how much more would he neglect a part of it? (arg. D.28.2.29 [D.28.2.*De liberis et postumis heredibus instituendis vel exheredandis* (The institution of children and postumi as heirs and their disherison).29 **Scaevola**, *in the sixth book of Questions*: Aquilius Gallus established that posthumous grandchildren can be instituted as heirs in the following manner: "If my son should die while I am still alive, and if, after my death, within ten months following the months in which my son died, a grandchild, whether a boy or girl, shall be born to me through him, let them be heirs."]; D.36.1.22 [D.36.1. *Ad senatus consultum Trebellianum* (The senatus consultum Trebellianum).23 (22) **Ulpianus**, *in the fifth book of Disputations, book 5*: A woman, who had two sons under the patria potestas of their father and subsequently married another man, instituted her later husband as her heir and requested him to restore her inheritance to her children after the death of their father or to the one who survived them. When the children were emancipated by their father, it was said that the stepfather had returned the inheritance. Later, one of the sons died while the father was still alive. The question arose whether the son who survived could claim the part of the inheritance that had been returned to his brother as if it had been prematurely given. Scaevola relates that the deified Marcus judged on a similar case in his lecture hall: A certain Brasidas, a Spartan, a praetor, separated from his wife with his sons, and if they had come into his power through the death of their father, he left a fideicommissum and emancipated them. After the emancipation, they claimed the fideicommissum. Therefore, the deified Marcus decided that the fideicommissum should be reinstated to them, understanding the mother's intent. She had deferred the fideicommissum until the father's death because she did not believe he would emancipate them. If she had hoped he would emancipate them, she would not have deferred the fideicommissum until his death. According to these, I was saying that it should be inferred that the decree of the deified Marcus applies to the presented question and that the fideicommissum was correctly discharged to both parties.]; D.50.17.62 [D.50.17. *De diversis regulis iuris antiqui* (Various rules of early law). 62. **Julianus**, *in the sixth book of Digest*: An inheritance is nothing other than the succession to every right possessed by the deceased person.], C.6.25.3 [C. 6.25. *De institutionibus seu* *substitutionibus sub condicione factis* (Concerning appointments, substitutions or trusts, made upon condition). 3. If your mother appointed you her heirs upon condition of your emancipation, and if before the wish of the decedent was carried out, your father was sentenced to deportation1 or died, you, being released from the paternal power by his death, or in some other manner, acquired the right to enter on the inheritance together with its belongings.]; C.8.54.5 [C.8.54. *De donationibus quae sub modo vel condicione vel ex certo tempore conficuntur* (Concerning gifts made subject to a duty, or upon condition or for a definite time).5. If a mother made a gift to her daughter in her father's power, upon condition that she should be emancipated within two years, (then) though she, having become sui juris, did not hold it (the gift) (strictly) under the wish of her mother, still having become sui juris in some manner, namely by the death of the husband (of the mother) and father (of the daughter), she can firmly hold and claim the gift left in pattern of a legacy.].

On the other hand, a condition is necessary for the act when the act cannot exist in its specific form without this given condition. For example, a disinheritance after the burial cannot happen without the condition prescribed by Aquilius Gallus[99] in D.28.2.29 [D.28.2.*De liberis et postumis heredibus instituendis vel exheredandis* (The institution of children and postumi as heirs and their disherison).29 Scaevola, *in the sixth book of Questions* see above, in this theorem 21.]. Alternatively, even if an act can exist in its specific form without this condition, it cannot exist without any condition in general.

Such are acts that are naturally conditional, like substitution[100], D.28.6.23 [D.28.6.*De vulgari et pupillari substitutione* (Normal and pupillary substitution).23 **Papinianus,** *in the sixth book of Replies, book 6*: If someone appoints multiple heirs and writes as follows: "And I substitute them all reciprocally," then, after one of them has entered upon the inheritance and the condition of substitution has been fulfilled, with another heir rejecting their

[99] Berger, *ad vocem Aquilius Gallus*, "Aquilius Gallus, Gaius. One of the most creative jurists under die Republic, praetor in 66 B.C. His name is linked with the introduction of the Stipulatio Aquiliana and the Actio Doli.".

[100] Leibniz (1665-1667?), *Methodus*, AA VI 2, p. 18, "Substituere est dare secundo, si primus non acquiret. Mutuo substituti simul pure instituuntur" [To substitute is to give to a second if the first does not want to accept. Mutually the substitutes are established in the same way unconditionally.] (e.t.).

share, the entire portion will go to the survivors, because they will be seen as substituted reciprocally for every possible reason. For when someone appoints heirs and writes in this manner: "And I substitute them reciprocally," those will be seen as substituted who have become heirs.], (D.28.6.8.pr. does not preclude [D.28.6.*De vulgari et pupillari substitutione* (Normal and pupillary substitution).8 **Ulpianus**, *in the fourth book to Sabinus*: When someone substitutes children who have not yet reached puberty, they usually do so either unconditionally or under a condition. Unconditionally, it is done as follows: "If my son should pass away before reaching puberty, let Seius be the heir," whether this Seius has been appointed as an heir and also substituted for the child not yet at puberty, it does not have any condition attached to it, or if he has been only substituted. However, if it has been appointed under a condition and he substitutes it, that is, "if he will be my heir," there will be no heir arising from the substitution unless he has already been appointed as an heir. A similar case is this substitution: "whichever of the above-mentioned individuals will be my heir." It contains the same condition as the previous one.]), according to *Crispinus ad pr., n. 6. I. eod.*[101], *Alciatus, de V. S. lib. 3 n. 19*[102].

Franciscus Duarenus in tit. del C. I. c. 1[103] disagrees; indeed, it contains this: if one does not have it, let the other have it! Likewise, the surety (*fideiussio*) in the new law, whenever one does not waive the *beneficium ordinis*

[101] Jean Crespin (c. 1520–1572), *Imperatoris Iustiniani Institutiones libri IIII, studio I. Crispini et I Pacii.* (the edition I consulted is Amstelodami, 1642), p. 121 "6. Substitutionem generaliter definire possumus institutionem conditionalem in subsidium prioris heredis deficientis". [We can generally define substitution as the conditional institution that replaces the first heir who fails, e.t.].

[102] Andrea Alciato (1492–1550), *De verborum et rerum significatione* (the edition I consulted is Lugduni, 1572), pp. 112-113, "19. Item vulgaris substitutio hac formula concipitur: Si Titius heres non erit, tunc Seius esto: & tamen pupillarem in se habet". [Similarly, ordinary substitution is conceived according to this formula: If Titius is not heir, let Seius be heir and, in any case, it contains within itself the pupillary <substitution>].

[103] François Douaren (1509–1559), *D. Francisci Dvareni IC celeberrimi Omnia Quae Quidem Hactenus Edita Fuerunt Opera.* (Francofurti, 1592) in Tit, VII De Conditionibus Institutionum, cap. I, p. 411, "Sed ego dixi substitutionem vulgarem quae ita sit, Si Titius Heres non erit, Seius heres esto, fieri sub condicione posse, aliquando etiam pure fieri posse". [But I said the ordinary substitution, which is in this way, If Titius is not heir, let Seius be heir, it can be done under condition, sometimes it can also be done pure].

or excussionis[104], it indeed contains: If the principal debtor does not pay, I shall pay. See Nov. 4 [Auth. praesente C. de fideiuss. Nov. 4, (*Ut creditor primo debitores principales convenient, et secundo loco, si illi non solvendo esse reperiantur, mandatores vel constitutae pecuniae reos vel fideiussores.*) That creditors must first sue the principal debtors, and they may sue mandators, guarantors of money agreed to be paid on a day fixed, and sureties (by stipulation: only if the former are found to be insolvent.) Preface. We have deemed it best, on account of its importance in settling continuously recurring questions, to revive and make effective an ancient law which in an unknown manner had fallen almost out of use, and to do so not merely in its ancient form—for it was defective in some respects—but to amend it in a manner that is proper and pleasing to God. c. 1. So if any one makes a loan of money to another for which a surety, by stipulation and mandate and by promising to pay another's existing debt, is also responsible, the lender shall not, at the beginning, sue such surety, and shall not, while neglecting the principal debtor, make trouble for the intercessors, but he shall first sue the party who received the money and contracted the debt. If he recovers his debt from him, he shall refrain from troubling the others. For what has the o do with outsiders, if he is paid by the party who received the money? If, however, he is unable to recover the debt or any part of it from the principal debtor, he may have recourse against the surety, for the remainder which he cannot recover from the former. And this applies when neither the principal debtor nor the surety are absent. But if the surety is in the same jurisdiction, and the principal debtor is not, it would be harsh to send the creditor to some other place, and he may immediately demand payment from such surety. A suitable amelioration must, however, be provided in this matter. The ancient law did nothing in that respect, although the great Papinianus showed the means. If the creditor, therefore, sued such surety, and the latter wants to produce the principal debtor in court, the judge presiding in the cause must give them time to do so, so that such principal debtor may first be compelled to sustain the burden of the action, and so that the former may be held liable only in the reserve. And the presiding judge must lend his assistance in this respect to the surety, for it is just that this should be done, so that they may in the meantime be released by the principal debtor so produced. But if the time fixed passes by—for the judge must also fix such time—(and the debtor is not produced), then the surety, mandatory or guarantor, must sustain the burden of the action and

[104] Berger, *ad vocem Beneficium excussionis*, "Beneficium excussionis (or ordinis). Both terms coined in literature. Justinian gave a surety the right to compel the creditor who had sued him before the principal, to sue the principal first.".

pay the debt, the rights of action over against the principal debtor passing to them.].

The *stipulatio poenalis*[105], let's consider: if you do this or you don't, do you promise to give to that extent? See *Julius van Beyma, Tr. de stipulatione poenali*[106].

The *in diem addictio imperfecta*[107] indeed contains this: if you pay the price on the agreed day, let the bought thing be yours (D.18.2.2pr., 4pr. [D.18.2 *In diem addictio.* 2 **Ulpianus**, *in the twenty-eighth book to Sabinus*: pr. See above in definition 21. 4 **Ulpianus**, *in the twenty-eighth book to Sabinus*: pr. When there is a conditional sale, Pomponius denies that the buyer can acquire it through usucapion, and he also states that the fruits do not belong to him.]). The succession agreement (*pactum successorium*[108]), which is always associated with a

[105] Leibniz, note 98, AA VI 2, p. 18, "Stipulatio poenalis est, quae hoc continet: si hoc facies (non facies), dare spondes?, seu simplicius: est cum quis promittit se daturum, si certi aliquid faciat vel non faciat" [The stipulatio poenalis is the one that contains this: if you do this (or you won't do it), do you promise to give?, or more simply: it is when someone promises that he will give, whether or not he does a certain thing]. About *Stipulatio,* see note 43 above; Berger, *ad vocem Stipulatio poenae,* "A stipulatio concerning the payment of a penalty by a debtor if he failed to perform his obligation as agreed upon. The penalty settled in the stipulatio might serve either as a substitute for the losses suffered by the creditor (in such a case he might sue the debtor tor the payment of the penalty without proving the amount of his actual losses) or as a mere penalty (poenae nomine) to be paid beside the indemnification for effective losses.".

[106] Julius van Beyma (1539-1598) (1645), *Commentaria in varios titutlos juris...item... de poenali stipulatione.* Leovardeiae, 599-612.

[107] Berger, *ad vocem Addictio in diem,* "An agreement between buyer and seller giving the latter the right to declare the sale annulled if, within a certain time, he received an offer of higher price (adiectio) for the object sold. In such case the first buyer had the possibility to increase his bid and to keep the thing." Leibniz (1665-1667?), note 98, AA VI 2, 18, "In diem addictio imperfecta est, quae hoc continet: si statuta die pretium solves, ea res tibi emta esto.". [The in diem addictio imperfecta is the one that contains this clause: if you pay the price within the established term, the thing sold shall be yours.].

[108] Leibniz (1665-1667?), note 98, AA VI 2, p. 18, "Pactum successorium mutuum seu confraternitas est, cum ego do tibi, si praemoriar, seccessionem in bona mea, et tu vicissim mihi, si tu praemorieris, in tua" [The reciprocal succession agreement or brotherhood is when I give you the succession in my assets and you reciprocally to me, if you predecease, in yours].

condition of death, see infra theorem 38. *Sponsio*[109] or *pactum certariorum*[110], *eine Wette* (in German in the text, a bet, e.n.), see *Paride dal Pozzo tr. de Ludis n. 36*[111] and *Petrus Santerna, tr. peculiari de Assecurationibus et Sponsionibus mercatorum*[112], e.g. if the king of the Parthians lives, D.12.1.37 [D.12.1.*De rebus creditis si certum petetur et de condictione* (Things credited giving rise to fixed claims and the condictio). 37 **Papinan**, *in the first book of Definitions*: When a condition is attached to the present time, the stipulation is not suspended, and if the condition is true, the stipulation is binding, even if the contracting parties are unaware of the existence of the condition. For example, 'If the King of the Parthians is alive, do you promise to give me a hundred?' The same rule applies when the condition is attached to the past.]). If that pregnant woman gives birth to a male, do you promise to give to that

[109] Leibniz (1665-1667?), note 98, AA VI 2, 18, "Sponsio est conventio mutua utrinque conditionalis collata in rem seu praeteritam seu futuram, e.g. in evenutm cujusdam certaminis, seu serii seu ludicri inter ipsos spondentes (hinc *sponsio aleatoria, Spielwette, statutio praemii, wetter unter spielenden*) aut alios.". [The sponsio is the reciprocal convention, conditional for both parties, handed over to an event both past and future, for example, to the outcome of a certain dispute, both serious and for fun, between the promissors themselves (hence the aleatory sponsio, bet on a game, the establishment of an award, bet between gamblers) or others]; Berger, *ad vocem Sponsio*, "(From *spondere*) The earliest form of an obligation under ius civile assimued through an oral answer (*spondeo* to the future creditor's question (*spondesne?*). The *sponsio*, conceived in this broader sense, was in the course of time absorbed by the *stipulatio*. In a narrower sense sponsio denoted the obligation of a surety- who equally through exchange of question and answer obligated himself to pay what another had promised; see adpromissio. This function of the *sponsio* was probably the earlier one.".

[110] Leibniz (1665-1667?), note 98 above, AA VI 2, 18, "Sponsio dicitur pactum certatorium, quia fit inter certantes vel potius inter dispuntantes et sibi invicem contradicentes seu proprio seu alieno, vel de alia quadam historia" [Sponsio is called the pact of those who contend because it occurs among contenders or rather disputants who mutually contradict each other regarding a dispute, whether it is their own or someone else's, or some other story.].

[111] Paride Del Pozzo (1410–1493) (1489/94), *Tractatus Paridis de Puteo de Ludo*, in *Tractatus universi iuris ... in unum congesti... T. VII* (Venetiis: Franciscus Zilletus, 1584), pp. 153-154, n. 36, "Sponsio super futuris quae in consilio Dei sunt, ut mors, vita, victoria etc. an valeat. Conditionis solus cuentus habetur pro causa.".

[112] Pedro De Santarém (1460-1521), *Tractatus de assecurationibus et sponsionibus mercatorum* (Venetiis, 1552).

extent? Then the other, and you, if female, even in the same extent? And each one responds to the other, 'I promise,' in the same way as the game in *Opitium der Poetischen Walder, lib. 1, p. 4*[113].

[113] Martin Opitz (1597-1639), *Poetische Walder*, in *Welthliche Poemata*, Der andere Theil. (Amstelodami, 1645).

CHAPTER V

[Multiplication of the Terms and Interpretation of Quantity]

Definitions

And these are the things examined on interpretation in general, simply, without ordered arrangement, for the one and the manifold, the whole and the part.

Let's come to the multiplication of the terms and the interpretation of quantity that, since it consists of general, maximally metaphysical rules, applied only to the law, we appropriately introduced to the special treatment of the partial propositions and terms in them.

Firstly, we will explain the terms we will use: every disposition in which they have been placed, they are either

26. ONE UNIT, i.e. the undivided, or

27. MANIFOLD, facts resulting from division (in both ways, either formally or in fact, when the unit represents the manifold, or vice versa, as stated in theorem 23). An individual unit in nature can become manifold, meaning it has parts that are homogeneous among themselves and with the whole, which are otherwise referred to as similar. The whole is referred to as

28. DIVISIBLE (since, in a different sense, although it is truly divisible, it is not legally divisible due to the incommensurability of the parts).

However, if the parts are heterogeneous among themselves and in relation to the whole, that is, dissimilar, the whole is called

29. INDIVISIBLE, *adde* after definition 40, D.32.11.23 [D.32.*De legatis et fideicommissis* (Legacies and *fideicommissa*). 11. **Ulpianus**, *in the second book of Fideicommissa, book* 2: 23. If something

is left undone in a public work, the divine Marcus and Lucius Verus decreed that each heir is liable for the whole amount. However, they granted a time limit to the coheir within which they should contribute to the completion of the work. After that time, they intended that only Procula's share would be charged to the coheir for their portion of the expenses. (according to Schepers, it shoud be law 24 not 23, probably mistprints, e.n.): 24. Therefore, the deified Marcus ruled in a rescript that the same applied to a statue, a servitude, and other things not admitting division.]; D.35.1.112. pr. [D.35.1. *De condicionibus et demonstrationibus et causis et modis eorum, quae in testamento scribuntur* (Conditions, designations, explanations for and modalities of provisions in wills). 112 **Pomponius**, *in the twelfth book of Letters*: Such conditions as "if they have made a monument," for example, cannot exist for multiple individuals unless they all fulfill the condition simultaneously.]; D.35.2.81.1 [D.35.2.*Ad legem Falcidiam* (The lex Falcidia).81 **Gaius**, *in the eighteenth book of Provincial Edict*: 1. Dowry falls outside the lex Falcidia, obviously because the woman gets back her own property.].

The indivisible part is commensurable with the remaining parts and consequently with the whole, and the proportion of them can be expressed in another number either *effabilis* [commensurable, expressible, rational, e.n.] as 2, or *surdus* [incommensurable, irrational, e.n.] as e.g. the square root of 2[114]. Just as in geometry (where the term "commensurable" is used in a broader sense that includes rational numbers), each line is commensurable with every other line, each surface with every other surface, and so on. However, when considering heterogeneous parts, like angles, points, lines, surfaces, and wholes, they are incommensurable with each other. There is no relation between an angle of contingency and a rectilinear angle, nor is there any comparison between space and motion or time. In physics and law, the concept of quantity or fungible[115] goods, are divided into individual species.

[114] For of the meaning of the words *numerus effabils* as rational number and *numerus surdus* as irrational number, according to the Leibniz's speech, see G.H.R. Parkinson, "Philosophy and logic", in Nicholas Jolley (ed.), *The Cambridge Companion to Leibniz* (Cambridge, 1995), p. 206.

[115] AA VI 1, Quaest. XV, "7...vel quantitativum, quo refert res fungibiles,

For example, a piece of gold, no matter how small, can be proportionally related to a mass of gold of any size because every piece of gold is gold, just as every piece of land is land, D.30.34.15 [D.30.*De legatis et fideicommissis* (Legacies and *fideicommissa*).34 **Ulpianus**, *in the twenty-first book to Sabinus*: 15. But even if someone leaves the following legacy to Titius: "I give and bequeath a plot of land for him," it seems to me that it can be said that he will have a share. For it seems that by the designation of land, he did not refer to the entire estate but to a part, as even a part of an estate is properly called an estate.].

However, a part of a human is not a human, so we cannot determine the measure of a human in relation to a hand or how much more a human is worth compared to a hand (see Question 15 of the Philosophical Questions[116]).

In certain cases, divisible conditions can be distributed among several parts. For instance, in the scenario of Titius and Caius being heirs, if they give 100 thalers to Sempronius, each of them will give 50 thalers, resulting in a total of 100 thalers. Money itself is divisible D.35.1.23 [D.35.1.*De condicionibus et demonstrationibus et causis et modis eorum, quae in testamento scribuntur* (Conditions, designations, explanations for and modalities of provisions in wills).23 **Julianus**, *in the forty-third book of Digest*: If someone is ordered to give ten to two heirs and to have a plot of land for himself, it is truer that he cannot split the condition, lest the legacy also be split. Therefore, even if he gives five to one heir, he will not claim any part of the land, unless, when the other heir also approaches the inheritance, he pays the remaining five, or if the other one abandons the inheritance, he gives the full ten to the one who alone approaches the inheritance.], although it can become indivisible when allocated for the expenses of an indivisible work, D.35.1.112.2 [D.35.1.*De condicionibus et demonstrationibus et causis et modis eorum, quae in testamento scribuntur* (Conditions, designations, explanations for and modalities of provisions in wills).112 **Pomponius**, *in the*

quae a JCtis quantitates dicuntur" [or quantitative, by which we refer to fungible things, which are called quantities by jurists.].

[116] AA VI 1, Quaest. XV, "1. Totum et Pars a JCtis distinguitur ...". [The whole and the part are distinguished by Jurists.].

twelfth book of Letters: 2. The question also arises regarding this: a plot of land is bequeathed to certain individuals, provided they deliver a specific amount of money for the burial and transportation of the body to another region. Because unless both have given, neither of them has a legacy, since the condition cannot be fulfilled unless both do. However, we usually interpret these cases more leniently so that when a plot of land is bequeathed to two people, if they have given ten, the legacy must also be given to the one who has given a part.]. However, I refer to the very concept as the

30. DIVISIBLE OR INDIVISIBLE DISPOSITION when the Condition is divided, whether the Conditioned is also divided or not, as stated in aforesaid D.35.1.23 [D.35.1.*De condicionibus et demonstrationibus et causis et modis eorum, quae in testamento scribuntur* (Conditions, designations, explanations for and modalities of provisions in wills).23 **Julianus**, *in the forty-three book of Digest*, see above in definition 29.]. Furthermore, a part can be categorized as either

31. RELEVANT or IRRELEVANT. If a part is fulfilled independently without necessitating the fulfillment of the whole, it is not fulfilled in vain and should not be reiterated. It serves a purpose D.29.2.74.1 [D.29.2. *De adquirenda vel omittenda hereditate* (Taking up or failing to take up an inheritance).74 **Paulus**, *in the twelfth book to Plautius*: 1. But if someone believes they have been ordered to give five when they have been ordered to give ten, and they give five, they do not fulfill the condition but make some progress. If they later fulfill the remainder, it might be considered as if the condition were fulfilled by the contribution of the remaining five from others.] and does not impede the rest D.40.5.23.3 [D.40.5.*De fideicommissariis libertatibus* (Grants of freedom by *fideicommissa*).23 **Papinianus**, *in the ninth book of Replies*: 3. Even the freedom granted by way of a fideicommissum, given by a father to his son after a certain age, should be restored on the day specified, if the son has not yet reached that age. This rule, established by a specific legal principle, has not been extended to other fideicommissa left behind.].

In D.29.2.74 [D.29.2.*De adquirenda vel omittenda hereditate* (Taking up or failing to take up an inheritance).74 **Paulus**, *in the twelfth book to Plautius*: 1, see above in this definition 31.], when someone pays 5 instead of 10, their ignorance does not harm them as long as they rectify their mistake. Conversely, in D.40.5.23.3 [D.40.5.*De fideicommissariis libertatibus* (Grants of freedom by *fideicommissa*).23 **Papinianus**, *Replies, book 9*: 3, see above in this definition 31.], the fulfillment of the whole is not hindered by the fulfillment of a particular condition, *adde* D.35.1.40.pr. [D.35.1.*De condicionibus et demonstrationibus et causis et modis eorum, quae in testamento scribuntur* (Conditions, designations, explanations for and modalities of provisions in wills).40 **Javolenus**, *in the second book* of *Posthumous Works of Labeo*: pr. On the days when your neighbor obstructs you from using the public road when you wanted to fulfill a condition and does not stand in your way, these days will not be counted towards fulfilling the condition.].

Multiple elements can be either disjointed, connected, or linked.

32. DISJOINTED are either A or B. For instance, consider Titius, who may either give 10 or ascend to the Capitol, resulting in receiving 100. However, every disjunctive statement can be resolved into a dual conditional statement with a negative Condition and an affirmative Conditioned. For example, "Let it be either A or B" is equivalent to saying: "If A is not, then let B be; if B is not, then let A be." Consequently, a conditional stipulation, such as promising to give Pamphilus if one fails to deliver, is tantamount to a pure promise of giving Pamphilus, D.45.1.115 [D.45.1.*De verborum obligationibus* (Verbal obligations).115 **Papinianus**, *in the seond book of Questions*: I have stipulated as follows: "Do you promise to stand in a specific place; if you do not stand, do you undertake to pay fifty gold coins?" If a day in the stipulation has been omitted in error, while the aim of the stipulation was that you stand on a specific day, the stipulation will be incomplete. This is no different from if I had stipulated that a certain weight or number was to be measured without adding the weight or number, or if I had stipulated that an island be built without specifying the location, or if I had stipulated the transfer of a property without mentioning the name. However, if from the beginning the purpose was that you stand on any day, and if you do not stand, you pay the money, as if the stipulation was conceived conditionally in this way, it will have legal force, and it will not be committed until it is declared that it is impossible for the person to fulfill the promise of standing.]. On the contrary,

in the legacies of fungibles[117] [such as a legacy of slave, without any further identification, see note 112, e.n.] or option [among several], each individual seems to be bequeathed under the condition of not choosing the others D.40.9.3 [D.40.9 *Qui et a quibus manumissi liberi non fiunt et ad legem Aeliam Sentiam* (Manumitted persons not free and the lex Aelia Sentia).3 **Gaius**, *in the second book on Legacies in the Urban Edict*: If an option has been given to a man, or if a legatee is described indistinctly as "a man," the heir cannot diminish or destroy the right of election by manumitting certain slaves or all of them. For, in the case of slaves, the option or election is in a way considered as granted to each one individually, subject to the condition.]; D.33.5.9 [D.33.5. *De optione vel electione legata* (The legacy of an option or choice).9 **Julianus**, *in the thirty-second book of the Digests*: When a legacy is made in the following manner: "I give Stichus to Titius if he does not choose Pamphilus, and to the same Titius, Pamphilus, if he does not choose Stichus," it is similar to if the legacy had been made in this way: "I give Stichus or Pamphilus to Titius, whichever of them he may choose.], *Alciatus tr. de Stipul. Divid. n. 16*[118]. Moreover, when multiple parties stipulate individually, promising to give to me if you do not give to them, it is said to anticipate the action (similar to believing in two opposing parties) D.45.1.9 [D.45.1.*De verborum obligationibus* (Verbal obligations).9 **Pomponius**, *in the thirty-second book to Sabinus*: If Titius and Seius have separately stipulated, "do you promise to give me that farm, if you have not given it to him," there will be an intention of giving it to either until an action is received; and therefore there will be an action of the occupant.], which raises some doubts, as discussed in theorem 4 above.

[117] Berger, *ad vocem Legatum generis*, "A legacy of fungibles (see genus) and not of some individually designated thing (species). The legacy of a slave, without any further indication, was such a legacy. Normally the testator set in his testament who had to make the choice from among the things of the same kind (slaves, horses) belonging to the estate: the heir, the legatee or a third person. The jurists did not agree about the solution in the case the testator did not entitle any person to make the selection. Apparently the rules varied according to the form in which such a legacy (legatum) was left. The Justinian law favored the choice by the legatee.".

[118] Andrea Alciato (1492–1550), *Tractatus de stipulationum divisionibus*, T. de legibus 2, 3, 4 de verborum obligatione scholia, in *Opera*. (Basileae, 1558), vol. III, pp. 820-41.

33. They are CONJUNCTED, for example, let A and B be, and the conjunctive proposition is resolved into two unconditional affirmatives: let A be, let B be, which, for the sake of brevity, are reduced to only one. *Corsetti, in his treatise De verbis geminatis, number 8*[119], refers to the conjunctive condition as "comitative." They are conjuncted in succession: first, let A be, then let B also be conjuncted. They are disjuncted in succession: let A be, if A could not, let B be. Where B has been added only as a reserve, refer to theorem 30 below. This well-ordered disjunction is present in every substitution, D.28.6.1.1 [D.28.6. *De vulgari et pupillari substitutione* (Normal and pupillary substitution). 1 **Modestinus**, *in the second book of Pandette*: 1. The substitution of an heir is either simple or double, as follows: "Let Lucius Titius be the heir: if Lucius Titius is not my heir, then let Seius be my heir." "If he is not the heir, or if he is the heir and dies before reaching puberty, then let Gaius Seius be my heir."].

34. CONNECTED are those which are mutually consequent or necessary between them.

(35. The REQUIREMENT, on the other hand, is what, "without which," the requiring cannot be, in this way: if A is not, let B not be! The consequent is what, when an inference is placed, is placed in this way: if B is, let A be). The designation will be as follows: if B is, let A be; if A is, let B be or as follows: if A is not, let B not be; if B is not, let A not be. One designation, in fact, follows from another, and every necessary is the consequent of that to which it is necessary, and vice versa, see above theorem 2. Commonly, on the other hand, a conjunction is given by a connection, but not vice versa. A connection, indeed, is not presumed because not even from words that conjoin two individuals, for example, Titius and Caius (or with Caius), saying, "Be heirs!" it follows that one cannot be an heir without the other, and it would be

[119] Antonio Corsetti (c.1450–1503) (1499), *De verbis geminatis*, in, *Tractatus universi iuris ... in unum congesti...* T. XVIII (Venetiis: Franciscus Zilletus, 1584), p. 267, n. 8, Conditio comitiva utriusque partis veritatem requiret.

very burdensome, I.2.20.17 [I.2.20. *De legatis* (Of Legacies). 27. If a testator gives a legacy of female slaves along with their offspring, the legatee can claim the latter even if the mothers are dead, and so again if a legacy is given of ordinary slaves along with their vicarii or subordinates, the latter can be claimed even if the former are dead. But if the legacy be of a slave along with his peculium, and the slave is dead, or has been manumitted or alienated, the legacy of the peculium is extinguished; and similarly, if the legacy be of land with everything upon it, or with all its instruments of tillage, by the alienation of the land the legacy of the instruments of tillage is extinguished.]; D.28.5.29 [D.28.5.*De heredibus instituendis* (Institution of heirs).29. **Pomponius**, *in the fifth book to Sabinus*: In this clause, "quisque" signifies everyone: and for this reason, Labeo writes, if it is written as follows: "Titius and Seius, however much each of them shall have had as my heir in part, is to be my heir," unless everyone has written the testator as their heir, neither of them can be an heir, because the discourse pertains to the action of all, and in this, I think the intention of the testator should be considered. However, it is more reasonable that the one who has named the testator as their heir shall be an heir to that extent, and the one who has not named the testator shall not be admitted to the inheritance.]; D.28.7.2.1 [D.28.7.*De conditionibus institutionum* (Conditions on institutions).2 **Ulpianus**, *in the sixth book to Sabinus*: 1. see above in theorem 10.], D.30.52.pr., 62, 121 [D.30.*De legatis et fideicommissis* (Legacies and *fideicommissa*). 52 **Paulus**, *in the fourth book to Sabinus*: If all the slaves have been bequeathed to someone with a peculium, even those slaves who have no peculium are owed. 62 **Paulus**, *in the forty-first book on Edict*: If a female slave has been bequeathed along with her children, and the female slave alone, if there are no children, and the children alone, if there is no female slave, are owed. 121 **Marcianus**, *in the third book of Rules*: If someone bequeaths to both Titius and Maevius, and one of them is admitted to the bequest without the other, for instance, when the praetor orders "that the unborn child with the children be put into possession," even if there are no children, the the unborn child will be put into possession.]; D.31.89.2 [D.31.*De legatis et fideicommissis* (Legacies and *fideicommissa*). 89 **Scaevola**, *in the fourth book of Replies*: see above in theorem 12.]; D.32.10, 29.2 [D.32.*De legatis et fideicommissis* (Legacies and *fideicommissa*).10 **Valens**, *in the second book of Fideicommissa*: If I have bequeathed you and the one who comes from my three children for my funeral, one hundred gold coins, the bequest is not reduced in your case if no one comes. 29 **Labeo**, *in the second book of The Posthumous Works epitomized by Javolenus*: 2. When a bequest is made as follows: "My heir shall give Seia as much money as I have received from Titius' estate," Labeo believes that what the testator has recorded in his accounting books as having received from that estate has been bequeathed. Furthermore, he denies that the legatee should provide a stipulation of guarantee to the heir if, by chance, the heir has been subsequently condemned for a debt of that estate. I hold the opposite view because what the heir is about to give for a debt of that estate cannot be considered as having been received by the heir. Alfeno Varo wrote that the same view seemed right to Servius, and that is also true.]; D.33.8.3, 4 [D.33.8.*De peculio legato* (The legacy of a peculium). 3 **Paulus**, *in the fourth book addressed to Sabinus*: But if a female slave, together with her own children, is bequeathed, even if she dies or is sold or manumitted, her children will still belong to the legatee because two separate bequests have been made. 4 **Gaius**, *in the eighteenth book On Provincial Edict*: But even if a slave is bequeathed together with his substitutes, the bequest of the substitutes continues even after the slave's death, alienation, or manumission.]; D.35.1.33.4, 81 pr., 112.1 [D.35.1. *De condicionibus et demonstrationibus et causis et modis eorum, quae in testamento scribuntur* (Conditions, designations, explanations for and modalities of provisions in wills). 33 **Marcianus**, *in the sixth book of Institutes*: 4. What, then, if someone has written as follows: "I give Stichus and Pamphilus to Titius if they will be mine when I die," and one of them has been alienated? Can either of them be claimed by the legatee? It is agreed that they can be claimed, for this statement, even though it is in the plural, should be understood in place of it, just as if he had said separately: "Stichus, if he is mine when I die.". 81 **Paulus**, *in the twenty-first book Questions*: pr. "Julius Paulusus to Nymphidius: You asked whether, if it were provided in a will as follows: 'If Stichus shall have given his accounts, let him be free along with his concubine, and let ten (items) be given to her as heir,' the woman would be free if Stichus died before rendering his accounts, either as a mother or as having something else. And you also asked whether the same should be understood regarding the legacy. When liberty is granted on condition of rendering accounts, it appears that this condition of rendering accounts is understood in such a way that the person is ordered to render the rest if they have any, with good faith toward their own act. If there are none, they will be considered to have received liberty absolutely. And if, after entering upon the inheritance, they died, they will be seen to have received the legacy on the same condition. But if, while they still have something left, they died, under the same condition, it seems that Stichus received liberty on condition while his concubine received it absolutely. And it will not be inapt to say that Stichus was manumitted on condition, while his concubine was manumitted absolutely, and that this union pertains not to joining the condition, but to indicating the relationship. 112 **Pomponius**, *in the twelfth book of Letters*: 1. Likewise: 'If Titius has furnished one hundred to

Symphorus and Januarius, I bequeath him a plot of land.' Would the legacy lapse with Symphorus's death? But this should also be interpreted in such a way that each of them should have furnished it while alive. But with a lenient interpretation, it should be said that if, not long after Symphorus's death, Januarius should furnish one-half, he would follow as legatee for one-half of the land.]; D.40.4.13.3 [D.40.4.*De manumissis testamento* (Testamentary manumissions). 13 **Ulpianus**, *in the fifth book of Disputes*: 3. But even if a female slave has been ordered to be free with her children, even if she has none, she will be free. Or if she indeed has them, but her children cannot attain to freedom, the same must be said. And even if she herself cannot be free, her children will nevertheless attain to freedom. For the addition 'with her children' does not constitute a condition unless you suggest to me that there was another intention on the part of the testator; then indeed these words are to be taken as a condition. But the fact that they do not constitute a condition is evident from the edict of the praetor, by which it is provided, 'I shall order the unborn child to be in possession with the children'; for he is content, although there are no children, to put the unborn child in possession according to the edict.]; D.40.7.13.2, 31.1 [D.40.7. *De statuliberis* (Statuliberi). 13 **Julianus**, *in the forty-third book of Digest*: 2. If two slaves have been ordered to be free after giving their accounts, and they have given their accounts separately, they can unquestionably fulfill the condition separately as well. But if their actions have been so intertwined that they cannot be separated, one of them, by ceasing his part, will necessarily hinder the freedom of the other. The condition will not be considered fulfilled in the other person's case unless the remaining amount, calculated based on their accounts, has been paid in full either by both of them or by one of them. 31 **Gaius**, *in the thirteenth book on Lex Julia et Papia*: 1. And therefore, when it was asked whether, "Stichus, after giving his accounts, should be free with his concubine" or if Stichus could be free if he died before the condition concerning his concubine was fulfilled, Julianus said that the question is similar to the one concerning legacies, "I give to X together with Y," whether, if one of them fails, the other should be admitted to the legacy. He finds it more to his liking as if it were written, "I give to X and Y." There is also another question, whether the condition is also linked to the concubine. He thinks it would be more reasonable. Therefore, if Stichus has nothing else, she should be immediately free, but if he has other assets, he must pay her money. However, it is not allowed to give it from his own peculium because those who are primarily ordered to give money for their freedom are permitted to do so.].

Continuing, any conjunction is either

37. [So in the numbering of the Latin text, e.n.]. VERBAL, when multiple things are set in the same speech or proposition, or real when multiple things are set in the same disposition or the same thing is assigned to multiple persons[120], which is called

38. CONCURRENT CLAIMS on the same asset, in accordance with D.30.84.12 [D.30.*De legatis et fideicommissis* (Legacies and *fideicommissa*).84 **Julianus**, *in book thirty-three of the Digest*: 12. Concerning those to whom a slave is bequeathed in the following manner: "I give and bequeath a single slave to Titius and Maevius," it is certain that they do not have a claim to the same slave, just as they would not have a claim when a bequest is made in the following way: "I give and bequeath a slave to Titius; I give and bequeath another slave to Maevius."].

However, if, nevertheless, in the same speech, for example, a testament or formulary, multiple things are set not in the same sentence, they are indeed not connected by words; nevertheless, the same things are to be examined, specifically in which case they are placed, either without interruption or with distance, the use of which will be seen later. From this, it is evident that the CONJOINED INDIVIDUALS[121] (*conjuncti*, that is, individuals conjoined by law) are either conjoined by means of words alone (*conjuncti verbis*), or thing alone (*conjuncti re*), or both in a mixed manner (*conjuncti mixti*), according to D.50.16.142 [D.50.16.*De verborum significatione* (Meaning of expressions).142 **Paulus**, *in the sixth book on the Lex Julia and Papia*: In three ways conjunction is understood: either through the thing itself, or through the thing and words, or through words alone. There is no doubt that those are conjoined whom the combination

[120] Berger, *ad vocem Concursu partes fiunt*, "When the same thing (inheritance, legacy) or the same right is assigned to several persons all share equally therein, unless the testator disposed otherwise.".

[121] Berger, *ad voces Coniunctim*, "Jointly. Heirs instituted coniunctim: became co-heirs with equal shares. A condition imposed coniunctim upon several persons is binding on all Ant. *Disiunctim, Separatim*,"; *Coniunctio*, "An institution of several heirs for the same estate or of several legatees for the same thing in common. The estate (or legacy) became common property of the coheredes (or collegatarii). The heirs or legatees thus awarded are termed coniuncti.".

of names and the matter itself unites, as in the case of "Let Titius and Maevius be heirs to half each," or "Let Titius and Maevius be heirs," or "Let Titius with Maevius be heirs to half each." However, let's consider whether, even if you remove these conjunctions "et" (and), "que" (that), and "cum" (with), they should still be regarded as conjoined, as in "Let Lucius Titius, Publius Maevius be heirs to half each," or "Let Publius Maevius, Lucius Titius be heirs." "Let Sempronius be heir to half" in such a way that Titius and Maevius may come into half and seem conjoined both through the thing itself and verbally. "Lucius Titius be heir to half. Let Seius be heir to the portion for which I have instituted Lucius Titius as heir. Let Sempronius be heir to half." Julianus suggests that it may be doubted whether three halves were created or whether Titius was appointed as the heir to the same half with Gaius Seius. But because Sempronius is also written as the heir for half, it is more likely that two were compelled and jointly appointed as heirs to the same half.], although only verbal conjunction (*conjunctio verbalis*) is said to be a conjunction (*conjunctio*), according to D.7.2.1 [D.7.2.*De usu fructu adcrescendo* (The accrual of usufruct).1 **Ulpianus**, *in the seventeenth book to Sabinus*: 3. In some cases, however, even if the parties are not jointly entitled, a usufruct left by way of legacy may still accrue to one of them, for example, if the usufruct of a whole estate is left to me separately and is left to you in similar terms. For, as Celsus in the eighteenth book of his Digest and Julianus in the thirty-fifth book state, by virtue of our concurrent rights, we both hold shares. The same result would also follow in the case of the bare ownership; for if one party repudiated, the other would have the entire estate. However, in the case of usufruct, there is this further point to be made: Even when a usufruct has been created and afterward lost, it may nonetheless admit of the right of accrual. In fact, all the authorities have agreed on this point in the writings of Plautius, and, as Celsus and Julianus eloquently state, a usufruct is created and left by legacy every day and not, like the bare ownership, only at the time when an action can first be brought to recover it. Thus, as soon as either party finds that there is no one else whose right is concurrent with his, he will have exclusive enjoyment of the whole usufruct; and it makes no difference whether the legacy was joint or several.].

39. CONNECTED BY MEANS OF WORDS ALONE (*CONIUNCTI VERBIS*) when only one is the proposition, but manifold are the things, which MANIFOLD things are either separate, e.g. I give, leave as legate to Titius and Caius, to the first Stichus, to the latter Dama; or are

40. united, i.e. parts of a whole, and the UNITED are either heterogeneous, e.g., I give, leave as legate to Titius and Caius my home, to the first the upper floor, to the latter the downstairs; or are homogeneous, in which case is said a completely divisible whole, see supra definition 28.

The HOMOGENEOUSES, again, are either unequal or equal.

UNEQUAL, e.g., I give, leave as legate to Titius and Caius the Cornelianus plot of land in double to the first more than to the latter.

EQUAL, e.g., I give, leave as legate to Titius and Caius the Cornelianus plot of land in in equal parts. So, it appears that the nature of the *conjuncti verbis* those who restrict it to a single ritual phrase: in equal parts, because they do not find another example in the Laws, the few that we have, after the immense ancient jurisprudence. In the same way that if I wanted to restrict the laws to Titius and Sempronius and to such fictitious figures, since only they were mentioned. And for what reason for such a conjunction the equality of the parties is necessary, and why it is not allowed a double proportion of them or a triple or a similar? They, exactly, did not pay attention to this sentence pattern: "in equal parts", that is used for this reason, because it can express with a brief expression. In fact, if the testator wanted to assign double to one more than another, he cannot speak like that: I give, leave as legate the Cornelianus plot of land to Titius and Caius, in uneven parts or in double parts or in double proportion of the parts, because this way it cannot be understood which of the two should have more, which of the two less. Yea indeed, I believe that they are *coniuncti verbis* too to which one thing indivisibly has been assigned in one sentence, but in another clarifier of the first <sentence> it becomes the assignment of the parts, e.g. in this way, I give, leave as legate to Titius and Caius the Cornelianus plot of land, and shortly thereafter, I want Titius to be satisfied with the third part of the Cornelianus plot of land. Other conceptions of the *coniuncti verbis* formed *Albericus Gentilis* by himself, in a certain letter sent to *Hugo Donellus*[122], which was inserted in the posthumous pamphlets of the latter by his brother, *Scipione Gentile* (1563-1616), <he> affirms that only then by those words they are coniuncti, because the speech becomes silly once it is omitted one or the other [of the beneficiaries, Titius or Caius, e.n.], thing which does not fit with the examples of the jurisconsults.

41. CONNECTED BY MEANS OF THING ALONE (*CONIUNCTI RE*) are solely, when only one thing is assigned to more persons but with a different speech or proposition, e.g. I leave as legate Stichus to Titius, I leave as legate Stichus to Caius. Therefore

42. CONNECTED BY MEANS OF BOTH (*CONIUNCTI MIXTI*) are: I leave as legate Stichus to Titius and Caius. From the foregoing, therefore, the following

Theorems

emerge, in which we will operate in such a way that we conceive them in a general manner but apply them specifically to different situations.

(22) *Multiple things that are separate form one uncertain entity.*

For example, let there be either A or B. I argue that it is sufficient for only one of them to exist. Whether you say, "if A does not exist, let it be B," or conversely, "if

[122] Alberico Gentili (1552 – 1608) to Hugo Donellus (1527-1591), Oxonii, V. Id. Feb. 1583, edited by Pieter Burman Senior (1668-1741), in appendix to *Epistolae Marquardi Gudii etc.* (Ultrajecti, 1697), p. 336, "Et quo si alterum nominatorum amoveo, insulsam hanc relinquis orationem, Titio fundum aequis partibus lego" [And from this, if I remove one of the named, leave this sentence meaningless, I leave as legate this land to Titius in equal parts, e.t.].

B does not exist, let it be A," according to definition 32. Only one of them is required, as stated in D.31.27 [D.31. *De legatis et fideicommissis* (Legacies and *fideicommissa*).27 **Celsus**, *in the thirty-fourth book of the Digest*: If this or that thing is bequeathed, it is one legacy. If this or that thing has been bequeathed under contradictory conditions, we hold it to be one legacy. It makes no difference if the heirs and the legatee are different persons, for example, if the legacy is so written, "if Nerva shall become consul, let my heir Titius give a farm to Attius; if Nerva shall not become consul, let my heir Seius give one hundred to Maevius."]; D.35.1.26 [D.35.1. *De condicionibus et demonstrationibus et causis et modis eorum, quae in testamento scribuntur* (Conditions, designations, explanations for and modalities of provisions in wills). 26 **Julianus**, *in the eighty-sixth book of Digest*: see above in theorem 6.].

From this, *Osvaldus Hilliger*[123] concludes that it may not be entirely correct to call it a concourse of actions indicating a choice, since where only one, even though uncertain, action is admissible, there is no concourse. Specifically, it is enough for only one of the disjunctive conditions to exist, I.2.14.11 [I.2.14. *De heredibus instituendis* (Of the institution of the heir).11. If an institution is made to depend on two or more conditions, conjunctively expressed,—as, for instance, 'if this and that shall be done '— all the conditions must be satisfied: if they are expressed in the alternative, or disjunctively—as 'if this or that shall be done'—it is enough if one of them alone is satisfied.]; D.28.7.5 [D.28.7.*De conditionibus institutionum* (Conditions on institutions).5 **Paulus**, *in the second book to Sabinus*: If multiple conditions are imposed on the heir simultaneously, all of them must be observed because they are considered as one; if they are separate, then any one of them.]; D.35.1.78.1 [D.35.1.*De condicionibus et demonstrationibus et causis et modis eorum, quae in testamento scribuntur* (Conditions, designations, explanations for and modalities of provisions in wills).78 **Papinianus**, *in the ninth book of Replies*: 1. When two conditions are imposed in a disjunctive manner, if one of them fails, it does not harm the situation, as long as the other condition has been fulfilled, even if it occurs afterward. It doesn't make a difference whether the conditions are conditional on someone's choice or on chance.]; C.6.25.6 [C.6.25.*De institutionibus seu substitutionibus sub condicione factis* (On the Institutions and Substitutions Made under a Condition). 6 In general, we prescribe that if someone made the

[123] Osvaldus Hilliger, see note 5 above in *Preface*.

following disposition: if the son or daughter dies intestate or without children or without a will or without getting married, and if this son or daughter had children or got married or made a will, the same son or daughter will possess the hereditary assets, and there will be no place for substitution or restitution. However, if none of these cases occurs, then the condition will be valid, and the assets will be restituted according to the expressions of the will, thus providing a certain limit to the uncertainty of succession. What will be said if he or she made a will but did not have children? Perhaps, based on the previously mentioned provision, his or her children should be deprived of almost all of the paternal inheritance? Let us close this harsh path to avoid causing anyone to go astray, and let this law, favorable to both fathers and children, be valid forever. By doing so, we also provide for other individuals, even if they are unrelated, applying this law to them as well if the need arises. Furthermore, considering the wise opinion of the eminent mind of Papinianus that in the case where a father has substituted his children without mentioning children that may be born to them, the substitution vanishes if the person burdened with it becomes a father and leaves offspring. As it is not likely that the father, if he had thought of grandchildren, would have made such a substitution, we believed, out of humanity, that this judgment should be given greater latitude. So, if someone has natural children and has left or given them a share within the measure we have established, burdening them with substitution without mentioning their children, the substitution itself will be nullified, excluding the children. Those who are called to the substitution cannot enter into this share, but this share will be transmitted to the children, daughters, grandchildren, great-grandchildren of the deceased, of both sexes, and the substitution will only apply if the children have died without legitimate offspring. In short, what was said about legitimate children will also apply to natural children. These provisions will also apply to legacies and trusts. 6 The Emperor Justinian. If a man left anything to his daughter upon condition that she would have children by her then husband, and she had no children by him, but had children by another marriage, then let her have what was left her, although her father specially mentioned the matrimony then existing.].

However, even if the condition appears to be fulfilled when it does not depend on the *conditionarius* (see below theorem 60), if there are multiple disjoints regarding the thing and simultaneously under condition (for example, whoever of my two cousins marries Tullia shall be the heir!), it is sufficient that only one of them exerts the maximum effort to obtain the marriage. Even if she does not want it, he will still be the heir, as stated in D.28.7.23, 24 [D.28.7.*De conditionibus institutionum* (Conditions on institutions). 23 **Marcellus**, *in the twelfth book of the Digests:* see above in theorem 16. 24. **Papinianus**, *in the sixth book of Responses*: "The one of my brothers who marries our cousin Titia shall inherit two-thirds; the one who does not marry her shall inherit one-third." If the cousin Titia died while the testator was alive, both, when they come to inherit, shall have half, as it is true that they were appointed heirs, but they were distinguished concerning the more advantageous portion based on the marriage event.].

When a condition, which is likely not added, equates to a fulfilled condition, it follows that if one of the two disjunctively inserted conditions is likely not added, the whole disposition is unconditional, D.35.1.26 [D.35.1. *De condicionibus et demonstrationibus et causis et modis eorum, quae in testamento scribuntur* (Conditions, designations, explanations for and modalities of provisions in wills).26 **Julianus**, *in the eighty-second book of the Digests*: see above in theorem 6.]; D.28.7.8.5 [D.28.7.*De conditionibus institutionum* (Conditions on institutions).8 **Ulpianus**, *in the fiftieth book of the Edict*: 5. But if he has been appointed under the condition of swearing an oath or giving ten thousand, that is, under an alternative condition, in such a way that he either fulfills the condition or swears something else, it should be examined whether it is necessary to remit the condition because he can easily fulfill one of the two conditions. However, it is truer that the condition should be remitted to avoid that for some reason, the condition leads him to swearing in another way.].

However, if they were added conjunctively (D.28.7.8.4 [D.28.7. *De conditionibus institutionum* (Conditions on institutions).8 **Ulpianus**, *in the fiftieth book to the Edict*: 4. If someone has been appointed under the condition of taking an oath and, furthermore, under another condition, it should be examined whether the condition is remitted to him, and it is the preferable opinion that the condition of taking an oath should be remitted, although he must observe the other condition.]), on the contrary, if only one is the conditional disjunct of a disjunctive disposition, the whole disposition would be unconditional. For example, if you promise to give Stichus or a gem, and the gem if the ship will have arrived from Asia. I believe that the whole disposition would be suspended by this condition. Neither Stichus nor the gem can be demanded separately, but both, so that the debitor (see below definition 57) chooses what he wants to pay. However, the gem cannot be demanded before the ship arrives from Asia, and neither can Stichus.

From the same source, it follows that a conjunctive negative is contrary to a disjunctive affirmative. For example, if you have not given a man or a plot of land, do you promise to pay one hundred. Both actions must be performed to prevent the *stipulatio* from becoming operative, D.28.5.86(85) [D.28.5. *De heredibus instituendis* (The institution of heirs). 86 (85) **Scaevola**, *Scaevola in the second book of Replies*: Lucius Titius, who had a brother, made the following provision in his will: "Let my brother Titius be my heir in equal shares (ex asse). But if Titius refuses to be my heir or, which I detest, dies before he enters into my inheritance or does not have a son or daughter born of himself at the time of entering into my inheritance, then my slaves Stichus and Pamphilus shall be my free heirs and shall share equally." The question posed is whether, when Titius enters into the inheritance and does not have children at the time of entering, Stichus and Pamphilus can be considered free heirs through substitution. The next question is whether, if they cannot be free heirs through substitution, they should be regarded as having a share in the inheritance. The answer provided is that it seems the testator did not intend to appoint anyone as an heir alongside his brother, whom he explicitly appointed as his heir in equal shares (ex asse). Therefore, if the brother enters into the inheritance, Stichus and Pamphilus will not be heirs. Furthermore, the testator did not want them to be heirs if the brother passed away before entering into the inheritance, leaving children behind. The testator's wise decision is evident because he preferred his brother as the heir, not just over the substitutes but also over his brother's children.]; D.34.5.13.2 [D.34.5.*De rebus dubiis* (Dubious cases).13 **Julianus**, *in single book On Ambiguities*:When we formulate a stipulation like this: "Do you promise to pay a sum of one hundred if you do not give the slave or the land?" Both the one and the other act must be performed to avoid the penalty of the stipulation. In other words, if one of the two acts is performed, it will be as if neither has been performed, and the stipulation will be effective. The same principle evidently applies when several specific things we want to be done are proposed, and we formulate the stipulation as follows: "Do you promise to deliver Stichus, Dama, and Erote, or pay a sum of ten if any of them does not appear?" It is necessary that all of them are presented for the stipulation to be fulfilled. To clarify this further, let's assume the stipulation is framed as follows: "Do you promise to pay a sum of ten if you do not present Stichus, Dama, and Erote?" Without a doubt, it is necessary that all of them are presented equally.]; C.6.25.6 [C.6.25. *De institutionibus seu substitutionibus sub condicione factis* (On the Institutions and Substitutions Made under a Condition). 6, see above in this theorem 22.].

It is enough, indeed, that only one does not happen, as stated in D.45.1.129 [D.45.1.*De verborum obligationibus (Verbal obligations)*.129 **Scevola**, *in twelfth book on Questions*: If someone stipulated as follows: "Do you give the sum of ten if the ship arrives, and Titius becomes a consul?" The payment will not be made unless one of the two events occurs. Similarly, in the opposite case, if it was stipulated like this: "Do you promise to give if the ship does not come, and Titius is not made a consul?" It is required that neither of the two events happens. Likewise, if it is written like this: "If neither the ship comes nor Titius is made consul." But if it is phrased as follows: "Will you give if either the ship comes or Titius is made a consul?" It is sufficient if one of the two events occurs. Conversely, if the stipulation is formulated as follows: "Will you give if the ship does not come or Titius is not made a consul?" It is enough that one of the events does not happen.].

Only one, therefore, is enough, but it has not been defined.

However, it has been determined by chance.

An act *inter vivos* of two disjunctive conditions consists of only one simple action when one of them is impossible. For example, if you undertake to give a hippocentaur or have a man sued, it is as if someone had only stipulated that a man be sued, D.45.1.16, 97, 126.3, 128 [D.45.1. *De verborum obligationibus* (Verbal obligations). 16 **Pomponius**, *in the sixth book to Sabinus*: If you owe me Stichus or Pamphilus and one of the two becomes mine for some reason, you owe me the remainder of the debt. 97 **Celsus**, *in the twenty-sixth book of Digests*: If I stipulated as follows, "will you appear; if you do not appear, will you deliver a heffalump," it is as if I had just stipulated; "will you appear?". 126 **Paulus**, *in the third book on Questions*: If I have stipulated that you will appear and give me an "ippocentaurus," and you do not appear, it will be the same as if I had simply stipulated that you would appear. 128 **Paulus**, *in the tenth book of Questions*: If two stipulate jointly, so that the stipulation of the one is valid, of the other invalid, the invalid stipulator cannot properly receive payment, because he is being paid in respect of his own, not the other's, obligation and his is invalid. Similarly, if there is a stipulation for Stichus or Pamphilus, which is valid as regards one, the other, who belonged to the creditor, cannot properly be given in payment, even if he should cease to belong to him. Both were mentioned as objects of the obligation, not of payment.].

(23) *If many represent only one, they are deemed to be only one, and conversely, if only one represents many, he is deemed to be many.*

It is said to represent that right which one does not have for oneself, but in the capacity of the person being represented. Let there be individuals b. Titius and c. Caius, who represent solely A. Sejus, for example, the father. Suppose that these individuals, b. and c., concur with D. Sempronius at the Cornelian plot of land denoted as E. I argue that b. and c. should be considered as only one (and the plot of land can be divided into two parts, one belonging to b. and c., and the other to D.). For if they were considered as two, the plot of land would be divided into three parts, of which b. and c. would receive two, and D. would receive the third part. However, if A. were to concur with D., A. would receive only half, as demonstrated independently in theorem 26. And since b. and c. would receive more than A., the representatives would receive more than the represented, which is absurd.

The same demonstration shows that if A. represents B. and C., they should not be considered as one but as two. Otherwise, the representative would receive less than the represented, which is absurd. These two theorems, which are particularly notable, have been demonstrated more accurately in a mathematical manner, following the given construction.

The entire right known as the Representation in matters of successions depends on these theorems. Meanwhile, this usage is also observed. Refer to D.35.1.56 [D. 35.1. *De condicionibus et demonstrationibus et causis et modis eorum, quae in testamento* scribuntur (Conditions, designations, explanations for and modalities of provisions in wills).56 **Javolenus**, *in the fourteenth book of the Letters*: see above in theorem 17.] for an example of the first case, and an example of the latter case is seen in the instance of a slave belonging to multiple masters, who is deemed to have the status of multiple slaves, D.30.81.1 [D.30.*De legatis et fideicommissis* (Legacies and *fideicommissa*).81 **Julianus**, *in the thirty-second book of the Digest*: If something has been bequeathed to a common slave, one master can accept the bequest, while another can refuse it. In this respect, regarding this cause of acquisition, a common slave is considered as if they were two slaves.]; D.31.20 [D.31.*De legatis et fideicommissis* (Legacies and *fideicommissa*).20 **Celsus**, *in the nineteenth book of the Digest*: Proculus agreed with me, or so I learned from my father, that a legacy left to a slave held in common, if one of the masters rejects it, it does not accrue to the other. This is because it is not a joint legacy, but parts are bequeathed; because, if both vindicated it, each would have a part of the legacy in proportion to his share in the slave.]; D.35.1.44.8 [D.35.1.*De condicionibus et demonstrationibus et causis et modis eorum, quae in testamento scribuntur* (Conditions, designations, explanations for and modalities of provisions in wills). 44 **Paulus**, *in the ninth book to Plautius*: 8. If a legacy has been bequeathed to two slaves under the condition of giving, some say that the condition cannot be fulfilled in parts, but the money must be given all at once. However, I believe the opposite.]; D.45.3.1.4 [D.45.3. *De stipulatione servorum* (The stipulation of the slaves). 1 **Julianus**, *in the fifty-second book of Digest*: 4. A common slave represents the person of two slaves. Therefore, if my slave, who is common to both me and you, stipulates in one set of words, the legal effect is the same as if two separate stipulations had been made, one in the name of my slave, and the other in the name of your slave. We should not think that I acquire only a half share, and the other half goes to no one. For the character of a common slave is of such a nature that in a case where one of his masters can acquire and one cannot, he is considered as if he belonged only to the one for whom he has the capacity to acquire.].

(24) The continuous discrete is manifold.

Indeed, since it is discrete, it is divided into intervals, and divided parts are manifold according to definition 27.

Therefore, if 10 annuities are left as a legacy or brought into a condition, it is not a single legacy but as many as there are years, D.7.4.27 [D.7.4. *Quibus modis usus fructus vel usus amittitur* (The ways in which a usufruct or a right of use is lost). 28 not 27, evidently, e.n., **Paulus**, *in the thirteenth book to Plautius*: If a usufruct has been bequeathed for alternating years, it cannot be lost due to non-use, because there is a plurality of legacies.]; D.33.1.4, 11 [D.33.1. *De annuis legatis et fideicommissis* (Annual legacies and *fideicommissa*). 4 **Paulus**, *in the sixty-second book to the Edict*: see above in theorem 10. 11 **Paulus**, *in the twenty-first book of Questions*: When a legacy is made payable annually, it is generally agreed that there are multiple legacies, and each legacy is examined separately for the right to claim it.]; D.35.1.101.4 [D.35.1. *De condicionibus et demonstrationibus et causis et modis eorum, quae in testamento scribuntur* (Conditions, designations, explanations for and modalities of provisions in wills).101 **Papinianus**, *in the eighth book of Responses*: 4. see above in theorem 16.]; D.35.2.1.16 [D.35.2. *Ad legem Falcidiam* (The Lex Falcidia).1. **Paulus**, *in sole book on the Lex Falcidia*: 16. Put the case of a legacy year by year to Titius; the legacies being both several and conditional, there will be scope for the edictal security, "to restore the excess received."]; D.36.2.10, 20 [D.36.2. *Quando dies legatorum vel fideicommissorum cedat* (When a legacy or a *fideicommissum* vests). 10 **Ulpianus**, *in the twenty-third book to Sabinus, book 23*: When something is left as legacy year by year, it is understood to be not a single legacy but but several. 20 **Marcianus**, *in the sixth book of Institutes*: If a legacy is made with a specification of years, like 'Ten to Titius for up to ten years,' Julianus, in the thirtieth book of the Digest, writes that it makes a difference: if it is a legacy for the purpose of maintenance of the legatee, then these are considered multiple legacies, and the legacy of future years does not pass to the heir if the legatee dies. However, if the legacy was not for maintenance of the legatee but was divided into installments for the relief of the heir, Julianus states that, in this case, the legacy is treated as a single legacy for all the years. If the legatee passes away within the ten-year period, the legacy for future years also passes to his heir. This opinion is correct.].

(25) The number of dispositions corresponds to the number of things included in the condition.

(From this, it is not the conditioned aspect, but the multitude of conditioners that multiplies the disposition), as stated in D.4.8.21 [D.4.8. *De receptis: qui arbitrium receperint ut sententiam dicant* (Matters referred to arbitration and those who have undertaken to arbitrate in order to make an award). 21 **Ulpianus,** *in the thirteenth book of the Edict*: However, if he has been appointed regarding multiple disputes that have nothing in common and has made an award with reference to one and not yet about the others, has he ceased to be arbiter? Therefore, let us see whether he can change the award he has already given for the first dispute. What is of particular relevance is whether the terms of the reference to arbitration provided that he makes an award for all cases together or not. In the former case, he could change (for he has not yet made his award), but if he was to make an award for each individual case, the position is as though there are several distinct arbitrations, and therefore he ceases to be arbiter with respect to the matters relating to the dispute in question.]; D.31.2 [D.31.*De legatis et fideicommissis* (Legacies and *fideicommissa*). 2 **Paulus,** *in the seventy-fifth book on Edict*: Whenever several things are expressed by name in a legacy they are several legacies. But if furniture or silver or peculium or equipment is bequeathed, it is one legacy.]; C.8.53.34.3 [C.8.53. *De donationibus* (Concerning gifts). 34.3 If anyone, moreover, bestows many bounties at various times on the same person, neither of which alone exceeds the legal limit, but if added and heaped together in the manner aforesaid is larger than the legal amount, it would seem not to be right to add them together and so find a method by which to render them void and of no effect; they should, on the contrary, be considered as separate gifts, each treated according to its own nature and as not requiring registration.]; D.45.1.29, 75.9 [D.45.1.*De verborum obligationibus (Verbal obligations).* 29 **Ulpianus,** *in the forty-sixth book to Sabinus*: We should know that in stipulations, there are as many stipulations as there are amounts, and there are as many stipulations as there are objects or species. Accordingly, it happens that when a single sum or item is introduced, which was not in the preceding stipulation, there is no novation, but it brings about two stipulations. Although it has been agreed that there are there are as many stipulations as sums of money, and as many stipulations as there are objects, if someone stipulates money that is present or a pile of money, there are not as many stipulations as there are individual coins, but rather it is a single stipulation because having a stipulation for each individual coin is absurd. The stipulation for legacies is also considered to be one, even if there are several items or multiple legacies. Similarly, a stipulation for an entire household or all the slaves is one. Likewise, a stipulation for a four-horse chariot or sedan chair carriers is one. But if someone has stipulated this and that, there are as many stipulations as there are individual items. 75 **Ulpianus,** *in the twenty-second book on Edict*: 9. Whoever stipulates for the capital sum and interest, if any, is thought to stipulate both for a certain and for an uncertain thing, and there are as many stipulations as there are several objects.].

Because the things are the subjects, while the rest are predicates.

The principal subject is the main element, while the predicates are the accessories.

The same entity as a single occurrence cannot exist in multiple subjects, but the same subject can have multiple incidental attributes. However, when it comes to numerical measurement or unity, it is preferable to consider it based on the principal and definite aspect rather than the accessory and variable aspect.

(26) *If something must be combined with several things, it is allocated to each of them, or rather, it belongs to all of them from the beginning.*

This principle is reiterated in numerous passages, particularly in relation to the right of accrual (*jus adcrescendi*[124]), D.7.2.3.1 [D.7.2. *De usu fructu adcrescendo* (The accrual of usufruct). 3 **Ulpianus**, *in the seventeenth book to Sabinus*: 1. Celsus writes that if two property owners of a plot of land transfer ownership while reserving the usufruct, and one of them loses the usufruct, it rejoins the bare ownership, but not in its entirety. Instead, the usufruct is associated with the portion each of them had initially conveyed. In short, it must return to the share from which it was originally separated.]. Other laws commonly reinforce this principle.

On the contrary, if one of the conjoint individuals is not concurrent—either due to incapacity or unwillingness—and the others do not acquire any portion on behalf of the absent person, especially if the absent person does not actually exist D.30.15.1, 16.pr.

[124] Berger, *ad vocem Ius adcrescendi*, "The law of accrual under which the portion of a co-owner increases, as, for instance, if a co-owner manumits a common slave, the manumission being void, the other co-owner acquires full ownership over the slave (Justinian ordered the slave freed). In the law of succession, the share of a co-heir increases when the other co-heir fails to take his share under the win or on intestacy.".

e 2 [D.30. D.35.1. *De condicionibus et demonstrationibus et causis et modis eorum, quae in testamento scribuntur* (Conditions, designations, explanations for and modalities of provisions in wills). 15 **Paulus**, *in the third book to Sabinus*: 1. If someone has bequeathed an amount to "his daughters", including a posthumous one among them, if the posthumous daughter was not born, the entire amount will be due to the surviving daughter. 16 **Pomponius**, *in the fifth book to Sabinus*: If a thing is bequeathed jointly to two persons, though one of them is not in existence, then I think it true that only a part is due to the other. 2. If a legacy has been left to Titius and the posthumous children of the testator and no posthumous child is born, Titius shall vindicate it all. Even if the testator had intended equal shares to be given to Titius and the posthumous children and even if he expressly stated this intention, the whole legacy is due to Titius if no posthumous child is born.].

However, when the possibility remains for one of the two to concur, all bequests are kept intact for that individual. Consequently, with the condition of the co-heir suspended, only one does not receive the entire inheritance (*Ant. Fab. dec. 49 err. 10*[125]).

Nevertheless, in the case of a legacy of usufruct granted to several individuals, the usufruct may suitably be enjoyed by only one person on a daily basis while others are concurrently instituted D.7.2.6.2 [D.7.2.*De usu fructu adcrescendo* (The accrual of usufruct).6 **Ulpianus**, *in the seventeenth book to Sabinus*: 2. If the usufruct of an estate is left by way of legacy to me absolutely and to you subject to a condition, it can be said that the usufruct of the whole estate belongs to me in the meantime and that if I undergo a change of civil status, I lose the whole usufruct. However, if the condition is fulfilled, then should I have undergone a change of civil status, the whole usufruct goes to you; but if there has been no change in my status, the usufruct must be shared between us.]. This understanding aligns with the same law D.7.2.1.3 [D.7.2. *De usu fructu adcrescendo* (The accrual of usufruct).1. **Ulpianus**, *in the seventeenth book to Sabinus*: 3. In some cases, however, even if the parties are not jointly entitled, a usufruct left by way of legacy may still accrue to one of them, for example, if the usufruct of a whole estate is left to me separately and is left to you in similar terms. For, as Celsus in the eighteenth book of his

[125] Favre, see note 28 above, p. 1171, Decad. XLIX, Err. 10, De pluribus haeredibus institutis uno pure, alio sub condicione an pure institutus, totum interim habeat, an partem.

Digest and Julianus in the thirty-fifth book state, by virtue of our concurrent rights, we both hold shares. The same result would also follow in the case of the bare ownership; for if one party repudiated, the other would have the entire estate. However, in the case of usufruct, there is this further point to be made: Even when a usufruct has been created and afterward lost, it may nonetheless admit of the right of accrual. In fact, the authorities quoted by Plautius are all in agreement on this point, and, as Celsus and Julianus elegantly put it, a usufruct is created and left by legacy every day and not, like the bare ownership, only at the time when an action can first be brought to recover it. Thus, as soon as either party finds that there is no one else whose right is concurrent with his, he will have exclusive enjoyment of the whole usufruct; and it makes no difference whether the legacy was joint or several.].

Nevertheless, when only one person is not fulfilling, the entire condition can be fulfilled and all that was subject to the condition can be obtained by the others D.40.4.13.1 e 2 [D.40.4.*De manumissis testamento* (Testamentary manumissions).13 **Ulpianus**, *in the fifth book of Disputes*: 1 So too can we ask what more was specified in a condition granting freedom to two craftsmen or painters if they had painted a room or built a ship; was it the testator's wish to make the action of one of them a condition for the freedom of the other? If so, the failure of one may make the other unable to fulfill the condition, when he is prepared to perform. If the testator showed by written or spoken words that he was content for either to perform, there is no difficulty; then by his own performance either of them will advantage both himself and his fellow, or himself alone, in accordance with what appears to have been the wish of the testator. 2. This problem is also discussed in the case where a man has given freedom to two slaves on condition of their rendering accounts. In fact, Julianus discusses whether the fact that one is ready to do so and the other not bars the freedom of both; he is perfectly right in saying that if their accounts were separate, the one who renders his accounts does enough to obtain freedom, but if they were jointly responsible, neither seems to have complied with the condition, unless he discharged arrears due from both. In regard to arrears, we ought to take it that the actual account books should be handed over.]; D.35.1.74 disturbs <on this point>, from which the Doctors persuaded themselves that the right of accrual is not granted to those who are admitted to a legacy based on a special right, namely by the will of the law, contrary to the testator's will. [D.35.1. *De condicionibus et demonstrationibus et causis et modis eorum, quae in testamento scribuntur* (Conditions, designations, explanations for and modalities of provisions in wills).74 **Papinianus**, *in the thirty-second book of Questions*: A usufruct was left to a woman and Titius on condition that the woman did not marry. In the event of the woman's marrying, Titius, so long as he lives and his position is unchanged, will have his share of the usufruct. For the woman will be understood to receive, by the concession of the statute, only so much of the usufruct as she would have received if she had complied with the condition. And it would avail her nothing if Titius, not meeting the condition, repudiated the legacy.]

For example, if the testator writes as follows: "I bequeath to Titius and Sempronia, if she does not marry". The conditional clause is understood as not added, according to theorem 38. If the woman marries, she will still have half of the legacy, but she will not have the right of accrual to the other half of Titius, in case he is missing, according to the opinion of the Doctors. However, Alciato rightly criticizes this, and it certainly results in deception of the laws. The laws have abolished this condition so that marriages are not hindered to the detriment of the state, but despite this rule, marriage can still be impeded if the woman chooses celibacy to have the advantage of accrual, while perhaps indulging in fickle desires. In effect, it will be as if a condition of widowhood has been added to the portion that was assigned to Titius, which is rightly considered as not added. Therefore, regardless of the condition, the woman will still have the right to the portion that Titius is missing, which is the right of accrual.

Even if the law were against us, we would not be greatly concerned due to obvious reasons. Nevertheless, the law does not contradict us. Let us examine its words and provide an explanation. The words outside the parentheses are the words of the law, and the words inside the parentheses are ours: The usufruct is bequeathed to the Woman and Titius if the Woman does not marry (This condition affects both the Woman and Titius according to the testator's intention, but according to the will of the laws, the condition is considered as not added for both of them. It is for the

Woman so that marriages are not hindered by the temptation of celibacy, and for Titius so that the Woman does not gain something through a fictitious fulfillment, and fiction does not surpass truth, which would happen if the condition does not apply to the person of the woman but applies to the person of Titius. Therefore) if she marries as long as Titius is alive and in the same status (e.g., not deported or enslaved) (in short, as long as Titius himself concurs for the legacy of usufruct and is capable of receiving it) the Woman will have a portion (only) of the usufruct (because Titius, as a concurrent, will have the remaining portion). Thus, the woman is granted only as much as the law allows, as if she had obeyed the condition.

(From these words, I deduce two conclusions contrary to the Doctors: 1. The condition should also be considered as not added with respect to Titius; otherwise, the woman would receive more than if she had truly obeyed. 2. In the absence of Titius, the woman's portion increases; otherwise, she would have less than if she had truly obeyed. And she must have, based on these words, an equal share.)

Even if Titius, who lacks the condition (in reality, even if not in legal effect, as otherwise how could he reject the legacy that he does not possess, according to D.50.17.3 [D.50.17. *De diversis regulis iuris antiqui* (Various rules of early law). 3 **Ulpianus**, *in the third book to Sabinus*: The power of refusal belongs to someone who is in a position to be willing.], although the following words suggest that he can reject it), rejects the legacy (and thus does not concur), it will not benefit the woman (or grant her more than if she had truly obeyed, as she would have received the whole in that case). And this interpretation is in complete harmony with the very obscure law but is entirely contrary to the common interpretation. Furthermore, fiction should not surpass truth, as stated in D.40.7.4.2 [D.40.7 *De statuliberis* (Statuliberi).4 **Paulus**, *in the fifth book to Sabinus*: 2. If a man's freedom is ordered after he has served Titius as a slave for a year, he will not become free immediately on Titius's death but only after passage of the year, since the grant seems to be not merely conditional but subject to a time clause, and it is actually absurd that he should become free when he is not fulfilling the condition, earlier than he would have been, had he fulfilled it.].

Therefore, in light of these facts, it is clear that it is futile to introduce any right of accrual or non-decrease in the case of *conjuncti re*. It is evident that nothing accrues to them when one of them is lacking because they retain only what they have. This is also the reason why the portion of the other increases (that is, does not decrease) without any burden or added condition, according to D.35.1.30 [D.35.1. *De condicionibus et demonstrationibus et causis et modis eorum, quae in testamento scribuntur* (Conditions, designations, explanations for and modalities of provisions in wills). 30 **Julianus**, *in the first book From Minicius*: If an entire estate was bequeathed to me separately and unconditionally, and to you under a condition; and you were to die before the condition is fulfilled, I will not need to fulfill the condition. Even if the condition remains unfulfilled, the portion you would have claimed will be added to mine.].

Moreover, the right of the lacking party does not pass to the other, as the former did not have the right acquired yet, but rather the right remains undivided for the other. Indeed, it is too generous to argue that nothing decreases, as stated in D.32.10 [D.32.*De legatis et fideicommissis* (Legacies and *fideicommissa*). 10 **Valens**, *in the second book of Fideicommissa*: see above in definition 35.], but shall we invent a separate right of non-decrease? It is already contained in the right of every individual regarding any property, that no one can take away or diminish it unless they have a greater or equal right. Therefore, it will be permissible to establish rights such as the right of retention, non-burdening, non-injury, etc., which is both absurd and useless. And in verbal conjunction, it is not properly the right of accrual, but only a presumed substitution, as we will show below. Hence, we could easily do without this mother of confusions.

(27$_1$) Parties are determined by the concurrence of interested individuals to the same asset, and they are of equal size, as stated in D.30.33, 79, 85

[D.30.*De legatis et fideicommissis* (Legacies and *fideicommissa*). 33 **Paulus**, *in the third book of the Rules*: If the same thing has been left as legacy to multiple individuals, if it was bequeathed jointly, and one of them claims it while the other takes action based on the will, the one who acts according to the will shall receive no more than their share. However, if the legacy was made separately, and it is abundantly clear that the testator, after revoking the first legatee, intended to refer to the second legatee, then only the second legatee may receive the legacy. If there is no clear indication of the testator's intent, then all of them may share the legacy equally, unless the testator made it explicitly clear in the written provision that they wanted each of the two legatees to receive the entire thing. In this case, the one who first initiated the action regarding the legacy or fideicommissum shall be assigned the value in money, and the other party shall receive the thing. The choice between the thing and the money value is reserved for the party who first initiated the legal action regarding the legacy or fideicommissum, with the provision that, once a choice is made, they cannot switch to the other option. 79 **Julianus**, *in the fifth book of Digest*: If anyone in his will directs that ten are to be given to Titius and Seius, these words admit of no ambiguity; he who said ten is taken to have meant ten each. 85 **Paulus**, *in the eleventh book to Plautius*: A farm was bequeathed to two persons conjointly. One of them obtained the value of his part through a personal action. Should the other wish to vindicate the whole farm, he is prevented by a defense of fraud from the half because the deceased wished the legacy to come to them once only.]; D.31.88.6 [D.31.*De legatis et fideicommissis* (Legacies and *fideicommissa*). 88 **Scaevola**, *in the third book of Replies*: 6 In the testament of Lucius Titius, it is stated: "I wish my small estate to be given to my freedmen and freedwomen, and those whom I have manumitted in this will, and to Seia, my fosterling, so that it shall not pass to anyone not bearing the family name, until the property comes into the hands of one person." I inquire whether Seia holds a share in common with the freedmen or if she can claim half of that small estate for herself. I respond that the testator's intention is clear, as he includes everyone under the term "to the manly shares," indicating that all of them should share equally.]; D.32.80 [D.32.*De legatis et fideicommissis* (Legacies and *fideicommissa*). 80 **Celsus**, *in the thirty-fifth book of Digest*: Appointing heirs jointly or leaving legacies jointly means that the whole inheritance and the whole of the legacies are given to each individually but shared concurrently.]; D.45.1.56 [D.45.1.*De verborum obligationibus* (Verbal obligations). 56 **Julianus**, *in the fifty-second fook of Digest*: One who has thus stipulated, "Do you promise to give me and Titius thesum of ten?" is always presumed to have stipulated a single sum of ten for himself and for Titius; in the same way as he who leaves a legacy to Titius and to Sempronius, is not otherwise presumed to have bound commonly to both of them the sum of ten.].

This theorem holds significant importance and has been derived with subtlety by ancient jurists from the nature law itself. Now, let us proceed to demonstrate this theorem using a specific type of demonstration that simultaneously clarifies and proves it. This phenomenon inherently possesses a physical principle rooted in the nature of motion.

Consider Body A, upon which two bodies B and C simultaneously exert a uniform impetus, one along the BA axis and the other along the CA axis. The angle BAC is bisected by the straight-line AD, which diverges from the two moving bodies B and C. Let lines be extended as follows: BA extended to point E and CA extended to point F. I affirm that Body A will advance along the line AD.

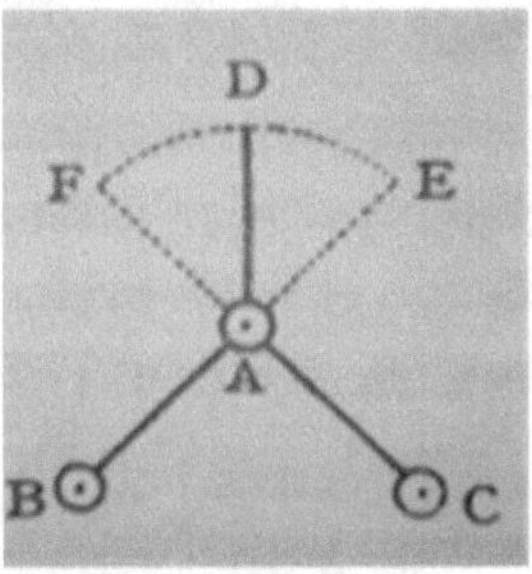

When a body is propelled, it moves along the continuous line of the impelling force. In this case, the continuous lines of the impelling bodies are AE and AF. Therefore, if Body A had been solely pushed by B, it would have moved along line AE, or if solely pushed by C, it would have moved along line AF. However, with both forces acting, Body A will not remain stationary because it is being impelled, and although it is being impelled by multiple forces in the same direction (not opposing), it will not be moved along either of the continuous lines of the impelling bodies. This is because the forces acting on them are uniform, and there is no reason for Body A to be moved in one direction rather than the other. Nothing happens without a cause, and even less so will Body A be moved along both lines, as it cannot occupy multiple positions simultaneously. Furthermore, no line other than AD, which is the only line intersecting between AE and AF, will be moved because all other lines deviate towards one or the other direction. However, as there is no reason for this deviation, only the line AD, which bisects the angle EAF by construction, will be moved. That which was to be demonstrated.

Now, let us apply this theorem to a juridical context.

The two converging bodies can be compared to the motions BA and CA. The object of convergence is the inclination of the motion line of A towards the lines of the converging bodies. The greater this inclination, the smaller the angle. Therefore, when the inclination is maximized, the angle becomes zero, and both the motion of A and the motion of any impelling body occur along a straight line. This occurs when one impelling body alone exerts force without the concurrence of another. This is similar to the acquisition of a whole in law and, specifically, the absolute acquisition of the larger part, namely the entirety, when there is no other concurrent factor. Conversely, what does not concur results in the absolute acquisition of the smaller part, which is nothing. In the case of multiple concurrent motions, the inclination is divided, and when there is a uniform impetus towards the motion of the impelling bodies, both sides and parts have the same angle and inclination. Therefore, in legal matters involving multiple parties with equal entitlement to the same asset, the asset is divided in a way that assigns an equal share to each party.

(27_2) However, the parts are formed by concurrence when the thing is divisible; intellectual, that is, the thing becomes common when it is indivisible.

Because when the thing is divisible, it consists of homogeneous parts, as per definition 28.

Therefore, it does not matter to which part you assign them. But when it is indivisible, it consists of dissimilar parts, as per definition 29.

Therefore, since an exact ratio between the parts and the whole is not possible, as definition 29 shows, and even the exact division cannot be established, the strict rule is that the whole thing belongs to both or is common. (However, in equity, the judge may establish any division if someone refuses to be in the common ownership.)

For example, let's consider two things: 100 Thalers and Stichus. If 100 Thalers are common to two persons, half will be 100, that is, 50 Thalers or 100 semithalers. And since all Thalers are similar to each other, according to the assumption, the division is straightforward. But it is different with the servant Stichus. Since half of Stichus is not Stichus, no matter how you divide him, Stichus cannot be divided. However, by mental division, as many partial Stichus are imagined as there are owners, according to Theorem 25.

Now, let us apply this to our conditions.

If one condition or one conditioned thing is assigned to multiple conditioners or persons, it is divided into parts if those parts are homogeneous, as stated in D.30.81.1 [D.30.*De legatis et fideicommissis* (Legacies and *fideicommissa*). 81 **Julianus**, *in the thirty-second book of Digest*: 1.see above in theorem 23.], D.33.2.30 [D.33.2. *De usu et de usu fructu et reditu et habitatione et operis per legatum vel fideicommissum datis* (Right of use, usufruct, income, right o f habitation, and services given by legacy or fideicommissum). 30 **Javolenus**, *in the second book from the Posthumous Works of Labeo*: see above in theorem 16.]; D.35.1.44.8, 56 [D.35.1. *De condicionibus et demonstrationibus et causis et modis eorum, quae in testamento scribuntur* (Conditions, designations, explanations for and modalities of provisions in wills). 44 **Paulus**, *in the ninth book to Plautius*: 8, see above in theorem 23. 56 **Javolenus**, *in the fourteenth book of the Letters*: see above in theorem 17.].

Likewise, a condition that is attributed to multiple persons in general is understood to apply to all individuals, as it is not apparent to whom it has been specifically assigned, as stated in D.35.1.39 [D.35.1 *De condicionibus et demonstrationibus et causis et modis eorum, quae in testamento scribuntur* (Conditions, designations, explanations for and modalities of provisions in wills). 39 **Javolenus**, *in the first book of Posthumous Works of Labeo*: A condition that pertains to a class of individuals and not to specific and named persons, is considered to affect the entire will and all the instituted heirs. However, a condition that has been adapted to specific individuals, we should relate only to the particular degree by which these individuals were instituted.].

(28) A disposition is divisible if both the condition and the conditioned are divisible.

(As mentioned in D.33.1.10 [D.33.1. *De annuis legatis et fideicommissis* (Annual legacies and *fideicommissa*). 10 **Papinianus**, *in the eighth book of Replies*: "To Seius, a most faithful friend, if he wishes, as he was involved in my affairs, I want him to be involved in the same way as my sons, to be provided with six aurei annually, and to be given the dwelling he uses." Nevertheless, it was decided that annual support should still be provided to Seius for his share in the inheritance of the surviving daughter, even though two out of Titia's three sons had passed away, with the other heirs instituted in their lives, as they would receive both labor and money for the division.], since both the task and money are divisible).

Indeed, since the condition and the conditioned are all parts of the disposition, as defined in definitions 1 and 14, and if all the existing parts are divisible, then the whole is divisible according to definitions 28 and 29. The same disposition will be divisible.

However, on the contrary, if the conditioned and the nature of the thing put in the disposition is indivisible, the disposition is indivisible according to D.45.1.72.pr. [D.45.1.*De verborum obligationibus* (Verbal obligations). 72 **Ulpianus,** *in the twentieth book on Edict*: Stipulations are not divided when the things themselves cannot be divided, such as roads, rights of way, water pipes, and other servitudes. I believe the same applies when someone stipulates for the performance of something, such as the delivery of land, digging a ditch, constructing an island, carrying out works, or anything similar; the division of these would invalidate the stipulation. However, Celsus reports in the thirty-eighth book of the Digest that Tubero believed that if we stipulated for something to be done, and it was not done, then money should be given, and in this case, the stipulation could be divided. According to Tubero, Celsus says that it can be argued that a claim should be made for the fair valuation of the performance.].

More precisely, even if only the condition is indivisible, but only in that case, according to D.32.11.23 [D.32.*De legatis et fideicommissis* (Legacies and *fideicommissa*).11 **Ulpianus,** *in the second book of Fideicommissa*: 23 If something has been left undone in the construction of public works, the divine Marcus and Lucius Verus responded in a rescript to Procula that each coheir is jointly responsible. However, they established a time limit for the coheir, within which they should contribute to the completion of the work. After this time, they intended to attribute the entire cost for that part to the coheir Procula.]; D.35.1.112 [D.35.1 *De condicionibus et demonstrationibus et causis et modis eorum, quae in testamento scribuntur* (Conditions, designations, explanations for and modalities of provisions in wills). 112 **Pomponius,** *in the twelfth book of Letters*: pr., see above in definition 29.]; D.40.4.13.2 [D.40.4. *De manumissis testamento* (Testamentary manumissions). 13 **Ulpianus,** *in the fifth book of Disputes*: 2.see above in theorem 26.].

(29) *In the case of last wills, a divisible testamentary disposition is divided through an act when there is an underlying cause for division.*

Indeed, for a disposition to be divided, it implies that a part of the conditioned is fulfilled because a part of the condition is fulfilled, as defined in definition 30.

However, this does not necessarily follow from the words of the disposition, in which the connection is not between parts but between wholes. Therefore, it does not apply unless it is derived subsidiarily from the presumed will of the testator, who prefers the fulfillment of their entire will rather than just a part.

Nevertheless, they still prefer the fulfillment of a part rather than nothing, whenever the complete fulfillment is not possible. Therefore, if someone is commanded to give 10 to the heir and keep a plot of land for themselves, it is not allowed to offer 5 to that person and demand half of the land from the unwilling heir, as stated in D.35.1.23, 56 [D.35.1. *De condicionibus et demonstrationibus et causis et modis eorum, quae in testamento scribuntur* (Conditions, designations, explanations for and modalities of provisions in wills). 23 **Julianus**, *in the book forty-three of Digest*: see above in definition 29. 56 **Javolenus**, *in the fourteenth book of the Letters*: see above in theorem 17.]; D.29.2.74.1 [D.29.2. *De adquirenda vel omittenda hereditate* (Taking up or failing to take up an inheritance).74. **Paulus**, *in the twelfth book to Plautius*:1. see above in definition 29.].

However, if a part of the conditioned is destroyed, for example, if half of the land is acquired by another through uninterrupted possession (*usu capta*[126]) D.35.1.44.9 [D.35.1. *De condicionibus et demonstrationibus et causis et modis eorum, quae in testamento scribuntur* (Conditions, designations, explanations for and modalities of provisions in wills). 44 **Paulus**, *in the ninth book to Plautius*: 9. If a part of the legated thing has been acquired by usucaption, I am in doubt whether it should be returned in its entirety, and it can be argued that it should be returned in part according to the testator's intention.], it is sufficient to fulfill an

[126] Berger, *ad vocem Usucapio*, "Acquisition of ownership of a thing belonging to another through possession of it (possessio) for a period fixed by law. Further requirements ot usucapio under ius civile were (a) bona fides (good faith), i.e., the possessor's honest belief that he acquired the thing from the owner (while, in fact, he acquired it from a non-owner, a non dommo), and through a transaction which legally was suitable for the transfer of ownership (while, in fact, it was not, if, e.g., the thing which was a res mancipi was conveyed by traditio). Good faith was required on the part of the possessor only at die beginning of his possession. If he lost later his good faith by getting knowledge of the true situation, the completion oi the usucapio was not impaired; (b) a just cause (iusta causa, also called iustus titulus) ; see [voice] Pro in connection with possession. Such a just cause was either an act of liberality (donatio) of the owner or an agreement with him (a purchase) which would justify the acquisition of ownership if Aere were not a defect in the transaction itself ("e.g., traditio of a res mancipi instead of mancipatio) or in the person of the transferor (a non-owner). [...].".

equal part of the condition, thus reducing the burden accordingly, as mentioned in D.35.1.43.3, 62.1 [D.35.1. *De condicionibus et demonstrationibus et causis et modis eorum, quae in testamento scribuntur* (Conditions, designations, explanations for and modalities of provisions in wills). 43 **Paulus**, *in the eighth book to Plautius*: 3. Neratius writes in his first book of Responses that if, out of two written heirs, one is asked to return the inheritance to you and you are required to give a specific sum to Titius, and the heir, in making the restitution, avails himself of the benefit of the Falcidian Law, not unjust that your liability to Titius be correspondingly reduced. 62 **Terentius Clemens**, *in the fourth book on Lex Julia et Papia, book 4*: 1. If something was left to someone who does not take the whole share if had given something to the heir, the question arises whether they can obtain what they gave for the purpose of fulfilling the condition as part of the legacy (as if they did not receive what they had spent) or whether it is outside of it and not obtain more from the testator's assets just because it was a conditional legacy, no more than they would have received if the legacy had been without conditions. And Julianus rightly writes that they will obtain as much as they are obliged to give for the purpose of fulfilling the condition, and it does not matter whether they were instructed to give it to the heir or a stranger because, with the calculation that is always directed *ad hominem*, no more of the granted share will accrue to them.]; D.35.2.32.4 [D.35.2.*Ad legem Falcidiam* (The lex Falcidia). 32 **Maecianus**, *in the ninth book of Fideicommissa*: 4. If Titius' share had been reduced by twenty legacies due to the Lex Falcidia, and he was also instructed to return five to Seius, our Vindius says that only as much should be deducted from the five for Seius' share as was deducted from Titius' twenty. This opinion is more equitable and reasonable; for the legatee is to be liable on fideicommissa on the pattern of the heir; he is to be allowed to offset the burden on himself even though, as legatee, he cannot invoke the lex Falcidia directly; this, unless the testator specifically make the the fideicommissum one of "everything which [Titius] takes under the will."]; D.36.1.65(63).12 [D.36.1.*Ad senatus consultum Trebellianum* (The senatus consultum Trebellianum). 65 (63) **Gaius**, *in the second book of Fideicommissa*: 12. If Titius is asked to return the inheritance to Maevius, and Maevius to give a certain amount to Seius, and Titius has benefited from a fourth to be retained against Maevius, Neratius writes that it is also less fair for Maevius to provide for Seius so that he does not suffer a loss himself.]; D.39.6.20 [D.39.6. *De mortis causa donationibus et capionibus* (Gifts and acquisitions *mortis causa*). 20 **Julianus**, *in the first book to Urseius Ferox*: A plot of land was left as a legacy to someone who could not receive more than a part of it on the condition that he gave ten to the heir. He does not have to give the whole of that sum in order to get only part of the land, but only a part of it in proportion to the amount of the legacy that he secures.].

On the other hand, if a part of the condition cannot be fulfilled without fault on the part of the *conditionarius*, they still receive a part of the conditioned. For instance, if someone is directed to give 10 to two heirs and keep a plot of land, and one of the heirs is deceased, if they give 5 to the surviving heir, they will still have half of the land, as stated in D.35.1.23 [D.35.1.*De condicionibus et demonstrationibus et causis et modis eorum, quae in testamento scribuntur* (Conditions, designations, explanations for and modalities of provisions in wills).23 **Julianus**, *in the forty-third book of Digest*: see above in definition 29.]. Refer also to the definition 34 mentioned earlier, where we stated that a connection is not presumed. However, these conditions are true only when the whole disposition is divisible, as also indicated in this theorem.

Furthermore, it should be noted that the term "part" is used ambiguously, sometimes referring to a part of a thing and other times to a part of a sentence. Certain parts of a sentence are not parts of a thing or an act but are merely circumstances. For example, in the sentence "If you ascend to the Capitolium on the kalends," the kalends are not a part of the ascent but a circumstance. Therefore, when multiple things are connected in a sentence, they are sometimes placed as distinct entities. For example, "Titius and Caius are heirs," where they are considered as separate parts. Even if Titius does not exist in reality, the division still takes place, and Caius remains as the heir. In this case, it is true that what is useful is not invalidated by what is useless, as stated in D.28.5.34 [D.28.5. *De heredibus instituendis* (The institution of heirs). 34 **Papinianus**, *in the first book of Definitions*: An inheritance is not correctly left with an initial or final term, but once the defect regarding the term is removed, the institution of the heir remains.]; D.28.7.8.4 [D.28.7.*De conditionibus institutionum* (Conditions on institutions). 8 **Ulpianus**, *in the fiftieth book to the Edict*: 4 see above in theorem 22.].

Additionally, if a divisible part of the condition is missing, it does not invalidate the rest, as mentioned in D.33.4.12 [D.33.4. *De dote praelegata* (*Praelegatum* of dowry).12 **Scaevola**, *in the third book of Replies*: A husband had received the dowry in cash and in valued goods. He made the following legacy to his wife: "If my wife Seia displays and delivers to my heir all the items described in the dowry inventory, I want her to receive the sum of the dowry I received from her father, plus ten denarii." Many items from the dowry were consumed through use and no longer existed when the husband passed away. It was questioned whether the legacy was due, given that it was made under an impossible condition. Scevola answered: The condition is considered fulfilled if what remained of the dowry items came into the possession of the heir.].

However, there are cases where things are placed in such a way that they affect each other, as in the example of Titius giving 100 to Caius. In this scenario, Titius and Caius are not parts of the disposition but rather correlations. Therefore, if Caius does not exist in reality, the condition becomes impossible. In such cases, it cannot be resolved into two propositions, and there is no room for division, as an impossible circumstance renders the condition itself impossible.

The topic can be further illustrated using the analogy of numbers.

Numbers can be connected as two parts of a single whole, such as 2 + 3 = 5 in addition (similarly for subtraction), or as two factors of a single product, such as 2 x 3 = 6 in multiplication (similarly for division). If the number 0 is added, for example, 2 + 0, the result is 2. However, if a number is multiplied by 0, the product is 0, as in 2 x 0 = 0. On the other hand, circumstances are connected to each other like a multiplier to what is being multiplied, not merely through comparison, but in a way that they mutually affect and penetrate each other. It is relevant to note that when a condition is assigned to several individuals, it is not necessary for only one of them to wait for the others (which is not even necessary when a divisible condition exists, see the explanation of theorem 26). Instead, if one fulfills a part, they receive a corresponding part of the conditioned, as stated in D.35.1.56 [D. 35.1. *De condicionibus et demonstrationibus et causis et modis eorum, quae in testamento scribuntur* (Conditions, designations, explanations for and modalities of provisions in wills).56 **Javolenus**, *in the fourteenth book of the Letters:* see above in theorem 17.]. Moreover, the freedom of one individual is a part of the freedom of two, as indicated in D.40.4.11.1 [D.40.4. *De manumissis testamento* (Testamentary manumissions). 11 **Pomponius**, *in the seventh book to Sabinus*: 1. "Let Stichus and Pamphilus be free; if they give 10", one can become free by giving five, even though the other has given nothing.].

These statements hold true when a divided condition divides the conditioned and vice versa. However, sometimes a divided condition does not divide the conditioned. In such cases, it is necessary to consider whether this lightens the burden of the condition or not, as per the theorem.

(30) A part of a condition, whether orderly conjunctive or disjunctive, when fulfilled disorderly, does not alleviate the burden of the condition.

Let's consider an orderly conjunctive condition: If Titius gives 10 to Caius first, and then to Sempronius. Alternatively, an orderly disjunctive condition: If Titius gives 10 to Caius, or if he cannot, to Sempronius. If Titius gives 10 to Sempronius first, I affirm that those 10 do not fulfill the condition, and nothing has been accomplished. However, if they have been given to Caius first, or if Caius falls into that condition such that those 10 cannot be given to him, then once again that money must be given to Sempronius. This is because the order is derived from the condition, based on the hypothesis and definition 34 [correction: it should be definition 33]. Therefore, it must also hold true for theorem 16, which states that if a part is disorderly fulfilled and cannot be repeated, such as when Titius first manumits Stichus, then Davus, if Titius first manumits Davus, the condition fails. This is because freedom can only be given to Davus once, and it is impossible to subsequently first manumit Stichus and then manumit Davus. Thus, according to definition 36, the condition fails under strict terms of the law.

When a partial fulfillment is allowed, it does not divide the disposition but rather alleviates the condition, as stated in D.40.7.3.5 and 6 [D.40.7 *De statuliberis* (Statuliberi).3 **Ulpianus,** *in the twenty-seventh book to Sabinus*: 5. If ordered to give ten and set free, and he gives five, he does not attain freedom unless he gives the whole ten. In the meantime, the owner of the five coins can legally claim them by vindicatio. But if the remaining sum is paid, even this initial payment, ownership of which had not been previously transferred, is then alienated. Therefore, the transfer of the initial sum remains pending. However, it should be noted that the coins do not retroactively become the property of the recipient but only become his from the moment when the remaining sum has been paid. 6. If he has given more than he was ordered to, let's say he was ordered to give ten but gave twenty, whether he counted it out or gave it in a bag, he attains freedom and can reclaim the excess.].

(31) *Only those connected by means of words alone (coniuncti verbis) are presumed to be mutually substituted in the same legal position.*

This does not derive from the law of nature or nations but from a Roman decree (*placitum*[127]). Nevertheless, it has a rationale: individuals connected by means of words alone (*conjuncti verbis*) occupy a middle ground between individuals not connected to each other in a testament and those connected by means of thing alone (*coniuncti re*). The vacant part indeed accrues to those connected by means of words alone, ensuring that they

[127] Berger, *ad vocem Placitum*, "What private individuals agreed upon, an agreement. The term is less frequently used than its syn. pactum. With reference to legislative provisions placitum denotes either a statutory norm (placitum legis) or that of an imperial constitution (placitum principis).".

are not lowered to the level of the above-mentioned individuals not connected to each other. However, they also bear their own burden[128] to prevent them from being equated with those connected by means of thing alone, as stated in theorem 26.

Nevertheless, even among these individuals connected by means of the thing alone (*coniuncti re*), there is no right of accretion. It is not the person that accrues to the thing, but rather the thing to the thing, specifically the portion to the portion, when considering the precise meaning of the word. This can be seen in cases of alluvion. However, in this case, the thing cannot accrue to the thing since they are not connected through the thing itself (*coniuncti re*).

Let's see if it is permissible to delve a bit deeper into the topic.

There are two phenomena that I observe in the case of individuals connected by means of words alone (*coniuncti verbis*):

the vacant part of one is added to the other with its burden, for example, in a condition, which is clearly stated in many passages. See meanwhile, regarding the condition, D.35.1.54.1 [D.35.1. *De condicionibus et demonstrationibus et causis et modis eorum, quae in testamento scribuntur* (Conditions, designations, explanations for and modalities of provisions in wills). 1) 54 **Javolenus**, *in the second book from Cassius*: 1. The same thing is left to two people, if they give the heir one hundred; if one of them gives fifty, he acquires his share of the legacy, and the share of the defaulter will accrue to him subject to its condition.], although it is also extended to co-heirs in C.6.51.10 [C.6.51.*De caducis tollendis* (Concerning abolishing lapses (escheats).1.10. Now this being settled, we find that in the preceding part of this constitution we made mention in several places of joint beneficiaries, and we have thought it necessary to consider

[128] While the *coniunctum verbis* would see its hereditary burdens increase in proportion to the vacant quotas that ultimately, he acquires; *coniunctum re* is liable for the deceased's debts by reason of the only their shares of succession, see Biondi, note 45 above, p. 659.

this subject with greater care and treat it in greater detail, so that this subject, too, may be clear to all. 10a. Bequests are left not only jointly but also severally. When coheirs have all been appointed or substituted jointly or all severally, a lapsed bequest consisting of a part or parts of an inheritance, belongs, subject to all of its burdens, to the other coheirs in proportion to the parts inherited by them, even though some of them are already deceased. 10b. And this applies even to those who are unwilling to accept the lapsed portion, if they have accepted their portion for which they were originally appointed, since it is absurd to accept part and refuse part, as has also been provided by decisions of our majesty. 10c. If the heirs and substitutes are mixed in kind, some having been appointed jointly and others severally, and the portion of one of those appointed jointly lapses, this portion, with its burden, shall go only to those who were appointed jointly with him, in proportion to the amount inherited by each. 10d. If, however, a portion of one of those who were appointed severally lapses, this portion, with its burden, goes not only to those who were appointed severally, but to all alike, those who are appointed jointly and severally, in proportion to their inheritance. 10e. The distinction is made because those who are appointed jointly constitute one person, as it were, on account of the unity in the appointment, and hold the portion of the joint heirs with them as their own, but heirs appointed severally have, by reason of the very words of the testator, been separated and have indeed their own, but cannot alone claim another's property, but receive it jointly with all their coheirs. The foregoing provisions are made only for heirs.].

(2) Individuals connected by means of words alone are preferred over individuals connected by means of the thing alone (*coniuncti re*), for example, I give as a legacy to both Titius and Caius the plot of land in equal parts; I give as a legacy to Sempronius the same plot of land. If Titius dies, his portion is added not to Sempronius but to Caius. The reason for these provisions can perhaps be expressed more concisely by saying: it is assumed that the testator mutually replaced them. We have confirmed this in the same theorem 31 and its demonstration.

D.31.61.1 [D.31.*De legatis et fideicommissis* (Legacies and *fideicommissa*).61 **Ulpianus**, *in the eighteenth book on Lex Julia et Papia*: 1. Julianus indeed says that if one of the legitimi heredes repudiates his share, when fideicommissa were left as a charge on him, the co-heir is not to be obliged to deliver the fideicommissa; for the share belongs to the co-heir unencumbered. But in consequence of a rescript of Severus, according to which fideicommissa left charged on the appointed heir are due from his substitutes, a co-heir too, like a substitute, will get the accruing share with its encumbrance.], is not contradictory, as the substitutes:

1) must also accept a burden along with the thing, as stated in D.30.74 [D.30.*De legatis et fideicommissis* (Legacies and *fideicommissa*).74 **Ulpianus**, *in the fourth book of Disputations*: It is true that our emperor ruled in a rescript with his father that where the testator laid a charge on an appointed heir, it should be held that he meant it to apply to the substitute. This, however, must be taken to be the case where it is clear that the testator had no different intention. It will be gathered from many indications whether a testator was unwilling that a legacy or, fideicommissum charged on the heir should be due from the substitute. And what if he has left charged on the substitute the delivery to the fideicommissary or legatee of another thing, which he had not left charged on the appointed heir? Or if there was a definite reason why he should leave a legacy charged on the heir, which did not apply to the substitute? Or if he chose as partial substitute a beneficiary to whom he had left a fideicommissum charged on the appointed heir? It must therefore be said that the rescript applies where the testator's intention is obscure.]; D.31.61.1 [D.31.*De legatis et fideicommissis* (Legacies and *fideicommissa*).61 Ulpianus, *in the eighteenth book on Lex Julia et Papia*: see above in this theorem 31.]; C.6.49.4 [C.6.49. *Ad senatus consultum Trebellianum* (As to the Trebellian senate decree).4 We think that you needlessly fear that you will lose the benefit of the portion of the inheritance left you as a trust on the ground that the grandmother of the testator (and yours) who was appointed part-heir and was requested to transfer it to you (as a trust), fraudulently repudiated the inheritance, so that her portion might go to another grandson, her coheir, upon who the payment of the trust was not specifically imposed, and on the ground that the grandmother, ordered to enter on the inheritance which (she said) she suspected as insolvent, died before she did so and before she did nay act as heir. For it was long ago ordered by the divine Antoninus, our predecessor, that, in view of the testator's intention, the trust must also be carried out by the substitute (her heir), the request for him to do so being implied. Nor need you fear the retention of the (Falcidian) fourth, which your grandmother, who repudiated the inheritance, and who was ordered to accept it, though suspected as insolvent (as she said), could not retain.].

2) They are preferred over connected ones (*coniuncti*), as in D.28.6.39.2 [D.28.6.*De vulgari et pupillari substitutione* (Normal and pupillary substitution).39 **Javolenus**, *in the first book*

from the Posthumous Works of Labeo: 2. A certain person had appointed four heirs and had provided a substitute to all the heirs except one; that one to whom no one had been substituted and one of the others had died during the lifetime of the head of the household. Ofilius and Cascellius [when consulted] replied that the share to which no one had been substituted went to the substitute also, and their view is correct.].

(32) *If two contrary conditions are added separately to the same conditioned party, the disposition is unconditional.*

However, if they are added together, it is null. Let's consider it this way: either A will be or A will not be, and let B be.

I affirm that this disposition is unconditional, just as if I said: let B be. The separate conditions in this context are contradictory, and only one of the contradictory conditions can be true. Therefore, only one condition must exist, as it is sufficient for one of the disjunct conditions to exist, according to theorem 26. The condition that must necessarily exist is treated as if it is not added, as proven independently based on theorems 17 and 64. Thus, the disposition is unconditional, as stated in D.12.6.60. pr. [D.12.6. *De condictione indebiti* (The condictio for money not owed). 60 **Paulus**, *in the third book of Questions*: Julianus argued that a true debtor, while the lawsuit was still pending and the judgment not yet finalized, couldn't claim a repayment after making a payment. He believed that such a debtor wouldn't have the right to claim a repayment, whether they were acquitted or convicted. Even if they were acquitted, they would still remain a debtor by nature. He compared this situation to someone who made a promise, whether a ship arrived from Asia or not, because the origin of the obligation to pay was dependent on one cause or the other.]; D.18.6.8.1 [D.18.6. *De periculo et commodo rei venditae* (Risk and benefit of the thing sold). 8 **Paulus**, *in the thirty-third book to the Edict*: 1. If a sale is made in the following manner: "that slave is bought, whether a ship from Asia has arrived or not," Julianus believes that the sale is immediately completed because it is clear that it has been agreed upon.]; D.28.2.10 [D.28.2.*De liberis et postumis heredibus instituendis vel exheredandis* (The institution of children and postumi as heirs and their disherison). 10 **Pomponius**, *in the first book to Sabinus*: Most conveniently, someone who is not yet born can be instituted as an heir in the following manner: "whether I am alive or dead when he is born, let him be the heir," or even unconditionally, making mention of neither time. If either event has been omitted and a child is born in the event which has been omitted, he breaks the will, because this son is not regarded as being even conditionally appointed as heir, being born in the very event which has not been covered by the will.]; D.35.2.87.3 [D.35.2. *Ad legem Falcidiam* (The lex Falcidia). 87 **Julianus**, *in the sixty-first book of Digest*: 3. If you were initially appointed as an heir for one-quarter, and Titius for another quarter, and then you were additionally appointed for half of the inheritance conditionally, and the deceased left legacies and freedoms, the freedoms will be granted, and the legacies will be paid in full even before the condition is fulfilled. In fact, if the condition is fulfilled, you become the heir, and the legacies and freedoms are valid; if the condition fails, both you and Titius will be heirs. Now, if you're asking whether, according to the Falcidian law, it's appropriate to combine your quarter and your half when the condition is fulfilled and calculate the three quarters concerning the legatees to whom you were appointed in the purely appointed heirship, we will respond that the two shares are to be merged.]; D.36.2.13 [D.36.2. *Quando dies legatorum vel fideicommissorum cedat* (When a legacy or a *fideicommissum* vests). 13 **Pomponius**, *in the sixth book to Sabinus*: A legacy in these terms "whether such a thing be done or be not done, I give and bequeath" does not pass to the heir unless one or other event have happened in the life of the legatee; for nothing can be due before there is some ground upon which it is due, nor will the legacy be due in all events merely because one or other must happen; for a legacy such as "let my heir give when he shall die" is certain to be due; yet it does not pass to the heir of the legatee if he die in the life of the heir.]; D.40.7.37 [D.40.7 *De statuliberis* (Statuliberi).37 **Gaius**, *in the sole book of Problems*: If it is written in this manner: "I give Stichus to Titius so that he may manumit him; if he does not manumit, Stichus shall be free," Stichus is immediately free.].

Consequently, if someone is partly instituted unconditionally and partly under a condition in the same will, and they do not have a concurrent heir, it is considered that they have been unconditionally instituted for the entire inheritance *(ex asse hereditario)*, as specified in D.28.5.33 [D.28.5. *De heredibus instituendis* (The institution of heirs).33 **Gaius**, *in the second book on Wills according to the Edict of Urban Praetor*: If someone has written his will as follows, "Titius is to be the heir for one-half, and the same Titius for the other half if the ship comes from Asia" as the heir will accept under the unconditional institution, although the condition imposed on the other is still unfulfilled, he becomes heir to the whole inheritance, that is to say, even if the condition is not fulfilled, as the fulfillment of the condition is of no advantage to him; because indeed there is no doubt that if someone has been instituted heir in respect of a half share and no one else besides him, he is regarded as being instituted heir to the whole inheritance.]; D.29.2.52.1, 53 [D.29.2.*De adquirenda vel omittenda hereditate* (Taking up or failing to take up an inheritance). 52 **Marcianus**, *in the fourth book of Institutes*: 1. A person who has been instituted heir unconditionally to one share and conditionally to another as sole heir, if he has accepted the inheritance, will be heir to the whole estate even while the condition is unfulfilled, because whtever happens he is going to be sole heir, unless he has a substitute with regard to the conditional share. 53 **Gaius** *in the fourteenth book on Lex Julia et Papia*: If someone has been appointed as the heir in two parts, one purely and the other under a condition, and they have accepted the unconditional appointment and later the condition arises, that part also belongs to their heir.].

Regardless of whether the condition exists or not, they have the portion burdened by the testator's words, maintaining the right of non-decrease, as if they were connected to themselves.

(33) If several conditions are separately added to the conditioned party itself[129]*,*

[129] I prefer to footnote this long parenthetical sentence placed by the Author in the text, for better readability of the theorem: "(For if they have been contextually subordinated to each other, no change or suspension of the will is assumed, but rather the combination of both conditions is understood, as stated in D.40.4.*De manumissis testamento* (Testamentary manumissions).45 **Modestinus**, *in the book of Pandectae*: What is commonly said, that when freedom is given under multiple conditions, the lightest condition should be considered, is true if the conditions are given separately; but if they are given together, unless all are fulfilled, there will be no freedom.; D.35.1.*De condicionibus et demonstrationibus* (Conditions, designations, explanations for and modalities of provisions in wills). 89 **Valens**, *in the first book on Fideicommissa*: This concerns not only those provisions that are more frequently given under various conditions, but also those that initially are given in a pure and simple manner, then later under condition. Therefore, what is ordered to the heir to give in a pure and simple manner or what is bound in a pure and simple manner, when, after a certain period of time, it is bound under condition, the second provision is valid; if it is given initially under condition, and later bound in a pure and simple manner, it is due immediately. If, however, concerning what has been bequeathed purely and simply as a legacy with immediate real effect, the heir has been obligated or

for example, "if A will be, let B be! And in another passage, if C will be, let B be!", in the context of institution and freedom status (*statuliberi*), they are considered as disjunctive, or rather, only one of them is uncertain, so that it is sufficient for only one to be fulfilled.

This is also what is stated in the Laws, that in such a case, in matters of freedom, a condition is regarded as the slightest, not entirely slight, but rather the one that leads more easily to freedom, as mentioned in D.35.1.35, 51pr., 87, 88 [D.35.1. *De condicionibus et demonstrationibus et causis et modis eorum, quae in testamento scribuntur* (Conditions, designations, explanations for and modalities of provisions in wills). 35 **Pomponius**, in the *sole book of Rules*: In the matter of liberty, the most benevolent construction is to be placed upon a condition imposed thereon, however weighty or severe its content. 51 **Modestinus**, *in the fifth book of Distinctions*: Where a slave is bidden to be free under separate, disjunctive conditions, he may choice that condition which to him appears least burdensome; where, on the other hand, a legacy is so bequeathed, the legatee must honor the condition last mentioned. 87 **Valens**, *in the first book of Fideicommissa*: The rule is that in the case of legacies, one looks to the last stated condition but, in grants of liberty, to the most benevolent. 88 **Gaius**, *in the first book of Fideicommissa*: that is, to the one most to the slave's benefit.].

It means the condition that is fulfilled first, as they say in the matter of inheritance institutions, as stated in D.28.5.27.2 [D.28.5. *De heredibus instituendis* (The institution of heirs). 27 **Pomponius**, *in the third book to Sabinus*: 2. But if several institutions have-been made in respect of the same share under diverse conditions, whatever condition is first satisfied will bring about the result we specified above, where the same person is instituted unconditionally and conditionally.]; D.28.7.17

requested through fideicommissum to give it under condition, it is as if the same thing is bequeathed with the addition of a subsequent written provision, so that it may either be claimed immediately against whoever possesses it, if the legatee desires, or, when the condition is fulfilled, it may be demanded in court from the heir, unless subsequently it has been written with reference to the legacy formulated first, such as: 'if such a thing is done, my heir shall give Stichus to such a person, to whom I have bequeathed it.' Then indeed, it will be considered that he wrote this with the intention to revoke the legacy for immediate execution and to give it under condition; and if he claims the thing before the condition is fulfilled, the defense of fraud may take place.)".

[D.28.7.*De conditionibus institutionum* (Conditions on Institution).17 **Florentinus**, *in the tenth book of Institutes 10*: If several institutions have been made in respect of the same share under different conditions, the condition which has been fulfilled first will rule the institution.].

In legacies and *fideicommissum* (and even if freedom is granted through it, according to D.35.1.90 [D.35.1. *De condicionibus et demonstrationibus et causis et modis eorum, quae in testamento scribuntur* (Conditions, designations, explanations for and modalities of provisions in wills).90 **Gaius**, *in the first book of Fideicommissa*: When freedom is granted by fideicommissum, under a variety of conditions, one looks to not the most benevolent but the last, since the later wish prevails; a rescript of the deified Antoninus agrees.]; D.40.4.5 [D.40.4.*De manumissis testamento* (Testamentary manumissions).5 **Pomponius**, *in the third book to Sabinus*: In the case of freedom (manumission) clauses, the most lenient (easiest) wording should be considered, so that, if there are multiple conditions, the one that is more favorable to the slave's freedom should be understood. However, in the case of freedom clauses in fideicommssa provisions, the most recent wording is considered.]), and in tutelage (D.26.2.8.3 [D.26.2. *De testamentaria tutela* (Testamentary tutelage).8 **Ulpianus**, *in the twenty-fourth book to Sabinus*: 3. In the appointment of a tutor (*tutoris dationem*), should the easiest or the most recent condition, as in the case of a legacy, be considered? For example, "Titius, when he is able, shall be the guardian" versus "Titius, if a ship comes from Asia, shall be the guardian." Julianus rightly wrote in the twentieth book of the Digests that the most recent piece of writing should be considered.]) settled in the last will, according to D.28.6.16 [D.28.6. *De vulgari et pupillari substitutione* (Normal and pupillary substitution). 16 **Pomponius**, *in the third book to Sabinus*: If a person who has left a legacy of a slave in his will, then, in relation to a substitute to his son, has ordered him to be free, the slave will be free, the legacy being treated as revoked; for in the case of a legacy also, in these wills the last thing written must be considered, just as would happen in the same will (or in a will and confirmed codicil).]; D.30.12 [D.30.*De legatis et fideicommissis* (Legacies and *fideicommissa*).12 **Pomponius**, *in the third book to Sabinus* 3. See above in theorem 14.], D.35.1.35, 51, 87, 88 [see above in this theorem 33.].

In contracts, those conditions are joined, and both must be fulfilled.

The rationale for this is as follows: a conjunctive condition, which is a certain double condition, holds less significance than a simple certain condition, and the latter holds less significance than a disjunctive condition, which is only one uncertain condition. This has been demonstrated independently in theorem 67.

Similarly, contracts receive no favoritism, while legacies, tutelages, institutions of heirs, and freedoms receive varying degrees of favoritism. Therefore, the value of the conditions' favoritism should be distributed accordingly.

Furthermore, if we consider the matter according to strict law, two conditions should always be understood as being inserted together. Hence, in contracts, they are deemed conjunctive, in legacies only one certain condition is considered, and it is the most recent one, αἱ δευτέραι γὰρ φροντίδες σφοώτεραι [in Greek in the text, "second thoughts are somehow wiser"[130]] as expressed in D.34.4.16, 17 [D.34.4.*De adimendis vel transferendis legatis vel fideicommissis* (The ademption of legacies and *fideicommissa*).16 **Paulus**, *in the sole book of The Law of Codicils*: There is no difference between the erasure and the ademption of a provision. 17 **Celsus**, *in the twenty-second book of the Digest*: Nothing prevents the correction, alteration, or cancellation of an earlier provision by a later one.]; D.35.1.90 [D.35.1. *De condicionibus et demonstrationibus et causis et modis eorum, quae in testamento scribuntur* (Conditions, designations, explanations for and modalities of provisions in wills).90 **Gaius**, *Fideicommissa, book 1*: see above in this theorem 33.]; C.6.36.3 [C.6.36. *De codicillis* (Concerning codicils).3. Since you state that the mother of your minor wards made two codicils, at different times and with discordant provisions, there is no doubt that what she stated in the older codicil is revoked by the later codicil, in which she expressed the secrets of her wish, if the tenor thereof differs from the former and contains a contrary wish.].

[130] αἱ δεύτεραί πως φροντίδες σοφώτεραι, it is a verse from Euripides' Hippolytus, 437, "second thoughts are somehow wiser" [Stephen Esposito (ed.), *Euripides. Medea, Hippolytus, Heracles, Bacchae.* (Indianapolis. Indiana, 2004), 111].

In institutions of heirs, only one uncertain condition is deemed.

Based on all of these, it follows as a concise corollary: if someone is unconditionally instituted in a single will in one passage and conditionally in another, they should be understood as unconditionally instituted, as stated in D.28.5.27.2, 68 (67) [D.28.5. *De heredibus instituendis* (The institution of heirs).27 **Pomponius**, *in the third book to Sabinus*: 2, see above in this theorem 33. 68 (67) **Pomponius**, *in the second book to Quintus Mucius*: If a will has been written as follows, "let Tithasus be heir if he has climbed the Capitol; let Tithasus be heir," the second statement will be preferred; for it makes a fuller grant than the first.].

However, if in one passage they are unconditionally bequeathed, and in another passage under condition, the same bequest is considered conditional if the previous one was unconditionally bequeathed, and vice versa, if the previous one was under condition, it is considered unconditional, according to D.35.1.40.2, 89 [D.35.1. *De condicionibus et demonstrationibus et causis et modis eorum, quae in testamento scribuntur* (Conditions, designations, explanations for and modalities of provisions in wills). 40 **Javolenus**, *in the second book of Excerpts from Labeo's Posterior Works*: 2. see above in theorem 14. 89 **Valens**, *in the first book of Fideicommissa*: But this applies not only to those dispositions made commonly under diverse conditions but also to those which are made first without qualification and then subjected to a condition. Suppose, then, that the heir is requested to give or a legacy is made without qualification and then the same is afterward left subject to a condition; the latter disposition prevails; but should the first disposition be conditional, the second unqualified, the latter takes effect. If, though, a conditional heir be charged or requested required to deliver a legacy immediately, the case will be as if the same legacy were made with the previously inserted rider; the legacy [per vindicationem] can be claimed immediately, if he so choose, by the legatee or he may seek it from the heir when the latter's condition has been fulfilled, that is, unless, with a reference to the earlier bequest, a later one be written so: "Let my heir give to 'X,' if he shall have done this or that, the Stichus whom I bequeathed to 'Y'." In this case, the testator shows himself as revoking an existing bequest and making a conditional other one; then if [the new legatee] claim before the satisfaction of the condition, he may be met with the defense of bad faith.].

They are indeed like two conditions, where one is valid and the other is null. In the institution of heirs, the one that is fulfilled first holds validity, whereas in legacies, the one that is written subsequently prevails.

(34) *If from an unconditional proposition a conditional proposition is subtracted, the residue is a contrary conditional proposition.*

For example, "I bequeath 100 to Titius; if the ship does not arrive from Asia, I bequeath to Sempronius the 100 that I had bequeathed to Titius". It is the same as if I had said: If the ship arrives from Asia 100 for Titius; but if not, I bequeath to Sempronius, D.12.1.36 [D.12.1. *De rebus creditis si certum petetur et de condictione* (Things credited giving rise to fixed claims and the *condictio*).36 **Javolenus**, *in the first book of Letters*: Following my request, you made a stipulation with Atius under a condition for the sum of money that you owed me unconditionally. Since, during the pending condition, your obligation to me remains in the same state as it would be if you had stipulated with me for the money under the opposite condition, will my legal action be in vain if I request it while the condition is pending? I replied: There is no doubt that my money, for which I myself stipulated without any condition, remains owed to me, even if the condition regarding the same money stipulated by Atius at my request has not yet been fulfilled. This is because, in essence, it's as if no other stipulation had taken place. However, in the uncertainty of the fulfillment of the event claimed as a condition, I cannot demand it through legal action. This is because, with the uncertainty of whether something is owed based on the stipulation with Atius, it is considered that I would be requesting it before the appropriate time.]; D.34.4.7, 10, 14 [D.34.4.*De adimendis vel transferendis legatis vel fideicommissis* (The ademption of legacies and *fideicommissa*).7 **Ulpianus**, *in the twenty-fourth book to Sabinus*: If a testator bequeaths something under a condition to one person that he bequeathed purely to another, it is not understood that he has completely revoked the first bequest but only in the sense that the condition of the second bequest is fulfilled. On the other hand, if the testator intended to completely revoke the first bequest, it must be said that the bequest is taken away from the first legatee. 10 **Julianus**, *in book thirty-seventh book of Digest*: If a legacy made to Tiberius unconditionally is revoked under a condition, and Tiberius dies while the condition is pending, even though the condition is not fulfilled, the legacy will not belong to Tiberius' heir. In fact, the legacy revoked under a condition is as if it had been made under the opposite condition. 14 **Florentinus,** *in the first book of the Institutes*: Legacies whose concession is invalid are not confirmed by fullfillment. An example would be a situation in which a man is designated as the heir, an unconditional legacy is given to his slave and this is then conditionally adeemed, since an unconditional legacy, if conditionally adeemed, is regarded as a legacy given under the opposite condition and is, by virtue of that interpretation, confirmed. But the purpose of fulfillment is to prevent, not to lead to, a legacy being owed.]; D.35.1.107 [D.35.1. *De condicionibus et demonstrationibus et causis et modis eorum, quae in testamento scribuntur* (Conditions, designations, explanations for and modalities of provisions in wills).107 **Gaius,** *in the sole book of Cases*: It sometimes happens that a seemingly conditional legacy is to be construed as without qualification; for example, it is left under the same condition as that under which the heir is instituted. So, also, if the legacy be, "if the heir accepts the inheritance." Conversely, a legacy, apparently unconditional, becomes treated as conditional; put the case that there be a conditional ademption of a legacy bequeathed subject to the converse condition.]; D.36.2.6 [D.36.2. *Quando dies legatorum vel fideicommissorum cedat* (When a legacy or a *fideicommissum* vests).6 **Paulus,** *in the third book to Sabinus*: see above in theorem 17.]; D.40.7.13.5 [D.40.7 *De statuliberis* (Statuliberi).13 **Julianus,** *in the forty-third book of Digest*: 5. A testamentary provision is written as follows: "Stichus shall be free when he reaches the age of thirty; if he has not given a sum of ten, Stichus shall not be free." This writing should be understood to mean that Stichus will be free if he has given the sum of ten and has reached the age of thirty. This is because the revocation of freedom or a bequest made under a condition adds the condition to the bequest or freedom that was previously granted.].

For indeed, two conditions contrary to each other are like complements to an unconditional disposition, as stated in theorem 32. Moreover, if you take a part from the whole, the remaining part serves as a complement to the whole, according to the commonly held opinion [κοινὴν ἔννοιαν in Greek in the text, e.n.]. Therefore, when the conditional is subtracted from the unconditional, it is necessary that the remaining part be constituted by a contrary condition, which is precisely what needed to be demonstrated.

However, it should be noted that, if the condition of revocation is such that it cannot exist unless the thing unconditionally reaches the intended recipient, it seems that it has been given not under a suspensive contrary condition, but rather under a resolutive contrary condition, as seen in D.34.4.3.4 [D.34.4.*De adimendis vel transferendis legatis vel fideicommissis* (The ademption of legacies and *fideicommissa*).3 **Ulpianus**, *in the twenty-fourth book to Sabinus Sabinus*: 4 see above in theorm 15.].

Similarly, if a slave is unconditionally bequeathed to someone, and the legatee is requested by a third party to unconditionally return the slave, and subsequently the legatee is required to grant freedom to the slave under a condition, it was decided that the slave should be promptly delivered to the fideicommissarius or the third party, but with a resolutive condition.

Alternatively, it is necessary to provide assurance that once the condition exists, the slave will be returned, so that the legatee can manumit them, as stated in D.40.5.47.3 [D.40.5.*De fideicommissariis libertatibus* (Grants of freedom by *fideicommissa*).47 **Julianus**, *in the forty-second book of Digest:* 3. When fideicommissary and conditional freedom is given to a slave legated, he should not be delivered to the legatee without guarantee that he will be redelivered if the condition is realized.].

Therefore, why was it not decided elsewhere that when something is unconditionally given but conditionally revoked, it is understood to be given under that resolutive condition or rather under a contrary limitation, which, in my opinion, seems more suitable to the nature of the case? Or if this decision was not made elsewhere, why was it made here?

It is of great importance, indeed, whether something is given under a resolutive condition or under a suspensive condition.

(35) *If from a conditional proposition is subtracted all of its condition, the remainder is pure.*

Because, if from conditional proposition is removed all of its condition, the residual condition is null.

And when the condition is null, the disposition is unconditional, according to the definition 1, D.35.1. 53 [D.35.1.*De condicionibus et demonstrationibus et causis et modis eorum, quae in testamento scribuntur* (Conditions, designations, explanations for and modalities of provisions in wills).53 **Modestinus**, *in the sole book in the On <legal> remedies*: If someone has ordered that a servant be freed, and if he has presented the accounts to the heir, and later forbade him from presenting the accounts, as if to make the liberation pure and simple, freedom is granted to him based on the will.]; D.34.4.3.9 [D.34.4.*De adimendis vel transferendis legatis vel fideicommissis* (The ademption of legacies and *fideicommissa*).3 **Ulpianus**, *in the twenty-fourth book to Sabinus*: 9. Let's examine whether the condition of a legacy, inheritance, or statuliber can be removed. Julianus says, "Removing the condition from freedom does not makes it is due." Even Pomponius, in the seventeenth book of his Questions, generally states that a condition cannot be removed. He argues that a condition is not granted but added, and what has been added cannot be removed, just as one cannot remove what has been given. However, it is better to follow the sense rather than the words and say that conditions, just as they can be added, can also be removed.].

Chapter VI

[Form of the Partial Propositions]

Definitions

From the general interpretation, let us now turn to the specific form and subject matter of partial propositions. The form, just like in any proposition, also exists in the conditioned proposition, either in terms of quantity or sign, and in terms of quality or copula, or in both.

A proposition is divided, in terms of quantity, into universal and particular.

An indefinite proposition, indeed, does not exist in reality or even in our thoughts, but only in words, when we omit the sign that is nevertheless understood in our minds.

However, a singular proposition is not equivalent to a particular one, but rather to a universal one. This goes against the common opinion of logicians, as we have demonstrated in our *Dissertation on combinatorial art,* which is enriched not only with new ideas but also with knowledge, in problem 2 of the 23rd [but 24[131],e.n.] section.

131 AA VI I, pp. 181-182, "24. We cannot undoubtedly approve those who have equated singular propositions with particulars [e.g., Johannes Hospinianus (1515-1575), a professor of logic at the University of Basel, cited by Leibniz in the omitted passage of this paragraph in the Ars Combinatoria, e.n.]. (....) Although it is commonly believed, we actually judge everything differently, in a truer way. For instance, a proposition such as 'Socrates is the son of Sofroniscus,' if resolved according to the method of Johannes Raue [1610-1679, a professor of eloquence and logic at the Ritterakademie in Sora-Soroe (Denmark); one of his works is *Prior fundamentalis controversia pro logica novissima* (Rostock, 1638), e.n.], takes the form: 'Whoever Socrates is, he is the son of Sofroniscus.' It is not incorrect to say that every Socrates is a son of Sofroniscus, even though he is unique. (We are not referring to the name itself, but to the individual). It is similar to saying, 'I bequeath all the clothes I have to Titius.' Who would doubt that even though I have only one, it belongs to him? Thus, according to jurists, the universal always subsists in the singular,

Nevertheless, when a universal term is used, a singular term can be more precisely added, including identifying circumstances such as the subject, object, place, and time, as discussed in theorem 36 below. In terms of copula or quality, a proposition is divided into affirmative and negative I.3.15.4 [I.3.15. *De verborum obligatione (Verbal contract)*.4, see above in theorem 6.]. The highest degree of negativity is

43. Mere negative propositions. They are not certain to be true unless the subject ceases to exist, for example: "Titius will not drink wine." We cannot be sure if he will abstain or not, if the opposite becomes impossible, or until he is deceased. Although, even if all wines were to be removed from nature, he would still be unable to drink further. Nevertheless, there is no need to fear this, and in moral matters, we give little attention to the fact that these things may not occur or may not occur easily,

D.3.4.7 [D.3.4. *Quod cuiuscumque universitatis nomine vel contra eam agatur* (Actions in the name of or against any body corporate).7 **Ulpianus**, *in the tenth book to the Edict*: Just as the praetor has granted action in the name of the citizens of a municipality, so too he has rightly deemed it proper to provide in the edict against them. Furthermore, I believe that an action should be granted in favor of their delegate, who has incurred expenses for a public matter, against the citizens of a municipality.]; Carpzov, p. II. c. VI, def. 17 [referring to Benedikt Carpzov (d. 1666), *Jurisprudentia Forensis Romano Saxonica* (Franofurti, 1638), p. II. c. VI, def., 17, Collegio per mortem collegiatorum dissoluto bona Collegii Superiori seu Magistratui accrescunt]. In fact, the term 'every' does not imply a multitude of singulars, but rather the inclusion of singulars. So, even if Socrates did not have a brother, we would still say correctly: every Socrates is a son of Sofroniscus. What about the proposition: 'Is this man learned?' From this, we can rightly conclude: Peter is this man; therefore, Peter is learned. 'This,' on the other hand, is a singular sign. In general, therefore, we dare to assert that every singular proposition, according to the mode in the syllogism, must be treated as universal, just as every indefinite proposition must be treated as particular.
On this passage from the *Combinatorial Art*, referred to by Leibniz in the text, see Gabriel Nuchelmans, "Judgment and proposition," in Daniel Garber, Michael Ayers (eds.), *The Cambridge History of Seventeenth-Century Philosophy*, vol. I (Cambridge, 2003), pp. 119-120; for the influence of Raue's logic on Leibnizian thought, see Maria Rosa Antognazza, *Trinità e Incarnazione. Il rapporto tra filosofia e teologia rivelata nel pensiero di Leibniz* (Milano, 1999), 68 onwards. (English transl. by Gerald Parks, New Haven: Yale University Press, 2007).

even though they are absolutely possible. Furthermore, the negative species is considered

44. indefinite, meaning it is not defined in place and time. This is commonly understood by the rule that a negative proposition cannot be proven, as exemplified in the *Quaest. Phil. q.* 2[132].

45. Therefore, based on the quality, a proposition is divided into true and false; determined and indeterminate, and the true determinate proposition is called necessary, while the false determinate proposition is

46. Impossible (whose species is strictly erroneous, as mentioned in D.35.1.72.7 [D.35.1. *De condicionibus et demonstrationibus et causis et modis eorum, quae in testamento scribuntur* (Conditions, designations, explanations for and modalities of provisions in wills).72 **Papinianus**, *in the book eighteen eighteen of Questions*: 7. Cassius and Caelius Sabinus stated that erroneous condition is impossible, such as: "Panfilus will be freed if he pays what I owe to Titius," when nothing is owed to Titius. If, after making the will, the testator paid the sum that was owed, it is considered that the condition did not occur.]), the circumstance of which, in fact, does not exist in reality in one way or another. For example, if Titius were to go to Utopia, the statement "be heir!" would be erroneous D.30.104.1 [D.30.*De legatis et fideicommissis* (Legacies and *fideicommissa*).104 **Julianus**, *in the first book to Urseius Ferox*: 1 see above in theorem 19.], D.35.1.6.pr., 27 [D.35.1. *De condicionibus et demonstrationibus et causis et modis eorum, quae in testamento scribuntur* (Conditions, designations, explanations for and modalities of provisions in wills). 6 **Pomponius**, *in the third book to Sabinus*: see above in theorem 16. 27 **Alfenus Varus**, *in the fifth book of Digest*: A man wrote in his will that he wished to be erected to himself a monument like that of Publius Septimius Demetrius in the via Salaria; should this not be done, he imposed a bulk fine on his heirs. When it was discovered that there was no monument of Publius Septimius Demetrius but that there was one of Publius

[132] A VI 1, p. 77, "6. Generaliter igitur cum negans probare non potest, sive sit penitus, sive moraliter impossibile, onus probandi contrarium, trasfert in eum qui si ita esset videtur posse" [In general, therefore, when those who deny cannot prove, because both de facto and morally impossible, the burden of proving the opposite falls on those who, in such a situation, it seems good that they can].

Septimius Dama, which it was suspected that the testator intended as the model of his own memorial, the heirs asked what sort of monument they should erect and, assuming that they erected none because they could not identify the intended model, whether they would incur the penalty. The reply was that if it could be discerned which monument the testator sought to identify, even though he misdescribed it, they should build on the model which he thought that he had identified; if, however, the testator's intention could not be ascertained, the penalty would be ineffective because the model he requested to be copied never existed.; still they would certainly have to erect a monument appropriate to the wealth and standing of the deceased.]; D.40.5.41.16 [D.40.5.*De fideicommissariis libertatibus* (Grants of freedom by *fideicommissa*).41 **Scaevola**, *in the fourth book of Replies*: 16. "Let Spendophorus be free, after my daughter has married within the family, if he has satisfactorily rendered to her accounts of his administration"; the daughter died without reaching puberty in the father's lifetime, and Seius became the heir by substitution; given that Spendophorus did not administer the affairs of the pupilla and ceased to administer the affairs of the head of the household in his own lifetime, and that Titia, if she were alive, would have been over twelve, would he be free under the will? He replied that if he had not administered affairs of which he owed accounts to the heir, he would be free according to the things exposed.], D.40.7.26.1 [D.40.7.*De statuliberis* (Statuliberi).26 **Modestinus**, *in the ninth book of the Rules*: 1. If it was ordered that a slave should conquer freedom on rendering accounts, he will still be free, even though he had no accounts of his administration to render.].

Similarly, an erroneous demonstration is also referred to as erroneous D.35.1.33 [D.35.1. *De condicionibus et demonstrationibus et causis et modis eorum, quae in testamento* scribuntur (Conditions, designations, explanations for and modalities of provisions in wills).33 **Marcianus**, *in the sixth book of Institutes*: An erroneous designation, for example, description as a brother, sister, grandson, or anything of the like, does not deemed to the disadvantage of a legatee, trust beneficiary , or instituted heir; this is observed by the spirit of the civil law and in rulings of the deified Severus and Antoninus.].

Impossibility can be absolute or relative, depending on the context.

Relative impossibility can arise from a specific circumstance, such as a certain time, resulting in the current situation being impossible at that time and state.

However, once changed, it becomes possible (Theorem 40). It can also be based on a certain rule of action, which is why we term it politically impossible, as engaging in such an action would be foolish. In law, something is considered impossible when, after observing the law as a rule of action, it cannot exist (Theorem 38). It is a true indeterminate proposition that

47. Contingent, the false indeterminate that

48. Possible; possible, according to the degrees of possibility, something is said to be easy or difficult, of which we will discuss further when we address the value of the conditions. This division into determinate and indeterminate is akin to the division into theorems, namely, true propositions based on terms, and observations, that is, true propositions based on sensory perception and inductive reasoning. The former pertains to reason, e.g., the whole is greater than its part; the latter pertain to matters of fact, such as the given existence of a world, as well as all historical propositions.

The observations, however, can be of the past, present, or future. And there are some who hold the opinion that not all additions of these varieties are equally appropriate.

They argue that a motive pertains to the past and a punishment to the future D.35.1.12 [D.35.1. *De condicionibus et demonstrationibus et causis et modis eorum, quae in testamento scribuntur* (Conditions, designations, explanations for and modalities of provisions in wills).12 **Ulpianus**, *in the twenty-four book to Sabinus*: If it was bequeathed in this way: "Since my eldest son took from my chest the sum of ten, my younger son, as the heir, shall take a sum of ten," the legacy is due because it was left to equalize the condition of the sons. Certainly, this is a motive because the motive relates to the past and the penalty to the future.]; D.34.6.2 [D.34.6. *De his quae poenae causa relinquuntur* (Legacies made by way of penalty).2 **Marcianus**, *in the sixth book of Institutes*: It is the purpose of the testator that distinguishes a condition from a penalty and the question of whether a given clause is a penalty, a condition, or a transfer is decided on the basis of the wishes of the deceased. The deified Severus and Antoninus stated this in a rescript.].

The condition of a future fact is a specification of a past fact, D.35.1.34.1 [D.35.1. *De condicionibus et demonstrationibus et causis et modis eorum, quae in testamento scribuntur* (Conditions, designations, explanations for and modalities of provisions in wills).34 **Florentinus**, *in the eleventh book of Institutes*: 1. Between particularization and condition, there is this distinction: Particularization generally relates to what has happened, condition to what is to happen.]; D.30.6 [D.30.*De legatis et fideicommissis* (Legacies and *fideicommissa*).6 **Julianus**, *Digest, book 33*: see above in theorem 14.]. But just as the specification can be in a future fact, D.34.2.34 [D.34.2. *De auro argento mundo ornamentis unguentis veste vel vestimentis et statuis legatis* (Legacies of gold, silver, toilet equipment, jewelry, perfumes , clothing or garments, and statues).34 **Pomponius**, *in the ninth book to Quintus Mucius*: Quintus Mucius writes that if the head of a household had bequeathed all his gold to his wife, the gold that he had given to the goldsmith for the purpose of creating something, or the gold that would be owed to him if the goldsmith failed to repay it, is not owed to the woman. Pomponius: This statement is partially true and partially false. It is undeniably true concerning the owed amount. For example, if he had stipulated a certain weight of gold, the gold owed to him under that stipulation does not belong to the wife, as it hasn't yet become his property. He bequeathed gold that was already his, not gold for which he had a legal claim. In the case of the goldsmith, it's incorrect when he has provided gold to the goldsmith with the intention that something should be crafted from it. In such a scenario, even though the gold may be in possession of the goldsmith, there has been no change in ownership. It still belongs to the person who provided it, and he is only considered liable for the goldsmith's labor. This leads us to the conclusion that the gold is still owed to the wife. If, however, he provided gold to the goldsmith with the condition that a specific item should be crafted for him, but not necessarily from the same gold, then, insofar as the ownership of that gold has transferred to the goldsmith, considering it as if an exchange had been made, that gold, too, will not pass to the wife.]; the condition can be in a past fact, D.28.3.16 [D.28.3.*De iniusto rupto irrito facto testamento* (A will which has not been lawfully made, or which has been broken or rendered ineffectual).16 **Pomponius**, *in the second book to Quintus Mucius*: When we institute an heir in the second will, whether purely or under a condition (provided the condition could have actually occurred, even if it did not), the prior will is nullified. However, the type of condition that is established is of great importance. Conditions may be formulated in the past, present, or future. A condition framed in the past, such as "if Titius was consul," would mean that if this condition is true, i.e., if Titius was indeed a consul, then the heir is instituted in such a way that the previous will is nullified, and in this case, they would become the heir. If Titius was not a consul, the prior will is not nullified. For a condition expressed in the present, like "if Titius is a consul," the result is the same: if Titius is indeed a consul, the heir can be instituted, and the previous will is nullified; if Titius is not a consul, the heir cannot be instituted, and the prior will remains valid. As for future conditions, if they are possible and could potentially occur, even if they haven't happened yet, they lead to the nullification of the prior will. However, if future conditions are impossible, such as "Titius will be the heir if he touches the sky with a finger," they are considered equivalent to conditions not set at all, as they are impossible.]; D.45.1.122.4 [D.45.1. *De verborum obligationibus* (Verbal obligations). 122 **Scaevola**, *in the twenty-eighth book of Digest*: 4. Agerius, a son of a family, stipulated with Publius Maevius' slave, promising to give whatever amount his father owed to Publius Maevius. After his father's death, before the amount and nature of the debt had been determined, it was questioned whether Agerius would be held responsible if an action had been taken against his father's heir or another successor and the debt had been established. The response was that if the condition had not been fulfilled, the stipulation was not binding.]; D.40.4.51.1 [D.40.4.*De manumissis testamento* (Testamentary manumissions).51 **Papinianus**, *in the fourteenth book of Replies*: 1. In regard to a testamentary provision "Slaves who have not been a cause of offense shall be free," it was deemed that a condition had been added, the interpretation of which should be such that it does not appear that the testator intended to grant freedom to those whom a penalty has restrained or who have been removed from the duty of serving or managing business.].

Although a moral condition must be uncertain, see theorem 17, dissenters infer from this that it can only be applied to future facts. However, this does not necessarily follow.

For certain past and present events, there is also uncertainty. For example, if the world was founded in the fall or not, we ignore which of the two contradictory events is true, although we know that one of them must be true. Similarly, in future events, we know that after the sixth millennium has passed, the world will either be burnt or not, although we are uncertain about which of the two possibilities is truer. And this, in truth, is based on our knowledge.

But if you consider the nature of things themselves, the truth or falsehood of not only past events but also future events is certain, see D.5.1.28.5 [D.5.1.*De iudiciis: ubi quisque agere vel conveniri debeat* (Actions: where a man should sue and be sued).28 **Paulus**, *in the seventeenth book to Plautius*: 5. If the head of a household passes away, leaving behind one son and a pregnant wife, it would be incorrect for the son to demand half of a debt from the debtors. This is the case even if, later on, only one son is born, as it was still possible for more children to be born. The laws of nature may have made it certain that only one child was in the process of being born, but Cassius and Sabinus argued that only a quarter of the debt should be claimed. This is because it was uncertain whether three children might be born. Instead of focusing on the laws of nature, where everything was definite and what was meant to happen would certainly occur, we should consider our own lack of knowledge.].

Nor do laws preclude, which seem to indicate that a condition cannot be applied to a past event, see I.3.15.6 [I.3.15.*De verborum obligatione* (Verbal obbligations).6 Conditions relating to past or present time either make the obligation void at once, or have no suspensive operation whatever. Thus, in the stipulation 'Do you promise to give so and so, if Titius has been consul, or if Maevius is alive?' the promise is void, if the condition is not satisfied; while if it is, it is binding at once: for events which in themselves are certain do not suspend the binding force of an obligation, however uncertain we ourselves may be about them.]; D.12.1.37[133], 39 [D.12.1. *De rebus creditis si certum petetur et de condictione* (Things credited giving rise to fixed claims and the *condictio*). 37. **Papinianus**, *Definitions, book 1*: se above in theorem 21. 39 **Papinianus**, *in the first book of Definitions*: So, a condition holds power when it pertains to the future.]; C.6.61.3.13 (?) [C.6.61. *De bonis, quae liberis in potestate constitutis ex matrimonio vel aliter adquiruntur, et eorum administratione* (Concerning property which children under

[133] In the Latin text, L. quotes l. 37 and l. 39 de R.C. According to Armgardt (note 27 above in *Introduction*, 63), l. 37 R.C. usually corresponds to D.34.7, *De regula Catoniana* (Catonian rule); however, l. 37/39 in *De regula Catoniana* does not exist. In my view, l. 37 R.C. refers to D.12.1.37, as in the text above, although in the following quote, *De rebus creditis* is abbreviated as R. Cr. This is also how Boucher interprets it (note 56 above in *Introduction*, 131, n. 565).

paternal power acquired through marriage or otherwise and the management thereof).3. [13. does not exist! It seems a misprint in latin text, e.n.] The statement in prior constitutions, that a father does not acquire a prenuptial gift from a daughter under paternal power, nor a dowry through a son3, is hereby confirmed with this addition, that if the son or daughter die while still under paternal power, leaving children surviving, their property shall go to the children by right of inheritance and not to the father by right of peculium,4 nor does such property become that of the grandfather, through his grandchildren. 1. And if, moreover, a grandchild dies without children, leaving surviving his father as well as his grandfather, the ownership of property which such child acquired through the mother or through the maternal line, shall not go to the grandfather, but to the father, provided that the usufruct in such cases also shall belong to the grandfather while living.]; D.28.7.10.1 [D.28.7.*De conditionibus institutionum* (Conditions on institutions).10 **Ulpianus**, *in the eighth book on Disputes*: 1. If we suppose someone instituted as follows, "let him be heir if I have appointed him heir by codicil," the institution is valid even in the case of a son who is in parental power, whereas a condition which is related to the past or which [is related] to the present, such as, "if the king of the Parthians is alive," "if a ship is lying in the harbor," is null.]; D.35.1.34.1 [D.35.1. *De condicionibus et demonstrationibus et causis et modis eorum, quae in testamento scribuntur* (Conditions, designations, explanations for and modalities of provisions in wills).34 **Florentinus**, *in the eleventh book of Institutes*: 1: see above in definition 48.]; D.28.5.70(69) [D.28.5. *De heredibus instituendis* (The institution of heirs). 70 (69) **Proculus**, *in the second book of the Letters Letters*: see above in definition 10.]; D.45.1.100, 120 [D.45.1.*De verborum obligationibus* (Verbal obligations).100 **Modestinus**, *in the eight book of Rules*: A condition which refers to the past and not merely to the present either destroys the obligation or has no delaying effect. 120. **Papinianus**, *in the thirty-seventh book of Questions*: If I had stipulated in this way: "Do you undertake to give this sum of one hundred aurei?" even though this expression is clearly heard as "provided that they are one hundred aurei," the addition of these words does not constitute a condition, since if they are not one hundred aurei, the stipulation is void. Nor is language considered akin to a condition when it does not refer to the future but to the present, even if the contracting parties are unaware of the truth of the matter.].

For, if the condition is compared to what is in the past and present, with regard to what is in the future, it approaches more closely to the nature of a pure condition, for the right is transmitted and carried back by it, as stated below in theorem 68. However, this is contrary to the nature of other conditions in Last Wills, which neither transmit nor carry back. The reason for this is that a condition that has already existed or failed, and even if it is suspended until it is certain whether it has occurred or failed, it still makes no difference. For this reason, for they approach very much like unconditioned propositions, are called pure. The disposition of contingent propositions, and the determination of their truth or falsity based on the differences between past, present, or future, is called

49. Event, whose state either becomes true and consequently necessary, because what is done cannot be undone[134], and so it is said that it

50. Occurs, or becomes impossible, and so it is said that it

51. Fails, D.35.1.30 [D.35.1. *De condicionibus et demonstrationibus et causis et modis eorum, quae in testamento scribuntur* (Conditions, designations, explanations for and modalities of provisions in wills).30 **Julianus**, *in the first book From Minicius*: see above in theorem 26.], and no further hope remains that the person, once the condition is unfulfilled, will live, D.35.1.31 [D.35.1. *De condicionibus et demonstrationibus et causis et modis eorum, quae in testamento scribuntur* (Conditions, designations, explanations for and modalities of provisions in wills).31 **Africanus**, *in the second book of Questions*: see above in theorem 19.].

52. The condition pends before the event, as stated in D.7.1.35 [D.7.1.*De usu fructu et quemadmodum quis utatur fruatur* (Usufruct and the way in which a man may exercise it). 34 **Julianus**, *in the first book to Urseius Ferox*: If usufruct has been bequeathed but the heir named in the will accepts the inheritance later, to ensure that the bequest is acquired later, he will also be responsible for this, as Sabinus deemed appropriate.]; D.12.1.36 [D.12.1. *De rebus creditis si certum petetur et de condictione* (Things credited giving rise to fixed claims and the *condictio)*.36 Javolenus, *in the first book of the Letters*: see above in theorem 34.]; D.12.6.16 [D.12.6.*De condictione*

[134] Titus Maccius Plautus (c. 254 – 184 BC), *Aulularia*, IV, X, v. 741, Factum est illud; fieri infectum non potest [it is done; it cannot be undone, (e.t.)].

indebiti (The *condictio* for money not owed). 16 **Pomponius**, *in the fifteenth book to Sabinus*: see above in theorem 6.]; D.36.2.8 [D.36.2. *Quando dies legatorum vel fideicommissorum cedat* (When a legacy or a *fideicommissum* vests).8 **Ulpianus**, *in the twenty-fourth book to Sabinus*: Because freedom is not granted until after entry into the inheritance, it has seemed fairer that the day of the legacy should not expire earlier; otherwise, the legacy would be useless if its term expired before freedom was acquired. This happens when a legacy is bequeathed to a slave in a pure manner and he is ordered to become free under a condition, and the condition is still pending after accepting the inheritance.]; D.42.4.14.1 [D.42.4. *Quibus ex causis in possessionem eatur* (The grounds on which missio in possessionem granted). 14 **Paulus**, *in the second book of the Questions*: 1. If a person granted missio in possessionem[135] for the preservation of legacies be not allowed to take it, the measure of damages will be the value of the legacy, even though it be subject to a condition which may not be realized; for it is in his interest that he has security.].

It is said to be suspended, as mentioned in D.10.2.34 [D.10.2. *Familiae erciscundae* (The action for dividing an inheritance). 34 **Papinianus**, *in the eighth book of Replies*: When slaves are being appraised during the division of an inheritance among co-heirs, the common perspective is that their valuation is not for the purpose of buying them but rather for the purpose of dividing them. Consequently, if they pass away before a condition linked to them is fulfilled, they are considered lost both to the heir and the fideicommissarius.]; D.35.1.72.4 [D.35.1. *De condicionibus et demonstrationibus et causis et modis eorum, quae in testamento scribuntur* (Conditions, designations, explanations for and modalities of provisions in wills).72 **Papinianus**, *in the eighteenth book of Questions*: 4. "If Seia marries with Titius's consent, my heir shall give her a plot of land." While Titius is alive, she can accept this bequest even without Titius's consent, and it appears that the law aims not to impose any hindrance to the marriage. But if Titius dies while the testator is still alive, even if the condition fails, as it would have been suspended in any case, the woman will be assisted.].

See supra definition 7, which properly pertains to the conditioned party.

Similarly, what we properly stated as "pends" pertains to the condition, and applies to the conditioned party, D.12.6.60.1 [D.12.6.*De condictione indebiti* (The *condictio*

[135] A legal process for taking possession of the estate (e.n.).

for money not owed). 60 **Paulus**, *in the third book of Questions*: 1. However, in the case where someone, with the intention of making a novation, has promised, with a stipulation under condition, what he owes without condition, the majority <of jurists> believes that he can demand what has been paid pending the novation, since it is still uncertain for which obligation he is paying; and the same applies even when, for example, different persons have promised with an unconditional stipulation and <then> under a condition, with the intention of novating, the same amount owed. But this case is different <from the first one>, because, indeed, in the unconditional stipulation, and in that of the conditional novation, it is certain that the debtor is the same.].

However, sometimes a condition is said to pend when it has indeed occurred or failed, but its certainty is still uncertain. In such cases, it would be more accurate to say that it is suspended.

53. A proposition is contrary to another proposition when it cannot be both true and false at the same time, as stated in D.46.5.8.1 [D.46.5.*De stipulationibus praetoriis* (Praetorian stipulations).8 **Papinianus**, *in the fifth book of Questions*: 1. A legacy is left to Titius and Maevius under incompatible conditions; security must be given to each, since each anticipates the legacy as the testator desired.]; D.50.17.121 [D.50.17. *De diversis regulis iuris antiqui* (Various rules of early law). 121 **Paulus**, *in the thirteenth book to Edict*: Who does not do what he ought to do, seems to do the opposite, because he does not do; and he who does what he ought not to do, does not seem to do what he was ordered to do.]. Add theorem 34.

The Scholastics would call it contradictory, for it is contrary to the former propositions when it cannot be true and false simultaneously, but it can be false at the same time.

This is also assumed in D.28.5.87(86) [D.28.5. *De heredibus instituendis* (The institution of heirs). 87 (86) **Maecianus**, *in the seventh book of Fideicommissa*: There is no longer any doubt that even *sui heredes* can be named as heirs under this condition, that they become heirs if they wish to, and, in the event that they do not become heirs, that whomever one prefers may be substituted for them. There is also no dispute that in this scenario it is unnecessary to disinherit the son under the opposite condition. First, this would be required only when it is not within his power to become his father's heir, given that the event of the condition is dependent on external factors for the person waiting for it to be fulfilled. Furthermore, although in general the son should be disinherited under the opposite condition, in the case at hand, not even a suitable condition could be identified. Imagine trying to formulate this condition in words: "if he desires, he shall be heir," what other words could be conceived of except these: "if he does not desire to be heir, he shall not be heir"? It is evident how ridiculous that would be.]; D.34.5.13.3 [D.34.5. *De rebus dubiis* (Dubious cases).13 (14) **Julianus**, *in the sole book of Ambiguities*: 3. The question of how to formulate the stipulation 'if this or that is not done' or in this way 'if nothing among what has been included to be done is not done' is important. Even if one of the two events had truly occurred, this does not imply that the other event has not occurred. In fact, both events can be true even if they are contradictory to each other. This happens because the meaning is not taken from the whole, but from a part of it. If one part is true, it makes the entire statement true. Conversely, two statements containing conflicting events are both false, such as if some of the children have died at a young age and some at an adult age. In this case, both the statement that all the children have died at an adult age and the statement that all the children have died at a young age are false. This occurs because the meaning is taken from the whole, and if there is something false in the whole, it makes the entire statement false. So, it is important to consider the subject of the question. For example, when we formulate 'if this or that is not done,' the question is whether one thing has been done or not. In this case, the effect is that neither of the two things has been done. On the other hand, with 'if nothing is done,' the question is whether something has been done or not. In this case, the effect is that both things have been done. Therefore, it is not useful in one case to claim that something has not been done if something has indeed been done, and likewise, it is not useful in the other case to claim that something has been done if nothing has actually been done.].

From these definitions flow now

Theorems

(36) *A moral negative condition that is indefinite over time should be regarded as a general condition because pertaining to time.*

Contra Sabinus[136] D.45.1.115.1, 2 [D.45.1. *De verborum obligationibus* (Verbal obligations). 115 **Papinianus**, *in the second book of Questions*: 1. However, if you had stipulated in this way: "you promise to give one hundred aurei if you do not ascend to the Capitol" or "if you do not go to Alexandria," the stipulation will not be immediately binding, even if you could have ascended to the Capitol or reached Alexandria, but only when it becomes certain that you will not be able to ascend to the Capitol or go to Alexandria. 2. Again, if someone stipulates as follows, "if you do not give Pamphilus, do you promise that one hundred will be paid," Pegasus gave an opinion that the stipulation took effect only when it was no longer possible for Pamphilus to be. But Sabinus held the view, based on the intentions of the parties, that once the slave could be given, an action could be brought on the stipulation at once, and was postponed only so long as failure to give was not the fault of the promisor. He relied on the analogy of a legacy of provisions. For Mucius wrote that if an heir could hand over the provisions bequeathed and did not, he was at once liable for the sum of money mentioned in the legacy. This is accepted, as a matter of convenience, in view of the intention of the deceased and the nature of the subject matter. The view of Sabinus can therefore be accepted, on condition that the stipulation is framed not conditionally, for example, "if you do not convey Pamphilus, do you promise to pay one hundred," but a s follows, "do you promise that Pamphilus will be conveyed; if not, that such-and-such an amount will be paid." This is undoubtedly the true position if the proved intention was that if the slave was no tgiven, both slave and money should be owing. But even if the wording is such that on failure to transfer the slave, only the money is owing, the same solution can be defended, because the proved wish was that either the slave should be transferred or the money claimed.].

Indeed, let it be a moral negative condition indefinite over time: for example, "if Titius does not become consul", as defined in definition 27.

I affirm that it should be understood as follows: If Titius will never become consul. Otherwise, it should be understood as follows: if Titius will not become consul in the end, which is necessary because he cannot

[136] Leibniz is referring here to Sabin, the founder of one of the two significant schools of Law in Rome, namely the Sabinian school, which existed during the 1st and 2nd centuries CE. The Sabinian school stood in opposition to the Proculean school; see about, Paul du Plessis, note 53 above, p. 45.

become consul at any time. However, this necessity is not moral, according to theorem 17, because contradicts the premise. Nevertheless, if it is a conditional power granted to a slave and added to their freedom, although it is not entirely specific in time, it is also not entirely universal. It appears to be fulfilled when, for the first time, they could conveniently act inappropriately in relation to it but did not do so. For instance, if Stichus does not ascend to the Capitol, they shall be free! As soon as they could but did not do so, they become free, according to D.40.4.17.1 [D.40.4.*De manumissis testamento* (Testamentary manumissions).17 **Julianus**, *in the forty-second book of Digest*: 1. In this testament clause "Pamphilus should be free, but he must be accountable to my sons," it was questioned whether the freedom was given under a condition. I replied that the freedom was indeed granted and that the addition "but he must be accountable" did not constitute a condition for the freedom. However, because the clear intention of the testator was expressed, Pamphilus should be compelled to be accountable.].

The reason for this is that other such conditions are considered fulfilled only upon the death of the person, as explained in theorem 15 above. However, in that case, a guarantee must be given by the conditional party that they will not make mistakes in relation to it in the future. But since a slave cannot provide such a guarantee, another way, as I described, has been found to assist them.

(37) The opposite of the necessary is impossible.

Because, being the necessary definitely true, e.g. that man is an animal, according to definition 46, its contrary that man is not an animal will be definitely false, according to definition 53, that is impossible, according to definition 47, see D.45.1.7 [D.45.1.*De verborum obligationibus* (Verbal obligations).7 **Ulpianus**, *in the sixth book to Sabinus:* see above in theorem 17.].

Hence the impossible condition of not doing, e.g. if you do not touch the sky with a finger, is the opposite of the necessary, D.28.5.51(50).1 [D.28.5. *De heredibus* instituendis (The institution of heirs). 51 (50) **Ulpianus**, *in the sixth book of Rules*: 1. If an impossible condition, consisting in not doing something, has been attached to the institution of an heir, according to the view of every authority, he will be heir, just as if he had been instituted unconditionally.]; D.45.1.50 [D.45.1.*De verborum obligationibus* (Verbal obligations). 50 **Ulpianus**, *in the fiftieth book To the Edict*: see above in theorem 16.].

(38) What is impossible in law, although under other respects by its own nature is about to make better the position of someone, has not to be executed, simply has to be equated to the <naturally> impossible.

D.28.7.15 [D.28.7.*De conditionibus institutionum* (Conditions on institutions).15 **Papinianus**, *in the sixteenth book of Questions*: A son who was under parental authority, instituted as heir in writing under a condition that the Senate or the Emperor disapprove, shall render his father's will invalid, as if the fulfillment of the condition were not in his power. This is because acts that offend our compassion, our dignity, our sense of decency, and, to express it in general terms, that go against good morals, are to be believed as acts we cannot even perform.], for example, if someone were to make a testament like this: "Titius, if he kills Sempronius, shall be the heir!" This is legally impossible, according to the explained definition 46, because, even without considering natural law, it cannot occur. I affirm that both the lawmaker and the magistrate have a definite obligation to ensure that Titius does not profit from the murder of Sempronius and that he does not become the heir, regardless of whether he kills Sempronius or not. It is indeed the duty of the legislator, as well as the magistrate, to prevent violations in the Republic, that is, any actions against the law, to the extent possible. On the other hand, the prevention of a violation involves removing the incentive, and the incentive for a violation is the profit derived from it. Therefore, the lawmaker must take care, and laws must be enacted in such a way that no profit is gained from a violation. Consequently, even if the condition is fulfilled, it should be considered as not fulfilled, either because it cannot be effectively fulfilled or because, in terms of the effect, it is equivalent to the impossible. What was to be demonstrated.

The same principle applies even if it is impossible under civil law. However, although it is possible to seek a relaxation of this impossibility from the ruler, it is difficult to do so. Moreover, because it is harmful to the state, legal scholars consider it as impossible, as *Zasius noted in ad l. cum serv., § fin. de L. 1 n. 6*[137]. (Just as, on the other hand, we refer to something as impossible when it goes against the law, Vergil also referred to a truly impossible act as "Nefas" [an impious act, e.n.]: *Nefas quem neque fas igni cuiquam nec sternere ferro - Aeneid, Book 7*[138]).

From this example, it becomes evident, as I will mention in passing, that *Hermann Conring* (1606-1681), a highly perceptive scholar in civil principles, has correctly emphasized that the purpose of strictly prescribed laws (those that are not merely principles of law) can be sought for the benefit of the Republic. In fact, the virtue of citizens is the primary aim of legislation. Without it, self-sufficiency would prevail, and extreme poverty is highly condemnable.

As a corollary, it follows that in the case of a simply impossible condition in last wills, where it is not included, as stated in Theorem 63, the same principle, or something

137 Ulrich Zasius (1461–1536), *Commentarium ad Pandectas* (Basileae, 1537), in *Opera omnia*, vol. 2. (Francofurti, 1590), p. 190, § Constat cum l. seq. [i.e. D.30.*De legatis et fideicommissis (Legacies and fideicommissa)*.39 ULPIAN, ULPIAN, *in the twenty-first book to Sabinus*: pr. Cum servo, e.n.]. "6, Patrimonium principis legari non potest."; see also Alexandre Thiercelin, "Conditions, conditionnels, droits conditionnels: L'articulation du jeune Leibniz (II e Partie)", in *Studia Leibnitiana*, 2009, Bd. 41, H. 2, p. 137.

138 Vergil (70–19 BC) (29 et 19 BC), *Aeneid*, 7, 691-2 "Nefas quem neque fas igni cuiquam nec sternere ferro [That no one is allowed to knock down on ground neither with fire nor with iron, ed. transl.]", see also Henry Rushton Fairclough [1862–1938] (ed. and transl.), *Virgil. Aeneid, VII-XII.* The Minor Poems. (Cambridge: Harvard University Press, 1918), 50-51, "whom none may lay low with fire or steel.".

akin to it, applies to impossibilities in law, which are said to have been remitted, as per D.28.7.9, 14, 15 [D.28.7. *De conditionibus institutionum* (Conditions on institutions). 9 **Paulus**, *in the forty-fifth book To the Edict*: Conditions that are introduced in the will and go against good morals, such as, "if he does not ransom his father from enemies," "if he does not provide sustenance to his ancestors or his patron," are to be released. 14 **Marcianus**, *in the fourth book of the Institutes*: Conditions that are written in opposition to the edicts of the emperors, laws, or other provisions that have the force of law, or that are contrary to good morals, or derisory, or have modalities that the praetors disapprove of, are considered as if unwritten. The inheritance or legacy is acquired as if the condition had not been added to the inheritance or legacy. 15 **Papinianus**, *in the sixteenth book of Questions*: see above in this theorem 38.]; D.29.1.29.2 [D.29.1.*De testamento militis* (The soldier's will).29 **Marcellus**, *in the tenth book of Digest*: 2. The Edict of the praetor by which he remits an oath to instituted heirs and legatees applies even to the wills of soldiers, as it applies even to fideicommissa, and likewise, if the condition was shameful.]; D.35.2.88 [D.35.2.*Ad legem Falcidiam* (The lex Falcidia).88 **Africanus**, *Questions, book 5*: A person who had 400 [aurei] left 300 [aurei] in his will, then bequeathed you a property worth 100 aurei under the condition "if the lex Falcidia has no application to [my] will.". The question is raised: what is the legal status of this? I said that this question belongs to those paradoxes that are treated among dialecticians. In fact, whatever we establish as true, it will be found to be false. For if we say that the legacy given to you is valid, the lex Falcidia operates, and therefore it will not be payable due to the condition being absent. On the other hand, if, because the condition fails, the legacy will not be valid, there will be no place for the Falcidian law. Furthermore, if lex Falcidia does not operate, with the condition in existence, the legacy to you will be payable. However, since it is clear that the testator's intention was not to diminish the other legacies for the sake of your legacy, it is more appropriate for us to establish that the condition of your legacy has failed.]; D.38.17.2.44 [D.38.17. *Ad senatus consultum Tertullianum et Orphitianum* (Senatus consultum Tertullianum and Orphitianum). 2 **Ulpianus**, *in the thirteenth book to Sabinus*: 44. It can be a nice question for consideration whether the constitution falls into suspension where a large legacy has been left to a pupillus under the condition that "he has had no tutors," and for that reason his mother has made no application on his behalf, lest he should fail to fulfill the condition. And I submit that it lapses if the loss is less than the amount of the legacy. And this question is treated by Tertullian in the case of municipal magistrates. And he submits that an action should be granted against them insofar as more was entailed in the loss than in the legacy. Unless, perhaps, one submits that a condition of this nature should be crossed out as contrary to public policy as many others have been, or, by hairsplitting over the wording, one has calculated against the mother the fact that she failed to make application for curators. But imagine that the condition has been expressed in full; will the mother not be pardoned? Or is it to be held against her that she did not petition the emperor to have the condition struck out? And I submit that it should not be held against her.].

Conversely, even though it may seem that a simply impossible condition in a soldier's testament is not remitted, but rather renders the disposition void, it is evident that an impossible condition in law is remitted, as stated in D.29.1.29.2, 3 [D.29.1.*De testamento militis* (The soldier's will).29 **Marcellus**, *in the tenth book of Digest*: 2 see above in this theorem 38. 3. It is agreed that bonorum possessio contra tabulas in respect of the share owed to him should be given to a person's father, who in an emancipation had himself become manumitter, with the exception of that property which the son had acquired on military service in respect of which he has unfettered *testamenti factio*.].

Furthermore, our theorem holds true for acts that are contrary to the laws of nature (commonly known as transgressions) as stated in D.28.7.9, 15, 14 [D.28.7. *De conditionibus institutionum (Conditions on institutions)*. 9 **Paulus**, *in the forty-fifth book to the Edict*: see above in this theorem 38. 14 **Marcianus**, *in the fourth book of Institutes*: see above in this theorem 38. 15 **Papinianus**, *in the sixteenth book of Questions*: see above in this theorem 38.]; D.45.1.35 [D.45.1. *De verborum obligationibus* (Verbal obligations). 35 **Paulus**, *in the twelfth book to Sabinus*: If I stipulate that something be done which nature does not allow to be done, the obligation does not exist, just as when I stipulate that something be given which cannot be given, unless it has been in someone else's power whether the thing could be done or not.], as well as for acts that violate civil law, including those that defy its explicit provisions (referred to as prohibited) as stated in D.28.7.14 [D.28.7.*De conditionibus institutionum* (Conditions on institutions). 14 **Marcianus**, *in the fourth book of Institutes*: see above]; an example of this can be found in D.35.2.88 [D.35.2. *Ad legem Falcidiam* (The lex Falcidia).88 **Africanus**, *in the fifth book of Questions*: see above in this theorem 38.].

It also applies to acts that comply with the literal wording of the law but circumvent its intended purpose (referred to as fraud on the statute), D.1.3.29, 30 [D.1.3. *De legibus senatusque consultis et longa consuetudine* (Statutes, senatus consulta, and long-established custom).29 **Paulus**, *in the sole book to the Lex Cincia*: It is a contravention of the law if someone does what the law forbids, but fraudulently, in that respect the words of the law but evades its sense. 30 **Ulpianus**, *in the fourth book to the Edict*: Fraud on the statute is practiced when one does what the statute does not wish anyone to do yet which it has failed expressly to forbid. And what separates "words from meaning" separates cheating from what is done contrary to law.]; D.28.6.43 [D.28.6.*De vulgari et pupillari substitutione* (Normal and pupillary substitution).43 **Paulus**, *in the ninth book of Questions*: A question arises from this scenario: A man, who had a mute and pubescent son, obtained from the emperor the privilege of appointing a substitute for his mute son and designated Titius as the substitute heir. Subsequently, the mute son marries and has a son after his father's demise. I am inquiring about the testament's validity. In response, it should be noted that imperial privileges are typically interpreted by the emperors themselves. However, for those discerning the emperor's intentions, one could argue that the privilege was intended to remain in effect as long as the testator's son remained in the same condition, just as, under civil law, the will of a pupillus ceases with puberty. Hence, the emperor may have acted in accordance with the law concerning individuals unable to make a will due to infirmity. If the testator had made a substitution for an insane son, we would similarly conclude that the will becomes invalid upon the son's recovery of sanity, as he would then be capable of making his own will. If we were to assume that the emperor's privilege remained valid, it would unjustly deprive a person of sound mind of testamenti factio capacity. Consequently, it must be acknowledged that the substitution is also invalidated when a sane suus heres is introduced into the agnatic family. This applies regardless of whether the son himself designated another heir subsequently or if a suus heres was acquired by legal means. It is improbable that either the father or the emperor had contemplated this scenario or intended to disinherit the child born later. The method by which the imperial privilege influences testamenti factio, whether favoring one or multiple parties, is immaterial.]; D.28.7.7 [D.28.7.*De conditionibus institutionum* (Conditions on institutions). 7 **Pomponius**, *in the fifth book to Sabinus*: In cases where an individual has appointed heirs with the requirement that they provide each other with guarantees, assuring the payment of the specified legacies in the will, it is established that this condition is considered void. The reason behind this is that such a condition is designed to circumvent legal provisions that forbid certain individuals from receiving legacies. Even if a guarantee had been provided, the promisor would still need to be shielded by a legal defense within the lawsuit itself.]; D.35.1.37, 64.1 [D.35.1. *De condicionibus et demonstrationibus et causis et modis eorum, quae in testamento* scribuntur (Conditions, designations, explanations for and modalities of provisions in wills). 37 **Paulus**, *in the sole book on the Fufia Caninia Law*: see above in theorem 15. 64 **Terentius Clemens**, *in the fifth book on Lex Julia et Papia*: 1. If the disposition is written as follows: "If she does not marry in Aricia," it is necessary to examine whether it has been so arranged to circumvent the law, because if the woman is in circumstances where she cannot easily marry elsewhere, what was written to circumvent the law shall be null by operation of law. Indeed, the interpretation should favor the law that aims at public benefit, namely the one that was enacted to increase the population.]; C.6.25.2 [C.6.25. *De institutionibus seu substitutionibus sub condicione factis* (Concerning appointments, substitutions or trusts, made upon condition). 2. If you did not fulfill the condition under which you were appointed as heir in the testament of your mother, the substitute takes your place. Nor does it appear that she attempted to pledge you to widowhood under pretense of arranging a dishonorable marriage, since her purpose in wanting to join you in marriage to the son of her sister, your cousin, was entirely commendable. 1. Nor are you entitled to special relief, since it appears form the contents of your petition, that it is not your cousin's fault that the last wish of your mother, the testatrix, has not been complied with.].

Acts that are in fraud on the statute are considered as not included, as stated in D.28.7.7 [D.28.7.*De conditionibus institutionum* (Conditions on institutions). 7 **Pomponius,** *in the fifth book to Sabinus*: see above.]; D.34.9.10 [D.34.9. *De his quae ut indignis auferuntur [Legacies taken away on grounds of unfitness]*. 10 **Gaius,** *in the fifteenth book on the Lex Julia et Papia*: A person who, whether through a formal written agreement or a simple spoken promise, covertly commits to delivering an item bequeathed in a will or any other asset to an individual prohibited by law from receiving it is engaging in a deceptive actin fraud of the statute.].

I.2.23.1 contrasts on point [I.2.23. *De fideicommissariis hereditatibus* (Of trust inheritances).1. Legacies or inheritances given by trust had originally no binding legal force, because no one could be compelled against his will to do what he was merely asked to do. As there were certain classes of persons to whom testators were unable to leave inheritances or legacies, when they wished to effect these objects they used to trust to the good faith of some one who had this kind of testamentary capacity, and whom they asked to give the inheritance, or the legacy, to the intended beneficiary; hence the name 'trusts', because they were not enforced by legal obligation, but only by the transferor's sense of honesty. Subsequently the Emperor Augustus, either out of regard for various favourites of his own, or because the request was said to have been made in the name of the Emperor's safety, or moved thereto by individual and glaring cases of perfidy, commanded the consuls in certain cases to enforce the duty by their authority. And this being deemed equitable, and being approved by the people, there was gradually developed a new and permanent jurisdiction, and trusts became so popular that soon a special praetor was appointed to hear suits relating to them, who was called the trust praetor.] where it is mentioned that in the past, it was customary for people to leave things as *fideicommissa* to those whom they could not legally leave them to, and that Augustus approved of this practice. However, it is argued that some laws are beneficial to the Republic and should not be evaded, but rather assisted through interpretation, D.35.1.64.1 [D.35.1. *De condicionibus et demonstrationibus et causis et modis eorum, quae in testamento scribuntur (Conditions, designations, explanations for and modalities of provisions in wills).* 64. **Terentius Clemens,** *in the fifth book on Lex Julia et Papia*: 1.see above in this theorem 38.].

Other laws are deemed futile and excessively intricate but tolerated for specific reasons. For example, certain laws of ancient Romans intricately limited the power to bequeath a thing more than the will of the testator, and therefore were rightfully circumvented through *fideicommissa.*

I have noticed that this distinction was indeed utilized in another practical case regarding conditions and proves to be of considerable utility. In the vicinity of Leipzig, a peasant woman disinherited her son, who was a cleric, under the condition that he would only inherit his *pars legitima*[139] if he agreed to share it with

[139] Berger, *ad vocem Pars (portio) legitima,* "The share of an inheritance due to an heir who would succeed under the law on intestacy (heres legitimus, ab intestato). The fourth part of the pars legitima (quarta legitimae partis) had to be left certain heirs among the next relatives (descendants, ascendants, and later, consanguineous brothers and sisters) in any form. Otherwise, i.e., if the share left to them was less than

his sisters according to the *Gerade*[140] tradition. Although this appeared to be an attempt to circumvent the Saxon Law on inheritance for clerics, the jurors of Leipzig, without hesitation, ruled that this arrangement with the specified condition was valid. This decision was supported by the distinguished Mr. Bornius, a current alderman and former juror of Leipzig, in his publication entitled "Dissertation on the Law of Gerade"[141]. The rationale behind this judgment can be explained by these principles, which are not always readily apparent: the law concerning the transmissibility of the *Gerade* to clerics was upheld not for the benefit of the state, but due to ancient customs. In the past, clerics employed various cunning methods to advance their positions of power whenever the opportunity arose. Generally, it was deemed acceptable and even necessary to find ways to circumvent such stringent laws, which results in C.6.51.1 [C.6.51.*De caducis tollendis* (Concerning abolishing lapses (escheats).1.1. And as the Papian law was, in many respects, corrected by former emperors and at last fell into desuetude, so, too, it shall lose its hateful vigor in its application to escheats (*caduca*) by us, inasmuch as it was displeasing even to the great jurists who found many ways to avoid the occurrence of lapses (*caduca*).]. This is because an inconspicuous evasion causes less disruption to the republic than a direct change in legislation.

This also applies to that condition which, although not against the law, goes against morality and is deemed contrary to good morals, which encompasses other conditions in a broad sense, D.28.7.15 [D.28.7.*De conditionibus institutionum* (Conditions on institutions).15 **Papinianus**, *in the*

the required fourth, or if they were not mentioned in the testament at all or were unjustly disinherited, they had the querela inofficiosi testamenti which might lead to the rescission of the whole testament.".

140 Nils Jansen, "Testament formalities in Early modern Europe", in Kenneth G. Creid, Marius J. De Waal, Reinhard Zimmermann (eds.), *Comparative Succession Law*. I, (Oxford, 2011), p. 31, "parts of the household that were regarded as the property of women and exclusively transferred to women".

141 Jakob Born (1638-1709), *De gerada disputatio iuridica*, (Lipsiae, 1665).

sixteenth book of Questions: see above in this theorem 38.], more strictly referring to immoral actions D.28.7.9 [D.28.7.*De conditionibus institutionum* (Conditions on institutions*)*. 9 **Paulus**, *in the forty-fifth book to the Edict*: see above in this theorem 38.]; Pauli. Sent. III 4, 15[142]; strictest in cases that are against the customs of people, D.50.16.42 [D.50.16. *De verborum significatione* (Meaning of expressions).42 **Ulpianus**, *in the fifty-seventh book to the Edict*: "Probum" is the same thing as "obprobrium." It is sometimes something which is inherently disgraceful, and sometimes it is considered as such by convention and the customs of society. For example, theft or adultery is inherently disgraceful, but but to be condemned to undertake tutelage is not by nature shameful but is so by custom of the community. Anything that can happen to an honorable person is not inherently disgraceful.]; X.1.5 [X.4.1. *De sponsalibus et matrimoniis* (Concernig the promise of marriage and marriage).5. Si sponsus de futuro ante copulam ad remota se transfert, sponsa libere cum alio contrahit: si tamen per eam stetit, quo minus matrimonium perficeretur, sibi poenitentia imponitur [If the future bridegroom leaves for distant lands before the carnal union, the bride linearly contracts marriage with another: if however, it depended on her that the marriage was not completed, a penance was imposed on her.]; against one's own Republic, *Cornelio Nepote praef. Vit.*[143], as well as a turpentine condition, D.28.7.15 [D.28.7.*De conditionibus institutionum* (Conditions on institutions).15 **Papinianus**, *in the sixteenth book of Questions*: see above in this theorem 38.]; D.23.3.79.1 [D.23.3.*De iure dotium* (The law of dowry). 79 **Labeo**, *in the sixth book of the Posthumous Works*

[142] Julius Paulus, *Receptarum sententiarum libri V* (Parisiis, 1558), l. III, tit. IIII, p. 64, "[15] Conditiones contra leges & decreta principum, vel bonos mores adscripta nullius momenti sunt, veluti, si uxorem non duxeris, si filios non susceperis, si homicidium feceris, si barbaro habitu processeris et his similia." [The conditions contrary to laws and decrees of the prince, or against good morals, are of no significance. For example, if you do not marry, if you do not have children, if you commit murder, if you adopt a barbarian appearance, and similar conditions.].

[143] Cornelius Nepos (c. 110–c. 25 BC], *Vitae excellentium imperatorum, Autoris Praefatio*, "[…] Hi, si didicerint, non eadem omnibus esse honesta atque turpia, **fed** omnia majorum institutis judicari; non admirabuntur, nos, in Graiorum virtutibus s exponendis, mores eorum secutos. […]"; Engl. tr. by Robert Arrol, *Cornelius Nepos's, Lives of Excellent Commanders* (Edimburgh, 1744), pp. 2-3, "[…] If these People understood once, that the same things are not honourable scandalous with all People; but that all things are judged of by the usages of our Forefathers they will not wonder that we, in relating the noble quaalifications of the Greeks, have follow ed their Fashions. […].".

Epitomized by Javolenus: 1. A father pledged to provide a dowry of one hundred gold coins for his daughter, with the condition that it should be paid "at the most suitable time." Ateius mentioned that, following Servius' interpretation, the father should deliver the dowry promptly, as long as he could do it without facing dishonor and loss of reputation.].

Such conditions indicate an imperfection in the law and are always considered illicit according to human laws, D.50.17.144 [D.50.17. *De diversis regulis iuris antiqui* (Various rules of early law). 144 **Paulus**, *in the book sixty-second to the Edict*: Not everything which is lawful is honorable.]. For it is also the responsibility of the legislator's prudence to ensure that in certain matters, people strive to shake off the yoke not through penalties but by being less constrained, seeking to restrain themselves out of a sense of modesty.

The condition of an oath (*iureiurandi*[144]), on the other hand, when it is defined as shameful D.35.1.20, 26 [D.35.1. *De condicionibus et demonstrationibus et causis et modis eorum, quae in testamento scribuntur* (Conditions, designations, explanations for and modalities of provisions in wills). 20 **Julianus**, *in the twenty-seventh book of Digest*: Marcellus notes: We do not doubt that base conditions are to be renounced; among them are particularly conditions of oath-taking. 26 **Julianus**, *in the eighty-second book of Digest*: see above in theorem 6.], should not be considered inherently shameful, but rather as an incentive towards disgrace. The frequency of oaths gradually encompasses the readiness to swear and commit perjury. Therefore,

[144] Berger, *ad vocem Iusiurandum*, "An oath. There were two kinds of oaths, one during a iudicial trial (iusiurandum in iure, iusiurandum necesarium, iusiurandum in litem), the other sworn extrjudicially upon agrrement of the parties engaged in a dispute (iusiurandum voluntarium). The prmissory oath of a freedman was of specific character."; *ad vocem Iusiurandum voluntarium*, "An extrajudicial oath. It is opposed to the iuramentum necessarium since it is voluntary and is based on an agreement of the parties engaged in a controversy. 'An oath contains a kind of transaction and has a greater authority than a judgement' (D.12.2.2). When the claimant swore to uphold his claim, he had a pretorian action (actio ex iureiurando or iureiurandi) against the debtor. When the debtor denied his debt under oath, he might oppose an exceptio iusiurandi when sued by the creditor. The attribute 'voluntarium' is a creation of Justinian – D.12.2.".

the *iuramentum calumniae*[145], administered prior to any lawsuit, which elsewhere tarnishes the reputation of deceitful procurators with countless perjuries, has been abolished in the Saxon court by appropriate decision.

However, it is permissible to fulfill the condition of an oath, D.29.3.62 [D.29.2.*De adquirenda vel omittenda hereditate* (Taking up or failing to take up an inheritance).62 **Javolenus**, *in the first book From the Posthumous Works of Labeo*: Antistius Labeo says that a person instituted thus, 'if he has sworn an oath, let him be heir', although he has sworn, nevertheless, will not be heir immediately, before he has done some action as heir, because by swearing he is regarded, rather, as having [only] stated his intention. I think that he has sufficiently acted as heir if he swore as heir; Proculus has the same opinion, and this is the law applied.].

Neverthless, if someone does not wish to fulfill it, it shall be remitted to them, D.28.7.8 [D.28.7. *De conditionibus institutionum* (Conditions on institutions).8 **Ulpianus**, *in the fiftieth book to the Edict*: pr. Clauses in a will that require an oath are disapproved by the praetor. This is because he aims to ensure that a person who receives something under the condition of swearing an oath should neither forfeit the inheritance or legacy for failing to fulfill the condition nor be compelled to take a demeaning oath. The praetor's decision ensures that the recipient of a bequest under the condition of swearing an oath should accept it in the same manner as those without this condition, which is justifiable. This approach accommodates individuals with different attitudes toward oaths – some may readily swear, while others, out of deep religious reverence or superstition, are hesitant. The praetor's intervention ensures that neither the former exploits nor the latter loses what has been bequeathed to them. If a testator genuinely desired an act to be performed under the sanctity of an oath, they could have included this condition, allowing recipients to gain the bequest by fulfilling the requirement or failing to do so by not swearing the oath.]; D.29.1.29.2 [D.29.1.*De testamento militis* (The soldier's will).29 **Marcellus**, *Digest, book 10*: 2, see above in this theorem 38.];

145 Berger, *ad vocem Iusiurandum Calumniae*, "An oath demanded by the defendant from the plaintiff to the effect that he does not sue for mere chicanery (non calumniae *causa* agere) or by the plaintiff from the defendant that he does not deny the plaintiff's claim for a similar purpose. In Justinian's law both and their advocates had to take the iusiurandum calumniae. C.2.58.; Calumnia iurare: to swear of bringing an accusation without resorting to forgery [e. t.], Cael. in Cic. Fam., 8,8,3.".

D.35.1.20 [D.35.1. *De condicionibus et demonstrationibus et causis et modis eorum, quae in testamento scribuntur* (Conditions, designations, explanations for and modalities of provisions in wills). 20 **Julianus,** *Digest, book* 27, see above in this theorem 38.].

D.35.1.97 does not preclude [D.35.1. D.35.1. *De condicionibus et demonstrationibus et causis et modis eorum, quae in testamento scribuntur* (Conditions, designations, explanations for and modalities of provisions in wills). 97. **Paulus,** *in the second book to Neratius*: see above in theorem 15.]. I respond by affirming that nothing else is stated there than the fact that municipalities can indeed swear, and there is no doubt about their ability to do so.

Once the condition of the oath is waived, its object, namely that which someone had to swear to guarantee, is not waived, because it was the testator's intention, and the laws did not object. Therefore, the remaining question is whether the object of the oath (e.g., if Titius swears to build me a sepulcher, let him be my heir; the object of the oath is to build the sepulcher) should be understood as a condition or as a limit (*modus*). Nevertheless, the testator did not intend to burden the heir to the extent of building the sepulcher before accepting the inheritance, but through the oath, there was at least a certain obligation for the heir to build the sepulcher in due course.

Although the caution of an oath (*cautio iuratoria*[146]) has been removed by the laws, the testator's intention can still be satisfied if another personal or real guarantee is provided, which achieves the same result, according to definition 21, by transforming the object of the oath condition into a limit (*modus*), D.28.7.8.6 [D.28.7.*De conditionibus institutionum* (Conditions on institutions). 8 **Ulpianus,** *in the fiftieth book to the Edict*: see above in theorem 6.]; D.35.1.26 [D.35.1. *De condicionibus et demonstrationibus et causis et modis eorum, quae in testamento scribuntur* (Conditions, designations, explanations for and modalities of provisions in wills).26 **Julianus,** *in the eighty-*

146 Berger, *ad vocem Cautio iuratoria* "The strenghtening of an obligation by oath.".

second book of the Digests: see above in theorem 6.]; refer to theorem 15.

From this very fact, however, as the marvelous interconnection of more deeply understood things reveals, it is further inferred that although a real guarantee is to be provided for juratory caution in other cases, the necessity of swearing has nonetheless remained for slaves D.38.1.7. pr., 2 [D.38.1. *De operis libertorum* (The services of freedmen). 7 **Ulpianus**, *in the twenty-eighth book to Sabinus*: For an oath to be binding, he who swears it must be a freedman, and he must swear in return for his freedom. 2. But to be bound, he must swear after manumission; and whether he has done so immediately or after an interval, he is bound.]; D.40.4.36 [D.40.4. *De manumissis testamento* (Testamentary manumissions). 36. **Paulus**, *in the seventh book to Plautius*: I granted freedom to a slave through my will with the following provision: "If he takes an oath to provide my son Cornelius with ten days of labor, he shall be emancipated." The legal aspect of this situation is brought into question. It's important to understand that the slave satisfies the condition by swearing the oath. However, he is not obligated to fulfill the ten days of labor unless he takes the oath after being emancipated.]; D.40.7.13.3 [D.40.7.*De statuliberis* (Statuliberi). 13 **Julianus**, *in the forty-third book of Digest*: 3. A man whose freedom has been ordered, "if he has sworn to climb the Capitol," will become free as soon as he has taken the oath, although he has not climbed the Capitol.]; D.40.12.44.2 [D.40.12. *De liberali causa* (The suit for freedom).44. **Venuleius**, *in the seventh book on the Actions*: 2. A legal action based on the concept of workdays can be pursued against an individual who swore an oath before attaining puberty, as long as they were capable of swearing an oath, but this action can only be pursued after they have reached puberty. However, even before reaching puberty, the individual can provide services, such as acting as an attendant who informs their master about the names of people they encounter or working as a stage actor.]; D.46.4.13 [D.46.4.*De acceptilatione* (Formal releases). 13 **Ulpianus**, *in the fiftieth book to Sabinus*: A more accurate perspective is that the duty of providing services, which is established through an oath and placed upon a freedman, can be fulfilled by means of a formal exoneration or release.].

Because a condition or something analogous to it must be fulfilled before one becomes free (for once someone is made free, they cannot be compelled into slavery due to the irrevocability of liberty), and thus, the condition of servitude is so harsh that D.40.12.44 explicitly commands it [D.40.12. *De liberali causa* (The suit for freedom).44. **Venuleius**, *in the seventh book on the Actions*: While there used to be uncertainty regarding whether a person was obligated to their patron based on the conditions imposed during manumission, whether as a slave or upon becoming a freedman, the more accurate viewpoint is that such an obligation exists only after achieving freedom. Consequently, it is a common practice to extract an oath from slaves so that, once they become free individuals, a sense of religious obligation might prompt them to take a second oath, provided that this second oath or promise is made immediately after manumission.]. However, a slave cannot provide caution (since where there is no obligation, there is no confirmation of it through caution, and a slave has no obligation). Therefore, the only option remaining is for the slave to swear. Nevethless, it seems to us that the above-mentioned D.38.1.7.pr. and D.46.4.13 oppose us in this very matter, stating that if a slave swears, it does not create any obligation. Therefore, in order for an obligation to be contracted, it is necessary for a freedman to swear. Anyway, the matter remains intact, for I concede that the obligation arising from a slave's oath is merely natural and does not give rise to legal action. Since the testator did not demand any other caution from the slave except the bond of religion, the heir should also be satisfied with that. Moreover, the fear of perjury, entailing a lifelong infamy, and even public penalties for perjurers come into play.

And thus, we have spoken more diligently about the condition of oath, as it shares many similarities with the condition of changing religion. For example, if Titius is to be the heir upon his return to the Roman church, it is not inherently disgraceful, since anyone is permitted to embrace a belief they consider to be truer. Moreover, once a lasting religious peace has been established, with regard to political implications, the act of changing religion within the authorized denominations—formerly limited to the Pontifical and Augsburg Confessions, and now including the Reformed—is considered a neutral action, just like an oath. However, just as the ancient jurists deemed it vile to swear an oath to a person, especially when motivated by a deceitful intention to obtain money, it is much more contemptible to change one's religion for the sake of an inheritance or legacy. It is presumed that the one who made such a change, upon becoming aware of the condition imposed upon them, committed this despicable act. But you would certainly have doubts as to whether such a condition is vitiated or vitiates, that is, whether the disposition is unconditional or null.

This is indeed very similar to mercenary (*captatoriae*[147]) conditions. Indeed, there is an attempt to caught not other people's money, but their opinion or mindset, which is far more valuable than money.

A MERCENARY condition, on the other hand, is presumed to have been added with the purpose that someone may leave something in their final will, and it invalidates or renders the disposition null, D.28.5.71(70) [D.28.5. *De heredibus instituendis* (The institution of heirs). 71 (70) **Papinianus**, *in the sixth book of Replies*: The senate condemned as mercenary not those institutions which have brought about dispositions based on mutual affection, but those containing a condition aimed at violating the privacy of another person's wishes.] (for the dishonest person is indeed concerned about the inheritance of a living person, D.28.6.2.2 [D.28.6.*De vulgari et pupillari* substitutione (Normal and pupillary substitution).2 **Ulpianus**, *in the sixth book to Sabinus*: 2. Sometimes the instituted heir must be bound to accept the inheritance for the sake of the will of the impubes also, so that fideicommissum under the secundae tabulae is validated, as, say, where the pupillus has already died; but if he is still alive, Julianus thinks that someone who is concerned about the inheritance of a living man is wicked.]), D.34.8.1 [D.34.8.*De his quae*

[147] Berger, *ad vocem Captatorius*, "A disposition in a will by which the testator instituted an heir or bequeathed a legacy on the condition that the beneficiary shall grant a gift to another person in his will was called captatoria institutio (*scriptura*) or *captio*. Such a disposition was not valid.".

pro non scriptis habentur (Provisions deemed not to have been written). 1 **Julianus**, *in the seventy-eighth book of Digest*: Suppose an individual includes in their will an inheritance or legacy for themselves. The question arises as to whether this inheritance or legacy should be considered as if it was never included. Now, what happens if such an appointment is subject to a substitution? My response is as follows: "The portion of the inheritance in question should go to the substitute. When the Senate established penalties under the Lex Cornelia for those who include an inheritance or legacy for themselves, it seems to have disapproved of this practice to the same extent as appointments of the following nature: "Let Titius be my heir to the extent that he has declared in his will that he has appointed me as his heir." Consequently, both types of appointments are treated as if they were never written into the will.]; D.45.1.61 [D.45.1. *De verborum obligationibus* (Verbal obligations). 61 **Julianus**, *in the second book to Urseius Ferox*: A stipulation was formulated in the following manner: "Do you commit to giving me a certain amount if you do not designate me as your heir?" This stipulation is invalid since it goes against ethical principles.]; C.2.4.34 [C.2.4. *De transactionibus* (Concerning compromises).34. Since you state that you either by way of a gift or compromise knowingly remitted the debt due you from your brother on account of his management as guardian, and (since) no fraud is perpetrated on one acting voluntarily, you complain of fraud in vain, nor is anyone bound the promise of his own inheritance (to another), to carry out what he agreed to do.]; C.8.38.4 [C.8.38. *De inutilibus stipulationibus* (Concerning invalid stipulations). 4. It is manifest that you have no right of action on that document, because, contrary to good morals, the stipulation was entered into as to a future inheritance, since everything contained in a pact or stipulation which is contrary to good morals is void.].

All so that last wills be not forced, but be free what does not return, the faculty of free choice.

On the other hand, a condition added for the past is not mercenary, for example, "if Titius instituted me as his heir, be my heir!", D.28.5.29, 72(71), 82(81).1 [D.28.5. *De heredibus instituendis* (The institution of heirs).29 **Pomponius**, *in the fifth book to Sabinus*: see above in definition 35. 72 (71) **Paulus**, *in the fifth book on the Lex Julia and Papia*: "However, those instituting provisions are not considered as captatory, as when someone institutes an heir in this manner: 'To the extent Titius has instituted me as an heir, from that extent Maevius shall be the heir,' because the institution is transferred to the past, not the future.". 82(82).1. **Paulus**, *in the ninth book of Questions*: "If a testator has written as follows: 'To the extent that I would have been instituted as an heir by Titius, from that extent Sempronius shall be my heir,' this is not a captatory institution. Clearly, when the testament has been recited, it will appear void, having removed all suspicion of a captatory institution from the testator himself.]; D.28.7.20 [D.28.7.*De conditionibus institutionum* (Conditions on institutions). 20 **Labeo**, *in the second book of The Posthumous Works epitomized by Javolenus*: see above in theorem 16.].

The expression "he will have appointed" [*habuerit* <*scriptum*>, in the Latin text, e.n.] in the mentioned D.28.5.29 is ambiguous, capable of being interpreted both before and after, that is, for the past and for the future, but in case of doubt, it should be interpreted in the most favorable way. For this reason, reciprocal testaments are also not mercenary, as they are directed towards the present, C.6.21.11 and *Gothofredus* mentions this as well[148].

On the other hand, mercenary conditions vitiate, but they are not vitiated. I believe this because mercenaty conditions, in themselves, are not unlawful, nor are they directly contrary to the interest of the Republic.

However, they instill uneasiness in one of the parties involved and restrict their last will, as it is important for it to remain free for the tranquility of minds. This leads to the effect that the disposition is void, which is what the testator seems to desire more than an unconditional one, as the condition serves as the aim for the one

148 Denis Godefroy, note 68 above, t. II, (sub, C.6.21.*De testamento militis* (Concerning the testament of a soldier).11. c. 491, "Captatoria autem non est, quae remunerandae iam factae institutionis causa D.28.5.71, quae fit mutuatis affectionibus: ita enim forte legendum in D.28.5.70, id est placata testatoris offensa D.29.6.3 et lex ultima huius tituli (C.6.21.18) ut mutuari affectionem testatoris sit placabilibus verbis testatorem provocare ad mutandam exheredationem: ad legatum relinquendum poenitenti.". [It is not mercenary that is done to remunerate an institution that has already been created D.28.5.71, that is done out of mutual affection: therefore perhaps it will have to be read in D.28.5.70, that is, once soothed the displeasure of the testator D.29.6.3 and the last law of the same title (C.6.21.18), so that mutuari affectionem testatoris means reducing him with words of pacification to revoke the disinheritance and leave the legate to those who have repented.].

imposing it, the means for the one to whom it is directed; the conditioned on contrary, see infra theorem 46. In the remaining cases, indeed, in which the testator intended something inherently harmful to the Republic, it was deemed appropriate, as if in place of a penalty, that the condition, which nonetheless is the testator's intention, should be considered as not added.

Therefore, upon careful consideration, it appears to me that we must doubt whether the condition of having to change religion vitiates or is vitiated. And indeed, the response thus far is the latter and this seemed appropriate to the jurists, whose passages *Dr. Zieglerus, disp. de Condit., n. 75*[149], mentioned. However, since the testator is somehow being punished, despite intending good rather than evil, regardless of their religion, I would argue that the contrary opinion is more accurate, namely that the disposition is void.

Although perhaps the first opinion is more beneficial to people of our own religious group, as priests often leave something to us more frequently than we leave to them; nevertheless, in these matters, we must judge without partisan bias.

From these principles, as if from a theorem, I deduce this rule. If a grave evil (*malitas*), as I call it, according to D.4.2.5 [D.4.2. *Quod metus causa gestum erit* (Acts done under duress). 5 **Ulpianus**, *in the eleventh book to the Edict*: Labeo says that duress is to be understood not as any alarm whatever but as fear of a serious evil.], of a legally reprehensible condition or that which inherently leads to a grave evil, is intended by the settlor, the condition is vitiated, meaning it is considered as not added. Just as a penalty for the disposer, whose

[149] Kaspar Ziegler, see note 8 above in *Preface*, LXXV, "[...] Sed enim stabimus nos potius ex partibus Wittebergensium, Jenensium, Coburgensium & aliorum, qui talem conditionem pro turpi adeoque pro non scriptam habuerunt & pronunciarunt.". [But indeed, we will rather stand on the side of the parties of Wittemberg, Jena, Coburg, and others, who considered and pronounced such a condition as disgraceful and therefore as unrecorded]..

purpose is the condition, and the conditioned is the means to that bad purpose of harming the recipient of the condition (*conditionarius*).

If, on the contrary, it has not been desired by the settlor, and a serious evil has only resulted by chance, however, the same harm befalls the recipient who fulfills the said condition; there the conditioned party is vitiated, which is precisely the intention of the recipient, and consequently, the disposition. It is the same thing in fact that the condition vitiates, and the conditioned or the disposition be vitiated.

I have not included this theorem in the order and in the number of theorems, since mine, just as a hypothesis, is also only a conjecture, not founded on the laws in terms. However, it does not mislead.

Hence, indeed, the condition of celibacy and divorce does not vitiate, but rather they are vitiated. This is because widowhood, celibacy, or divorce are inherently detrimental to the Republic and are considered evils. If the settlor, such as a testator, directly intended these conditions, they are rightly regarded as penalties and deemed as not added. Regarding the condition of celibacy, or *if you do not marry*, please refer to D.35.1.22, 62.2, 63.1, 72.5, 74, 79.4 [D.35.1. *De condicionibus et demonstrationibus et causis et modis eorum, quae in testamento scribuntur* (Conditions, designations, explanations for and modalities of provisions in wills). 22 **Julianus**, *in the thirty-fifth book of Digest*: In cases where a legacy is bequeathed to a woman with the condition that she remains unmarried, and she is additionally bound by an honor obligation to transfer it to Titius if she does marry, the appropriate legal principle dictates that even if she marries, she is entitled to the legacy and is not obliged to fulfill the secondary requirement. 62 **Terentius Clemens**, *in the fourth book on Lex Julia et Papia*: 2. What is the legal stance when an individual leaves a legacy to his wife spanning several years, with the condition that she does not marry outside of their children's presence? Julianus's response was that the woman could both marry and receive the legacy. However, if the condition had been phrased as "if she does not marry away from our children under the age of puberty," the provision would not apply. In this case, the emphasis would be on the guardianship of the children rather than the widow's marital status. 63.**Gaius**, *in the third book on Lex Julia et Papia*: 1. Now, let's consider the bequest with the condition "if she marries Titius." It is undeniable that if she could marry Titius respectably, she would forfeit the legacy unless she fulfilled the condition. However, if Titius, as a husband, would disgrace her, it can be argued that the law permits her to enter into any marriage of her choice. Someone instructed to marry Titius is, in essence, prohibited from marrying anyone else. Therefore, if Titius proves unworthy, the situation is effectively the same as if the condition were stated more broadly as "if she does not marry." However, from a technical standpoint, our current condition is more restrictive than if it simply said "if she does not marry." She is not allowed to marry anyone else at all and is directed to marry Titius, even though she cannot do so honorably. 72. **Papinianus**, *in the eighteenth of Questions*: 5. Suppose the will states, "Upon my death, I bequeath the estate to Maevia, provided she remains unmarried." In this case, it could be argued that even if she gets married, she should immediately inherit the legacy. The reason for this is that the will does not specify whether a particular or an indefinite time frame is associated with the condition. 74 **Papinianus**, *in the thirty-second book of Questions*: If a usufruct is granted to a woman and Titius with the condition that the woman does not marry, and she does marry, Titius will continue to enjoy his portion of the usufruct as long as he lives and his circumstances remain the same. This is because, under the statute, it is assumed that the woman will only receive that portion of the usufruct she would have obtained had she fulfilled the condition. If Titius fails to meet the condition, it wouldn't benefit the woman if he renounced the legacy. 79 **Papinianus**, *in the first book of Definitions*: 4. There is no validity in a provision written to impede marriage, contrary to the spirit of the statute, for instance, "let the heir give one hundred to the father, Titius, if the daughter in his power does not marry" or "let the heir give to a son-in-power if his father does not take a wife."]; D.45.1.134 [D.45.1.*De verborum obligationibus* (Verbal obligations).134 **Paulus**, *in the fifteenth book of Replies*: Titia, who had a son from a previous relationship, entered into a marriage with Gaius Seius, who had a daughter of his own. During their marriage, they made an agreement that their respective children should be engaged to each other. A formal document was created, and it included a penalty clause to prevent either spouse from obstructing the proposed marriage. Subsequently, Gaius Seius passed away while still married to Titia. However, his daughter declined to go through with the marriage. The question arises: Are the heirs of Gaius Seius bound by the terms of the stipulation? In response, Paulus stated that the stipulation in question went against moral principles. Therefore, any legal action based on it could be met with the defense of fraud. It is considered inappropriate for the institution of marriage, whether existing or intended in the future, to be enforced through the use of a penalty clause.], (*If he/ she marries by the choice of Titius*, D.35.1.72.4 [D.35.1. *De condicionibus et demonstrationibus et causis et modis eorum, quae in testamento scribuntur* (Conditions, designations, explanations for and modalities of provisions in wills). 72 **Papinianus**, *in the eighteenth book of Questions*: 4. see above in definition 52.]), law 3 and the whole title of C.6.40 [C.6.40. *De indicta viduitate et de lege Iulia miscella tollenda* (Concerning enforced widowhood and repeal of the law Julia Miscella[150]; Miscellaneous Julianus law). In particular, 3. It is clear that, according to the intent of the enactment recently promulgated concerning the law Julia Miscella, not only is that law repealed as to women, but as to men as well. 1. Lest credulous men, however, continue to doubt, we expressly ordain that the law Julia Miscella and the senate decrees made concerning it, as well as the Mucianian promise introduced in connection with such marriages (contemplated by said law) shall be abolished not only as to women but also as to men. 2. But as we find certain cases mentioned in Ulpianus's Sabinian books to which the law Julia Miscella does not apply, we ordain, in order that none many think that the law applicable to these cases is also repealed, that if anything is left to women in these words: "If she shall be a widow," or "while she shall be a widow," or "as long as she shall be a widow," or if, on the contrary, anything is left to husbands thus: "If they shall lose their wives," or "whenever they become widowers" - in all such cases they may claim and legally take what is left them. For the property is not in such cases left to women to remain widows or to men to remain widowers, so that the law Julia Miscella, which is already abolished, could not even previously have had any application. But as soon as the condition happens, the bequest in favor of such persons may be claimed immediately, since such bequest - left in a lump sum or as an annuity - seems to be left upon condition, so that it might be a solace

[150] Berger, *ad vocem Lex Iulia Miscella*, "The name occurs twice in Justinian's enactments. "Miscella" is not a proper name as sometimes assumed. It is an adjective, syn. with saturus (see Leges Saturae). The specific provision referring to it (nullity of a legacy bequeathed by a husband to his wife on the condition that she remain unmarried after his death) is found in the Lex Iulia de Maritandis Ordinibus, Called 'miscella' by Justinian because of its various intermingled provisions. —C. 6.40.".

in grief.], adde *Antonium Hottomannum Rit. Nup. c. 22*[151] and *M. Vetranium Maurum tr. de iure trium Liberorum*[152].

If she marries Titius, it is valid, C.6.25.1 [C.6.25.*De institutionibus seu substitutionibus sub condicione factis* (Concerning appointments, substitutions or trusts, made upon condition).1, see above in theorem 1.]; D.35.1.91 [D.35.1. *De condicionibus et demonstrationibus et causis et modis eorum, quae in testamento scribuntur* (Conditions, designations, explanations for and modalities of provisions in wills).91 **Maecianus,** *in the second book On Fideicommissa*: see above in definition 19.].

Likewise, *in order to marry Titius* D.35.1.71.1 [D.35.1.*De condicionibus et demonstrationibus.* (Conditions, designations, explanations for and modalities of provisions in wills).71 **Papinianus,** *in the seventeenth book of Questions*: 1. A bequest of one hundred is left to Titius on the condition that he marries the widow Maevia. This condition cannot be set aside, and neither can the stipulation be voided. It's important to note that this view does not contradict the fact that if someone promises money in case there is no marriage to Maevia, the praetor would not grant an action. There's a distinction between being coerced into a marriage by the threat of a penalty and being invited to marry through a provision in a will.].

Likewise, *if she does not marry Titius,* D.35.1.64 [D.35.1. *De condicionibus et demonstrationibus et causis et modis eorum, quae in testamento scribuntur* (Conditions, designations, explanations for and modalities of provisions in wills). 64 **Terentius Clemens,** *in the fifth book on Lex Julia et Papia*: Julianus said that in this way, a bequest given with the condition "if Lucius Titius does not marry" should not be valid.].

[151] Antoine Hotman (d. 1596), *Observationum ad veterem nuptiarum ritum pertinent liber singularis* (Parisiis, 1585), p. 57, cap. XXII, De usu ac legis Miscellae interpretatione.

[152] Marcus Vetrianus Maurus, *De Jure liberorum liber singularis* (Lugduni, 1558); Berger, *ad vocem Ius liberorum,* "Parents of several children enjoyed certain privileges, first introduced by the Augustan legislation (lex Iulia et Papia Poppea). Fathers might claim exemption (excusatio) from public charges and from guardianship to which they were called by law (tutela legitima). The most important application of ius liberorum concerned women. A freeborn wroman with three children and a freedwoman with four children (ius trium vel quattuor liberorum) were freed from guardianship to which women were subject (tutela mulierum) and had a right of succession to the inheritance of their children. The women's ius liberorum was applied even when the children were no longer alive.—C. 5.66; 8.58.—See Senatusconsultum Tertullianum.".

Likewise, *when she will marry* D.35.1.10, 68 [D.35.1. *De condicionibus et demonstrationibus et causis et modis eorum, quae in testamento scribuntur* (Conditions, designations, explanations for and modalities of provisions in wills). 10 **Ulpianus**, *in the twenty-third book to Sabinus*: "To my daughter when she shall marry" is a condition that the testator will find fulfilled by the mere occurrence of marriage, without specifying a time. Therefore, if she marries during the testator's lifetime after the will is made, the condition is considered satisfied. This is especially true because it's a condition that can be met once and for all. However, not all marriages fulfill this condition. For instance, if a girl who is not of marriageable age is taken to her husband's house, it does not meet the condition. Similarly, if she is married to someone to whom she is forbidden to marry, the same applies. There is some doubt as to whether she can satisfy the condition by a subsequent marriage as if her earlier marriage did not occur. If the testator had the first marriage in mind, it can be argued that the condition has failed. However, a more lenient interpretation suggests that a condition not yet fulfilled has not failed. 68 **Javolenus**, *in the second book to Cassius*: Consider a legacy with the condition, "if she marries." If the woman is already married, and the testator is aware of this, we should anticipate a subsequent marriage. It doesn't matter whether this second marriage takes place during the testator's lifetime or after their death.].

The condition of widowhood is valid according to the laws of the Novels, with the increasing influence of the monastic way of life prevailing at that time, Nov. 22.43, 44 [Nov. 22.*De iis qui secundas nuptias contractent. (Concerning those who marry a second time)*. c.43. see above in theorem 15. c.44. We accordingly ordain that if a man forbids his wife, or a wife forbids her husband—for the same rule applies to both—to remarry and bequeath some property (to the surviving spouse) on that account, such surviving spouse may elect to remarry and renounce the bequest, or to honor the decedent, abstain from another marriage and receive the bequest. 1. In order that the matter may not be in suspense and the return of the property may not finally have to be exacted, it has seemed advisable to us to provide that the bequest should not be turned over (to the surviving spouse) within a year, unless by reason of priesthood conferred upon such surviving spouse, there remains no hope of a second marriage. 2. After the lapse of a year, the beneficiary may receive such bequest, but not unconditionally even then. If the property is immovable, he or she must give a pledge of property—one that is implied being also granted by this law—and must take an oath that he or she will, in case of a second marriage, return the property in like condition and will also return the income received therefrom in the meantime. 3.

If the bequest consists of movable property, and the beneficiary of such bequest has an abundance of other property, it shall be turned over to him or her under the same oath and pledge. Any fungible property must be returned in the condition in which it was received or the damages thereto made good. 4. In case of money, it must be returned with such interest as he was able to receive thereon, which is to be determined by the oath of the party who must return such money. If he (or she) did not let it out at interest, but used it, four per cent per annum shall be paid. 5. If the recipient of such bequest is poor, he must be asked to give a surety. If he cannot give such surety, he shall receive what was left him upon taking the oath and giving the pledge aforesaid. 6. But as soon as he remarried, the property shall be reclaimed, no matter in whose possession it may be and shall be considered as never having been bequeathed at all. This shall apply to every case of restitution, whether the property is movable or immovable. 7. If it is gold that was bequeathed, and the beneficiary has no surety and does not have sufficient property, the principal amount will be retained by the party who was to pay it (upon order of the decedent), but he must pay four per cent interest thereon to such beneficiary, and shall do so until such beneficiary enters into a second marriage—in which case restitution of income must also be made—or until it becomes clear that the latter can no longer enter into another marriage, either by a priesthood being conferred upon him—in which event the bequest will be turned over to him—or by death. In the latter case the heirs of the beneficiary will receive the bequest and will not be compelled to restore any interest. 8. The foregoing rules shall apply not only when one spouse leaves some property to the other under the above mentioned condition, but also when some one else wants to leave some property to the husband or wife upon such condition, and in such event, too, the various situation, shall, as to giving and restoring such bequests, be governed according to their nature and according to the laws relating thereto. We change the constitution already enacted by us in regard to the Miscellaneous Julian Law only this far; in all other respects they shall remain as we have enacted them. 9. The assurances (oath, pledge and surety) provided to be given by us, must be given, in case the property is left as a trust or legacy, to the heirs or their substitute or those, in a ward, by whom the property is to be delivered (to the beneficiary); in case of a gift in contemplation of death they must be given to the heirs. But if anyone is appointed as heir, upon the foregoing condition, for a whole inheritance, he must give such assurances to his substitutes, if any, or to the intestate heirs, so that the law may be perfect in every respect. If the testator, however, has provided that the party whom he appoints as heir, either for part or for all of his property, or to whom he leaves a legacy or trust or makes a gift in anticipation of death, then the wish of the decedent shall be followed; for it is our special desire to carry out the wishes of testators when not in conflict with law], see *Paganino Gaudenzi, tr. De moribus seculi Justinianei*[153].

Likewise the condicion of divorce is vitiated, C.6.25.5 [C.6.25.*De institutionibus seu substitutionibus sub condicione factis* (Concerning appointments, substitutions or trusts, made upon condition). 5. You are to be blamed, more than your mother. For she could not, if she wanted you to be her heir, order you to do something which she had no power to order, namely for you to dissolve the matrimony with your husband. 1. But you approved her wish by divorcing him. However, even though such condition were permissible to be made, marital peace should be preferred to gain. Since good morals forbid that such condition should be complied with, you could have retained your marriage in effect without prejudice to you. You may, therefore, return to your husband, knowing that you will retain the inheritance from your mother, despite such return, since, forsooth, you would have retained it even though you had not left him at all.]; C.6.46.2 [C.6.46. *De condicionibus insertis tam legatis quam fideicommissis et libertatibus* (Concerning conditions attached to legacies, trusts and manumissions). 2. See above in theorem 15.].

Furthermore, for the same reason, conditions that violate freedom are remitted.

Hence, if someone were to bequeath in the following manner: "so that he does not abandon my monument, I give as a legacy 100," the limit, the condition is considered as if not written. And the legatee receives what was assigned, D.35.1.71.2 [D.35.1. *De condicionibus et demonstrationibus et causis et modis eorum, quae in testamento* scribuntur (Conditions, designations, explanations for and modalities of provisions in wills). 71 **Papinianus**, *in the seventeenth book of Questions*: 2. An amount of one hundred is bequeathed to Titius under the condition that he does not abandon my tomb or establish his residence in a specific city. In this case, it can be argued that there is no room for an obligation that encroaches upon one's freedom. However, our approach is distinct when it comes to the freedmen of the deceased.].

153 Paganino Gaudenzi (1595–1649), *Liber de Justinianaei seculi moribus nonnullis: cum ejusdem dissertatione de successione foeminarum* (Argentorati: typis et sumptibus Friderici Spoor, 1654).

And in agreements of the same nature, such a stipulation, "if you live here and not there, and promise to give 100", is void.

And if the condition is not met, as well as he receives it here, in the same way, he retains 100 there.

Similarly, on the other hand, the condition of bearing a name is comparable to diminished freedom. Although, if the name is reputable the praetor expects the heir to bear it, he does not, however, demand it, D.36.1.7 [D.36.1.*Ad senatus consultum Trebellianum* (The senatus consultum Trebellianum).7 **Maecianus**, *in the fourth book on Fideicommissa*: However, it is important to consider the costs associated with undertaking the journey. If the institution were, for instance, "if he has given ten to Titius," he would only be obligated if the money were actually offered to him. Additionally, the person's health and social status must be taken into account. For example, what if an individual suffering from an illness were instructed to accept the inheritance in Alexandria, or to bear the name of a testator known for grave robbing?].

Instead, to those who do not wish to bear the name, he grants possession of goods and *actiones utiles*[154]. These individuals, for whom the condition is considered fulfilled through fiction and leniency alone, do not become heirs but rather possessors of goods (*bonorum possessores*[155]) according to D.36.1.65(63).10

[154] Berger, *ad vocem Actiones utiles*, "Actions introduced through the activity of praetors and jtirists by a modificadon of an already existing formula to cover legal situations and transactions for which the original formula did not soffice. The mechanism of the actiones utiles contributed considerably to the development of the law. The original action is called directa. —See Actiones directae.".

[155] Berger, *ad vocem Bonorum possessio*, "The law of succession introduced by the praetors as a system of inheritance parallel to that of the jus civile, in order to correct certain iniquities (iniquitates) in the latter. Laterally bonorum possessio means the possession of an estate given by the praetor to a person (bonorum possessor) without regard to whether or not he had the right of succession in the specific case under the civil law (jus civile). Practically the bonorum possessor had a legal position similar to that of a universal successor without being called heres, since that term is reserved to those who succeeded into the entire property of the deceased under the ius civile. An old rule says: praetor heredes facere non potest (= the praetor cannot make heredes, Gai Inst.

[D.36.1.*Ad senatus consultum Trebellianum* (The senatus consultum Trebellianum).65 (63) **Gaius**, *in the second book on Fideicommissa*: 10. If the condition is to assume a specific name, as required by the praetor, it is generally considered acceptable to comply with it, especially when the name belongs to a respectable person. The praetor typically does not require such a condition for infamous or disgraceful names. However, if the individual refuses to adopt the specified name, Julianus suggests that the condition should be waived. In such cases, useful actions may be granted, or bonorum possessio secundum tabulas may be awarded, allowing the individual to acquire these actions and subsequently transfer them in accordance with the senatus consultum.]. This is not contradicted by D.31.88.6 [D.31.*De legatis et fideicommissis* (Legacies and *fideicommissa*). 88 **Scaevola**, *in the third book of Replies*: 6, see above in theorem 27_1], D.35.1.108 [D.35.1. *De condicionibus et demonstrationibus et causis et modis eorum, quae in testamento scribuntur* (Conditions, designations, explanations for and modalities of provisions in wills). 108 **Scaevola**, *in the nineteenth book of Digest*: A man bequeathed his house to all his freedmen with the condition that they must reside in it, not abandon his name, and, in the event that only one survivor remained, that individual would inherit the house. Additionally, he expressed his desire for his freedmen to receive the Sosian estate. The question raised was whether the condition of "not abandoning my name" also applied to the subsequent legacy of the Sosian estate. The response was affirmative.].

Imposing a name on a person is one thing, while preventing it from being transferred to individuals outside the family (*exire de nomine familiae*) is another. Nevertheless, the heirs, if the name was respectable, obeyed the testator, and in any case, Augustus commanded his heirs to bear his name according to *Suetonius, in Aug. c. ult.* [156].

Z22; lust Inst. Z92), but he might give a person factual possession of the inheritance and thus create a legal situation similar to that of the civil heres. [...].".

156 Suetonius, *De XII Caesaribus libri VIII, Augustus*, "101 Heredes instituit primos: Tiberium ex parte dimidia et sextante, Liviam ex parte tertia, quos et ferre nomen suum iussit."; Engl. tr., in Donna W. Hurley (2011), *Svetonius, The Caesars*. (Indianpolis, IN: Hackett Publishing, 2011), p. 111, 101.2 Augustus named as heirs of the first-degree Tiberius for two-thirds of his estate and Livia for one third, and he ordered them to bear his name.

Similar to the conditions discussed thus far is the one that *infringes upon the jurisdiction of the magistrate.* Thus, in stipulations, if someone stipulates a penalty for something that is already prohibited by the magistrate, that the stipulation is null, D.45.1.10 [D.45.1. *De verborum obligationibus* (Verbal obligations).10 **Pomponius**, *in the third book to Sabinus*: see above in theorem 1.]. Although C.6.46.2 appears to contradict it [C.6.46.2 *De condicionibus insertis tam legatis quam fideicommissis et libertatibus* (Concerning conditions attached to legacies, trusts and manumissions.).2, See above in theorem 15.].

Also, for this reason, perhaps, the bequests made in the form of penalties were once considered reprehensible, see the whole title of C.6.41 [C.6.41. *De his quae poenae nomine in testamento vel codicillis relinquuntur* (Concerning those things which are provided in a will or testament as punishment).], D.30.43.2 [D.30.*De legatis et fideicommissis* (Legacies and *fideicommissa*). 43 **Ulpianus**, *in the twenty-first book to Sabinus*: 2. The bequest can be made dependent on the will of others but not on that of the heir.]; Fragm. Ulpiani. Tit. 25§16 [If the heir declares the inheritance to be burdensome, he is compelled by the praetor to enter into and restore it in its entirety, such that both he and the person receiving the inheritance are granted legal actions, just as if it had been restored to him according to the Trebellian senatorial decree. And this is ensured by the Pegasian senatorial decree.].

However, D.35.1.6, 27 and D.31.3.3 oppose [D.35.1. *De condicionibus insertis tam legatis quam fideicommissis et libertatibus* (Concerning conditions attached to legacies, trusts and manumissions.). 6 **Pomponius**, *in the third book to Sabinus*: see above in theorem 16. 27 **Alfenus Varus**, *in the fifth book of Digest*: see above in definition 46.]; [D.31.*De legatis et fideicommissis* (Legacies and *fideicommissa*). 3 **Paulus**, *in the fourth book to Plautius*: 3. A legacy expressed as "my heir shall be obliged to provide, unless he ascends to the Capitol" is legally valid, even if the heir has the option to ascend or not to ascend.].

Neverthless, the above-mentioned D.30.43.2, Fragm. Ulpiani. Tit. 25§16, have been changed (*mutatum*), according to C.6.41.1 [C.6.41 *De his quae poenae nomine in testamento vel codicillis relinquuntur.* (Concerning those things which are provided in a will or testament as punishment). 1. We abolish a useless observance of ancient laws which hinder the wishes of testators from becoming effectual, and direct that wishes of testators shall not be invalidated under the pretext that provisions for leaving or taking away bequests by way of penalty are invalid. But a testator may, in order that his wishes may be carried out, direct money to be given or a penalty to be inflicted on whomsoever he wishes, either by depriving them of inheritances, legacies, trusts or manumissions, or by directing the first receiver of a gift to transfer it to others, or to give some other property to others, if the heir, legatee or donee of liberty does not comply with his directions. 2. If a person so ordered, however, to do something which is forbidden by law, or is disgraceful or impossible, he may ignore the order of the testator without prejudice.].

Some here, specifically, refer to a frivolous condition that has no relevance whatsoever, for example, "if you put your right foot out of the house first". But considering that it is in the very interest of the one imposing the condition to require obedience, I don't believe the condition should be considered as not being added. It doesn't contradict the fact that the condition of throwing money into the sea is remitted, see in theorem 48 below, because not only it is useless but also harmful. This concerns to the condition inserted out of hate, which invalidates, such as the condition of death, for instance, "if Titius were to die before Sempronius, you promise to give 100" C.2.3.19, 30 [C.2.3. *De pactis* (Concerning informal agreements).19. Although among civilians a writing, which provides that he who survives shall have the property of the other, does not even appear as an effective gift in contemplation of death; still as the wished of a soldier, in respect to the last breath of life, and concerning the disposal (*decreto*) of his property, in any manner, in contemplation of death, reduced to writing, has the force of a last will and testament, and since you state that you and your brother, as you went into the danger of battle, made a mutual pact with each other, on account of the common danger from death, to the effect that the property of the person whose life should be ended by fate should belong to the survivor, if that condition has arisen, it is perceived that you receive the benefit of your brother's property, pursuant to his wish, confirmed as it is by the ready indulgence expressed in the imperial enactments. 30. We have been asked by the lawyers in Caesarea in regard to this question: Two or more persons, in hopes that an inheritance would perhaps come to them by reason of blood relationship, entered into pacts as to such hoped-for inheritance, in which it was specifically declared that if their relative should die leaving them the inheritance, certain specified things should obtain as to the inherited estate; or if perchance the benefit of the inheritance should come to only some of them, then certain pacts should be in force. It was doubted whether these pacts should be held valid.].

Even slavery is equated with death D.50.17.209 [D.50.17. *De diversis regulis iuris antiqui* (Various rules of early law). 209 **Ulpianus**, *in the fourth book on Lex Julia et Papia*: We compare slavery closely with death.]: "if Titius were to be enslaved", it would be impious to entertain such an expectation, as stated.in I.3.19.2 [I.3.19. *De inutilibus stipulationibus* (Of invalid stipulation).2. Precisely the same a principle applies where a man stipulates for the delivery of a thing which is sacred or religious, but which he thought was a subject of human ownership, or of a thing which is public, that is to say, devoted in perpetuity to the use and enjoyment of the people at large, like a forum or theatre, or of a free man whom he thought a slave, or of a thing which he is incapable of owning, or which is his own already. And the fact that a thing which is public may become private property, that a free man may become a slave, that the stipulator may become capable of owning such and such a thing, or that such and such a thing may cease to belong to him, will not avail to merely suspend the force of the stipulation in these cases, but it is void from the outset. Conversely, a stipulation which originally was perfectly good may be avoided by the thing, which is its object, acquiring any of the characters just specified through no fault of the promisor. And a stipulation, such as 'do you promise to convey Lucius Titius when he shall be a slave?' and others like it, are also void from the beginning; for objects which by their very nature cannot be owned by man cannot either in any way be made the object of an obligation.]; D.18.1.34.2 [D.18.1.*De contrahenda emptione et de pactis inter emptorem et venditorem compositis et quae res venire non possunt* (Conclusion of the contract of purchase, special terms agreed between the vendor and purchaser, and things which cannot be sold).34 **Paulus**, *in the thirty-third to the Edict*: 2. It is not permissible to intentionally purchase a free person, and transactions or agreements with a clause like "when he becomes a slave" are also prohibited. This stands, even though we have stated that it's possible to engage in transactions involving future events, as it goes against ethical principles to anticipate such a possibility.]; D.45.1.83.5 [D.45.1.*De verborum obligationibus* (Verbal obligations).83 **Paulus**, *in the seventy-second book to the Edict*: 5. A stipulation will not be legally binding if it pertains to sacred or religious items, public utilities meant to last indefinitely (e.g., a forum or basilica), or a free person. Even though sacred items can be secularized, public utilities can be converted for private use, and a free person can become a slave, stipulations involving these subjects are not valid. For example, if someone promises to deliver a secular item or a slave like Stichus, the obligation is discharged if the item becomes sacred without the promisor's involvement or if Stichus gains his freedom. The obligation won't be reinstated even if, by legal means, the sacred item becomes secular again or if Stichus, who was previously free, is reduced to slavery. The reason for both the release and the reinstatement is the possibility of delivery. If the owner disassembles a ship promised in a stipulation and then rebuilds it using the same planks, the obligation is reinstated because it is still considered the same ship. However, in the case of a freeman, the possibility of becoming a slave was not initially considered. Stipulations with a freeman, like "do you promise to deliver him when he becomes a slave," or regarding a plot of land changing from sacred to secular, are not valid because the obligation cannot be immediately fulfilled. Stipulations should only involve matters that are possible to fulfill. We don't usually wait for misfortune to occur, especially for things that can't be immediately put to use and come under our ownership. Concerning the ship, if it was dismantled with the intention of repurposing the planks for another use, then the first ship has been destroyed, and the reconstructed one is considered different. However, if the planks were all reassembled with the purpose of rebuilding the same ship, it's not regarded as destroyed, and it's still considered the same ship upon reconstruction. The question arises whether the same principle applies to praetorian stipulations where security is taken for the restoration of an object and whether the object remains the same when it is rebuilt.].

However, in modern times, the concept of a confraternity [*confraternitas*, but the term here has the meaning of a succession agreement among nobles, e.n] includes the condition of death, or a succession agreement (*pactum successorium*), as explained by *Gothofredus*[157] in the mentioned C.2.3.19 [*De pactis* (Concerning informal agreements): see above in this theorem 38.].

[157] Godefroy, note 68 above, comments on this under C.2.3.19, "An agreement made between two parties for reciprocal succession is not valid; therefore, would such a donation be valid only among soldiers? Papone, in Book 20 of the Arrests, Arrest I, states that in practice it is currently accepted in France, especially among the nobility, that one person can appoint the other as an heir in the community of all goods. Hotman, in counsel 1, writes that similar donations made mutually among the living are valid, especially for the preservation of families, or if they are made among relatives and agnates, fol. 7 and fol. 48 and following. By common opinion, the same author states that this law

Additionally, the granting of a fief belonging to a living person, known as *gratia expectativa*[158], is delimited by *Gerhardus* in *c. 1 §si quis de Feud.*[159], requiring the consent of Titius. C.2.3.19 opposes. *Baldus in d. c. 1 and H. Pistor 2 quaest. 25*[160] set different limitations: unless the thing can be transferred to the *conditionarius* through means other than succession. *Contra, Vulteius* in *1 Feud. 7 n. 48*[161]. More precisely, it can be said that the old rules have fallen into disuse, especially where the fear of deceptions is absent.

(39) Impossible is that which has an impossible circumstance.

The reason and use of its subject matter have been expounded in theorem 29, adde definition 46. From

extends to pagans due to the common custom of all nations, where a similar society (*confraternitas*) was formed and contracted in Germany in the year 1373 between the Duke of Saxony and the Landgrave of Hesse, and another at a different time between the Duke of Saxony and the Margrave of Brandenburg, and in France, such a donation was formed among the lords of Alegre, in Italy among the lords of Molza, and in brief, these agreements are considered valid everywhere, as reported by Cino, Baldo, Castrense, Saliceto on the law *Si pater 5. infr. De inofficioso.* Hippolytus, Singulari 150 and 333. Tiraquello, on the law Si unquam, num. 10. infr. De revocandis donationibus. Minsinger, Book 2. Observ. 33. I have mentioned this on the law 5 infr. De pactis conventis.".

158 A grant of benefice not yet vacant. Regarding gratia expectativa feudalis, refer to Armgardt, note 27 above in *Introduction*, 74, n. 229. As for gratia expectativa canonica, the term 'expectativa canonica' in the strict sense refers to the right granted by the Pontiff to an ecclesiastic for a determined or indeterminate benefit or charge that is currently occupied but will become available in the future. [e. t.]», Anna Ravà, *Aspettativa canonica*, in *Enciclopedia del diritto*. (Milano, 1958), III, p. 247.

159 Gerhardus Nigrus or Niger, *De feudis libri V. Quorum primus est Gerardi Nigri* […] cum notis Iac. Cujacii. (Lugduni, 1566), p. 25, § Si quis de manso.

160 Baldo degli Ubaldi (1327–1400), *Baldi Perusini, in usus feudorum commentaria* […]. (Lugduni, 1585), p. 14, § Si quis de manso; Hartmann Pistoris (d. 1603), *Quaestionum illustrium juris tum communis tum Saxonici libri IV.* Liber secundus. (Lipsiae, 1621), p. 544, Quaestio XXV, De investitura facta de feudo vassalli adhuc viventis, in casum quo is defunctus fuerit.11. Investitura de feudo viventis adhuc, etiam possessore non consentiente, concedi potest.

161 Hermann Vulteius (1555–1634), *Libri II de Feudis eorundemque Jure.* (Marpurgi, 1602), Liber I, cap. 7, p. 174, n. 48.

which the condition, whose term has expired, has not been fulfilled, D.31.11 [D.31.*De legatis et fideicommissis* (Legacies and *fideicommissa*).11 **Pomponius**, *in the seventh book From Plautius*: Labeo's view is that a statuliber cannot receive a legacy from the testator's heir without being granted his freedom, even if his freedom is in question under the terms of the will. This is because, without the grant of freedom, the slave would effectively be considered the heir's property. However, if the heir includes the same condition in the legacy as was stated in the testator's will regarding the slave's freedom, then the legacy is considered valid. Even if the slave was originally meant to be set free upon the heir's death, it is clear that the heir can rightfully leave a legacy to the slave without granting him freedom, since it would be redundant to grant him freedom under the heir's will when he already has that freedom under the testator's will. For example, if the testator's will states, "Let my heir give Stichus or Pamphilus, whichever he chooses, to Titius, provided that on the day when my will is read, he says which he wishes to give." If the heir fails to specify whether he prefers to give Pamphilus or Stichus, it is my opinion that he becomes liable as if he were instructed to give either Pamphilus or Stichus, and he must give the one that the legatee, Titius, selects. If the heir initially expresses a preference to give Stichus and Stichus passes away before the due date of the legacy, the heir is released from his obligation. However, if one of the slaves dies before the legacy matures, the heir remains obligated to provide the surviving one. Once the heir has made a choice and expressed his intention to give a particular slave, he cannot alter his decision. Julianus concurs with this interpretation.]; D.40.5.41.12 [D.40.5. *De fideicommissariis libertatibus* (Grants of freedom by *fideicommissa*).41 **Scaevola**, *in the fourth book of Replies*: 12. If they failed to complete the accounts within the timeframe indicated in the condition but later provided them, can they still achieve freedom? The response was that if their failure to meet the specified deadline was due to their own negligence, then the mere intention to submit the accounts after the designated time will not grant them their freedom.]; D.40.7.23 [D.40.7. *De statuliberis* (Statuliberi). 23 **Celsus**, *in the twenty-second book of Digest*: pr.: "If Stichus has given one hundred within a quinquennium, let him be free"; he will not give to a third party or to the heir or the purchaser after the quinquennium], adde theorem 42.

(40) What is impossible at present is perfectly possible.

D.35.1.58, 59.1, 104 [D.35.1. *De condicionibus et demonstrationibus et causis et modis eorum, quae in testamento scribuntur* (Conditions, designations, explanations for and modalities of provisions in wills).58 **Pomponius**, *in the tenth book of Miscellaneous Readings*: A legacy is given to another's slave woman, "when she marries." Proculus says that the legacy is valid because she could be manumitted and marry afterward. 59 **Ulpianus**, *in the thirteenth book on Lex Julia et Papia*: 1. What, then, if he does not die but ceases to be a citizen? Suppose a legacy to someone, "if he becomes consul," and he be deported to an island; is it to be said that the legacy is not destroyed in the interim, because he could be restored to citizenship. I think this the more acceptable view. 104 **Paulus**, *in the fourteenth book of Replies*: A person, deported after the opening of the will but then restored, can claim a fideicommissum, the condition of which is satisfied after his recovery of Roman citizenship.].

For just as he who can do, if can, already can D.50.17.174 [D.50.17. *De diversis regulis iuris antiqui* (Various rules of early law). 174 **Paulus**, *in the eighth book to Plautius*: One who can bring it about that he can satisfy a condition is regarded as already able to do so.]; likewise, that which can happen if it can, can already happen. Although its possibility is of a lower grade.

(41) *At the moment in which it is occurring, a condition still pends, i.e. it has not yet occurred.*

Because what happens, it is not yet happened, if something is, it has not yet been arg. D.1.5.15 [D.1.5. *De statu hominum* (Human status). 15 **Tryphoninus**, *in the tenth book on Disputes*: see above in theorem 16.], where those who, by the fact alone that giving birth to them the mother is set freed, they are deemed to be born of a slave, and for this they are slaves. Likewise, we are deemed alive while we are dying, D.39.6.42.1 [D.39.6. *De mortis causa donationibus et capionibus* (Gifts and acquisitions mortis causa). 42 **Papinianus**, *in the thirteenth book of Responses*: 1. see above in theorem 19.]; D.40.4.18.1 [D.40.4. *De manumissis testamento* (Testamentary manumissions).18 **Julianus**, *in the second book to Urseius Ferox*: 1, see above in theorem 19.].

(42) *A negative condition occurs at the last moment of the possibility of a contrary affirmative*

Because an affirmation and a denial can not be simultaneously true, therefore, as long as one of them is impossible, the other, e.g. the denial becomes necessary, according to the theorem 37. By the fact alone, on the other hand, while it becomes necessary, it occurs, according to definition 50. What was to be demonstrated.

On the other hand, becoming impossible its circumstance, <the condition> becomes impossible, according to the theorem 39 [30 in the text, but it is a misprint, e.n.] it is evident that for the destruction of the thing or the conditional person, the negative condition occurs, e.g. if you will have not manumitted Stichus. With the death of Stichus, his manumission becomes impossible, <but> being necessary the manumission < for the non-fulfillment of the condition>, the condition, therefore, occurs D.35.1.103 [D.35.1. *De condicionibus et demonstrationibus et causis et modis eorum, quae in testamento scribuntur* (Conditions, designations, explanations for and modalities of provisions in wills). 103 **Paulus**, *in the fourteenth book of Questions*: Consider this legacy: "Grant it to Titius after a decade, if he refrains from demanding a guarantee from the heir." If Titius passes away before the completion of the ten-year period, his legacy transfers to his own heir, as the condition is met by his death through his demise.], *adde* theorem 15.

(43) *If a condition has been fulfilled more than expected, it has been fulfilled perfectly*

Because the lesser is included in the greater, D.50.17.120 [D.50.17. *De diversis regulis iuris antiqui* (Various rules of early law).120 **Paulus**, *in the twelfth book of Edict*: No one leaves a greater benefit to his heir than he himself had.], < an excessive act > is equated to those which occur, when <condition> it is deemed as not added, D.35.1.74 [D.35.1 *De condicionibus et demonstrationibus et causis et modis eorum, quae in testamento scribuntur* (Conditions, designations, explanations for and modalities of provisions in wills). 74 **Papinianus**, *in the thirty-second book of Questions*: see above in theorem 26.], see supra theorem 27 [but it is 26, e.n.], likewise when the betrothal[162] is

[162] D.23.1. *De sponsalibus (On mariages)*1. **Florentinus**, *Institutes*: Betrothal is the announcement and mutual promise of marriage in the future.

pretended to produce legal effects through sexual intercourse X.4.1.30 [X.4.*De sponsalibus et matrimoniis* (Concerning betrothal and marriage).1.30, Sponsalia de futuro transeunt in matrimonium per carnalem copulam subsecutam, sed not per nisum carnalis copulae tantum. (Mutual promise of marriage in the future, turns into marriage, for later sexual intercourse, but not for the attempt only of the sexual intercourse.)].

Chapter VII

[Subject Matter of The Partial Propositions: Persons]

Definitions

Subject Matter follows soon after the form of the partial propositions; it contains in itself: persons, chap. 7 here, things chap. 8, and the state or event added as condition [see infra definition 71, e.n.], that is the conditioned, and the circumstances of place or time, chap. 9.

The person referred to in the conditional provision, that is, the conditional person is either

54. PRINCIPAL, such as are those among them the transaction is managed; or not quite less principal, which is called as

54[a]. THIRD. The principal person is either the conditionator or the conditional debtor (*debiturus*), who shall give the thing in condition when the condition occurs (see definition 57), or the *conditionarius*.

55. A CONDITIONATOR is the person whose conditional disposition in a declarative act of last will is valid. In last wills, the testator is the conditionator. In *inter vivos* acts, it refers to someone who promises something under a condition, such as the debtor in verbal contracts.

And since the words of a judge's sentence are considered the words of the party, the condition of the promisor is that which has been imposed on him, according to *Baldus in law 74, § 1, on Eviction.*[163].

[163] Baldo Degli Ubaldi (1327–1400), *Commentaria in primam et secundam Digesti veteris partem* (Venetiis, 1615), p. 171, sub D.21.2.74.1 ...factum iudicis reputatur factum partis... [D.21.2. *De evictionibus et duplae stipulatione* (Evictions and the stipulation for double the price) 74 **Hermogenian**, *in the second book of the Epitome of Law*: 1. If a pledge is sold by order of the judge, taken by virtue of his office, for a dispute decided

Therefore, it is evident that the one to whom something has been conditionally imposed in the sentence seems to be the conditionator. Hence, the speaker is not always the conditionator, as is evident in the case of a judge, nor is the one who makes a sale proposal always the conditionator, as the contrary is true in the case of the debtor in a stipulation. Moreover, just as the *Auctor*[164] is divided into first and second in D.21.2.4 on eviction [D.21.2. *De evictionibus et duplae stipulatione* (Evictions and the stipulation for double the price).4 **Ulpianus**, *in the thirty-second book to the Edict*: It has been asked whether one selling a slave ought to give a verbal guarantor against eviction, what might commonly be called a second guarantor of the purchaser. The tradition is that this it not indispensable, unless the parties have specifically provided otherwise.], therefore

56. CONDITIONATOR, also, is either the FIRST or the SECOND. There, with a declaration of intent, the provision, however, is valid to an extent that it assigns only a revocable right, here also a vested right (which in what they differ we will explain infra definition 77); e.g. in a conditional legate the testator is the conditionator of first degre. The heir is the second conditionator, because the testator does not yet assign a vested right, we must wait, indeed, for the acceptance of the inheritance, which if it does not follow, makes the legate ineffective.

In other cases, the first conditionator coincides with the second. In fact, in *inter vivos* acts immediately by way of promise, a vested right is assigned; in the institutions

by judgment and it is then evicted, an action for purchase will be granted against the one who was released from the payment of the price, not for what corresponds to his interest as a buyer, but only for the amount of the price and the related interest, taking into account the fruits; of course, provided there was no necessity for them to be returned to the one who evicted the thing.].

164 Berger, *ad vocem Auctor*, "[...] Auctor is also used for the predecessor in title who transfers his right on another (a seller, for instance) and through the transaction assumes the guaranty that the acquirer will not be evicted from the thing transferred.".

of heir the testament gives a revocable right, the death of the testator a vested right.

57. The conditional debtor (*debiturus*) is someone who will give the conditioned thing when the condition occurs. For example, in legacies, the testator is the one who sets the condition, but they are not the one conditionally obliged; instead, it is the heir. In the institutions of the heir, there is no conditional debtor.

In *inter vivos* acts, the conditional debtor and the one who sets the condition coincide.

58. A *CONDITIONARIUS* is someone to whom a conditioned thing is owed when the condition exists. Examples of conditionarii are the heir in institutions, the legatee in legacies, and the stipulator in verbal contracts.

59. PENDING is the term used for a right whose *conditionarius* is disjunctive; that is, when a right belongs to two individuals, and each of them is subject to a condition that is contrary to the condition of the other. Therefore, the ownership (*dominium*) of the disputed thing is suspended, with each litigant being subject to the condition of victory, while the outcome of only one remains uncertain so far.

Similarly, the ownership of a bequeathed thing is also suspended while a condition is pending, D.36.3.5 [D.36.3. *Ut legatorum seu fideicommissorum servandorum causa caveatur* (That a *cautio* be given for the security of legacies or *fideicommissa*). 5 **Papinianus**, *in the twenty-eighth book of Questions*: The heir was taken captive by the enemy, and later the condition of a legacy, which had been established through the edictal stipulation, was met. I maintained that the oral guarantors were not responsible during this interval since there was neither a valid claim nor an individual to whom the stipulation's terms could be applied.]. As for paternal authority I.1.12.5 [I.1.12. *Quibus modis ius potestatis solvitur* (Of the modes in which paternal power is extinguished).5. Again, capture of the father by the enemy makes him a slave of the latter; but the status of his children is suspended by his right of subsequent restoration by postliminium; for on escape from captivity a man recovers all his former rights, and among them the right of paternal power over his children, the law of postliminium resting on a fiction that the captive has never been absent from the state. But if he dies in captivity the son is reckoned to have been independent from the moment of his father's capture. So too, if a son or a grandson is captured by the enemy, the power of his ascendant is provisionally suspended, though he may again be subjected to it by postliminium. This term is derived from limen and post, which explains why we say that a person who has been captured by the enemy and has come back into our territories has returned by postliminium: for just as the threshold forms the boundary of a house, so the ancients represented the boundaries of the empire as a threshold; and this is also the origin of the term limes, signifying a kind of end and limit. Thus, postliminium means that the captive returns by the same threshold at which he was lost. A captive who is recovered after a victory over the enemy is deemed to have returned by postliminium.].

60. CONDITIONAL TRANSMISSIBLE RIGHT is one that has been arranged in such a way that it is owed to the heirs of the *conditionarius,* as well as against the heirs of the conditional debtor. This means that not only the conditional debtor and the *conditionarius* are clearly defined, but also their heirs.

61. The third person mentioned in the conditional disposition mostly pertains not to the conditioned thing, but to the condition itself. And this person can be either active, passive, or neutral, but only as a circumstance. In an active sense, there are cases where a person is matched in such a way that if they do not desire it, the condition does not occur D.20.4.9.1 [D.20.4. *Qui potiores in pignore vel hypotheca habeantur et de his qui in priorum creditorum locum succedunt* (Priority in pignus or hypotheca and displacing an earlier creditor).9. **Africanus,** *in the eighth book of Questions*: 1. He also took the view that a conditional creditor should be protected against one to whom a debt was later incurred, unless the condition was one which could only be fulfilled with the debtor's consent.]. For example, if Titius were to go to Alexandria. In other cases, the condition occurs when the person desires it, and it is said to fall within their power (61[a]). For example, if Titius were not to ascend the Capitolium. And this third person can be either God alone, in which case it is called a

62. CASUAL CONDITION. For example, if the sky will be clear tomorrow, something that pagans attribute to chance but we rightfully attribute to God. Or it can be a person, and then we say

63. EXPOSED (*exposita*) [DEPENDENT ON THE HUMAN WILL] (that is, not excluded from the human capacity to condition events).

64. POTESTATIVE (otherwise known as the common, D.35.1.11.1 [D.35.1. *De condicionibus et demonstrationibus et causis et modis eorum, quae in testamento scribuntur* (Conditions, designations, explanations for and modalities of provisions in wills).11. **Paulus,** *in the fourth book to Sabinus*: see above in theorem 1.]) if the man in whose power it falls is himself a *Conditionarius*. The famous division of the condition into casual, potestative, and mixed is generally understood so that the term "potestative" is considered equivalent: it includes both what is exposed and what falls into the power of a third party, or even the debtor himself (arg. from the above-mentioned D.20.4.9.1).

However, not only the Doctors very often, but also the law 7 in C. 6.51, [C. 6.51.7 *De caducis tollendis* (Concerning abolishing lapses (escheats), see above in theorem 14.] in which the foundation of this division is found, and D.35.1.78.1 [D.35.1.*De condicionibus et demonstrationibus et causis et modis eorum, quae in testamento scribuntur* (Conditions, designations, explanations for and modalities of provisions in wills). 78 **Papinan,** *in the ninth book of Replies*: 1. see above in theorem 22.], restrict the potestative to what falls within the power of the recipient [who is about to acquire the right e.n.], i.e., the *conditionarius*, according to our terminology.

But since a condition can be granted to a person or to chance, and the former can be granted to a third party, or to the debtor, or to the recipient (D.28.5.23.2 [D.28.5. *De heredibus instituendis* (The institution of heirs). 23 **Pomponius,** *in the forst book to Sabinus*: 2. Furthermore, if the heir is incapable of fulfilling a condition that is beyond his control, such as one dependent on the actions of another person or an external event, e.g., "if a certain individual becomes consul," then, at the request of the creditors, the praetor will stipulate that unless the inheritance has become available to the heir within a specified period and has been assumed by him, the creditors will be permitted to take possession of the deceased's assets. In the interim, the praetor will allow any urgent matters to be managed through agents and authorize the sale of such assets.]; D.35.1.60.pr [D.35.1. *De condicionibus et demonstrationibus et causis et modis eorum, quae in testamento scribuntur* (Conditions, designations, explanations for and modalities of provisions in wills).60 **Paulus**, *in the seventh book on Lex Julia et Papia*: pr. Conditions based on factual events can be classified into three categories: those that involve something being given, done, or occurring, and their opposites, which entail something not being given, done, or happening. Among these, conditions related to giving and doing are concerned with the individuals who receive something or with others.]), when the term "potestative" is used more accurately, that famous subdivision will be narrower than what was originally divided, and therefore we have added the term "exposed".

Nevertheless, it is inevitable that the ancient writers have sometimes referred to what depends on vicarious as potestative condition, as when the Doctors say that potestative is not withdrawn (arg. from the D. 20.4.11.1 [D.20.4.*Qui potiores in pignore vel hypotheca habeantur et de his qui in priorum creditorum locum succedunt* (Priority in pignus or hypotheca and displacing an earlier creditor).11 **Gaius**, *in the sole book on Action on Mortgage*: 1. Would our stance be identical if a mortgage is provided as security for a conditional stipulation, and while the condition remains undetermined, another creditor offers an unconditional loan using the same collateral? If the condition is subsequently met, should the second creditor be prioritized? I have reservations about this. When the condition is satisfied, the initial commitment is regarded as if it had been made without any conditions. This appears to be the more sound resolution.]), where, however, it depends on the debtor, or sometimes as a casual condition (D.28.5.23.2, arg. 30 [D.28.5. *De heredibus instituendis* (The institution of heirs).23 **Pomponius**, *in the forst book to Sabinus*: 2, see above in definition 64; 30. **Ulpianus**, in the twenty-first book to the *Edict*: The Emperor Severus stated in a rescript that a slave subject to a pledge could be appointed *necessarius heres* to his master, but on condition that he first is prepared to satisfy the creditor.]; C.6.51.7 [C.6.51.*De caducis tollendis* (Concerning abolishing lapses (escheats).7: see above in theorem 14.] and C.6.27.6 [C.6.27.*De necessariis et servis heredibus instituendis vel substituendis.* (Concerning the appointment and substitution of slaves, as compulsory heirs). 6, see above in theorem 3.]).

Whether a condition is potestative depends, on the other hand, on the fact, D.28.5.4.1 [D.28.5. *De heredibus instituendis* (The institution of heirs).4 **Ulpianus**, *in the fourth book to Sabinus*: 1. I believe it's appropriate to assert the following general principle: Whether the condition was within the person's control or not is essentially a factual matter. Even a condition like "if he has reached Alexandria" could be one that's beyond his control due to adverse weather conditions, or it could be within his control if it's imposed on someone operating only a mile from Alexandria. Similarly, a condition such as "if he has given ten to Titius" could lead to complexities if Titius is away on an extended journey. Therefore, it's advisable to consider this as a case-specific question and rely on the general principle.] and on the will of the testator, D.35.1.4 [D.35.1. *De condicionibus et demonstrationibus et causis et modis eorum, quae in testamento scribuntur* (Conditions, designations, explanations for and modalities of provisions in wills). 4 **Pomponius**, *in the third book to Sabinus*: If a legacy be made to those to whom a patron owes legacies, the praetor must ensure that the condition is obeyed so that proportionate advances are made to both the patron and the instituted heirs for the purpose of honoring the condition.].

That condition: "if he will prove he is my son" is not a potestative condition, D.35.1.83 [D.35.1. *De condicionibus et demonstrationibus et causis et modis eorum, quae in testamento scribuntur* (Conditions, designations, explanations for and modalities of provisions in wills).83 **Paulus**, *in the twelfth book of Replies*: Lucius Titius made the following will: "If Aurelius Claudius, born of such-and-such woman, establish before a judge that he is my son, let him be my heir." Paulus's opinion was that the supposititious son was instituted under a condition beyond his own power to realize and thus that the will was of no effect.].

The mixed condition was omitted for this reason, as it is always either purely casual or purely exposed in reality, which even *Angelo de Gambiglioni, tr. de testam. gloss. 58 n. 12*[165], admitted.

[165] Angelo de Gambiglioni (d. 1465), *Tractatus Ang. De Gambillionis de Aretio in materia testamentorum.* (Papie,1512) fol. 30, Glo. Item reliquit... decem (58), "[...] Notandum est quod triplex est genus conditionis, una potestativa; alia cusalis, alia mixta. Et ista ultima est duplex, alia pendente a voluntate mea: et a viribus fortunae: ut l. si pater Co. Inst et

65. The MIXED, indeed, is CASUAL, mostly occurring when the exposed event is left to chance. For example, "if you go to Alexandria", here, if the winds will allow you to achieve the desired outcome while sailing, it is left to chance, C.6.25.4 [C.6.25. *De institutionibus vel substitutionibus seu restitutionibus sub condicione factis* (Concerning appointments, substitutions or trusts, made upon condition).4. If a father appointed his son, whom he had in his power, as heir upon a condition, the fulfillment of which was not in the power of the son, nor disinherited him in case of default (in said condition), his testament does no seem to be valid. Since, moreover, you say that you were appointed heir, while you were across the sea and lived far away, made you his heir on condition that you should have returned to your fatherland, which was in the province of Mauritania, and you also say that your were not disinherited in case you should not return, it is manifest that non-fulfillment of the condition might have been brought about through many circumstances, not voluntary on your part, but so that you could not fulfilled it fortuitous; and you are nor, therefore, forbidden to enter on the inheritance.].

66. MIXED EXPOSED is that which, if the casual event will occur, is within human control. For example, if you give 10, I imagine that you have 100 ready. Therefore, to fulfill the condition, both paying and avoiding the uncertainties of fate are within your power. However, if you postpone it, it can happen that you, by some chance, are robbed of resources, in vain trying to grasp the adversity of a hostile fortune.

67. HONORED (*honoratus*) is the third party to whom, by the power of the disposition, it is of interest that the condition occurs. For example, "if you give 100 to Titius, let him be the heir!", I refer to Titius as the honored party for the sake of distinction. Otherwise, the term 'honored' is attributed to the same *conditionarius* in C.6.51.7 [C. 6.51. *De caducis tollendis* (Concerning abolishing lapses (escheats)).7: see above in theorem 14.].

subst. sub cond. facti.". [It should be noted that there are three types of conditions: one is potestative, another is casual, and another is mixed. The latter is twofold, some dependent on my will and others on the forces of fate, as in C. 6.25.4.].

In testamentary laws, they are defined as those which fall under mortis causa, as seen in the entire title D.39.6. *Gifts and acquisitions mortis causa*. Additionally, refer to D.35.2.30.7, 67.pr., 91, where it is stated that what was given to the heir for the fulfillment of a condition is not imputed to him according to the Falcidian law[166], but to

[166] Berger, *ad vocem Lex Falcidia*, "Lex Falcidia. (40 B.C.) Provided that legacies (legata) should not exceed three quarters of the testator's estate. A minimum of a fourth part (quarta Falcidia. Falcidia) was reserved to the heir appointed in the testament. In the case of several heirs each ot them had to receive at least one fourth of the share assigned to him. The part of the legacy exceeding three-quarters was void; an heir sued by the legatee for the surplus could oppose the exceptio legis Falcidiae. The value of the estate at the time of the testator's death was decisive. Later changes did not count. The tendency of the law was to prevent the refusal of an inheritance, charged with exorbitant legacies, by the testamentary heir. Imperial legislation introduced substancial reforms. Antoninns Pius extended the quarta Falcidia to intestate inheritance if the owner disposed in a codicil over more than three-fourths of the estate by fideicommissa. The application of the law was in some exceptional cases excluded, as with regard to a soldier's testament or to legacies in favor of piae causae (for charitable purposes). —Inst. 2.22; D. 35.2; C 6.50.". D. 35.2. *Ad legem Falcidiam (The lex Falcidia)*. 30 **Maecianus**, *in the eighth book on Fideicommissa*: 7. While it is true that assets provided to the heir for the purpose of fulfilling a condition are not considered under the Lex Falcidia, nonetheless, Celsus and Julian found it appropriate to include anything that a person is obligated to take from the person to whom they are instructed to convey the estate. This obligation should be accounted for. Consider a scenario where an heir is instructed to sell certain items at a specified price. Here, there is no explicit condition for fulfillment, but rather, a fixed price for the items is introduced. In this context, a question has been raised: should the fideicommissary be compelled, even against their wishes, to pay the amount and accept the inheritance, as if this obligation were in line with their honor? This seems unlikely since the formulation appears to be intended for their benefit rather than to their detriment. 67 **Terentius Clemens**, *in the fourth book on Lex Julia et Papia*: pr. In cases where an individual is bequeathed more than what they are legally entitled to, and the lex Falcidia becomes applicable, the initial step is to calculate the Falcidian deduction. This calculation is done to determine what portion is due to the recipient, but only if it does not surpass the legal limits. [Armgardt, see note 27 in *Introduction*, 79, n. 245, H. Schepers corrects in 76 pr.: **Gaius**, *in the third book Praetor's Edict, Legacies, book* 3: Items provided by a co-heir, legatee, or statuliber to fulfill a condition are not subject to the lex Falcidia, as they are received due to the event of death. However, if an heir receives coins from a freedman's peculium, these coins are attributed to his share since he acquires them not due to the death but based on his role as an heir.] 91 **Marcian**, *in the thirteenth book of Institutes*: The quarter of the inheritance allotted to the heir according to the lex Falcidia includes what he acquires in his role as the heir itself and excludes items received as legacy, fideicommissum, or for fulfilling conditions, as these do not factor into his share. In

the Trebellian senatusconsultum[167].

Ultimately, the condition based on individuals is either transferable (*ambulatoria*), i.e., its fulfillment is not linked to a specific person, as stated in D.40.7.34. pr. [D.40.7.*De statuliberis* (Statuliberi). 34 **Papinianus**, *in the twenty-first book of Questions*: pr. If a condition for a slave's freedom was set as giving ten to the heir, and the heir subsequently emancipated the statuliber, and then the heir passed away, the heir of the heir is not entitled to receive the payment. This is because the rule stipulating payment to the heir of the heir is applicable only when the previous heir would have received the payment as the owner. In this particular case, we have what we might term a "transferable condition." Essentially, there are two grounds for fulfilling the condition concerning the original heir in their capacity as the heir; one is their status as the owner, and the other as the designated beneficiary. The former title transfers to every successive owner to whom the slave is transferred in an unbroken line, while the latter title pertains solely to the person designated as the beneficiary.], or linked to a specific person (*cohaerens personae*), as stated in D.34.4.24 [D.34.4.*De adimendis vel transferendis legatis vel fideicommissis* (The ademption of legacies and *fideicommissa*).24 **Papinianus**, *in the eighth book of Replies*: see above in theorem 12.], meaning that it may or may not exist when individuals are replaced. See our theorem in this regard.

cases where an inheritance is transferred under a fideicommissum, any legacies will be attributed to the heir's share. However, if the heir is directed to transfer the inheritance in exchange for a sum of money, that amount will be considered part of his share, as ruled by the deified Pius. Yet, anything received by the heir from legatees to fulfill conditions will not be considered in the Falcidian calculation. For example, if the deceased left land valued at one hundred, and a legatee gives the heir fifty, the computation will consider it as a legacy of one hundred, with the fifty lying outside the inheritance and not affecting the heir's share.

[167] Berger, *ad vocem Senatusconsultum Trebellianum*, "(A.D. 56.) Ordered that 'if an inheritance was delivered over to anyone on account of a fideicommissum, the actions which would lie at ius civile for, or against, the heir, should also be given in favor of, or against, him to whom the inheritance has been made over.'. (Gaius, Inst. 2.2.53). The pertinent actions were proposed in the praetorian edict as actiones utiles. — D. 36.1; C. 6.49.".

Theorems

(44) *For the conditionator, it is required that the conditioned thing be within their power.*

Indeed, everything that falls under a disposition must exist in the realm of nature, D.50.17.135 [D.50.17. *De diversis regulis iuris antiqui* (Various rules of early law). 135 **Ulpianus**, *in the twenty-third book on Edict*: Things which are impossible to give or which are not in the nature of things are regarded as not added <to a property>.], and in commerce, D.18.1.34.2 [D.18.1.*De contrahenda emptione et de pactis inter emptorem et venditorem compositis et quae res venire non possunt* (Conclusion of the contract of purchase, special terms agreed between the vendor and purchaser, and things which cannot be sold).34 **Paulus**, *in the thirty-third to the Edict*: 2, see above in theorem 39.]; D.45.1.83.5 [D.45.1.*De verborum obligationibus* (Verbal obligationts). 83 **Paulus**, *in the seventy-second book to the Edict*: 5.see above in theorem 39.].

So that if it is not already mine, at least it can potentially come under my control. In such a case, based on the same expectation, I am allowed to make arrangements regarding something that is not yet mine. (However, having the expectation of acquiring a sacred thing or a free person is dishonest, as in above-mentioned law).

Therefore, one can promise someone else's property, but only under a condition, D.20.4.7.1 [D.20.4. *Qui potiores in pignore vel hypotheca habeantur et de his qui in priorum creditorum locum* succedunt (Priority in pignus or hypotheca and displacing an earlier creditor).7 **Ulpianus**, *in the third book of Disputations*: 1. I mortgage in your favor my future assets and also specially mortgage certain land, should it become mine, in favor of Titius. I then acquire the land. Marcellus thinks that both creditors have concurrent mortgages. It makes little difference that the debtor paid with his own money, since property purchased with money subject to a mortgage is not for that reason alone subject to the mortgage.].

Additionally, one can bequeath or promise someone else's property under a condition, since its ownership may cease to belong to them, D.18.1.61 [D.18.1 *De contrahenda emptione et de pactis inter emptorem et venditorem compositis et quae res venire non possunt* (Conclusion of the contract of purchase, special terms agreed between the vendor and purchaser, and things which cannot be sold).61 **Marcellus**, *in the twentieth book of Digest*: I think that it is possible for me to make a conditional purchase of my own thing, since there may be an expectation that it will cease to be mine.]; D.31.41.2 [D.31.*De legatis et* fideicommissis (Legacies and *fideicommissa*).41 **Javolenus**, *in the seventh book of Letters*: 1 [§ 2 does not exist, e.n.] 1. I have been charged with a legacy in my capacity as the heir, and it pertains to my wife with the following condition: "Whatever has been received by Seius on behalf of Titia as her dowry, let my heir Seius give an equivalent amount to Titia." I inquired whether expenses could be deducted, similar to how they might be allowed in a dowry claim. He replied: I have no doubt that when a legacy is granted to a wife in the form of "I request my heir to provide her with whatever has come into your possession," the entire dowry, without considering expense deductions, is owed to the woman. However, this same principle cannot be applied to a case where the will is from someone other than a husband who has dedicated a dowry to his wife. In the latter instance, "whatever has come into your possession" effectively stands in for an appraisal. But in the former scenario, when a husband dedicates a dowry to his wife, it is understood that he bequeaths as much as the wife would have the right to claim in a dowry lawsuit.]; D.45.1.31, 98 [D.45.1. *De verborum obligationibus* (Verbal obligations). 31. **Pomponius**, *in the twenty-fourth book to Sabinus*: If I stipulate my own property conditionally, the stipulation is valid if the property is not mine at the time when the condition comes into force. 98. **Marcellus**, *in the twentieth book of Digest*: I believe I can make a conditional stipulation regarding something that belongs to me. For instance, I can stipulate for a right of way over a property, even if I don't own the property at the time of the stipulation. If this weren't the case and I made a conditional stipulation for someone else's property and then acquired it without cost, the stipulation would immediately become void. The same would happen if the owner stipulated conditionally for a right of way, and the land was subsequently sold; the stipulation would lose its effect right away. This is the view of those who believe that even when they have a legitimate claim, it becomes invalid when they no longer have the right to sue.].

(45) For the conditionarius, it is required that they have the legal capacity to acquire the thing under condition.

At least when a vested right arises from it, it does not matter that they were not capable at the time of making the will, as long as they become capable afterward,

D.28.5.60(59).4 [D.28.5. *De heredibus instituendis* (The institution of heirs). 60 (59) **Celsus,** *in the sixteenth book of Digest*: 4. If the instituted heir was a Roman citizen at the time of writing the will, then was interdicted from fire and water, he becomes heir, if he has returned before the time of the testator's death or, if he was instituted heir under a condition, at the time when the condition is fulfilled. The same rule also in legacies and in bonorum possessiones.]; D.35.1.59, 104 [D.35.1. *De condicionibus et demonstrationibus et causis et modis eorum, quae in testamento scribuntur* (Conditions, designations, explanations for and modalities of provisions in wills). 59 **Ulpianus,** *in the thirteenth book on Lex Julia et Papia*: A legacy fails if the person to whom it was left under a condition dies. 104. **Paulus,** *in the fourteenth book of Questions*: A person, deported after the opening of the will but then restored, can claim a fideicommissum, the condition of which is satisfied after his recovery of Roman citizenship.].

The Catonian rule[168] does not apply to conditional cases, D.34.7.4 [D.34.7. *De regula Catoniana* (The Catonian rule).4 **Ulpianus,** *in the tenth book to Sabinus*: It is agreed that the Catonian Rule does not apply to conditional appointment of heirs.].

(46) The condition of the conditionator and the debtor is an additional condition included for the benefit of the conditionarius.

This important theorem emerged as a necessity in theorem 38, where we established the foundation for distinguishing whether a reprehensible condition vitiates or is vitiated. If it were to vitiate, the *conditionarius* would be punished, and if it were to be vitiated, the conditionator would be punished. Thus, we clearly observed from whose side the transgression occurred and concluded that punishment should be imposed accordingly. On the other hand, it is evident that the conditioned thing is beneficial to the *conditionarius,* while the condition itself is detrimental to them. The same condition, however, benefits the debtor, as it allows for

[168] Berger, *ad vocem Regula Catoniana,* "(Also sententia Catoniana.) A rule concerning legacies. "A legacy which would have been void if the testator died at the time of making the testament, is invalid whenever he shall have died" (D. 34.7.1 pr.). This rule, whose author was one of the two Catones (see Cato), was in later classical law not fully valid.".

the delay of payment until the condition is fulfilled. In cases where the conditionator and the debtor coincide, except in the case of last wills, the same can be said about the conditionator. In last wills, the potestative condition, which is under the power of the *conditionarius,* serves as the goal for both the conditionator and the testator. It serves as a means for the *conditionarius* to achieve the conditioned outcome. Conversely, as mentioned earlier, the conditioned thing is the purpose for the *conditionarius* and, indeed, the means for the testator to attract the *conditionarius* towards fulfilling the condition, adde *Vultej. in Consil. Marp. T. 1 p. 124*[169]

Therefore, the testator must ensure that the fulfillment of the condition benefits the *conditionarius* more than it harms them. Indeed, who would not find amusement in a disposition such as "if you have successfully returned my son captured by Algirians, receive 10 florins," when accomplishing this with only 10 florins is impossible! Or another example, "if you have given 100, receive 100!", D.35.2.65 [D.35.2.*Ad legem Falcidiam* (The lex Falcidia). 65 **Paulus**, *in the sixth book on Lex Julia et Papia*: Let's consider a scenario in which land valued at fifty is bequeathed with the condition that the legatee must give fifty to the heir. Many believe that this legacy is valid because the act of giving fulfills the condition, and the Lex Falcidia applies in this case. However, if the legacy is simply fifty gold pieces, and the legatee is required to give fifty, then it can be argued that the legacy serves no purpose and seems ridiculous.], which is considered derisory, D.28.7.14 [D.28.7. *De conditionibus institutionum* (Conditions on institutions). 14. **Marcianus**, *in the fourth book of Institutes*: see above in theorem 38.], as stated in theorem 63.

[169] Hermann Vulteius (1555–1634), *Consiliorum sive responsorum doctorum et professorum facultatis juridicae in academia Marpurgi* (Marpurgi Cattorum, 1606), T. 1, p. 124, C. XV, "284Conditio etiam et causa finalis in idem recidere censentur Tiraquellus etc. […]. 285 Causa vero eiusmodi, ut ampliat, ita etiam restringit et coartat obligationem […]. 286 ideoque hic locum habet, quod cessante causa cessat effectus.". [284. The condition and the final cause are also believed to coincide in the same thing, Tiraquellus, etc. [...]. 285. But such a cause, such as it expands, at same time restricts and reduces the obligation [...]. 286 Therefore, here it takes place that if the cause ceases, also the effect ceases].

These examples are reminiscent of testamentary tables of unknown origin: "let my mother be the heir," "I give and bequeath my daughter to Charidem, entrusting her with a generous dowry," or "I give my mother to Nicostratus for her care and sustenance." However, these dispositions have been carried out, as can be seen.

Our theorem also has another application: it infers from disjunctive conditions that the choice belongs to the *conditionarius*, and from disjunctive conditioned things that the choice belongs to the debtor. This is because anyone burdened with an option presented in a disjunctive manner should have the choice. The other party can only demand one uncertain option. See theorem 22 for further details. The theorem also applies to theorem 20.

(47) *The conditionator under suspensive condition is a conditionarius under resolutive condition and vice versa.*

That is, the one who owes a thing to another under a suspensive condition, meanwhile owns the thing under a resolutive condition, compare the definitions 21, 22, 23.

A notable example exists in the case of an heir, insofar as he possesses a thing bequeathed under a condition. While the condition is pending, the legatee appears to be the conditional owner because, according to Emperor Justinian's decree, once the distinction among legatees is abolished, ownership directly passes to the legatee. Both personal and real actions are available to the legatee. The mere existence of the condition alone cannot confer ownership. However, in the meantime, the heir is also the owner, D.10.2.12 [D.10.2. *Familiae erciscundae* (The action for dividing an inheritance). 12 **Ulpianus**, *in the nineteenth to the Edict*: 2. Any property left as conditional legacy is considered part of the inheritance and, therefore, belongs to the heirs until the condition is satisfied. It is included in the inheritance division process and can be adjudicated along with any related items. If the condition is fulfilled, the property is taken from the person to whom it was assigned. If the condition is not met, it reverts to the heirs who were originally charged with it. This same principle applies to a statuliber who, in the interim, remains the property of the heirs but gains his freedom once the condition is fulfilled.]; D.7.6.4 [D.7.6. *Si usus fructus petetur vel ad alium pertinere negetur* (The actions for claiming a usufruct or denying that another has a right to one). 4 **Julianus**, *in the thirty-fifth book of Digest*: An estate was left as a legacy to Titius under reservation of the usufruct, and the usufruct of the same estate was left to Sempronius, subject to a condition. I said that in the interim the usufruct was at one with the bare property, even although the general rule is that when an estate is left as a legacy under reservation of the usufruct, the usufruct remains with the heir. The reasoning behind my opinion is that when an owner leaves an estate as a legacy under reservation of the usufruct and leaves the usufruct to another by way of a legacy subject to a condition, it is not his intention that the usufruct should remain with the heir.]; D.29.5.1.4 [D.29.5.*De senatus consulto Silaniano*[170] *et Claudiano*[171]*: quorum testamenta ne aperiantur* (The senatus consultum Silanianum and the senatus consultum Claudianum; those whose wills may not be opened). 1 **Ulpianus**, *in the fiftieth book to the Edict*: 4. The term "slaves" includes individuals who have been left by legacy under certain conditions. During the interim period, these slaves are considered part of the heir's property. Even when the condition is eventually fulfilled and they are no longer part of the heir's property, during the interim, they are still viewed as such. This same principle applies to statuliber, who follow a similar pattern.].

Otherwise, the failure of the condition would constitute a means of acquiring ownership for the heir. Meanwhile, the legatee is the owner under a suspensive condition, and the heir is subject to a resolutive condition

[170] Berger, *ad vocem Senatusconsultum Silanianum,* "(AD. 10.) When a master of slaves was assassinated and the murderer could not be found, all slaves who lived widi him "under the same roof" were subjected to torture and eventually condemned to death. A slave who revealed the murderer was declared free by die praetor's decree.".

[171] Berger, *ad vocem Senatusconsultum Claudianum,* "3. (AD. 52.) Contained among other things the provision that a free woman living in a conjugal union with a slave (contubernium) became a slave (and her children as well) if after three warnings by the slave's master she continued her relation with the slave. She was then attributed to the slave's master as his slave. Later legislation gradually modified the penalties of this senatusconsultum. There were still some other senatusconsulta in the times of Claudius. —Inst. 3.12 ;D. 29.5: C. 7.24; 9.11.".

Therefore, there are not two owners of the same thing; rather, there are distinct kinds and degrees of ownership. This can be understood as follows: when a person has passed away, similarly, when there is an estate at hand, all individuals who come together to share in the deceased's goods should be regarded as a single person. And since the institution of an heir is the primary element of a will, the heir, participating in universal succession, holds the principal position, while the others, participating in singular succession, hold subordinate positions.

Consequently, the legatee is considered to approach the heir and obtain the ownership assigned to them. Just as the usufructuary and the owner are assumed to have a shared possession of an item, D.7.1.25.4 [D.7.1. *De usu fructu et quemadmodum quis utatur fruatur* (Usufruct and the way in which a man may exercise it). 25 **Ulpianus**, *in the eighteenth book to Sabinus*: 4. If a slave held in usufruct enters into a stipulation to transfer the usufruct, whether without specifying a particular person or explicitly on behalf of the owner, the acquisition benefits the owner. This situation is similar to when a slave is co-owned by two individuals, and if that slave stipulates on behalf of one owner for something that the owner already possesses, the stipulation is invalid because a person cannot stipulate for something that is already their property. However, if the slave stipulates for the same thing on behalf of the other owner, the acquisition benefits the latter entirely.], similarly, once the inheritance has been accepted, both the legatee and the heir can be seen as distinct individuals. While the condition is in effect, the legatee has the right to request a division and assert their own claim, as stated in Theorem 56, at the end.

However, during the pendency of the condition, since the prohibition specified by the condition takes precedence over common ownership, the heir is reminded by Justinian's legislation, in C.6.43.3.2 [C.6.43. *Communia de legatis et fideicommissis et de in rem missione tollenda* (Common rules concerning legacies and trusts and concerning abolishing the granting of the right to enter on an inheritance).3.2. And while our majesty has heretofore in many cases looked after the interests of legatees and beneficiaries of a trust, as we have given them the right to a personal action, an action in rem (*vindicatio*) and a hypothecary action and have abandoned the dark error of putting in possession of property (*missio in rem*), we now come to the present law.], not to alienate the property.

If the heir does so, the validity of the sale remains pending. Since the termination of the giver's right dissolves the receiver's right, as stated in D.20.6.3 [D.20.6.*Quibus modis pignus vel hypotheca solvitur* (Ending a pignus or hypotheca).3 **Ulpianus**, *in the eighth book of Legal Disputes*: see above in definition 21.], any onerous acts of the heir that prejudice the legatee, such as alienation, pledging, or imposition of servitude are nullified D.7.4.16 [D.7.4.*Quibus modis usus fructus vel usus amittitur* (The ways in which a usufruct or a right of use is lost).16 **Ulpianus**, *in the fifith book of Legal Disputes*: If a usufruct is left to me by a legacy subject to a condition and in the meantime it is with the heir, the latter can leave the usufruct by way of legacy to a third party. The consequence is that if the condition governing the legacy to me is met, the usufruct left by the heir comes to an end. However, if I lose the usufruct, it will not revert to the legatee, to whom it was bequeathed in absolute terms by the heir. The reason is that the legal position of joint legatees cannot arise from different wills.], D.8.6.11.1 [D.8.6. *Quemadmodum servitutes amittuntur* (How servitudes are lost).11 **Marcellus**, *in the fourth book of Digest*: 1. Land was left as a legacy subject to a condition, and the heir subjected it to certain servitudes. If the condition is met, the servitudes will be extinguished. If the servitudes had been created in favor of the land that was the subject of the legacy, let us consider whether they would go to the legatee. The better opinion is that they would.]; D.30.81. pr. [D.30.*De legatis et fideicommissis* (Legacies and *fideicommissa*).81 **Julianus**, *in the thirty-second book of Digest*: pr. If an heir, who was entrusted with the inheritance of a plot of land subject to a condition, had, during the pending of that condition, bequeathed the land to someone else under a different condition, and subsequently, when the condition specified in the initial will was fulfilled, the condition set in the heir's bequest was also satisfied, the ownership of the land does not transfer from the first legatee.]; D.35.1.105 [D.35.1. *De condicionibus et demonstrationibus et causis et modis eorum, quae in testamento scribuntur* (Conditions, designations, explanations for and modalities of provisions in wills).105 **Pomponius**, *in the fifth book of Letters*: A testator left a plot of land with a condition attached to it. While the condition was still pending, the heir transferred it to another person. Upon the fulfillment of the condition mentioned in the original will, the first legatee will not lose ownership of the land. Furthermore, the heir will not have the authority to consecrate any part of the land or establish a servitude over it. In fact, any servitude that may have been previously established will be terminated upon the condition's satisfaction.]. (Hence, if there is a dispute concerning the inheritance, it is preferable for the legatees to be subject to a resolutive condition or provide guarantees, D.35.1.44.6 [D.35.1. *De condicionibus et demonstrationibus et causis et modis eorum, quae in testamento scribuntur* (Conditions, designations, explanations for and modalities of provisions in wills).44 **Paulus,** *in the ninth book to Plautius*: 6. Let's say I am appointed as the heir, and a dispute arises regarding the inheritance. If a legatee wants to ensure that they will return the legacy if I am deprived of the inheritance, they should also provide security for the return of what they have received.], *adde* the whole title D.44.6. *De litigiosis* (Property subject to litigation).

However, the gratuitous acts of the heir remain valid, as stated in D.8.6.11.1 [D.8.6. *Quemadmodum servitutes amittuntur* (How servitudes are lost).11 **Marcellus,** *in the fourth book of Digest*: 1, see above in this theorem 47.]. It appears that the heir has acted on behalf of the legatee, D.3.5.39 [D.3.5. *De negotiis gestis* (Unauthorized administration).38 (39) **Gaius,** *in the third book on Verbal Obligations*: Paying on behalf of someone else, even without their awareness and consent, relieves them of their obligation. However, it is not permissible for a third party to demand payment of someone else's debt without their consent. Both the principles of natural justice and civil law support the idea that we can assist and improve another person's situation without their knowledge and agreement, but we cannot act in a way that would harm or worsen their position.].

Therefore, the *exceptio rei judicatae*[172] can benefit the legatee but cannot harm them, as argued in D.10.2.7

[172] Berger, *ad vocem Exceptio rei iudicatae,* "An exception opposed by the defendant and based on the fact he had been sued for the same thing (eadem res) in a previous trial and a judgment had been passed in the matter. Identity of the plaintiffs was not necessary since the exceptio might be used against the successor of the claimant in the trial. There was a maxim: "Good faith does not permit that the same thing be claimed twice" (D. 50.17.57). The most important point in the application of this exception was the idendity of the claims (eadem res). A similar exceptio was the exceptio rei in iudicium deductae which was available when in the first trial a judgment had not been rendered but the joinder of issue (litis contestatio) had been reached. —D. 442.—.".

[D.10.2.*Familiae erciscundae* (The action for dividing an inheritance). 7 **Venuleius**, *in the seventh book on Stipulations*: If a co-heir is appointed subject to a condition or is in enemy hands, and the other heir claims that he is heir, brings an action to support his claim, and wins it; but later the condition is met or the co-heir returns by postliminium. Ought the other heir to share the benefits of his victory with him? For without doubt an action on the judgment for the full amount is available to him. The co-heir should be given a choice; that is to say, either the benefits should be shared or the heir who has qualified as heir or has returned to his city since his co-heir's victory should be given the opportunity to go to law. The same rule is to be followed if a posthumous son is born subsequently. For such people should not be accused of failing to claim earlier, seeing that they have only qualified for the inheritance after their coheir's victory.].

What we said about inheritance is generally true, that while the condition is pending, the thing belongs to the conditionator, and even though the *conditionarius* possesses it, he cannot acquire ownership through long use (*usucapere*[173]), D.41.4.2.3 [D.41.4. *Pro emptore* (Usucapion as purchaser). 2 **Paulus**, *in the fifty-fourth book to the Edict*: 3. Sabinus argues that if an item is sold with a condition that the sale will be void if the price is not paid by a specified date, usucapion (acquiring ownership through possession, e.n.) will not occur if the price has not been paid. However, we should also examine whether this provision should be considered a condition or, rather, a pact. If it is regarded as a pact, it involves the dissolution of the contract rather than its execution.].

Nevertheless, the conditionator can demand the thing back if he provides security when the condition occurs, as stated in D.44.4.5 [D.44.4.*De doli mali et metus exceptione* (The defense of fraud and that of duress).5 **Paulus**, *in the seventy-first to the Edict*: If you owe me ten without any conditions, and later I bequeath this amount to you subject to a condition, the heir, in the meantime, could claim that sum. In this case, the heir should not be prevented by the defense of fraud because the condition itself might not be fulfilled. The heir would need to initiate a stipulation for the legacy, but if the heir doesn't provide this guarantee, they can be barred by the defense of fraud. It's in the legatee's best interest to hold onto the sum rather than having the

[173] Berger, *ad vocem Usucapio*, "Acquisition of ownership of a thing belonging to another through possession of it (possessio) for a period fixed by law. [...]".

hereditary estate subjected to a missio in possessionem, concerning fraud, malice, and exceptions.], and if he makes a payment while unaware that the condition is pending, he can claim reimbursement. D.12.6.16 [D.12.6.*De condictione indebiti* (The *condictio* for money not owed). 16 **Pomponius**, *in the fifteenth book to Sabinus*: In conditional debts, a mistaken payment before fulfillment of the condition can be recovered but not once the condition has been met.].

(48) The person honored can be in a worse legal position compared to the legatee, not better.

Otherwise, what someone cannot achieve as a legatee, they will indirectly achieve as a person honored, leading to a fraud on the statute, D.39.6.9 [D.39.6. *De mortis causa donationibus et capionibus (Gifts and acquisitions mortis causa)*. 9 **Paulus**, *in the third book to Sabinus*: Anyone who can accept legacies is allowed to make acquisitions mortis causa.].

D.35.1.55 [D.35.1. *De condicionibus et demonstrationibus et causis et modis eorum, quae in testamento scribuntur* (Conditions, designations, explanations for and modalities of provisions in wills). 55 **Javolenus**, *in the thirteenth of Letters*: Land is bequeathed to Maevius under the condition that he gives two hundred to Callimachus, who lacks testamentary capacity according to the testator. Maevius is required to fulfill the condition by giving the two hundred for the land to become his own, even if he doesn't make Callimachus the owner of the coins. The manner in which Maevius is instructed to give, whether to a specific person, place, or even to throw it into the sea, doesn't affect the fact that what is due under the will won't be received by the designated person due to the death of the donor.] does not contradict this, where it is stated that if Maevius leaves a bequest of 100 to Callimachus, but Callimachus does not have the legal capacity to make a valid will (*non habet testamenti factionem*[174]), he cannot receive the bequest and, therefore, cannot acquire a right by reason of death (*mortis causa*). So, what is the applicable law in this case?

The Jurisconsult responds that Maevius must comply with the condition and give 100 to Callimachus,

174 Berger, *ad vocem Testamenti factio*, see note 87 above.

even though the money does not become the property of Callimachus but is merely assigned to him as if it were thrown into the sea. *Meyer*, in *Collectiones Argumentorum*, objection number 14[175], argues that it has been absolutely believed that the Jurisconsult claimed that the money was thrown into the sea. The response is that both possibilities exist, but they differ in that the throwing of money into the sea is remitted (for the sake of public utility, as it would not benefit anyone later, see *Eman. a Costa Commentarius ad L. Gallus number 20*[176]), whereas the deposit of money with Callimachus is not remitted. Since the money does not become Callimachus's property, it can be reclaimed by Maevius.

From this, it is clear that the person honored cannot be in a better legal position than the legatee. Let us examine whether there are cases where the person honored is in a worse legal position. Indeed, there are such cases. For example, if the heir, passing over the will (*omissa causa testamenti*), takes possession of an inheritance without a valid will (*ab intestato*), in this situation, the person honored is in a lower position than the legatee, as the Pretor does not provide assistance to the person honored, D.29.4.8 [D.29.4. *Si quis omissa causa testamenti ab intestato vel alio modo possideat hereditatem* (Where someone, passing over a will, takes possession of an inheritance on intestacy or in some other way). 8 **Ulpianus**, *in the fiftieth book To the Edict*: see above in theorem 6.]. This is diametrically opposed to D.29.4.1.8 in the same law [D.29.4. *Si quis omissa causa testamenti ab intestato vel alio modo possideat hereditatem* (Where someone, passing over a will, takes possession of an inheritance on intestacy or in some other way).1 **Ulpianus**, *in the fiftieth book to the Edict*: 8. A beneficiary who, designated as the heir subject to a specific condition, had the capability to meet the condition but chose not to, and subsequently inherits through intestacy, should be held accountable under the

175 Justus Meier (1566–1622), *Collegium Iuridicum Argentoratense totius jurisprudentiae absolutum systema exibens*. T. 2. (Argentorati, 1657), 698, sub D.35.1.55, n. 14.VII.

176 Emanuel a Costa (d. 1563, 1564?), *Commentarium in § Et quid si tantum, L. Gallus FF. De Liberis et posthumis* (Coimbricae, 1548), p. 8, n. 20.

edict. This is because conditions of this nature should be treated as though they carry no weight.].

It is Ulpianus who speaks in both cases, which is a remarkable inconsistency. I could provide a reconciliation if I were to resort to specific cases, but I prefer to remain silent rather than say foolish things.

(49) *The heir and legatee can collude in fraud against the person honored, unless the latter is a coheir.*

We cannot provide a reason for this theorem because, if we consider strict law, there seems to be no privilege for the coheir in this regard. However, I believe that equity (*aequitas*[177]) should provide assistance even to an outsider (*extraneus*[178]). But this is how it was deemed right by the Jurisconsult. Let's consider the following scenario: The testator wrote: "My heir must give 100 to Titius if Titius gives 50 to Maevius". Titius and the heir make an agreement in which the legatee returns the bequest to the heir and, for another reason or pretext, they stipulate that 80 should be given to Titius unconditionally, disregarding the original condition. In this way, the heir gains 20, and Titius gains 30. The question arises whether Maevius has any remedy against this stratagem. The answer is no, as stated in D.35.1.57 [D.35.1. *De condicionibus et demonstrationibus et causis et*

[177] Berger, *ad vocem Aequitas (aequum)*, "Related to justice *(iustitia, iustum)* but distinguished from the positive law, ius. One of the fundamental principles which direct orshould direct the development of law; it is the corrective and creative element in such development. A law which is guided by the aequitas is ius aequum, its antonym is ius iniquum. In the legal sphere aequitas may be realized either by interpreting the existing law or by supplementing it where an exact legal provision is missing. Aequitas, as the word itself indicates, implies the element of equality. Transferred into the province of law it postulates equal treatment of all according to the conceptions nurtured in the social (common) conscience of the people which change, of course, when social and economic condition undergo a change. The Roman aequitas fulfilled its functions in the development of the Roman law.".

[178] Here the term *extraneus* is not in the meaning of *heres extraneus*, Berger, *ad vocem Extraneus*, see note 45 above.

modis eorum, quae in testamento scribuntur (Conditions, designations, explanations for and modalities of provisions in wills).57 **Pomponius,** *in the ninth book to Quintus Mucius*: The inquiry has been raised regarding a scenario where a slave is instructed to attain freedom by providing a certain number of days' work to an *extraneus* (individual outside the household). Should such a condition be interpreted in a manner analogous to our views on monetary transactions rather than services rendered? The guiding principle we adhere to is that just as it is acknowledged that if a slave contributes from his peculium to an *extraneus,* he will be granted freedom, similarly, if he performs services for the *extraneus,* freedom should be a logical outcome. In such a situation, the heir would be prudent to prohibit the performance of services. This way, the slave would indeed achieve liberty, but the *extraneus* would not reap the benefits of his services.], where it is considered a wise action (I believe this is similar to what Christ said, that the sons of the world are wiser in their generation than the sons of light). Similarly, in D.40.7.3.3 [D.40.7. *De statuliberis* (Statuliberi).3 **Ulpianus,** *in the twenty-seventh book to Sabinus*: 3. The slave seeking freedom achieves liberation not only if hindered from fulfilling a directive to provide something but also if barred from executing an order, such as ascending the Capitol or traveling to Capua when instructed to fulfill an obligation there. This is because someone impeding the slave from embarking on such tasks is presumed to be more focused on obstructing freedom rather than utilizing the slave's services.].

The situation is different when a coheir is involved D.40.7.3.3 [D.40.7. *De statuliberis* (Statuliberi).3 **Ulpianus,** *in the twenty-seventh book to Sabinus*: 4. However, if one of the inheritors prevents the slave from delivering what was instructed to a fellow heir, the slave still attains freedom. In this case, the heir to whom the slave was directed to give, thereby gaining freedom, can initiate a legal action (familiae erciscundae). The co-heir causing the obstruction will then be compelled to compensate the heir, representing the share in the slave's freedom that was hindered.].

However, D.12.4.3.9 contradicts this idea [D.12.4. *De condictione causa data causa non secuta* (The condictio for nonreciprocation).3 **Ulpianus,** *in the twenty-sixth book to the Edict*: 9. Despite the statuliber being permitted to fulfill his condition using his peculium, the heir has the authority to prevent any payments in order to safeguard the money. In such a scenario, if the statuliber is restrained from complying with the testator's directives, he achieves freedom through the constructive fulfillment of the condition, while the coins are also preserved. However, the individual intended by the testator to receive payment can pursue an "actio infactum" against the heir to ensure the testator's intentions are honored.]. In that law, an *actio in factum*[179] is granted to the injured party against the heir, without making any distinction based on greater equity. As for reconciling these laws, let others work on that[180].

(50) *According to the pure law, a vested conditional right is transmissible, while an unvested right is not transmissible.*

On the other hand, a vested right is one that cannot be taken away by the will or actions of others. And because such a right has, so to speak, become united with the person, it is rightfully transmitted to the heir. Therefore, a conditional right is not transmitted through the last will.

[179] Berger, *ad vocem Formula in ius concepta,* "Ant. formula in factum concepta. The distinction is based on the contents of the intentio in the procedural formula. When a question of law is raised, as, for instance, when the plaintiff claims the ownership over a thing or another right, under Quiritary law, or when he sues for the performance of an obligation by the defendant under civil law (dare oportere), there is in the intentio a direct or indirect reference to a legal transaction or relation protected under ius civile. In a formula in factum, however, the intentio mentions the fact from which the piaintiff draws his claim and the judge is authorized to condemn the defendant if the fact in question is proved. The formula in factum is adapted to the particular circumstances of the case, for instance, when a freedman summons his patron to court, or when a person summoned to court does not appear or give a guaranty. The substantial difference between the two kinds of formulae is that in the formula in factum the condemnation of the defendant is connected with a fact from which his liability is derived, whereas in the formula in ius the establishment of a specific right of the claimant either over a thing or to a performance by the defendant effects the condemnation of the latter. In the creation of formula in factum the jurists and the judicialmagistrates (the praetors) equally co-operated. Granted first in specific cases the formula in factum gradually entered into the praetorian edict in the form of an announcement of the praetor that he was willing to grant an action in certain situations, not proteoed hitherto by the law. The formulae in factum were an important factor in the development of the ius honorarium.".

[180] This passage, on my view, disavows the alleged "mathematicity" of Leibnizian legal thought.

However, if the *conditionarius* dies while the condition is pending (it is different if the debtor dies, leaving his obligated heir, D.35.1.65 [D.35.1. *De condicionibus et demonstrationibus et causis et modis eorum, quae in testamento scribuntur* (Conditions, designations, explanations for and modalities of provisions in wills).65 **Paulus**, *in the sixty-second to the Edict*: When a legacy is bequeathed under a condition, should the heir, away from whom it has been so left, die while the condition is still pending, he leaves his own heir charged.]), the conditioned right becomes null and void D.28.5.60(59).6 [D.28.5. *De heredibus instituendis* (The institution of heirs). 60 (59) **Celsus**, *in the sixteenth book of Digest*: 6. If a testament is formulated in the following manner: "Let Titius be designated heir for one-third; let Maevius be designated heir for one-third. If a ship arrives from Asia by three days before the first of the month, let Titius be designated heir for the remaining share." Let's examine whether Titius doesn't immediately become the heir for half of the estate. In this case, two heirs have been appointed, with Titius inheriting either half or two-thirds. Therefore, at least one-sixth is in a state of uncertainty. If the condition is fulfilled, Titius becomes the heir for two-thirds; if not, that one-sixth transfers to Maevius. However, if Titius passes away before the "condition is met and then the condition is fulfilled, that one-sixth will still go to Maevius, not to Titius's heir. This is because when it was still uncertain whether the one-sixth belonged to Titius or Maevius, Titius died, and it cannot be considered as granted to someone who did not exist at the time of the grant.]; D.30.65.1 [D.30. *De condicionibus et demonstrationibus et causis et modis eorum, quae in testamento scribuntur* (Conditions, designations, explanations for and modalities of provisions in wills).65 **Gaius**, *in the first book on Legacies, To the Edict of the Praetor*: 1, see above in theorem 17.]; D.32.11.6 [D.32.*De legatis et fideicommissis* (Legacies and *fideicommissa*).11 **Ulpianus**, *in the second book on Fideicommissa*: 6. The phrase "when he wishes" might imply an extension for the duration of the fideicommissum obligor's life. However, if this individual passes away before fulfilling the obligation, the responsibility falls upon their heir to fulfill it. Yet, if the fideicommissary dies before the heir makes a decision[181], it is considered that the fideicommissary has not transferred anything to the heir. It is evident that the bequest was conditional, and the fideicommissary passed away while the condition of the bequest was still pending.], D.35.1.31, 40.2, 59, 69 [D.35.1. *De condicionibus et demonstrationibus et causis et modis eorum,*

[181] It seems like an incoherent statement: how can the heir of the fideicommissary make a decision before the fideicommissary dies?

quae in testamento scribuntur (Conditions, designations, explanations for and modalities of provisions in wills). 31 **Africanus**, *in the second book of Questions*: see above in theorem 19. 40 **Javolenus**, *in the second book of Excerpts from Labeo's Posterior Works*: 2. see above in theorem 14. 59 **Ulpianus**, *in the thirteenth book on Lex Julia et Papia, book 13*: A legacy fails if the person to whom it was left under a condition die. 69 **Gaius**, *in the thirteenth book on Lex Julia et Papia*: In a note on Labeo, Proculus observes that a bequest, "I give and bequeath to Titius, if he wants it," would go to the legatee's heir only if the legatee himself had wished to have it; for the condition is considered to pertain to the legatee himself.].

Similarly, a postponed right with an uncertain date of acquisition, as mentioned in Theorem 14, C.6.51.7 [C.6.51. *De caducis tollendis (Concerning abolishing lapses (escheats)* 7 see above in theorem 14.], when it will be acquired, is also nullified. However, if it is given unconditionally, with only the power to demand being suspended, then it is transmitted, C.6.53.5 [C.6.53. *Quando dies legati vel fideicommissi cedit* (When a legacy or trust vests). 5: see above in theorem 14.].

A conditional postponed right, given during one's lifetime, is transmitted to the heirs of the creditor, even if the *conditionarius* dies while the condition is pending I.3.15.4 [I.3.15.*De Verborum Obligatione* (Of verbal obligation).4, see above in theorem 6.]; I.3.19.25 [I.19.*De Inutilibus Stipulationibus* (Of invalid stipulations). 25. If a man stipulates for performance on the fulfilment of a condition, and dies before such fulfilment, his heir can sue on the contract when it occurs: and the heir of the promisor can be sued under the same circumstances.]; D.45.1.57 [D.45.1. *De verborum obligationibus* (Verbal obligations). 57 **Julianus**, *in the fifty-third book of Digest*: If someone promised, "ten to be paid if Titius become consul" although the promisor die while the condition is unfulfilled, he bequeaths the obligation to his heir.].

Ultimately, the thing itself is transmitted and passes with its legal condition D.35.1.60.1 [D.35.1. *De condicionibus et demonstrationibus et causis et modis eorum, quae in testamento* scribuntur (Conditions, designations, explanations for and modalities of provisions in wills).60 **Paulus**, *in the seventh book on Lex Julia et Papia*: 1.The imperial treasury has to comply with the same conditions as does the person from whom some bequest comes to it; it thus claims the bequest subject to its burden.], D.29.5.9 [D.29.5. *De senatus consulto Silaniano et Claudiano: quorum testamenta ne aperiantur*

(The senatus consultum silanianum and the senatus consultum claudianum; those whose wills may not be opened).9 **Gaius**, *in the seventeenth book on Provincial Edict*: When the caduciary property of a deceased person is assigned to the imperial treasury because of an unavenged death, an action is given against it for the legacies; and <grants of> freedom are ratified, made to those, of course, who are excepted from the senatus consultum.]; D.49.14.6 [D.49.14.*De iure fisci* (Rights of the imperial treasury).6 **Ulpianus**, *in the sixty-third on Edict*: The imperial treasury, when it succeeds to the legal right of a private person, enjoys that person's rights as regards the period before its succession; but after it has succeeded, it will have its own privilege. But [is it privileged] as soon as the title begins to belong to it, or after it has sued the debtor, or after the title has been registered among those of the debtors? And, indeed, the imperial treasury sues for interest due to itself, even if the sums due are trivial from the time when it sues the particular debtor who admits [his liability]. But as regards the privilege, there are differing rescripts; my own view, however, is that there is scope for privilege from the time when the title has been registered among those of the debtors.], just like the *statuliber* (freed slave), see definition 70 at the end.

However, giving a right to the heir of the honored person is useless D.35.1.94 [D.35.1. *De condicionibus et demonstrationibus et causis et modis eorum, quae in testamento scribuntur* (Conditions, designations, explanations for and modalities of provisions in wills).94 **Hermogenianus**, *in the first book of Epitome of Law*: see above in theorem 19.], except when given by a slave to obtain his freedom (Theorem 60).

CHAPTER VIII

[Subject Matter of The Partial Propositions: Things]

Definitions

Let us now turn from individuals to things that are derived from or brought into a conditioned state. However, things that cannot be derived into a conditioned state, or in other words, cannot be subjected to conditions, are called.

69. Inconditionable. On the other hand, conditionable things include inheritances, legacies, money, etc., which I will discuss shortly. This also extends to conditional freedom, and the person themselves is referred to as

70. Statuliber, whom I define as a slave manumitted under a suspensive condition in a testament. I call him a slave, for he is the pure slave of the heir, D.31.11 [D.31.*De legatis et fideicommissis* (Legacies and *fideicommissa*).11 **Pomponius**, *in the seventh book From Plautius*: see above in theorem 39.]; D.40.7.9, 15. [D.40.7.*De statuliberis* (Statuliberi).9 **Ulpianus**, *in the twenty-eighth book to Sabinus*: No one should be unaware that in the meantime the statuliber is the slave of the heir; for this reason it will be possible to surrender him noxally. But he will still be able to hope for freedom after the surrender, nor will the surrender deprive him of the hope of freedom. 15. **Africanus**, *in the ninth book of Questions*: If, upon the death of the heir, the statuliber had contributed a substantial amount to the inheritance as instructed, such as by settling debts or supporting the household, he believed that the individual would promptly attain freedom.].

However, under a resolutive condition (see definition 21 and following), or rather not fully, hence the person who owes a slave is not released by giving a statuliber, D.12.6.63 [D.12.6. *De condictione indebiti* (The *condictio* for money not owed). 63 **Gaius**, *in the sole book of Cases*: Neratius recounts a case where there is no recovery of what has been given because, although the giving effects no discharge, what is given is owed. So, suppose one is bound to give a certain slave and gives him when statuliber. There he does not get his discharge because he fails to transfer the entire property in the slave to the stipulator; but he cannot recover, because what he gives he does owe.]; D.46.3.38.2 [D.46.3.*De solutionibus et liberationibus* (Performances and releases).38 **Africanus**, *in the seventh book of Questions*: 2. An action on the peculium was brought against the [slave's] master; judgment going against him, he paid; [Julianus] said that sureties accepted for the slave are also released and that a proof that the same money can be paid on several counts is that when security for satisfaction of a judgment is given and the defendant, defeated in the action, pays, he and his sureties are released not only from the action to enforce a judgment but also from the stipulation. And very similar is it that when the possessor of an inheritance, thinking himself heir, pays, the heir is not thereby released in that case because it happens that [the possessor] pays in his own name money not due from him and can reclaim it.].

The right under a resolutive condition is indeed weaker. If, however, someone promises that a statuliber will appear at trial in the same situation, once the condition has been fulfilled, he appears as free, and the effects of the stipulation are lost, D.2.9.6 [D.2.9. *Si ex noxali causa agatur, quemadmodum caveatur* (How provision for a guarantee may be made where a noxal action is brought).6 **Paulus**, *in the eleventh book to Sabinus*: But if a promise is made that a statuliber will appear, he is held to appear in the same legal condition, although he appears when free, because the chance of freedom was involved in his original condition.].

The same legal condition, indeed, in which he was at that time, that is, the statuliber status under terms or conditions, has led him to the condition in which he is now, that is, full freedom. The statuliber, as if already a free man, should be punished, D.48.18.14 [D.48.18. *De quaestionibus* (Investigations).14 **Modestinus**, *in the eighth book of Rules*: A statuliber discovered in a delict is, as an indication of his expected freedom, to be penalized not as a slave due to the uncertainty of his status but as a free person.]; D.48.19.9.16 [D.48.19.*De poenis* (Punishments).9. **Ulpianus**, *in the tenth book on Duties of Proconsul*: 16. The deified Pius wrote to Salvius Marcianus in a rescript that a statuliber should be punished as a freeman.]. However, D.40.7.29. pr. [D.40.7. *De statuliberis* (Statuliberi).29 **Pomponius**, *in the eighteenth book to Quintus Mucius*: pr. Statuliber scarcely differ at all from the rest of our slaves. Consequently, concerning legal actions stemming from wrongdoing, unauthorized management, or contracts, statuliberi possess an identical status as the rest. Likewise, in public trials, they are subject to the same penalties as other slaves.] strongly opposes this, although efforts can be made to reconcile those who believe that there can be contradictions in capital punishment.

Therefore, we have called the statuliber:

1. a slave,

2. manumitted, whereby fideicommissaria freedom is excluded when the manumission is entrusted to another person, and the slave to whom fideicommissaria freedom is granted is the freedman (*libertus*[182]) of the manumitter or the one to whose trust the testator has committed. However, the statuliber is *libertus Orcinus*[183], D.40.7.2. pr. [D.40.7.*De statuliberis* (Statuliberi).2 **Ulpianus**, *in the fourth book to Sabinus*: pr. A man who acquires the status of a statuliber is so circumstanced that if he transferred to another owner, his hope of freedom is not affected by the alienation; if he be usucapted, he retains his status, and if he be manumitted, he does not lose the hope of becoming freedman of the deceased testator. But a slave does not obtain this status unless at least one of the heirs instituted has entered on the inheritance; if he is alienated or usucapted or manumitted at an earlier stage, his hope of the freedom arranged lapses.]. The slave who is instituted with freedom is also excluded, D.40.7.2.3 [D.40.7. *De statuliberis* (Statuliberi).2 **Ulpianus**, *in the fourth book to Sabinus*: 3. If in the first will a slave should be conditionally freed and instituted heir as to half the estate, would he obtain the status of a statuliber with effect that on entry by the heir he would be usucapted retaining his status? Inasmuch as he would have received freedom from himself, he cannot obtain the status of a statuliber. If, indeed, the conditional institution should fail in which case according to Julianus he secures freedom at least, it must be said that he obtains the status of a statuliber, since he is thought to have received freedom not from himself, but from the co-heir.], for he receives freedom from himself and therefore does not require manumission. He can remain in his own slavery

182 *Libertus*, see note 47 above.

183 *Libertus Orcinus*, see note 47 above.

without harm[184], and he is the freedman of his ex-master (*suus libertus*[185]), see D.28.5.6.4 [D.28.5. *De heredibus instituendis* (The institution of heirs).6 **Ulpianus**, *in the fourth book to Sabinus*: 4 aee above in theorem 3.].

Also, refer to what we have discussed in the dissertation *De Casibus perplexis*, § 15.[186]

3. The third requirement is that he be manumitted through a testament.

Indeed, nobody can be conditionally manumitted by *vindicta* by means of an *inter vivos* act; it is called a legitimate act (*actus legitimus*), as stated in theorem 52 below. It should be noted here that the freedom granted through a testament differs greatly from a legacy, in fact, it is opposed to it D.10.2.12.2 [D.10.2. *Familiae erciscundae* (The action for dividing an inheritance).12 **Ulpianus**, *in the nineteenth book to the Edict*: 2. The thing that is left as legacy under a condition temporarily belongs to the heirs. Therefore, it becomes subject to the judgment for dividing an inheritance and can be adjudicated, with its own legal justification, of course. This means that, with the condition fulfilled, it is removed from the person to whom it was adjudicated, or if the condition fails, it reverts to those heirs by whom it was left. The same principle applies to a statuliber, who is temporarily considered part of the heirs' estate but, when the condition is fulfilled, attains freedom.]; D.35.1.47, 51, 81, 86, 87 [D.35.1. *De condicionibus et demonstrationibus et causis et modis eorum, quae in testamento scribuntur* (Conditions, designations, explanations for and modalities of provisions in wills). 47 **Marcellus**, *in the fourteenth book of Digest*: see above in theorem 3. 51 **Modestinus**, *in the fifth book of Distinctions*: see above in theorem 19. 81 **Paulus**, *in the twenty-first book Questions*: pr., see above in definition 35. 86 **Maecianus**, *in the third book on Fideicommissa*: Our Julianus argued that if a slave, tasked with giving ten and gaining freedom, were freed by the testator

[184] W. W. Buckland, Peter Stein (rev.), *A text-book of Roman Law from Augustus to Justinian* (Cambridge, 1963), p. 88, "Apart from any special obligation to operae and munera undeertaken, a libertus was boud to support is patron in need, according to his means. The obligations were not all one way. The libertus must not be treated as a slave.", therein, note 17, "Libertus cannot be compelled to live with patron C.6.3.12.".

[185] *Suus Libertus*, see note 47 and 48 above.

[186] See note 52 above.

during the testator's lifetime, they could not receive a legacy given to them with freedom unless they fulfilled the testamentary condition. Similarly, they would have to fulfill the condition for their purchaser if they were sold. However, this would apply only in cases where the legacy could be acquired exclusively with freedom, even if the condition was not explicitly imposed on the legacy, such as when the legacy was tied to the moment of liberation. 87 **Valens**, *in the first book on Fideicommissa*: The rule is that in the case of legacies, one looks to the last stated condition but, in grants of liberty, to the most benign. 88 **Gaius**, *in the first book on Fideicommissa*: That is, to the one most to the slave's advantage.]; D.39.6.8, 19, 20.3 [D.39.6. *De mortis causa donationibus et capionibus* (Gifts and acquisitions mortis causa).8 **Ulpianus**, *in the seventh book to Sabinus*: pr. One who has renounced an inheritance for a certain sum of money acquires this sum mortis causa, whether the inheritance passes to a substituted heir or to an intestate heir. This is because anything received due to the death of a person is acquired mortis causa. Julianus adopted this view, and it is the legal principle that we also follow. Indeed, even what we acquire from a statuliber or a legatee for fulfilling a condition is acquired mortis causa. Julianus states that what a father gives due to the death of his son or relative is acquired mortis causa.19 **Julianus**, *in the eightieth book of Digest*: If something was given to a son-in-power due to death, and the donor recovered health, the son-in-power will have an action against the father for peculium. However, if the head of a household receives a gift mortis causa and then allows himself to be adopted, the property itself can be reclaimed by the donor. The case of someone who receives a gift mortis causa and then gives it to somebody else is not similar, since the donor would in that case bring a condictio against the latter not for the property, but for its value. 20.3 does not exist in D.39.6, e.n.], the whole D.40.7 *De statuliberis* (Statuliberi) (although it is said to be included in it, in D.50.16.80 [D.50.16. *De verborum significatione* (Meaning of expressions). 80 **Paulus**, *in the ninth book to Plautius*: In the case of a general revocation of legacies, even liberty which has been granted is included according to the intention of the Law of the Twelve Tables.]).

If we carefully examine it, the grant of freedom is nothing other than the removal of constraints, as freedom consists merely in the absence of constraints. On the other hand, legacies contain something positive, except for the *legatum liberationis*[187], which is very similar to the granted freedom.

Finally, it is required that the slave be manumitted by testament, but under a suspensive condition, as has been mentioned previously. Thus, once established as a statuliber, the slave cannot be prejudiced, for they are alienated along with their legal status, as stated in D.40.7.2 [D.40.7. *De statuliberis* (Statuliberi).2 **Ulpianus**, *in the fourth book to Sabinus*: pr., see above in this definition 70.]; C.7.2.13 [C.7.2. *De testamentaria manumission* (Concerning testamentary manumission).13. It is certain that freedom granted upon condition, cannot be taken away by the heir. Alienation or usucaption (prescription) cannot prejudice anyone, to whom a bequest of liberty is made upon condition, so as to prevent him, upon the happening of the condition, from acquiring his freedom.].

The contrary does not hold in D.40.7.30 [D.40.7.*De statuliberis* (Statuliberi).30 **Javolenus**, *in the seventh book of Readings*: If someone has been ordered to be free in the following manner, "Stichus, if the heir does not alienate him, let him be free," even if he is a statuliber, he can still be alienated.], where the slave ceases to be a statuliber upon alienation, because that was precisely the condition of freedom, if it is not alienated.

Theorems

(51) Anything pertaining to the fact cannot be subject to condition

This theorem is evident from the definition of moral conditional disposition, in which a certain right should be disposed of, according to definitions 8 and 9. Therefore, since possession is a fact, which is evident from many texts and has been extensively discussed in *Papponius's* dissertation on possession[188], it is not capable

[187] Berger, *ad vocem Legatum liberationis*, "A legacy by which a testator released a legatee who was his debtor, from the debt.".

[188] Girolamo Papponi (1533 – 1605), *Disputatio juridica. Possessio iuris ne fit an facti. Contra Joannem Bolognetum* (Venetii, 1600)

of being conditional. Although *Antonius Faber* seems to disagree in the *Codex Sabaudico, lib. I, tit. 2 def. 57 n. 2*[189], it is usually understood by him and others that the word "possession" signifies the right derived from it.

Similarly, the rights of blood (*jura sanguinis*) are unconditionable, as stated by Master *Carpzov* in *Respons. VI, 8, 77, 12*[190]. Likewise, the assertion or proposition in which a factual matter is narrated. Thus, an oath cannot be made under a condition, nor can a confession or an *acceptilatio*[191], as a confession is made about a payment, D.46.4.4.5 [D.46.4.*De acceptilatione* (Formal releases).4 **Ulpianus**, *in the thirty-fourth to Sabinus*: 5. A formal release made as from a

[189] Antoine Favre, *Codex Fabrianus Definitionum Forensium* (Genevae, 1674, first ed. 1628), 17, Lib. I, tit. 2, def. 57, n. 2, "Nemo enim dubitat, quin sicut dominium ita & possessio transferri in alium sub condicione possit, ita uti ne prius amissa translatave quam condicio secuta sit.". [No one indeed doubts that just as ownership, so too possession can be transferred to another under condition, in such a way that it is not abandoned or transferred before the condition is fulfilled].

[190] Benedict Carpzov (1595-1666), *Responsa iuris electoralis* (Lipsiae, 1642), 1461, lib. VI, tit. 8, resp. 77, n. 12, "Agnationem vero, eiusque jura conditionalia dicere, ridiculum foret, cum conditiones omnes a libera paciscentum voluntate dependeant. [...]. Sanguinis autem jura nulli, ne eius quidem, qui leges condendae facultatem habet, potetatis suum subjectae, l. iura sanguinis 8 ff. de Reg. jur.". [It would be ridiculous, however, to define agnation and related rights as conditional, since all conditions depend on the free will of those who enter into a deed. [...] On the other hand, the rights of blood are not subject to the authority of anyone, not even those who, in truth, have the right to write a law, according to law iura sanguinis 8 ff. de Reg. jur.].

[191] For the concept of *acceptilatio* in Roman law, see GAI [Institutiones], 3, p. 169, "Item per acceptilationem tollitur obligation. Acceptilatio autem est veluti imaginaria solutio. Nam quod ex verborum obligatione tibi debeam, id si velis mihi remittere, poteris sic fieri, ut patiaris haec verba me dicere: QUOD TIBI EGO PROMISI, HABESNE ACCEPTUM? et tu respondeas: HABEO. The word later took on the meaning of debt remission. Berger, *ad vocem Acceptilatio*, "An oral form of dissolving oral obligations, according to the rule that obligations contracted verbis had to be dissolved in the same way (orally). The stipulatory debtor asked his creditor: 'What I promised to you, have you received it (habesne acceptum)? The latter answered 'I have (habeo).'. Later, Greek words were admitted. In order to dissolve an obligation other than an oral one by acceptilatio which was the safest form of receipt, the parties transferred the obligation into a stipulatio to which an acceptilatio was afterwards applied. This extension of acceptilatio was introduced by the jurist Aquilius Gallus who composed the formula of the novating stipulatio called stipulatio aquiliana.".

certain date is of no value; for such release should effect discharge as does performance.]; D.50.17.77 [D.50.17.*De diversis regulis iuris antiqui* (Various rules of early law).77 **Papinianus**, *in the twenty-eighth book of Questions*: see above in theorem 17.]. Also, a tutor cannot conditionally exercise his authority or interpose a confession regarding his consent, even if the act is conditional, according to D.26.8.8 [D.26.8.*De auctoritate et consensu tutorum et curatorum* (The authority and consent of tutors and curators).8 **Ulpianus**, *in the forty-eighth book to Sabinus*: Even if a contract is concluded with a pupillus under a condition, the tutor must grant authorization purely and simply. Indeed, for the conditional contract to be confirmed, the authorization must be interposed not under a condition but purely and simply.].

Furthermore, because possession and acts of possession, such as *traditio* (transfer of ownership), proper investiture of a fiefdom (excluding abusive cases), *aditio hereditatis* (entry into an inheritance), D.50.17.77 [D.50.17.*De diversis regulis iuris antiqui* (Various rules of early law).77 **Papinianus**, *in the twenty-eighth book of Questions*: see above in theorem 17.], *depositio*[192] (deposit), and *pignoris oblatio* (offer of pledge), are unconditionable, as stated by *Negusantius* in *de pignor., V, 3, 2, 10*[193]. Even though the right of pledge itself can be contracted under a condition, according to D.13.7.11.2 [D.13.7.*De pigneraticia actione vel contra* (Pignus: the actions for and against the pledgee).11 **Ulpianus**, *in the forty-eighth book to Sabinus*: 2. If, as one who is about to give you money, I take a pignus from you and then give you none, I will be liable to the actio pigneraticia even before there is any performance on your part. The same is true if, regarding to the money for which the pledge was given, the debt is released or a

[192] Berger, *ad vocem Depositio in sede*, "A debtor who wants to pay his debt and was unable to do so because the creditor refused to accept the payment, was absent or unable to accept it or was uncertain (as for instance, when the heirs of the original creditor were yet unknown) might deposit the sum due in a temple (in aede sacra) or in a public office (in loco publico) designated by an official [...].".

[193] Antonio Negusantius, see note 61 above, V, 3, 2, [Secunda pars tertii membri quintae partis principalis, e.n.], p. 10, "Tertio requiritur oblatio sit pura et non contineat conditionem extrinsecam [...].". [Thirdly, it is required that the offer be pure and does not contain an extrinsic condition.].

condition is not met or an effective pact is made that no suit shall be brought for the money.].

According to the force of this theorem, it seems that a servitude, at least according to the hypothesis of the old Juriconsults, cannot admit a condition, D.8.1.4 [D.8.1. *De Servitutibus* (Servitutes).4 **Papinianus**, *in the seventh book On Legal Questions*: see above in definition 25.].

For it consists of a perpetuated constitution, which pertains to a fact, D.7.2.1.3 [D.7.2. *De usu fructu adcrescendo* (The accrual of usufruct).1 **Ulpianus**, *in the seventeenth book to Sabinus*: 3.see above in theorem 25.].

(52) Legitimate acts are unconditionable.

Legitimate acts, that is, solemn acts, in which it was intended for the sake of decorum that they should not be left uncertain by the addition of a condition.

However, when the authority is not so harmed by the tacit addition of a condition, it is often accepted, D.50.17.77 [D.50.17. *De diversis regulis iuris antiqui* (Various rules of early law).77 **Papinianus**, *in the twenty-eighth book of Questions*: see above in theorem 17.]. For explicit conditions are harmful, while unexpressed conditions are not, as seen in theorem 17. Examples of such acts were those involving the transfer of *jus Quiritum* or *mancipium*[194],

[194] Berger, *ad vocem Mancipatio*, "In historical times a solemn form of conveyance of ownership of a res mancipi, accomplished in the presence of five Roman citizens as witnesses and of a man whd held a scale (libripens), with a prescribed ritual and the solemn utterance of a fixed formula by the transferee (the buyer when the mancipatio involved a sale). The formula was: 'I declare that this slave (this thing) is mine under Quiritary law and be he (it) bought by me with this piece of bronze and the bronze scale.' The assertion was not denied by the transferor. The transfer of ownership over a res mancipi could be achieved only in this way, otherwise the transferee did not acquire Quiritary ownership, but only possession which might lead to such an ownership through usucapio. The transaction was perhaps originally called mancipium (from manu capere = to grasp with the hand, which was one of the decisive gestures performed during the act). Mancipatio was also applied for other purposes as, e.g., to make a donation, to constitute a dowry, to hand over a thing to another as a trustee, fiduciae causa (see fiducia). In all these instances the external aspea of the act

and were carried out through fictitious sales, known as *Legis actiones*[195]. These acts could not be done through a *procurator*[196] and were performed once, using specific words (*certis verbis*[197]), and so on.

was that of a sale although the "price" paid was fictitious, a small coin being given as compensation (mancipatio nummo uno). In the further development other legal transactions were perfomed in the form of mancipatio such as the transfer of power over the wife to the husband, emancipating a child (see emancipatio), making a testament per aes et libram, or constituting a servitude. Various clauses might be added to the oral formula of the mancipatio, except the restriction of the transfer by a condition or term (see Actus legitimi). Such additional declarations of transferor were covered by the term nuncupatio. Later, specific duties of the parties were assumed by stipulatio. The increasing use of written documents deprived the mancipatio of its importance. In Justinian's law it does not appear any more. Mention of it in classical texts, accepted into Justinian's codification, was omitted and substituted in the formless traditio; mancipare was replaced simply by dare.

[195] Berger, *ad vocem Legis Actio*, "The earliest form of Roman civil procedure about which we are relatively well informed. Its characteristic feature was the tipe of prescribed oral formulae which were used in the stage of the trial before the magistrate (see in iure). Changes in the prescribed words by one of the parties might result in their losing the case. There were five legis actiones: sacramento, per iudicis arbitri postulationem, per condictionem, per manus iniectionem and per per pignoris capionem (see the following items). This form of civil procedure was later superseded by the formulary process with written formulae (see formula) which was the classical Roman procedure. The fundamental source on legis actio is Gaius' Institutes, completed in part by a few parchment sheets discovered in 1933, the so-called Gaius Florentinus (see Institutiones Gai), which throws new light on some problems connected with the procedure under legis actio.".

[196] Berger, *ad vocem Procurator*. (In private law.) "One who administers another's affairs under his authorization (mandatu)" (D. 3J. 1 pr.). Wealthy people used to have a general manager (administrator) of their property, a procurator omnium bonorum, whose activity for his principal was practically unlimited (alienations were excluded), unless specific restrictions were imposed on him concerning certain kinds of transactions. He was designated as a general agent ad res administrandas datus (= appointed for the administration of the property). Normally such an agent was a freedman (sometimes even a slave). Procuratorship was distinguished from MANDATUM (in a technical sense) which referred to an authorization to perform a certain act whereas the procurator omnium bonorum acted either under a general authorization or, at times, as a negotiorum gestor and for an absent principal. The procurator unius rei (= for one affair) is a later creation.".

[197] Berger, *ad vocem Verba certa ac (et) sollemnia*, "Words the use of which is prescribed for the validity of an act concluded (e.g. stipulatio, acceptilatio, dictio dotis, confarreatio, appointment of a cognitor in a trial, etc. In the early law, the use of words other than the certae ac solemnae,

Regarding these acts, D.50.17.77 [D.50.17. *De diversis regulis iuris antiqui* (Various rules of early law).77 **Papinianus**, *in the twenty-eighth book of Questions*: see above in theorem 17.], upon which our theorem is based, states: "Legitimate acts that involve a specific day or condition are completely invalidated by the addition of time or condition". This is found in the Florentine Pandects[198]. The Haloander edition[199] reads:"'which do not involve"; *Cujacius*, in his 15th observation[200], defends the former reading, while *Fr. Hottomannus*, in his *Illustr. Quest. 32, fol. 210 sqq.*[201], supports the latter.

However, both readings ultimately lead to the same conclusion. In the former reading, "do not involve" means "they are not capable", and the meaning is that legitimate acts cannot include a condition and, if added, they are invalidated. In the latter reading, "they involve" is the same as "they receive", and the meaning is: if legitimate acts (by their very nature unconditionable) still receive a de facto condition from someone, the entire act is invalidated.

rendered the whole transaction void. Gradually, minor changes became permissible. For the development of the stipulatio the most typical act performed by the use od certa et solemnia verba.".

198 Berger, *ad vocem Florentina*, see note 22.

199 Emperors (Rome) & Gregorius Haloander (1501-1531). *Digestorum seu Pandectarum libri quinquaginta. Editi ... per G. Haloandrum, etc.* (Noribergae, 1529).

200 Jacques Cujas, see note 26 above, Lib. XV, obs. 16, "[...] cum in l. 77 D. de regul. iur. non sit legendum qui non recipiunt, quasi scilicet alii sint, qui recipiant, sed ut Florentiae, qui recipiunt, id est quibus aperte adiicitur dies vel conditio". [since in D. 50.17.77 it is not to be read as 'in which they do not fit,' as if there were others who do fit, but as in the Florentine edition, 'in which they do fit,' that is, in which a day or condition is explicitly added.].

201 François Hotman, *Francisci Hotomani I.C. Clarissimi Quaestionum illustrium*. (Hanover, 1595), p. 303, question 34 [note 32, as quoted in the text], "Itaque Papinianus non dixit Actus legitimi non recipiunt diem vel conditionem [...]". '[Therefore, Papinian did not say that legitimate acts do not admit a term or condition.]

Furthermore, the following are mentioned in D.50.17.77: *mancipatio*[202], which Justinian removed from the Corpus Juris, *acceptilatio*[203], as discussed earlier in theorem 51 and in D.46.4.4 [D.46.4. *De acceptilatione* (Formal releases).4. **Pomponius**, *in the ninth book to Sabinus*: There can be no conditional formal release.], the acceptance of inheritance (*hereditatis aditio*[204]), as mentioned earlier in the aforesaid

[202] Berger, *ad vocem Mancipatio*, "In historical times a solemn form of conveyance of ownership of a res mancipi, accomplished in the presence of five Roman citizens as witnesses and of a man whd held a scale (libripens), with a prescribed ritual and the solemn utterance of a fixed formula by the transferee (the buyer when the mancipatio involved a sale). The formula was: 'I declare that this slave (this thing) is mine under Quiritary law and be he (it) bought by me with this piece of bronze and the bronze scale.' The assertion was not denied by the transferor. The transfer of ownership over a res mancipi could be achieved only in this way, otherwise the transferee did not acquire Quiritary ownership, but only possession which might lead to such an ownership through usucapio. The transaction was perhaps originally called mancipium (from manu capere = to grasp with the hand, which was one of the decisive gestures performed during the act). Mancipatio was also applied for other purposes as, e.g., to make a donation, to constitute a dowry, to hand over a thing to another as a trustee, fiduciae causa (see fiducia). In all these instances the external aspea of the act was that of a sale although the "price" paid was fictitious, a small coin being given as compensation (mancipatio nummo uno). In the further development other legal transactions were perfomed in the form of mancipatio such as the transfer of power over the wife to the husband, emancipating a child (see emancipatio), making a testament per aes et libram, or constituting a servitude. Various clauses might be added to the oral formula of the mancipatio, except the restriction of the transfer by a condition or term (see *Actus legitimi*). Such additional declarations of transferor were covered by the term nuncupatio. Later, specific duties of the parties were assumed by stipulatio. The increasing use of written documents deprived the mancipatio of its importance. In Justinian's law it does not appear any more. Mention of it in classical texts, accepted into Justinian's codification, was omitted and substituted in the formless traditio; mancipare was replaced simply by dare.".

[203] See note 189 above.

[204] Berger, *ad vocem Aditio hereditatis*, "The acceptance of an inheritance by an heir (heres) appointed in a last will or inheriting under the law. Only a certain category of heirs (see heres voluntarius) was obliged to declare expressly their willingness to accept the estate, whereas the nearest relatives belonging to the family of the testator (heres necessabius, heres suus et necessarius) acquired the inheritance automatically under the law (ipso iure) without any particular formality. The anncient form of aditio hereditatis was cretio, later forms were: acting as an heir (pro herede gerere) and an informal declaration of intent (aditio nuda voluntate). An acceptance once made was irrevocable. —D. 29.2; C. 6.O".

theorem, and the appointment of a tutor (*tutoris datio*[205]), D.26.1.6.1 [D.26.1. *De tutelis* (Tutelages). 6 **Ulpianus**, *in the thirty-eighth book to Sabinus*: 1. It appears reasonable that a tutor cannot be designated by the governors of a province subject to a condition, and if such an appointment occurs, it should be considered void. Pomponius concurs but contends that the supplementary clause employed by the governors, "I appoint a tutor, if he gives security," does not constitute a condition. Instead, it serves as a reminder that the tutelage can be conferred upon the individual only if they provide security. In other words, the person is not permitted to administer the tutelage unless they assure the safety of the property.].

(53) Public law (Ius publicum[206]) *is unconditional.*

Since every condition is referred either to chance or to the power of man, as stated in the above definitions 61 and following, both of these are inappropriate for public law, which should not depend on the actions of private individuals and certainly not on chance. And if you were to argue that what is entrusted to chance is attributed to God, it would still be a temptation of God (*temptatio Dei*[207]), as in common trials (*purgationes vulgares*[208]). Therefore, the appointment of a guardian is unconditional, as stated in the previous theorem 52, the exercise of jurisdiction, D.5.1.35 [D.49.4.*Quando appellandum sit et intra quae tempora* (When an appeal is to be made and within what times).35 **Javolenus**, *in the tenth book of Letters*: 1.

205 Berger, *ad vocem Tutor dativus (datus)*, "A guardian appointed by a magistrate: in Rome by the praetor urbanus (see lex Atilia). in the provinces by the governor under the Lex lulia et Titia. Under die Principate consuls and praetors appointed guardians, and from the time of Marcus Aurelius a special praetor was concerned with tutelary matters; see praetor tutelarius. The term tutor dativus refers sometimes to a tutor ap pointed in a testament. —D. 26.5; C. 5.47.".

206 Berger, *ad vocem Ius publicum*, "The law which is concerned with the existence, organization (status) and finctioning of the state [...]".

207 See Saint Thomas Aquinas (1225 –1274) (T.F. O Meara, O.P., M. J. Duffy, O.P.), *Summa Theologiae.* Vol.4°. Superstition and Irreverence. (Cambridge, 2006): pp. 86-87, Question 97, Tempting God. Man can't test God.

208 It was a trial by ordeal, see Alexander Mansfield Burrill (1806–1869), *A Law Dictionary and Glossary*, 2. (New York, 1870) *ad vocem Vulgaris Purgatio.*

The lawsuit cannot be pending or concern matters that may come into obligation in the future in the same way that the obligation of the surety can be pending or prepared for the future. I believe, indeed, that no one will doubt the fact that a surety can be accepted before the obligation of the debtor arises; however, it is not possible to accept the institution of a lawsuit before something is owed.".], the judgment (*sententia*), D.49.4.1.5 [D.49.4.*Quando appellandum sit et intra quae tempora* (When an appeal is to be made and within what times).1 **Ulpianus**, *in the first book on Appeals*: 5. Two or three days will be reckoned for filing an appeal from the day the judgment is rendered. What then, if the judgment is pronounced under a condition? Do we compute the time to appeal from the day of the judgment, or from the day the condition of the judgment occurred? Indeed, a judgment should not be considered under a condition, but if it were pronounced as such, what would happen? It is certainly advantageous that the periods for filing an appeal should be immediately calculated.], excommunication, X.2.28.37 [X.2.28. *De Appellationibus, recusationibus et relationibus* (On appeals, recusations and petitions).37. The judgement with penalty of *interdictum* is not suspended by a subsequent appeal.]; X.5.39 [X.5.39. *De sententia excommunicationis* (On the judgement with penalty of excommunication).].

And because canon law (*ius sacrum*[209]) also pertains to public matters, it was appropriate that it too be unconditional, as stated in X.3.12.1 [X.3.12. *Ut ecclesiastica beneficia sine deminutione conferantur* (In order the ecclesiastical benefits be granted without diminution).1. Rubrum sufficit pro summario, vel summa sic secundum Abbatem: Occulta collatio beneficii, licet sit suspecta, bene valet, dummodo alias legitime facta probetur. [...] [the title of the chapter [*rubrum, red,* was the way to indicate the title of the chapter, because it was written in red ink, e.n.] is sufficient as a summary such as summarized by the Abbot: the conferral of a benefit does not made public, however suspicious, has value, as long as it is proven that it was legitimately granted

[209] Here *ius sacrum* is in the sense of canon law; for the meaning of ius sacrum in Roman law, Berger, *ad vocem Ius sacrum*, "Strictly connected with ius divinum and ius pontificium. It embraces "the legal principles and institutions which are connected with the relations of men to gods, with questions of cult, sacrifices, temples, consecration, graves, and sacerdotal functions, whenever they may occur. The jurists Servius Sulpicius and Trebatius wrote on the subject of the ius sacrum. In oldest times the ius sacrum exercised a considerable influence on private law. the knowledge of legal rules and their interpretation and applicability having been a monopoly of the priests.".

elsewhere.], confer without opposition, X.3.5.11 [X.3.5.*De praebendis et dignitatibus* (On praebends and dignities).11. The prelate and the chapter can impose a just burden on the vacant prebend, which the prebendary must comply.]; X.1.6.4 [X.1.6. *De Electione et electi potestate* (The election and the power of the elected).4 To the elected archbishop, the apostolic see does not transmit the pallium, if he has not previously taken an oath of fidelity and obedience.]; X.3.4.4 [X.3.4. *De Clericis non residentibus in ecclesia vel praebenda* (On not resident clerics in the church and on the prebend).4. The unconfirmed <bishop> presented to a church, if it appears that he did not want to reside, must not be appointed by the superior; the confirmed which does not reside for just cause, on the other hand, is deprived <of the prebend> without the right of appeal.].

These are external conditions mentioned in the quoted definitions and add Clem.3.3.1.pr. [Clem.3.3. *De concessione praebendae et ecclesiae non vacantis* (On the granting of a prebend and a non-vacant church): A conditional decree before the event of the condition does not affect the power of the ordinary or of another conferring <the benefit>, otherwise, when the time of acceptance of the benefit is added with a decree. And he who requests or receives a vacant benefit from the executor is believed to have accepted it; this vacant benefit is assumed <as > known to those who have the expectation, from which it follows that it is considered publicly known in the place where the benefit is located.].

However, these canons should be understood in relation to the ordinary, VI 1. 6. 2 [VI 1. 6. *De electione et electi potestate.* 2: Vota conditionalia et alternativa et incerta[210] in electionibus reprobantur et habentur pro non adiectis, et recidunt in pure consentientes. (On the election and the power of the elected. 2: Conditional, alternative, and uncertain votes are disapproved in elections and are considered as if not given, and they fall under pure consent).]. C.16.q.7.c.20. [Let no cleric obtain a church from the laity.].

The Supreme Pontiff has reserved for itself the power to confer benefits under suspensive conditions and effective from a specific date (*ex die*), as stated in C.7.q.1.c.42. [Qui metu hostilitatis ad alium locum transierit postea

[210] Henricus Pirhing, S.J., *Synopsis Pirhingiana seu SS. Canonum Doctrina.* (Romae, 1849), p. 66, "vota conditionata (eligo Caium, si eum etiam decanus elegerit); alternativa (eligo Titium vel Caium); incerta (eligo eum, in quem decanus consentit).".

ad suam ecclesiam redire oportet. (It seems a wrong quotation, not conferring with the text).].

Here we encounter a theological question regarding the subject and a juridical one concerning the predicate.

However, because the nature of the predicate may also determine the resolution, we are permitted to examine it, namely whether baptism can be conditional. The canons, in cases where the validity of an infant's baptism is doubtful, deemed it appropriate to administer the following form: *"If you have already been baptized, I do not baptize you; if you have not been baptized, I baptize you in the name, etc."* (see X.3.42.2 [X.3.42.*De baptismo et eius effectu*.2 (On baptism and its effects). If plausibly is doubted, whether anyone has been baptized, can be baptized with the formula indicated here [see it in the text, e.n.]; D.68.c.2 [D.68.c.2. (in the end): [...] as well as if it is doubtful whether he hadn't been before baptized, achieves the grace of baptism, whether the same person has been baptized, <the formula> does not concern the repetition of baptism, but the guarantee of salvation.]).

The theologians in our region hold the opposite opinion (see *Brochmand. System. Theol. Loc. de Baptismo, c. 6, § ult. cas. 7*[211]). The addition of a condition does not appear necessary since the condition is already inherent in the law itself (theorem 17). A repeated baptism is considered invalid according to the canonists' view (as baptism impresses an indelible mark), but due to the fear of committing a sin, a good intention prompts the inclusion of this condition. While the second baptism may not have a positive effect on the one being baptized, it does have a negative effect on the one performing the baptism. However, in this particular case, given the presence of uncertainty, it does not seem necessary to

[211] Jaspers Rasmussen Brochmand (1585-1652), *Universae Theologiae Systema*. T. 2. (Francofurti ad Moenum, consulted 1668 edition), p. 448, Casus conscientiae VI An infantes expositii, de quibus certo non constat an sint baptizati, baptizari debeant? § ult., "Nec obstare debet metus iterandi Baptismus: non quod nescitur esse factum, pro iterandi haberi non habet." [Nor should the fear of repeating Baptism hinder: for what is not known to have happened must not be regarded as to be repeated].

resort to scrupulousness, so as not to leave an infant without baptism. In the sight of God, who scrutinizes the hearts, if one acts sincerely, a mental and verbal declaration are considered equivalent. Not to mention that the canons have omitted the condition in a similar example. For instance, when it is unknown whether a church has been consecrated, it should be consecrated without condition, purely, D.1.c.16.1 [D.1.*De consecratione* (On consecration) c.16.1: Whenever you doubt the consecration of churches, that there are no certain documents or witnesses, from whom you have news of the consecration, know that those <churches> are to be consecrated; nor does such insecurity entail repetition, since it is not shown that has been repeated what one does not know if has happened.] ; D.1 c. 18 [D.1 *De consecratione* (On consecration) c. 18: The part of the Church and the altars about which it is doubtful their consecration have to be consecrated, and the superfluous altars have to be demolished.].

(54) It is therefore unconditionable anything that is commanded under the law relating to the quality of citizen.

Therefore, it is evident that the *legitima*[212] share is unconditionable; it cannot be increased or diminished, not even under a potestative condition. The condition is considered as if not added, C.3.28.32 [C.3.28. *Concerning an unjust testament* (De inofficioso testamento.).32. Since we decided in former sanctions that if less than the legal portion be left to those who by virtue of ancient laws could bring an action to set aside a testament as unjust, this deficiency should be supplied, and not furnish the occasion for annulling the testament, we think we should add at present that if the rights of heirs who were permitted to bring such actions appear to be diminished by reason of certain conditions, deferments or other provisions involving delay, condition, or other

[212] Berger, *ad vocem Pars (portio) legitima*, "The share of an inheritance due to an heir who would succeed under the law on intestacy (heres legitimus, ab intestato). The fourth part of the pars legitima (quarta legitimae partis) had to be left certain heirs among the next relatives (descendants, ascendants, and later, consanguineous brothers and sisters) in any form. Otherwise, i.e., if the share left to them was less than the required fourth, or if they were not mentioned in the testament at all or were unjustly disinherited, they had the querela inofficiosi testamenti which might lead to the rescission of the whole testament.".

burden, such condition, deferments, or other provisions involving any burden whatever, shall be void, and the matter in connection with the will shall proceed as though no such addition had been made to the testament.]. D.35.1.83 and C.6.25.4 oppose [D.35.1. *De condicionibus et demonstrationibus et causis et modis eorum, quae in testamento scribuntur* (Conditions, designations, explanations for and modalities of provisions in wills). 83 **Paulus**, *in the twelfth book of Replies*: see above in definition 64.]; [C.6.25. *Concerning appointments, substitutions or trusts, made upon condition.* (De institutionibus vel substitutionibus seu restitutionibus sub condicione factis.).4, see above in definition 65.].

Nicol. Vigelius in Method. Iur. Controv. Præfatione dè Rat. Legendi, column. 9[213], argues that D.35.1.83 e C.6.25.4, have been repealed by the aforementioned C.3.28.32.

However, it is not necessary to resort to that just yet. In D.35.1.83 and C.6.25.4, it is simply stated that if a father appoints the son as heir under a non-potestative condition, the testament is invalid, as the son is clearly passed over (*praeteriit*). If, in fact, he appoints only under a potestative condition, under the contrary condition he does not appoint, that is, he passes over <the son>. In this case the testament becomes null and unjust, D.28.3.1 [D. 28.3.*De iniusto rupto irrito facto testament* (A will which has not been lawfully made, or which has been broken or rendered ineffectual).1 **Papinianus**, *on the first book of Definitions*: A will is said to be either not legally made when the legal formalities are lacking, or of no effect when a son who was under the father's power has been omitted; or it is broken by another will under which there can be an heir or by the addition of a *suus heres* to the agnatic family; or it is rendered ineffectual by the non acceptance of the inheritance.]; D.28.5.4 [D.28.5. *De heredibus instituendis* (The institution of heirs).4 **Ulpianus**, *in the fourth book to Sabinus*: A *suus heres* also can be instituted under a condition; but a son is a special case because he cannot be instituted under any sort of condition. But he can be [instituted] under such a condition as it is in his own power to satisfy; for on this there is agreement among all authorities. But does the institution only have effect if he has met the condition or even if he has not met it and has died? Julianus thinks that a son instituted

[213] Nikolaus Vigel (1529–1600), *Methodus juris controversi* (Basileae, 1616) *Praefatio de Ratione legendi*, col. 9.

under this sort of condition, even if he has not fulfilled the condition, has been removed; and, therefore, if the son so instituted has a co-heir, he ought not to wait until the son meets the condition, although if he would make the father intestate by not meeting the condition, undoubtedly he ought to wait, and this view seems acceptable to me, so that [a son] instituted under such a condition a s it is in his option [to satisfy] does not make his father intestate.]; except for the condition: "if he will want to be the heir," which does not deprive the son of anything but rather grants him the freedom to not be a necessary heir[214] (v. infra about tutor theorem 58 at the end), D.28.5.87(86) [D.28.5. *De heredibus instituendis* (The institution of heirs). 87 (86) **Maecianus**, *in the seventh book of Fideicommissa*: see above in definition 53.]; D.28.7.10, 12, 28 [D.28.7. *De conditionibus institutionum* (Conditions on institutions).10. **Ulpianus**, *in the eighth book on Disputes*: see above in definition 17. 12 **Hermogenianus**, *in the third book of Epitome of Law*: The phrase "let Publius Maevius, if he wishes, be heir" introduces a condition specific to a necessarius heres. If Publius Maevius chooses not to accept the inheritance, he does not assume the role of heir. This condition is particularly relevant when the designation of an heir is voluntary. In such cases, adding these words becomes redundant, as the voluntary nature of the designation implies that even without this addition, an individual who chooses not to accept the inheritance would not become the heir. 28 **Papinianus**, *in the thirteenth book On Questions*: see above in theorem 1.]; D.28.2.16, 29 [D.28.2.*De liberis et postumis heredibus instituendis vel exheredandis (The institution of children and postumi as heirs and their disherison)*.16 **Africanus**, *in the fourth book on Questions*: If a son has been instituted heir, omitting any postumus, and substituted to the son is a grandson born of him, if the son dies in the meantime, should no postumus be born, the grandson will be suus heres both to his father and to his grandfather. But if no one has been substituted to the son and he alone has been instituted, then, because at the time when he dies it becomes certain that no one will be heir under that will, the son himself will become heir to his intestate father, just as usually happens when a son who has been instituted heir under a condition which it will be in his own power to fulfill, dies before he fulfilled it. 29 **Scaevola**, *in the sixth book on Questions*: see above in theorem 21.]; D.35.1.83 [D.35.1. *De condicionibus et demonstrationibus et causis et modis eorum, quae in testamento scribuntur* (Conditions, designations, explanations for and modalities of provisions in wills).83 **Paulus**,

[214] See note 45 above.

in the twelfth book of Replies: see above in definition 64.]; C.6.25.4 [C.6.25.*De institutionibus vel substitutionibus seu restitutionibus sub condicione factis* (Concerning appointments, substitutions or trusts, made upon condition).4. see above in definition 65.].

Furthermore, to be considered as passed over, the laws require the presence of a non-potestative condition, D.28.7.15, 28 [D.28.7. *De conditionibus institutionum* (Conditions on institutions).15 **Papinianus**, *in the sixteenth book of Questions*: see above in this theorem 38. 28 **Papinianus**, *in the thirteenth book On Questions*: see above in theorem 1.] and the mentioned passages. Otherwise, it is considered mere disobedience of the son.

Hence, the difference between C.3.28.32 and D.35.1.83 and C.6.25.4, becomes clear. In the former, the condition is added to the *legitima* share, while in the latter, it is added to the inheritance. In the former, the potestative condition is rejected, but in the latter, it is allowed. Therefore, in the former case, nothing prohibits the condition be vitiated, whereas in the latter case, it vitiates the testament.

This brings us to the point that a condition cannot be added to the inheritance if it has already been given unconditionally in the testament. If it was given conditionally, the condition cannot be removed or changed by a codicil, I.2.25.2 [I.2.25. *De codicillis* (Of codicils).2. An inheritance can neither be given nor taken away by codicils, nor, accordingly, can a child be disinherited in this way: for, if it were otherwise, the law of wills and of codicils would be confounded. By this it is meant that an inheritance cannot directly be given or taken away by codicils; for indirectly, by means of a trust, one can very well be given in this manner. Nor again can a condition be imposed on an instituted heir, or a direct substitution be effected, by codicils.]; D.29.7.6 [D.29.7. *De iure codicillorum* (The law of codicils).6 **Marcianus**, *in the seventh book of Institutes*: The deified Severus and Antoninus stated in a rescript that a mother who, when she instituted her children as heirs unconditionally, imposed a condition of emancipation in a codicil, achieved nothing, because it is not possible either to impose a condition on the instituted heir in a codicil or make a substitution to the direct heir.]; D.28.7.27.1 [D.28.7.*De conditionibus institutionum* (Conditions on institutions). 27

Modestinus, *in the eighth book of Replies*: 1. The heir, who was solely and simply instituted in the will, had a condition imposed by the de cuius within the codicils. The question arises whether it is necessary for the designated heir in the will to fulfill this condition. Modestinus provides the answer: it is not necessary because, in the codicils, the inheritance cannot be revoked. On the other hand, it is understood that the de cuius had contemplated the revocation of the inheritance in the event of non-compliance with the condition.].

Since the inheritance cannot be given or taken away by codicils, if a condition is attached to it in case of non-fulfillment, it is deemed fulfilled according to theorem 6, see lord V.[innius].

(55) *All other rights and acts accept conditions.*

For example,

ownership D.12.1.8 [D.12.1. *De rebus creditis si certum petetur et de condictione* (Things credited giving rise to fixed claims and the condictio). 8 **Pomponius**, *in the sixth book From Plautius*: see above in definition 7.], D.7.1.12, 70.1 [D.7.1. *De usu fructu et quemadmodum quis utatur fruatur* (Usufruct and the way in which a man may exercise it). 12 **Ulpianus**, *in the seventeenth book to Sabinus*: The passage Leibniz provided here does not explicitly mention conditions in the legal sense, mistake in quoting? e.n. 70 **Ulpianus**, *in the seventeenth book to Sabinus*: 1. During the transitional period before the young animals are assigned and the deceased ones are substituted, the question arises: who has ownership rights over these young animals? Julianus, as mentioned in his thirty-fifth Digest book, suggests that the ownership of these animals is in suspense. Consequently, if they are designated as replacements, they are attributed to the bare owner; however, if no such allocation occurs, they are deemed to be owned by the usufructuary. This perspective is considered valid.]; D.8.4.18 [D.8.4. *Communia praediorum tam urbanorum quam rustichusrum* (Rules common to both rustic and urban estates).18 **Paulus**, *in the first book of the Handbook*: It is established that multiple co-owners, even if not establishing servitudes simultaneously, may impose or acquire servitudes in a way that all previous acts are confirmed by the latest act, as if all co-owners had established them simultaneously. Therefore, if the individual who initially performed the act of establishment has died or another form of succession has occurred, or if they have alienated their share in some way, and subsequently another co-owner performs the act of establishment, nothing will have been accomplished. This is because when the last co-owner completes the act of establishment, the acquisition of the servitude is not considered retroactive. It happens almost as if all others had already performed the act when the last one does so; hence, this act will still be pending until the new co-owner, in turn, performs the act of establishment. The same principle applies even if a servitude is established in favor of one of the owners, and then any of these events befalls another co-owner. Consequently, even if the opposite occurs, and any of those events happens to the one who did not perform the act of establishment, all must start anew with the act of establishment. They are granted only a period within which what they can do collectively can be done at different times, and thus, a servitude cannot be established for the benefit of one only, nor can one alone establish it. The same holds true if one establishes the servitude with an inter vivos act, and the other through a legacy. If all co-owners establish the servitude through a legacy, and their inheritance is accepted simultaneously, it can be said that the legacy is effective. However, if accepted at different times, the moment of acquiring the legacy becomes ineffective. It is not established that acts of the deceased remain pending in the same way as those of the living.]; D.39.6.29 [D.39.6. *De mortis causa donationibus et capionibus* (Gifts and acquisitions mortis causa). 29 **Ulpianus**, *in the seventeenth book on Edict*: If something was given as a gift in contemplation of death, and the donor regained their health, let us examine whether they have the actio in rem. If the donor intended for the donee to have the property at the time of their death, without a doubt, the donor can make a vindicatio after the death of the donee; if, however, the donor himself died, then the donee can make it. But if the donor intended for the donee to have the property immediately, with the condition of returning it in case the donor regains health, returns from battle, or from a journey, it can be argued that, upon the occurrence of any of these events, the donor is entitled to the actio in rem, but in the meantime, the action belongs to the donee. If the donee dies before the donor, the donor will still be granted the actio in rem.]; C.4.54.1 [C.4.54. *De pactis inter emptorem et venditorem compositis* (Pacts made between the purchaser and the seller).1. If you sold land under the agreement that, unless the price were paid within a definite time, the (female) purchaser would lose the earnest money and that ownership should revert to you, the condition of the contract must be carried out.]. Although a conditional deed (*titulus*) does not transfer ownership, according to *Tiraquell. De const.*

Poss., p. 2 ampliat. n. 3, 4[215]; *Wesembec. tr. de pac. n. 10*[216];

payment (*solutio*[217]), D.46.3.16 [D.46.3. *De solutionibus et liberationibus* (Performances and releases).16 **Pomponius**, *in the fifteenth book to Sabinus*: If a receipt is given to the debtor under a condition, once the condition is verified, the debtor is considered liberated from that moment. Ariston stated that this holds true even if the payment is made with an object. Indeed, he expressed it as follows: If someone promised a sum under a condition and gave it with the provision that the condition is fulfilled, the sum is considered paid; upon the fulfillment of the condition, he is liberated, and it doesn't matter if the money became the property of the creditor before that.];

improper grant of a feud, see *Rosenthal, c. 6, concl. 23*[218];

215 André Tiraqueau (1488-1558), *De Jure constituti possessorii* (Parisiis, 1553), p. 2, ampliatio 15, 3; Berger, *ad vocem Constitum possessorium*, "Not a classical term. In literature it denotes the legal situation of a person who transferred possession (possessio) of a thing to another but continued to hold it (detinere) under another title. Possessory protection is consequently given to the new possessor. A constitutum possessorium took place when the seller of an immovable remained therein as a tenant [...].".

216 Mattheus Wesembeck (1531-1586), *Commentaria quae olim paratitla in pandectas iuris civilis et codici Iustiniani libros* (Antverpiae, 1621), p. 211, in *commentum ad D. Lib. XVIII, tit. I De contrahenda emptione*, n. 10.

217 Berger, *ad vocem solutio*, "In a broader sense solutio indicates any kind of liberation of the debtor from his debt. Obligations contracted in a specific form (litteris, verbis) had to be extinguished in a similar form; see prout quis- quisque. Thus, a literal obligation (litterarum obligatio) was extinguished by expensilatio, a stipulatio by a parallel oral form, the acceptilatio. In a narrower sense solutio denotes the payment, the fufillment of an obligation. Payment could be made by anyone, not only by the debtor himself, but even without bis knowledge and against his will. The creditor was not obliged to accept a part of the debt nor another thing in lieu of that which was actually due (aliud pro alio) Failure to pay at the term fixed produced for the debtor the disadvantages of a default (see mora debitoris). A creditor who refused the acceptance of the payment could also be in default (in mora) see mora creditoris. —D. 46.3; C. 8.42; 11.40.".

218 Heinrich von Rosenthal (d. 1625), *Tractatus et synapsis totius juris feudalis conclusionibus et sentantia in capita duodecim...digestus* (Francofurti ad Moenum, 1624), p. 187, c. 6, conclusio XIX [not XXIII, such as in text, e.n.] "Feudi promissio, et investitura abusiva, tam pure, quam sub condicione et in diem fieri, et condicione pendente, nec laicus, nec clericus poenitere potest.". [The promise of a feud and the abusive investiture* can be made both unconditionally and under conditions,

partnership, D.17.2.1, 70, 75 [D.17.2. *Pro socio* (Partnership).1 **Paulus**, *in the thirty-second book to the Edict*: A partnership can be established either indefinitely, lasting as long as the involved partners are alive, or for a specified duration, starting from a particular moment or under certain conditions. 70 **Paulus**, *in the thirty-third book To the Edict*: No association of partnership is formed for all time. 75 **Celsus**, *in the fifteenth book of Digest*: Should a partnership be established based on shares to be determined by Titius, and Titius passes away before making the decision, the venture cannot proceed. This condition was explicitly stipulated, indicating that the partnership would only be formed according to the terms determined by Titius.]; the mortis causa gift, D.39.6.10 [D.39.6. *De mortis causa donationibus et* capionibus (Gifts and acquisitions mortis causa).10 **Ulpianus**, in the twenty-fourth to *Sabinus*: It is recognized that a replacement can be designated for an individual to whom a gift in contemplation of death has been granted, with the latter committing to give it to another person if they are unable to accept it or under certain conditions.];

surety, D.46.1.6.1, 16 [D.46.1. *De fideiussoribus et mandatoribus* (Sureties and mandators).6 **Ulpianus**, *in the forty-seventh book to Sabinus*: 1. And it is of little relevance whether I bind the surety unconditionally, as from a certain date or under a condition. 16 **Julianus**, *in the fiftieth book of Digest*: A surety cannot be bound to someone with whom there is no pre-existing obligation to fulfill a promise. Therefore, if a slave, belonging jointly to Titius and Sempronius, specifically contracted with Titius and asked for a surety bond as follows: "Do you undertake to give this to Titius or Sempronius?" Titius may indeed demand from the surety, but Sempronius' role seems to be interposed only for the purpose of obtaining payment from him before a contested legal dispute and in the absence of Titius, who may be unaware or unwilling.];

purchase, I.3.23.4 [I.3.23. *De emptione et venditione*.4. A sale may be made conditionally as well as absolutely. The following is an example of a conditional sale: "If Stichus meets with your approval within a certain time, he shall be purchased by you for so many aurei."]; D.18.1.7 [D.18.1 *De contrahenda emptione et de pactis inter emptorem et venditorem compositis et quae res venire non*

including immediate execution and pending conditions. Neither cleric nor layperson can retract or repent.]. * Francesco Foramiti (1760-1843), *Enciclopedia legale*. (Venezia, 1839) III, ad vocem Investitura feudale (feudal law), (...) improper <investiture> is also called abusive or ceremonial, it is an immission into real possession only, combined with some external ceremony to make the act more solemn (e.t.).

possunt (Conclusion of the contract of purchase, special terms agreed between the vendor and purchaser, and things which cannot be sold).7 **Ulpianus**, *in the twenty-eighth book to Sabinus*: The sale of a slave under the condition "if he shall have settled his accounts to his master's satisfaction" is contingent. Contingent sales only become effective when the condition is fulfilled. The question arises whether the mentioned condition pertains to the master's personal satisfaction or the satisfaction of an honorable person. If we adopt the former interpretation, the sale is void, similar to a case where someone sells based on their own discretion or promises in a stipulation, "I will give ten if I want to." Obligations cannot be subject to the arbitrary decision of a contracting party. Consequently, the earlier jurists determined that the judgment of an honorable person, not the master, should be considered. Thus, if the accounts were satisfactory but the master refused or if he feigned non-acceptance after accepting them, the condition for purchase would be fulfilled, allowing the vendor to be sued through the action on purchase.];

lease D.19.2.20. pr. [D.19.2. *Locati conducti* (Lease and hire).20 **Paulus**, *in the thirty-fourth book to the Edict*: [but is pr., not §1 such as in the text, e.n.]. Like purchase, lease also can be contracted under a condition.];

mandate D.17.1.3 [D.17.1.*Mandati vel contra* (The action on mandate or the counteraction).3 **Paulus**, *in the thirty-second book to the Edict*: Additionally, in a lawsuit grounded on a mandate, another factor is considered: At times, the condition of the mandator cannot be enhanced, occasionally it is possible to improve it, but it can never be deteriorated.];

the vow, C.32.q.8.c.1 [C.32.q.8.c.1 *De matrimonio* (On marriage). q.8.c.1: No one must dissolve from the vow of continence, even if an infidel has offered to become a Christian.]; the right of action (to claim the legacy), C.6.53.5 [C.6.53. *When a legacy or trust vests.* (Quando dies legati vel fideicommissi cedit.). 5: see above in theorem 14.].

Can anyone comprehensively describe all these cases?

(56) An irrevocable thing cannot be given under a resolutive condition or a limit (modus).

To give something under a resolutive condition or a limit means that once the condition is met or the limit is not fulfilled, the holding ends or the thing is revoked, def. 21, 22, 25. On the other hand, it implies that an irrevocable thing has been revoked.

However, such is the nature of freedom that once it is given, it cannot be taken away. Therefore, nobody can be free for a certain period or under a resolutive condition, or be a slave under a suspensive condition, D.40.4.33, 34, 52 [D.40.4.*De manumissis testamento* (Testamentary manumissions).33 **Paulus**, *in the twelfth of Questions*: Freedom cannot be given for a period. 34 **Paulus**, in the seventy-fourth book to the *Edict*: Hence, if it were provided, "let Stichus be free for ten years," the addition of the period serves no purpose. 52 **Paulus**, *in the twelfth book of Questions*: The emperors to Missenius Fronto: "A soldier's will contains a grant of freedom in these words: 'I wish' or 'order my slave Stephanus to be free'; freedom is due to him when the inheritance is entered on, and therefore the words subjoined, 'so however that he should remain with my heir so long as he is young; if he has refused or disdained to comply, he should be held in the status of slavery' are not effective to revoke the freedom which is due." The same rule is observed in the case of civilian wills too.].

Nevertheless, if a limit added to freedom is potestative, it becomes an obligation, and the one who has been made free is compelled by a judge's order to fulfill it, D.40.4.44 [D.40.4.*De manumissis testamento* (Testamentary manumission).44 **Modestinus**, *in the tenth book On Responses*: see above in definition 7.].

Similarly, once someone becomes an heir, they never cease to be so, meaning that the inheritance cannot be given for a certain time, and therefore not under a resolutive condition, D.28.5.34 [D.28.5. *De heredibus instituendis* (The institution of heirs).34 **Papinianus**, *in the first book of Definitions*: see above in theorem 29.].

Still, there is a different rule in the testament of a soldier, D.29.1.15.4, 19.2, 41. pr. [D.29.1. *De testamento militis* (The soldier's will).15 **Ulpianus**, *in the forty-fifth book to the Edict*: 4. A soldier can make someone heir up to a particular time and someone else heir thereafter, or from or to the fulfillment of a condition. 19 **Ulpianus**, *in the fourth book of Disputations*: 2. Where one person had been appointed heir by a soldier up to a certain time and another person from that time the question arises whether the later heir is bound to pay legacies charged on the earlier heir.

And I think that he is not bound, unless it is proved that the wishes of the soldier were otherwise. 41. **Tryphoninus**, *in the eighteenth book of Disputations*: pr. A soldier can designate an heir with the following formulation: "Let Titius be heir during his lifetime, and Septicius after his death." However, if the designation is made in the following manner, "Let Titius be heir for a period of ten years," without providing a substitute, the situation after ten years will result in intestacy. Since we've established that soldiers can appoint an heir from a specific time until a certain time, the implication is that, before the designated heir assumes the inheritance, there is an interim period of intestacy. The privileges granted in terms of managing a share of the estate also apply within the same scope for a specified period, even if that period is of significant duration.]; C.6.21.8 [C.6.21. *De testamento militis* (Concerning the testament of a soldier).8. The law is certain that a soldier has the right to appoint a person as heir for a limited time.].

It has been questioned whether ownership (which is revocable not by law but by delivery) can be under a resolutive condition, so that once the condition occurs, it is dissolved by law. Some think that once the condition occurs, the ownership of the possessor is not dissolved, but only the right over the thing (*jus ad rem*[219]) is given to another until delivery takes place, arg. C.4.54.3 [C.4.54. *Pacts made between the purchaser and the seller* (De pactis inter emptorem et venditorem compositis).3. If a person has sold land under the agreement that it should be restored to him unless the

[219] Harold J. Berman, *Law and Revolution II. The impact of the Protestant Reformations on the Western Legal Tradition* (Cambridge, MA: Harvard University Press, 2003), p. 116 (and ft. 49), "The concept of jus ad rem, not to be found in the Institutes, had been invented by the scholastic jurists of the twelfth century and had become an integral fundamental concept of European law". According to Berman, it is due to the German jurist Johann Apel (1486–1536) [*Methodica dialectices ratio ad Jurisprudentiam adcommodata Authore Johanne Apello.* (Noribergae, 1535); Id., *Isagoge per dialogum in quattuor libros Institutionum D. Iustiniani Imperatoris Authore Johanne Apello.* Wratislaviae, 1540) e. n.], the criticism and reworking of the subdivision of right such as, "declared in Justinian's Institutes, into "persons", "actions", and "things". The author of the Institutes did not define these terms in a satisfactory way and did not in fact organize his exposition around them. Apel contended, first, that the category "persons" is incidental to "things". He then went on to divide "things" (*res*) into "right in a thing" (*ius in re*), to which he applied the term "ownership" (*dominium*), and "right to a thing" (*ius ad rem*), to which he applied the term "obligation" (*obligatio*), under which he also subsumed "actions".".

remainder of the purchase price should be paid within a fixed time, he does not have the right to bring a real action (vindicatio) if he did not give mere permissive possession, but he has an action on the sale.], *Vasquius ill. controv. c. 69*[220]. Because ownerships of things are transferred not by pacts but by deliveries, C.2.3.20 [C.2.3.*De pactis* (Concerning informal agreements*)*.20.The ownership of property is transferred by delivery and usucaption (prescription), but not by naked pacts.], for example, "I sell you the plot of land Cornelianus, but it is immediately agreed between us that the fund is again mine once you do not fulfill something within two years". Here, those famous jurists say that, once the two-year period has passed, only a personal action (*actio personalis*[221]) of sale (*ex vendito*[222]) is allowed, but I believe also a real action

[220] Fernando Vasquez de Menchaca (1512-1569) (1668), *Illustrium controversiarum, aliarumque usu frequentium*. Francofurti, 259, p. II, lib. III, cap. 69, n. 2, Dominium rei venditae et traditae non trasfertur, si fides non est habita de pretio.

[221] Berger, *ad vocem Actiones in personam*, "Actions in which the plaintiff based his claim on a contractual or delictual obligation of the defendant.".

[222] Berger, *ad vocem Emptio venditio*, "A purchase and sale, i.e., a contract by which a thing is exchanged for money. The terminology emptio venditio indicates the two elements of the contract: an emere by the buyer (emptor) and a vendere by the seller (venditor). The Roman sale was a consensual contract concluded when the parties by simple consent (nudo consensu) agreed upon the thing to be sold and the price (pretium) to be paid therefor, without further formality. The sale contract itself did not transfer ownership of the thing sold to the buyer. To accomplish that another legal act was necessary (mancipatio, in iure cessio, traditio). The vendor had only to hand over the thing to the buyer to make the latter possess and enjoy it peacefully (ut rem emptori habere liceat). The buyer had to pay the price in money, either immediately or later, according to the agreement. The exchange of one thing for another is not a sale, but a permutatio. Anything may be the object of a sale (merx) except things excluded from private transactions (res cuius commercium non est). Non-corporeal things (a servitude, an usufruct) may be sold, as well as future things (see emptio spei, emptio rei speratae). The price must be fixed in an unequivocal way (pretium certum) and be real, i.e., corresponding to the true value of the thing (verum), not ficticious (e.g., as a device to cover a prohibited donation). Sale was a contract bonae fidei; the pertinent actions were actio venditi (ex vendito) against the buyer for payment of the price and actio empti (ex empto) against the seller if he did not fulfill his obligations, failed to deliver the thing sold, for example, or to take care of it (custodia) in the period between the conclusion of the sale and delivery so that the thing perished or deteriorated. The seller was not liable for accident (casus). See periculum rei venditae. Special rules settled the liability of the vendor when the

(*actio realis, in rem*[223]).

However, in this case, the ownership is not transferred by a pact, but the matter should be understood more accurately. While the seller hands over the plot of land, by that act alone, the ownership is transferred, but modified by a covenant so that the seller retains conditional ownership and grants unconditional ownership to another, but under a resolutive condition, i.e., not yet fully effective. Therefore, once the condition is met, it becomes evident that the unconditional ownership remains with the seller, which was previously uncertain.

buyer was later evicted from the thing by a third person. See evictio, stipulation duplae. Warranty against hidden defects in the thing sold was originally stipulated expressly by the seller; besides, the actio empti, as a bonae fidei actio, gave the opportunity to take into consideration defects fraudulently concealed by the seller. The edict of the aediles curules, as the supervisors of the markets established particular provisions for the sale of slaves and domestic animals. Above all, the seller had to inform die buyer of any defect or disease that was not apparent to the buyer. He was liable for all allegations (dicta et promissa) be may have made about special qualities of tbe slave or animal or the lack of secret defects (even those unknown to himself). Two actions lay against him, either the actio redhibitoria for the rescission of the sale (the seller being obliged to return the price and the buyer to restore the thing with accessories) or the actio quanti minoris (named also aestimatoria) by which the buyer claimed restitution of a portion of tbe price paid, corresponding to the lesser value. The principles of the aedilian edicts were later extended to all kinds of sale. Throughout the classical period no written document was required for die validity of a sale contract. When made, it served only for purposes of evidence. Justinian ordered some formalities for written sales, when according to the will of the parties, the written form was a requirement for the validity of the sale (instrumentum emptionis, instrumentum emptionale). Until the formalities were accomplished, with the assistance ot a notary (tabellio), the parties could rescind the sale. Many reforms in the law of sale were introduced by Justinian. — Inst 323; D. 18.1; 18.5; 19.1; C. 4.38; 40; 44; 45; 49; 54; 58.—.".

[223] Watson, note 32 above, Glossary, *Actio in Rem* (Real Action), "An action asserting ownership of property, or other related though more limited rights over it, for example, a servitude [sewitus q.v.1. Such an action lay against anyone withholding the property.".

Certainly, in a pact of *lex commissoria*[224], the *rei vindicatio*[225] is granted more securely, C.4.54.4 [C.4.54. *De pactis inter emptorem et venditorem compositis* (Pacts made between the purchaser and the seller).4. A person cannot enforce the agreement of forfeiture (*commissoria*) made in connection with a sale if he does not elect, after the time fixed for the payment of the price to ask for the recovery of the property but prefers to sue for the interest on the purchase price.].

And within the day of the better offer (*in diem addictio*), the pact allows that the thing belongs to the seller only for a certain period, until a better condition is offered, D.18.2.4.3 [D.18.2 *In diem addictio*.4 **Ulpianus**, *in the book twenty-eight book to Sabinus*: 3. Marcellus, in his fifth book of the Digest, asserts that in the case of an absolute sale subject to a defeasible condition, specifically an in diem addictio, if a superior offer is presented, the land is no longer bound by a pledge if the purchaser had pledged it. This implies that the purchaser holds ownership during the interim period; otherwise, the pledge would not be enforceable.], add D.6.1.41 [D.6.1. *De rei vindicatio* (*Vindicatio* of property).41 **Ulpianus**, *in the seventeenth book to the Edict*: pr. If a person bought under to this condition, that if a better offer is made, the sale should be rescinded, then once such an offer has been made, the buyer cannot bring an action in rem. But even if someone has a right to an estate subject to in diem addictio, then, before it happens, he can bring an action in rem; after it has happened, he cannot.].

The quoted texts should be added to the previous theorem 55, which discusses the conditionability of ownership. Also, see theorem 47 for further reference.

(57) *The risk of deterioration or loss of a conditional thing lies with the conditionarius once the disposition is perfect.*

224 Berger, *ad vocem Commissoria lex*, "(In a pledge.) An agreement between creditor and debtor by which the former becomes owner of the pledge if the debtor fails to pay the debt at the date fixed. Constantine forbade such agreement. —C.8.34.".

225 Watson, note 32 above, Glossary, *Vindicatio*, "A term commonly used for the action claiming ownership of property, its full title being rei vindicatio. I t was sometimes also used to cover other kinds of mainly real actions [actio i n rem q.v.1. See D.6.1."-

Referring to D.18.6.8. pr., 10 [D.18.6. *De periculo et commodo rei venditae* (Risk and benefit of the thing sold). 8 **Paulus,** *in the thirty-third book to the Edict*: pr. It is crucial to determine the point of perfection in a sale, as it establishes the party responsible for bearing the risk associated with the item. Once the sale is perfected, the purchaser assumes the risk. The sale is considered perfect when the item is identified, its nature and quantity are defined, the price is agreed upon, and there are no conditions attached. In cases where the sale is conditional and the condition remains unsatisfied, there is no valid sale. However, if the condition is fulfilled, Proculus and Octavenus argue that the risk shifts to the purchaser, a view endorsed by Pomponius in his ninth book. If either the seller or the buyer passes away while the condition is pending, their heirs become liable upon the condition's realization, treating the sale as if it were retroactively binding from the initial agreement. If the item is delivered while the condition is still pending, the purchaser cannot acquire ownership through usucapion. In case the item ceases to exist during the pending condition, any paid price must be refunded, and the fruits gained during this period belong to the seller (similarly applicable to conditional stipulations and legacies). If the item exists when the condition is satisfied but has deteriorated, it can be argued that the purchaser assumes the risk. 10. **Ulpianus,** *in the eighth book of Disputations*: If it be agreed in a conditional sale that the thing shall be at the purchaser's risk, I think that the pact is valid.]; D.46.2.14 [D.46.2.*De novationibus et delegationibus* (Novations and delegations).14 **Ulpianus,** *in the seventh book of Disputes*: In cases where a simple obligation is promised conditionally through novation, the novation does not take effect immediately but only upon the realization of the condition. For instance, if Stichus is the subject of the obligation and passes away while the condition is pending, novation would not occur since the object of the obligation no longer exists when the condition is satisfied. Therefore, Marcellus contends that even if Stichus is made the object of a conditional obligation after a culpable delay, the delay is purged, and it does not extend into the subsequent obligation.]; I reiterate, only once the disposition has been perfected, as argued by D.23.3.10.5 [D.23.3.*De iure dotium* (The law of dowry).10 **Ulpianus,** *in thirty-fourth book to Sabinus*: 5. Hence, the inquiry arises as to whether the woman is responsible for the loss incurred if slaves, whose value was assessed before the marriage, perish. It logically ensues that she is, as the sale is contingent, and if death occurs while the condition is unresolved, it renders the sale null. Consequently, the woman experiences a loss in this scenario, given that the sale had not yet been finalized.], please also consider what we have discussed in theorem 68 regarding the retroactive effect of the condition (*retrotractio*).

Chapter IX

[The State or Motion that Must Occur or Fail in Conditioned Part]

Definitions

Above, at the beginning of Chapter 7, we stated that the matter of partial propositions consists of persons, things, what is included in propositions, and the circumstances of place and time. Chapters 7 and 8 address the topics of persons and things. As for what is included in the conditioned part, it is covered in the treatment of things.

Therefore, it remains that:

71.The conditioned part refers to the state or motion that must occur or fail. For example, if Titius ascends the Capitolium, the act of ascending becomes the conditioned part, and so on.

In terms of this, the condition is divided into:

72. Either of fact or legal. This division is sometimes equivalent to the division into extrinsic and voluntary, as stated in D.35.1.21 [D.35.1. *De condicionibus et demonstrationibus et causis et modis eorum, quae in testamento scribuntur* (Conditions, designations, explanations for and modalities of provisions in wills).21 **Julianus,** *in the thirty-first book of the Digests*: see above in definition 12.], see the earlier definitions 8, 9.

However, in this context, it is the same as saying that one condition is based on pure physical facts, while the other is based on a significant fact that has legal effectiveness. In this sense, what is purely a matter of fact is denied from passing to heirs or owners, as stated in I.3.17.2 [I.3.17. *De stipulatione servorum* (Of stipulations made by slaves).2. When, however, what is stipulated for is permission to do some specific act, that permission cannot extend beyond the person of the promisee: for instance, if a slave stipulates for permission to cross the promisor's land, he cannot himself be denied passage, though his master can.]; D.35.1.44.pr. [D.35.1. *De condicionibus et demonstrationibus et causis et modis eorum, quae in testamento scribuntur* (Conditions, designations, explanations for and modalities of provisions in wills).44 **Paulus**, *in the ninth book to Plautius*: pr., see above in theorem 19.] (although there, the rule is misused since the act of giving is not purely a fact). It is also mentioned in D.46.3.31 [D.46.3.*De solutionibus et liberationibus* (Performances and releases).31 **Ulpianus**, *in the seventh book on Disputes*: see above in theorem 19.], and supported by Theorem 19. Furthermore, services cannot be performed by another person, D.40.7.39.5 [D.40.7. *De statuliberis* (Statuliberi).39 **Javolenus**, *in the fourth book From the Posthumous Works of Labeo*: 5, see above in theorem 19.], supported by Theorem 12.

Nevertheless, even though the one who gives also creates, D.50.16.18 [D.50.16.*De verborum significatione* (Meaning of expressions).18 **Paulus**, *in the ninth book to the Edict*: "Munus" is understood in three ways: first, as a gift, whence we talk of munera being given or sent; second, as a burden, and when this is remitted release from military service or a munus is as a result called immunity; third, as a duty, whence we talk of military munera and call some soldiers performers of the munera; and, therefore, we talk of municipes because they undertake civil munera.].

The term "to give" sometimes signifies the transfer itself, from one person to another, D.35.1.44.pr. [D.35.1. *De condicionibus et demonstrationibus et causis et modis eorum, quae in testamento scribuntur* (Conditions, designations, explanations for and modalities of provisions in wills).44 **Paulus**, *in the ninth book to Plautius*: pr., see above in theorem 19.]. It also applies to the person who cannot make something their own, D.35.1.55 [D.35.1. *De condicionibus et demonstrationibus et causis et modis eorum, quae in testamento scribuntur* (Conditions, designations, explanations for and modalities of provisions in wills).55 **Javolenus**, *in the thirteenth of Letters*: see above in theorem 48.]. Nevertheless,

73. "To give" in common usage means to accomplish all that is within our power, so that something may be added to another person's possessions. Therefore, a physical action is not required from the one compensating, D.40.7.20.2 [D.40.7.*De statuliberis* (Statuliberi).20 **Paulus**, *in the sixteenth book to Plautius*: 2. But if he was ordered to give ten to the heir and the heir should owe that sum to the slave, the slave will be

free, should he wish to set off one sum against the other.] or from the one credited D.30.81.5 [D.30.*De legatis et fideicommissis* (Legacies and fideicommissa).81 **Julianus**, *in the thirty-second book of the Digest*: see above in theorem 16.], even though it is said that they gave in the quoted passages.

Furthermore, the acceptance of the other person is not required; it is sufficient to exert the maximum effort to fulfill the condition (see theorem 69). This means offering, as mentioned in D.35.1.45 [D.35.1. *De condicionibus et demonstrationibus et causis et modis eorum, quae in testamento scribuntur* (Conditions, designations, explanations for and modalities of provisions in wills).45 **Paulus**, *in the sixteenth book to Plautius*: see above in theorem 16.].

For a statuliber, it is sufficient to deposit the money, D.40.7.4.pr. [D.40.7.*De statuliberis* (Statuliberi).4 **Paulus**, *in the fifth book to Sabinus*: pr. When the heir was absent on public business, the statuliber with the cash must wait until the return of the person to whom the money is to be given, or deposit it in a temple under seal, so he attains freedom at once.]. Therefore, anyone who refuses without reason is complaining without ground, C.6.46.7 [C.6.46. *De condicionibus insertis tam legatis quam fideicommissis et libertatibus* (Concerning conditions attached to legacies, trusts and manumissions).7. If several persons were ordered to fulfill a condition, it was doubted by Ulpianus whether all should jointly fulfill it, or whether each is compelled to do so as though imposed on him alone. 1. It appears to us that each should fulfill the condition, and each respectively receive that portion of the benefit destined for him, so that those who have complied with the directions, receive what is due them by reason thereof, while those who have failed to do so may blame themselves, if they are barred from receiving anything.].

Regarding the condition of rendering accounts, the question arises whether it pertains more to giving or doing. Rendering accounts, in essence, is nothing other than having to pay the remainder to the entitled person, and thus, it is a form of giving as desired in D.35.1.32 [D.35.1. *De condicionibus et demonstrationibus et causis et modis eorum, quae in testamento scribuntur* (Conditions, designations, explanations for and modalities of provisions in wills).32 **Africanus**, *in the ninth book of Questions*: Rendering accounts is nothing more than discharging balances; still if through the culpability of both statuliber and heir, but without bad faith on the slave's part, less be paid than is due and the accounts be deemed rendered in good faith, the slave will be free. Did we observe differently, no one conditionally manumitted would ever attain liberty, if an underpayment were made through oversight. [Julianus] says that this holds good if, when a slave is directed to render accounts, he so renders accounts through error but without guile that the master is also in error over the computation.].

Caesius believes, in *l. 1§2 n. 23 V.O.*, that rendering accounts primarily involves doing[226], but there is a distinction between showing accounts (*edere*) and rendering accounts (*reddere rationes*). and rendering accounts. Additionally, along with the preparation of

[226] The name *Caesius* might be a misprint for Ulrich Zasius (see Boucher, note 56 above in *Introduction*, 199, n. 953; Armgardt, note 27 above, in *Introduction*, 96, n. 314), author of *De verborum obligationibus* (Basileae, 1540). On p. 42 of this book, in note 23 of the commentary to l. 1§2 V.O (D.1. *De verborum obligationibus* (Verbal obligations) 2, Paulus, *in the twelfth book to Sabinus*), Zasius actually writes: "...facere & dare sunt duo diversa, sed facere est potentius quo in ratione reddenda, unde rationem reddere, qui est casus mixtus, reputabitur pro obligatione faciendi, licet habeat in se datione." [Doing and giving are two different things, but doing is preponderant in accounting, so accounting, which is a mixed case, will be considered an obligation of doing, even though it contains giving within itself]. A significant passage of the Digest which better illustrates the difference between *edere* and *rationes reddere* is in l. 89§2 V.[erborum] S.[ignificationibus] <D.50.16.89. Pomponius, *in the sixth book to Sabinus*>: "There is a great deal of difference between *edere* and *reddi rationes*." See also Jacques Cujas, *De verborum significationibus commentarius* (Francofurti, 1595), therin 201, ad l. 89§2, "unde queritur quid sit edere, quid reddere rationes. Reddere rationes est reliqua solvere, pariare, seu parem rationem facere, & edere rationes legendas, cognoscendas, dispungendas. [...] Atqui edere tantum iubetur, non continuo reliqua solvere debet, sed chartas, & instrumenta debet offerre legenda, & dispungenda.". [So, it is asked what it means to disclose, show (*edere*), and what it means to give back what remains (*reddere rationes*). To give back what remains (*reddere rationes*) means to settle a balance, i.e., to pay or settle a bill, and to show the accounts which need to be read, understood, and verified. However, now it is only commanded to disclose and show (*edere*), without an immediate requirement to make payment. Instead, one must present papers and documents to be read and verified.]. For the sake of completeness, I add that Titus Caesius was a Roman jurist enumerated by Pomponius among the ten disciples of Servius Sulpicius in D.1.2.44. Caesius is nowhere expressly mentioned in the Digest (see William Smith (ed.), *A Dictionary of Greek and Roman Biography and Mythology* (London, 1880), *ad vocem T. Caesius*; Richard A. Baumann, *Lawyers in Roman Transitional Politics*, Munchen, 1985, 70).

accounts, which is a form of doing, it also includes the act of giving back the remaining amounts to be fulfilled, as specified in D.50.16.89 [see footnote 226]. Therefore, the condition of rendering accounts is a combination of giving and doing, D.40.7.6.7 [D.40.7.*De statuliberis* (Statuliberi).6 **Ulpianus**, *in the twenty-seventh book to Sabinus*: 7. Suppose a man's freedom was ordered, subject to the condition not of his giving ten, but of his rendering accounts, would this condition pass to the buyer? It is sure in other cases that only those conditions pass to the buyer which consist in giving, not in doing, for example, teaching a boy his letters; conditions of the latter sort are tied indissolubly to the particular persons named; but a condition that accounts are to be rendered insofar as it involves payment of sums due, consists in giving money, though insofar as it involves handing over the actual books of accounts, elucidating them by questions, balancing, and then checking and scrutinizing them, it means having done something. Would the man not then attain freedom by actually giving to the purchaser any sums due, whereas the other actions concern the heirs? So, in my opinion, it remains for the heir to require rendering of the accounts and the sums due are to be paid over to the purchaser with effect that the condition is divided; so too Pomponius writes in the eighth book of Sabinus.].

The condition of doing can be either intrinsic or extrinsic.

The intrinsic condition relates to intellect, for example, if someone has believed or similar situations, or it can pertain to the will, such as if someone wants. This is explained by jurist *Ziegler in n. 40 de condit*[227].

On the other hand, the extrinsic condition includes the intrinsic condition; for instance, if you will do something, it implies the intrinsic condition of wanting to do it.

[227] Kaspar Ziegler, see note 8 above in *Preface*, states, "XL. Potestativa conditio rursus vel tota voluntati ipsi inest v.g. Si Volueris vel tota non inest, sed extrinsecum aliquod insuper respicit. Illa intrinseca, haec extrinseca non male vocari potest.". The potestative condition, on the contrary, either resides entirely within the same will, for example, if you wish, or it does not reside entirely but takes into account something extrinsic in addition to this. Appropriately, the former can be called intrinsic, and the latter can be called extrinsic.

Otherwise, they differ, just like the distinction between tacit and express conditions, as stated in D.28.5.69(68) [D.28.5. *De heredibus instituendis* (The institution of heirs). 69 (68) **Pomponius**, *in the seventh book to Quintus Mucius*: see above in theorem 17.].

However, ‹the following laws› mix together and equate D.31.1pr. [D.31.*De legatis et fideicommissis* (Legacies and fideicommissa).1 **Ulpianus**, *in the ninth book to Sabinus*: pr. To make a legacy subject to someone else's discretion is like imposing a condition. For what difference is there between lefting something to me "if Titius should mount to the Capitol" and "if he should wish?".], D.35.1.52 [D.35.1. *De condicionibus et demonstrationibus et causis et modis eorum, quae in testamento scribuntur* (Conditions, designations, explanations for and modalities of provisions in wills).52. **Modestinus**, *in the sevent book of Distinctions*: It is possible for explicitly stated things to pose a hindrance, even if they could be implicitly understood and pose no obstacle. For instance, someone is given a legacy as follows: "I give and bequeath ten to Titius, if Maevius goes up the Capitol." For although it lies in Maevius's discretion whether he goes up the Capitol and so to wish the legacy to be given to Titius, the testator could not effectively have used the formulation: "If Maevius so wishes, I give ten to Titius"; for one cannot leave a legacy at another's pleasure. Hence, the expression "what is said, does harm; what is not, does not."], D.40.5.46.2 [D.40.5.*De fideicommissariis libertatibus* (Grant of freedom by Fideicommissa).46 **Ulpianus**, *in the sixth book of Disputations*: 2. However, if it is formulated as "I desire Stichus to gain freedom, if this should be the wish of Seius contingent upon the desire of Seius," I believe the freedom grant can be considered valid, as it resembles a condition similar to a legacy being contingent on Titius ascending the Capitol. But if it should be so drafted, "I wish Stichus to be free, if this should be the wish of Seius," in my view the grant of freedom can be said to be effective, since it is rather a condition analogous to a legacy to me being made conditional on Titius climbing the Capitol.].

The extrinsic condition of doing attributed to the *conditionarius*, i.e., the potestative condition, requires either absolute submissiveness or at least obedience, or the highest intent to obey when inserted, even if the will is not compliant. This is what is meant as

74. The command (*iussum*), in the neutral gender, is indeed used, D.29.2.62.1 [*D.29.2.De adquirenda vel omittenda hereditate* (Taking up or failing to take up an inheritance).*62* **Javolenus**, *in the first book From the Posthumous Works of Labeo: 1.* Where a slave instituted heir had been alienated after receiving instructions from his master to accept the inheritance but before he accepted, new instructions from the later owner, and not the instructions of the earlier one, are required.]. Juriconsults make use of the command formula (*iussus est*, e.n.), as seen in D.35.1.44. pr. [D.35.1. *De condicionibus et demonstrationibus et causis et modis eorum, quae in testamento* scribuntur (Conditions, designations, explanations for and modalities of provisions in wills).44 **Paulus**, *in the ninth book to Plautius*: pr., see above in theorem 19.], and in countless other passages."

75. "To depend on someone" (*per aliquem stare*) or not to depend *(non stare*) means that, when someone exerts their maximum effort, the event can or cannot occur. It depends on the person who, despite being able to achieve it, does not want to; it does not depend on the person who wants to achieve it and exerts their maximum effort, or rather, they want it with an effective will but cannot. There are numerous texts containing this formula, see, for for example, D.33.1.13 [D.33.1. *De annuis legatis et fideicommissis* (Annual legacies and fideicommissa).13. **Scaevola**, *in the fourth book of Replies*: see above in theorem 16.]; see *per heredem steterit* it was dependent on the heir D.40.7.34 [D.40.7. *De statuliberis* (Statuliberi).34. (...Quid ergo, si neget se reliqua traxisse atque ideo, quia per heredem steterit, ut accipiat rationes, liberum factum, heres autem neque se fecisse moram et reliqua debere statuliberum contendat?...) **Papinianus**, *in the twenty-first book of Questions*: 1. What, then, if the statuliber denies that he has dragged out paying the arrears and claims that he has become free, since it was the responsibility of the heir to receive the accounts, whereas the heir contends that he made no delay and the statuliber owes arrears?] to which it pertains, that formula of the ancients *per te non fieri*: that nothing will be done by you, D.45.1.50 [D.45.1.*De verborum obligationibus (Verbal contracts)*.50... (In illa stipulatione: "per te non fieri?" non hoc significatur nihil te

facturum, quo minus facere possis, sed curaturum, ut facere possis.) **Ulpianus**, *in the fiftieth book To the Edict*: pr. see above in theorem 16.].

Theorems

(58) *The condition of wanting frees the principal person, to whom it is attributed, from the burden of the conditional disposition.*

This theorem must be proved and explained simultaneously.

The principal persons are the conditional debtor (*debiturus*) or the conditionator on one side and the *conditionarius* on the other side, as in definition 54. The burden, on the other hand, for the conditionator arises from the conditional disposition, which is the conditionated or the necessity to fulfill it for oneself or for the heir. The burden for the *conditionarius* is the condition itself or the necessity to fulfill it. Both cases are based on theorem 46. Therefore, the condition of wanting is first attributed to the debtor, for example, if I want or if the heir wants, Titius will have 100, or if you want, you promise to give 100. I argue that the condition ensures that the heir or the promisee is not obligated to fulfill the condition, thus removing their burden, and rendering the disposition void, as stated in D.30.43.2 [D.30.*De legatis et fideicommissis* (Legacies and *fideicommissa*).43 **Ulpianus**, *in the twenty-first book to Sabinus*: 2. see above in theorem 38.].

However, it is different when it comes to "to anyone of my freedmen you wish" (*cui ex illis volueris dato*), or "to one of the two you wish", (*utri voluerit, heres dato*). In these cases, the person is compelled to make the choice D.31.24 [D.31.*De legatis et fideicommissis* (Legacies and fideicommissa).24 **Ulpianus**, *in the second book on Fideicommissa*: Cum quidam ita fideicommissum reliquisset: "Rogo restituas libertis meis, quibus voles", Marcellus putavit posse heredem et indignum praeferre. At si ita:"his quos dignos putaveris", petere posse ait eos qui non offenderint. Idem ait, si neminem eligat, omnes ad petitionem fideicommissi admitti videri quasi iam praesenti die datum, cum sic relinquitur "quibus voles" nec ulli offerat. Plane si ceteri defuncti sunt, superstiti dandum vel heredi eius, si prius quam peteret decessit. Scaevola autem notat: si omnes petere potuerunt, cum nulli offertur, cur non et qui decesserunt, ad heredem transmiserunt, utique si uno petente iam eligere non potest, cui det? Videtur enim Marcellus, cum fideicommissum ita relinquitur **ex libertis cui volueris**, arbitrari, nisi offerat cui heres velit et statim offerat sine aliquo scilicet intervallo, statim competere omnibus petitionem: cum igitur omnibus competat, merito notatus est, cur superstiti soli putet dandum, nisi forte antequam iustum tempus praetereat, quo potuit eligere cui potius offerat, ceteri decesserint.24 **Ulpianus**, *in the second book on Fideicommissa*: When someone had bequeathed a fideicommissum with the wording, "I request that you grant to those of my freedmen whom you desire", Marcellus believed that the heir could even choose an unworthy freedman. However, if the wording were, "to those whom you deem worthy", Marcellus stated that only those who had not committed an offense could make the claim. He further expressed that if the heir chooses no one, all could be considered eligible to claim the fideicommissum as if it were for immediate payment, especially when it is bequeathed "to those whom you wish," and the heir does not offer it to anyone. Clearly, if the others have passed away, it should be given to the surviving one or to the heir of the survivor if the latter passed away before making the claim. Nevertheless, Scaevola raised an objection: If all can claim when it is not offered to anyone, why wouldn't all those who have passed away transmit the claim to their heirs, so that the heir, with only one claimant, would not be without the option to choose the beneficiary? Marcellus appears to believe that when a fideicommissum is bequeathed "to anyone among my freedmen that you wish," unless the heir offers it to someone they wish and makes the offer immediately without delay, the claim becomes immediately open to everyone. Therefore, a valid objection arises: Why does he think the legacy is due only to the survivor, unless it turns out that the others have passed away before a reasonable time has elapsed for the heir to make a choice regarding to whom they would prefer to offer it?].

Yet, it is not permissible to say "whichever of them he wishes, be him Tutor" (*utri voluerit, Tutor esto*). D.26.2.23 [D.26.2. *De testamentaria tutela* (Testamentary tutelage).23 (Tutor ita recte non datur: "Illi aut illi filiis meis, utri eorum volet, Titius tutor esto"; quid enim dicemus, si Titius constituere nolit, utri ex filiis tutor esse velit?). **Africanus**, *in the eighth book of Questions*: pr. It is not correct to appoint a tutor in this manner: "Let Titius be tutor to 'A' or 'B,' my sons, whichever of them he wishes." For what shall we say if Titius is unwilling to decide to which of the sons he wishes to be tutor?].

What if he does not want to make the choice? But why is he not compelled to make the choice in this case? Or "when he wishes" (*cum volueris*)? In that situation, the choice is given to the person, whereas here, only the time is given, and the time expires with death D.32.41.13, 11.6 [D.32.*De legatis et fideicommissis* (Legacies and fideicommissa).41 **Scaevola**, *in the twenty-second book of Digest*: 13. Scaevola responded: If a designated heir has been instructed to return the inheritance to another at his discretion, he cannot be compelled to fulfill the fideicommissum in the interim. Claudius: In any case, it is presumed to be granted [for discharge] after the death of the heir. 11 **Ulpianus**, *in the second book on Fideicommissa*: 6. However, this 'when he wishes' has a certain scope, as long as he who the fideicommissum has been left to is alive: but if before he gives, he should die, his heir takes charge. But also, if the fideicommissary, before the heir appoints, should die, it seems that he has transferred nothing to his heir: for it is undoubtedly a conditional legacy, and it appears that the fideicommissary is considered to have died with the condition of the legacy pending.], D.40.5.17 [D.40.5.*De fideicommissariis libertatibus* (Grant of freedom by fideicommissa).17 **Scaevola**, *in the twenty-first book of Digest*: The words "when you think fit to manumit" are an effective grant of fideicommissary freedom.]; D.32.11.7 [D.32.*De legatis et fideicommissis* (Legacies and fideicommissa).11 **Ulpianus**, *in the second book of Fideicommissa,*: 7. But although fideicommissum worded, "if you should wish," may not be due, it will be due if the wording is "if you judge it good," "if you think it suitable," "if you hold it," or "shall hold it advantageous." For here he has not left full choice to the heir but has committed a trust to him as an upright man.].

However, only the fideicommissum is valid unless the heir refuses (*nisi haeres noluerit*), D.32.11.5 [D.32. *De legatis et fideicommissis* (Legacies and fideicommissa).11 (Sic fideicommissum relictum: "*nisi heres meus noluerit*, illi decem dari volo" quasi condicionale fideicommissum est et primam voluntatem exigit: ideoque post primam voluntatem non erit arbitrium heredis dicendi noluisse) **Ulpianus**, *in the second book of Fideicommissa*: 5 A fideicommissum expressed as "unless my heir declines, I want him to pay ten to such a person" resembles a conditional fideicommissum. It stipulates that the heir must express willingness at least once. Once the heir has shown willingness, they are no longer at liberty to claim that they refused.]. Conversely, the same fideicommissary freedom can be granted if the heir wishes, D.40.5.46. pr. [D.40.5. De *fideicommissariis libertatibus* (Grant of freedom by *fideicommissa*).46 **Ulpianus**, *in the sixth book of Disputations*: pr. The liberty of the fideicommissary can be granted as follows: "I entrust you, my heir, with a fideicommissum to emancipate Stichus if you so desire," even though the effectiveness of any other provision in the will doesn't hinge on the approval of the heir.].

There are also examples in which an act is declared invalid because it was entrusted to the judgment of the party making the promise D.18.1.7 [D.18.1 *De contrahenda emptione et de pactis inter emptorem et venditorem compositis et quae res venire non possunt* (Conclusion of the contract of purchase, special terms agreed between the vendor and purchaser, and things which cannot be sold).7 **Ulpianus**, *in the twenty-eighth book to Sabinus*: see above in theorem 55.]; D.44.7.8 [D.44.7.*De obligationibus et actionibus* (Obligations and actions).8 **Ulpianus**, *in the four-seventh book to Sabinus*: No obligation is created if it is subject to a condition "if I wish"; for that which you cannot be obliged to give unless you so wish is as if it has not been expressed. For neither is the heir of a promisor "who never wished to give" liable, because such a condition never comes into existence against the promisor himself.], D.45.1.17, 46.3, 108 [D.45.1. *De verborum obligationibus* (Verbal obligations).17 **Ulpianus**, *in the twenty-eighth book to Sabinus*: A stipulation is not valid when a condition is delegated to the judgment of the party making the promise. 46 **Paulus**, *in the twelfth book to Sabinus*: 3. However, the stipulation "do you promise to give, if you wish" is clearly invalid. 108 **Javolenus**, *in the tenth book of Letters*: 1. No promise can be valid if it lies wholly within the choice of the promisor.].

However, if I demand solemn promise from you "when you wish" *(cum volueris)*, the *stipulatio* is said to be invalid (quite strictly) if you die before making the decision D.45.1.46.2 [D.45.1.*De verborum obligationibus* (Verbal obligations).46 **Paulus**, *in the twelfth book to Sabinus*: 2. If I stipulate with the words "when you wish," some say the stipulation is invalid, others that it is invalid only insofar as if you die before you make the decision, which is true.].

And so, we have seen that when the condition of wanting is satisfied, it releases the obligor from the obligation that must be fulfilled.

Let's see how the same condition exonerates the conditionarius from the condition to be fulfilled and renders the disposition unconditional, such as: "if you wish, be heir!" (*si volueris, heres esto*), which is an unconditional disposition (*pura dispositio*), D.35.1.69 [D.35.1. *De condicionibus et demonstrationibus et causis et modis eorum, quae in testamento scribuntur* (Conditions, designations, explanations for and modalities of provisions in wills).69 **Javolenus**, *in the second book to Cassius*: In a note on Labeo, Proculus observes that a bequest, "I give and bequeath to Titius, if he want it," would go to the legatee's heir only if the legatee himself had wished to have it; for the condition is considered to pertain to the legatee himself.]; D.28.7.12 [D.28.7.*De conditionibus institutionum* (Conditions on institutions).12 **Hermogenianus**, *in the third book of the Epitome of Law*: The expression "allow Publius Maevius to be the heir, if he desires," establishes a condition in the case of a necessary heir. If Publius Maevius does not wish to become the heir, the condition is not fulfilled, and he does not inherit. In the case of a voluntary heir, such phrases are redundant because, even without them, someone who does not wish to inherit would not become the heir.].

Similarly: "if you wish, be free!" (*si volueris, liber esto*), D.40.5.46.1 [D.40.5.De *fideicommissariis libertatibus* (Grant of freedom by *fideicommissa)*.46 **Ulpianus**, *in the sixth book of Disputations*: 1. Of course, freedom can also be given to a man in the terms: "if this should be the wish of Stichus.".].

"If you want, I give and bequeath to you" (*si volueris, tibi lego*) is called conditional disposition in the laws, D.30.65.1 [D.30.*De legatis et fideicommissis* (Legacies and *fideicommissa*).65 **Gaius**, *in the first book on Legacies, To the Edict of the Praetor*: 1, see above in theorem 17.], D.35.1.69 [*De condicionibus et demonstrationibus et causis et modis eorum, quae in testamento* scribuntur (Conditions, designations, explanations for and modalities of provisions in wills).69 **Javolenus**, *in the second book to Cassius*: see above in this theorem 58.], and "if I want, I promise" (*si volueris, spondeo*), *Cujacius*[228] affirms that it will have the same effect as D.45.1.17 [D.45.1.*De verborum obligationibus* (Verbal obligations).17 **Ulpianus**, *in the twenty-eighth to*

[228] Jacques Cujas, *Ad titulum de verborum obligationibus*, in *Opera*, T 6. (Prati, 1584), col. 722," Stipulatio inutilis est si interrogatus quis respondeat, si voluero, l. a Titio, in fi. inf. hoc tit.".

Sabinus: see above in this theorem 58.], but the condition itself, "if you want" (*si volueris*) in legates, is only extrinsic due to the denied passage before the legatee declares that he wanted, see supra theorem 10.

Let's examine the condition attributed to a third party (which depends on a third party, i.e., which is contingent on a third party), the institution of the heir cannot be determined by the third party's will, but it is vitiated, D.28.5.32, 69(68) [D.28.5. *De heredibus instituendis* (The institution of heirs).32 **Gaius**, *in the first book on Wills according to the Edict of Urban Praetor*: This institution "whom Titius has wished" is defective for the reason that it has been left to the decision of someone else; for the old authorities have laid down constantly enough that the rights themselves created under wills should stand up by themselves and not depend on the decision of someone else. 69 (68) **Pomponius**, *in the seventh book to Quintus Mucius*: see above in theorem 17.].

However, if this bequest is valid, "if Titius wishes, I give and bequeath 100 as a legacy" (*si Titius voluerit, tibi 10 lego*), there is a strong disagreement among the laws; Modestinus denies it, D.35.1.52 [D.35.1. *De condicionibus et demonstrationibus et causis et modis eorum, quae in testamento scribuntur* (Conditions, designations, explanations for and modalities of provisions in wills).52, **Modestinus**, *in the sevent book of Distinctions*: see above in this theorem 58.]; but Ulpianus directly contradicts Modestinus' conclusion with his arguments, D.31.1 [D.31.*De legatis et fideicommissis* (Legacies and *fideicommissa*).1 **Ulpianus**, *in the ninth book to Sabinus*: pr., see above in this theorem 58.]. Ulpianus also states in general that a bequest can be made conditional on the will of another, except in the case of an heir, D.30.43.2 [D.30.*De legatis et fideicommissis* (Legacies and *fideicommissa*).43 **Ulpianus**, *in the twenty-first book to Sabinus*: 2. See above in theorem 38.].

"A tutor can be appointed through a testament, subject to the condition that he wishes to accept" (*Tutor si voluerit, testamento dari potest*), D.26.2.23.1 [D.26.2. *De testamentaria tutela* (Testamentary tutelage). 23 **Africanus**, *in the eighth book of Questions*: 1. This is the correct way to appoint a tutor: "Let Titius, if he is willing, be tutor to 'A,' my son."], because otherwise he is obliged. This gives him the freedom, just like the necessary heir, see supra theorem 54.

Finally, "If at the moment of death, he has expressed his wishes" (*si cum morietur voluerit*), a last will is the will of the living not revoked, D.31.77.10 [D.31.*De legatis et fideicommissis* (Legacies and *fideicommissa*).77 **Papinianus**, *in the eighth book of Replies*: 10. (A filia pater petierat, ut cui vellet ex liberis suis praedia **cum moreretur** restitueret: uni ex liberis praedia fideicommissi viva donavit. Non esse electionem propter incertum diem fideicommissi certae donationis videbatur: nam in eum destinatio dirigi potest, qui fideicommissum inter ceteros habiturus est remota matris electione) A father had requested from his daughter that, upon her death, she should return the estate to whichever of her children she wished. While still alive, she gifted the estate of the fideicommissum to one of her children. It appeared that there was no choice due to the uncertain date of the definite donation, for the designation can be directed towards the person who is to receive the fideicommissum among others, with the mother's choice removed.].

(59) *In a potestative condition from the last will, obedience or rather the intention to obey is understood to be included in the condition.*

The testator, indeed, is like a superior towards those who receive from the testament, just as a superior tends to reward someone who, not by chance or unknowingly, but with a definite intention of doing good, has done something. Therefore, someone who fulfills the condition by chance does not appear to have complied with the will of the testator, D.35.1.2 [D.35.1. *De condicionibus et demonstrationibus et causis et modis eorum, quae in testamento scribuntur* (Conditions, designations, explanations for and modalities of provisions in wills). 2 **Ulpianus**, *in the fifth book to Sabinus*: Some conditions can be fulfilled at any time, even during the testator's life, for instance, "if the ship comes from Asia"; for, whenever the ship shall have arrived, the condition is seen to be satisfied; others can be satisfied only after the testator's death, for example, "if he shall have given ten," "if he goes up the Capitoline hill"; now for someone to be regarded as complying with such a condition, he must know of its insertion in the will; should he have done by chance what is requested, he is not considered to have complied with the testator's wishes.].

(60) *The potestative condition from the last will is an order, that is, if its non-fulfillment does not depend on the conditionarius, it is deemed fulfilled.*

Because we interpret last wills very benevolently according to theorem 20, it is better for a part of the disposition, namely the condition, to exist than nothing at all. When the condition cannot occur, it is as if the *conditionarius* is obeying, which the superior sometimes considers as a fact. This theorem is very common in this argument but is often confused with theorem 16, from which we have carefully distinguished it.

See, for example, D.12.4.3.9 [D.12.4. *De condictione causa data causa non secuta* (The *condictio* for non reciprocation).3 **Ulpianus**, *in the twenty-sixth book to the Edict*: 9, see above in theorem 49.]; D.28.7.20, 23, 27 [D.28.7. *De conditionibus institutionum* (Conditions on institutions).20 **Labeo**, *in the second book of The Posthumous Works epitomized by Javolenus* 2: see above in theorem 16. 23 **Marcellus**, *in the twelfth book of the Digest Digest*: see above in theorem 16. 27 **Modestinus**, *in the eighth book of Replies*: An individual designated the heir in his will under the following condition: "if he throws my mortal remains into the sea." Since the appointed heir did not fulfill the condition, the question arose as to whether he should be excluded from the inheritance. Modestinus gave a response that the heir should be praised rather than accused because he did not cast the testator's mortal remains into the sea in accordance with the testator's will, but instead handed them over for burial, in memory of the human condition. However, first and foremost, it must be determined whether the person who imposed such a condition was of sound mind. Therefore, if this suspicion can be dispelled by clear reasons, the legitimate heir cannot in any way validly contest the inheritance against the heir designated in writing in the will.]; D.30.54.1, 92.1 [D.30.*De legatis et fideicommissis* (Legacies and fideicommissa).54 **Pomponius**, *in the eighth book to Sabinus*: 1. If Titia was left a legacy on the condition that she marry according to the evaluation of Seius, and if Seius died while the testator was still alive, and she got married, the legacy is due to her. 92 **Julianus**, *in the thirty-ninth book of Digest*:1.If one of the heirs, with the aim of paying the inherited debts, has bought from the co-heirs their shares of an entailed estate, fixing the price according to the income of that estate in the presence and with the consent of the person to whom the entail was due, it seems fitting that not the estate itself but its price should be given to the entailed heir. Marcellus notes: I believe that the heir should be listened to, if they prefer to give the estate.]; D.31.34.4, 76.6, 88.3 [D.31. *De condicionibus et demonstrationibus et causis et modis eorum, quae in testamento scribuntur* (Conditions, designations, explanations for and modalities of provisions in wills).34 **Modestinus,** *in the tenth book of Replies*: 4. If a fideicommissum has been left to a freedman on condition of his not leaving the testator's children and their tutors have prevented him from fulfilling the condition, it is unjust that since he is blameless, he should forego the profit from the fideicommissum. 76 **Papinianus,** *in the seventh book of Replies*: 6. A mother left a legacy to a tutor not legally appointed. If he consents to be confirmed by the praetor's decree, and the praetor does not consider him fit, he will not be refused an action for the legacy. 88 **Scaevola,** *in third book of Replies*: 3. "Whoever shall be my heir or heirs, Lucius Eutychus, in addition to what I appointed him as heir for, shall take from the estate and have for himself along with Pamphilus, whom I declare to be free, the entirety of the instrumental assets of the blacksmith's workshop, in order to continue the business activity there." Lucius Eutychus died while the testatrix was still alive; his share of the inheritance belonged to the co-heir. I raise the question of whether Pamphilus, named in the same will, can be admitted to the petitory action for the share of the instrumental assets, even though the workshop can no longer be operated as the testatrix intended. I gave the opinion that he should be admitted.]; D.35.1.6, 14, 31, 40, 56, 78, 81, 84 [D.35.1. *De condicionibus et demonstrationibus et causis et modis eorum, quae in testamento scribuntur* (Conditions, designations, explanations for and modalities of provisions in wills).6 **Pomponius,** *in the third book to Sabinus*: see above in theorem 16. 14 **Pomponius,** *in the eighth book to Sabinus*: A legacy provides: "If Titius establishes statues in the town, he shall inherit"; Titius is willing to set up the statues, but the townspeople refuse to provide him with a location. Sabinus and Proculus assert that he will become the heir, and they argue that the law applies similarly in the case of legacies. 31 **Africanus,** *in the second book of Questions*: see above in theorem 19. 40 **Javolenus,** *Posthumous Works of Labeo, book 8*: pr., see above in definition 31. 56 **Javolenus,** *in the fourteenth book of the* Letters: see above in theorem 17. 66 **Modestinus,** *in the tenth book of Replies*: An heir manumitted a statuliber to whom he was demanded to transfer a fideicommissum on the happening of a condition. The answer of Herennius Modestinus was that although he had manumitted the statuliber, he would be obliged to make over the fideicommissum left under the same conditions only when satisfied of their realization or if it were his own fault that they were not complied with. 78 **Papinianus,** *in the ninth book of Replies*: When either a pupillus or his tutor impedes the fulfillment of a condition inhering in the person of the pupillus, the condition is deemed to be fulfilled in the general law of both legacies and manumissions. 81 **Paulus**, *in the twenty-first book of Questions*: pr., see above in definition 35. 84 **Paulus**, *in his fourteenth book of Replies*: see above in theorem 16.]; D.36.2.5.5 [D.36.2. *Quando dies legatorum vel fideicommissorum cedat* (When a legacy or a *fideicommissum* vests).5 **Ulpianus**, *in the twentieth book to Sabinus*: 5. Even if the condition is not left unfulfilled due to the legatee's actions but rather due to the actions of the heir or the person instructed to fulfill the condition, the legacy becomes effective. In such cases, the condition is treated as if it has been fulfilled. For instance, if I am instructed to give ten to the heir, and he refuses to accept it, the legacy is considered vested. However, if a legacy is bequeathed to me on the condition that I marry Seia and she refuses to marry me, the legacy is still deemed to vest because the non-fulfillment of the condition is not a result of my actions but rather the actions of another party.]; D.40.5.39.3 [D.40.5. *De fideicommissariis libertatibus* (Grant of freedom by *fideicommissa*).39 **Paulus**, *in the thirteenth book of Replies*, §3 doesn't exist, print mistake? (e.n.)]; C.6.25.1 [C.6.25. *De institutionibus vel substitutionibus seu restitutionibus sub condicione factis* (Concerning appointments, substitutions or trusts, made upon condition).1. see above in theorem 1.]; C.6.37.8 [C.6.37. *De legatis* (Concerning legacies).8. His oath as a soldier (religio sacramenti) deprived Marcellus, whom you state to have been appointed as your guardian by your father, in his testament, of the right to manage the guardianship. But that does not prevent him from acquiring a legacy (given to him as compensation); nor is he justly barred from claiming it, since he is forbidden to manage such guardianship even should he wish to do so.]; C.6.45.1 [C.6.45. *De his quae sub modo legata vel fideicommissa relinquuntur* (Concerning legacies and trusts which are left subject to a duty *(sub modo)*.1. In legacies or trusts, a definite purpose is treated the same as a condition. But if it is not your fault that you do not comply with the testator's wish, but the fault of him whom you were directed to marry, you are not prevented from retaining the property left you.]. Also see VI.5.12, 41, 66 [VI.5.12. *On the rules of law*. 41: It should not be imputed to the person for whom it does not stand if they fail to do what should have been done through them. 66. When it does not stand to the person to whom it pertains for the condition to be fulfilled, it should be considered as if it had been fulfilled.].

Even if the condition cannot be maintained, the bequest can still continue. For example, I give freedom to Stichus and bequeath sustenance if he remains with my son. If the son cannot keep him or dies shortly after, sustenance is still owed to Stichus as long as he is alive, by express rescript[229] from Emperor Antoninus.

See D.32.30.5 [D.32.*De legatis et fideicommissis* (Legacies and *fideicommissa*).30. **Labeo**, *in the second book of Posthumous Works, Epitomized by Javolenus*: 5. "My heir shall give the sum of two hundred per year to my wife, for as long as she stays with my son in Capua"; the son went to live in a different place from the mother. I have considered that if both of them had lived in Capua, the bequest would have been owed to the mother, even if they had not lived together; if, however, the son had moved to another town, only [the bequest] related to one year would be owed, however short the period they had lived together might have been; Trebazio also asserts this. Let's see now if with these words 'for as long as she stays with my son in Capua' a condition is expressed, or if that expression should be considered something superfluous. I do not approve that it is superfluous. However, if the fact of not living with the son is not due to an obstacle on the part of the woman, the bequest is owed to her.]; D.33.1.20. pr. [D.33.1.*De annuis legatis et fideicommissis* (Annual legacies and *fideicommissa*).20 **Scaevola**, *in the eighteenth book* of *Digest*: pr. A gentleman left an annual legacy with the following terms: "provided they dwell with my designated mother who is instituted as a partial heir." The question arose as to whether, in the event of the mother's demise, the specified condition was considered unfulfilled, thereby relieving any obligation for provisions such as food or clothing. In response, it was asserted that based on the circumstances presented, such provisions were indeed owed.]; D.34.1.13.1, 2, 20.3 [D.34.1. *De alimentis vel cibariis legatis* (Aliment or legacies of provisions).13. **Scaevola**, *in the fourth book of Replies*: 1. Emperor Antonius Pius to the freedpeople of Sestia Basilia: Although the words of the will state that sustenance and clothing are bequeathed to you as long as you reside with Claudius Justus, I, however, believe that the deceased intended for the bequest to

[229] Berger, *ad vocem Rescripta principum*, "Written answers given by the emperor to queries of officials (relatio, consultatio, suggestio) or to petitions of private persons (preces, libellus, supplicatio). The rescripta were issued either on the petition itself in the form of a subscriptio or in a separate letter (epistulae principum). A rescript expressed the emperor's opinion upon a legal question or a decision in a specific case. It often gave rise to a legal innovation when the emperor's view introduced a new legal rule which, although in principle binding only in the case for which it was issued, nevertheless, because it emanated from the emperor's authority, easily could acquire a general binding force. In particular, when a specific rule was repeatedly expressed by various emperors (phrases like imperatores saepe rescripserunt, saepe [saepissime] rescriptum est, and the like, occur frequently in juristic writigs), it became law in fact.".

be provided even after Justus's death. He replied: This provision should be understood in a way that the obligation to provide sustenance remains perpetual. 2. Similarly, when consulted about this provision: "I want them always to remain with you," I ask if, having the freedmen of the heir stayed with him for a long time but having left him due to the severe servitude he imposed on them, they should receive the sustenance that he refuses to give them if they do not perform the service he demands. He replied: According to the circumstances presented, sustenance is owed to them. 20 **Scaevola,** *in the third book of Replies*: 3. Following the establishment of her son as the heir, a mother has bestowed freedom upon her slave Pamphilus through a fideicommissum. Additionally, she has bequeathed him five aurei annually for sustenance and an empty allowance for clothing, contingent upon his continued residence with her son. I inquire whether provisions are still owed in the event of the son's demise. He has expressed the view that if the condition has been met, the obligation persists even after the son's death.]; C.6.37.1 [C.6.37. *De legatis* (Concerning legacies).1. A legacy was required to be given in a formal manner; but any informal declaration of intention, even a nod, might be enough to constitute a trust.]. [230]

Although there may be doubt regarding the testator's intention, D.35.1.84 [D.35.1. *De condicionibus et demonstrationibus et causis et modis eorum, quae in testamento scribuntur* (Conditions, designations, explanations for and modalities of provisions in wills).84 **Paulus,** *in the fourteenth book of Replies*: see above in theorem 16.], also consider D.35.1.101.[D.35.1. *De condicionibus et demonstrationibus et causis et modis eorum, quae in testamento scribuntur* (Conditions, designations, explanations for and modalities of provisions in wills). 101 **Papinianus,** *in the eighth*

[230] C. 6.42. (*De fideicommissis* (Concerning trusts). 22. There is not doubt that, when (the proper number of) witnesses have been called, a trust may be left by letter, by a note, even by word of mouth, or by a nod. Andrew M. Riggsby, note 59 above, p. 119; David Carey Miller, note 59 above, p. 67, "This is the most important form of personal servitude and the other forms are derivatives of it. The personal servitudes [such as use, habitation, e. n.] were so designated because they featured a vesting of all or part of the beneficial interest of the right of ownership in a person other than the owner, the right being personal to that,"; ID., ibidem, p. 208, "The law of actions is the last of the three in the institutional scheme, and is quite different from the subject that precede it. While the earlier subjects are concerned with substantive rules and principles, the law of actions is concerned with redress. It is not quite the same as 'the law of procedure', however; it often includes matters that might easily have been treated under law of persons or of things. This is because actions evolved as a subject over time when procedure was not distinct from substantive law.".

book of Replies: A father, through his will, designated his daughter Severiana Procula to be the wife of his relative Elius Philippus. He left as a fideicommissum to his daughter a plot of land if she married Elius Philippus; and if she did not marry him, he wished that the property would be given to Elius Philippus. The young girl died before reaching puberty. The response is: Since in the conditions stipulated in wills, one must consider the intent rather than the words; thus, it should be understood that the fideicommissum was left to Elio Philip in the event that Procula, the deceased's daughter, did not wish to marry him. Therefore, since she died before reaching puberty, it is considered that the condition has not been fulfilled.].

In exceptional cases, this principle applies to wards (*pupilli*[231]) as well. If a tutor prevents the fulfillment of the condition, it is deemed as if it were fulfilled, D.35.1.78 [D.31.1.*De condicionibus et demonstrationibus et causis et modis eorum, quae in testamento scribuntur* (Conditions, designations, explanations for and modalities of provisions in wills).78 **Papinianus**, *in the ninth book of Replies*: see above in this theorem 60.].

The favor of freedom is also significant. If the condition of freedom is assigned to the heir, it is considered an order that the heir must execute. If there is a delay, the condition is deemed fulfilled, D.40.5.41.1 [D.40.5. *De fideicommissariis libertatibus* (Grants of freedom by *fideicommissa*).41 **Scaevola**, *in the fourth book of Replies*: 1, see above in theorem 16.].

Similarly, if an honored *extraneus* dies without giving anything to anyone, it results in freedom.

[231] Berger, *ad vocem Pupillus*, "One below the age of puberty (impubes) who ceased to be under the power of his father by the latter's death or through emancipation (D. 50.16.2.39 pr.). An impubes who became sui iuris was under guardianship (tutela impuberum). In a broader sense pnpillus is used of all who are below the age of puberty, hence aetas pupillaris — the age below puberty. A pupillus could not alienate property or assume an obligation without the consent of his guardian (auctoritas tutoris). The opinions of the jurists were divergent as to whether a pupillus could acquire possession; some required the guardian's cooperation. Justinian declared the acquisition valid when the pupillus was beyond the age of infancy. In Justinian's Law, the property of a pupillus was not accessible to usucaption. —D. 26.8; 27.2; C 5.49; 50.".

However, this does not apply to a legatee whose condition fails for the same reason, D.35.1.94 [D.35.1. *De condicionibus et demonstrationibus et causis et modis eorum, quae in testamento scribuntur* (Conditions, designations, explanations for and modalities of provisions in wills).94 **Hermogenianus**, *in the first book of Epitome of Law*: see above in theorem 19.], D.40.7.20.3, 39.4 [D.40.7.*De statuliberis (Statuliberi)*.20 **Paulus**, *in the in the sixteenth book to Plautius*: 3. A directive was issued for a slave to provide ten units of currency to secure his freedom, and the intended recipient passed away. According to Sabinus, the slave would attain freedom if he had the funds ready, as it was not his fault that he couldn't give them. However, Julianus asserts that, in line with the principle favoring freedom, the slave would rightfully gain freedom, even if he acquired the sum later. Nevertheless, this freedom is acquired through a legal principle rather than the provisions of a will. Therefore, if a legacy was also made to him and the intended recipient of that legacy has died, he would indeed secure freedom but not receive the legacy. Julianus maintains the perspective that this places him in a similar position to other legatees. 39 **Javolenus**, *in the fourth book From the Posthumous Works of Labeo*: 4. "If Stichus has given one thousand coins to Attia, let him be free." Attia died in the testator's lifetime. Labeo and Ofilius answered that Stichus could not be free. Trebatius took the same view if she died before the will was made; if later, he would be free. There is reason in the opinion of Labeo and Ofilius, but under the law now in force, the slave is free under the will.].

If the prescribed time to meet the condition has elapsed without fault before the person could know it, it does not harm, but the time is extended, D.29.5.3.31 [D.29.5. *De senatus consulto Silaniano et Claudiano: quorum testamenta ne aperiantur* (The senatus consultum Silanianum and the senatus consultum Claudianum; those whose wills may not be opened).3 **Ulpianus**, *in the fiftieth book on Edict*: 31. If persons instructed to meet a condition within a prescribed time limit from the date of the death have failed to do so because of ignorance and if the reason for their ignorance was that the tablets [of the will] could not be opened for fear of the senatus consultum, they are protected in the matter of fulfillment of the condition.]; D.40.5.41.12 [D.40.5.*De fideicommissariis libertatibus* (Grant of freedom by *fideicommissa*).41 **Scaevola**, *in the fourth book of Replies*: 12.see above in theorem 39.].

If the time limit is determined by a specific number, for example, within 100 days, the last day is crucial, so to speak, not the inclusive ones. For example, suppose that if I am detained by robbers during the last 10 days, those days will not be considered to have passed, and thus the time will effectively be extended for me, D.35.1.40.pr. [D.35.1. *De condicionibus et demonstrationibus et causis et modis eorum, quae in testamento scribuntur* (Conditions, designations, explanations for and modalities of provisions in wills).40 **Javolenus**, *in the second book of Posthumous Works of Labeo*: pr.see above in definition 31.].

The presence of D.28.7.6 does not contradict this, as in that case, the condition is impossible from the beginning [D.28.7.*De conditionibus institutionum* (Conditions on institutions).6 **Ulpianus**, *in the ninth book to Sabinus*: If a person was instituted with these words, "if he had erected a monument after the testator's death, in the three days next after his death," where the monument cannot be completed in three days, it will have to be held that the condition disappears, as being impossible.].

It is required that it does not depend on the *conditionarius*, that is, there is no default or negligence. Justinian also established in that if, for example, bandits steal money that a statuliber gives to the heir for his freedom, the slave still becomes free C.6.46.7 [C.6.46. *De condicionibus insertis tam legatis quam fideicommissis et libertatibus* (Concerning conditions attached to legacies, trusts and manumissions.).6, [not 7 as in the text, e.n.]. Someone in his testament left freedom to his slave upon condition that he should furnish to his heir a certain number of solidi (gold pieces) or some other property or a substitute-slave, and the slave (so benefited), who did not live in the same place as the heir, upon learning of this master's will, hastened to the heir with what he had been directed to deliver to him, but the property which he carried with him was lost on the way through an attack by robbers or by an incursion of enemies. It was questioned by the ancients whether the slave would lose his freedom on account of his inability to give what he was directed to give, by reason of the unfortunate accidents above mentioned. 1. Settling the doubt of the ancients, we have decided that the slave shall have his liberty, but the heir or a stranger shall not be deprived of the benefit which they were to receive by reason thereof. 1a. By whatever cause, therefore, the slave is hindered (from delivering what he was directed to deliver) whether by the heir or someone else to whom the slave was to give something, or by fortuitous circumstances, he shall, nevertheless, receive his liberty, unless he himself refused to comply with the condition; but he shall, nevertheless, after receiving his freedom, be liable to the heir or to someone else to whom he was ordered to give - unless the latter fail to accept the property brought - and when it has once been refused by him, they cannot again lay claim thereto - and must give all that he was ordered to give, whether that be a substitute slave, if he exists, or his value, computed at not more than fifteen solidi, or whether it be some other property, if that exists, and if it does not exist, then its value.]. However, later, he remains obligated to the heir for the amount imposed by the testator.

This is related to our theorem, that heirs are not obliged to return the honorarium to an advocate if it did not depend on the advocate himself and if he was intercepted by death before he could argue the case, D.19.2.38 [D.19.2. *Locati conducti* (Lease and hire). 38 **Paulus**, *in the sole book of Rules*: A man who leases out his work should receive wages for the entire term if he is not responsible for his labor not being rendered.], D.50.13.1.13 [D.50.13.*De variis et extraordinariis cognitionibus et si iudex litem suam fecisse dicetur* (Various and extraordinary judicial examinations and if a judge is said to have neglected his duty.).1 **Ulpianus**, *in the eighth book of All Seats of Judgment*: 13. The deified Severus prohibited a fee to be claimed back from the heirs of an advocate after his death, because it was not his fault that he did not plead the case.].

(61) *The opinion of a certain person in last wills is considered to be the judgment of a good man* (arbitrium boni viri[232]).

Therefore, if the condition is that Titius deems it good, it is deemed as if not added, D.30.75. pr. [D.30.*De legatis et fideicommissis* (Legacies and *fideicommissa*).75 **Ulpianus**, *in the fifth book of Disputations*: pr. If a legacy or a fideicommissum has been left as follows: "if my heir if my heir should see fit", "if he approved it", "if he thought it right", both the legacy and the fideicommissum will be due, since the thing was more entrusted to him as to an honest man, than referred to the mere will of the heir.]; D.32.11.7 [D.32. *De legatis et fideicommissis* (Legacies and *fideicommissa*).11 **Ulpianus**, *in the second book on Fideicommissa*: 7. See above in theorem 58.]

[232] Berger, *ad vocem Arbitrium (arbitratus) boni viri*, "The judgement, opinion of an honest, upright man to whom a controversial point has been submitted.".

(where the distinction can be observed between these: "if you wish" and "if you consider it good," or between the words of understanding and will), D.40.5.14, 41.2, 46.3 [D.40.5.*De fideicommissariis libertatibus* (Grant of freedom by *fideicommissa*). 14 **Modestinus**, *in the tenth book of Replies*: see above in theorem 1. 41 **Scaevola**, *in the fourth book of Replies*: 2. A testator entrusted to the faith of the guardian, appointed with the will for his children, the manumission of the slaves belonging to that same guardian. This guardian was relieved of the guardianship. The question arises as to whether the guardians who, in place of the excused guardian, administer the guardianship are obliged or not to grant freedom to those same slaves. The response is that, based on the circumstances presented, even the instituted heirs are considered tasked with granting freedom. 46 **Ulpianus**, *in the sixth book of Disputations*: 3. However, if the wording is "if it should be the wish of the heir," the grant will not take effect; freedom will only be granted at his discretion, provided the testator has made everything contingent upon the heir's desire. Conversely, if the testator has granted discretion to the heir as a person of good judgment, there is no doubt that freedom is owed. In fact, it has been established that freedom is due under the formula: "I request you to manumit if you think fit," as this is understood to mean "if you, as a person of good judgment, think it fit." I also believe that freedom is due when expressed as "if you should approve my wish," as well as in phrases like "if he has earned your favor" or "if he has not offended you," implying judgment as a person of good character. Similarly, "if you have approved of him" or "if you have not disapproved of him" or "if you have thought him deserving" are also considered grounds for granting freedom. Indeed, when a testator established a fideicommissum in Greek, stating, "I wish freedom to be given to such and such a man if this has your sanction," the deified Severus ruled through a rescript that the fideicommissum might be implemented.].

Because it is as if it were the judgment of a good man, as mentioned in D.30.75. Moreover, the last will itself is considered equivalent to the judgment of any good man, as stated in D.32.43 [D.32.*De legatis et fideicommissis* (Legacies and *fideicommissa*).43 **Celsus**, *in the fifteenthbook of Digest*: Suppose a father instructed that a dowry be granted to his daughter at the discretion of her guardian. Tubero contends that this should be interpreted in the same manner as if it had been bequeathed at the discretion of an honest and fair-minded individual. Labeo poses a question: How can one determine the appropriate dowry for the daughter of a specific individual at the discretion of an upright person? Tubero responds by stating that it is not challenging to assess based on the social status, financial situation, and number of children of the testator.].

In contracts, if Titius does not consider it good, Justinian established that it should be deemed as if it were lacking, I.3.23.1 [I.3.23. *De Emptione et Venditione* (Of purchase and sale).1. It is necessary that the price should be settled, for without a price there can be no purchase and sale, and it ought to be a fixed and certain price. For instance, where the parties agreed that the thing should be sold at a price to be subsequently fixed by Titius, the older jurists doubted much whether this was a valid contract of sale or not. The doubt has been settled in the following way by our decision; if the third person named actually fixes the price, it must certainly be paid, as settled by him, and the thing must be delivered, in order to give effect to the sale; the purchaser (if not fairly treated) suing by the action on purchase, and the vendor by the action on sale. But if the third person named will not or cannot fix the price, the sale will be void, because no price has been settled. This rule, which we have adopted with regard to sales, may reasonably be extended also to contracts of hire.]; C.4.38.15 [C.4.38. *De contrahenda emptione* (Concerning contracts of purchase).15. Emperor Justinian to Julianus, Praetorian Prefect. A great doubt arose among the ancient jurists as to a sale where a man brought property with the understanding that the price should be the valuation put upon the property by (say) Titus. 1. Settling this doubt, we order that if a sale is made at a valuation to be fixed by some other person, such sale shall be valid whether in writing or oral, upon condition that if the person named fixes the price, it must be paid as fixed by him, and the sale shall be carried into effect, provided that if such contract shall be reduced to writing, it must be duly completed and executed according to the provisions of our law. 2. But if the person appointed will not or cannot fix the price, then the sale shall be held for naught, as one where no price is fixed, and there shall be no further speculation or conjecture in the future, whether the contracting parties had a definite person or (merely) a good man in view to fix the price, since we deem the latter entirely unlikely and by this sanction remove that consideration from such contract. We order that these provisions shall also apply in leases of the kind.].

The D.19.2.25 is in agreement, unless it has been interpolated by a Tribonian norm [D.19.2. *Locati conducti* (Lease and hire). 25 **Gaius**, *in the tenth book on Provincial Edict*: If the rental amount is pledged at the discretion of an unspecified third party, no lease contract is deemed to be established. However, if the agreement states "as much as Titius estimates it to be," the lease is valid with the provision that if Titius, the specified person, does indeed determine the rent, then the agreed-upon rent must be paid, and the lease must be executed in accordance with his estimation. If, however, Titius is unable or unwilling to set the rent, the hiring arrangement becomes void, under the premise that no rent has been determined.].

On the other hand, if the judgment of a person who has an interest in the condition is deduced, it is sometimes understood as the judgment of a good man, as D.18.1.7 [D.18.1 *De contrahenda emptione et de pactis inter emptorem et venditorem compositis et quae res venire non possunt* (Conclusion of the contract of purchase, special terms agreed between the vendor and purchaser, and things which cannot be sold).7 **Ulpianus**, *in the twenty eighth book to Sabinus*: see above in theorem 55.], and sometimes the act is considered as imperfect, as in D.18.1.35 [D.18.1 *De contrahenda emptione et de pactis inter emptorem et venditorem compositis et quae res venire non possunt* (Conclusion of the contract of purchase, special terms agreed between the vendor and purchaser, and things which cannot be sold). 35 **Gaius**, *in the tenth book on Provincial Edict*: 1. It is established that no agreement is reached when the seller tells the buyer, "You shall purchase for the amount you choose to offer, or what you consider fair, or at your own valuation of its worth."].

The same principle applies when the judgment of another person is added, such as a modifying circumstance. For example, if you marry according to Titius' judgment, as stated in D.35.1.28 [D.35.1. *De condicionibus et demonstrationibus et causis et modis eorum, quae in testamento scribuntur* (Conditions, designations, explanations for and modalities of provisions in wills).28 **Paulus**, *in the second book of the Epitome of Alfenus Digest*: An individual bequeathed the following provision to his daughter: "If my daughter, Attia, marries as instructed by Lucius Titius, let my heir grant her a specified number of coins." Since Titius passed away before the testator, Attia got married. The query arose regarding whether the bequest was owed to her, and the response was in the affirmative.].

Thus, we have explained the deduction in a condition.

Let us now add something about the circumstance of time to complete our classification.

(62) A repeatable condition, known to the testator, is rendered void before the testament.

When the testator is both aware of an event and expresses a desire for the same event to occur, it is assumed that they want it to happen again, D.35.1.9, 11.1, 68 [D. 35.1.*De condicionibus et demonstrationibus et causis et modis eorum, quae in testamento scribuntur* (Conditions, designations, explanations for and modalities of provisions in wills).9 **Ulpianus**, *in the twentieth book to Sabinus*: We adhere to the principle that when a husband who makes a legacy to his wife upon the condition of her having children, he typically does not consider the offspring she may have already given birth to.. 11 **Paulus**, *in the fourth book to Sabinus*: 1. Understand that ordinary conditions, such as "if he ascends the Capitol" and similar requirements, should be fulfilled after the testator has passed away if they are intended for the will to be executed. On the other hand, uncommon conditions, like "if Titius becomes consul," can be fulfilled even during the testator's lifetime. 68. **Gaius**, *in the thirteenth book on Lex Julia et Papia*: Consider a legacy that is contingent on the condition "if she marries." If the woman is, to the knowledge of the testator, already married, one must anticipate a subsequent marriage. It is immaterial whether her second marriage occurs during the testator's lifetime or after his death.]; D.31.45.2 [D.31.*De legatis et fideicommissis* (Legacies and *fideicommissa)*.45 **Pomponius**, *in the eighty-second book to Quintus Mucius*: 2. If a father, through his will, instructs his heir to give a specific amount of aurei to his daughter upon her marriage, and it turns out that the daughter was already married at the time of making the will, without her father's knowledge and in his absence, the legacy remains valid and is owed. However, if the father was aware of the existing marriage, it is presumed that he intended a different marriage, and the obligation does not apply.].

I refer to it as "repeatable" because if it is not inherently repeatable and the testator is aware of this, it appears that they have included an impossible condition, which in last wills is considered as not added according to theorem 63. Therefore, it is deemed fulfilled, D.35.1.11 [D.35.1. *De condicionibus et demonstrationibus et causis et modis eorum, quae in testamento scribuntur* (Conditions, designations, explanations for and modalities of provisions in wills).11 **Paulus**, *in the fourth book to Sabinus*: pr. If the condition stipulated in the will has already occurred, as known to the testator, one must await its recurrence, if possible. If the testator is unaware, the bequest is immediately payable.].

Furthermore, the testator must be aware, as if they are unaware of its occurrence, it is considered satisfied. Perhaps if they had known, they would not have mentioned it, D.35.1.10.1, 11.pr. [D.35.1. *De condicionibus et demonstrationibus et causis et modis eorum, quae in testamento scribuntur* (Conditions, designations, explanations for and modalities of provisions in wills).10 **Ulpianus**, *in the twenty-third book to Sabinus*: 1. Suppose a legacy "if the ship comes from Asia" and, unknown to the testator, the ship has already arrived at the time that the will is made; the condition should be held to be satisfied. One should hold likewise of a legacy "when he shall come of age.". 11 **Paulus**, *in the fourth book to Sabinus*: pr., see above in this theorem 62.].

Importantly, the condition must occur before the testament, as it may validly occur at any time after the testament, even while the testator is still alive, D.35.1.2, 10.pr., 61, 68 [D.35.1. *De condicionibus et demonstrationibus et causis et modis eorum, quae in testamento scribuntur* (Conditions, designations, explanations for and modalities of provisions in wills).2 **Ulpianus**, *in the fifth book to Sabinus*: see above in theorem 59. 10 **Ulpianus**, *in the twenty-third book to Sabinus*: see above in theorem 38. 61 **Ulpianus**, *in the eighteenth book on Lex Julia et Papia*: When an individual leaves a bequest to his wife contingent upon her bearing children, there arises uncertainty regarding whether the testator is specifically considering only those offspring born after his demise or also those conceived during his lifetime but after the will's creation, provided he passes away while the marriage is ongoing. Nevertheless, the equitable course is to assert that the entitlement applies to any children born, whether during the husband's lifetime or after his death. 68 **Javolenus**, *in the second book to Cassius*: see above in theorem 38.]; D.40.4.18 [D.40.4. *De manumissis testament* (Testamentary manumissions).18 **Julianus**, *in the second book to Urseius Ferox*: see above in theorem 19.]; C.6.25.7 [C.6.25. *De institutionibus vel substitutionibus seu restitutionibus sub condicione factis* (Concerning appointments, substitutions or trusts, made upon condition).7. We ordain generally, that if anyone uses the words: "If my son or daughter should die intestate" or "without children" or "without marriage," (the property given shall go to a substitute) and such son or daughter either has children, or marries or makes a testament [Blume explains, i.e., if either of the conditions are fulfilled, see therein n. 4] , he or she may firmly retain the property left him or her, and a provision for substitution or restitution shall not apply in such case. If, however, none of these things happen, the condition is effective, and the property must be surrendered (to the substitute) according to the wording of the testament, in order to end the uncertainty of the succession of the decedent by a definite substitution or restitution. Who could approve of the view, that if he or she does not, perchance, make a testament, but has posterity, his (or her) children should, on account of narrow construction of words, be altogether cheated out of their paternal inheritance? In order to block a path so devoid of love, and that no one may wander astray, we enact this sanction and ever-enduring law, pleasing alike to father and children, and by which example we also come to the assistance of others, including outside heirs, for whose benefit like provisions have been made.].

This is because, when it is established that the testament has not been revoked, it is deemed that the testator died immediately after the testament was made, through the use of the Catonian rule[233]. Thus, even if the condition occurs after the testament while the testator is alive, it is understood to occur at the moment of their death.

The time of the testament and the time of death are linked through a legal fiction, where either the testament is retroactively associated with the moment of death or the death is associated with the moment of the testament, assuming the testator's will has not been revoked. Consequently, any condition that is unfulfilled while the testator is still alive is deemed to have been unfulfilled from the beginning, D.28.7.8.7 [D.28.7.*De conditionibus institutionum* (Conditions on institutions).8 **Ulpianus**, *in the fiftieth book to Edict*: 7. see above in theorem 1.]. This applies particularly to conditions that occur before the testament, D.40.7.39.4 [D.40.7. *De statuliberis* (Statuliberi).39 **Javolenus**, *in the fourth book of the Posthumous Works of Labeo*: 4. see above in theorem 60.], serving the purpose of preserving the testator's intentions.

As to whether someone can validly fulfill a condition before knowing that the testator has commanded it,

233 Berger, *ad vocem Regula Catoniana*, see note 168 above.

see theorem 59. Two time-related aspects that should be noted are: firstly, the date added to the condition of freedom should not be understood as the starting point of the time period, but rather as the range within which it must occur. For example, if Stichium gives [something] on the calends, it means that the gift can occur both before and on the calends, D.40.4.41.1 [D.40.4.*De manumissis testament* (Testamentary manumissions).41 **Pomponius**, *in the seventh book From Plautius*: 1. However, if the conditions outlined in the will state, "Grant freedom to my slave Stichus if he pays or secures the payment of one thousand coins to my heir within one, two, or three years following my death," the liberation of the slave is not permitted until the completion of three years, unless immediate payment or security in cash is made. In this case, the heir is entitled to compensation for expediting the man's emancipation through an early settlement of the funds.]; secondly, the computation of a temporary condition is made, in cases of doubt, from the day when the disposition is fully executed, that is, when it grants the acquired right, such as in legacies from the acceptance of the inheritance, D.35.1.46 [D. 35.1. *De condicionibus et demonstrationibus et causis et modis eorum, quae in testamento scribuntur* (Conditions, designations, explanations for and modalities of provisions in wills).46 **Paulus**, *in the third book to Vitellius*: If a statuliber is instructed to make a payment, for instance, within a hundred days, and no specific starting date is mentioned for this period, the duration commences upon the acceptance of the inheritance. It would be illogical for the period to conclude before someone accepts it. The same principle applies to anyone directed to provide something to an heir. Consequently, the timeframe for fulfilling a condition also begins for a legatee upon the acceptance of the inheritance.].

Chapter X

[Legal Effectiveness of the Conditional Disposition]

Definitions

So far, we have discussed the form and parts of conditional propositions, as well as the form and parts of their components. We have also explored the effectiveness and legal force of each.

Now, we turn to the overall effect of the entire disposition or conditional proposition, which is the right.

The right can be null, conditional, or unconditional. These categories differ like numbers: zero, fraction, and integer. They vary based on the following causes: impossibility, contingency, and necessity. The scheme can be represented as follows:

Impossible Condition,	Contingent Condition,	Necessary Condition
0	½	1
Null Right,	Conditional Right,	Unconditional Right

Just as a fraction lies between zero and an integer, a conditional right lies between null and unconditional. And just as fractions vary, with those closer to zero being below ½ and those closer to one being above ½, the estimation of a conditional right varies, ranging from being close to unconditional to being close to null.

The foundations of this matter, which have not been previously explored, are based on philosophical principles, which we will present in Theorem 66 shortly.

It is worth noting that a conditional right is akin to a conceived one, the pure like one already born. For instance, when someone becomes a slave, they are deemed to "die" D.50.17.209 [D.50.17. *De diversis regulis iuris antiqui* (Various rules of early law). 209 **Ulpianus**, *in the fourth book on Lex Julia et Papia*: see above in theorem 38.]. Therefore, when someone becomes free, they are considered to be "born". Hence, a statuliber is like an embryo (*conceptus est*). A conditional right is distinct from an unconditional right D.50.17.169.1 [D.50.17. *De diversis regulis iuris antiqui* (Various rules of early law).169 **Paulus**, *in the second book from Plautius*: 1, 1. What is pending is not regarded as already in being.].

Furthermore, regarding its parts, where someone who already possesses an unconditional right does not perform any juridical act by conditionally acquiring it again, D.18.5.7.pr. [D.18.5. *De rescindenda venditione et quando licet ab emptione discedere* (Rescission o f a sale and the circumstances i n which a purchase may be departed from).7 **Paulus**, *in the fifth book of Questions*: pr. If I buy again conditionally what I have already bought unconditionally, the second sale is without effect.], refer to the previous theorems 32 and 34.

However, it cannot be said that a testator who conditionally bequeaths something has bequeathed it in part D.28.5.57(56) [D.28.5. *De heredibus instituendis* (The institution of heirs). 57 (56). **Paulus** *in the single book on the second testament*: An individual can appoint an heir in the following manner: "If I pass away prior to reaching my seventieth year, designate so-and-so as my heir." In this case, the person should not be considered as having made a part will but rather as having established an heir under a specified condition.]. Dividing a good (*res*) is different from dividing an expectation (*spes*).

Although an unconditional right is more comprehensive than a conditional right, sometimes it is preferable for something to occur conditionally when it cannot occur unconditionally, see Theorem 44, add D.28.5.38 [D.28.5. *De heredibus instituendis* (The institution of heirs).38 **Julianus**, *in the thirtieth book On the Digest*: A man who bequeaths the slave Pamphilus to his underage son, from whom he has removed inheritance rights, can establish Pamphilus as an heir for a portion after the son's demise. This is analogous to a situation where a person leaves a slave to Sempronius in a legacy and subsequently designates Sempronius as an heir for a portion following Sempronius's death.]; D.34.7.4 [D.34.7. *De regula*

Catoniana (The Catonian rule).4 **Ulpianus**, *in the tenth book to Sabinus*: see above in theorem 45.]; D.35.1.104 [D.35.1. *De condicionibus et demonstrationibus et causis et modis eorum, quae in testamento scribuntur* (Conditions, designations, explanations for and modalities of provisions in wills).104 **Paulus**, *in the fourteenth book of Replies*: A person, deported after the opening of the will but then restored, can claim a fideicommissum, the condition of which is met after his recovery of Roman citizenship.]; D.26.2.10.4 [D.26.2.*De testamentaria tutela* (Testamentary tutelage).10 **Ulpianus**, *in the thirty-sixth to Sabinus*: 4. A slave belonging to someone else can be designated as a tutor using the expression: "If he becomes free, appoint him as the tutor." Moreover, indeed, even if the appointment is made without specifying a condition, the implication is that the condition "when he becomes free" is inherent. Additionally, anyone can seek fideicommissary freedom for a slave not from their own household based on these grounds. After all, it matters little whether the appointee is one's own slave or another's, as the acquisition of freedom is undertaken for the ward's benefit and the greater good of the public. Consequently, freedom through fideicommissum can be asserted for this individual as well, provided the testament does not explicitly oppose it.]; D.30.29 [D.30.*De legatis et fideicommissis* (Legacies and *fideicommissa*).29 **Paulus**, *in the sixth book on the Lex Julia et Papia*: see above in theorem 17.].

77. Furthermore, a right can be either revocable or vested. The latter belongs to a person and cannot be removed, except by their own actions. The former is structured in a way that it remains dependent on the will of another, not in a positive sense (otherwise, there is no right, but merely an expectation – for instance, until someone wishes to make a donation to me), but rather in a negative sense, and such a revocable right is acquired through the Last Will.

Consequently, it does not require acceptance since it is not yet vested. Hence, a petition that has not been submitted to a superior does not grant a vested right to the petitioner, but it can be revoked by the college, as stated X.1.5.4 [X.1.5 *De postulatione praelatorum*.4. Archipiscopus in archipiscopum postulatur. Et ex quo postulatio praesentata est papae, non possunt postulantes ab ea accedere: sed debet superioris iudicum expectari. (The archbishop is proposed for the office of archbishop. Once the postulation has been presented to the Pope, the postulants cannot withdraw from it; instead, they must await the judgment of the superior authorities.)].

In the case of a Last Will, upon the death of the testator, the heir has a vested right, while the legatee acquires their right only upon the acceptance of the inheritance by the heir, at which point the heir becomes obligated to them.

The slave, likewise, does not attain the status of a freeman except through inheritance, as indicated in D.40.7.2. pr. [D.40.7. *De statuliberis* (Statuliberi).2 **Ulpianus**, *in the fourth book to Sabinus*: pr. see above in definition 70.], add a similar theorem 62.

Moreover, a vested right cannot be taken away even by the Prince; see *Petr. Anton. de Petra, Tractatus de jure quæsito per principem non tollendo*[234].

78. Furthermore, a conditional right can be either simple or time-bound.

A simple conditional state nothing more than, "You shall have 100!" if it is true that a ship will come from Asia.

On the other hand, a time-bound conditional should be interpreted as follows: "You shall have 100 only when the ship arrives from Asia". In this case, the ship's arrival serves not only as the condition but also as the time limit for the payment.

There is a significant difference between these two situations: a simple condition merely suspends the right, while a time-bound condition also defers it. See D.36.2.6.1 [D.36.2. *Quando dies legatorum vel fideicommissorum cedat* (When a legacy or a *fideicommissum* vests).6 **Paulus**, *in the third book to Sabinus*: 1, see above in definition 12.], which is of great importance in the doctrine of retroactivity.

[234] Pietro Antonio Pietra, *Tractatus de jure quesito per principem non tollendo*. (Venetiis, 1590).

79. They say that a conditional right is retroactive when the condition, once fulfilled, is treated as if it had been fulfilled right from the beginning, at the same moment when the provision was made. This concept is used in the context of creditors' disputes, tax matters, and other situations, as will be evident later. Moreover, in cases where retroactivity is attributed to the condition, it is not necessary for the condition to have actually occurred; it is sufficient to have certainty about it. For example, if Titius promises to pay you 100 if he does not go to Alexandria within two months, and he falls seriously ill or even swears that he will not go to Alexandria, you will be immediately obliged to pay the 100.

Commonly, retroactivity in conditions is explained through a legal fiction, as if the condition, upon occurrence, is deemed to have already occurred from the outset of the provision.

However, this is unnecessary because the conditionated is immediately owed once the condition occurs, as the very words of the promise infer – they assure 100 without delay if the ship comes from Asia. In this context, I imagine a respected prophet in the Republic, whose predictions are never wrong, and whose counsel the magistrates often rely upon to resolve doubts concerning matters of fact without any risk of deception. This prophet is akin to figures in literature, such as Sophocles' Thyresias among the Thebans in 'Antigone,' Homer's Calchas among the Greeks, and Virgil's Cassandra among the Trojans. Yet, the Scriptures provide more authentic examples. For the sake of clarification and to demonstrate the nature of retroactivity, I imagine this esteemed prophet foretelling the arrival of a ship, and because his words are regarded as fact, I will then have grounds for a legal action. This, in essence, means that the condition is retroactive – that is, the conditionated's fulfillment depends not on time but on the truth of the condition. Therefore, the syllogism goes as follows: if the ship comes from Asia, I will have 100 according to the disposition of the conditionator, but since this is already true (due to the prophet's words), I can now demand the sum.

80. An act is considered eventual when solemn actions are performed that pertain to the eventual act, but the effectiveness of the act is suspended by a condition. This situation often occurs, such as in an appeal or during a *litis contestatio*[235], *p. 1 const. d. Elect. Augusti 13*[236]. Consequently, acts concerning a matter under dispute remain eventual, as evidenced in the work of the esteemed *Thomas Tr. de concess. litigios. alien.*[237]

Similarly, in the case of a legate thing with a pending condition, add theorem 47, suppose someone is designated as an heir with the condition that he manumits a hereditary slave. If the heir validly performs the act of manumission before he officially becomes the heir, and if the manumission is effective only after the heirship is established, it may seem that the act is legally perplexed and void. However, it is accepted based on the intention of the party, allowing the solemn act of manumission to be executed, while the effectiveness of the manumission is suspended until the heirship takes effect. This allowance is justified as the acceptance and the heirship follow immediately, without any interruption.

The opinion of Labeo supports this notion, D.28.7.20.1 [D.28.7. *De conditionibus institutionum* (Conditions on institutions). 20 **Labeo**, *in the second book, from the Posthumous Works epitomized by Javolenus*: 1. If someone is ordered to manumit a slave from the inheritance and thereby become the heir, even if,

[235] Berger, *ad vocem Litis contestatio*, "The final act in the proceedings in iure, by which, after the appointment of the judge (iudex), the controversial issues are established and submitted to the latter for the examination of the facts and for judgment. […].".

[236] Kurfurst August. *Constitutiones und Verordungen*. (Dresdae,1572).

[237] Johann Thomasius, *De concessa litigiosi alienatione*. (Jenae, 1650)

upon manumission, no valid legal act is completed, they will still be considered the heir. It is true, indeed, that the slave has been manumitted. However, after acceptance [of the inheritance], the freedom granted to the slave is validated according to the testator's intention.].

Furthermore, when a codicillar clause is present, the testament becomes an eventual codicil[238], as outlined in the work of *Dn. Tabor in his dissertation on De clausul. Codicill.*[239]

Theorems

(63) *The impossible condition renders a right null and void, as a general rule and according to pure law.*

As the condition cannot exist by hypothesis, the conditioned act cannot come into existence, as per theorem 6.

However, on the other hand, this same condition is contained in the conditioned act, so that the right belongs to the *conditionarius*, as in definitions 5 and 9.

Based on this theorem, in all inter vivos acts, the impossible condition vitiates the act I.3.19.11 [I.3.19.

[238] Berger, *ad vocem Codicilli*, "Codicilli. A written document containing dispositions of a testator to be valid after his death (mortis causa), but not the institution of an heir which was permissible only in a testament. The recognition of codicilli is somehow connected with the institution of fideicommissa (under Augustus). Distinction is made between codicilli testamento confirmati (a codicil confirmed in a later or earlier testament) and non confirmati (not mentioned in a testament). While the former codicil might contain various dispositions (legacies, muinmissions, appointment of a guardian) and was considered as a part of a testament (pars testamenti), the latter was reserved for fideicommissa only. There were also codicilli ab intestato, i.e., codicilli in which the testator charged his heirs on intestacy with fideicommissa. In classical law no specific form was required for codicilli. Later imperial legislation required the presence of witnesses. Justinian introduced even oral codicilli. A testator might dispose in his testament that in case of its invalidation because of formal deficiencies, it should be treated as a codicill—Inst. 2.25; D. 29.7; C. 6.36.".

[239] Johann Otto Tabor (1604-1674), *Dissertatio de clausola codicillari* (Argentorati, 1647).

De inutilibus stipulationibus (Of invalid stipulations), see above in theorem 17.]; D.44.7.1.11, 31 [D.44.7.*De obligationibus et actionibus* (Obligations and actions). **Gaius**, *in the second book of Golden Words*: 11. Again it is well known that a stipulation made subject to an impossible condition is invalid. 31 **Paulus**, *in the twelfth book to Sabinus*: Not only are stipulations which are dependent on an impossible condition of no validity, but other contracts too, such as sales, lettings, in which an impossible condition has been introduced are equally of no validity; for in a matter which contains the consent of two or more persons, the intent of everyone is looked at, and in a transaction of this sort their contemplation is without doubt of a kind that when inserting a condition which they realize was impossible, they had in mind that nothing should be done.]; D.45.1.7, 69 [D.45.1.*De verborum obligationibus* (Verbal obligations).7 **Ulpianus**, *in the sixth book to Sabinus*: see above in theorem 17. 69 **Ulpianus**, *in the sixth book to the Edict*: If a man is dead he cannot be produced and no penalty is incurred far something that is impossible, just as if someone who stipulated for the delivery of Stichus, now dead, stipulates for a penalty if he is not delivered.]; D.46.1.29 [D.46.1.*De fideiussoribus et mandatoribus* (Sureties and mandators).29 **Paulus**, *in the eighteenth book to the Edict*: If I stipulate under an impossible condition, no guarantee can be taken.].

In this context, derisory promises were often made, as stated in the previous theorem 46, which are abundant in ancient history. For example, if someone came to Lemnos from Athens with the wind of Boreas, when Athena receives the northernmost winds from Lemnos, *Cornel. Nep. Miltiad. c. 1*[240]. The oracle responded to Croesus that he would win if a mule reigned over the Medes, but in reality, Cyrus was born

[240] Cornelius Nepos [c. 110 BC – c. 25 BC], *De excellentibus ducibus exterarum gentium. Miltiades*, I, "Illi irridentes responderunt, tum id se facturos, quum ille, domo navibus proficiscens, vento Aqui- lone venisset Lemnum; hie enim ventus, a septen- trionibus oriens, adversum tenet Athenis proficiscentibus. 6. Miltiades, morandi tempus non hab- ens, cursum direxit, quo tendebat, pervenitque Chersonesum."; Engl. transl. by John Clark, *Cornelius Nepos. Lives of excellent commanders.* (London, 1825), c. 1, Miltiades, "they bantering him, replied, that they would then do it, when he, coming by ship from, home, should arrive at Lemnus with the wind called Aquila. For this wind arising from the north, is full against those that come from Athens. Miltiades having no time to stay, steered on his course to the place he was bound for and came to the Chersonese.".

to a noble Mede mother and an unknown Persian father (*Herodotus, l. 1*[241]). There was also an oracle that claimed Florence could be conquered only if oxen were seen flying around the city walls, and this happened when the besiegers represented an ox on their flags. Pope Sylvester, according to legend, obligated himself to the devil if he celebrated mass in Jerusalem, although there was actually a chapel or shrine in Rome that they referred to as Jerusalem, unbeknownst to Sylvester. When he conducted the divine function there, the devil fiercely claimed his right. Another oracle stated that Constantinople could only be captured by an Angel, and it became a reality when the Latin enemies entered through a tower named after an Angel.

In similar vein, when Philippus Valesius, King of France, besieged Cassel, the townspeople hung woolen roosters on the walls and claimed that the town would be taken when the roosters sang (*Frossard. lib. 1*[242]). However, such derisive situations often turned to the detriment of those who made them.

Similar to derisory conditions, indeed it is the same, as stated in D.30.122.2 [D.30.*De legatis et fideicommissis* (Legacies and *fideicommissa*).122. **Paulus**, *in the third book of Rules*: 2. He to whom a property was bound under the condition that he would give a hundred to the heir, if the price of the property equals what he was ordered to give to the heir, is not compelled to carry out the entail left to his charge, as nothing is considered taken by will by one who disburses as much as he receives.]; D.35.2.65 [D.35.2.*Ad legem Falcidiam* (The lex Falcidia).65 **Paulus**, *in the sixth book on Lex*

[241] Herodotus [c.484 - c. 425 AC], *The histories*, Engl. Transl. by A. D. Godley, (Cambridge. Harvard University Press, 1930), Clio, I, 55, "After his gifts to the Delphians, Croesus made a third inquiry of the oracle, for he wanted to use it to the full, having received true answers from it; and the question which he asked was whether his sovereignty would be of long duration. To this the Pythian priestess answered as follows: [2] "When the Medes have a mule as king, Just then, tender-footed Lydian, by the stone-strewn Hermus Flee and do not stay, and do not be ashamed to be a coward.".

[242] Jean Froissard (c. 1337-c. 1405), *Les Croniques de France*. I, Lutetiae Parisiorum, 1495).

Julia et Papia: see above in theorem 46.] likewise, it is so difficult that it is almost impossible, D.40.7.4.1 [D.40.7.*De statuliberis* (Statuliberi).4 **Paulus**, *in the fifth book to Sabinus*: 1. A man is not statuliber whose freedom is deferred to a time so distant that the person to be manumitted could not survive until then, or if [the testator] added a condition so difficult, or rather virtually imposible, that his freedom could not accrue, for example, that he should have given the heir one thousand, or that his freedom was ordered only on his deathbed; such a grant of freedom is ineffective, as Julianus too writes, since there is not even an intention that it should be given.].

For example, if someone were to grant freedom to a slave on the condition that they give millions to the heir, i.e., an enormous sum, far exceeding the savings of an ordinary slave (*peculium*[243]), such a condition is not to be sought for.

Now, taking advantage of this occasion, we need to discuss the addition: "when you die, have it!".

These words seem more like a derisive condition or rather a postponement.

Indeed, a usufruct cannot be left as a legate in this manner, as it is considered a personal right, D.35.1.79.3 [D.35.1. *De condicionibus et demonstrationibus et causis et modis eorum, quae in testamento scribuntur* (Conditions, designations, explanations for and modalities of provisions in wills).79 **Papinianus**, *in the first" book of Definitions*: 3. The legacy of a usufruct may be ineffective where the beneficiary dies; still the device of the Mucian undertaking has point where a usufruct is bequeathed with a condition that something be not done.]; C.6.61.8 [C.6.61. *De bonis quae liberis in potestate constituendis ex matrimonio vel aliter adquiruntur et eorum administratione* (Concerning property which children under paternal power acquired through marriage or otherwise and the management thereof.). 8.l.fin. Moreover, when slaves are given to unemancipated children, either during marriage or by outsiders, upon condition to immediately manumit them, the paternal authority shall not be a hindrance to do so. For how can a usufruct be acquired in a right

243 Berger, *ad vocem Peculium*, "A sum of money, a commercial or mdustrial business, or a small separate property granted by a father to his son or by a master to his slave, for the son's (or slave's) use, free disposal, and fructification through commercial or other transactions. [...].".

existing but a moment? If it is necessary to set the slave free the moment possession of him is acquired, what kind of a usufruct in him can be acquired for the father?].

Similarly, no one can be legally commanded to be free in such a manner as "when you die", D.40.4.17. pr., 61.pr. [D.40.4.*De manumissis testamento* (Testamentary manumissions).17 **Julianus**, *in the forty second book of Digests*: pr. Liberty, which is granted at the end of life, such as "Let Stichus be free when he dies", is to be considered of noeffect. However, this clause, "Let Stichus be free if he does not ascend the Capitol", should be understood as "if he does not ascend the Capitol when he first has the opportunity": for in this way, Stichus will achieve freedom if he refrains from ascending the Capitol when given the chance. 61 **Pomponius**, *in the eleventh book of Letters*: pr. I know that some, wishing to ensure that their slaves never attain freedom, have been accustomed to write in this way: "Let Stichus be free when he is dying". But Julianus also says that freedom, which is granted at the end of life, is of no significance, since the testator is understood to have written in this manner more for the purpose of preventing freedom than of granting it. Therefore, even if it is written in this way: "Let Stichus be free if he does not ascend the Capitol", it is of no significance if it appears that the testator intended to confer freedom at the end of life, and there is no place for Mucian's caution.]; D.40.7.4.1 [D.40.7.*De statuliberis* (Statuliberi).4 **Paulus**, *in the sixth book on Lex Julia et Papia Sabinus*: 1, see above in this theorem 63.].

However, despite this, it still has an effect in cases where transferable objects are concerned. In such cases, the legatee receives the bequest in the last moment of life and transfers it to the heirs, as described in D.36.2.4 [D.36.2. *Quando dies legatorum vel fideicommissorum cedat* (When a legacy or a fideicommissum vests).4 **Ulpianus**, *in the nineteenth book to Sabinus*: see above in theorem 6.]; D.35.1.72.5, 79 [D.35.1. *De condicionibus et demonstrationibus et causis et modis eorum, quae in testamento scribuntur* (Conditions, designations, explanations for and modalities of provisions in wills).72 **Papinianus**, *in the eighteenth book of Questions*: 5. "I give the estate, on my death, to Maevia, if she has not married." It can be said that even if she does marry, she will be admitted immediately to the legacy. For it is not proved whether a specific or a nonspecific period has been written into the legacy. 79 **Papinianus**, *in the first book of Definitions*: "When Titius passes away, instruct my successor to bestow upon him a sum of one hundred". The legacy is direct, as it is delayed not by a condition but by a temporal gap; for the condition is inevitable.], and this is why the praetor, who does not concern himself with trivial matters, takes care of momentary acquisitions as well, D.50.17.127 [D.50.17. *De diversis regulis iuris antiqui* (Various rules of early law).127 **Paulus**, *in the twentieth book to the Edict*: When the praetor gives an action against an heir, it is sufficient as far as he is concerned, if it came to him even for a moment by deception of the deceased.].

Regarding the condition "if you will not have done" its effectiveness is equivalent to "when you will have died". Since, if you will not have done something, it cannot be determined while you are alive, as mentioned in I.3.15.4 [I.3.15. *De verborum obligatione* (Verbal obligation).4, a stipulation is conditional, when performance is made to depend on some uncertain event in the future, so that it become actionable only on something being done or omitted: for instance, "Do you promise to give five aurei if Titius is made consul?" If, however, a man stipulates in the form "Do you promise to give so and so, if I do not go up to the Capitol?" the effect is the same as if he had stipulated for payment to himself at the time of his death. The immediate effect of a conditional stipulation is not a debt, but merely the expectation that at some time there will be a debt: and this expectation devolves on the stipulator's heir, supposing he dies himself before fulfilment of the condition.]; D.36.1. 67 (65.)1 [D.36.1.*Ad senatus consultum Trebellianum* (The senatus consultum Trebellianum). 67 (65) **Maecianus**, *in the fifth book of Fideicommissa*: 1. Should the testator have directed his heir to return the inheritance to a woman in the event of her marriage, we would assert that if the heir claims the inheritance is questionable, he must be compelled to accept it and return it to the woman, even if she is already married. Julianus supports the same stance in situations involving other conditions that can only be fulfilled at the conclusion of the individual's life. According to this perspective, the heir should only return the inheritance after a caution has been provided to the concerned parties by those to whom he was instructed to return it under these specified conditions.] (see supra th. 15). It is also noted that if a third-party dies, the condition is still met, as mentioned in D.35.1.40.2 [D.35.1. *De condicionibus et demonstrationibus et causis et modis eorum, quae in testamento scribuntur* (Conditions, designations, explanations for and modalities of provisions in wills).40 **Javolenus**, *in the second book of Excerpts from Labeo's Posterior Works*: 2.see above in theorem 14.].

We previously mentioned that, according to strict adherence to the law, an impossible condition renders the disposition void.

However, in last wills, it is accepted that the condition itself is nullified, and the disposition becomes unconditional, possibly due to the leniency afforded to last wills, as explained in D.28.7.1, 6 [D.28.7.*De conditionibus institutionum* (Conditions on institutions). 1 **Ulpianus**, *in the fifth book to Sabinus*: It is established that an institution made under an impossible condition or with some other blunder is not vitiated. 6 **Ulpianus**, *in the ninth book to Sabinus*:see above in theorem 60.]; D.28.5.46(45), 51(50).1 [D.28.5. *De heredibus instituendis* (The institution of heirs). 46 (45) **Alfenus**, *in the second book of the Digests epitomized by Paulus*: "If both Maevia, my mother, and Fulvia, my daughter are alive, then designate Lucius Titius as my heir." Servius expressed the view that even if the testator never had a daughter, but his mother survived, Titius would still be the heir. This is because anything impossible stipulated in a will holds no legal force.". 51 (50) **Ulpianus**,*in the sixth book of Rules*: 1. If an impossible condition, consisting in not doing something, has been attached to the institution of an heir, according to the view of every authority, he will be heir, just as if he had been instituted unconditionally.]; D.28.3.16 [D.28.3.*De iniusto rupto irrito facto testamento* (A will which has not been lawfully made, or which has been broken or rendered ineffectual).16 **Pomponius**, *in the second book to Quintus Mucius*: see above in definition 48.]; D.30.104.1 [D.30.De *legatis et fideicommissis* (Legacies and *fideicommissa*).104 **Julianus**, *in the first book to Urseius Ferox*: 1, see above in theorem 19.], D.33.4.12 [D.33.4.*De dote praelegata* (Praelegatum of dowry).12 **Scaevola**, *in the third book of Replies*: see above in theorem 29.].

I believe this principle can be extended to gifts mortis causa, as argued in D.39.6.18.3 [D.39.6. *De mortis causa donationibus et capionibus* (Gifts and acquisitions mortis causa).18 **Julianus**, *in the sixtieth book of Digest*: 3. Where someone has received mortis causa a slave who is liable to noxal surrender or under some other obligation, he is to be taken as having received as much as the slave can be sold for. The same rule can be applied in the case of a plot of land which is encumbered in order to discover the value of the gift.], where conditions are equated to last wills.

The same principle is allowed in canonical law for betrothals, see the whole title of X.4.5. *De conditionibus appositis in desponsatione vel in aliis contractibus* (On the conditions attached to marriage vows and other contracts).

Furthermore, we have demonstrated that impossible conditions in law are treated the same as impossible conditions in fact, as stated in the above theorem 38.

Perplexed conditions also exist, which occur when a condition is possible in itself, but not when considered alongside the conditioned, resulting in mutual obstruction between the condition and the conditioned, D.28.5.44(43) [D.28.5. *De heredibus instituendis* (The institution of heirs). 44 (43) **Paulus**, *in the first book on Lex Aelia Sentia*: Because they hinder each other.]. In such cases, it is unclear which one precludes the other D.46.1.5 [D.46.1. *De fideiussoribus et mandatoribus* (Sureties and mandators).5 **Ulpianus**, *in the forty-sixth book to Sabinus*: Julianus asserts, in a general sense, that a person who is the heir of the person for whom he was a surety is relieved of his ancillary liability and becomes liable only in his capacity as heir. He concludes by stating that when a surety succeeds to the position of heir of the person for whom he was a guarantor, he is released from his guarantor's liability and is now bound as a principal debtor. On the other hand, a principal debtor who succeeds another principal debtor incurs liability on two fronts. In such a scenario, it's not obvious that one obligation is being extinguished. This clarity can be achieved in the case of a principal debtor and a guarantor because the former's liability is more extensive. In situations where there is deifference the obligations, it is possible to determine that one obligation extinguishes the other. However, when both obligations carŕy equal weight, it is challenging to establish why one would take precedence over the other in being extinguished. Julianus illustrates this by relating it to a case where he aims to show that there is no novelty in the existence of two obligations in one person. Such a scenario does exist. If an individual, bound by a promise, becomes the heir to another individual similarly bound by the promise, he bears two obligations. Similarly, if a party to a stipulation becomes the heir of another stipulatory promisee, he bears two obligations. Clearly, if action is taken on either of these obligations, he terminates both. This is evidently because the nature of the two obligations is identical, so when one is brought into question, the other is also consumed.].

For further examples, refer to our dissertation on *perplexed cases* in section 13[244] and following.

The perplexed conditions also encompass those that go against the nature of marriage. These conditions invalidate the entire act, X.4.5.7 [X.4.5. *Concerning conditions added in betrothal or in other contracts.* If a disgraceful or impossible condition is added to the contract of marriage, it is considered as not added, unless it is against the essence of marriage, as then it vitiates the contract. This chapter is noteworthy and highly citable.]. For instance, when someone says, "I will marry you if I don't find a more beautiful woman" (*Damas de Brocard, membr. 3, n. 10*[245]). The condition "I will marry you if I don't find a better woman" is valid only when a fixed time is added (*Bartholomeus Brixiensis, qu. Vener. 38*[246]).

"I will marry you, if I will have known you [sexually e.n.]", what is the law? Once the intercourse has happened, some others believe that only the betrothal becomes unconditional *(purificatus)*; the intercourse, indeed, makes the betrothal unconditional, but it

[244] AA VI, I, p. 235, "XIII. An incompatible condition is one that is contrary either directly, for example, 'if you will not be the heir, be the heir,' where someone substitutes themselves (l. 9 § fin. D. de V.P.S. Casus 1), or indirectly. For instance, a testator, who has already exhausted three-quarters of the legacies, leaves 100 to Titius, 'if the Falcidian law is not applicable in his will,' which condition is incompatible with such a legacy due to the testator's own act (l. 88 D. ad L. Falc.), and here, in a concise sense, the meaning is obscure, as Dn. Rebhan has quasi-reduced it to syllogisms in Hodeg. Jur. p. 294.".

[245] Damasus (1210 – 1215), *De brocardis*, in (1584), *Tractatus illustrium in utraque tum Ponrificii, tum Caesarei Iuris facultate Iuriconsultorum, duce et auspice Gregorio XIII*, voll. 18. Venetiis, vol. 18, f. 511, membr. 3, n. 10, "Quando autem apponitur contra substantiam matrimonii conditio vitiat matrimonium: ut si dicatur contraho tecum usque dum pulchriorem inveniam: nullum est matrimonium [...] When, however, a condition is added against the essence of marriage, it vitiates the marriage. For example, if it is stated, 'I marry you until I find a more beautiful person,' the marriage is null and void.".

[246] Bartholomaeus Brixiensis [b. probably in the second half of the 12th century at Brescia; died 1258], *Quaestiones veneriales* in (1572), *Quaestiones selectae variorum variae*, Lugduni, 149, Quaestio 38, "Solutio. T. dicit quod talis conditio apponi potest, dummodo fiat ad certum tempus.... The solution. Thomas says that such a condition can be added, provided it is done for a specific period of time.".

makes the condition as if not added, X.4.1.30 [X.4.1 *On Betrothals and Marriages*. 30. Betrothals about the future (*sponsalia de futuro*[247]) are transformed into a marriage through subsequent physical copulation, but not through the mere attempt of physical copulation.]. It is as if a novation[248] has been made, but only in the second intercourse there is the marriage, according to X.4.5.6 [X.4.5. *Regarding the conditions attached to marriage promises and other contracts*. 6. Whoever enters into a promise of marriage with an honorable condition, and before the condition's occurrence, has sexual relations with the promised spouse, renounces the condition.]. However, according to *Brunellus de Sponsal. concl. 30*[249], it happens immediately with the first one.

[247] Göran Lind, *Common Law Marriage*. Oxford (2008), the whole Chapter 3 *Informal marriages in Canon Law*, in particular,109, "If *Sponsalia de future* was followed by copula carnalis, it was presumed that copula ipso facto included a *sponsalia de presenti* and that relationship, consequently, was a marriage". While the *sponsalia de presenti* created an indissoluble marriage, the *sponsalia de futuro* only referred to a future marriage and as such were considered a dissolvable engagement by mutual consent of the involved parties. It was presumed that the carnal copula after the *sponsalia de futuro* included the *sposalia de praesenti* and thus rendered the *sponsalia de futuro* a valid marriage. Lind emphasizes that the distinction between *sponsalia de praesenti* and *sponsalia de futuro* was introduced by Peter Lombard, there p. 105. Jakob Anton Zallinger Zum Thurn (1735-1813), *Institutiones Juris Ecclesiatici. Liber III, Decretalia*. Romae, 1872), p. 387, "Olim tamen, ante decretum concilii tridentini de matrimoniis clandestinis et nunc etiam in locis ubi illud decretum non viget, siquis sponsalia de futuro sponsam carnaliter cogno[ve]rat praesumebatur consensum de praesenti in matrimonium praestitisse, et quidem praesumptione juris et de jure contra eam non admittebatur probatio, c. 5 et c. 30.".
However, in the past, before the decree of the Council of Trent on clandestine marriages and even now in places where that decree is not in force, if anyone had carnal knowledge of his betrothed with a promise of marriage in the future, it was presumed that he had given present consent to the marriage, and indeed, this presumption was accepted as a legal presumption and as a matter of law, proof to the contrary was not admitted, c. 5 and c. 30 [of the decree].

[248] Berger, *ad vocem Novatio*, "The transformation and transfer of a former obligation into a new one (D 46.2.1 pr.), i.e., an existing obligation is extinguished and substituted by a new one. [...].".

[249] Joannes Brunellus (f. XVI cent.), *Tractatus insignis de sponsalibus et matrimoniis* in *Tractatus illustrium in utraque tum Ponrificii, tum Caesarei Iuris facultate Iuriconsultorum, duce et auspice Gregorio XIII*. voll. 9. (Venetiis, 1584), conclus. 30, fol. 32, "Matrimonium contractum per verba de praesenti est solubile per ingressum religionis. Et post copulam non, textum est etc." [A marriage contracted through *verba de praesenti* is

What is the law if an adulterous husband promises to a raped maid servant: 'I will marry you if my wife dies'? See *Dn. Richter Jenenses decisiones*[250].

(64) A necessary condition renders the right unconditional.

For whatever is necessary in itself, it is considered as if not added in a disposition, theorem 17. Therefore, a necessary condition is also to be regarded as not added. By the definition 1, if a condition is considered as not added, the disposition becomes unconditional. Consequently, the right derived from it will also be unconditional, I.3.19.11 [I.3.19. *De inutilibus stipulationibus* (Of invalid stipulations).11, see above in theorem 17.].

Also, in this context, we have the condition commonly known as "negative impossible" or rather as "consisting in a not doing", where the action itself is impossible, and the condition requires future inactivity, for example, "if you have not touched the sky with your finger, be the heir". Such a condition should be classified more as necessary rather than impossible negative, despite being labeled so by laws, D.28.5. 50 (51).1 [D.28.5. *De heredibus instituendis* (The institution of heirs). 51 (50) **Ulpianus**, *in the sixth book of Rules*: 1, If an impossible condition, consisting in not doing something, has been attached to the institution of an heir, he will be heir according to the opinion of every authority, just as if he had been instituted unconditionally.]; D.45.1.7 [D.45.1. *De*

dissolvable by entry into religious life. And after the consummation, it is not [dissolvable], it is stated in the text [of the law etc.].

250 Christoph Philipp Richter (d. 1673), *Centuria variorum juris decisionum.* (Jenae, 1673), p. 158, Decisio LXXXVIII, Virginem vel honestam viduam stuprans, eam vel in uxorem ducere, vel dotare, infantique alimenta praestare tenetur, n. 63 [If someone violates a virgin or an honorable widow, he is obligated either to marry her, provide a dowry, or support the child, according to number 63], "Fustigatio dictata fuit quidam marito, qui vivente priore coniuge rem habuit cum ancilla, & stupratae sub conditione, su uxor decederet, matrimonium promisit." [The flogging was dictated to a certain husband who, while his previous spouse was alive, had a relationship with a maid and, under the condition that his wife would pass away, promised marriage].

verborum obligationibus (Verbal obligations).7 **Ulpianus**, *in the sixth book to Sabinus, book 6*: see above in this theorem 64.].

Please refer back to supra theorem 17 for further comparison.

(65) An uncertain condition renders the right unconditional.

A conditional right is an intermediate state between an unconditional right and no right at all (null). The uncertain condition lies between the necessary and the impossible in terms of our ability to determine it. Therefore, when a necessary condition makes the right unconditional (theorem 64) and an impossible condition makes it null (theorem 63), an intermediate uncertain condition makes the right conditional. This is what we had to demonstrate, D.46.2.9.1 [D.46.2. *De novationibus et delegationibus* (Novations and delegations).9 **Ulpianus**, *in the forty-seventh book to Sabinus*: 1. One who stipulates under a condition which is bound to eventuate is deemed to make an unqualified stipulation.].

The uncertainty may pertain to the past, present, or future, as mentioned in definition 48. Refer also to our discussion about "uncertain if" (*incertus an*) in definition 20 and theorem 14.

However, even if a condition is uncertain, it must still be provable (*certificabilis*) in its nature, so that its truth and consequently its impact on the conditioned party become evident. A condition that is not provable in the senses, for instance, if it involves a theoretical question, such as whether the void exists or if angels have a tenuous body, lacks provability. The resolution of such questions cannot be proven.

Even things that someone may have believed to have demonstrated, like the Peripatetic view that a raw material exists, but an entity with an infinite quantity does not require confirmation through an oath, as

Cicero mentioned in *Academ. quaest. p. 48,* edited by *Gothofredus*[251]

Moreover, universals and indefinites are not perceptible in the senses. For example, if one makes a promise under a condition without specifying anything in particular, such a condition cannot be ascertained, as it were ἄσημος [inintelligible, in Greek in the text, e.n.]. As a result, the promise (*sponsio*) is null.

However, in last wills, such a condition is considered impossible and deemed as not added, D.28.5.36 [D.28.5. *De heredibus instituendis* (The institution of heirs).36 **Ulpianus**, *in the eighth book of Disputations*: If an individual designates an heir with the condition, "let him inherit in the same portion as the one I assign to Titius in a codicil," even if no specific portion has been allocated in the codicil, the appointed heir will inherit as if formally instituted without the specification of a share.]; C.6.25.8 [C.6.25. *De institutionibus seu substitutionibus sub condicione factis* (Concerning appointments, substitutions or trusts, made upon condition). 8. If anyone appoints an heir under this condition: "If he shall become consul," or "praetor," or appoints his daughter as heir upon condition: "if she shall marry," and if during the testator's lifetime such heir shall become consul or praetor, or finishes his office as such, or the daughter is married, but divorced from her husband, the condition - solving all doubt among the ancients - shall be considered fulfilled, without reference whether that happened in the lifetime of the testator, or at the time of , or after his death. This shall also apply to legacies, trusts and manumissions, lest, if we construe such provisions too technically, the wishes of testator will be defeated.].

(66) Conditional right establishes something in existence.

It is commonly said that a condition does not establish anything in existence, but we have demonstrated the opposite in many ways. Now, as we have shown above (definition 76), just as existence is

[251] *Auctores Linguae Latinae in unum redacti corpus, adiectis notis Dionisii Gothofredi,* (S. Gervasii, 1602), cap. II, p. 554, "413. Infinitatem. Cicero Academic. At hoc Anassimandro populai et sodali suo non persuasit. In eum infinitatem rerum atque natura dixit esse, e qua omnia gignetur.". [But Anaximander did not convince his people or his fellow citizens of this. For he said that there is an infinity of things and of nature, from which all things are generated.]

like a fraction compared to the whole, so is conditional right to unconditional right.

In fact, a conditional right is included in assets (*jus conditionale est in bonis*), so it is not necessarily preserved in the cession of all rights, *Baldus*[252] in comment to C.4.10.6 [C.4.*De obligationibus et actionibus* (Concerning obligations and actions).6. The same Emperors and the Caesars to Mauricus. If your debtor paid you by a debt due him from his own debtor and made you procurator for our own benefit in connection therewith, you may pursue the special or general pledge which you have. If these, however, were sold by prior creditors to whom they were pledged, you can see that they cannot be demanded back from the purchasers thereof.], except if it is added: as much as we can <dispose of that right>, *Cravetta vol. 2 cons. 227*[253].

The same is true in business: an asset has as much value as the uncertainty that the conditional event can occur, as described in D.35.2.55, 73.1 [D.35.2. *Ad legem Falcidiam* (The lex Falcidia).55 **Marcellus**, *in the twentieth book of Digest*: A yearly sum of ten is left to Titius, and a judge is conducting a Falcidian calculation between the heir and the remaining legacies. If Titius is alive, the judge must evaluate the potential value of the legacy, considering the uncertainty surrounding the duration of Titius's life. However, if Titius is deceased, the sole consideration is the extent of the heir's obligation under that specific bequest. 73 **Gaius**, *in the eighteenth book on the Provincial Edict*: 1. Considerable uncertainty surrounded debts with pending conditions at the deceased's death. The question arises: should the conditional amount be included in the creditor's assets and deducted from the debtor's? Our principle dictates that the anticipated amount of the obligation is considered an addition to the stipulator's assets and a reduction from the debtor's assets. Alternatively, the issue can be resolved through the establishment of security, leading to one of two outcomes: either an account is settled as if the debt were unconditional or as if nothing

[252] Baldo degli Ubaldi, *In Quartum et Quintum Codicis libros Commentaria* (Venetiis, 1577), sub Tit. De actionibus et oblig., 21, lex VI, Cedi an possit hypothecaria sine personali.

[253] Aymon Cravetta, *Aymonis Cravettae Consiliorum sive responsorum: Tomi Prioris Prima, Secunda et tertia Pars*. (Francofurti ad Moenum, 1624), 56, Cons. CCXXVII, n.11 seems, "sexto arguitur, nam generalis dispositio non comprehendit maiora expressis.". [It is being argued against the sixth, for the general provision does not encompass greater things than those expressly stated].

were owed. Subsequently, heirs and legatees engage in reciprocal agreements wherein, if the condition materializes, the heir commits to rectifying any shortfall, or the legatees undertake to refund any excess amount received.].

This aspect can be likened to a gamble (*alea*), although Terentianus denies that he bought hope (*spes*) for a price, D.18.1.8.1 [D.18.1 *De contrahenda emptione et de pactis inter emptorem et venditorem compositis et quae res venire non possunt* (Conclusion of the contract of purchase, special terms agreed between the vendor and purchaser, and things which cannot be sold).8 **Pomponius**, *in the ninth book to Sabinus*: 1. At times, a sale is recognized even in the absence of a tangible item, particularly when the acquisition involves a form of uncertainty or chance. This is evident in transactions like buying the potential catch of birds or fish, or the anticipation of receiving a gift. The agreement remains valid even if the expected outcome does not materialize, as it is essentially a purchase of expectancy. In the instance of largesse, if there is any dispossession from the acquired items, legal action for the purchase will not be valid. This is because the parties are presumed to have entered into the contract with the understanding of such a possibility.].

This idea fits well in this context, as a conditional right is often referred to as "hope," as seen in I.3.15.4 [I.3.15 *De Verborum Obligatione* (Verbal obligation).4, see above in this theorem 66.], D.50.16.54 [D.50.16.*De verborum significatione* (Meaning of expressions).54 **Ulpianus**, *in the sixty-second book on the Edict*: Conditional creditors encompass individuals who not only currently lack an action but anticipate acquiring one in the future, or those who harbor the expectation that they might have one.].

From a conditional right, one can be considered a creditor, if the conditional right arises from a transaction inter vivos, as D.44.7.42 [D.44.7.*De obligationibus et actionibus* (Obligations and actions).42 **Ulpianus**, *in the twenty-first book to the Edict*: see above in theorem 6.]; D.45.1.54 [D.45.1.*De verborum obligationibus* (Verbal obligations).54 **Julianus**, *in the twenty-second book of Digest*: Stipulations are at times made with specific individuals in mind, and at other times, they are more general in nature. In particular stipulations, the agreement needs to be divided between the individuals involved and their respective heirs, with each party entitled to specific portions of the whole. In the case of generic stipulations, a division is made based on quantity. For example, if someone stipulated for both Stichus and Pamphilus and left two heirs with equal shares, each heir is owed a half share in both Stichus and Pamphilus. Similarly, if the stipulation was for two slaves, each heir is entitled to one slave.]. It can be donated, C.8.54.3 [C.8.54. *De donationibus quae sub modo vel condicione vel ex certo temporo conficuntur* (Concerning gifts made subject to a duty, or upon condition or for a definite time.).3. In case a gift is made subject to the duty that after a certain time the property given should be turned over to another, it was provided by the authority of the ancient law that in case that he to whom the benefit of such bounty was given2 had no stipulation, and the agreement was not carried out, the author of the bounty of his heirs should have a right of an action in personam (*condictio*).], can be assigned, according to the eminent scholar *Shacher, in de cess. act. diss. 7. Th. 28*[254].

It can also be secured through pledges and guarantors, D.20.1.28 [D.20.1. *De pignoribus et hypothecis et qualiter ea contrahantur et de pactis eorum* (Formation and terms of pignus and hypotheca). 28 **Paulus**, *in the third book of Questions*: A conditional legacy was left to a son-in-power, and, as security for it, his father took a mortgage over property belonging to the heir. If the condition was fulfilled after the father's death or the son's emancipation, the legacy is now owed to the son, and neither father nor son can sue for possession of the mortgaged property. The son has now acquired a right of action and cannot claim any right over the property mortgaged from the preceding period. The same is said of a surety.]; D.36.3.1.11, 5.2 [D.36.3.*Ut legatorum seu fideicommissorum servandorum causa caveat* (That a *cautio* be given for the security of legacies or *fideicommissa*).1 **Ulpianus**, *in the seventy-ninth book of Edict*: 11. If a legacy or fideicommissum is bequeathed with the condition that, should the beneficiary lose it, it is to be given to them again, we need to examine whether the beneficiary can request security for the subsequent legacy or fideicommissum. There are several considerations, such as whether the legacy or fideicommissum is currently due, how frequently it is due, and whether the legatee should provide security to ensure they do not lose it. A rescript from the deified Pius to Junius Mauricus addresses these issues, stating that, based on the facts presented, the legacies or fideicommissa under the testament of Clodius Felix should be paid to Clodius Fructulus without any obligation for him to provide security against dissipating any part of them. The rescript clarifies that the fideicommissum imposed on the heir by the

254 Quirin Schacher (1597–1670), *Disputatio septima. De cessione actionum, exhibens actiones cessibiles, sive materiam cess. [ionum]* (Lipsiae: excusa per Timotheum Hönium, 1645).

testator does not require Fructulus to secure the initial legacies, nor does it obligate the heir to restore the same amount without limit for every loss. Instead, the legacies are considered as being left to Fructulus once again by fideicommissum. Therefore, if he consumes anything after receiving this subsequent fideicommissum, the heir is not at further risk. This rescript indicates that the legatee is not required to provide security to the heir to safeguard the legacy. On the other hand, whether the heir should furnish security for the second legacy or fideicommissum is a matter of debate. The opinion is inclined towards the view that the heir should not be required to provide security since it is within his power not to lose what has been bequeathed to him. Although, if viewed solely as a disposition on condition, it might be argued that security should be demanded. 5 **Papinianus**, *in the twenty-eighth book of Questions*: 2. If someone claims that the entitlement to request or file a lawsuit for a legacy or fideicommissum is delayed due to a condition or until a future date, and seeks security for this reason, while the heir argues that the demand is baseless and denies that such a bequest exists, the party requesting security cannot be considered unless they present a written document that substantiates their assertion that the legacy or fideicommissum was indeed bequeathed to them.] , D.46.1.16.5, 29 [D.46.1.*De fideiussoribus et mandatoribus* (Sureties and mandators).16 **Julianus**, *in the fifty-third book of the Digests*: 5. see above in theorem 6. 29 **Paulus**, *in the eighteenth book of Edict*: see above in this theorem 63.].

It can be validly discharged by a formal release (*acceptum ferri*), D.46.3.16 [D.46.3.*De solutionibus et liberationibus* (Performances and releases).16 **Pomponius**, *in the fifteenth book to Sabinus Sabinus*: see above in theorem 55.]; D.46.4.12, 21 [D.46.4.*De acceptilatione* (Formal releases).12 **Pomponius**, *in the twenty-sixth book to Sabinus*: An obligation that is contingent upon a condition or set to become due at a specific time can be effectively discharged through a formal release. However, this is only permissible when it is evident that the discharge is contingent upon the fulfillment of the condition or the occurrence of the specified date. 21 **Venuleius**, *in the eleventh book of Stipulations*: If I, through novation, enter into a stipulation for a legacy bequeathed to me under a condition and provide a formal release before the condition is fulfilled, according to Nerva the Younger, even if the condition is later satisfied, there will be no action either on the basis of the will, due to the novation, or on the stipulation, which has been nullified by the release.]; D.50.17.77 [D.50.17.*De diversis regulis iuris antiqui* (Various rules of early law). 77 **Papinianus**, *in the twenty-eighth book of Questions*: see above in theorem 17.].

With this right, someone can be granted possession of assets (*mitti in possessionem*[255]), D.42.4.6, 11 [D.42.4. *Quibus ex causis in possessionem eatur* (The grounds on which missio in possessionem granted). 6 **Paulus**, *in the fifty-seventh book to the Edict*: A creditor is normally granted missio in possessionem of assets, even though money be promised him under a condition. 11 **Paulus**, *in the eighth book to Plautius*: If a legacy or fideicommissum is bequeathed to a son-in-power under a condition, we must acknowledge that both the son-in-power and his head of household are entitled to missio in possessionem. This is because both individuals have an expectation of benefit.].

However, D.42.4.14.2 opposes this opinion [D.42.4. *Quibus ex causis in possessionem eatur* (The grounds on which missio in possessionem granted).14 **Paulus**, *in the second book of Questions*: 2. A conditional creditor, however, is not granted missio in possessionem because possession is arranged to one who can sell the property under the edict.].

We respond that, there [D.42.4.6, 11], the conditionarius is allowed to enter into possession, but according to the first decree[256] of the praetor, here [D.42.4.14.2] it is excluded, as per the second decree. The reason for this is clearly stated in D.42.4.14.2: only those who are allowed to sell goods through an edict can be granted entry into possession, a privilege that is only given to those who have entered into possession through a second edict.

Moreover, an appointed person, even if the condition is pending, can possess the goods according

[255] Arangio-Ruiz, see note 32 above, p. 144, *missio in possessionem* is the term used to describe an act of authority by a magistrate, based on criteria established in the edict, that grants private individuals access to the mere detention or actual possession of specific goods or a group of goods. This can vary in duration and comes with administrative control powers, which may differ from case to case.

[256] According to the first decree of the praetor, the interested person has only the detention of the good, together with the owner. If the owner did not comply with the order issued by the magistrate, it would be transferred to missio in possessionem ex secundo decreto, granting full possession to the creditor with the right to sell the good received. (see Arangio-Ruiz, note 32 above, pp. 144, 222); conditional creditor, as Leibniz notices, is not included in the latter case.

to the will, D.37.11.2.1, 5, 6 [D.37.11.*De bonorum possessione secundum tabulas* (Bonorum possessio according to will).2 **Ulpianus**, *in the forty-first book to the Edict*: 1. If a son is appointed as an heir under a condition, Julianus consistently argues that the bonorum possessio, in accordance with the terms of the will, belongs to him as if he were the specifically named heir. This holds true regardless of the nature of the condition, even if it involves a scenario such as "if a ship arrives from Asia." Even in cases where the condition is not fulfilled, the praetor, having granted him bonorum possessio as per the terms of the will, must still safeguard the son. This protection is extended as if he had received bonorum possessio contrary to the terms of the will. Such safeguarding is deemed necessary, particularly for someone who has been emancipated. 5 **Ulpianus**, *in the fourth book of Disputations*: In the case where an individual is appointed as an heir under a condition, and upon receiving bonorum possessio in accordance with the terms of a will, the condition proves unsuccessful, there are instances where the property is required to be relinquished to the possessor. For example, if an emancipated son has been designated as an heir under a condition, and the condition is not fulfilled, Julianus notes that the son still obtains bonorum possessio as stipulated in the will. Similarly, if the individual in question would be the bonorum possessor in the case of intestacy, he is also entitled to protection, a principle that aligns with our observation of this rule. 6 **Ulpianus**, *in the eighth book of Disputations*: Lastly, those heirs conditionally instituted, who have been effectively instituted, can apply for bonomm possessio while the condition is still pending and not yet met; but, if someone has not been effectively instituted, an ineffectual institution is of no avail for the purpose of seeking *bonorum possessio.*].

However, a conditional right does not novate, except in specific cases, D.46.2.14. pr., 31 [D.46.2.*De novationibus et delegationibus* (Novations and delegations).14 **Ulpianus**, *in the seventh book of Disputations*: When an obligation to deliver something is initially promised unconditionally and is later redefined conditionally through novation, the novation doesn't take immediate effect but only when the specified condition is fulfilled. Consequently, if the subject of the obligation is, for instance, Stichus, and Stichus passes away while the condition is pending, novation wouldn't occur since the entity (Stichus) doesn't exist at the time when the condition is met. In line with this, Marcellus argues that even if there is a regrettable delay in making Stichus the subject of a conditional obligation, the delay is rectified, and it doesn't carry over into the subsequent obligation. 31 **Venuleius**, *the third book of Stipulations*: If I stipulate for the delivery of a certain item and subsequently stipulate under a condition for the same item from the same person with the intention of novation, the effectiveness of the novation requires that the item continues to exist unless it is the fault of the promisor for not providing it. Therefore, if you are supposed to give me a slave and you negligently delay the delivery, you remain liable even if the slave dies. However, if, while you are already in delay, I stipulate from you for the same slave before his death, and the slave then dies before the condition is met, novation occurs. This is because you are already bound by stipulation to provide the slave to me.], nor can it be novated, D.46.2.8.1 [D.46.2.*De novationibus et delegationibus (Novations and delegations)*.8 **Ulpianus**, *in the forty-sixth book to Sabinus*: 1. If legacies or fideicommissa are made the subjects of a stipulation with the intent of novation, novation will occur immediately if they were left without qualification or as of a certain time. However, if they were left conditionally, novation will only take place upon the fulfillment of the condition. In other scenarios, when someone stipulates for a specific time, novation happens immediately if that is the intention, as it is certain that the designated day will arrive at some point. On the other hand, when stipulating under a condition, novation doesn't occur immediately but rather when the condition is satisfied.].

Finally, the question arises whether a conditional right gives rise to an action, or if it is nullified by an exception. This does not seem to be the case.

The praetor did not grant the action if it was evident from the very foundation of the parties that it should not be granted. This is explicitly stated in D.42.7.14 where it is deemed inappropriate to sell the goods of a debtor under a suspensive condition, as it is not yet possible to sue them. [D.42.4. *Quibus ex causis in possessionem eatur* (The grounds on which missio in possessionem granted). 7 **Ulpianus**, *in the fifty-ninth book to the Edict*: 14. If an individual with a conditional or time-bound liability goes into hiding, his property should not be sold. This is because there is no distinction between a person who is not a debtor and a debtor who cannot be sued at the moment. The same principle applies when the individual is not a debtor at all or when his adversary has a claim that can be countered with a defense.]. The same is confirmed in D.50.16.213 where it is mentioned that, when a condition is pending, neither has the day for the payment arrived, nor the day on which the money can be claimed [D.50.16. *De verborum significatione* (Meaning of expressions). 213 **Ulpianus**, *in the first book of Rules*: see above in theorem 6.].

(67) A conditional right derives its value from the conditionated object, the probabilities of the condition's existence, and ultimately from itself.

Little has been said about the valuation of a conditional right, but we believe this argument deserves examination.

Although a conditional right is, in fact, illiquid and therefore cannot be offset against an unconditional right, arg. D.16.2.7 [D.16.2. *De compensationibus* (Set-off). 7 **Ulpianus**, *in the twenty-eighth book to the Edict*: If a debt is not due for payment until a specific date, it cannot be used as a subject for set-off before the arrival of that day, despite the obligation to pay it.], a conditional right can be offset by another conditional right if their conditions are the same or commensurable. By "commensurable", I mean conditions that both depend on a fungible thing, for instance, Titius owes Caius 100 if he receives 1000, whereas Gaius owes Titius 500 if he receives 50. After offsetting, it becomes clear that Titius owes Caio 450.

Moreover, a conditional right can be evaluated while the condition is pending D.42.4.14.1 [D.42.4. *Quibus ex causis in possessionem eatur* (The grounds on which missio in possessionem granted).14 **Paulus**, *in the second book of the Questions*: 1. see above in definition 52.]; D.35.2.55, 73.1 [D.35.2.*Ad legem Falcidiam* (The lex Falcidia).55 **Marcellus**, *in the twentieth book of Digest*: see above in theorem 66. 73 **Gaius**, *in the eighteenth book on the Provincial Edict*: 1, see above in theorem 66.]. It can be valued as much as it can be, according to these laws.

In the context of having to undertake an inventory of goods, whether in the judgment *familiae erciscundae*[257] or in the *lex Falcidia*[258], the question arises about how to handle assigned legacies and conditional debts.

[257] Berger, *ad vocem Actio familae erciscundae*, "Action among coheirs (cohehredes) in order to bring about division of the commom property inherited.".

[258] See note 164.

Proculus, indeed, suggested that they should be estimated as much as possible D.35.2.45 [D.35.2. *Ad legem Falcidiam* (The lex Falcidia).45 **Paulus**, *in the sixtieth book to the Edict*: In those legacies that have been left under a condition, Proculus thought that, when the question arises concerning the Lex Falcidia, the legacy included as much as the amount for which they could be sold. If this is so, then the deduction can also be made in such a way that it is deemed to be owed by virtue of the legacy as much as the value for which the claim can be sold. However, this opinion is not approved; therefore, the matter will be better regulated through guarantees.], add the quoted D.35.2.73.1.

However, the Sabinians[259] took a safer approach, considering that with proper guarantees, the conditional right could be deemed, for the time being, either pure or null (see the quoted D.35.2.45). Thus, the Lex Falcidia calculation does not apply during that interim period, D.35.2.53 [D.35.2. *Ad legem Falcidiam* (The lex Falcidia).53 **Celsus**, in *the seventeenth book of Digest*: If a Falcidian account is in progress concerning conditional legacies, those legacies, even if presently bequeathed, cannot be claimed in their entirety.].

From these considerations, it is evident that estimating a conditional right is generally beneficial.

We will now explain the foundations of the estimate, which we have set forth in the following three theorems: the conditioned, the hope of the condition, and the nature of the conditional right itself.

The nature of the conditional right is such that one aspect is vested while the other is revocable (see supra definition 77), and furthermore, one aspect is retroactive with a time limit (definitions 78, 79), and yet another aspect is transferable while the other is personal (supra definition 60).

A conditional right derived from a last will is revocable; however, when it arises from a covenant, it is vested (citing definition 77). Similarly, the former is transferable while the latter is not (theorem 50).

Finally, the former is retroactive, and the latter is subject to a time limit (infra theorem 68). Consequently, since a vested, transmissible, and retroactive right is

[259] See note134.

more extensive than one subject to a condition or time limit (retroactive but deducting the interest accrued in the intermediate period until the condition occurs or the time limit expires, it is evident that a conditional right by covenant is more extensive than a right descending from the last will, D.35.2.66) [D.35.2.*Ad legem Falcidiam* (The lex Falcidia).66 **Ulpianus**, *in the eighteenth book on Lex Julia et Papia*: Regarding the Lex Falcidia, it is important to note that when something is bequeathed under a condition or for a specified period, the actual value may be less than the nominal amount. For instance, if ten units are bequeathed to someone under a condition that is fulfilled, say, after ten years, the bequeathed amount is not considered as the full ten units. The passage of time and the interest accrued during the interval reduce the effective value from the original ten units.].

Although the laws may favor the last will (theorem 20), this preference applies only to the interpretation of the testator's words and not to the legal effect to be attributed per se.

Another essential aspect in evaluating a conditional right is the conditioned factor.

Here, the rule is that all other things being equal, a conditional right is greater when the conditioned factor is more significant. For example, suppose there are two bequests: If the ship comes from Asia, I leave a legacy of 100 to Seius and 200 to Caius. It is evident that Caius' right is greater, although it is possible that the difference in the conditions may make a conditioned factor with a higher nominal value of lesser practical value.

For instance, consider two more legacies: I leave a legacy of 100 to Titius if he ascends to Capitolium, and I leave a legacy of 200 to Caius if my cousin, captured by Tripolitanians, returns. In this case, I affirm that the legatee of Titius is greater than that of Caius.

Therefore, let us now turn to the estimation of Seius' conditional right, which is the third but the main fundamental. The entire estimation relies on the logical doctrine of degrees of probability[260], although, to the best of my knowledge, it has not been precisely treated by any, despite its significant practical utility, not only here but also when presumptions must be considered.

Let this be the general rule: the greater the probability of the occurrence of a condition, the greater the value of the conditional right. From this, it is immediately clear that the potestative condition is of greater value than the casual one because the fulfillment of the former is certain, provided you want it. The resulting conditional right should be assessed based on the gravity or triviality of the same event deduced in the potestative condition.

Furthermore, it follows from this that the more the condition can be hindered by someone to whom it is detrimental, and the more the condition can be taken advantage of by someone to whom it is advantageous, the more significant the condition becomes and holds greater value in the former case, and lesser value in the latter.

From this, it follows also that: a condition remitted to the debtor is of lesser value, remitted to the case is intermediate (for indeed, it does not concern God), and remitted to the conditional recipient is of greater value.

Finally, the greater the breadth of the condition, or the more ways it can exist, the greater its value; on the other hand, the greater the length of the condition, the more requirements are needed to fulfill it (for we traverse the entire length of the road, but as for the width, we can cover whatever we want), the lesser its value.

That quantity is called extensive, this intensive, based on this foundation, the disjunctive conditional right is of greater value, and the conjunctive is of lesser value.

[260] The doctrine that will never be elaborated by Leibniz. See about his *Noveaux essays sur l'entendement humain*, note 71 above, AA VI, 6, IV, 2, §14.

Moreover, all other things being equal, the negative condition is considered more valuable than the affirmative condition because the affirmative can only exist in a moment, while the negative extends almost infinitely.

(68) When a condition occurs, the conditional right is retroactive to the time of the disposition, according to the normal law.

Let there be, indeed, any conditional disposition: if the ship comes from Asia, Titius shall have 100. Since this provision contains nothing else but that the conditioned event must be true, without any added delay, if the condition is true, that is, if we can already be certain of the ship's arrival, it implies that we need not wait for that time, and if the ship comes, he shall have it! Let us imagine, for the sake of explanation, a prophet of proven reputation in the Republic saying: the ship comes, and the conclusion follows: therefore, he shall have it! Why then, should it not be requested, as the words do not include any postponement? However, since such prophets do not exist, it becomes evident that a conditional right should also be retroactively traced. Indeed, a delay or time limit is one thing, and a condition is another, D.36.2.6.1 [D.36.2. *Quando dies legatorum vel fideicommissorum cedat* (When a legacy or a *fideicommissum* vests). 6 **Paulus**, *Sabinus, book 3*: 1.see above in definition 12.].

Additionally, it is different when the money begins to be owed and when the day arrives on which the money can be claimed D.50.16.213 [D.50.16. *De verborum significatione* (Meaning of expressions). 213 **Ulpianus**, *in the first book of Rules*: see above in theorem 6.]. Therefore, correctly, in agreements, the time of the contract is considered, not the time when the condition is fulfilled D.50.17.144.1 [D.50.17. *De diversis regulis iuris antiqui* (Various rules of early law).144 **Paulus**, *in the sixty-second book to the Edict*: 1. In stipulations, the time at which we contract is considered.].

Consequently, if a slave or a *filius familias* promises something in a stipulation under suspensive condition while still under paternal power, and once manumitted, the condition is satisfied, the property is acquired either from the father or from the master, which is different from what happens in bequeaths for the last will, where those goods are owed to the manumitted one, D.45.1.78 [D.45.1.*De verborum obligationibus* (Verbal obligations).78 **Paulus**, *in the sixty-second book to the Edict*: If a son-in-power who stipulated subject to a condition were emancipated and then the condition was fuflfilled, his father can bring an action, because in stipulations we look to the moment when the contract is made.]; D.50.17.18 [D.50.17. *De diversis regulis iuris antiqui* (Various rules of early law). 18 **Pomponius**, *in the sixth book to Sabinus, book 6*: In the case of things which go to our heir on our death, having been left to us, we get by means of ourselves their benefit for those in whose power we are; the case is different where we have made a stipulation; for even if we stipulate under a condition, we get for them in every way even if the condition arises when we have been freed from the power of our master.].

For the same reason, once the condition occurs, the interim fruits are owed to the *conditionarius*, as in the case of *addictio in diem*[261], where if someone offers a better condition, the first purchaser must also return the fruits, D.18.2.6 [D.18.2 *In diem addictio*. 6 **Ulpianus**, *in the twenty-eighth book to Sabinus*: When it is said that interim fruits go to the first purchaser, that holds good whenever there appears no purchaser who makes a better offer or a false purchaser; but if there be a genuine second purchaser, it is established that the first purchaser must return the fruits, but to the vendor. So wrote Julianus in the forty-eighth book of his Digest.]; D.41.4.2.4 [D.41.4. *Pro emptore* (Usucapion as purchaser). 2 **Paulus**, *in the fifty-fourth book to the Edict*: 4. In the case of a sale made with an "in diem addictio," meaning unless someone makes a better offer, Julianus contends that the sale is concluded, the produce becomes the property of the buyer, and usucapion begins. Other legal scholars argue that such a sale is also subject to a condition, but Julianus maintains that it

[261] D.18.2 *In diem addictio*. 1. **Paul**, *in the fifth book to* Sabinus: In diem addictio takes the following form: "Let the land be sold to you unless someone makes a better offer before the first of January next, by which event the land departs from the owner.". Berger, *ad vocem Addictio in diem*, see note 107.

is not conditionally contracted but rather defeasible conditionally. According to him, this perspective is the correct and accurate opinion.].

And if someone lends money under a suspensive condition, and immediately afterward, another lends money unconditionally, and the debtor becomes poor with the condition of the first occurring after the credit of the second, nevertheless, the one who made the credit under the condition is deemed to precede and consequently is considered to be preferred, as it is taken into account the same time of the contract D.20.4.11.1 [D.20.4.*Qui potiores in pignore vel hypotheca habeantur et de his qui in priorum creditorum locum succedunt* (Priority in pignus or hypotheca and displacing an earlier creditor).11 **Gaius**, *in the sole book on the Action on Mortgage*: 1. Would we hold the same view if a mortgage is provided to secure a stipulation with a condition, and while the condition remains undetermined, a second creditor extends an unconditional loan using the same collateral? In the event the condition is subsequently fulfilled, does the second creditor take precedence? I am inclined to think not. When the condition is met, the initial commitment is treated as if it had been made without any conditions. This, in my opinion, is the more fàvorable resolution.].

An exception is made for the case where the condition was in the power of the debtor, D.20.4.9.1 [D.20.4.*Qui potiores in pignore vel hypotheca habeantur et de his qui in priorum creditorum locum succedunt* (Priority in pignus or hypotheca and displacing an earlier creditor).9 **Africanus**, *in the eighth book of Questions*: 1. He also took the view that a conditional creditor should be protected against one to whom a debt was later incurred, unless the condition was one which could only be met with the debtor's accord.], add. *Dan. Moller Com. in const. elect. p. 1 const. 28 n. 72*[262]; this opinion is well-grounded.

Indeed, if it is within the debtor's power, the right is not yet vested in the *conditionarius* or creditor. Therefore, only the occurrence of the condition is required, which is why it cannot be retroactive. Also, when a sale is made under a conditional contract, while the condition is pending, the interim risk falls on the purchaser, as if the

[262] Daniel Moller, see note 44.

sale, which is deemed valid after the event (condition occurs), were considered perfect from the time of the initial agreement, D.18.6.8. pr. [D.18.6. *De periculo et commodo rei venditae* (Risk and benefit of the thing sold). 8 **Paulus,** *in the thirty-third book to the Edict*: pr., see above in theorem 57.], add. supra theorem 57.

Moreover, if a formal release is granted to someone who owes under a suspensive condition in the meantime, when the condition subsequently materializes, he is considered to have been already released, D.46.3.16 [D.46.3. *De solutionibus et liberationibus* (Performances and releases).16 **Pomponius,** *in the fifteenth book to Sabinus*: see above in theorem 55.].

Furthermore, from this follows that with regard to the conditional contract, the gabell has to be paid to the exciseman or publican who held the position at the time of the contract, not the one who holds the position at the moment when the condition occurs (*Bertachin, tract. de Gabell, part. 5 n. 1*[263]).

So, with regard to engagements, it is questioned whether, if a condition is added, the marriage is still postponed until the condition occurs. *Joh. Brunell. in tr. de Sponsal. concl. 36 n. 2*[264] affirms this, but *Thomas* and *Bonaventura in Magistr. IV sent. Dist. 29; Distinctio XXVIII*[265] deny it, and rightly so. Betrothals are similar to

[263] Johannes Bertachini (1489), *Tractatus de Gabellis*. Venetiis, 10, pars. 5, n. 11 [not 1, such as in the text, e.n.], "[...] quod gabella debet solvi tempore contractus non tempore existentis conditionis.". The tax must be paid at the time of the contract, not at the time when the condition occurs.

[264] Johannes Brunellus, see note 250 above, p. 37, concl. 33 [not 36 such as in the text: concl. 36 does not exist, e.n.], n.2, "Conditio suspendit quando est talis, cuius praexistentia est necessaria ad esse matrimonui, ut cum Christianus dicit Iudeae vel infideli, contraho tecum matrimonium si facta fueris Christiana, sine qua conditione non tenet matrimonium [...].". [The condition suspends when it is such that its existence is necessary for the existence of the marriage, as when a Christian says to a Jew or an unbeliever, "I contract marriage with you if you become a Christian," without which condition, the marriage does not hold.]

[265] Saint Thomas Aquinas (c. 1252), *Scriptum super sententiis Magistri Petri Lombardi (Commentary on the Sentences of Master Peter Lombard)*,

contracts, so they should be judged in favor of marriage. Why delay a situation that is certain and risk causing scandal and disputes when there is no doubt? Not to mention that this retroactivity is supported by true law, so it is necessary to rule in its favor until it can be shown that the contrary was introduced by civil law.

This, however, pleased the authors of civil law, that if a time limit has been added to the condition, it is understood to be inherent to the conditioned, so that even though the condition is certain, the specified time must still be awaited. For example, if you have not given Stichus by the Kalends, you promise to give 10; Stichus dies before the Kalends and thus fulfills the condition, but he cannot be given on the Kalends. However, the specified time must be awaited, D.2.11.10.2 [D.2.11. *Si quis cautionibus in iudicio sistendi causa factis non obtemperaverit* (If anyone does not honor a promise given on account of appearance in court).10 **Paulus** *in the first book to Plautius*: 2. A person who intended to take legal action for insult secured an agreement requiring the opposing party to appear in court. However, after the agreement took effect, the promisse passed away before the legal dispute could progress. It is established that the heir of the deceased individual cannot pursue legal action based on the agreement because such agreements are specific to the nature of the legal claim, and the right to bring an action for insult does not transfer to the heir. Although the agreement made to ensure the appearance in court does pass to the heir, it does not apply in this scenario. If the deceased had abandoned the insult claim and wanted to pursue the agreement, they would not have been allowed to do so. The same principle

https://aquinas.cc/la/en/~Sent.IV.D29.Q1.A3.Q2.4 "Or else it is a contingent condition, such as the giving of money or the parents' approval. And then the judgment is the same about this kind of consent as about consent that is given in words speaking of the future, and so it does not cause marriage"; Saint Bonaventure (1217/1221-1274), (beginnings of XIII cent.) *Commentaria in quattuor libros sententiarum magistri Petri Lombardi*, 691, Quaestio III, *Utrum consensus conditionatum faciat matrimonium, Conclusio*], *Distinctio XXVIII [not XIX such as in latin text, e.n.]*, in, PP. Collegii a San Bonaventura (ed.), *Opera Omnia*, vol. 2. (Quaracchi, 1885) "The conditioned [part] expressed in words speaking of the future does not constitute marriage, only a promise of marriage. On the other hand, in general, it is not valid if the condition is made as a penalty or as a dishonest limit of the contract and against the essence of marriage. If the condition is made with words speaking of the future, even then it does not constitute marriage if the condition is on a contingent future.". [e.t.]

applies if the person against whom the insult action was intended has passed away, and the agreement has taken effect. In such cases, the heir cannot be held liable under the agreement, as Julianus notes. According to this perspective, even if there are guarantors involved, legal action cannot be taken against them upon the death of the defendant. Pomponius echoes this sentiment, adding that the exception is if the defendant did not die after a significant amount of time had passed, as the plaintiff would have been able to engage in legal proceedings with the defendant had they appeared in court.]; D.35.1.4.1 [D.35.1. *De condicionibus et demonstrationibus et causis et modis eorum, quae in testamento scribuntur,* (Concerning conditions and precise designations, their reasons and kinds, which are written in wills).4 **Pomponius**, *in the third book to Sabinus*: 1, see above in definition 19.]; D.40.7.4.1 [D.40.7 *De Statuliberis* (Statuliberi). 4 **Paulus**, *in the fifth book to Sabinus*: 2. See above in theorem 26.]; D.45.1.8 [D.45.1. *De verborum obligationibus* (Verbal obligations).8 **Paulus**, *in the second book to Sabinus*: see above in definition 25.].

The legal scholars believe that the quoted D.45.1.8 opposes, and they invent many unreasonable things (ἄλωγα, in greek in the text, e.n.). Indeed, it is not the task of science to discover differences between cases; it is the task of science to demonstrate why the difference in circumstances leads to different legal outcomes.

However, *Cujac. p. 2 obs. 9*[266] clearly supports what was in question. He affirms that in D.45.1.10 [D.45.1. *De verborum obligationibus* (Verbal obligations). 10 **Pomponius**, *in the third book to Sabinus*: see above in theorem 1.], the time limit was not added to the condition (i.e., according to our style, to the conditioned part) for payment when, on the contrary, it can be asserted in any case. This is precisely what the juriconsults want to convey - that the term has been derived from the condition to the conditioned. It seems to me there is no contradiction. For in D.45.1.10, it is stated that it cannot be demanded before it is certain that Titius cannot come, yet nowhere is it added that if it is certain, then it can be demanded immediately, even

[266] Cujas, note 26, L. I, cap, XXII [not p. 2 obs. 9 as in the text, but this seems to be a citation error; in Cujas' book we find an "observatio" on D.45.1.8, not D.45.1.10, e.n.].

if the Kalends of May have not yet arrived. The Doctors derive this argument a contrario sensu (argument from the contrary), which often leads to antinomies, but indirect authority is of no importance as it yields to direct authority.

The D.40.7.3.14 presents a stronger contrast, [D.40.7. *De statuliberis* (Statuliberi).3 **Ulpianus**, *in the twenty-seventh book to Sabinus*: 14. Consider a scenario where a slave is instructed to provide a set amount annually for three consecutive years, and instead of waiting for the designated day, the slave presents the entire sum to the heir at once. Alternatively, if the slave gives ten in the first year and offers twenty in the second year, what would be the outcome? The more compassionate perspective would be to grant the slave freedom in both situations. This is because both the slave, by achieving freedom sooner, and the heir, by forgoing delay and accepting the full amount immediately, demonstrate foresight and willingness to act in a mutually beneficial manner.], but the favor of the right of freedom prevailed over the precepts of the right, although we cannot fully reconcile[267] it with the D.40.7.4.2 [D.40.7.*De statuliberis* (Statuliberi).4.**Paulus**, *in the fifth book to Sabinus*: 2. see above in theorem 26.].

Here, one cannot disregard a certain type of inverted promise or stipulation, once deemed invalid, which was allowed in all cases by Justinian's constitution, despite having been prohibited by Leo in dowries. In this form, the time limit of the conditioned comes before the end of the condition; for example, "if the ship does not arrive within two years, you promise to give 10 today," I.3.19.13.14 [I.3.19.*De inutilibus stipulationibus* (Of invalid stipulations).13. Formerly, a man could not stipulate that a thing should be conveyed to him after his own death, or after that of the promisor; nor could one person who was in another's power even stipulate for conveyance after that other's death, because he was deemed to speak with the voice of his parent or master; and stipulations for conveyance the day before the promisee's or promisor's decease were also void. Stipulations, however, as has already been remarked, derive their validity from the consent of the contracting parties, and we therefore introduced a necessary emendation in respect also of this rule of law, by providing that a

[267] Thus, a logical solution may be elusive, e.n.

stipulation shall be good which bargains for performance either after the death, or the day before the death, of either promisee or promisor. 14. Again, a stipulation in the form: 'Do you promise to give to-day, if such or such a ship arrives from Asia to-morrow?' was formerly void, as being preposterous in its expression because what should come last is put first. Leo, however, of famous memory held that a preposterous stipulation in the settlement of a dowry ought not to be rejected as void, and we have determined to allow it perfect validity in every case, and not merely in that in which it was formerly sanctioned.]; D.12.1.40 [D.12.1. *De rebus creditis si certum petetur et de condictiones* (Things credited giving rise to fixed claims and the condictio).40 **Julianus**, *in the thirteenth book of Digest*: An oath imposed on a debtor operates as a release for a pledge, resembling a formal discharge in its effect. It establishes a lasting defense and, therefore, when a creditor seeks a penalty, they should be thwarted, and any payments made can be reclaimed. In essence, resorting to an oath brings an end to disputes on all aspects of a matter.]; D.45.1.64, 126 [D.45.1. *De verborum obligationibus* (Verbal obligations).64 **Africanus**, *in the seventh book of Questions*: A stipulation was made in the following manner: "If Titius becomes consul, do you commit to giving ten each year from that moment?" After three years, the condition was fulfilled. There is a legitimate question as to whether one could legally pursue a claim for this time period. The response asserted the validity of the stipulation, asserting that payment was deemed due for each year that passed before the condition was met. The argument maintains that when Titius became consul, ten units were owed for each year, accounting for the intervening period as well. 126 **Paulus**, *in the third book of Questions*: If I stipulate thus, "if Titius becomes consul, do you promise ten annually from this day," and the condition is fulfilled three years later, thirty can then be claimed.]; C.6.23.25 [C.6.23. *De testamentis: quemadmodum testamenta ordinantur* (Concerning testaments: In what manner testaments are executed). 25 The fault attached to an expression inverted in order, which was directed to be disregarded in the recent constitution of Leo, in connection with dotal documents, must also be disregarded in all other contracts and in all testaments, and gives rise to no defense. Hence a stipulation and other contracts, as will as a will of a testator, shall be valid notwithstanding such fault, and the right thereunder shall accrue after the happening of the condition stated, or after the day fixed.][268].

[268] Note by Fred H. Blume (1875-1971): "A question in the form I do you promise today, if such or such ship arrives tomorrow is an expression inverted in order, because what should come last is put first. Hence a stipulation based thereon was formerly void. But, by a law of Leo this rule was changed as to dotal documents, and the amount promised

So far, we have discussed inter vivos acts.

As for the last wills, it must be understood that a conditional inheritance is retroactive when the condition occurs, not only under the *ius commune*, but also to prevent it from appearing as if it belonged to no one in the interim period D.29.2.54 [D.29.2.*De adquirenda vel omittenda hereditate* (Taking up or failing to take up an inheritance).54 **Florentinus**, *in the eight book of the Institutes*: Whatever the time at which an heir accepts an inheritance, he is understood to have succeeded to the deceased as from the time of death.]; D.45.3.28.4 [D.45.3. *De stipulatione servorum* (The stipulation of the slaves). 28 **Gaius**, *in the third book on Verbal Obligations*: 4. The inquiry has been raised regarding whether a slave who is part of an inheritance can make an agreement on behalf of a future heir. Proculus asserted that this is not possible, as at the time of the agreement, the slave did not belong to the prospective heir. On the contrary, Cassius argued that it is permissible, contending that whoever eventually becomes the heir should be regarded as succeeding the deceased from the moment of death. This line of reasoning is supported by the notion that once the mourning period concludes, household slaves are considered to be under the ownership of the heir from the time of the death, even if the heir is officially determined later. Consequently, it is evident that the stipulation made by the slave accrues to his benefit.]; D.50.17.138, 139 [D.50.17. *De diversis regulis iuris antiqui* (Various rules of early law).138 **Paulus**, *in the twenty-seventh book to the Edict*: Every inheritance, although it is entered into later, is regarded as existing at the instant of death. 139 **Gaius**, *in the sole book on Urban Praetor's Edict*: All actions which perish with death or the passage of time remain intact once the trial has started.].

However, a conditional bequest, as weak as it may be compared to other bequests, is not transferred (see supra theorem 50), and therefore, it is not retroactive.

So, if a conditional bequest is made to a son or a slave, and the condition occurs after they are no longer under the power of their father or master, the bequest will be due to them and not to the father or master, because conditional legacies are not transferred, which

became due on the arrival of the day fixed or the happening of the condition. Justinian extended the provision of Leo so as to apply to all contracts and documents. Inst. 3.19.14.".

is the same reasoning presented in D.50.17.18 [D.50.17. *De diversis regulis iuris antiqui* (Various rules of early law).18 **Pomponius,** *in the sixth book to Sabinus*: The legacies left to us that pass to our heir upon our death, we acquire for those in whose power we are, through our own actions in the same manner; it is different from what we have stipulated. For, stipulating under a condition, we acquire for them in every way, even if the condition arises after we have been freed from the authority of our master.][269]; add C.6.46.5 [C.6.46. *De condicionibus insertis tam legatis quam fideicommissis et libertatibus* (Concerning conditions attached to legacies, trusts and manumissions).5 If it is shown that your wife was in her father's power at the time of her marriage, the trust which was left her "when she should marry," belongs to her father, if there is nothing else to prevent the vesting of it at that time.].

These points are supported by frequent references in the laws, indicating that while a condition is pending, the legacy belongs to the heir (see supra theorem 47).

Furthermore, even if a bequest is unconditional in its effect, for example, whether the thing is done or not, it will still be deemed to have a time limit inserted into the bequest, allowing one of the two events to be expected. If the legatee dies in the meantime, the bequest will not be passed on to the heir, as if it were postponed to an uncertain day, D.36.2.13 [D.36.2. *Quando dies legatorum vel fideicommissorum cedat* (When a legacy or a *fideicommissum* vests).13 **Pomponius,** *in the sixth book to Sabinus*: see above in theorem 32.]. However, this seems excessively harsh and irrational to me.

What should be said about the institutions concerning the heir in this case, others may determine. As we mentioned earlier, the institutions appear to be retroactive, and thus the inheritance will be owed to the father or the master. Here, an interesting question

[269] Boucher, note 56 above in *Introduction*, 244, n. 1223, has criticized Leibniz for not adequately demonstrating that conditional legacies do not retroact. According to this critique, Leibniz should have argued, in line with D.50.17.18, that the inheritance does not retroactively transfer to a person who becomes *sui iuris* if the condition is fulfilled after their liberation from *alieni iuris* status. This would avoid an incorrect interpretation of retroactivity.

arises: while a conditional bequest is not retroactive, if a mortgage is established as security during the pending condition, when the condition is fulfilled, it becomes retroactive, giving priority to the party with a superior right, as affirmed in D.20.4.9.2 [D.20.4.*Qui potiores in pignore vel hypotheca habeantur et de his qui in priorum creditorum locum succedunt* (Priority in pignus or hypotheca and displacing an earlier creditor).9 **Africanus**, *in the eighth book of Questions*: 2. An heir pledged his estate, comprising assets subject to a conditional bequest, and subsequently mortgaged the same assets to secure a loan. The condition attached to the legacy was met. In this case as well, he believed that the initial mortgagee should be safeguarded.].

Although in cases where a bequest and a covenant are mixed, the vulnerability of the bequest prevails, for example, when someone promises a conditional bequest in a stipulation, if the legatee dies while the condition is pending, it does not pass on to the heirs, D.36.3.1.11 [D.36.3. *Ut legatorum seu fideicommissorum servandorum causa caveat* (That a *cautio* be given for the security of legacies or *fideicommissa*).1 **Ulpianus**, *Edict, book 79*: 11 see above in theorem 66.]. However, this appears to be highly questionable.

Both conditional tutelage, in other cases and in this one, are similar to a bequest in that when the condition is met, they are not retroactive, D.27.1.45.1 [D.27.1. *De excusationibus* (Excuses).45 **Tryphoninus**, *in the thirteenth book of Disputes*: 1, see above in definition 25.].

Even an eventual act is not retroactive, which means during a *litis contestatio*[270], it is permissible to amend the petition, *Moller. part. 3 const. 3 fol. 11*[271].

For further information on retroactivity in general, *Joh. Baptista Costa tr. pecul*[272] has covered the topic.

[270] See note 236 above.

[271] Moller, see note 44 above.

[272] Johannes Baptista Costa, *Tractatus de retroactione seu de fictione translativa* (Venetiis, 1606)

But if the condition fails, the disposition is considered null from the beginning D.18.6.8. pr. [D.18.6. *De periculo et commodo rei venditae* (Risk and benefit of the thing sold).8 **Paulus**, *in the thirdy-third book to the Edict*: pr., see above in theorem 57.] and therefore it is also necessary for the term to be retroactive, as the failure of a condition and the existence of a term are the same thing (see supra def. 21, 22, 23, 24).

So, if a plot of land were sold according to the *lex commissoria*[273], once the day has passed, the fruits are still owed to the seller, D.18.3.4.1 [D.18.3. *De lege commissoria* (The forfeiture clause).4 **Ulpianus**, *in the thirty-second book to the Edict*: 1. Neratius's assertion that the buyer may at times keep the profits is reasonable, as the buyer forfeits the amount of the price already paid. Therefore, Neratius's compassionate perspective applies when the buyer has made some partial payment of the price.], add D.35.1.79.2 [D.35.1. *De condicionibus et demonstrationibus et causis et modis eorum, quae in testamento scribuntur* (Concerning conditions and precise designations, their reasons and kinds, which are written in wills).79 **Papinianus**, *in the first book of Definitions*: 2. A person who receives a legacy by making the Mucian promise is obligated to return any income derived from it to the heir if the stipulation is enforced due to a breach of the promise on the legatee's part. The legatee is compelled to make this commitment from the very beginning.].

However, it is different in the *addictio in diem*[274], where if the sale is unconditional, the buyer gains the fruits, subject to the condition of resolution; but if it is minimally conditional, then the buyer gains neither the fruits nor the risk.

(69) If the condition is not fulfilled, the disposition is said to be vitiated.

It is said that a disposition is vitiated when it has no legal effect, D.28.7.1 [D.28.7. *De conditionibus institutionum* (Conditions on institutions).1 **Ulpianus**, *in the fifth book to Sabinus*: see above in theorem 63.]; D.50.17.77 [D.50.17. *De diversis regulis*

[273] See note 224 above.

[274] See note 107 above.

iuris antiqui (Various rules of early law).77 **Papinianus**, *in the twenty-eighth book of Questions*: see above in theorem 17.].

Similarly, a condition is said to be vitiated when it has no legal effect, in which case the disposition is not vitiated but becomes unconditional, although D.28.7.8 expresses it improperly by stating that what was left under condition is disapproved when, in fact, only the condition is disapproved [D.28.7. *De conditionibus institutionum* (Conditions on institutions).8 **Ulpianus**, *in the fiftieth book to the Edict*: pr., see above in theorem 38.]. The condition, on the contrary, vitiates; on the other hand, it is also said that something is vitiated, D.22.1.20 [D.22.1. *De usuris et fructibus et causis et omnibus accessionibus et mora* (Interest, fruits, incidentals, accessions, and delay).20 **Paulus**, *in the twelfth book to Sabinus*: It is evident that unlawful interest presented as capital is not owed, yet the demand for the actual capital is not invalidated as a result.], when it removes the conditionated from the same stability in case of contention, as it happens in impossible conditions (theorem 63), or when, due to its legal ineffectiveness, it nullifies the conditionated itself, which is done in captatory conditions (supra theorem 38).

If, therefore, a condition is not fulfilled, the disposition is vitiated

or extinguished, D.2.14.27.2 [D.2.14. *De pactis* (Pacts).27 **Paulus**, *in the third book to the Edict*: 2. If someone, after entering into an agreement not to pursue legal action, later consents to bring a lawsuit, the initial agreement is annulled by the subsequent one. This annulment does not occur by operation of law, as a stipulation is extinguished by another stipulation. Stipulations are related to legal matters, while pacts are factual. Consequently, the defense provided by the earlier agreement is negated by a counter-statement. Similarly, the prior pact does not benefit guarantors for the same reason. However, if the pact is such that it extinguishes an entire legal action, such as a claim for insult, the plaintiff cannot revive the action by later agreeing to sue. This is because the initial action is extinguished, and the subsequent pact cannot effectively reinstate the legal claim. Actions for insult derive from the insult itself, not from a pact. The same principle applies to contracts made in good faith, where a pact extinguishing the entire obligation, as in the case of a sale, does not revive the previous obligation but creates a new contract. On the other hand, if the pact subtracts something from the contract without extinguishing it entirely, the later pact can renew the original contract. This also applies to actions for dowry. For instance, if a woman initially agrees for the immediate restoration of the dowry and later agrees to its restoration only after the legally allowed time, the dowry reverts to its proper legal status. It is not accurate to claim that the condition of the dowry worsens due to the pact. When the action for the dowry returns to the legal position defined by its inherent nature, its legal status is not worsened but restored to its proper form. This interpretation is supported by our Scaevola.],

or is destroyed,

or is deemed ineffective,

although it is also said to be ineffective from the beginning, D.44.7.44.3 [D.44.7. *De obligationibus et actionibus* (Obligations and actions).44 **Paulus**, *in the seventy-fourth book on the Praetor's* Edict: 3.see above in definition 20.].

Because indeed, if a condition is impossible, the disposition is null, as mentioned in theorem 63. And if it is pending, the disposition is in suspense, according to theorem 6. Therefore, if it becomes impossible or remains unfulfilled (per definition 51), the disposition will also become null or be vitiated I.2.17.2 è [I.2.17. *Quibus modis testamenta infirmantur* (Of the modes in which wills become void).2. Again, a subsequent will duly executed is a revocation of a prior will, and it makes no difference whether an heir ever actually takes under it or not; the only question is whether one might conceivably have done so. Accordingly, whether the person instituted declines to be heir, or dies in the lifetime of the testator, or after his death but before accepting the inheritance, or is excluded by failure of the condition under which he was instituted—in all these cases the testator dies intestate; for the earlier will is revoked by the later one, and the later one is inoperative, as no heir takes under it.], D.28.6.8 [D.28.6.*De vulgari et pupillari substitutione* (Normal and pupillary substitution). 8 **Ulpianus**, *in the fourth book to Sabinus*: see above in theorem 21.]; D.28.5.87 (86) [D.28.5. *De heredibus instituendis (The institution of heirs)*. 88 (87) **Hermogenianus**, *in the third book of the Epitome o f Law:* If, in a situation where Primus is appointed heir to six shares and Secundus to eight, Tertius is designated heir for the remaining share or without specifying any portion, Tertius would possess five twelfths of the inheritance. This calculation arises from distributing the inheritance into twenty-four shares, resulting in five twelfths for Tertius, as if he had been appointed for ten shares. However, it appears to be an error to cite the appropriate legal provision; it should be corrected. 87 (86) **Maecianus**, *in the seventh book on Fideicommissa*: see above in definition 53.]; D.27.7.2. pr., 28 [D.28.7. *De conditionibus institutionum* (Conditions on institutions). 2 **Ulpianus**, *in the sixth book to Sabinus*: pr.: When a will includes the phrase "let that slave, if he is mine" (or "who is mine"), "when I die, be heir," the interpretation of "mine" becomes a subject of inquiry. If, indeed, the testator has transferred the usufruct of the slave, the slave still remains the property of the testator. However, if the testator has conveyed a share in the slave, the question arises whether the condition on the institution is invalidated. The more accurate perspective is that the condition does not fail unless there is clear and indisputable evidence that the testator intended these words to be included as a condition signifying this: "if the entire slave remains in his ownership." In such a case, if a share has been transferred, the condition is deemed to have failed. 28 **Papinianus**, *in the thirteenth book of Questions*: see above in theorem 1.]; D.35.1.33.3 [D.35.1. *De condicionibus et demonstrationibus et causis et modis eorum, quae in testamento scribuntur* (Conditions, designations, explanations for and modalities of provisions in wills).33 **Marcianus**, *in the sixth book of Institutes*: 3. If someone bequeaths an item under the condition that it is their property at the time of their death, and it is subsequently determined not to be in their possession at that time, not even its value is considered as being bequeathed.]; C.6.43.3 [C.6.43. *Communia de legatis et fideicommissis et de in rem missione tollenda* (Common rules concerning legacies and trusts and concerning abolishing the granting of the right to enter on an inheritance).3 If an option to pick out a slave or other property was left to one, two or more persons, or if the option to pick out a slave or other property was left to one person, but that person died leaving several heirs, it was doubted by the ancients what the legal situation was, if the legatees or the heirs of the legatee should disagree, and each should want to choose a different slave or different property.]; C.6.51.2, 6 [C.6.51. *De caducis tollendis* (Concerning abolishing lapses (escheats).2. And since bequests left in last wills were held to lapse in three different ways, it is proper to state the times and the names thereof, so that it may be known what is abolished and what is reformed. 7. If any bequest is left on condition, which either depends on chance, or on the will of the donee, or is mixed, that is to say, the outcome of which depends on a chance-event of nature, on the wish of the person honored, or on both, or on the arrival of an uncertain day, the outcome of the condition under which it was left or the arrival of the uncertain day, must be awaited, so that it may vest when the condition is fulfilled or the uncertain day arrives. And if he too who receives a benefit under a testament dies in the meantime, or if the condition fails during his lifetime, such bequest which on that account did not remain in force, we direct, become the property of those who were directed to pay it, unless a substitute or joint beneficiary, whether that is an heir or legatee, has been appointed; for in such event, the latter will receive it, since the law is certain that a substitute may be appointed in instituting heirs, giving a trust, or making gifts in anticipation of death.].

Likewise, a disposition is vitiated if the conditionated is vitiated, because the conditionated is the principal element, not a secondary addition, and the entire disposition refers to the conditionated (add supra theorem 17 at the end). On the other hand, the conditionated is vitiated whether it is inevitable or impossible; for example, if one leaves as a legacy to Titius the right to breathe freely or if one leaves a bequest for the islands around the poles. However, since this stems not from the doctrine of conditions but from the nature of business in general, there is no need to explain it with a particular theorem.

We note one thing: the cases in which the conditioned is impossible or necessary, not in itself, but as connected with a condition, were explained in the *dissertation on perplexing cases in sections 13, 14, 15, 16, 17*[275].

However, when the disposition is rendered ineffective, the conditionated passes to the substituted, D.28.5.27, 33 [D.28.5. *De heredibus instituendis* (The institution of heirs). 27 **Pomponius**, *in the third book to Sabinus*: Should I appoint you as the sole heir without conditions for one half share and with a condition for the other, while also naming a substitute for you, Celsus asserts that if the condition remains unfulfilled, the substitute will inherit that share. 33 **Gaius**, *in the second book on Wills according to the Edict of Urban Praetor*: see above in theorem 32.]; D.35.1.26.1, 30, 54 [D.35.1. *De condicionibus et demonstrationibus et causis et modis eorum, quae in testamento scribuntur* (Conditions, designations, explanations for and modalities of provisions in wills). 26 Julianus, *in the eighty-second book of the Digests*: 1, If the same item is bequeathed

[275] AA VI, 1, pp. 240-242.

unconditionally to one person and subject to a condition for another, or if one person is unconditionally named as heir and another conditionally, then, in the event of the condition not being fulfilled, the portion of the legacy or inheritance will also pass to the heir of the person to whom the legacy or inheritance was unconditionally granted, provided that their inheritance has been accepted. 30 **Julianus,** *in the first book From Minicius*: see above in theorem 26. 54 **Javolenus,** *in the second book From Cassius*: Imagine someone specifies legacies without any conditions to be given on a date in the first, second, and third year, and bequeaths the money to someone when they reach the age of puberty. In his Commentaries, Gaius [Cassius] states that this legacy is payable on the first, second, and third year after reaching puberty. I disagree; the condition is introduced to postpone a legacy that would otherwise be immediately due; however, the age of puberty indicates a specific point in time.]; C.6.25.2. [C.6.25. *De institutionibus seu substitutionibus sub condicione factis* (Concerning appointments, substitutions or trusts, made upon condition). 2 see above in theorem 38.].

The *conjuncti re*[276] have the entirety (whole), as mentioned in D.28.5.60(59).6 [D.28.5. *De heredibus instituendis* (The institution of heirs). 60 (59) **Celsus,** *in the sixteenth book of Digest*: 6, see above in theorem 50.], and what was mistakenly given to fulfill a condition can be recovered (*confici*) according to D.12.6.67 [D.12.6. *De condictione indebiti* (The *condictio* for money not owed). 67 **Scaevola,** *in the fifth book of Digest*: Stichus obtained his freedom under the assumption that the man he considered his owner had bequeathed it to him, with the condition of paying the heirs ten units annually for ten years. He fulfilled this obligation for eight years. Upon discovering that he was actually freeborn, he ceased payments for the remaining years. His status as freeborn was confirmed. The question arises: Can he reclaim the money paid to the heirs as undue, and if so, through what legal recourse? The answer is affirmative; he can recover the money, provided that the payment was not earned through his personal labor or derived from the possessions of the person he served in good faith.], the whole title C.4.6. *De condictione ob causam datorum* (Concerning *condictio* on the ground of what was given).

(70) If the condition occurs, the disposition becomes unconditional.

[276] See definition 41 above.

Because if the condition is necessary, the disposition is unconditional, as stated in theorem 64. Therefore, if the condition becomes necessary, that is, occurs, according to theorem 50, the disposition becomes unconditional, or rather, is made unconditional. This is what was to be demonstrated. We have already addressed the relevant texts on this matter, as mentioned supra theorem 1. The first and last theorems correspond to each other, just like a melody that begins and ends with the same pitch.

Moreover, the violation of the condition is considered equivalent to its occurrence, as when the disposition is regarded as not added, it also becomes unconditional. See examples mentioned supra theorem 38.

Thus, neither the condition of the one who fulfills it is better than that of the one who is merely assumed to have fulfilled it, i.e., for whom the condition is considered not added D.35.1.74 [D.35.1 *De condicionibus et demonstrationibus et causis et modis eorum, quae in testamento scribuntur* (Conditions, designations, explanations for and modalities of provisions in wills).74 **Papinianus**, *in the thirty-second book of Questions*: see above in theorem 26.], nor, conversely, is the condition of the assumed fulfillment better than that of the actual fulfillment D.40.7.4.2, 18 [D.40.7.*De statuliberis* (Statuliberi).4 **Paulus**, *in the fifth book to Sabinus*: 2 see above in theorem 26. 18 **Paulus**, *in the sole book on Grants of Freedom*: Should an individual instructed to provide ten units annually for three years offer twenty in the initial year, and if the heir declines this offer, the person does not immediately attain freedom. Even if the heir had accepted the offer, freedom would not have been achieved at that point.]. Refer to my arguments against the common opinion on the meaning of D.35.1.74 in theorem 26.

This pertains to the fact that the carnal union purifies the betrothal, just as if the condition had been fulfilled, X.4.1.30 [X. 4.1. *On Betrothals and Marriages*. 30. Mutual promise of marriage in the future, turns into marriage, for later sexual intercourse, but not for the attempt only of the sexual intercourse.].

The engaged parties are presumed to have, by a legal fiction, rescinded the condition through a novation.

This presumption does not allow any evidence to the contrary.

Once the disposition is purified and unconditional, the bequeathed item is transferred D.28.7.28 [D.28.7.*De conditionibus institutionum* (Conditions on institutions).28 **Papinianus**, *in the thirteenth book on Questions*: see above in theorem 1.]; D.36.2.13 [D.36.2. *Quando dies legatorum vel fideicommissorum cedat* (When a legacy or a *fideicommissum* vests). 13 **Pomponius**, *in the sixth book to Sabinus*: see above in theorem 32.], and the legatee becomes the rightful owner of the bequeathed object by law, D.31.80 [D.31.*De legatis et fideicommissis* (Legacies and fideicommissa).80 **Papinianus**, *in the first book of Definition*: The legacy confers ownership of the specific item to the legatee, just as the inheritance makes individual items part of the heir's estate. This implies that if the item is bequeathed without any conditions and the legatee does not reject the deceased's intention, the ownership, which belonged to the inheritance, directly passes to the legatee, never becoming part of the heir's estate.].

The legatee can rightfully claim it D.30.81.5, 6 [D.30. *De legatis et fideicommissis* (Legacies and *fideicommissa*).81 **Julianus**, *in the thirty-second book of the Digest*: 5, "I bequeath a farm to Titius under the condition that he gives ten to my heir." If he has owed ten to Titius and Titius gives him a receipt, he can vindicate the farm. 6, If Titius, to whom the servant Stichus had beenleft as legacy, passes away before realizing that the legacy pertains to him and leaves the same servant to Seius, if Titius's heir does not reject the legacy, Seius will claim ownership of Stichus.]; C.6.43.3.3 [C.6.43. *Communia de legatis et fideicommissis et de in rem missione tollenda* (Common rules concerning legacies and trusts and concerning abolishing the granting of the right to enter on an inheritance).3.3 And if, moreover, a legacy, universal or specific, is left upon condition or for uncertain period, or if a provision for substitution or restitution is attached thereto, the heir would do better even in these cases to refrain from selling or mortgaging the property covered thereby, lest he undergo the graver burden of eviction.];

and any delivery made by the heir to another party in the meantime is void, thus conferring no real rights, as all rights revert back to the legatee D.34.5.15 [D.34.5.*De rebus dubiis* (Dubious cases). 15 (16) **Marcianus**, *in the second book of Rules*: There are circumstances in which doubt arises, but subsequent events clearly determine what happened. For instance, if a property has been legated and, while the legatee is considering whether to accept the legacy, the heir transfers it to someone else: if the legatee decides to accept the legacy, the transfer is null and void; however, if the legatee rejects the legacy, the transfer is valid. The same principle applies if the heir lend money from the inherited estate that is the subject of a legacy: if the legatee does not reject the legacy, the heir has essentially lent money that does not belong to him; however, if the legatee rejects the legacy, the heir is considered to have lent his own money. So, what if the money has been spent? Certainly, A similar view will have to be taken, depending on the circumstances.].

Moreover, the occurrence of the condition makes the bequeathed item begin to be owed, D.28.7.8.8, 28 [D.28.7. *De conditionibus institutionum* (Conditions on institutions). 8 **Ulpianus**, *in the fiftieth book to the Edict*: 8. There is no need to approach the praetor to have this type of oath annulled; for it has been released once for all by the praetor and does not require to be released by individual [praetors]. And, therefore, it is regarded as released from the time when a legacy has vested even if the appointed heir does not know of this. And, therefore, in the case of the heir of the legatee, the view rightly approved is that if the legatee has died after the legacy has vested, his heir ought to bring the action on the legacy, as if an unconditional legacy had been left to the person to whom he had become heir. 28 **Ulpianus**, *in the fifth book to Sabinus*: If an institution reads, "let Titius be the heir if Secundus does not become the heir," and subsequently states, "let Secundus be the heir," it is understood that Secundus has been designated as the primary heir.]; D.36.2.5.2 [D.36.2.*Quando dies legatorum vel fideicommissorum cedat* (When a legacy or a fideicommissum).5 **Ulpianus**, *in the twentieth book to Sabinus*: 2. But if a legacy be left upon condition, it does not vest before the condition is met, not even if it be such a condition as is in the power of the legatee.]; C.6.51.7 [C.6.51.*De caducis tollendis* (Concerning abolishing lapses (escheats). 7, see above in theorem 14.].

The statuliber is legally considered free, arg. D.18.7.3, 9 [D.18.7. *De servis exportandis: vel si ita mancipium venierit ut manumittatur vel contra* (Slaves to be exported: the sale of slaves with a provision that they be, or not be, manumitted).3 **Paulus**, *in the fiftieth book to the Edict*: Titius sold a slave with a condition that if the slave remained in Rome, he could be subject to seizure; the buyer then resold the slave with the same condition. The slave escaped from the second buyer and stayed in Rome. I inquire whether the slave can be seized and by whom. I responded that in cases where the slave runs away, there is no doubt that the condition has not been violated, as the slave cannot remove itself from the ownership of its master, and a runaway slave does not remain. However, if the slave, with the consent of the second buyer, remains in breach of the condition, the original seller who established the condition has a stronger position. The second seller repeats the condition as a notice to their buyer and to absolve themselves from any responsibility, and they cannot in any way override the condition set by their own seller, whose conditions have already been fulfilled. If a penalty was promised, there will be two legal actions, but only the slave can be seized. However, if the first seller stipulated that if the female slave sold is forced into prostitution, she should be freed, while the second seller specified that in such a situation, she should be seized, the provision for freedom takes precedence over the one for seizure. Naturally, if the seizure condition was in the first sale and the freedom condition in the second, the more favorable interpretation would grant her freedom because each condition is tied to a slave, and, like seizure, freedom rectifies the wrongdoing.].

Finally, for someone who owes something under a suspensive condition, once the condition is fulfilled, and he becomes aware of it, he is immediately considered to be in default, just as the due date compels the creditor. I believe this was established because a reasonable time limit had already been granted to the debtor, and it is now fair for the debtor to remind himself.

The Doctors deduce this from D.22.1.18 [D.22.1. *De usuris et fructibus et causis et omnibus accessionibus et mora* (Interest, fruits, incidentals, accessions, and delay). 18 **Paulus**, *in the third book of Replies*: Having been evicted from agricultural lands, if initially an agreement was made for the seller to refund the price, subsequent interest after eviction must also be paid, even if the buyer delivers the fruits produced after the initiation of the property dispute to the adversary. The prejudice related to the intervening period of the legal process constitutes a loss borne by the buyer.]; C.8.37.12 [C.8.37. *De contrahenda et committenda stiplatione* (Concerning the contract of and defaults in a stipulation). 12. Clarifying an obscure point of the ancient laws which has given much occasion for protracted litigation up to this time, we ordain that if anyone promises under a stipulation to do or give something definite within a certain time, or to do what the promisee wishes, adding that he will pay a penalty if the promise is not fulfilled within the time fixed, he may know that he may not, in order to evade the penalty, object that no one reminded him, but he shall be subject to this penalty, according to the tenor of the stipulation without admonition, since he should himself keep his promise in mind, and should not ask that this be done for him by others.].

Index of Roman jurists, authors of the passages of the Digest cited by Leibniz

www.ingramcontent.com/pod-product-compliance
Lightning Source LLC
LaVergne TN
LVHW092116300926
849161LV00002B/150